Depression and Human Existence

Depression

and Human Existence

Edited by

E. James Anthony, M.D.
Washington University School of Medicine, St. Louis

Therese Benedek, M.D.
The Institute for Psychoanalysis, Chicago

Little, Brown and Company   •   Boston

To Our Children and Grandchildren

Contents

Preface

Depression as a phenomenon of human life is capable of various interpretations. The contributing authors have grappled with its protean manifestations and have responded to it as an affect, a feeling, a mood, a reaction, an illness, and a psychosis. They have attempted to describe it, to classify it, to study its origins, and to follow its course. As the editors, we are not concerned with minimizing the differences, homogenizing the constructs, or drawing facile conclusions based on superficial resemblances. We do point out, nevertheless, that the psychoanalytic contributions are more noteworthy for their commonality than for their divergences. A multiauthor book of this nature can be compared to the elephant in the parable of the blind men: each takes hold of a different segment of reality and interprets it logically in terms of his experience and, by doing so, helps to bring to this book a sense of the universal.

With these ideas in mind, we had two main aims in assembling this book. The first was to build bridges between neighboring disciplines so that the different workers could reach out and extract new sustenance for further growth, demonstrating that areas such as the biological and the psychological are not cut off from each other. The second aim was in the nature of an experiment. The hypothesis we hoped to test was whether depression could be regarded as a manifestation of existential factors in human life. Would a multiauthor book, its parts constructed independently, offer any support for such an assumption? Each contributor was invited to produce a chapter dealing with his particular field of interest and was given no guidance as to any centralizing or amalgamating idea. To what extent this hypothesis was confirmed is considered in the Epilogue. The test is a stringent one, since the chapters range from genetics to meta-psychology, with offerings from neurochemistry, sociology, cultural anthropology, and developmental and clinical psychoanalysis.

A book that is conceived and produced in this manner is very much in keeping with the current trend of psychiatry, which is struggling toward a clarification of a sociopsychobiological model. With an emphasis on the historical heritage, the book traces the gradual evolution of many of our current ideas. It makes its appearance at a point in history when psychoanalysis and the basic theories of modern science are meeting at a crossroad. Approaching the same junction are psychoanalysis as a science of the individual's psychological development and psychoanalysis as a tool for investigation of a psychiatric condition (not necessarily an illness) as it evolves from infancy to old age. Each phase of this evolution represents a complex interaction between the individual (his psyche and soma), his immediate milieu (the family), and the ambient sociocultural conditions. This necessarily complicates the view of depression as a simple phenomenon affecting the individual because of some manifest precipitating cause.

Because of the complexity of this model, the psychiatrist of today is expected to include in his investigating equipment a detailed knowledge of the genetic structure of the family, the developmental history of the patient, the moral, social, and cultural requirements under which he is trained to take his place in society, his physical functioning, and the impact of all these on his emotional state in health and illness. This multifactor approach is fast becoming the approach preferred by the contemporary psychiatric patient, at least in the Western world.

We are well aware that so-called psychiatric humanism is' on the fringe of medicine as a natural science and is even rejected by many physicians as basically nonmedical. Yet, psychoanalysis is considered a science rooted in biology, no matter how speculative the connection may appear. It is psychoanalysis that can help to encompass the diverse attempts at understanding the problem of depression, and it is psychoanalysis that throws light on the extent and difficulty of the problem. Genetics can only vaguely touch upon it, and neurophysiology and pharmacology can only struggle to disentangle the nerve pathways, the chemical mediation, and the functioning of the brain during normal and abnormal affective states. However, the "mysterious leap" between brain and mind, as Felix Deutsch termed it, remains as elusive as ever.

The juxtaposition of the approaches of various disciplines helps to highlight what is known, what is not known, and what is becoming known. All the disciplines are in various states of half-knowledge, and definitive statements are not easy to make. There are, nevertheless, a common theme and a common task to illuminate some portion of the theme, and the effort in any one discipline can only be helpful to the rest. As time progresses, the work will, we hope, become mutually complementary.

The book is written by psychiatrists and psychoanalysts for psychiatrists, psychoanalysts, and those in related disciplines. Behavioral scientists of all denominations are getting increasingly involved in the investigation of problems that afflict people in all societies and in all classes of life. Teachers are often perplexed by the chronically sad child in the classroom, pastoral counselors by the despair of some of their parishioners, and social workers by the profound feelings of hopelessness and helplessness that seize so many families as they become increasingly defeated by circumstances.

A multiauthor book such as this has one more feature: there are many contributors to thank for their collaboration in presenting their knowledge in the context of the book as a whole. Each of them has interpreted the editorial intention in his own way, and we are grateful for the expert knowledge that all of them have presented.

We also wish to record our personal debt to psychoanalysis for broadening our psychobiological horizons and for providing us with a frame of reference with which to incorporate knowledge from many different sources. If we look at things through psychoanalytic eyes, it is because our whole training and experience have been touched by this major influence in our lives.

Finally, we must acknowledge the work, less visible in the book itself but very visible in the manuscript, of our helpers, Carol Cordes and Darcy Gilpin, who typed and retyped the pages, constructed and reconstructed the table of contents, corresponded with contributing authors and our publisher, and, finally, helped in the arduous task of proofreading. Martha Kniepkamp, in St. Louis, had the additional task of preparing the final version for the publisher. She made herself quite indispensable to this task. P. G. Gordon's expertise in editing and preparing the manuscript and her helpfulness in communications between the editors and publisher deserve our gratitude. From our publisher we have received nothing but help, encouragement, and advice when these were needed. They were there at the beginning when the book was assessed, during the difficult middle phase when contributors appeared to develop a "negative communicative reaction," and, most helpfully, during the final phase, when deadlines were past.

We offer our ultimate words of gratitude to all those patients whom we were able to help work through a depressive illness and who in turn were able to help us understand the depressive experience.

E. J. A.
T. B.

Contributing Authors

E. James Anthony, M.D.
Blanche F. Ittleson Professor of Child Psychiatry, Director of the William Greenleaf Eliot Division of Child Psychiatry, and Director of the Harry Edison Child Development Research Center, Washington University School of Medicine, St. Louis; Training and Teaching Analyst, Institutes for Psychoanalysis, Chicago and St. Louis

Michael Franz Basch, M.D.
Associate Director, Center for Psychosocial Studies; Training and Supervising Analyst, The Institute for Psychoanalysis, Chicago

Therese Benedek, M.D.
Senior Staff Member Emeritus, The Institute for Psychoanalysis, Chicago

George L. Engel, M.D.
Professor of Psychiatry and Professor of Medicine, University of Rochester School of Medicine and Dentistry, Rochester, New York

Horacio Fábrega, Jr., M.D.
Professor of Psychiatry and Anthropology, Michigan State University College of Human Medicine, East Lansing

Jan Fawcett, M.D.
Professor and Chairman, Department of Psychiatry, Rush Medical College of Rush University; Chairman, Department of Psychiatry, Presbyterian–St. Luke's Hospital, Chicago

Sherman C. Feinstein, M.D.
Clinical Associate Professor, The University of Chicago Division of the Biological Sciences and Pritzker School of Medicine; Director, Child and Adolescent Psychiatry Training Program, Michael Reese Hospital and Medical Center, Chicago

Arnold I. Goldberg, M.D.
Clinical Associate Professor, The University of Chicago Division of the Biological Sciences and Pritzker School of Medicine; Attending Psychiatrist, Michael Reese Hospital and Medical Center, Chicago

Roy R. Grinker, Sr., M.D.
Chairman and Director, Psychiatric Institute of Michael Reese Hospital and Medical Center; Professor of Psychiatry, The University of Chicago Division of the Biological Sciences and Pritzker School of Medicine, Chicago

Edith Jacobson, M.D.
Visiting Professor Emeritus, Department of Psychiatry, Albert Einstein College of Medicine of Yeshiva University, New York

Arnold J. Mandell, M.D.
Professor and Cochairman, Department of Psychiatry, University of California, San Diego, School of Medicine, La Jolla

Mortimer Ostow, M.D.
Visiting Professor of Pastoral Psychiatry, Jewish Theological Seminary, New York

George H. Pollock, M.D., Ph.D.
Director, The Institute for Psychoanalysis; Professor, Department of Psychiatry, Northwestern University Medical School, Chicago

Arthur H. Schmale, Jr., M.D.
Professor of Psychiatry and Associate Professor of Medicine, University of Rochester School of Medicine and Dentistry; Psychiatrist and Physician, Strong Memorial Hospital, Rochester, New York

David S. Segal, Ph.D.
Associate Professor of Psychiatry, University of California, San Diego, School of Medicine, La Jolla

George Winokur, M.D.
Professor and Head of Department of Psychiatry and Director, State Psychopathic Hospital, The University of Iowa College of Medicine, Iowa City

Edward A. Wolpert, M.D., Ph.D.
Clinical Associate Professor of Psychiatry, The University of Chicago Division of the Biological Sciences and Pritzker School of Medicine; Director of Clinical Services, Institute for Psychosomatic Research and Training, Michael Reese Hospital and Medical Center, Chicago

Introduction

And the most tragic problem of philosophy is to reconcile intellectual necessities with the necessities of the heart and the will. For it is on this rock that every philosophy that pretends to resolve the eternal and tragic contradiction, the basis of our existence, breaks to pieces.

—*Unamuno*

EXISTENTIALISM AND ITS RELATION
TO PSYCHOANALYSIS

Existentialism derives from *existence*, a word with many connotations. Etymologically, it originates from the Latin *existere*, meaning to step forth, to emerge, to come into being, or to exist. *Existential* refers to a grounding in the experience of existence and to the empirically rather than the theoretically formulated concept. The term *existentialism* is defined by *Webster's Third New International Dictionary* as

an introspective humanism or theory of man that holds that human existence is not exhaustively describable or understandable in either scientific or idealistic terms and relies upon a phenomenological approach that emphasizes the analysis of critical borderline situations in man's life and especially of such intensely subjective phenomena as anxiety, suffering, and feelings of guilt in order to show the need for making decisive choices through a utilization of man's freedom . . . a theory stating that man's individual existence precedes his essence* and stressing his responsibility for fashioning his self.

The *American Heritage Dictionary* illuminates the philosophical meaning of "existential" by citing Paul Tillich: "anxiety is existential

---

* This is contrary to Plato, who maintained that the *idea* was prior to *existence* and that it was the essence of existence that changed with time and space. In the thirteenth century, Thomas Aquinas challenged this view and argued that if the immortal *ideas* were the essence of man, then man would be immortal. And six centuries later, Husserl was insisting that it was man's "flesh and blood that individuated the universal essence" [14].

in . . . that it belongs to existence as such and not to an abnormal state of mind." Our task in this Introduction is to show that depression is also an existential component of existence, different from yet interrelated with anxiety, and that it is not necessarily pathological.

These various definitions do not conflict with the basic tenets of psychoanalysis. A confrontation of psychoanalysis and existentialism is long overdue, and although we cannot attempt that larger task here, some comparisons and contrasts may help to sharpen the psychoanalytic view of existence.

Both disciplines base their approach on the fact of human existence, and both attempt to come to terms with the brute facts of life and death. Both, according to Barret [3], place emphasis on the individual in contrast to universal man. Both have been criticized for being literary productions, psychoanalysis as "second-rate literature" and existentialism as "poor poetry," and both have been dismissed by some as "mystical." Yet who can deny that the two come closer to the heart of life than the traditional psychologies and philosophies? This has been nicely put by Murdoch [19] in contrasting the two worlds of academic and existential philosophy: the academic world is one "in which people play cricket, bake cakes, make simple decisions, remember their childhood and go to the circus"; and the latter is a world "in which they commit sins, fall in love, say prayers or join the Communist party." The world of psychoanalysis, like the world of existentialism, contains the twin dreads of anguish and depression as an integral part of human experience. To be academically alive is not, therefore, synonymous with being authentically alive and marked by what Heidegger [13] has called the *existentialia*, or the basic categories of existence, namely, the mood that penetrates and permeates our whole being, the existential understanding that goes beyond our ordinary conceptual understanding, and language, whether spoken or silent, that is beyond talking and is rooted in being. Only in this existential sense can a person be said to exist, and without it there is no existence. The situation is summed up in Kierkegaard's little joke of the absentminded professor who is so abstracted from his own life that he hardly knows he exists until, one fine morning, he wakes up to find himself dead!

What goes on between people as portrayed by existentialism is also evocative of psychoanalysis.

Two people are talking together. They understand each other, and they fall silent—a long silence. This silence is language; it may speak more eloquently than any words. In their mood they are attuned to each other; they may even reach down into that understanding which lies below the level of articulation. The three—mood, understanding, and speech—thus interweave and are one [3].

This holds true for the experiential aspect of psychoanalysis in which intuition and empathy play a significant role in understanding the feelings of oneself and the other, even with silence. Experience is at the core of both disciplines. It is the business of neither to analyze anxiety and dread for the purpose of domesticating their immediate quality or of formalizing the terrors of existence of "being-in-inescapable-situations," as in the spirit of Greek tragedy. Both disciplines practice a return, in Husserl's words, "to the things themselves" rather than to the prefabricated conceptions that are often put in their place [14].

Existentialism has been as courageous in shunning the reassuring illusions of everyday life as has psychoanalysis. Each has confronted *nothingness* in its own specific ways. Heidegger opened up contemporary eyes to the horrors of nonbeing, and Freud to the fears of castration and death. Religion, as an alternative approach to the understanding of life and death, received very serious consideration from both sides. Freud concentrated on the obvious fact that religion does not keep its promises, although it endured because ordinary man had a need for "a system of doctrines and pledges that on the one hand explains the riddle of this world to him with an enviable completeness, and on the other assures him that a solicitous Providence is watching over him and will make up to him in a future existence any shortcomings in this life." [11]. Freud was uncompromising in his relentless pursuit of a rational understanding of the cosmos even though this entailed, as with Oedipus, "wisdom through suffering."

At times, perhaps not unconnected with the vicissitudes of his own life, Freud's pessimism came to the forefront as he envisioned the "dark, unfeeling and unloving powers" [10] that appeared to determine human destiny. Yet, in spite of this preoccupation with the long shadow cast by death, guilt, and fear on man's existence, compelling him to overcompensate with a self-defensive egotism, it was clear to Freud that Eros, not Thanatos, was victorious. Freud could not have functioned as an empathic therapist if his pessimism had been all-pervasive and persistent. Nor should Sartre's statement that "human life begins on the far side of despair" [23] be regarded as reflecting the existentialist position. Psychoanalysis, as Schafer [25] points out, is concerned not with pessimism but with a "tragic vision of man" as contrasted with the romantic view typified in so many of the humanistic ideologies. According to this view, man painfully struggles to the realization that he himself is always the unconscious saboteur of his luck, his love, and his life, and that he is constantly reenacting the pathos of the Oedipus complex. This sense of the tragic is not an invitation to pessimism and despair—which Klein

has referred to as the "products of a traumatized romanticism" [18]—
but involves the shedding of self-pity and the accepting of responsibility for one's life and one's decisions.

Existential philosophy deals with affects as experiential phenomena. The psychiatrist-philosopher Jaspers [15] carries us one step further in his phenomenology of the human condition, with its four
component parts of death, suffering, conflict, and guilt. The phenomenological approach attempts to dissect the affects and to find
qualitative and even quantitative shadings in the emotions. At the
heart of his existential position, man is concerned with man because
"in the world, man alone is the reality which is accessible to me . . .
man is the place at which and through which everything that is real
exists for us at all. To fail to be human would mean to slip into
nothingness. What man is and can become is a fundamental question for man" (Kaufman [16]). His tragic vision is summed up in
the statement: *"Grenzsituationen erfahren und Existieren ist
Dasselbe* [To experience inescapable situations and to exist are the
same thing"]. The major inescapable situation is death, the fear of
which is in two forms: the fear of nonexistence and the fear of nothingness. Life and death are interwoven intimately, as brothers living
with each other. The element of starkness is very much an integral
element of the philosophy: one stands face to face with life, and one
takes an authentic attitude toward death. The latter involves taking
death into oneself and considering it as a real possibility at any
moment.

Like other existential thinkers, Jaspers is deeply concerned with the
question of choice, which must be made consciously, without coer-
cion, compulsion, or condemnation. In this sense a man is the choice
that he makes, or to rephrase it in the transformed Cartesian axiom,
"Indem ich wahle, bin ich [I choose, therefore I am]" [15]. One is reminded here of the analytic process that attempts to carry the patient
metaphorically to the famous crossroads before Thebes, where, having
opened up all the dark mysteries to consciousness, it sets him in the
position of making a free choice.

Although existential philosophy and psychoanalysis are concerned
with the destiny of the individual in his human existence, they also
endeavor to develop universal explanatory concepts. The two major
parts of psychoanalysis, instinct and ego, can be considered in two
separate functional ways: the former in terms of the experiential
method and the discoveries stemming from it and the latter by the
conceptual method and the theories that have evolved from it. This
would seem to be a special case of bifurcation (a term first used by
Descartes and subsequently adopted by Whitehead [27] in his theory

of prehensions) in which there is a gap between actual and conceptual feeling, between experience and its explanation. Here the two
disciplines are at variance: existentialism looks fairly for the meaning
of the affective experience while psychoanalysis searches for the cause
in the past, the meaning in the present, and the forecast for the
future. Psychoanalysis is, therefore, a bipolar system in which the experiential and empirical quality of instinct is felt while, at the same
time, the causes and meanings and conjectures are built into a logical
framework of hypotheses.

One could, therefore, maintain that one aspect of Freud was intuitively existential but that he moved beyond this. His great discovery was a method that opened an observable way to the unconscious areas of the mind, namely analysis, and what followed were
attempts at understanding this momentous discovery. Others, in the
past, had examined themselves, but all their conclusions were predictable and were cast within a conventional framework of human
understanding. It was Freud who first took the apparently impossible
step through the encircling barriers of defenses built up by the individual and connected feelings with the unconscious layers of the
mind. It is in these respects that psychoanalysis is radically different
from existentialism.

Existential philosophers, excluding Heidegger and Jaspers, have
been criticized as being excessively morbid and preoccupied with
anxiety (the experience of their own neuroses), and the exclusion of
any reference to hope is a striking feature although hope must be
regarded as an existential concept. Hopelessness as an attribute of the
conservation-withdrawal type of depression has been regarded as a
primary affect, but hope is an attitude inherent in life instinct. It is
integrating in its function and projects into the future.

How does man face all the illusions, the losses, and the setbacks
of life without sinking into despair? The answer lies in the prevalence
and endurance of hope. Man cannot live without it, and the instinctual need for it is one of the sources of religion. Where does it
come from? It would be reductionistic to think of it as an outcome of
the infantile cycle of hunger and satiation. It is probably coterminous with life itself, a manifestation of the life energy directed toward
growth, toward becoming, toward the future. It could be regarded as
the psychic representation of this universal tendency. Only French
[9], among psychoanalysts, has paid attention to the influence of
hope in psychodynamic processes, regarding it as a factor in the integration of behavior.

In a remarkable nonanalytic work written almost sixty years ago by
Shand, a meticulous dissection of hope is carried out and its relation

to confidence, to anxiety, to disappointment, to despondency, and to despair is carefully defined. He begins with Locke's description of an impulse that is gratified or frustrated, in the latter instance giving rise to uneasiness. We feel a hope when the chances of gratification seem good; confidence when they seem certain; anxiety when there is doubt; disappointment when there is nonfulfillment; despondency when no progress is made toward attainment; and despair when hope is shut out, and attainment becomes impossible. Hope is the crucial tendency in human existence, according to him, and he quotes Amiel in support of this: "At bottom everything depends on the presence or absence of one single psychic element—hope" [1].

A more recent psychoanalytic view of hope sees it as somewhat more complicated than this. Schachtel [24] speaks of two types of hope, one embedded in the symbiotic unity that he refers to as magic hope and the other actively and realistically oriented toward the world. These are two profoundly different ways of feeling. Whereas magic hope is a wishful expectation that something will change for the better without oneself having anything to do about it, active hope is based on the attempt "to understand the concrete conditions of reality, to see one's own role in it realistically, and to engage in such efforts of thoughtful action as might be expected to bring about the hoped-for change." In this case, hope mobilizes energies for sustained action where attainment is a real possibility and not merely a fantasied one as with magic hope. The relation to time is also different. In magic hope the present is empty, boring, and futile, and the emphasis shifts to the future; but with realistic hope, the present receives its significance from the efforts one is making on one's own behalf.

PSYCHOANALYSIS AS AN EXPERIENTIAL AND THEORETICAL DISCIPLINE

There is no doubt that the essence of existential philosophy was experienced rather than conceived. Kierkegaard and Nietzsche almost destroyed themselves in the effort to formulate what they felt. They were pervaded by doubts and dreads, by fear and trembling, by the sickness unto death that frequently brought them to "the far end of despair" which was and is an emotionally taxing philosophy—"for most men," says Kaufmann, "are incapable of being existentialists with a full belly except perhaps for one or two years of their youth." [17].

For the past four decades those who practiced psychoanalysis have been required to undertake the experience themselves. This is, for the greater part, to deal with any emotional difficulties in themselves that might interfere with their work as analysts, but it also provides them with an experience comparable to that of their patients, which could have the important effect of enhancing their special tools of empathy and intuition. Unlike the theoretical constructs of psychoanalysis, which underwent almost continuous modification and refinement and were never completed, the original wholeness of Freud's self-analytic experience remained unquestionably valid. It did not take him long to realize that theoretical considerations can interfere with intuitive experience, and in several of his writings he pointed to the fact that knowledge was elaborated on another level of the mind. This understanding, however, does not help. The bifurcation of the mind was designed by evolutionary biology. It has taken many eons for the brain to develop and for consciousness eventually to emerge. This sequence related on the one side to the fact of existence and on the other to the experience that provided the ingredients for mental development.

The phenomenon perceived evokes the question "why" that is the primitive forerunner of knowledge of causality. Then the perceiver uses logic to "make meaningful connections" [15], and the knowledge that is subsequently developed helps to reassure the individual and to give him the feeling that he is mastering his world. During the development of the mind from prehistoric times, there must have come a time when simple causality was not in itself sufficient to satisfy the mind that pressed for fuller explanation. It was at some such hypothetical point that man began to be a producer and processor of meanings. How this actually came about is difficult if not impossible to reconstruct, but comparative philology and mythology offer some suggestions over and above speculation. When primitive man, for instance, was confronted with some awe-inspiring event, his first recourse was to name it and then, in a naive effort to explain it, to presuppose the action of a transcendental being, morphologically like himself but terrifyingly more powerful. According to Cassirer [5], not only religious conceptualization but speech, symbolization, and mythology all had a common origin in human experience.

ANXIETY AND HUMAN EXPERIENCE

Awe and anxiety are related phenomena; both are signals indicating a change in the homeostatic equilibrium. Anxiety is the human variation of the universal signal that alerts the organism to danger and (instinctively) organizes the system of species-specific and situationally adequate defenses. Awe is an affective state that often paralyzes the defenses by mobilizing a higher mental activity, for awe is an emotion in which dread is mingled with wonder and inspired by something majestic, sublime, and beyond human understanding. Such was probably the experience of those primitives who saw the transcendental power manifested in the lightning that struck the tree but allowed them to survive. Probably all religion, philosophy, and certainly psychology started with the experience of dread, which man needed to understand in order to master it.

What is *anxiety?* Is it an instinct, a drive, or an affect? Since it is the signal that alerts the organism to self-defense, fight or flight, it operates in the service of survival and must therefore be regarded as biological and instinctual. The organization of massive physiological defenses, however, could lend support to the thesis that anxiety is a drive. Finally, there are undeniable intrapsychic processes that are engineered by anxiety. Many authors today are quite content to label it an affect or even a primary affect. *Webster's Third New International Dictionary* focuses on the element of anticipation by defining it as uneasiness rising out of concern with what might happen; worry or apprehension about a possible future event. According to Shand, "the harassing effects of anxiety are frequently mentioned, but its uses are generally ignored." He allocates some important functions to anxiety: counteracting extravagant hopes, rendering us cautious and watchful, and hindering the development of overconfidence. It was psychoanalysis, however, that found new uses for anxiety.

In our highly complex mental apparatus, anxiety activates multiple physiological and mental responses to perception and then modifies that response *statu nascendi* in a variety of ways. It may relate to a current situation, to the past, or to an anticipation of the future. Since it is intuitively experienced and further elaborated by the creative activity of the mind, its manifold influences form an inexhaustible reservoir for research.

When one considers anxiety in its psychoanalytic context, one can catagorize it in terms of a signal function as in ego defense, in terms of flight reaction as in symptom formation and psychopathology generally, and in terms of its role in creativity. One of the earliest discoveries of psychoanalysis was the function of anxiety in symptom formation. The intrapsychic flight from the experience of anxiety was the motivation behind the symptoms and expressed their meaning. This unconscious process is actually closer to consciousness and the signal function that activates such primary structures as the ego defense mechanisms. The neurotic symptoms represented defenses against instinctual conflicts whereas the ego defenses gradually became charactcristic modes of dealing with emerging conflicts or intrapsychic tensions.

There is a third way in which the organism puts anxiety to use at the highest mental level of creativity. Whether this is in primitive myth making or in the mystic experiences of organized religion or in the scientific or artistic products of advanced civilizations, the expansion of the ego boundaries in such peak experiences comes from the mastery of manifest or subliminal anxiety. The creative religious philosophers who can be regarded as existential in their thinking, from St. Augustine to Kierkegaard, Tillich, and Buber, have all stressed, in one way or another, elements on the anxiety spectrum—awe, fear, dread, and despair. Kierkegaard, in two of his works, produced what are probably the best phenomenological descriptions of depressive anxiety, and his autobiographical references supply the psychodynamic etiology to account for it.

One can trace the same anxiety and awe in the depressions that haunted one of the greatest scientific minds of the seventeenth century. Pascal was well aware of the two worlds that opened up reverently to the thinking and intuiting mind. His *esprit de géométrie* was preoccupied with ideas and logical consequences whereas his *esprit de finesse* fought its way into more nebulous experiences. A sudden encounter with possible death brought him face to face with nothingness, making it no longer an abstraction but an experience. He saw himself, and man in general, occupying a middle position in the universe between the infinitesimal and the infinite, and he was filled with anxiety and awe [21].

Hope also has an important role in relation to anxiety, but it is still largely unexplored. Shand, in his classical monograph, tackles the association in some detail. He postulates a number of laws regarding the correlation of hope and anxiety; he is quick to point out that the two may not be felt at the same time but that the one makes possible the feeling of the other. In his fourth law Shand states that if anxiety succeeds in destroying hope, it not only destroys itself but generates despair. It is the presence of anxiety that inhibits the joyful element in hope. He goes on to say that hope has both a conservative and a creative tendency. It conserves the way to a new situation and is thus one of the "prospective emotions," and it tends to stimulate thought and effort along creative lines, harnessing instinctual energies. From the psychoanalytic point of view, hope represents that factor of mental life which not only provides reassurance against both internal and external onslaughts but diminishes the tragic, uncompromising, unendurable quality of the "dark" affects. It is one of the antidotes to the "dark, unfeeling, and unloving powers" that Freud believed determined human destiny.

ANXIETY AND AGGRESSIVENESS

Quite early in its development, advocates of psychoanalysis discovered the close relationship between anxiety and anger, and further observations led to the assumption that hostile impulses may not only cause fear of retaliation from the other against whom the aggression is directed but may also be transformed into their opposite by incorporated cultural requirements that may command us to love our enemy. Free show of aggression, therefore, involved a marked degree of contradiction that could either paralyze all activity or lead to what the ethologists have referred to as displacement behavior. The contradictions would be difficult to reconcile. Nature, with survival in mind (to phrase it teleologically), had equipped man and all other animals with the instinctual tendency and the accoutrement for attack that were clearly intended for use, while culture, influenced by the "social contract," prohibited the use. Such a discrepancy is conducive to a good deal of psychopathology. The psychobiological correlates of fight and flight are anger and fear, and the two are closely related. Cannon [4] originally demonstrated that the physiological responses that prepare the organism for fight also equip him for flight and that both entail a complex biochemical chain. This biochemical response to danger is not immediately an affect. It may be the first link in the sequence of neurophysiological processes, which interprets the internal or external perception as a signal of possible threat. It would thus seem that the aggressive potential is as inborn and as existential as anxiety.

Anger is the affect traditionally associated with aggression. When reference is made to aggression, it is generally being applied to aggressive behavior whether this be attacking or defensive. In carrying this beyond the descriptive level, aggression can be viewed as psychic energy (the counterpart of libido but with negative *Vorzeichen*), but it participates in the formation of all psychological structures from ego defense mechanisms to complex institutions such as the superego. Aggression, like libido, thus plays a role in every psychiatric or psychosomatic symptom formation.

In brief, the affects of anxiety and anger must be considered as existential and biological components of human life. Both participate in creating the disposition or the systematic affective disorder of depression.

ANXIETY AND DEPRESSION

Anxiety and depression, then, ought not to be regarded as equivalent psychic products nor as similar experiential phenomena. Anxiety is an activating agent. It turns the individual, man or animal, toward the environment the better to know what response to make and how. It facilitates perception, speech, and fantasy, and in this respect one could call it the biological stimulant. In fact, as long as it does not reach the level at which defense needs to be applied or attempted, it promotes mental functioning.

Phenomenologically, depression is the antithesis of all this. It turns vigilance inward and, by withdrawing attention from the environment, brings about a sense of isolation. Instead of activating mental processes, it slows down speech, limits fantasy, diminishes self-confidence, and reduces self-esteem. (Indeed, the "sickness unto death" described by Kierkegaard refers to a depressed condition characterized as *Verdruss*, which is an extreme *Argerlichkeit* with one's self and one's *Umwelt* because the person is unable to change himself or his ambience.)

This elaboration of unconscious signal affects into complex psychic structures is probably a human evolution, but emotional displays reflecting physiological changes in homeostasis are recognizable in the higher animals. Darwin [6] described imitative facial movements and postural changes in the body that are indicative of affects. In fact, love, hate, fear, rage, grief, and sorrow appear to be more intensely expressed in the body language of animals. Since man has at his disposal many shadings of emotional expression, he is not as direct and as unmistakably clear in the communication of affects. Of course we do not know what the animal feels, but it does respond to such signals for extraverted reactions as love, hate, fear, and rage by action. Whether or not it responds to loss and abandonment with introverted reactions of grief and sorrow as a means of self-protective withdrawal has become a major focus of study by ethologists in recent times. Animals may appear sad in such situations, but sadness per se is not an indicator of depressive illness in human beings and therefore would not be so for animals.

Man's capacity for grading his emotional responses is particularly noticeable in the manifestation of moods. Moods differ from affects in that they do originate in physiological and biochemical processes and are not amenable to analysis in terms of psychodynamic factors. Rather, they tend to be pervasive and nonlocalizable. As far as one can tell, under ordinary circumstances animals do not suffer from moods and certainly do not show the shadings of expression seen in humans. Animal studies, therefore, have only limited value in helping to clarify the many problems raised in this Introduction.

DEPRESSION AND THE CONSERVATION-WITHDRAWAL MECHANISM

Anxiety is an existential phenomenon and a biologically based system in the service of survival. Depression is a systemic disorder that differs from anxiety in many fundamental ways that have already been indicated. Yet, there are grounds for believing that the disposition for depression is existential. This is largely based on the pervasiveness of the conservation-withdrawal phenomenon, first conceptualized by Engel [7]. A long-term study of an infant born with atresia of the esophagus offered an opportunity for examining this far-reaching theoretical construct. The infant was fed through a gastric fistula, but she failed to develop physically and emotionally in spite of an adequate caloric intake because her mother, disturbed by the unusual physical condition, could not bring herself to relate to her. Monica was 15 months old when she was brought into hospital with an anaclitic depression. Her physicians arranged for her to have a sustained relationship with two adults, and during the period in which they cared for her she underwent a belated but otherwise normal psychic and somatic development. She became a friendly, smiling, even flirtatious child who showed only one peculiarity: her stranger anxiety was expressed not by crying but by withdrawal. She would turn her entire body away and often would fall asleep. On awaking, she would become friendly again only after the stranger had left the room. Years later, she still retained this tendency to turn away and insulate herself from unpleasant external stimulations. The behavior was first described as withdrawal depression but later was recognized as a defense mechanism and was renamed conservation-withdrawal (see Chapter 9).

The term conservation-withdrawal refers to "biological threshold mechanisms whereby survival of the organism is supported by processes of disengagement and inactivity vis-à-vis the external environment" [8]. It is not exclusively a human response but is manifested throughout the animal kingdom as animal hypnosis, catalepsy, death feint, tonic immobility, and the like.

The place of this type of defense reaction within the self-protective system of the organism has not received as much study as has anxiety. Although it also can be regarded as an existential attribute of living creatures, it belongs to the second line of defense, behind anxiety, and comes into action only if energy required for the first line is exhausted or becomes unavailable.

Both as affect and as a warning signal, anxiety has been well studied, and one could say that in some form and at some level it participates in every psychological process. Whether the conservation-withdrawal mechanism functions as a signal for depression is still an open question. One could regard it as an emergency signal indicating the need for an energy supply that is not forthcoming. Both anxiety and depression may be transformed by the setting in which they appear. Anxiety, for example, is modified in symptom formations and by other psychological processes; the conservation-withdrawal phenomenon is mitigated in typical depressive moods. The sad expression of the infant whose mother has just left the room soon changes as the infant begins to cry. The self-assertion is activated by signal anxiety, but the withdrawal signal may occur without the obvious need for conservation of energy. The withdrawal can be understood as an introversion or a turning in of energy toward the self as object. Individuals with a disposition to such a reaction respond with withdrawal from the environment and a guardedness against it even if the deficiency is not manifest. Engel and his collaborators consider hopelessness and helplessness as emotional indicators of the conservation-withdrawal mechanism.

DEPRESSIVE MOODS

Nostalgia is a typical example of mood. The word *nostalgia* itself comes from the Greek *nostos*, which did not initially mean the pronoun "we" but rather "home" or "nest." It is often translated as "homesickness" and is taken to denote a more or less intense longing for the primary object—mother, for childhood, or for the past in general or particular. The feeling may become painful and is accompanied by a sense of deprivation leading to sadness or depression but not necessarily to depressive illness. Proust's great autobiographical novel in the early part of the twentieth century is a veritable gold mine for the study of nostalgia in all its phases and variations [22]. He illustrates vividly how even painful memories can become a pleasurable preoccupation, how sensual experience can be retained almost unaltered in the memory so that sounds, smells, and tastes are reexperienced in an associative setting in all their pristine brilliance. Anthony [2] has called attention to these "screen sensations" in a clinical context. They may be associated with the pleasures of gratification or the pains of deprivation.

The nostalgic **mood pervaded Proust's life and** personality and almost took possession of his creative impulse. Even when eroticized, nostalgia retains its languid quality. There is never anything exuberant about it. It seems to reflect a reduced vitality. Is it possible that such a display of introversion or withdrawal may be a means of conserving energy? One can only recall the amount of time Proust spent in bed within his hermetically sealed chamber (allegedly to defeat his asthmatic attacks). So immersed was he within himself that his entire personality eventually became adapted to a lower level of energy consumption.

Boredom is another pervasive mood, but in contrast to nostalgia it is not eroticized. It is perceived as a deprivation but one that is self-administered. It is usually associated with feelings of emptiness and with wishes to fill the void, but the longing has no direction and no object. Fantasies are inhibited, and neither the internal nor the external world can arouse any lasting interest. Unlike the nostalgic mood, boredom is more characteristic of adults than of children. The healthy child is typically busy and involved in the world around him, but when he becomes either physically or psychologically unwell, he is a prey to boredom and will pester the adults around him to tell him what to do. He flits listlessly from one occupation to another, unable to settle to anything. According to Greenson, boredom is "a state of longing and an inability to designate what is longed for; a state of emptiness" [12].

Nostalgia and boredom may occur separately, alternately, or, especially with children, transiently together. The psychoanalysis of individuals suffering from pathological boredom reveals a higher than normal ambivalence toward the primary object—mother and reflects the excessive influence of the depressive constellation. The resulting increased tolerance of frustration generates conflicts in every phase of development.

These two depressive moods can be linked together in a single conceptual framework, the formulation for which might run as follows: if, within the object relationship, the positive pole of the ambivalence is dominant, the nostalgia may be eroticized; but if the negative pole is dominant, the aggressive cathexes, when introjected, will account for the hostility aimed at the self and at the mother. This creates a disposition that from time to time interacts with experience to produce the painful inactivity of boredom or depressive illness or both.

According to *Webster's Third New International Dictionary*, the word *boredom* has its origin in the verb "to bore" and means a piercing sensation of emptiness or nothingness. The German word *Langeweile* allows for a more benevolent interpretation. It signifies a long duration and introduces the distortion of time perception that is so characteristic of boredom. It is, for example, a normal experience to find that time spent in waiting appears longer than the clock shows. Ornstein [20] has expanded on the subjective experience of time, relating it to duration and duration to mood. The distortion of time experienced in pathological boredom may be due to the slowing down of the biological clock, which in turn may ensue from conservation-withdrawal.

What is being postulated here is that moods, like so many other basic psychological phenomena, also originate in biological processes. Time experienced in an active, object-directed mood would seem to be normal time. At such moments, one might even be able to tell the chronological time without looking at one's watch. In an elated mood, time seems to pass faster; when one is in a state of withdrawal (as may occur with nostalgia or boredom), time appears to pass slowly. These studies of time and experience lend support to Engel's hypothesis that conservation-withdrawal is a basic biological defense.

Boredom is a more complex mood than nostalgia. The synonyms emphasize different instinctual components of the mood. The English *weariness* refers to a degree of fatigue that implies the wish to leave it all since nothing has any meaning. The French *ennui* is a reference to the ambivalence connected with the primary gratification of food intake. A stronger expression of the same feeling is the synonym *nausée* which Sartre chose for the title of his existential novel. The German *Verdruss* and *Verdriessleikeit* refer to the angry feelings of internal frustration in which the individual has lost the ability to feel gratified; therefore, everything and everybody becomes *Wiederwertig*, that is, a contrary value or meaning; it implies something of the French *nausée*.

In his long discussion of emotions leading to "the sickness unto death," Kierkegaard chose the word *tedium* to express the exhausting monotony of all experience, which conduces to the "pain of emptiness." Neitzsche described the same sensation as *das durchbohreude Gefuhll des Nichts* and termed it *nihilism*.

One could add endlessly to these subtle illustrations of the profound interconnections between mood and language, but these examples of depressive moods will suffice to indicate the variety of instinctual and experiential factors that, beginning with the disposition to conservation-withdrawal, gradually build up into a depression as a systemic affective disorder.

If we turn again to Shand's encyclopedic survey of the affects shaping our lives, he gives the following description of moods:

The moods of emotion to which at times we are subject are caused by bodily states; and it is in these cases that the cause to which they are due is so different from the object to which they come to be referred. For while the cause is some state of the body, the object is something we invent to complete and justify the emotion. For it does not satisfy us to feel an emotion and not be able to refer it to anything in particular; and when a man is in an angry mood, there is scarcely anything, however unreasonable, to which he may not attribute it.

Shand goes on, as usual, to formulate a law that he considers common to all emotional moods: "All moods arise at first without a defined object, but there is an inherent tendency in them to search for one because an object is necessary to organize and direct their impulses." According to him, the mood tends to facilitate emotional reactions—for example, a despondent mood renders one susceptible to attacks of sadness and depression, to slower responses to stimuli, to a diminished sensibility to happiness, and to a weaker regard for hope and confidence.

Shand stresses the importance of bodily factors in the production of mood, citing the example written by Shinn of her little niece, who had such a joyous disposition that she "seemed to fill her days with an exuberant joyousness" [26]. But when she began to teethe, her mood changed radically, and she seemed like a different child—restless, fretful, ready to cry on the slightest occasion, and very demanding of attention and diversion.

Perhaps the most extraordinary thing about Shand's contribution is the way he anticipated much of the current work, even if his descriptions are couched in old-fashioned terminology. Here he is describing depressive reactions in terms of an energy system:

Our attempt to understand the system of sorrow through a study of its most conspicuous varieties of behavior has not disclosed its essential nature, because these varieties have been shown to be determined either by influence of some extraneous system, as anger or fear, or by variations of the amount of energy present in the organism. For we have to take into account of the facts that the degree of energy possessed by any individual may not only differ considerably from that which another possesses, but from that which he himself possesses at other times. If we suppose a sudden sorrow to overtake a man in whom there is little available energy to resist its depressing influence, it is obvious that it will have a more crushing effect than in the case of a man in whom there is a great store of such energy. In one case its influence may be unresisted; in the other, it may evoke a resistance so effective as to mask the depressing effect. The sorrow of a healthy child is often violent in its manifestations when things with which he is engrossed are taken from him: the sorrow of an energetic man is often restless, because there is present the energy to restore, where that is possible, the loss sustained.*

* From *The Foundations of Character* by A. F. Shand, 1920. Reprinted by permission of Macmillan International and Basingstoke.

We close this Introduction by echoing Shand's remark at the end of his careful analysis of the depressive moods and reactions: "To give a profound, comprehensive, and adequate interpretation of sorrow would tax the powers of the greatest minds, nor could it be accomplished by them until all the diverse effects of sorrow in the different systems of the mind had themselves been severally understood."

REFERENCES

1. Amiel, H. *Amiel's Journal; the Intimate Journal of Henri-Frédéric Amiel*. Translated by H. Ward. London: Macmillan, 1885.
2. Anthony, E. J., et al. Screen Sensations. *Psychoanal. Study Child* 16:211, 1961.
3. Barrett, W. *Irrational Man*. New York: Doubleday, 1958.
4. Cannon, W. B. *The Wisdom of the Body*. New York: Norton, 1939.
5. Cassirer, E. *An Essay on Man*. New York: Anchor Books, 1953.
6. Darwin, C. *The Expression of the Emotions in Men and Animals*. London: Murray, 1872.
7. Engel, G. L. *Psychological Development in Health and Disease*. Philadelphia: Saunders, 1962.
8. Engel, G. L., and Schmale, A. H. Conservation Withdrawal. In R. Porter and J. Knight (Eds.), *Physiology, Emotion and Psychosomatic Illness*. Amsterdam: Elsevier-Excerpta Medica, 1972.
9. French, T. M. *The Integration of Behavior*, vol. 1. Chicago: University of Chicago Press, 1952.
10. Freud, S. New Introductory Lectures on Psycho-Analysis and Other Works (1933). In *The Standard Edition of the Complete Psychological Works of Sigmund Freud*, transl. and ed. by J. Strachey with others. London: Hogarth and Institute of Psycho-Analysis, 1964. Vol. 22.
11. Freud, S. Civilization and Its Discontents (1930). *Standard Edition*. 1946. Vol. 21, p. 23.
12. Greenson, R. On boredom. *J. Am. Psychoanal. Assoc.* 1:7, 1953.
13. Heidegger, M. *Sein und Zeit*. Tübingen: Niemeyer, 1957.
14. Husserl, E. *Ideas: General Introduction to Pure Phenomenology*. Translated by W. B. Gibson. New York: Macmillan, 1952.
15. Jaspers, K. *The Way to Wisdom*. Translated by R. Mannheim. New Haven: Yale University Press, 1951.
16. Kaufman, W. (Ed.), *Existentialism from Dostoevsky to Sartre*. Translated by W. Kaufman. New York: Meridian, 1956, p. 141.
17. Kaufmann, W. *Critique of Religion and Philosophy*. New York: Doubleday-Anchor, 1961.
18. Klein, G. Is Psychoanalysis Relevant? In B. Rubenstein (Ed.), *Psychoanalysis and Contemporary Science*, New York: Macmillan, 1973.
19. Murdoch, I. *Sartre: Romantic Rationalist*. New Haven: Yale University Press, 1953.

20. Ornstein, R. E.   *On the Experience of Time.* Baltimore: Penguin, 1970.
21. Pascal, B.   *Pensées.* Translated by W. F. Trotter. New York: Dutton, 1958.
22. Proust, M.   *À la recherche du temps perdu.* Translated by F. A. Blossom. New York: Modern Library, 1932.
23. Sartre, J. P.   *No Exit and Three Other Plays.* Translated by S. Gilbert. New York: Knopf, 1958.
24. Schachtel, G.   *Metamorphosis.* New York: Basic Books, 1959.
25. Schafer, R.   The psychoanalytic vision of reality. *Int. J. Psychoanal.* 51:279, 1968.
26. Shinn, M. W.   *Biography of a Baby.* Boston: Houghton Mifflin, 1900.
27. Whitehead, A. N.   *Adventures of Ideas.* London: Cambridge University Press, 1939.

The Biological and Social Substrate

INTRODUCTORY COMMENTS

It is only within the last few decades that biological factors have been systematically investigated in the laboratory for their possible involvement in the causation of affective disorders. The current eagerness on the part of scientists (and funding agencies) to pursue this line of research is an indication of the hope invested in finding basic answers to a most perplexing group of mental disorders (and hope, as noted elsewhere in this book, is itself a most important ingredient in counteracting depression and despair). Although there are results that show consensus in some areas, serious investigators consider their own findings as merely steps in the right direction. All investigators wish and hope for a new approach that might open another avenue to the deeper reaches of the human brain, unraveling some of its complexity and, perhaps, in some remote future, linking its function to the psychological concomitants. During these years, cause for hope in this area has had its ups and downs; we are now undoubtedly in an era of new enthusiasm. The mechanisms of the human brain have been identified by radioactive labeling, electrical investigations, electron microscopy, enzyme studies, implanted electrodes, and other refined techniques. And although we are still far from correlating the new knowledge of brain function with our insights into mental function, the recent findings, as described by Fawcett and Mandell and Segal in Chapters 2 and 3, are both exciting and suggestive when considered in the context of the affective disorders.

The gap between the catalytic action of the enzyme monoamine oxidase in the brain associated with the clinical development of depressed emotional states, on the one hand, and Kierkegaard's analysis of the existential components of despair or Freud's description of the introjected lost object that "creates hell within the psyche," on the other, appears at first glance to be too large to be bridged from either side, but mediators are appearing on the scene. The reticular activating system (RAS) is now considered the great integrating mechanism of the brain without which any unity of response to the complex conditions of existence is impossible. The fact that the RAS also participates in the control of emotions, can be deactivated by the cortex, and recognizes the impingement of disturbing stimuli from the environment gives the system a central role in the genesis of affective disorders.

What Freud [1] termed biological psychiatry or "the psychological concomitants of biological processes" has moved further with the concept of the visceral brain described by Papez [3], who came closer to our empathic understanding when he raised the question: "Is emotion a magic product, or is it a physiologic process which depends on an anatomic mechanism?" and arrived at a revolutionary concept regarding the mechanism of emotion. It is the limbic system, or "visceral brain," Papez claims, that regulates the response to affect-provoking stimulation. He even suggested, on the basis of this reasoning, what psychiatrists and psychoanalysts have long believed: that "emotional expression and emotional experience may in the human subject be dissociated phenomena," adding that the processes originating within the visceral brain add emotional coloring to psychic processes in the cortex. It also seems to be responsible for the regulation of basic activities (fight, flight, flex, and feeling) in addition to the emotional impulses connected with them. Freud's dual perspective deriving from neuroanatomy and psychoanalysis would undoubtedly have made him empathetic to these mind-brain investigations.

Winokur's work is well known and demonstrates once again the importance of empirical research in providing a solid foothold for any subsequent theorizing or interpretation. The scientific approach to diagnostic classification is surely much needed in psychiatry, where people often use a term like depression to cover a multitude of syndromes. In keeping with the Maudsley-Renard tradition, Winokur prefers to deal with affective disorders as a whole rather than isolating elements of anxiety, depression, and elation, and placing them in a context of their own. His title therefore counterbalances the title of the book, which places special emphasis on one category of the affective disorders although it also deals with the others. The divisions into primary and secondary, bipolar and unipolar, and depression spectrum disease (reminiscent of the Kety-Rosenthal treatment of schizophrenia) and pure depressive disease are buttressed by research facts.

There are connecting themes in the growing body of research. The close relationship found between alcoholism and affective disorder has a psychodynamic link to Rado's work, in which alcoholism was seen as an equivalent of depression. The predominance of female depressives and the possible existence of X-linkage in manic-depressive disease lend support to Benedek's hypothesis that the potential for depression is rooted in the female procreative physiology (see Chapter 7).

The environment is understandably not given much prominence in genetic studies, and geneticists are inclined to regard it, with a somewhat jaundiced eye, as a rival etiological agent. Environmentalists have the same feeling about genetic causality and its explanatory shortcomings. Since the work of Waddington [4], it has been claimed that epigenetic theory has largely displaced genetic theory, and today it is hard to believe that any geneticist would conduct such a passionate love affair with genes as to turn his back completely on the environment. Winokur, as a clinician, seems equally aware of the rival claims, and his family studies offer a good connecting link between the two.

Cultural and sociological factors are epigenetic to the psychodynamic factors that motivate depressive illness in individuals. Discussing psychiatric conditions, such as depression, within the broad frame of culture and under various social conditions that influence the distribution, frequency, variety, and treatment modalities of the illness makes psychiatry modern in the best sense of the word, enabling it to play a critical role in appraising human existence under many different conditions in many different civilizations. As Fábrega puts it:

The psychological study of neuropsychiatric entities such as depression and schizophrenia in various cultures thus presents the researcher with an opportunity to probe the very essence of how culture articulates and rationalizes for man his unique position in the world. . . . When studying these neuropsychiatric entities, the researcher is placed in a strategic position to uncover elemental aspects about man's conception of his place in the world.

Fábrega rightly concludes that because these matters are so elemental, they need to be investigated especially rigorously. How rigorous one can be with "an almost illimitably plastic and responsive human organism," to quote Sir Aubrey Lewis [2], is debatable, but the aim is exemplary.

Psychoanalysis, struggling with its own complexity, can only benefit from examining the complexities of such researches. In becoming acquainted with the endeavors of scientists in adjacent fields, psychoanalysts can appreciate that even the harder behavioral sciences experience a great many problems with methodology and interpretation and cannot offer overall solutions for the complicated problems that beset human existence today. However, the bridges are there and ready to be used.

REFERENCES

1. Freud, S.   New Introductory Lectures on Psycho-analysis and Other Works (1933). In *The Standard Edition of the Complete Psychological Works of Sigmund Freud,* transl. and ed. by J. Strachey with others. London: Hogarth and Institute of Psycho-Analysis, 1964. Vol. 22.
2. Lewis, A.   *Inquiries in Psychiatry.* New York: Science House, 1967.
3. Papez, J. W.   Structures and mechanisms underlying the cerebral functions. *Am. J. Psychol.* 57:291, 1944.
4. Waddington, C. H.   *The Strategy of the Genes.* New York: Macmillan, 1957.

Heredity in the Affective Disorders

1

GEORGE WINOKUR

It is an undisputed fact that depressions and manias are familial disorders. Consider the case of Mr. U., who suffered a first depression in 1926. Forty-one years and seven depressions later he was hospitalized for his first mania in 1967. Of special interest is the fact that his mother had manias and depression; though his father was psychiatrically well, some kind of affective disorder was known in the paternal side of the family. This clustering of affective disorders in the family of a manic depressive is not a unique finding.

Familial does not necessarily mean genetic. Nutritional, infectious, and psychological circumstances could conceivably account for familial clustering of medical and psychiatric syndromes. Nevertheless, as the following material shows, it is very likely that familial does mean genetic in the case of the affective disorders. The data on the affective disorders are so striking that if we were not dealing with a psychiatric illness we would not question the genetic background. Only because of the special psychological quality of the affective syndromes do we even consider the possibility that the familial findings may be due to psychological problems. This chapter will deal with genetic studies of manias and depressions, or, more generally, the affective disorders. We will be dealing with only primary affective disorders, i.e. affective states that arise *de novo* after a period of good social functioning. Secondary affective disorders, which arise in the context of another psychiatric or medical illness, such as alcoholism, anxiety neurosis, or hysteria, will not be considered here. Generally the material will be relevant to severe affective disorders, i.e., those requiring the patient to enter a psychiatric hospital.

The first question that arises is whether the affective disorders should be separated as a group from the functional psychoses. Are schizophrenia and affective disorder aspects of the same illness or separate clinical entities? A considerable body of data supports the idea that schizophrenia and the affective disorders are separate noso-logical entities. Table 1 shows the incidence of affective disorders and

Table 1. Incidence of Affective Disorders and Schizophrenia in Parents and Siblings of Affective Disorder Patients and Schizophrenics

Probands	Parents and Siblings	
	Affective Disorder	Schizophrenia
Schizophrenia (N = 200)	5.5% ⎱ p < 0.0005	2.1% ⎱ p < 0.005
Affective disorder (N = 325)	13.5% ⎰	0.6% ⎰
(100 manics + 225 depressives = 325 total)		

schizophrenia among first-degree relatives in a blind family history study [20]. Three hundred twenty-five patients with affective disorders (100 manics; 225 depressives) and 200 schizophrenics, chosen accord-ing to strict diagnostic criteria, were compared [4]. The family his-tories in the charts were very complete; they were done in the years 1934 to 1944 at the Iowa Psychopathic Hospital. These family his-tories were evaluated without the investigators' knowing the diagnosis of the proband. From Table 1 it is apparent that there is a clear dif-ference between the family histories of affective disorder patients and schizophrenics.

If manic-depressive illness had a relationship to schizophrenia, one would expect some proportion of monozygotic twin pairs to show both illnesses. Although there is considerable concordance in twin pairs for schizophrenia and considerable concordance for manic-depressive ill-ness, manic-depressive disease and schizophrenia are not known to co-exist in a single monozygotic twin pair (see Table 2). The data of most

Table 2. Schizophrenia and Manic-Depressive Illness in Monozygotic Twins (Concordances Cited in Various Studies)

	Manic-Depressive	Schizophrenia
Manic-depressive	33 to 96%	0%
Schizophrenia	0%	6 to 69%

studies indicate an increased incidence of like illness in the families of both diseases, indicating that schizophrenia and manic-depressive disease are separate entities. Any study, familial or otherwise, showing a relationship between schizophrenia and manic-depressive illness must be suspect on the grounds of inadequate diagnostic criteria or methodological problems. Massive amounts of data can be marshalled in opposition to any assertion that schizophrenia and manic-depressive illness belong to the same diagnostic entity [13, 15].

A number of methodologies may be used to investigate the genetic background of an illness: family studies, twin studies, consanguinity studies, chromosome studies, association studies, and linkage studies. In addition, adoption studies and half-sib studies may be used to evaluate whether a genetic contribution is likely. Family studies and twin studies suggest but do not prove a genetic factor. Linkage and association studies are by their very nature the kinds of methods that would prove a genetic factor; they also give considerable information about transmission. Adoption studies and half-sib studies may indicate beyond a shadow of a doubt the presence or absence of a genetic factor; they have also the advantage that they lend themselves to an evaluation of the importance of genetic versus environmental factors [14]. Affective disorders have been investigated in many of these ways. First we will look at the genetic and familial backgrounds of patients diagnosed as having affective disorders. These are patients who present with manias or with primary depressions. We will attempt to differentiate the kinds of affective disorders by using familial and genetic methods.

FAMILY BACKGROUND IN AFFECTIVE DISORDERS

Several kinds of evidence may be used to support the idea that a disease of unknown etiology is genetic. Starting with a mixed group of primary affective disorders, we pursue the evidence that suggests a genetic factor. The first criterion suggesting a genetic background in a disorder of unknown etiology is the expectation that the risks for the same illness would be higher in family members of persons with the illness than in the general population. The incidence of manic-depressive illness in the general population varies between 0.36 percent and 2.5 percent [15], according to studies done in several European countries (e.g., Norway, Denmark, Sweden, United Kingdom, and Iceland). Almost invariably, more females than males are affected. Taking into account all affective states, however, which include patients diagnosed as manic-depressive disease, reactive or neurotic depression, bereavement, etc., the incidence is considerably higher; thus, in Iceland, where one of the most complete studies was done, the incidence for all affective states in the Icelandic population was 6.80 for both sexes, 5.20 for men, and 8.32 for women [5]. Compare this with the incidences in family members of affective disorder patients. Winokur and Pitts [21] found that in 366 affective disorder patients the incidence of affective disorder in the mothers was 22.9 percent and in the fathers 13.6 percent. Parents of 180 medically ill controls had a 1.7 percent incidence of affective disorder. Zerbin-Rudin [25] evaluated the results of 25 separate investigations and noted that the incidence of manic-depressive illness in parents, sibs, and children was 11.7 percent, 12.3 percent, and 16.0 percent, respectively. These data include some known and some probable manic-depressive psychoses as well as suicides. It seems clear that more affective illness is seen in the families of affectively disordered patients than in the general population.

Another finding that would suggest a genetic factor is a greater concordance of the illness in monozygotic than in dizygotic twin pairs. No study exists that contradicts this expectation in manic-depressive illness. Kallmann [6] found 96 percent concordance in monozygotic twins as opposed to 26 percent concordance in dizygotic twins. Slater and Cowie [15] found 50 percent concordance in monozygotic twins versus 23 percent concordance in dizygotic twins. Harvald and Hauge, studying the twin population of Denmark, found 60 percent concordance in monozygotic twins versus 5 percent concordance in dizygotic twins [reported in Kringlen, 7]. Price [11] reported on 12 monozygotic twin pairs in which the members of each pair were reared apart. Eight of the 12 pairs (67 percent) were concordant for affective illness.

A third finding that would suggest a genetic background is the observation that illnesses of the same functional system occur more frequently in families of patients with a particular illness than in the general population. In the case of affective disorders, "the same functional system" may be interpreted to mean "serving the same psychological function." Thus, we might look for other psychiatric syndromes to be overrepresented in the families of manic and depressive patients. In a recent study of depressive probands, 8 percent of the fathers and 11 percent of the brothers had either alcoholism or sociopathy [3]. The figures are higher than those for a control group reported by Robins [12]. Winokur et al. [23] studied 259 alcoholic probands and found a high significant overrepresentation of depressive illness in the family members compared with the general population. Åmark [1], studying a large group of male alcoholics, found that psychogenic psychoses (mainly psychogenic depression) were seen more frequently in relatives than would be expected in the general population. It appears, then, from the available data that alcoholism is quite likely to be related to affective disorder.

Finally, we consider adoption studies and half-sib studies. No adoption studies have been done in affective disorders, but there are some half-sib studies. Kallmann [6] reviewed the material in 96 involutional index families and found that half-sibs had an expectancy of involutional psychosis of 4.5 percent and full sibs an expectancy of 6.2 percent, both higher than the general population figures of .3 percent and .8 percent, respectively. For manic-depressive disease, Kallmann found that full sibs had a risk of 23 to 24 percent and half-sibs a risk of 13 to 17 percent. Assuming a random distribution of environmental factors, we would expect that half-sibs would have a lower risk for manic-depressive illness, since many of them would be the progeny of well parents. Likewise we would expect that the risk for half-sibs would be considerably higher than that for the general population.

One may conclude that the evidence favors the presence of a genetic factor in affective disorders. A logical next step is to assume that such a genetic factor is present and to proceed to look for specific kinds of transmission that might be associated with specific illnesses. It is not unreasonable to assume that the term affective disorders includes a very heterogeneous collection of patients and that more than one illness is present in the group.

In 1966 investigators from three countries, the United States, Switzerland, and Sweden, working independently uncovered evidence that the affective disorders consist of two separate disease entities. The approaches were quite dissimilar, which further strengthens the case for distinct disease entities. Winokur and Clayton [18] started with a group of 426 patients who were admitted to a psychiatric hospital and were diagnosed as having either mania or depression. Pursuing the idea that different illnesses might be inherited in different ways, these investigators divided patients into three groups, one in which two generations of affective disorders were seen (proband and parent or parent and sib), one in which the family history was negative for any kind of psychiatric illness, and a third (discarded) consisting of patients who did not have two generations of affective disorder but may have had some kind of psychiatric illness in the family. The family history positive group (two generations) was compared with the family history negative group (no family history of any kind of psychiatric illness); the data are given in Table 3. The two-generation group contained many patients who were manic at the time of admission; the family history negative group contained a minimal number of these. This suggested that there might be two types of psychiatric illness among the affective disorders.

Table 3.   A Comparison of Manic and Depressive Probands Grouped According to Family History (None Versus Two Generations of Affective Disorders)

	Family History Negative	Family History Positive
N	127	113
Onset before age 50	66%	75%
Index admission = first episode	43%	32%
Proband manic at index admission	1.6%	15%
($x^2 = 13.091$ with Yates correction; df $= 1$, P < 0.0005)		

Angst in Switzerland and Perris in Sweden in separate investigations approached the study of affective disorders in quite a different way. They compared familial illness in two types of patients, those who had only depressions and those who had both manias and depressions [2]. It is clear from their data that manic family members were most often found in the families of manic probands and were unusual in the families of simple depressive probands (see Table 4). Actually the first indication that there might be two illnesses, bipolar and unipolar, came from Leonhard, Korff, and Schulz [8], who noted that manic-depressive patients (bipolar) had more relatives with affective illness than did simple depressive (unipolar) patients.

Table 4.   Affective Disorders in Parents and Sibs of Manic-Depressive Probands and Probands with Depression Only

	Relatives with Mania (percent)	Relatives with Depression Only or Who Committed Suicide (percent)
Probands with Mania		
Angst	3.7	14.3
Perris	10.8	9.18
Probands with Depression Only		
Angst	0.29	11.4
Perris	0.35	14.2

It seems apparent that there are two affective illnesses: manic-depressive disease or bipolar illness, and depressive disease or unipolar illness.

MANIC-DEPRESSIVE ILLNESS (BIPOLAR)

Subsequently, Winokur, Clayton, and Reich [19] studied a group of patients admitted to a hospital for mania, in order to clarify familial transmission and clinical features of the illness. To accomplish this, a family study of 61 manic probands was undertaken. There were a number of striking findings. The modal illness was depression. A considerable number of the family members had had a mania, but most of the affectively ill family members had only depression (see Table 5).

Table 5.   Types of Illness Found in 167 Personally Interviewed First-Degree Relatives of 61 Manic Probands

Type	Percent
Depression only	17
Mania	10
Alcoholism	7
Undiagnosed	2
Psychiatrically well	63
	99

Of the first-degree relatives of 61 manic probands, 167 were personally interviewed. For many of the other relatives, who were either unavailable for interview or had died, family history data were available. The most reliable material, however, comes from the interviewed first-degree relatives. Table 6 presents the morbid risks for affective disorders of any kind in various classes of personally examined relatives.

A number of findings are of interest. Ill mothers outnumber ill fathers, and ill sisters outnumber ill brothers. Siblings and parents are equally ill. There are more ill female relatives than ill male relatives. Of special importance is the fact that there were no ill father–ill son pairs in this particular study. All of these things point to the possibility of X-linkage. An X-linked dominant transmission would involve more females than males showing the illness in the general population and in the family of a manic proband. It would involve manic fathers

Table 6.   Morbid Risks in Interviewed First-Degree Relatives of Manic Patients

	Number Interviewed	Number at Risk	Number Affectively Ill	Morbid Risk (percent)
Affective Disorder				
Mothers	35	33	18	55
Fathers	19	18	3	17
Sisters	45	33	17	52
Brothers	37	24	7	29
Sons	15	6	1	17
Daughters	16	6	5	83
Alcoholism				
Fathers	19	19	4	21

not being able to pass the illness to sons. Mothers, on the other hand, could give the illness equally to sons and daughters. All of these observations were made in the study of the 61 manic probands and their families. A further finding was of considerable significance: alcoholism appears overrepresented in the fathers of these manic probands.

Subsequent studies provided evidence of linkage, with a known marker on the X-chromosome. When two genes, each responsible for a separate trait, are close enough on the chromosome, they assort in a dependent fashion; this is called linkage. In two families, in which both color blindness and bipolar psychosis or manic-depressive illness existed, extended pedigrees were studied [19]. All of the family members who had an affective disorder were either color-blind themselves or were carriers of the gene (in the case of the females). Another study was accomplished using the Xg[a] blood system [24]. The result was positive for X-linkage but fell short of significance for a specific linkage with the Xg[a] blood system. Later observations made by Mendlewicz, Fleiss, and Fieve [9] indicate linkage of bipolar psychosis with the locus for proton and deutan color blindness.

In all fairness, it is important to note that the findings of all investigations have not supported the concept of X-linkage in manic-depressive illness. Perris [10] has published data that are against this possibility. It seems clear that the manic father may sometimes have a manic son. In our own experience this was very rare, and it was not seen at all in the above-mentioned studies. There are a number of possible explanations for this finding, however, even the rare cases. One is that paternity may be in question. Another possibility is that the

X-linked affective illness comes from the mother's side of the family; and, in fact, in many of the cases in which a manic father has a manic son, exploration of the mother's side of the family shows evidence of affective disorder. However, there are also cases in which paternity is not in question and the mother's side of the family is totally free of any affective disorder. The third possibility is that there is more than one type of bipolar psychosis and that these types are transmitted in different fashions, one type X-linked and another type transmitted in an autosomal fashion.

In summary, then, we might say that the genetic data and familial data strongly support separating from the vast group of affective disorders a particular entity that we might call manic-depressive illness or bipolar psychosis. This is an illness that manifests itself with manias and depression. Occasionally a patient will show only manias, but this could be simply an artifact of incomplete examination. The data suggest that a large group of these manic-depressive patients have an illness that is transmitted in an X-linked dominant fashion. In fact it may be better to call the illness an X-linked affective disorder than to call it bipolar psychosis or manic-depressive disease, since most of the ill family members have only depression. It appears that an affective disorder is transmitted in an X-linked fashion, but it may be that another kind of genetic factor is necessary to bring out the mania in an individual with the X-linked illness. The high degree of alcoholism in the families of bipolar patients suggests that alcoholism may be a clinical marker of another process that might conceivably bring out the mania in a person who has the X-linked affective disorder [16, 22].

DEPRESSIVE ILLNESS

Having separated out manic-depressive illness, we are left with a vast majority of affectively ill patients who exhibit only depression. Surely some of these are related to the bipolar patients, but this does not account for the large number that are seen in the hospitals and in the community. Certain things become quite apparent as one looks into patients who have simple depressive illnesses. In a recent study Dorzab et al. [3] reported that family members of rigorously selected depressive patients were more likely to be afflicted with depression than were persons in the general population. Zerbin-Rudin [26] collected data on twin pairs from series reported in the literature: of 20 monozygotic unipolar pairs, 9 or 45 percent were concordant; of 31 dizygotic same-sex pairs 9 or 29 percent were concordant.

In Price's study [11] of 12 monozygotic twin pairs reared apart (at least one member having an affective disorder), it appeared from his case descriptions that nine of the twin pairs had unipolar depressive illness. Four of the nine pairs or 44 percent were concordant for the illness. This was a minimal concordance rate because most of the individuals had not passed through the age of risk for an affective disorder. In view of the likelihood that depressive disease also has a genetic background, a study was done of a hundred patients diagnosed by conservative criteria as having depressive disease. Individuals admitted to the hospital for depression who had relatives with mania were excluded from the study. From this material it is possible to get a fairly good idea of the universe of hospitalized depressive patients as regards both family data and clinical data. Of the family members 129 were systematically and personally examined. Table 7 gives information

Table 7.   Affective Disorder and Alcoholism in Parents and Siblings of 100 Depressive Probands

	Number Ill	Prevalence Throughout Lifetime (percent)
Fathers (N = 100)		
Depression	9	9
Alcoholism	8	8
Mothers (N = 100)		
Depression	18	18
Brothers (N = 118)		
Depression	12	10
Alcoholism	6	5
Sisters (N = 116)		
Depression	17	15

about affective disorder and alcoholism in the parents and siblings of the depressive patients.

No significant alcoholism was found among female relatives. Of considerable interest is the fact that in the families of depressive probands females with depressive illness outnumber males. Alcoholism in the male family members makes up for the deficit in depression in males.

In order to determine whether there might be different types of depressive illness, we combined the systematic family study, family history material, and clinical material from two large studies [17]. The first of these concerns the hundred patients just described. The second study contains data on 345 depressive probands collected as part of another investigation. All the material in the latter group is family history material. No patient among the 345 depressive probands had ever had a mania. We divided the 445 probands, combined from the two studies, in groups according to sex and age of onset. Table 8 gives

Table 8. *Risks (Percent) for Alcoholism and Depression in First-Degree Relatives of 445 Depressive Probands by Sex and Age of Onset (Late, after Age 40; Early, before Age 40)*

	Relatives of Male Probands				Relatives of Female Probands			
	Early Onset (N = 75)		Late Onset (N = 75)		Early Onset (N = 149)		Late Onset (N = 146)	
	Male	Female	Male	Female	Male	Female	Male	Female
Depression	19	21	14	10	12	25	7	16
Alcoholism	6	3	3	−1	10	−1	5	−1
Either	25	24	17	10	22	25	12	16

material on the risks for depression and alcoholism in the four groups: early- and late-onset male probands and early- and late-onset female probands.

It is clear from Table 8 that there are major differences between groups. Early onset probands have more total illness than do late-onset probands. Male probands do not have differences in risks for depressive illness between male and female first-degree relatives, but female probands do show these differences. Male first-degree relatives of early-onset female probands have a high risk of alcoholism. Alcoholism is a lesser risk in male relatives of early-onset male probands and late-onset female probands. The lowest risk of alcoholism in male relatives is seen in the late-onset male group.

As one surveys the four groups of probands, it seems clear that the two groups that are the most different from each other are the early-onset females and the late-onset males. We have proposed that these two groups are prototypes of two separate illnesses, based on the idea that there is not only a different amount of illness in the family but also a difference in the qualitative aspects of illness in the families, i.e. the presence of alcoholism. The early-onset females are the prototype of an illness called depression spectrum disease. The reason for the name is that this illness frequently manifests itself as alcoholism in the male and as depression in the female. The late-onset male is the prototype of pure depressive disease. Here, alcoholism is an insignificant factor. Amounts of illness are less, and there is no increase in depressive illness among the female relatives. The differentiation of the two illnesses is based primarily on qualitative and quantitative differences in the family material. Clinical pictures of the two groups are not so distinct. Essentially the same criteria were used to bring all these patients into the study in the first place; thus, one would not expect in this kind of study to uncover significant clinical differences between early-onset females and late-onset males. What are needed to bolster this differentiation are subsequent clinical and follow-up studies indicating that age of onset and sex are relevant to differences in clinical biological variables.

SUMMARY

There are sufficient data in the literature to suggest a genetic factor in the affective disorder. Studies have suggested that there are two major kinds of affective disorders: manic-depressive disease (bipolar psychosis) and depressive disease (unipolar psychosis). Manic-depressive disease has a higher family incidence of affective disorder than does depressive disease. Evidence also exists that it may be X-linked. Linkage studies with color blindness support the concept of X-linkage in manic-depressive disease. Manic-depressive disease differs from depressive disease in number of episodes as well as age of onset, the former showing more episodes and an earlier age of onset.

Study of depressive disease as an entity suggests a strong possibility of a genetic factor being important in its etiology. Family data suggest the possibility of two types of depressive disease. The prototype of the first type, depression spectrum disease, is the early-onset female who becomes ill prior to the age of 40, shows a large amount of alcoholism among her male relatives, and an increase in depression in female relatives over male relatives. The other prototype, pure depressive disease, is seen best in the late-onset male who shows equal amounts of depression in male and female relatives and a lower amount of familial illness of all kinds than does the early-onset female. Further, alcoholism is relatively infrequently seen in male relatives of late-onset males. The importance of this differential is that it provides a framework for separation of patients into reasonable groups for further biological, psychological, and clinical studies.

REFERENCES

1. Åmark, C. A study in alcoholism. *Acta Psychiatr. Neurol. Scand.* (Suppl. 70), 1951, pp. 1-283.
2. Angst, J., and Perris, C. Zur Nosologie endogenes depressionen vergleich der ergebnisse Zweier untersuchungen. *Arch. Psychiatr. Nervenkr.* 210:373, 1968.
3. Dorzab, J., Baker, M., Cadoret, R., and Winokur, G. Depressive disease: Familial psychiatric illness. *Am. J. Psychiatry* 127:1128, 1971.
4. Feighner, J., Robins, E., Guze, S., Woodruff, R., Winokur, G., and Muzoz, R. Diagnostic criteria for use in psychiatric research. *Arch. Gen. Psychiatry* 26:57, 1972.
5. Helgason, T. The Frequency of Depressive States in Iceland as Compared with Other Scandinavian Countries. In E. S. Kristiansen (Ed.), *Depression. Acta Psychiatr. Scand.* (Suppl. 162) 37:162. Copenhagen: Munksgaard, 1961.
6. Kallmann, F. S. Genetic Principles in Manic-Depressive Psychosis. In J. Zubin and P. Hoch (Eds.), *Depression.* New York: Grune & Stratton, 1954.
7. Kringlen, E. *Heredity and Environment in the Functional Psychosis.* Norwegian Monographs on Medical Science. Oslo: Universitets Forlaget, 1967.
8. Leonhard, K., Korff, I., and Schulz, H. Die temperamente in den familien der monopolaren und bipolaren phasischen psychosen. *Psychiatr. Neurol.* (Basel) 143:416, 1962.
9. Mendlewicz, J., Fleiss, J., and Ficve, R. X-linked Dominant Transmission in Manic-Depressive Illness (Linkage Studies with the Xg^a Blood Group). Paper presented at the 63rd annual meeting of the American Psychopathological Association, New York, March 1973.
10. Perris, C. Genetic transmission of depressive psychoses. *Acta Psychiatr. Scand.* (Suppl. 203) 1968, p. 45.
11. Price, J. The Genetics of Depressive Behavior. In A. Coppen and A. Walk (Eds.), *Recent Developments in Affective Disorders: A Symposium. Br. J. Psychiatry* Special Publication No. 2. Ashford: Headley, 1968.
12. Robins, L. *Deviant Children Grown Up.* Baltimore: Williams & Wilkins, 1966.
13. Rosenthal, D. *Genetic Theory and Abnormal Behavior.* New York: McGraw-Hill, 1970.
14. Schucket, M., Goodwin, D., and Winokur, G. A study of alcoholism in half-siblings. *Am. J. Psychiatry* 128:1132, 1972.
15. Slater, E., and Cowie, V. *The Genetics of Mental Disorders.* London: Oxford University Press, 1971.
16. Winokur, G. Genetic findings and methodological considerations in manic-depressive disease. *Br. J. Psychiatry* 117:267, 1970.
17. Winokur, G., Cadoret, R., Dorzab, J., and Baker, M. Depressive disease, a genetic study. *Arch. Gen. Psychiatry* 24:135, 1971.
18. Winokur, G., and Clayton, P. Family History Studies: Two Types of Affective Disorder Separated According to Genetic and Clinical

Factors. In J. Wortis (Ed.), *Recent Advances in Biological Psychiatry*, vol. 9. New York: Plenum, 1967.

19. Winokur, G., Clayton, P., and Reich, T.   *Manic Depressive Illness.* St. Louis: Mosby, 1969.

20. Winokur, G., Morrison, J., Clancy, J., and Crowe, R.   The Iowa 500: II. A blind family history comparison of mania; depression and schizophrenia. *Arch. Gen. Psychiatry* 27:462, 1972.

21. Winokur, G., and Pitts, F. N., Jr.   Affective disorder: VI. A family history study of prevalences, sex differences, and possible genetic factors. *J. Psychiatr. Res.* 3:113, 1965.

22. Winokur, G., and Reich, T.   Two genetic factors in manic-depressive disease. *Compr. Psychiatry* 11:93, 1970.

23. Winokur, G., Reich, T., Rimmer, J., and Pitts, F. N., Jr.   Alcoholism: III. Diagnosis and familial psychiatric illness in 259 alcoholic probands. *Arch. Gen. Psychiatry* 23:104, 1970.

24. Winokur, G., and Tanna, V. L.   Possible role of X-linked dominant factor in manic-depressive disease. *Dis. Nerv. Syst.* 30:89, 1969.

25. Zerbin-Rudin, E.   Endogene Psychosen. In P. E. Becker (Ed.), *Humangenetik, ein Kurzes Handbuch*, vol. 2. Stuttgart: G. Thieme, 1967.

26. Zerbin-Rudin, E.   Zur Genetik der depressiven Erkrankungen. Paper presented at the Internationalen Arbeitstagung der Psychiatrischen und Neurologischen Klinik of the Free University of Berlin, "Das Depressive Syndrom," February 16-17, 1968.

Biochemical and
Neuropharmacological Research
in the Affective Disorders

2

JAN FAWCETT

There are a number of reasons for the psychiatric clinician to pursue the challenge of a more comprehensive understanding of the affective disorders. For one, the affective disorders have since our earliest recorded history been responsible for as much human suffering as any malady known. With the capacity to destroy hopefulness, the very essence of the human experience, and the will to live, the depressive mood threatens those ventures that promise to advance the human condition and promotes the meaninglessness, self-destructiveness, devaluation of human empathy, and violence that haunt our contemporary civilization. Those capable of tolerating an empathic encounter with a severely depressed individual for any length of time know that the psychic pain that may accompany the affective disorders is as excruciating as any type of pain that is part of the human experience.

A second reason for our attention to this problem is the frequency of the affective disorders. One survey determined the prevalence of affective disorders as 2 to 4 percent; a more recent study has estimated the prevalence of clinically significant depressive mood among persons 15 to 74 years of age at 15 percent [38, 64]. Other estimates suggest that 75 percent of psychiatric admissions are associated with depressive symptomatology, that 20 percent of medical patients have depression of clinical severity, and only that 50 percent of depressed individuals receive treatment for depression [64].

A third aspect of the affective disorders, which relates directly to the theme of this chapter, is their challenge to the mind-body duality that has characterized clinical thinking in psychiatry.

It is the goal of this chapter to demonstrate that knowledge accumulating in the study of the affective disorders is beginning to challenge the either-or thinking that reduces the depressed individual to the operation of a bundle of biochemical, behavioral, or psychoanalytic mechanisms, and to force us to integrate our conceptualizations in order to really understand our depressed patients. The therapeutic efficacy of the antidepressant drugs specifically commands that the clinician develop an understanding of the biochemical and neuropharmacological aspects of affective illness. No clinician who has observed the effect of one of these agents in relieving the torment of a severe depressive state can take the position that an understanding of these aspects of affective illness dehumanizes the depressed patient, when such knowledge is viewed within the context of the spectrum of empathic understanding, psychodynamic skill, and disciplined clinical thinking.

Both clinical descriptions and biochemical explanations can be traced back to Greek medicine, when melancholia was explained in terms of humoral theory as resulting from a predominance of "black bile." Even after psychiatry had recovered from demonology and was restored to the province of medicine, preoccupation with pathophysiological factors persisted.

Contemporary concepts of the psychobiology of depression were influenced by the introduction of electroconvulsive therapy (ECT) in 1934 and then by early studies of adrenal function in depressive illness in the early 1950s. This interest was stimulated by observations of the affective complications of adrenal steroid therapy and disorders of adrenal function such as Cushing's disease and Addison's disease, the availability of assays of adrenal steroids, and Selye's conceptualization of the role of the pituitary-adrenal axis in the organism's response to stress [64]. Early studies demonstrated a correlation of measures suggesting adrenal activation with depressive illness [18].

The efficacy of the monoamine inhibiting drugs (MAOI) and the tricyclic antidepressants (TA) in the treatment of depressive illness, demonstrated in the late 1950s, were the next great impetus to biochemical and neuropharmacological research in depressive illness. By the mid-1960s, knowledge of some of the pharmacological effects of the MAOI and TA drugs, along with evidence that reserpine can induce a depressive state and can affect the monoamine norepinephrine (NE) in the brain, led to formulation of the catecholamine hypothesis [6, 58]. Interest in another monoamine neurotransmitter, an indoleamine, serotonin or 5-hydroxytryptamine (5-HT), developed from similar kinds of evidence [10]. The catecholamine hypothesis stimulated a burst of research into the biochemistry and neuropharmacology of depression because it linked the function of monoamine neurotransmitters to the mechanisms of action of two different classes of antidepressant drugs. While other areas of biochemical research have been pursued, the central focus has remained the monoamines nor-epinephrine and serotonin.

DESCRIPTION AND CLASSIFICATION OF AFFECTIVE DISORDERS

Biochemical research in the affective disorders presents some specific problems of clinical description and classification. The term depression has been applied to a wide spectrum of mood states ranging from unhappiness or dysphoria, to normal grief and catastrophic reactions, to severe life stress through characterological depressions or anhedonic states, to discrete episodes of depression in the manic-depressive individual. While all of these states share the common feature of depressed mood, differences between the various states may be evident to the clinician. If patients with heterogeneous types of depressive illness are grouped for the study of biological variables, individual differences may cancel out any effect due to a given variable. On the other hand, if different types of depressions are compared with respect to a specific variable, contradictory findings may emerge. One investigator has suggested that the term *depression* be used to describe the range of life reactions that result in depressive mood while the term *melancholia* be reserved to designate a typical depressive syndrome with a cluster of typical symptoms [56].

It is obvious that limitations in our clinical definition of depressive illness could pose an obstacle to obtaining information on biochemical variables by the most sophisticated techniques. On the other hand, we must leave open the possibility that our methods of clinical description and classification do not adequately separate depressive subtypes. Depression may be analogous to fever. It is difficult to determine the etiology of a febrile illness on the basis of the fever characteristics alone, despite some typical patterns that have been observed (e.g., malarial fever, Pel-Ebstein disease). Ultimately, we may be forced to conclude that identical clinical syndromes are associated with different biochemical systems. This may explain why it is difficult to predict the response to antidepressant drug therapy in individual patients with similar types of depressive illness.

A review of the various approaches to the diagnosis and classification of affective disorders and an understanding of the problems involved in defining depressive syndromes is relevant to investigations of the psychobiology of depression. In considering various systems, we should keep in mind the purpose of classification. An effective classification has been designated as one that conveys information about similarities between members of a given group and predicts the future course of the illness. It may turn out that a diagnostic classification that is of great value in biochemical research is not as useful to clinicians, but as knowledge of biochemical factors and psychopharmacology advances, a single classification should be formulated that is useful to both the clinician and the clinical investigator.

In any serious effort to understand depression as an illness, signs and symptoms should be described in an attempt to classify various subtypes according to various criteria. The description of syndromes or subtypes of depression could provide a classification of depressive illness that would be useful in promoting understanding of the diagnosis, prognosis, and treatment outcome, and perhaps in permitting correlation of biochemical mechanisms with subtypes of depressive illness. The early work of Kraepelin [36] in separating psychiatric disorders into two groups (he termed them dementia praecox and manic-depressive psychosis) exemplifies such an attempt. He was able not only to separate the two groups in terms of clinical description but to show by follow-up studies that the two classes of illness had different prognoses.

Endogenous vs. Reactive Depression

Gillespie [21] in 1929 divided depressive illness into reactive depression and endogenous depression. This distinction was based on the presence or absence of a precipitating event in the history of the onset of the depression and included other characteristics found to correlate with either endogenous depression (age of onset and presence or absence of certain symptoms such as appetite loss, weight loss, early-waking insomnia, depressive delusions, diurnal variation of mood, loss of libido, and guilt) or reactive depression (onset prior to age 40 and insomnia associated with difficulty falling asleep, self-pity, absence of delusions, and weight loss) [21, 35]. The term *endogenous* suggested that the depressive illness resulted from some intrinsic change, probably a metabolic or other physical change within the patient, as opposed to the reactive depression, which was assumed to result from failure in psychological coping with accompanying disappointment. This classification has persisted, but it has been attacked on both methodological and clinical grounds. Despite the increasing criticism of this classification, studies using advanced statistical and sampling techniques and others relating classification to treatment outcome with somatic treatment (such as electroconvulsive therapy and antidepressant drugs) have continued to define a population of depressed patients roughly corresponding to the endogenous classification. The point is still argued whether the classes are discontinuous or simply extremes on a spectrum of symptoms [34].

It has been frequently asserted that "endogenous" is an unfortunate name for a classification of an illness for which the etiology has not been demonstrated. But at the same time, investigators have suggested that the endogenous group of patients would be the group in which one would be most likely to find biochemical mechanisms related to the etiology of the illness. Further criticism has come from clinical investigators studying the presence of precipitating events in patients with varying types of depressive illness. Many of these investigators suggest that stresses or precipitating events are present in the history of every patient with depressive illness, although it is also argued that groups of patients without depressive illness have an equal frequency of the same types of stressful events in their lives, suggesting that the nature of the stress itself is less important than the vulnerability of the individual in the development of a depressive illness [29].

Psychotic vs. Neurotic Depression

Another attempted classification of depressive illness is the one that has become the accepted standard for the American Psychiatric Association, the dichotomy of psychotic versus neurotic depression. The term psychotic depression here does not imply the presence of a psychosis as defined by a defect in the perception of reality but rather refers to the degree of functional impairment in an individual. Those individuals with severe functional impairment by a depressive illness are included in this category in the American Psychiatric Association's *Diagnostic and Statistical Manual of Mental Disorders*. It should be noted that many clinicians using the psychotic-neurotic dimension base their distinction on the presence or absence of psychotic thinking, such as delusions of poverty, guilt, or persecution, which might lead to a different classification of syndromes than that resulting from the official American Psychiatric Association diagnostic system or the endogenous-reactive criteria.

Factor-Analytic Classifications

An alternative approach to the classification of types of depressive illness is based on the use of various statistical techniques, such as factor analysis or cluster analysis, to group patients by predominant symptoms or other clinical characteristics. One of the earliest efforts to describe a group of depressed patients and to classify their illness into groups using factor-analytic techniques identified four types of depressive syndromes: (1) a group characterized by guilt, hopelessness, and psychomotor retardation, resembling the endogenous depression described earlier; patients in this group tended to respond favorably to ECT; (2) group characterized by agitation and clinging demands for attention; (3) one category of patients which showed relatively mild degrees of depressive affect but tended to be more angry and to dwell on physical symptoms and hypochondriacal preoccupations. These illnesses were found to follow the occurrence of precipitating events, and the patients in this group often had histories of schizophrenic symptoms or borderline psychotic traits. Patients in the last group (4), characterized by a high level of anger in addition to the presence of depressive affect, were found to be not withdrawn prior to the onset of their illness but narcissistic and overaggressive. These categories were based mostly on feelings, behavior, and histories [27].

Differential Responses to Drugs in Agitated, Retarded, and Hostile Types of Depression

A behavior rating scale used in attempting to characterize various types of depressive illness led to the definition of agitated, retarded, and hostile types of depression [47]. One study showed evidence of differential treatment response to major tranquilizers in the agitated group and to antidepressant drugs in the retarded group. Another recent effort to classify patients by types of depressive illness involves treatment response to the antidepressant drug amytriptyline. A multivariate cluster-analysis procedure was employed to group clinical ratings of a heterogeneous sample of depressed patients. One group, a "psychotic depression" group, was made up of older individuals with high scores for depressive delusions, guilt, retardation of movement, anorexia, and delayed insomnia. A second group, *"anxious depressives"* were moderately depressed with additional symptoms of anxiety, fatigue, obsessional symptoms, and depersonalization. This group had a high frequency of neurotic symptoms prior to the depressive illness. The third and fourth groups were both younger; the third group ("hostile") tended to show hostility in addition to depression, while those in the fourth group ("personality disorder") showed milder depression with marked fluctuations relating to environmental events and had histories of antisocial behavior. The psychotic depression group responded best to amytriptyline, and the anxious depressive group responded least; the hostile and personality disorder groups showed intermediate amounts of improvement with this treatment [49].

Primary vs. Secondary Depression

Another recent effort to classify depressive illness, proposed specifically for biological research purposes, demands that a patient's illness first meet depressive mood criteria and demonstrate the presence of a specified number of physiological or neuro-vegetative symptoms of depression before being designated as a case of affective disorder. The affective disorder is then characterized as a primary or secondary depression on the basis of the history. Primary depression is defined as a depressive episode occurring in the absence of other diagnoses except similar depressive or manic episodes. Secondary depression is defined as occurring in the context of another psychiatric illness, including schizophrenia, alcoholism, sociopathy, anxiety neurosis, and hysteria [55].

Recently, family studies described elsewhere (see Chapter 1) have resulted in subdividing the primary depression group into depression spectrum disease and pure depressive disease, based on the occurrence of depression in first-degree relatives. This classification is just now beginning to be utilized in clinical biochemical studies.

While these classifications by themselves may be inadequate in a total approach to the understanding of a patient from a therapeutic point of view, especially in instances where psychotherapeutic approaches are of great importance in the treatment plan, they are of potential value in decisions relating to chemotherapy and in attempts to relate biochemical findings to clinical subtypes. More specific, more adequate classifications of depressive syndromes will help to answer the question whether emerging biochemical factors in any way correlate with clinical symptoms or are observed independent of behavioral subtypes. More rigorous and universally applied systems of classification should at least obviate differences in clinical samples of patients as a cause of variance between studies in biochemical findings.

There is also an important need to develop and apply methods of behavioral measurement that will permit separation of trait variables from state variables in biochemical research involving depressed individuals. As will be noted more specifically later in this chapter, there have been a growing number of questions concerning whether biochemical findings in depressed patients are reflecting the illness itself or merely the patient's altered state as a result of the illness. A good example of this issue is the agitation or retardation aspect of depression. It is commonly found that patients with severe depressive illness show either intense anxiety and agitation or a state of slowed thought, speech, and physical movement called psychomotor retardation. Although these states are dichotomous in appearance, they are not necessarily mutually exclusive, since either might be present at different times in some depressed individuals. It is reasonable to ask whether the increased level of physical activity and excitation seen in agitation or the marked decrease in activity noted in psychomotor retardation is the source of abnormal biochemical findings or whether these findings are reflecting a basic disease process. Without good measures of these behavioral states at the time of the biochemical studies, these questions cannot be answered decisively.

More specific clinical measures and criteria for depressive illness will also permit a more specific appreciation of the possible application of biochemical findings in depressive illness. For instance, at present it is evident that most of the biochemical findings of interest in the field have been derived from the study of severe, hospital-based cases of the illness with symptoms more typical of the endogenous depression group. Whether these findings apply to the much greater number of patients seen in outpatient settings is not yet known. The use of more specific systems of classification may help to answer these questions. Thinking about patients with depressive illness in terms of various subtypes need not rule out an individual, empathic approach emphasizing psychodynamics or existential realities or the interpersonal field of the depressed individual. Sometimes, however, a more descriptive approach to the patient may help in assessing the indications for chemotherapy, partialing out the more biological aspects of the illness, determining the prognosis, and assessing the suicide risk.

The application of more specific clinical thought to depressive illness is probably one of the most important steps needed for advances in the approach to both treatment and research. With this background on the importance of clinical variables, let us proceed to an overview of the current status of biochemical research in affective illness.

THE MONOAMINE DEPLETION HYPOTHESIS

The possible role of altered metabolism of monoamine neurotransmitters in the brain in the etiology of some forms of depressive illness has become the dominant focus of biochemical research in depression over the past ten years. The term monoamine is used to represent several different neurotransmitters (norepinephrine—NE, serotonin—5-HT, dopamine—DA) released at nerve endings as a consequence of neuron firing and serving to stimulate the firing of other neurons whose dendritic processes are stimulated by transsynaptic diffusion of these chemicals. These substances all share one structural property, a terminal single amine (NH_2) group.

The current interest in monoamines is a direct consequence of the recognition of the effectiveness of the tricyclic (imipramine group) and monoamine oxidase inhibiting (MAOI) drugs introduced about 1958 for the treatment of depressive illness. The appearance of the catecholamine depletion hypothesis of depression in 1965 heralded an upsurge of research that included studies of NE and 5-HT metabolism in animal nervous systems (in vivo and in vitro) and clinical biochemical studies [6, 58]. The hypothesis stated that some types of depressive illness are related to a *depletion of NE at nerve endings of noradrenergic fibers in the hypothalamus*. The hypothesis was based on neuropharmacological evidence that the tricyclic antidepressant and MAOI drugs act by different mechanisms to increase functional NE in hypothalamic areas and that they can block the effects of NE-depleting drugs such as reserpine in animals. This body of observations was linked to the finding of a significant incidence of clinical depression in patients receiving reserpine for the treatment of hypertension [6, 58]. The catecholamine depletion hypothesis implies that a depressive state may be the result of a depletion of functional NE in hypothalamic tracts, which can be benefitted by the tricyclic and MAOI drugs acting to increase these levels of functional NE. The causes of the hypothesized depletion have not yet been determined. Other investigators, especially those working in England and other parts of Europe, have put forth evidence suggesting a similar or parallel role for the indole monoamine serotonin (5-HT) in depressive illness.

Before we review the evidence suggesting the possible role of monoamine neurotransmitters in depressive illness, let us give a capsule summary of the anatomy and metabolism of these neurotransmitters to introduce the terminology and to keep later discussions comprehensible to the clinician who has not closely followed this line of research. The reader who is familiar with this basic work may wish to skip the next few paragraphs.

New techniques for studying the neuroanatomy of the brain have in recent years permitted the localization of cell bodies, axons, and terminal endings of neurons releasing specific monoamine neurotransmitters making up systems or tracts that influence behavior. The definition of NE and 5-HT systems in the brain became possible through two basic techniques: the use of small lesions, which affect changes in the concentrations of these neurotransmitters, and the use of histochemical fluorescence-labeling techniques, which permit the differential visualization and mapping of NE and 5-HT systems in the brain [15, 43, 68]. Six monoamine systems—two NE systems, one 5-HT system, and three DA systems—have been identified in the rat brain. Significant species differences probably occur, but in view of the emphasis on NE and 5-HT metabolism in depressive illness it may be of value to review the tracts utilizing these neurotransmitters.

The *dorsal NE system* arises from cell bodies of the pontine nucleus locus ceruleus, ascends in the mid-reticular formation of the pons, and

at the junction of the mesencephalon and diencephalon (zona in-
certa) joins the ventral NE bundle in the *median forebrain bundle*. It
gives off branches to the anterior ventral thalamus, hypothalamus,
amygdala, and contralateral cortex while the bulk of its fibers terminate in the septal region and at terminals in the cortex and hippocampus. This system has been associated with the notion of a pleasure
center, based on repetitive bar-pressing behaviors of rats for self-
stimulation via electrodes implanted in this system. The *ventral NE
system* arises in cell bodies in the medulla and pons and ascends in the
mid-reticular formation, continuing in the mesencephalon in the
median forebrain bundle. It gives off terminals to the substantia grisea
centralis cerebri that are in contact with 5-HT nerve cells and to the
entire hypothalamus and amygdaloid cortex. Its specific functions are
unclear, but its proximity to the 5-HT system suggests a functional
relationship [68]. A lesion in the *ventral NE bundle* has resulted in
hyperphagia refractory to the anorexic effects of amphetamine.

Serotonin (5-HT) systems have been less clearly defined, but an
ascending system of 5-HT neurons arising from cell bodies in the
raphe nucleus of the mesencephalon, whose axons enter the median
forebrain bundle has been described. Widespread terminal fibers to
the suprachiasmatic nucleus, cortex, septum, caudate nucleus, anterior
perforated substance, interpeduncular region, pretectal area, thalamic
nuclei, most hypothalamic nuclei, amygdala, hippocampus, and
globus pallidus have been indicated by fluorescence techniques. Since
it is difficult to visualize 5-HT terminals with existing methods, they
may be even more widespread than we now know. Stimulation of the
raphe nuclei associated with this system produces calmness and EEG
patterns similar to those of normal sleep. Destruction of these nuclei
in the rat results in an increase in spontaneous motor activity, spontaneous rotary movements, and hypersensitivity to auditory stimuli.

The monoamine systems involving NE and 5-HT are summarized
here (evidence suggests that dopamine systems are not primarily related to affective disorders) as they have been mapped out in the rat
brain. One would expect that the behavioral significance of these
tracts might differ greatly in humans. It is important, however, to see
that specific systems involving NE and 5-HT can be traced in the
brain and that these systems appear implicated in certain behaviors
on the basis of stimulation or lesion experiments. These systems all appear to be involved primarily with subcortical functions especially associated with the hypothalamus and limbic system.

Turning to the metabolism of monoamine neurotransmitters, it is
helpful to have some knowledge of the basic steps in the synthesis and
degradation of NE and 5-HT in order to understand the implications

of the biochemical research relating to depressive illness and the pharmacology of antidepressant drugs. Figure 1 illustrates the pathways of synthesis and metabolic breakdown of norepinephrine (NE). The amino acid tyrosine is hydroxylated in a *rate-limiting* step by the enzyme tyrosine hydroxylase to form dihydroxyphenylalanine (dopa). Dopa is decarboxylated, forming dopamine (DA), which is also known to be a neurotransmitter in the basal ganglia, hypothalamus, and limbic system. DA is hydroxylated to form NE. Many studies of clinical depression and the pharmacology of the antidepressant drugs involve measurements of the breakdown products of NE. The break-

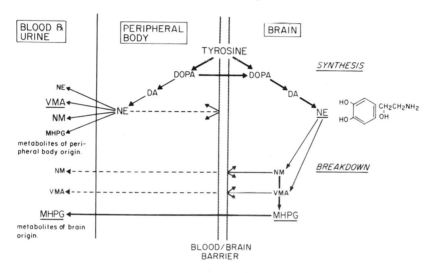

Figure 1.   Synthesis, breakdown, and excretion of norepinephrine.

down of NE occurs through an initial step of oxidative deamination by intracellular monoamine oxidase (MAO) to vanillylmandelic acid (VMA). NE may be further O-methylated by an extracellular enzyme catechol-O-methyltransferase (COMT) to form normetanephrine (NM). NM and VMA can be further metabolized to the metabolite 3-methoxy-4-hydroxy phenylglycol (MHPG). NE is broken down and excreted in the form of these three metabolites. NE metabolism is studied both grossly through determinations of levels of these substances in body fluids such as blood, urine, and cerebrospinal fluid (CSF) and at a cellular level through in vivo studies of preparations of noradrenergic nerve endings. The technique of studying cellular NE metabolism involves the subcellular fractionation of noradrenergic nerve endings (such as those in the NE systems outlined earlier) by a technique of ultra high speed centrifugation of brain tissue in a gradient of sucrose concentrations; this permits the separation of small "bags" of broken-off nerve endings called synaptosomes. Synaptosomes and their ultrastructure can be visualized in electron photomicrographs and preserved in in vivo preparations, allowing studies of metabolic dynamics of neurotransmitters and their interaction with various drugs.

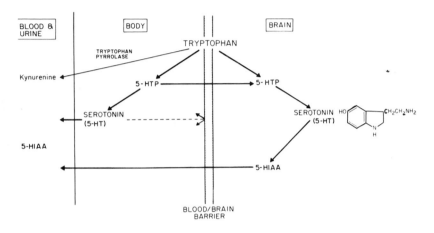

Figure 2.   Synthesis, breakdown, and excretion of serotonin.

Figure 2 summarizes the synthesis and breakdown of serotonin (5-HT). The amino acid L-tryptophan is hydroxylated to 5-hydroxytryptophan (5-HTP), which in turn is decarboxylated to form 5-hydroxytryptamine (5-HT), or serotonin. Serotonin is broken down to the metabolite 5-hydroxyindoleacetic acid (5-HIAA). Another pathway of excretion involves the conversion of tryptophan to kynurenine by tryptophan pyrrolase, an enzyme found in the liver. This appears to be a "throwaway" pathway for tryptophan that decreases the availability of tryptophan as a precursor of serotonin (5-HT). It is of interest, as will be considered later, that tryptophan pyrrolase activity is increased by adrenal cortical hormone activity.

Figure 3 illustrates a vastly simplified diagram of a noradrenergic nerve ending derived from its actual appearance in electron photomicrographs of synaptosome preparations; the figure also illustrates hypothetical receptor sites and the synaptic cleft separating the two. NE is portrayed as being released by electrical impulses from a protein-bound state in intracellular granules to a free functional state across the nerve ending membrane in the synaptic cleft, where it acts at receptor sites on dendrites of other neurons. Intracellular mitochondria containing monoamine oxidase are shown. The mitochondria, norepinephrine granules, and terminal membrane are all visible in electron photomicrographs. The synaptic cleft and receptor sites are hypothetical. Released NE is reuptaken by the terminal membrane and undergoes oxidative deamination intracellularly, producing the major breakdown product of NE, VMA. Extracellular NE is O-methylated by the enzyme COMT, found extracellularly to NM. A further breakdown product, MHPG, is also formed. The importance of this metabolite lies in the fact that MHPG may be the only breakdown product of NE that can diffuse out of the brain. The significance of NE and its metabolites, particularly MHPG, are reviewed on page 35.

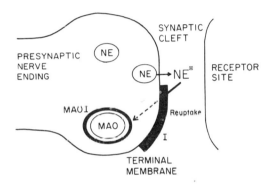

Figure 3. Terminal noradrenergic function (NE = norepinephrine; I = imipramine-like drug; MAO = mitochondria containing inactive metabolites; MAOI = monoamine oxidase–inhibiting drug).

The mechanisms of the antidepressant drugs are also illustrated in Figure 3. The tricyclic drugs, such as imipramine, block reuptake, thus increasing free functional NE by slowing its rate of intracellular inactivation. MAOI drugs increase available NE by inhibiting intracellular monoamine oxidase. The diagram illustrates in simplified form the present state of knowledge derived from electron photomicrographs of separated terminal nerve endings (synaptosomes) of noradrenergic fibers in the hypothalamic region of the brain. The illustrated mechanisms of antidepressant drug action are derived from in vivo and in vitro studies of isolated synaptosomal function using radioisotope-labeled precursors of NE and from studies of deaminated and methylated metabolites in animals pretreated with the antidepressant drugs. Further reference will be made to these studies in the following review of studies of NE metabolism and antidepressant drug effects on page 36.

An effort has been made to outline a basic neurochemical hypothesis of depressive illness related to the observed clinical effects of the two primary classes of antidepressant drugs and to the less commonly observed but documented depression-inducing properties of norepinephrine-depleting (and serotonin-depleting) drugs. The specific nerve systems that operate with NE and 5-HT neurotransmitters and that serve subcortical (basic drive) functions through connections with hypothalamic areas and the limbic system were reviewed here to illustrate that both the structure and the function of nerve systems utilizing these monoamines as neurotransmitters to regulate their function have been identified and are under study in lower mammals. The synthesis and breakdown of these monoamines and the affect of antidepressant drugs on the function and metabolism of these substances was briefly reviewed in anticipation of a review of clinical studies in humans.

Research involving humans requires a leap from a schematic concept of single cell function in which nerve endings (synaptosomes) can be visualized in electron microscope photographs to the measurement of breakdown products in peripheral body fluids as evidence for altered metabolism associated with depressive illness and with the action of various antidepressant drugs. This leap from "the cell" to total body metabolism of monoamines as a basis for inferences about altered monoamine metabolism in the brain, that miracle of complexity that we struggle to comprehend as it translates electrical and chemical energy into human feelings and behaviors, must be made with humility, perseverance, hope, and courage: our most advanced methods are still crude in light of the task. What follows is an attempt to present the most fruitful results of our efforts to understand the neurobiochemical substrate of one of man's most profound and painful experiences. To proceed in the studies, we must utilize approaches that are analogous to attempting to understand the function of the internal combustion engine by analyzing the composition of its exhaust products, without being able to look inside the engine. The methods even at this level are subject to many shortcomings, recognized and unrecognized, but they are all we have to study the biochemical basis of hopelessness, lifelessness, indecisiveness, panic, and dread that are sufficient at times to drive an individual to self-destruction, to the living death that we call depression.

MONOAMINE METABOLISM IN DEPRESSION

Studies relating monoamine metabolism and depression have for the most part focused on the catecholamines (NE and its metabolites) and the indoleamines (serotonin and its metabolites) since the wave of interest in these compounds began in the early 1960s. With the understanding that no definitive proof exists that altered monoamine metabolism is an etiological factor in even certain types of depressive illness, an attempt will be made to summarize the issues, conclusions, and implications at this time.

The investigations reviewed have in general been aimed at evaluating the hypothesis that depression is associated with a decrease in functional brain NE. This state could result from a wide range of factors, intrapsychic, environmental, or constitutional, operating through a number of possible mechanisms.

Catecholamines

STUDIES CORRELATING CATECHOLAMINE METABOLITES IN BODY FLUIDS
WITH DEPRESSIVE STATES

Early correlation studies of NE and its metabolies, NM and VMA, in general indicate decreased urinary excretion of these substances in retarded depressions and increases in agitated depressions and especially in manic states. Some of these studies suggested that the changes could be observed preceding the onset of mania or depression [4, 33]. Moreover, although these metabolites can be increased by physical activity, the available evidence does not support the conclusion that the observed changes can be accounted for by this variable. As with many biochemical studies of psychiatric illness, however, a major limitation of these studies is the fact that only a very small percentage of the metabolites measured represents NE metabolism in the brain; these metabolites are products of peripheral NE metabolism for the most part.

The finding that another metabolite of NE and NM, MHPG, may provide an index of the synthesis and breakdown of NE in the brain has therefore been of great interest. The assumption that urinary or CSF levels of MHPG may provide an indicator of brain NE metabolism has been based on radioisotope studies of brain metabolism in live mammals (cats, rats, and dogs). These studies suggest that 30 to 50 percent of urinary MHPG may originate in the brain as opposed to peripheral body metabolism of NE [42, 45]. Studies of MHPG excretion in a heterogeneous group of severely depressed patients revealed decreased MHPG excretion with no differences in NM and VMA excretion in about two-thirds of the patients as compared with nondepressed control subjects [40]. As long as MHPG is considered an indicator of brain NE metabolism, this finding tends to support the catecholamine depletion hypothesis in at least some cases of depression. Most of the subsequent studies of MHPG levels in urine and some though not all studies of MHPG levels in CSF of depressed patients have confirmed this finding [3, 4, 26, 33, 39, 42, 50, 61, 65, 66]. The question has also been raised whether the decreased MHPG levels might be artifacts of the decreased physical activity that is often associated with depression [50]. This objection has not been upheld by studies of agitated depressed patients and exercised subjects, who show changes in NE, NM, and VMA levels but no significant increase in MHPG levels [25, 60]. In addition, studies of MHPG levels in bipolar affective disorders have shown decreases in MHPG prior to the onset of depressive swings and increases in MHPG prior to the appearance of the manic state with its increased activity levels [4, 33]. Radiosotope studies in controls and patients tend to rule out peripheral factors as a cause of the decreased MHPG [42]. At this point, MHPG appears to be a promising metabolite for the study of altered NE metabolism in the brain in depressive illness.

In an effort to relate clinical features of depressive illness to drug response and altered MHPG levels, it has been found that patients with primary depressions have diminished MHPG excretion compared to patients with secondary depressions [39]. Other approaches have found that decreased MHPG levels tend to be correlated with bipolar and schizo-affective depressions [61, 62]. Despite early agreement in studies correlating decreased MHPG levels with depression and increased levels with mania, further studies are needed to replicate this correlation, and more data are needed to support the assumption that MHPG reflects the availability of functional NE in human brain (this is still questioned by some investigators) and to rule out other factors that might cause these changes, before the findings of these studies can be accepted as support for the catecholamine depletion hypothesis [66]. At this time, studies of MHPG levels appear to be a productive approach to relating clinical and metabolic aspects of depression.

DRUG EFFECTS AND NE METABOLISM IN DEPRESSIVE ILLNESS

An early study of NE metabolites in urine during the administration of the tricyclic antidepressant drug imipramine and MAOI drugs showed a decrease in the intracellularly formed deaminated O-methylated metabolite VMA, with a concomitant increase in the extracellularly formed O-methylated NE metabolite NM, related to the course of improvement during treatment with imipramine [59].

A correlation of therapeutic response to desipramine and imipramine in patients with low MHPG levels and a lack of improvement in patients with normal or increased MHPG levels suggested a further linking of biological subtypes of depression on the basis of brain NE metabolism with the mechanisms of the tricyclic drugs [19, 41]. A similar correlation between MHPG, mood response, and tricyclic response was seen in patients showing transient but definite improvement with dextroamphetamine [19]. Subsequent studies involving small groups of patients have for the most part confirmed a relationship of therapeutic response and low MHPG excretion [3, 57]. These two recent studies have suggested that depressed patients with normal or elevated MHPG may respond to another tricyclic antidepressant drug, amytriptyline. The findings of a relationship between a metabolite presumed to be an indicator of brain NE metabolism, MHPG, and antidepressant drugs presumed to act through their effect of increasing functional NE suggests the possibility of a biological classification of depressive illness and the prediction of therapeutic response to tricyclic antidepressant drugs. These exciting possibilities require further study and evaluation before they can be taken seriously.

Other drugs have been administered to depressed patients in attempts to alter the depressed state with agents known to have various effects on NE metabolism. The transient ameliorative effect of dextroamphetamine in depressed patients with decreased MHPG excretion and subsequent improvement with imipramine or desipramine therapy suggest a common mechanism of action shared by the two agents (blocking of NE reuptake).

Because dopa is a precursor of NE synthesis, it was expected that the effect of administering this substance might confirm the catecholamine depletion hypothesis by reversing depressive symptoms through a resultant increase in brain NE. Studies of the effects of dopa on depressive illness showed some improvement in a small proportion of unipolar depressions while bipolar patients showed transient symptoms of mania *without* relief of depressive mood. The failure of dopa to have a predictable effect may be explained by the possibility that dopa does not increase brain NE but does increase dopamine levels and perhaps acts in many mechanisms as yet unknown [23]. Lithium carbonate, a salt that may decrease functional brain NE by enhancing reuptake, can normalize a manic state, but it has also been shown to have a prophylactic effect on recurrent depressions, particularly in patients with a history of bipolar illness. There is some disagreement concerning the effect of lithium (which lowers urinary MHPG excretion) in acute depressive illness. Apparently a few patients do benefit from the use of lithium in the acute treatment of depression [24]. It does not appear, however, that lithium is an effective antidepressant in the majority of depressions [24]. The prophylactic effects of lithium in recurrent depression may stem from its regulatory effect on NE metabolism in brain. In summary, the finding of a relationship among low MHPG excretion, improvement in depression with tricyclics of the imipramine-desipramine group, and transient response to amphetamine with an absence of effect of these drugs in patients with high or normal MHPG associated with depression tends to fit with the catecholamine depletion hypothesis and suggests an explanation of other types of depressive illness (serotonin depletion, learned depressions).

THE INDUCTION OF DEPRESSIVE SYMPTOMATOLOGY
WITH NE-DEPLETING DRUGS

If a relative depletion of brain NE is one mechanism underlying depression, then it might be expected that drugs that cause a depletion of functional brain NE should produce symptoms of depression. The original formulation of the catecholamine depletion hypothesis was based on the observation of a 15 percent incidence of depression in patients receiving the drug reserpine in the treatment of hypertension [38]. More recently it has been claimed that the true incidence is closer to 3 to 6 percent and that the depression usually occurs in individuals with a history of spontaneously developing depression [46]. The production of depression following the withdrawal of dextroamphetamine in chronic users, which was associated with a decrease in MHPG excretion, provides another observation that appears constant with the catecholamine depletion hypothesis [62].

The administration of a drug, α-methyltyrosine, known to inhibit the production of NE through the inhibition of tyrosine hydroxylase, a rate-limiting enzyme in NE synthesis, should be a good illustration of the catecholamine depletion hypothesis. Clinical studies indicate that the drug initially produces sedation, followed by depression in some hypertensive patients. Hypomanic reactions have also been noted following its withdrawal [5, 46, 67]. It has been shown subsequently that α-methyl-para-tyrosine acted to decrease manic symptoms while tending to *increase* the severity of depressions in a small series of depressed patients. During these studies, a 50 percent decrease in VMA and MHPG excretion was observed [5]. α-methyl-para-tyrosine was also administered to nonhuman primates, resulting in changes in behavior and appearance resembling a state of retarded depression concomitant with a decrease in MHPG and VMA excretion [54].

Para-chlorophenylalanine, known specifically to deplete brain seroto-nin, had no similar effect despite evidence of decreased 5-HT turn-over [54]. In general, the observation of behavioral effects of drugs that would be expected to deplete brain NE lends evidence to the thesis that depressive symptomatology or the suppression of manic symptoms can be produced by brain NE depletion.

Other miscellaneous findings relating to the possible role of NE metabolism in depression include correlation studies of another amine found in brain, beta-phenylethylamine, which is excreted in decreased amounts by depressed patients and is found in increased amounts in manic patients. [56]. The excretion of this compound is also increased by both types of antidepressant drugs.

It is concluded at this time that there is evidence to support the catecholamine depletion hypothesis of depression. The evidence is based on generalizations of the role of MHPG as a possible indirect measure of brain NE from several animal species to man, in the ab-sence of crucial evidence as to what MHPG measured in peripheral body fluids indicates about brain NE metabolism in the human sub-ject. The evidence, though positive, is incomplete; confirming data are limited, and unexplained discrepancies in studies exist. While the present catecholamine depletion hypothesis may be vastly oversimpli-fied, it is clear that further studies in this area are needed.

Indoleamines

The catecholamine depletion hypothesis has also led to a great deal of interest in the indoleamine serotonin. This monoamine was found to be affected in the same way as NE by the tricyclic and MAO in-hibiting antidepressant drugs. At the present time, the growing litera-ture on 5-HT metabolism in depression tends to emphasize the effects of the MAO inhibiting drugs rather than the tricyclic compounds.

The literature on 5-HT and its metabolites in depression presents contradictory findings on several key points. These discrepancies prob-ably result from the large number of studies that have been done to replicate various findings. The review that follows will attempt to summarize the most salient findings from the studies of 5-HT metab-olism up to the present. From this literature and the findings relating catecholamine metabolism and depression there may be emerging a set of depressive syndromes involving NE, 5-HT, and perhaps other as yet undetermined biochemical systems. This may explain some of the discrepant biochemical findings and varied clinical responses of patients with similar-appearing depressive syndromes to various anti-depressant drugs.

STUDIES OF 5-HT METABOLITES IN BODY FLUIDS OF DEPRESSED PATIENTS

There have been a number of studies of 5-hydroxyindoleacetic acid (5-HIAA) in the urine and CSF of depressed patients. A majority of these studies show a pattern of decreased levels of 5-HIAA in urine and CSF in patients as compared with normal levels in nonpatients [2, 4a, 10, 13, 20, 30, 48, 69, 70, 71, 72]. There are contradictions, however: a few studies do not find decreased 5-HIAA levels in depressed patients. Studies attempting to relate 5-HIAA metabolism to depressive subtype have reported lower 5-HIAA levels in unipolar than in bipolar cases, and lower levels in psychotic depression than in reactive depression [2]. Some studies showing the decrease in 5-HIAA levels in CSF have shown persistently low values even after recovery [13]. Studies of urine excretion and CSF levels of 5-HIAA in manic patients have shown either elevated or normal values, and a recent study demonstrated an increase in CSF 5-HIAA levels in depressed patients under conditions of active exercise or "simulated mania" [50]. Further attempts to demonstrate reduced 5-HT production in the brain during depressive illness have employed the technique of administering the drug probenecid in sufficient doses to block the passage of 5-HIAA out of the CSF. Under these conditions of blockade, it is claimed, the rate of increase of 5-HIAA in CSF provides an estimate of the turnover rate of 5-HT in the brain [25, 69, 70]. Most of the studies employing this technique have demonstrated a significantly lower rate of accumulation of 5-HIAA. Variations in this rate of accumulation, it has been suggested, may indicate different subtypes of depressive illness. Further studies are needed to clarify the contradictory findings. One study compared the effects of 5-HTP versus placebo in ten patients with severe endogenous depressions. Each of the patients had been evaluated for rate of accumulation of 5-HIAA in CSF after blockade with probenecid. Three of the five patients receiving 5-HTP showed improvement; these three had abnormally low 5-HIAA accumulation in CSF when tested. Of the two patients not responding to 5-HTP, one showed normal 5-HT accumulation and one showed subnormal accumulation. No improvement was noted in the placebo group [70].

Another approach to studies of 5-HT metabolism in brain has been the assay of concentrations of 5-HT and 5-HIAA in various areas of the brain of suicide victims and comparing these levels with those determined in accident victims who died suddenly. Two studies of this type showed decreased 5-HT levels in the hindbrain of the suicides; a subsequent study did not find this difference but noted a decreased level of 5-HIAA [4a]. In none of the studies were significant differences in NE concentration measured in the brains of those dying from suicide as opposed to those dying from natural causes. The significance of these studies can be questioned in view of the numerous variables (prior medication, changes at death, age of victim) that could affect the results of the assays, but the findings across studies point to decreased levels of 5-HT and its metabolites in the brains of those presumed to have died as a result of severe depressive illness.

In general, then, a body of findings is accumulating that, despite differences and contradictions, continues to implicate a decrease in brain 5-HT in at least some types of depressive illness.

INTERACTION OF 5-HT METABOLITES, DEPRESSIVE SYNDROMES, AND ANTIDEPRESSANT DRUGS

Two studies have found a correlation between decreased urinary 5-HIAA excretion and response to MAO inhibiting drugs while another study has failed to demonstrate this relationship [20, 30, 48, 71]. One study showed that of patients receiving nortriptyline, the response of those with a CSF 5-HIAA levels below 15 ng per liter was considerably diminished even though the plasma nortriptyline level was well within the therapeutic range. It is of interest that nortriptyline differs from most tricyclic compounds in that it does not inhibit the reuptake of NE and 5-HT in the same way; NE is preferentially affected. That this compound has diminished efficacy in patients where CSF studies show a slowdown of 5-HT turnover would seem to support a specific relationship between antidepressant drug effects and the underlying 5-HT depletion associated with the syndrome.

BEHAVIORAL EFFECTS OF TRYPTOPHAN

There is a great deal of disagreement as to the effects of tryptophan, both combined with MAO inhibitors and alone, in depressive illness. Several studies have shown a potentiation of MAO inhibitors by tryptophan and 5-HTP, while other investigations have not confirmed this effect [11, 30, 72]. An antidepressant effect of tryptophan in depression was replicated recently in a double-blind study of this effect; other attempts to replicate the effect had failed [12]. It may be that tryptophan does have an effect in depressions related to serotonin metabolism but no effects in other types of depression. The finding that an amino acid in large doses might relieve certain depressions raises the interesting possibility that an individual with a known predisposition to "serotonin depressions" might prevent them by dietary changes during periods of increased psychological stress. The literature on serotonin and its metabolites in depressive illness, though replete with contradictory findings, continues to suggest that brain indoleamine metabolism may play a key role in some depressive syndromes. As in the case of the catecholamines, further research is needed to clarify the role of these monoamines in depressive illness.

Comprehensive Monoamine Hypotheses

The data available on the catecholamine depletion hypothesis at this point suggest that there are depressive syndromes in which mono-amine (NE or 5-HT) depletion plays a major role and that the effect of antidepressant medication is related to the type of depletion involved. As one might expect, it becomes clearer that no simple explanation will explain all depressive illness or even all of any one clinical subtype of depression. In other words, both of the monoamine systems, the catecholamines and the indoleamines, may play significant if not singular roles in subtypes of depressive illness that at this point are clinically indistinguishable.

The evidence available seems to suggest that both the catecholamine and indoleamine systems are related to the depressive syndrome itself and to the drugs that may effect a therapeutic response (various tricyclic drugs, MAO inhibitors, lithium, L-tryptophan, or even L-dopa) in certain instances. Observations point to monoamine depletion as one important factor in depressive illness and in the discrepancy in findings of some of the studies summarized. Other discrepancies may relate to the presence of factors not related to the monoamines.

We have reviewed correlation studies of metabolites as well as studies drawing inferences from the behavioral and biochemical changes resulting from the administration of antidepressant drugs or precursors of NE or 5-HT. There have been more recent trends toward the examination of the monoamine depletion hypotheses through the use of enzyme inhibitors and other agents that should result in the depletion of various monoamines in humans. A very recent review [46] of the effects of reserpine, which is believed to promote the release and depletion of monoamines, α-methyltyrosine, which is thought to deplete NE selectively by the competitive inhibition of the enzyme tyrosine hydroxylase (the rate-limiting enzyme that controls NE production), and para-chlorophenylalanine, which has the predominant effect of depleting 5-HT levels, reports that none of these drugs typically induces depressive states in humans as one would predict on the basis of the monoamine hypothesis. This review specifically questions the frequently repeated effect of reserpine in producing depressive symptomatology and asserts that the effect of reserpine is that of psychomotor retardation and dysphoric feelings rather than a true depressive state except perhaps in cases with a past history of depressive illness. The failure to produce depression reliably in humans casts doubt on the validity of the monoamine depletion hypotheses in the simple form thus far stated. On the other hand, despite predicted changes in metabolites of NE and 5-HT accompanying the administration of depletors and enzyme inhibitors that should result in the depletion of NE or 5-HT or both in brain, it certainly cannot be definitely established that brain levels of these monoamines were depleted by the dosages of the substances employed in the various studies. These studies, in the face of supporting studies, suggest that more complicated mechanisms involving monoamines or perhaps other neurotransmitters may be involved instead of changes in a single monoamine system.

Several extensions or modifications of the original monoamine depletion hypothesis have more recently been introduced, since findings suggest that simple single monoamine system malfunction is not comprehensive enough to account for the accumulating data. One such elaboration is the *permissive hypothesis*, which postulates that depletion of brain 5-HT, when superimposed on an existing state of indoleamine depletion, permits the development of a depressive illness. This hypothesis is based on the observation that 5-HT depletion as inferred from 5-HIAA measures in CSF and urine persists into the manic state and often does not return to normal levels in recovered depression patients [13]. The failure of L-dopa to reverse unipolar depressions, while it produces hypomanic episodes in patients with bipolar depression, fits with this hypothesis when one considers that L-dopa may deplete 5-HT. The recently reported ameloriative effect of tryptophan on mania as well as depressive syndromes in some studies also supports the permissive hypothesis [53]. Thus a precursor of 5-HT would correct the postulated depletion in both the manic and the depressive state, resulting in improvement in both cases.

Another elaboration of the monoamine depletion hypothesis, which is in no way mutually exclusive with the permissive hypothesis, is the *cholinergic-adrenergic hypothesis*, which asserts that depression results from a state of cholinergic dominance—that is, a predominance of acetylcholine neuron systems—and mania occurs in the presence of adrenergic dominance. This hypothesis is based on the antagonism of adrenergic drug effects such as methylphenidate excitement in test animals by physostigmine, a centrally acting acetylcholine esterase inhibitor (resulting in a potentiation of acetylcholine effect), and the blocking of mania symptoms for brief periods [31, 32]. It has also been pointed out by those investigators who proposed the hypothesis that tricyclic antidepressants have a cholinergic effect on brain. It has been noted that the drug iprindole, which lacks the capacity to increase noradrenergic effect by blocking the reuptake of NE shown by the tricyclic antidepressants, has an antidepressant effect. It has been suggested that in the absence of the capacity to increase noradrenergic activity, the antidepressant effect of iprindole may be due to its anticholinergic effects.

The evidence, though fragmentary, and at times contradictory, continues to point to the involvement of the monoamines in at least some depressive disorders. The catecholamines or indoleamines, or both systems in addition to an opposing cholinergic system, may be involved in different syndromes. The methods of studying these possible relationships have evolved from an initial heavy reliance on animal studies involving pharmacological interventions and correlation studies of monoamine breakdown products in blood and urine of humans to more reliance upon CSF measures of metabolites during interventions with mood-altering drugs, monoamine precursors, or specific inhibitors of steps in the synthesis of monoamines. While studies predicting outcomes of pharmacological interventions must be interpreted with caution because of possible unknown secondary effects of these agents and questions about the extent of effects in brain of a given dosage, this approach has extended the study of biochemical factors beyond the scope of earlier correlation studies.

While these two monoamine systems, catecholamines and indoleamines, have dominated neuropharmacological and biochemical research in depressive illness, other systems studied have been theoretically tied in with hypothetical changes in monoamine function. For example, recently another amine, phenylethylamine, has been measured in the body fluids of depressed patients and has been found to be correlated with mood, being present in greatly diminished amounts in severe depression and in increased amounts in mania [56]. How this compound, which resembles catecholamine products, fits into the monoamine story is not yet clear, but the substance, which resembles an endogenously produced amphetamine-like substance, presents yet another lead for further study.

While most of the research in monoamine metabolism has hinged on the notion of a depletion or excess of monoamines at receptor sites in brain, studies involving the possible role of thyroid function in depressive illness have led to the concept of *changes in receptor sensitivity to neurotransmitters* as a possible factor [52]. This line of research is based on the initial finding that small doses of thyroid hormone potentiate the effect of imipramine, resulting in an enhancement of its effect at least in females. Earlier in the history of biochemical research in depression and periodically since that time, there have been attempts to implicate thyroid function in depression; they have been inconclusive, despite evidence from animal studies that thyroid hormone is required for monoamine neurotransmitters to exert their effects. The initial demonstration of the therapeutic enhancement effect of thyroid hormone led to another revival of interest in this area as well as augmenting the receptor sensitivity notion. Further studies of thyroid function and depression have led to the finding that thyroid stimulating hormone (TSH), with its origin in the pituitary gland, has a transient antidepressant effect when administered to patients. The role of thyroid function needs further clarification at this point. Earlier observations of the insensitivity of depressed patients to the pressor effects of small but physiologically significant amounts of NE, and observations on the relative insensitivity of many depressed patients to amphetamines, further raise the receptor sensitivity issue [51].

Having reviewed the findings of research into the monoamines and related substances in depression, we will now consider some other lines of research involving other biochemical systems.

HYPOTHALAMIC-PITUITARY-ADRENAL FUNCTION AND ELECTROLYTE METABOLISM IN DEPRESSION

Prior to the introduction of antidepressant drugs and subsequent interest in monoamine metabolism in depression, adrenal cortical hormones became an object of investigation in some of the earliest biochemical studies of depressive illness, in the early 1950s, for several reasons. The introduction of methods for measuring 17-hydroxy-corticosteroids, a major breakdown product of the glucocorticoid hydrocortisone, was a major factor. Selye's studies of adrenal response to stress had led to his conceptualization of the general adaptation syndrome, which emphasized the role of adrenal gland function in adaptation to both physical and psychological stress. This presented an early model linking psychological events and physiological consequences, namely the pituitary-adrenal system, which supplemented the fight-flight reaction involving epinephrine release from the adrenal medulla described by Cannon [7]. At the same time adrenal cortical extract (ACE), the predecessor of the "miracle drugs" hydrocortisone and ACTH, had been identified and was rapidly coming into use. A number of cases of psychiatric complications occurred when adrenal steroids were exogenously administered to humans.

By the mid-1950s an increasing number of affective complications, especially depression, had been documented [18]. These observations, and a high incidence of depression in both Cushing's syndrome (a syndrome involving adrenal hyperfunction) and Addison's disease (a syndrome involving adrenal hypofunction) focused increasing attention on the possible role of adrenal cortical hormone metabolism in the etiology of depressive illness. Early correlation studies showed evidence of elevated levels of 17-hydroxycorticosteroid in the blood and urine of depressed patients. Studies over the next 20 years yielded contradictory results, as did more sophisticated studies of hypothalamic-pituitary-adrenal function [18]. While some studies continue to show varying abnormalities in adrenal corticosteroid levels, such as altered diurnal rhythms of adrenal function, research has focused increasingly on the possible significance of altered pituitary function. Changes in pituitary follicle-stimulating hormone (FSH) and growth hormone (GH) levels are being interpreted as reflecting basic disturbances in pituitary and ultimately hypothalamic function in depressive illness [8, 72]. Studies showing diminished feedback suppression of pituitary-hypothalamic function by tests employing exogenously administered synthetic steroids, though showing some contradictory results, have tended to uphold the finding of disturbances in suppression in a significant proportion of severely depressed patients, suggesting disturbances in hypothalamic function. As in the case of possible effects of alterations in adrenal cortical hormone secretion and metabolism in depressed patients, neither conclusive determination of the state of pituitary-hypothalamic function nor the significance of these findings for depressive illness has been clearly established. The suspicion that adrenal cortical hormone in brain function might relate to monoamine and electrolyte metabolism, as well as reflecting possible disturbances in hypothalamic function in depression, have resulted in continued interest in this system despite the absence of any definite consensus after over 20 years of research. For example, findings of adrenal activation under great stress in severe depressive illness and studies showing evidence of adrenal activation in depressed patients prior to suicide or serious suicidal behavior have kept alive interest in hypothalamic-pituitary-adrenal function among both clinicians and biochemical investigators despite the lack of consensus and the overshadowing of this area by monoamine studies.

Another area of interest that has developed over the past 15 years is research in altered sodium metabolism in brain in depressive illness. Early awareness of the possible importance of sodium metabolism in the functioning of the nervous system has led to several efforts to estimate the state of sodium metabolism in depressive illness with an emphasis on approximations of or inferences of changes in brain. Although again some contradictory results have been obtained and methods have been criticized, there is evidence from both indirect estimates in depressed patients and inferences based on the study of brain tissue obtained from patients who committed suicide as a result of depressive illness to suggest that intracellular sodium and water are increased in depressive illness [9, 72]. How these metabolic alterations relate to the presence of a depressive syndrome, whether they are primary to the neurochemical development of the state or epiphenomena is not known at present. Interest in electrolyte metabolism remains a viable, though peripheral, area of interest in psychobiological approaches to depressive illness. The possibility of an interrelationship among monoamine metabolism, hypothalamic function, adrenal hormone effect, electrolyte metabolism, and changes in brain excitability as measured by evoked potentials keep alive interest in these areas as they relate to depressive illness. At this time, however, these areas of investigation are clearly peripheral to the present focus, namely the possible role of altered monoamine metabolism in depressive illness.

ATTEMPTS AT INTEGRATION OF MECHANISMS OF DEPRESSION

Evidence that stress can result in measurable changes in NE levels in animals, depending on the nature of the stressor, is cited as evidence that profound psychological experience might be translated into alterations in monoamine metabolism similar to those found in patients with depressive illness. Thus, learning theory concepts, animal models of response to separation and to loss of control of reinforcements and punishments, and effects of stress on monoamine metabolism in animals can be used to extrapolate to possible mechanisms by which depression might occur in humans. Evidence of the increased incidence of depressive illness in families and monozygotic sibs of patients with unipolar or bipolar depression would lead us to expect depression to occur under varying severities of stress in individuals who may have genetic vulnerability expressed through enzyme response to depletion of monoamines, altered feedback control of monoamine metabolism, or altered receptor sensitivity to various monoamines that are present all the time or vary according to unknown cycles of vulnerability. Such theories, relying heavily on extrapolation from animal studies, point the way to general theories that allow integration of the entire range of evidence available at this time. These notions are doubtless oversimplified and subject to change, but they at least provide a set of concepts that bridge the islands of diverse observations.

Data from family studies, behavioral research, neurophysiology, and monoamine studies have been reviewed and interrelated in attempts to reach a theory of depressive illness that integrates clinical observations, psychodynamic theory, learning theory, and other psychological formulations of depressive illness with familial and biological evidence [1, 18, 72]. Among other things, such a theory will have to account for the responses of infants to separation from parents, the effects of separation and isolation on primates (who demonstrate similar behavioral responses), and reactions to perceived helplessness to obtain positive reinforcement in both humans and animals. As mentioned earlier, the observation that the anatomical substrate of the pleasure-reward system found in the median forebrain bundle is facilitated by NE release and a punishment function is inhibited by NE and facilitated by cholinergic activity in the periventricular system may provide a basis for tying in loss of reinforcement control to the experience of loss at the psychological level [1]. As investigations progress and new data come to light, it is hoped that general theories can be made more specific and that specific subtypes of depressive illness can be delineated. Only then will effective treatment specific to various types of depressive illness and perhaps even prevention of the illness in individuals identified as vulnerable become possible.

REFERENCES

1. Akiskal, H. S., and McKinney, W. T., Jr. Depressive disorders: Toward a unified hypothesis. *Science* 182:20, 1973.
2. Ashcroft, G. W., Brooks, P. W., Cumdall, A., Eccleston, E. C., Murray, L. G., and Pullar, I. A. 5-Hydroxyindole compounds in the cerebrospinal fluid of patients with psychiatric or neurological diseases. *Lancet* 2:1049, 1966.
3. Beckman, H., Jones, C. C., and Goodwin, F. K. Urinary MHPG and Response to Antidepressant Drugs. Scientific proceedings, annual meeting of the American Psychiatric Association, 1974.
4. Bon, P. A., Jenner, F. A., and Sampson, G. A. Daily variations of the urine content of 3-methoxy-4-hydroxy phenylglycol in two manic-depressive patients. *Psychol. Med.* 2:81, 1972.
4a. Bowers, M. B., Jr., Heninger, G. R., and Gerbode, F. Cerebrospinal fluid, 5-hydroxyindoleacetic acid and homovanillic acid in psychiatric patients. *Int. J. Neuropharmacol.* 8:255, 1969.
the urine content of 3-methoxy-4-hydroxy phenylglycol in two manic-depressive patients. *Psychol. Med.* 2:81, 1972.
5. Brodie, H. K. H., et al. Catecholamines and mania: The effect of alpha methyl-para-tyrosine on manic behavior and catecholamine metabolism. *Clin. Pharmacol. Ther.* 12:219, 1971.
6. Bunney, W. E., Jr., and Davis, J. M. Norepinephrine in depressive disorders. *Arch. Gen. Psychiatry* 13:483, 1965.
7. Cannon, W. B., and Rosenbleuth, A. *Autonomic Neuro-Effector Systems.* New York: Macmillan, 1937. P. 230.
8. Carroll, B. Endocrine Factors in Human Behavior. Paper presented

at the Fourth International Congress on Psychoendocrinology, Brain Information Service. University of California, Berkeley, September 1943.

9. Coppen, A.   Mineral metabolism in affective disorders. *Br. J. Psychiatry* 111:1133, 1965.

10. Coppen, A.   The biochemistry of affective disorders. *Br. J. Psychiatry* 113:1237, 1967.

11. Coppen, A., Eccleston, E. C., and Peet, M.   Total and free tryptophan concentration in the plasma of depressive patients. *Lancet* 2:60, 1973.

12. Coppen, A., Whybrow, P. C., Noguera, R., Maggs, R., and Prange, A. The comparative antidepressant value of L-tryptophan and imipramine with and without attempted potentiation by biothyronine. *Arch. Gen. Psychiatry* 26:234, 1972.

13. Dencker, S. J., U-Malm, B., Roos, E., and Werdinius, B.: Acid monoamine metabolites of cerebrospinal fluid in mental depression and mania. *J. Neurochem.* 13:1545, 1966.

14. Ebert, M. W., Post, R. M., and Goodwin, F. K.   Effect of physical activity on urinary 3-methoxy-4-hydroxy phenylglycol excretion in depressed patients. *Lancet* 2:766, 1972.

15. Falck, B.   Cellular Localization of Monoamines. In H. E. Himwich, and W. A. Himwich (Eds.), *Progress in Brain Research.* New York: Am. Elsevier, 1964. Vol. 8, p. 28.

16. Fawcett, J. A.   Schizophrenia. *Britannica Yearbook of Science and the Future.* Encyclopedia Britannica, 1973. P. 77.

17. Fawcett, J. A.   Unpublished data.

18. Fawcett, J. A., and Bunney, W. E., Jr.   Pituitary adrenal function and depression. *Arch. Gen. Psychiatry* 16:517, 1967.

19. Fawcett, J. A., Maas, J. W., and Dekirmenjian, H.   Depression and MHPG excretion. *Arch. Gen. Psychiatry* 26:246, 1972.

20. Gayral, L., Bierer, R., and Delhom, A.   L'excretion urinaire de l'acide 5-hydroxy-indolacetique dans les depressions et les melancolies sous l'influence du traitement par les inhibiteurs de la monamine-oxydase. In H. Brill (Ed.), *Neuropsychopharmacology.* Amsterdam: Elsevier-Excerpta Medica, 1967. P. 339.

21. Gillespie, R. P.   The clinical differentiation of types of depression. *Guys Hosp. Rep.* 2:306, 1929.

22. Goode, D. J., Dekirmenjian, H., Meltzer, H. Y., and Maas, J. W. Relation of exercise to MHPG excretion in normal subjects. *Arch. Gen. Psychiatry* 29:391, 1973.

23. Goodwin, F. K., Murphy, D. L., Brodie, H. K., and Bunney, W. E., Jr.   L-Dopa, catecholamines, and behavior: A clinical and biochemical study in depressed patients. *Biol. Psychiatry* 2:241, 1970.

24. Goodwin, F. K., Murphy, D. L., and Bunney, W. E., Jr.   Lithium carbonate treatment in depression and mania: A longitudinal double blind study. *Arch. Gen. Psychiatry* 21:486, 1972.

25. Goodwin, F. K., Post, R. M., Dunner, D. L., et al.   Cerebrospinal amine metabolites in affective illness: The probenecid technique. *Am. J. Psychiatry* 130:73, 1973.

26. Greenspan, K., Schildkraut, J. J., Gordon, K. K., Baer, L., Aronoff, M. S., and Purell, J.   Catecholamine metabolism in affective dis-

orders: III. MHPG and other catecholamine metabolites in patients treated with lithium carbonate. *J. Psychiatr. Res.* 7:171, 1970.

27. Grinker, R. R., Miller, J., Sabshin, M., et al. *The Phenomena of Depressions.* New York: Hoeber Med. Div., Harper & Brothers, 1961.

28. Heller, A., and Moore, R.   Effect of CNS lesions on brain monoamines in the rat. *J. Pharmacol. Exp. Ther.* 150:1, 1965.

29. Hill, D.   Depression: Disease, reaction, or posture. *Am. J. Psychiatry* 125:37, 1968.

30. Himwich, H. E.   Indoleamines and Depression. In H. E. Himwich (Ed.), *Biochemistry, Schizophrenia and the Affective Illness.* Baltimore: Williams & Wilkins, 1970. P. 230.

31. Janowsky, D., El-Yousef, M., Davis, J. M., and Sekerke, H. J.   A cholinergic-adrenergic hypothesis of mania and depression. *Lancet* 2: 632, 1972.

32. Janowsky, D., El-Yousef, M., Davis, J. M., and Sekerke, H. J.   Antagonistic effects of physostigmine and methylphenidate in man. *Am. J. Psychiatry* 130:1371, 1973.

33. Jones, F. P., Maas, J. W., Dekirmenjian, H., and Fawcett, J. A.   Urinary catecholamine metabolites during behavior changes in a patient with manic-depressive cycles. *Science* 179:300, 1973.

34. Kendall, R. E.   *The Classification of Depressive Illnesses.* New York: Oxford University Press, 1968.

35. Kiloh, L. G., and Garside, R. F.   The independence of neurotic depression and endogenous depression. *Br. J. Psychiatry* 109:451, 1963.

36. Kraepelin, E.   *Manic Depressive Insanity and Paranoia.* Translated by M. Barclay. Edinburgh: Livingstone, 1971.

37. Lehman, H.   Epidemiology of Depressive Disorders. In R. Fieve, (Ed.), *Depression in the 70's.* Amsterdam: Elsevier-Excerpta Medica, 1971. P. 21.

38. Lemieux, G., Davignon, A., and Genest, J.   Depressive states during *Rauwolfia* therapy for arterial hypertension. *Can. Med. Assoc. J.* 74: 522, 1956.

39. Maas, J. W., Dekirmenjian, H., and Jones, F.   The Identification of Depressed Patients who have a Disorder of Norepinephrine Metabolism and/or Disposition. In E. Usdin, and S. Snyder (Eds.), *Frontiers in Catecholamine Research—Third International Catecholamine Symposium.* New York: Pergamon, 1974.

40. Maas, J. W., Fawcett, J., and Dekirmenjian, H.   3-Methoxy-4-hydroxy phenylglycol (MHPG) excretion in depressive states: A pilot study. *Arch. Gen. Psychiatry* 19:129, 1968.

41. Maas, J. W., Fawcett, J. A., and Dekirmenjian, H.   Catecholamine metabolism, depressive illness, and drug response. *Arch. Gen. Psychiatry* 26:252, 1972.

42. Maas, J. W., Fawcett, J. A., Dekirmenjian, H., and Landis, D. H.   Catecholamine Metabolism and Depressive States: Current Studies. In T. Williams, J. Shields, and M. Katz (Eds.), *Recent Advances in the Psychobiology of the Depressive Illness.* Washington, D.C.: U.S. Government Printing Office, 1971.

43. Maas, J. W., and Garver, D. L.   Linkage of Basic Neuropharmacology. In A. M. Freedman, H. I. Kaplan, and B. J. Sadock (Eds.),

Comprehensive Textbook of Psychiatry. Baltimore: Williams & Wilkins, in press.

44. Maas, J. W., and Landis, D. H. In vivo studies of metabolism of norepinephrine in central nervous system. *J. Pharmacol. Exp. Ther.* 163:147, 1965.

45. Mannarino, E., Kirshner, M., and Mashold, B. S., Jr. Metabolism of C^{14} noradrenaline by cat brain *in vivo*. *J. Neurochem.* 10:373, 1963.

46. Mendels, J., and Frazer, A. Brain biogenic amine depletion and mood. *Arch. Gen. Psychiatry* 30:447, 1974.

47. Overall, J. E. Dimensions of manifest depression. *Psychiatr. Res.* 1:239, 1962.

48. Pare, C. M. B., and Sandler, M. Clinical and biochemical study of a trial of iproniazid in the treatment of depression. *J. Neurol. Neurosurg. Psychiatry* 22:247, 1959.

49. Paykel, E. S. Depressive typologies and response to amitriptyline. *Br. J. Psychiatry* 120:147, 1972.

50. Post, R. M., Kotin, J., Goodwin, F. K. and Gordon, E. K. Psychomotor activity and cerebrospinal fluid amine metabolites in affective illness. *Am. J. Psychiatry* 130:67, 1973.

51. Prange, A. J., Jr., McCurdy, L., and Cochrane, C. M. The systolic blood pressure response of depressed patients to infused norepinephrine. *J. Psychiatr. Res.* 5:1, 1967.

52. Prange, A. J., Wilson, I. C., Knox, A., et al. Thyroid-imipramine clinical and chemical interaction: Evidence for a receptor deficit in depression. *J. Psychiatr. Res.* 9:187, 1972.

53. Prange, A. J., Wilson, I. C., Lynn, C. W., et al. L-Tryptophan in mania. *Arch. Gen. Psychiatry* 30:56, 1974.

54. Redmond, D. E., Jr., Maas, J. W., Kling, A., and Dekirmenjian, H. Changes in primate social behavior after treatment with alpha-methyl-para-tyrosine. *Psychosom. Med.* 33:97, 1971.

55. Robins, E., and Guze, S. B. Classification of Affective Disorders. In T. A. Williams, M. M. Katz, and J. A. Shield, Jr. (Eds.), *Recent Advances in the Psychobiology of Depressive Illness*. Washington, D.C.: U.S. Government Printing Office, 1973.

56. Sabelli, H. C., and Mosnaim, A. D. Phenylethylamine Hypothesis of Affective Behavior. Paper presented at the annual meeting, American Psychiatric Association, Honolulu, May 1973.

57. Schildkraut, J. J. The catecholamine hypothesis of affective disorders: A review of supporting evidence. *Am. J. Psychiatry* 122:509, 1965.

58. Schildkraut, J. J. Norepinephrine metabolites as biochemical criteria for classifying depressive disorders and predicting responses to treatment—preliminary findings. *Am. J. Psychiatry* 130:695, 1973.

59. Schildkraut, J. J., Green, R., Gordon, E., and Durell, J. Normetanephrine excretion and affective state in depressed patients treated with imipramine. *Am. J. Psychiatry* 123:690, 1966.

60. Schildkraut, J. J., Keeler, B. A., Papousek, M., and Hartmann, E. MHPG excretion and clinical classification in depressive disorders. *Lancet* 1:1251, 1973.

61. Schildkraut, J. J., Keeler, B. A., Papousek, M., and Hartmann, E. MHPG excretion in depressive disorders: Relation to clinical subtypes and desynchronized sleep. *Science* 181:762, 1973.
62. Schildkraut, J. J., Watson, R., Draskoczy, P. R., and Hartmann, E. Amphetamine withdrawal: Depression and MHPG excretion. *Lancet* 2:485, 1971.
63. Secunda, S. K., Freedman, R. J., and Schuyler, D. *Special Report: 1973, The Depressive Disorders.* Bethesda, Md.: U.S. Department of Health, Education and Welfare, Health Services and Mental Health Administration, National Institute of Mental Health, 1973. P. 2.
64. Selye, H. Stress and general adaptation syndrome (Heberden oration). *Br. Med. J.* 1:1383, 1950.
65. Shopsin, B., Wilk, S., Gershon, S., Davis, K., and Suhl, M. Cerebrospinal fluid MHPG: An assessment of norepinephrine metabolism in affective disorders. *Arch. Gen. Psychiatry* 28:230, 1973.
66. Shopsin, B., Wilk, S., Sathananthan, G., Gershon, S., and Davis, K. Catecholamines and affective disorders revised: A critical assessment. *J. Nerv. Ment. Dis.* 158(5):369, 1974.
67. Sjoerdsma, A., Engelman, K., and Spector, S. Inhibition of catecholamine synthesis in man with alpha-methyl-tyrosine, an inhibitor of tyrosine hydroxylase. *Lancet* 2:1092, 1965.
68. Ungerstedt, U. Stereotaxic mapping of the monoamine pathways in the rat brain. *Acta Physiol. Scand.* (Suppl.) 367:1, 1971.
69. Van Praag, H. M., and Korf, J. Cerebral monoamines and depression. *Arch. Gen. Psychiatry* 28:829, 1973.
70. Van Praag, H. M., Korf, J., Dols, L. C. W., and Schut, T. A pilot study of the predicting value of the probenecid test in application of 5-hydroxytryptophan as antidepressant. *Psychopharmacologia* 25:14, 1972.
71. Van Praag, H. M., and Leijnse, B. Die Bedeutung der Monoaminoxydasehemmung als antidepressives Prinzip. I. *Psychopharmacologia* 4:1, 1963.
72. Whybrow, P., and Parlature, A. Melancholia, a model in madness: A discussion of recent psychobiologic research into depressive illness. *Psychiatr. Med.* 4:351, 1973.

3

Neurochemical Aspects of Adaptive Regulation in Depression: Failure and Treatment*

ARNOLD J. MANDELL
DAVID S. SEGAL†

Scientists who approach chemistry from behavioral disciplines such as psychoanalysis and experimental psychology may be misled by the apparent similarity of terms used by biological scientists and themselves when in fact the meanings often are disparate. For example, from the laboratories of basic biological scientists come reports of various kinds of depression of behavior, such as the significant retardation of spontaneous motor activity produced in rodents by the administration of reserpine. It may not be legitimate, however, to equate the phrase "depression of behavior" with depression as a human affective disorder.

The first efforts to match biochemistry to behavior were systematic studies of peripheral metabolic products in relation to various behavioral states in man. Attempts have been made to relate momentary alterations in blood hormone levels to anxiety or overstimulation and urinary excretion of catecholamines (CA) to work stress or competition. Other researchers have studied alterations in corticosteroids in the urine and blood in relation to various sorts of psychopathology, particularly affective disorders. Persons with an affective disorder manifest fluctuating corticosteroid levels in their blood and urine and abnormal amounts of both pituitary hormones and hormones released

* This work was supported by U.S. Public Health Service Grants DA-00265-03 and DA-00046-04 and Friends of Psychiatric Research of San Diego, Inc.
† National Institute of Mental Health Research Scientist, award number MH 70183-02.

from pituitary target organs such as the adrenal gland [33]. It is not clear whether these aberrations are epiphenomenal or play a role in the etiology of the mood disorder.

For years schizophrenia too has been pursued by searching for metabolic errors. Although this research has been characterized by premature claims and contaminated by uncontrolled variables, it goes on. Just now, Linus Pauling and his colleagues are using gas-liquid chromatography and mass spectrometry to look for patterns of metabolic excretion (most of which are as yet unidentified) that relate to personality disorder and psychopathology. Their work is just one example of the extremely sophisticated techniques of separation and identification that are being applied to the study of syndromes of aberrant human behavior.

Logic dictates that we regard deviations in peripheral metabolites as concomitants of coincidental psychological states, but we must be cautious about claiming that such empirical findings participate in a causal chain leading to mental illness. Most investigators cite realistic reservations readily enough and then often proceed to build complex theories around the assumption that the metabolic error is related directly to the psychopathology. As an example, Frohman et al. [11] have identified a circulating factor that alters the metabolism of red blood cells in the chicken. They have also demonstrated a factor that stimulates tryptophan uptake. Their initial empirical findings had correlational significance only, but correlation easily gives way to causation when we try to make sense out of our data, and Frohman et al. [12] now speculate that the correlational changes they have observed can be followed directly to the endogenous production of a hallucinogen.

We all engage in creative speculation, and within our own subspecialties it is safe enough because the other members know that is part of the ritual. But the fact is that, no matter how tentative, empirical inferences, once claimed, are inclined to operate at a very high theoretical level, and too easily seduce those beyond the inner circle. Another elaborate model of this kind, long espoused by Heath and Krupp [17], involves a circulating protein that alters the electrical activity of septal nuclei, but to which immunological properties have only recently been attributed. High-level theorizing from low-level peripheral metabolic indicators has probably done more to discredit biochemical research than anything else. That is not to say we should abandon the peripheral biochemical approach—only that we should hold our conclusions in check and avoid wearing blinders. A wide variety of neurometabolic diseases that can be picked up by examining the urine or blood reflect enzyme deficiencies resulting in more or less of a metabolite. Continued finding of such useful indices in pediatrics and internal medicine recommends use of the same approach to mental illness—with caution.

The technology necessary to study peripheral metabolites requires highly specialized scientists who often lack experience with the behavioral or diagnostic aspects involved. The biochemists and biologists who are looking at intervening variables are often aliens to the psychiatric and humanistic phenomenologists, and vice versa. Valid correlation between peripheral metabolites and various psychiatric syndromes would seem to require fusion of the scientific and humanistic epistemologies.

The second biochemical approach to mental illness is by way of what Schildkraut [35] has called the pharmacological bridge. The logic is as follows: Drugs that produce certain (objective or subjective) behavior in man also produce various kinds of measurable biochemical changes in the brains of animals. Those parts of the brain that are similar in man and animals (hypothalamus, brain stem, striatum) are often used for studies of the effects of acute or chronic administration of various drugs on transmitters, enzymes, intermediates, metabolites, etc. The drugs are also studied in clinical application, and the inference is made that biochemical changes similar to those observed in animals are responsible for the behavioral changes seen in man. A correlation between the reserpine-induced depression observed in man and metabolic changes in rodent brain is well established in neuropharmacology. Recently the effects of amphetamine on biological parameters in rat brain has been correlated with an effect of high doses or chronic administration of the drug on the behavior of man. A new dopamine hypothesis of schizophrenia [43] has grown from the juxtaposition of amphetamine-induced paranoid schizophrenia and the role of amphetamine in the facilitation of dopaminergic transmission in animals, particularly in relation to the specific capacity of antipsychotic drugs to block the receptors.

Similarly, another popular hypothesis asserts that certain indoleamines can be converted to their hallucinogenic dimethylated congeners by a brain enzyme system, and the regulation of this enzyme in rat brain is being studied by a number of scientists [2, 18, 19, 28, 29, 32]. Simultaneously, others are studying the effect of tryptophan loads plus monoamine oxidase inhibitors on the facilitation of indoleamine transmission in human brain, with or without concomitant administration of methyl donor amino acids [3, 20]. Because tryptophan loads plus monoamine oxidase inhibitors have been known to exacerbate schizophrenic symptoms in man, a relationship is drawn between the facilitated production of methylated indoleamines in animal brain and hallucinatory experience in man.

Although neuropharmacologists all over the world are using this rationale to study most of the drugs that have either been abused or used successfully to treat various psychiatric syndromes, traversing the pharmacological bridge is not without danger. The behavior of the animal is ignored in this equation because the difference in complexity of the neural substrate in human and animal brains might render inductions ridiculous. On the other hand, behavior itself alters brain chemistry, and it may be the behavioral change induced by the drug, rather than the drug itself, that is responsible for the brain changes in the animal. For example, it is conceivable that hyperactivity produces the same kind of brain change regardless of the stimulus.

The rationale of the pharmacological bridge may have application in new techniques that measure transmitter acid metabolites in the cerebrospinal fluid (CSF). The administration of probenecid blocks the pump that removes these metabolites from the CSF, allowing indirect measurement of the total metabolism of one or another transmitter as the metabolites accumulate in the CSF [7, 15, 42]. The assumption is that probenecid does not affect the pathway under study in any other way. The data may become suspect in light of recent evidence that certain rate-limiting enzymes in the biosynthesis of transmitters can be affected by the acid metabolites of the transmitters; perhaps the buildup of the metabolites changes the regulation of the pathway. Normative data for neurotransmitter metabolism in the CSF are incomplete. The mechanism of stop-flow analysis and its relationship to a variety of other physical variables (height, weight, race, etc.) await standardization.

On the other hand, an individual can serve as his own control in a before-after paradigm. Comparative CSF measurements are very useful, for example, in evaluating the biochemical correlates of the cyclic phases of a manic-depressive psychosis.

Another recent trend in strategies to traverse the abyss between behavior and biochemistry has to do with studies of peripheral tissue that contains enzymes similar to those of the brain. For example, some potential rate-limiting enzymes in the synthesis of biogenic amines, e.g. tyrosine hydroxylase, dopamine-β-hydroxylase, or tryptophan hydroxylase, can be studied in white cells and peripheral tissue. If the molecular-organic model holds, one could speculate that the same coding might be operative in expression and regulation at the periphery as in the brain; that is, drugs and other impinging variables, natural or induced, might alter peripheral enzymes as they do those in the brain [31].

The present foci of research, elaborated from one another over a quarter-century, constitute the experimental language in the juncture between behavior and biochemistry. We are still barred from direct study of the brain, but we are, so to speak, "casing the joint." In spite of the incredibly painstaking mapping of the brain by neuroanatomists and neurophysiologists, neurochemists, who heretofore lacked anatomical sophistication, often divided the brain grossly into anterior and posterior, or forebrain and hindbrain sections, or the like. Now we find very specific regional changes (sometimes only one millimeter apart) that attest to the heterogeneity and specificity of brain tissue. Simple biopsies of human cortex or random brain specimens (even when they are available) are not very revealing because the relevant changes may be occurring elsewhere—in the dopaminergic cell bodies of the substantia nigra or in the serotonergic nerve endings of the striatum. The more specific the dissection, the more likely it is that one will find a relatively consistent and distinct neurochemical change in response to any particular stimulus.

The fusion of sophisticated neuroanatomy and neurophysiology with neurochemistry is becoming a necessity for productive animal work in this area; the technological barrier to an understanding of the human brain may wait decades for resolution. The invasion of the human brain for research does not hold much therapeutic promise right now, and the direct neurochemical study of behavior depends upon the further evolution of our mechanical ingenuity. We just do not know whether we will measure absorbance or emission of some form of energy or collect samples in ways we have not thought of yet. In a brain it is possible to examine the enzymes and biogenic amines for up to two or three hours after death only, and this has been done in brains from suicide and heart attack victims [6]. But macromolecules disintegrate rapidly, and the artifacts surrounding the agonies of death could distort any data. So the myriad indirect approaches described seem justified by the technological and ethical barriers to direct study of the human brain.

The following neurochemical approach to depression brings together some of the strategies we have described: the pharmacological bridge (which is prominent), stop-flow analysis of CSF metabolites, and peripheral enzyme studies. We do not *know* whether our current hypotheses are true or not; they are consistent with a great array of data.

PRINCIPLES OF ADAPTIVE ENZYMATIC REGULATION

A few years ago we postulated adaptive regulation as a significant mechanism underlying the action of many psychotropic drugs [41]. Our data indicated that chronic administration of psychotropic drugs led to alterations in rat brain capacity to synthesize amines and to alterations in receptor sensitivity that seemed to counteract acute drug effects. For example, chronic administration of drugs that release or block reuptake of amines at central synapses decreased the activity of biosynthetic enzymes such as tyrosine hydroxylase and tryptophan hydroxylase. On the other hand, reserpine or receptor blockers such as the phenothiazines or propanolol increased those brain enzymes and led to functional supersensitivity of the receptors, at least in the CA systems. The latencies and durations of the changes in presynaptic enzyme activity and receptor function ranged from hours to weeks.

We thought we had a lead on a major paradox of clinical psychopharmacology: the time-to-efficacy of lithium, the phenothiazines, and the tricyclic antidepressants. The latencies corresponded to the time it took for compensatory macromolecular changes to occur in the rat brain. Perhaps the compensatory changes, rather than acute alterations in synaptic transmitter mobility, were responsible for the behavioral effects of the drugs. Devil's advocates suggested that those interesting shifts in indices of brain capacity to synthesize amines probably were mirror images that only confirmed the acute drug action, but we went on to imagine that depression *might* reflect pathological activation of central CA neurons that could be damped down by antidepressants and that would be exacerbated by the *Rauwolfia* alkaloids and the phenothiazines.

By careful regional dissection of rat brain we have specified regions in which cell bodies and nerve endings of various amine systems predominate. The chemical alterations that occur in these subcellular areas when parameters of drug dosage are carefully controlled involve several distinct mechanisms—mechanisms that appear to function as adaptive regulators of neurotransmission in the brain.

First, impairment of synaptic transmission in the rat brain by α-methyltyrosine or 6-hydroxydopamine (6-HODA) leads to supersensitivity of central CA receptors as reflected in behavioral response to chronic intraventricular infusion of low doses of CA. Some of this behavioral arousal, particularly in the case of 6-HODA, can be attributed to the loss of the presynaptic uptake mechanism, at least early on. Later changes, however, apparently involve the receptors. We blocked reuptake in controls with acute high doses of a tricyclic antidepressant. After two to three weeks of 6-HODA administration, behavioral sensitivity to CA infusion was much greater in the experimental animals than in controls treated with the tricyclic. It was also much greater than it had been shortly after the initial administration of 6-HODA [40].

Another mechanism has to do with alterations in the physical state of critical biosynthetic enzymes in the CA system, specifically tyrosine hydroxylase. At least two, possibly three models for the physical state of tyrosine hydroxylase in striatal synaptosomes can be demonstrated: an occluded state, a membrane-bound (allosterically activated) state, and an unbound soluble state [24, 25, 26, 27]. Certain acute drug effects seem to change the physical state and thereby the activity of this rate-limiting enzyme. For example, some aspects of enzyme activation by membrane binding can be mimicked in the presence of the specific mucopolysaccharide heparin. Fisher and Kaufman [10] have suggested that in the serotonergic system tryptophan hydroxylase may be regulated by membrane binding. Other factors that may be involved in intrasynaptosomal regulation of enzyme activity include product-feedback inhibition, cofactor supply, and substrate supply.

A third regulatory mechanism involves the uptake of amino acid precursors of biogenic amines. In the serotonergic system the uptake of radioactive tryptophan is inhibited by cocaine and stimulated by the acute administration of lithium or tryptophan loads; in turn, the rate of uptake influences the capacity of synaptosomes to convert tryptophan to serotonin [21, 23]. No one has yet found significant changes in tyrosine uptake associated with various drugs or environmental manipulations; so far it is doubtful that changes in the active uptake of tyrosine play a role in the normal regulation of CA biosynthesis.

Last, changes in the synthesis of the enzymes themselves in the cell body are apparently regulated either by feedback information from the postsynaptic cell or by the electrical firing rate of the presynaptic cell over certain lengths of time. Generally it takes days to weeks for alterations in the amount of enzyme to appear in the nerve ending [22, 23].

ADAPTIVE REGULATION AND THE CATECHOLAMINE HYPOTHESIS

Heretofore endogenous depressions have been attributed to a functional deficiency of brain catecholamines, and mania to an excess of the same amines [6, 34, 35]. Most of the supportive evidence for the so-called catecholamine hypothesis was gathered from attempts to elucidate the mechanism of action of psychotropic drugs in animals— drugs that are effective in treating mood disorders or that produce behavioral syndromes similar to natural disorders. Those studies involved primarily the examination of *acute* drug effects on CA storage, release, and reuptake at the synapse. Acute administration of drugs effective in treating depression was found to facilitate central CA transmission by altering one or more of these three mechanisms. Opposite alterations were claimed for drugs that precipitate depression [36].

The catecholamine hypothesis originated as a heuristic model, and it has generated much research. It has been challenged occasionally by suggestions that other amines, such as serotonin, might also affect mood [5, 13], that all depressive syndromes may not have a common etiology [14], and that mania may not reflect simply excess CAs [14], but generally the original model has held sway.

The prevailing concepts of psychotropic drug actions have been inferred from experiments performed on animals within hours of drug administration. *However, in man the behavioral effects of most of these agents are not discernible until days or weeks after initiation of treatment.* To assess the effects of psychotropic agents over a clinically relevant time period, we systematically studied the effects of *chronic* alterations in central CA transmission on various indices of CA biosynthesis. We have shown that conditions associated with reduced levels of central CA activity, e.g., chronic reserpine administration [41], thyroidectomy [9], and sensory isolation [37], significantly increase the specific activity of tyrosine hydroxylase in the midbrain. Preliminary results indicate that the chronic administration of amphetamine, pargyline, or imipramine, each of which initially enhances central adrenergic activity, decreases midbrain tyrosine hydroxylase activity. Compensatory changes in the amount or the activity of tyrosine hydroxylase or both seem to result from *prolonged* alterations in central adrenergic activity. We speculate that the functional significance of lasting drug-induced enzymatic changes lies here—in the production of a state of neurotransmission opposite to that caused by acute drug administration.

A BIOCHEMICAL THEORY OF AFFECTIVE DISORDER
INVOLVING ADAPTIVE REGULATION

Recently we compared the apparently delayed (adaptive) changes in tyrosine hydroxylase activity in various regions of rat brain after chronic administration of reserpine, which impairs transmission, and desipramine (DMI), which acutely potentiates transmission by blocking reuptake of the amine in the nerve ending [39]. We were particularly interested in the changes that occur one to two weeks after initiation of the drug regimen—to explain why tricyclics have their therapeutic effect weeks after they first block amine reuptake in the synapse. Chronic treatment with reserpine increased tyrosine hydroxylase activity in all the regions we studied; the activity reached 250 percent of control in the locus ceruleus. Such elevations were not present 24 hours after a single administration of reserpine. On the other hand, repeated administration of the tricyclic antidepressant DMI produced a significant decline in enzyme activity, the most pronounced reaching about 50 percent of control in the hippocampal cortex. No significant change in enzyme activity was observed 24 hours after a single administration of a large dose of DMI. These data are consistent with those from many of our previous studies, in which the independent variables were genetic strain, sensory isolation, selected drugs, or hormone levels [9, 37, 38, 41].

Imagine that a decrease in the firing rate of noradrenergic neurons compensates for the initial facilitation of transmission by the tricyclic antidepressant. In fact, a marked reduction in midbrain reticular activating system activity has been observed in cats about 30 minutes after injection of a tricyclic drug; the decrease persisted for 24 to 36 hours [44]. This (probably feedback-regulated) decrease in unit discharge rate may balance the facilitated transmission and account for the virtual absence of immediate clinical effects from tricyclics. Presuming, then, that the synthesis of enzymes is a function of the discharge rate of the cell over some critical time period, a change in firing rate *must be maintained* to produce macromolecular changes, much as the presence of an addicting drug must be maintained to produce tolerance. Data from peripheral systems [1] also suggest that the amount of tyrosine hydroxylase is some function of the firing rate, particularly over time. When a decrease in discharge rate is maintained by daily doses of a tricyclic there is a gradual decrease in tyrosine hydroxylase. In the presence of reserpine, in contrast, a marked increase in the presynaptic unit firing rate probably compensates for the impairment of transmission, and that increased rate would lead to an increase in tyrosine hydroxylase.

Evaluation of the net effects of drug treatments on central CA systems by analysis of CA acid metabolites in the CSF after the administration of probenecid is a promising possibility. Although the technique, as we have said, is not yet standardized, the preliminary findings may be relevant to the adaptive mechanism we are studying. Endogenous depressive patients apparently have low levels of catechol acids in their CSF [7, 15, 42]. However, chronic treatment with tricyclics reduces these abnormally low levels further [16], and the clinical response to tricyclic medication corresponds in time to the decrease in the accrual rate of CA metabolites after probenecid blockade. Decreased brain capacity for CA biosynthesis (decreased tyrosine hydroxylase) may also be reflected in the decrease in the accumulation of catechol acids in the CSF.

Integrating our findings with these and with others from the Laboratory of Clinical Science at the National Institute of Mental Health, we now suggest that the neurochemical model for depressive illness might be revised. Correlations between low catechol-O-methyltransferase (COMT) in red blood cells and clinical responsiveness to tricyclic antidepressant medication in a population of patients who suffer from unipolar endogenous depression [4, 8, 14] suggest the possibility that depression, particularly, unipolar depression, could be a manifestation of deficiency in COMT. Receptors might be sensitized if the capacity to remove CAs were lost with the lost COMT. A decrease in tyrosine hydroxylase would follow an initial endogenous compensatory decrease in spontaneous firing rate, resulting in low baseline measures of catechol acids in the CSF. Tricyclic treatment would initially potentiate transmission, which would decrease the firing rate and enzymatic activity still further, and certainly would not reverse the low catechol acids in the CSF. In other words, natural damping of sensitized receptors would be abetted by adaptive decreases in CA neuronal discharge and enzyme (perforce amine) synthesis after tricyclic potentiation of synaptic transmission.

CLINICAL IMPLICATIONS OF THE BIOCHEMICAL THEORY

The idea that the central CA systems might be functionally hyperactive in depressive states has precedents in classical theories of adrenergic function. Sleeplessness, weight loss, and persistent rumination are common experiences for people suffering from depression. The depression caused by reserpine fits our biochemical model in that the impairment of transmission provokes an increase in presynaptic neural activity, and the related increase in tyrosine hydroxylase activity results in the synthesis of more transmitter substance. We have also observed increased tyrosine hydroxylase activity in hypothyroid rats [9]; hypothyroidism, like chronic reserpine administration, is associated with depression in man.

Of course these speculations are risky in view of species differences in the complexity of mammalian brains, in the dynamics of pharmacology, and in the fine relationships between dose and efficacy, but the *questions* should be entertained: Could depression possibly be due to increased CA activity? Might tricyclics initially aggravate the hyperactivity and then achieve therapeutic effectiveness by invoking adaptive mechanisms such as those we have described? Curiously, in normal subjects several days of tricyclic administration has led to transient depression followed by a return to normal mood [30].

The efficacy of tricyclics in unipolar depressive illness in patients who manifest some deficiency of COMT hints at a syndrome of hyperactive central CAs in which the drug might protect the receptors by prompting compensatory mechanisms to further damp neuronal firing and enzymatic synthesis of transmitter substance. So we wonder if compensatory changes in biosynthetic enzymes are intrinsically related to the therapeutic action of psychotropic drugs.

Although hypothesis succeeds hypothesis, and proof of any of them is a long way off, it becomes increasingly important for even the most humanistic or psychoanalytically oriented psychologist or psychiatrist to be familiar with the principles and style of thought in neurochemical research. Modern psychiatry needs to contradict C. P. Snow's assertion that the capacities to comprehend the intuitive and the technological aspects of the world will never join.

REFERENCES

1. Axelrod, J.   Noradrenaline: Fate and control of its synthesis. *Science* 173:598, 1971.
2. Banerjee, S. P., and Snyder, S. H.   Methyltetrahydrofolic acid mediates N- and O-methylation of biogenic amines. *Science* 182:74, 1973.
3. Brune, G. G., and Himwich, H. E.   Effects of methionine loading on the behavior of schizophrenic patients. *J. Nerv. Ment. Dis.* 134: 447, 1962.
4. Bunney, W. E., Brodie, H. K. H., Murphy, D. L., and Goodwin, F. K.   Psychopharmacological differentiation between two subgroups of depressed patients. *Proc. Am. Psychol. Assoc.* 78 (5 Pt. 2):829, 1970.
5. Bunney, W. E., Carpenter, W. T., Engelman, K., and Davis, J. M. Brain serotonin and depressive illness. In T. A. Williams et al. (Eds.), *Recent Advances in the Psychobiology of the Depressive Illnesses.* Washington: U.S. Government Printing Office, 1972.
6. Bunney, W. E., and Davis, J. M.   Norepinephrine in depressive reactions. *Arch. Gen. Psychiatry* 13:483, 1965.
7. Coppen, A. J.   The chemical pathology of the affective disorders. *Sci. Basis Med.* pp. 189-210, 1970.

8. Dunner, E. L., Cohn, C. K., Gershon, E. S., and Goodwin, F. K. Differential catechol-O-methyltransferase activity in unipolar and bipolar affective illness. *Arch. Gen. Psychiatry* 25:348, 1971.

9. Emlen, W., Segal, D. S., and Mandell, A. J. Thyroid state: Effects on pre- and postsynaptic central noradrenergic mechanisms. *Science* 175:79, 1972.

10. Fisher, D. B., and Kaufman, S. The stimulation of rat liver phenylalanine hydroxylase by phospholipids. *J. Biol. Chem.* 247:2250, 1972.

11. Frohman, C., Dzajkowski, N. P., Luby, E. D., Gottlieb, J. S., and Sent, R. Further evidence of a plasma factor in schizophrenia. *Arch. Gen. Psychiatry* 2:263, 1960.

12. Frohman, C., Tourney, G., Beckett, P. G. S., Lees, H., Latham, L. K., and Gottlieb, J. S. Biochemical identification of schizophrenia. *Arch. Gen. Psychiatry* 4:404, 1961.

13. Glassman, A. Indoleamines and affective disorders. *Psychosom. Med.* 31:107, 1969.

14. Goodwin, F. K., Murphy, D. L., Brodie, H. K. H., and Bunney, W. E. L-DOPA, catecholamines, and behavior: A clinical and biochemical study in depressed patients. *Biol. Psychiatry* 2:341, 1970.

15. Goodwin, F. K., Post, R. M., Dunner, E. L., and Gordon, E. K. Cerebrospinal fluid amine metabolites in affective illness: The probenecid technique. *Am. J. Psychiatry* 130:73, 1970.

16. Goodwin, F. K., Post, R. M., and Sack, R. L. Clinical evidence for neurochemical adaptation to psychotropic drugs. In A. J. Mandell (Ed.), *Neurobiological Mechanisms of Adaptation and Behavior*. New York: Raven Press, in press.

17. Heath, R. G., and Krupp, J. M. The biologic basis of schizophrenia: An autoimmune concept. In O. Walaas (Ed.), *Molecular Basis of Some Aspects of Mental Activity*, vol. 2, p. 313. New York: Academic Press, 1967.

18. Hsu, L. L., and Mandell, A. J. Multiple N-methyltransferases for aromatic alkylamines in brain. *Life Sci.* 13:847, 1973.

19. Hsu, L. L., and Mandell, A. J. Stimulation of brain aromatic alkylamine N-methyltransferase activity by FAD and methylcobalamin. *Life Sci.* 14:877, 1974.

20. Kety, S. S. Possible relation of central amines to behavior in schizophrenic patients. *Fed. Proc.* 20:894, 1961.

21. Knapp, S., and Mandell, A. J. The effects of narcotic drugs on the brain's serotonin biosynthetic systems. *Science* 177:1209, 1972.

22. Knapp, S., and Mandell, A. J. Parachlorophenylalanine—its three phase sequence of interactions with the two forms of brain tryptophan hydroxylase. *Life Sci.* 11 (Pt. I):761, 1972.

23. Knapp, S., and Mandell, A. J. Short and long term lithium administration: Effects on the brain's serotonergic biosynthetic systems. *Science* 180:645, 1973.

24. Kuczenski, R. Soluble, membrane-bound, and detergent-solubilized rat striatal tyrosine hydroxylase: pH-dependent cofactor binding. *J. Biol. Chem.* 248:5074, 1973.

25. Kuczenski, R. Striatal tyrosine hydroxylase with high and low affinity for tyrosine: Implications for the multiple-pool concept of catecholamines. *Life Sci.* 13:247, 1973.

26. Kuczenski, R., and Mandell, A. J.   Regulatory properties of soluble and particulate rat brain tyrosine hydroxylase. *J. Biol. Chem.* 247: 3114, 1972.
27. Mandell, A. J., Knapp, S., Kuczenski, R. T., and Segal, D. S.   Methamphetamine-induced alteration in the physical state of rat caudate tyrosine hydroxylase. *Biochem. Pharmacol.* 21:2737, 1972.
28. Mandell, A., and Morgan, M.   An indole(ethyl)amine N-methyltransferase in human brain. *Nature* 230:85, 1971.
29. Morgan, M., and Mandell, A. J.   An indole(ethyl)amine N-methyltransferase in the brain of the chick. *Science* 165:492, 1969.
30. Oswald, I., Brezinova, V., and Dunleavy, D. L. F.   On the slowness of action of tricyclic antidepressant drugs. *Br. J. Psychiatry* 120:673, 1972.
31. Rimon, R., Mandell, A. J., Puhakka, P., and Vanalaincn, E.   Adrenergic blockades and cholinergic response in human CSF. In N. Kline (Ed.), *Factors in Depression.* New York: Raven Press, 1974.
32. Saavedra, J. M., Coyle, J. T., and Axelrod, J.   The distribution and properties of the nonspecific N-methyltransferase in brain. *J. Neurochem.* 20:743, 1973.
33. Sachar, E. J.   Psychological homeostasis and endocrine function. In A. J. Mandell and M. P. Mandell (Eds.), *Psychochemical Research in Man.* New York: Academic Press, 1969.
34. Schildkraut, J. J.   The catecholamine hypothesis of affective disorder: A review of supporting evidence. *Am. J. Psychiatry* 122:509, 1965.
35. Schildkraut, J. J.   Rationale of some approaches used in biochemical studies of the affective disorders; the pharmacological bridge. In A. J. Mandell and M. P. Mandell (Eds.), *Psychochemical Research in Man.* New York: Academic Press, 1969.
36. Schildkraut, J. J., and Kety, S. S.   Biogenic amines and emotion. *Science* 156:21, 1967.
37. Segal, D. S., Knapp, S., Kuczenski, R., and Mandell, A. J.   Effects of environmental isolation on behavior and regional rat brain tyrosine hydroxylase and tryptophan hydroxylase activity. *Behav. Biol.* 1:1, 1973.
38. Segal, D. S., Kuczenski, R., and Mandell, A. J.   Strain differences in behavior and brain tyrosine hydroxylase activity. *Behav. Biol.* 7:75, 1972.
39. Segal, D. S., Kuczenski, R., and Mandell, A. J.   Theoretical implications of drug-induced adaptive regulation for a biogenic amine hypothesis of affective disorder. *Biol. Psychiatry* 9:147, 1974.
40. Segal, D. S., McAlister, C., and Geyer, M. A.   Ventricular infusion of norepinephrine and amphetamine: Direct versus indirect action. *Pharmacol. Biochem. Behav.* 2:79, 1974.
41. Segal, D. S., Sullivan, J. L., Kuczenski, R., and Mandell, A. J.   Effects of long-term reserpine on brain tyrosine hydroxylase and behavioral activity. *Science* 175:847, 1971.
42. Sjostrom, R., and Roos, B. E.   5-hydroxyindolacetic acid and homovanillic acid in the cerebrospinal fluid in manic-depressive psychosis. *Eur. J. Clin. Pharmacol.* 4:170, 1972.

43. Snyder, S. H. *Madness and the Brain.* New York: McGraw-Hill, 1974.

44. Wallach, M., Winters, W., Mandell, A. J., and Spooner, C.   A correlation of EEG, reticular multiple unit activity and gross behavior following various antidepressant agents in the cat. *Electroencephalogr. Clin. Neurophysiol.* 27:563, 1969.

4

Cultural Influences in Depression

HORACIO FÁBREGA, JR.

Logical analysis discloses that the term disease as ordinarily used by investigators and lay persons signifies a person-centered, time-bound (i.e., persistent), undesirable deviation in a person. In a formal sense, the person who is diseased will usually be found to deviate both from group norms and from personal norms of the relevant characteristics. These, we emphasize, constitute necessary conditions for predicating that someone is diseased. In this formulation, then, we speak of different types of diseases, depending on the way we wish to characterize the person [25]. Throughout the history of man until the recent scientific revolutions, behavioral changes constituted the ultimate data or indicators that served to establish who was diseased. The person's thoughts and verbal reports regarding his well-being and the changes in the way he conducted his social life were factors that raised the possibility of disease, and they also contributed directly to the kind of diagnosis that he received.

In Western nations today most human diseases can be described as abstract biological entities. Special information about the structure and functioning of the human body, which in turn is analyzed within the framework of certain branches of biological science, serves to establish who is diseased and how someone is diseased. Although equally biological in its basic processes of inquiry and in its aims, psychiatry is the branch of medicine that continues to rely almost exclusively on purely behavioral data as the basis of disease definition and typing. Thus, while information derived from radiographic analyses, blood chemistries, and other specialized tests constitute the essence of disease making in other medical disciplines, psychiatrists persist in using mainly verbal reports and analyses of social conduct in their efforts to diagnose disease. Yet all human diseases are and always have been in the last analysis socially created entities, since socially derived and socially placed norms that we term scientific serve to delimit the criteria, characteristics, and boundaries of disease. Psychiatry shares with other medical disciplines these formal or generic premises regarding what disease is, but it is unique in that to a very large extent the content or material that clothes these diseases is rooted in social behavior.

This is the frame of reference I shall use in this and the following chapter to examine the human disease that today we call Depression. In depression we have an entity that appears to have been a preoccupation of medical thinkers and practitioners throughout recorded history. Persons showing certain distinctive behaviors believed to indicate mood changes of a melancholic sort have consistently been seen as diseased and as requiring treatment when these behaviors persisted. Why this is so is an important aspect of Western social and cultural history and must be seen as a component of the frame of reference to be adopted. However, given our aims in this book, historical processes that account for the epistemological and ontological status of depression can only be discussed tangentially.

The goal of this and the following chapter is twofold. On the one hand, we will review the components of a social-cultural frame of reference as it bears on medical, that is, disease-related matters. On the other hand, we will accomplish this by focusing on depression. During the analysis we will point to some of the information that we have and some that we need about depression. Empirical information about a domain or problem must be evaluated in the light of prevailing analytic premises and methods of procedure. Since our understanding of depression has evolved so rapidly, a great deal of earlier empirical data is of limited use. We will thus be forced to focus more on theoretical matters and on what needs to be done in this field of study.

A SOCIAL-CULTURAL FRAME OF REFERENCE

Although the existence of a particular psychiatric disease may be traced to highly discrete genetic and or biochemical factors, questions about the social-cultural bases of such a disease are pertinent. Familial amaurosis and phenylketonuria, for example, are terms for fairly specific changes and alterations in human functioning; and the mechanisms of these, it is to be emphasized, are well explained biologically. To be sure, the distribution of these alterations has a social-cultural basis: mating practices and dietary habits are governed by rules; hence, the distribution and even particular occurrences of amaurotic idiocy and phenylketonuria can be explained in terms of the social-cultural bases of such rules. Yet the fact that these terms are also disease labels can be viewed as essentially a social-cultural matter. They refer to human diseases precisely because certain norms and standards regarding social conduct prevail in our culture, and persons so labeled characteristically fail to meet these norms. Furthermore, for a variety of reasons, these particular failures are judged to be medical matters *by convention,* and there exist social prescriptions about how persons showing such behavioral failures should be treated. A social-cultural frame of reference, then, should encompass such basic matters as the reasons for the existence of norms and standards whose violations we call disease, even though the basis for or explanation of the behaviors in question is genetic or chemical.

A social-cultural frame of reference with respect to disease has traditionally been used to elaborate upon the prevailing biomedical definitions and conventions. In other words, given that specific changes or processes constitute disease *by definition,* how can we explain or better understand the phenomena in question by using formulations that draw on social and cultural factors? Classically this has involved viewing disease as an entity having extension in time and social space and inquiring whether certain characteristics of or factors involving disease (e.g., manifestations, causes, distribution) are related to variables we term social and cultural. When examined within such a frame of reference, features of disease typically have been examined comparatively—social groups of various sorts have been compared vis-à-vis aspects of disease.

The employment of a social-cultural frame of reference with respect to depression brings into focus a variety of theoretical considerations that need to be made explicit. I would like to examine two of these, each of which involves distinctions and dichotomies that although useful in many instances, in others may hinder or obscure understanding. The first involves the distinction between the biological and the social-cultural. Strictly speaking, of course, the meaning of the term biological is quite vague and should include broadly a consideration of how life forms developed phylogenetically and ontogenetically, which means that such development (and in particular, adaptation) of the form needs to be framed in terms of the modern synthetic theory of evolution [15, 72, 113]. When the life form is man, a consideration of his unique traits (e.g., language, thought, complex social organization) inevitably requires a discussion of factors one could describe as social, cultural, and psychological. Thus, the initial form of the first distinction above breaks down, and we are left with something such as genetic-organic versus environmental.

With regard to human behavior generally and human disease specifically, we note that the distinction genetic-organic versus environmental can in many instances serve a useful purpose in pointing to classes of phenomena and factors having an explanatory role. It is quite obviously meaningful and has been extremely productive to conduct investigations into the sources of variation of human behavior and disease using the concepts and methods of genetic theory. When the focus is a given individual or instance of disease, however, the distinction is less useful since the *logical* differences that articulate the distinction are difficult to separate in an *empirical* sense. Purely social and cultural considerations, such as dietary rules, family structure, social density, and behavior-regulating beliefs that indirectly affect the developing organism, have important constitutional or organic effects [31, 77]. And, in the domain of human disease, as Durell [19] has pointed out most lucidly, so-called genetic predispositions may involve vulnerabilities to environmental or physical factors (e.g., infections, toxins) whose incidence and prevalence is importantly influenced by other environmental factors of a social-cultural sort. These considerations suggest that in many instances we should use the distinction genetic-organic versus environmental less exclusively.

The second theoretical consideration to be discussed here touches more directly on medical matters and involves the opposition between a dimensional and a typological approach to human behavior generally and to disease in particular. Age, weight, and height are dimensions, whereas sex and ethnicity are types. In science generally, particularly in the physical sciences, one observes that central concepts and variables can be expressed in a mathematically continuous or discrete form. (Recently, Hage [36] has argued that we take a similar posture toward sociological constructs.) With regard to human behavior and psychopathology, one observes that empirically oriented investigators are prone to employ statistically derived concepts, such that persons or groups are characterized by high or low scores on X or Y factor. Implicit here is a view that people or groups show more or less of a particular dimension as opposed to falling into logical classes or types whose boundaries are sharp and whose membership criteria are relatively unambiguous.

This typological approach is often equated with the time-honored medical model in terms of which disease is articulated as an entity sui generis, having an existence of its own. Emphasis on natural histories of diseases serves to underscore the need for precise medical diagnosis as a basis for understanding the causes of disease and their effective treatment. In the light of this dichotomy, one observes that dimensional theorists are portrayed as though they eschewed the utility of medical diagnosis, whereas typologists and disease-oriented physicians are portrayed as though they were insensitive to the virtues of characterizing phenomena or persons by means of dimensional constructs [45, 128]. Needless to say, this alleged opposition can also obscure matters if one forgets that concealed by the metaphor of opposition are two general orientations to phenomena and disease that serve diverse purposes, have distinctive advantages, and can complement and enrich each other. There is much logic in subscribing to the position that distinct diseases occur in nature, each having a potentially separate natural history and requiring a unique program of therapy, and, at the same time, holding that the behavior of persons classified by means of such disease typologies can be described and explained by means of suitable dimensions. When one focuses on depression, the issue here under discussion touches tangentially on what Klerman [54a] describes as the unitary versus the pluralistic view. On the one hand, all depressions are said to share essentially a similar ontology, and what others refer to as types of depression are seen by the "unitarians" as merely different locations on a basic dimension or continuum. The alternative view is that several depressions exist, each a specific type, as it were, having distinct causes and perhaps requiring distinct courses of treatment [5, 22, 34, 53, 129].

ON THE DEFINITION AND PREVALENCE OF DEPRESSION IN WESTERN CULTURES

When contemporary researchers refer to depression as a psychobiological entity, they echo the convictions of clinicians of earlier eras who used the term melancholia to refer to changes in mood, characterological patterns, and bodily changes [56]. The term depression that because of Kraepelin [57] we now use to label certain affective disorders is obviously linked semantically with that of melancholia, which preoccupied Greek, medieval, and Renaissance practitioners [70, 120, 121, 122]. Contemporary dilemmas about the definition and classification of depression can also be seen as residues of the earlier, equally difficult task of specifying the features and bases for the melancholic type or the morbid condition melancholia.

I will here adopt for expository purposes the view that depression is a medical disease that has a singular and relatively unambiguous identity. The recent literature indicates that this is probably not the case, that instead various types of depression exist. However, sufficient problems persist regarding definition [37] that adopting a unitary view seems justified, especially since my aims are principally analytic. I will posit that a cluster of related changes that encompass a person's mood, appearance, actions, and bodily functioning, together indicate depression (or melancholia) and, furthermore, that this entity has been a constant preoccupation of the medical profession throughout recorded Western history. Each of these changes can be seen as or reduced to types of behaviors, which permits me to schematize my claim as follows:

$$\text{Depression (D)} = \sum_{i=1}^{n} Bi$$

where Bi refers to a distinctive type of behavior. Now, the recognition or singling out of an instance of depression is a social-cultural affair since it involves the judgment that behaviors or reports of a person are medically relevant (that is deviant, undesirable, in need of correction, and classifiable as disease). Fundamental questions regarding the prevalence of depression in Western cultures in terms of the above definition can be pursued. In this regard, one may ask: Why are such behaviors singled out as medically significant?

We can assume that perceptions of bodily changes come close to representing necessary conditions for judging that a state of disease exists [25]. Hence, any cluster of changes that includes bodily components is likely to be judged as medically relevant. But we are interested here in examining the nature of the association between disease and mood-related changes. Now, when in Western history man began to judge his mood state as separate from that of his body is obviously a difficult question to answer [27, 102, 114]. Let us assume that the notion of individual differences in temperament (a proto-personality typology) goes back to classic times and that such a notion was fused with ideas of bodily function and performance. Given this, we ask: Are altered mood-related behaviors a fundamental part of a disease melancholia or depression *because* of their frequent association with the perception of bodily changes and with behaviors that indicate diminished physical capacities? If so, then is this association due to a natural biological attribute of man to respond holistically? Or are people led to explain primary mood changes in terms of alleged bodily changes? Perhaps the perceptions of these bodily changes so alter the individual's sense of place in the world that the perceptions, in turn, prove unsettling to him in a psychosocial and emotional sense.

One must at least postulate that behaviors that suggest mood chances *by themselves* are, and have been under certain circumstances, sufficient conditions for the judgment that depression (or melancholia) prevailed, regardless of whether or not these behaviors were associated with or linked by the actor or significant others to existing bodily changes and functions. If this is the case, then why is it that behaviors suggesting or reflecting depressive moods when they persist and become encompassing have indicated undesirable deviations and ultimately disease? Is it the social or moral disarticulation that they metaphorically express, or is there built into our cultural rules and patterns the premise that persons should be happy or at least should be satisfied with their lot and carry out their social obligations with a positive or neutral disposition? Labeling failures in this domain as medical may have been our way of providing continuity of social organization. In short, the attempt to determine the prevalence of depression takes one to the basic issue of what behaviors are expectable or standard in *our* cultural system regarding mood, disposition, bodily performance, and social conduct, since it is in terms of this baseline that deviations representing disease are marked.

It should be clear that examining depression from this standpoint involves issues central to psychosomatic medicine and mind-body relations. A basic concern of persons espousing such a psychosomatic orientation centers on the perceptions and meanings that persons have about bodily matters, that is, how physiological function and dysfunction are registered in awareness and or behavior. We in Western culture have a language rich in lexical items that signify a domain of mind, mood, and motives, and we talk about, experience, and conduct social relations on the assumption that this domain is separate from but related to that of the body. This dualistic frame of reference is not universal, and we must inquire how the domains we term mind and body are reflected in behavior and articulated by members of linguistic communities that lack such a dualistic orientation and such a rich lexicon of the mind. In the light of these considerations, it is apparent that investigations aimed at evaluating how persons experience and express emotions and altered states of the body are much needed.

ON THE UNIVERSALITY OF DEPRESSION

Epidemiological and ecological studies involving contemporary nonliterate groups, together with evidence from the skeletal remains of ancient human groups, strongly suggest that diseases are endemic in human groups. Furthermore, all social groups have as part of their culture a medical nomenclature and taxonomy by which *they* define and label illnesses of various sorts (we shall use "illness" to signify natively defined entities). A great many, perhaps most, Western defined diseases can be uncovered among non-Western peoples, though of course the correspondence between these diseases and the native illnesses is a difficult one to ascertain.

Evaluating the prevalence of depression in non-Western cultures involves one in rather basic social-cultural considerations. A universal attribute of man, we assume, is that he has a concern about his bodily well-being and that he has feelings of various sorts. An experience that involves despondency, hopelessness, and disappointment, especially if it includes bodily disturbances, is likely to direct an individual to various persons or institutions to seek relief. Indeed, all societies provide for their members units and personnel whose function is precisely the fixing or reestablishing of a person's expressed disequilibrium. Given these considerations, it should be evident that how an individual defines such an experience is all-important as a basis for action. Interpretations and the action consequences associated with the experience thus determine how and what the actor does about it. In this light, the *language* of the individual can be seen as a device used to give meaning and significance to the experience. This meaning and significance can be seen as a program or map that behaviorally directs the person along culturally marked channels. In the case of depression, if its elaboration is in the religious sphere, religious preoccupations will be prominent and eventually religious personnel will be sought. If bodily components are prominent correlates, medical personnel will be visited. And if victimization is a prominent component, attorneys or witchcraft experts will be consulted, depending on the institutions the particular culture has singled out for the individual. Culture, in short, provides the basis for and meaning of the common experiences of man, and it also prescribes action and channels behavior under these conditions. Clearly, then, to *locate* depressed individuals, to be able to interpret actions and behavior reflecting disequilibrium, the investigator has to know the individual's culture and language.

Questions regarding the prevalence of depression in non-Western cultures may be pursued by examining our definitional formula:

$$\text{Depression} = \sum_{i=1}^{n} Bi$$

We may ask to what extent such a formula conforms to the rules embodied in the medical taxonomic systems of non-Western peoples, and to what extent related behaviors fall outside the domain of the medical. Thus, given an occurrence of depressive disease diagnosed by an informed outsider in terms of Western biomedical notions, are nonliterates also likely to judge that occurrence as an illness of some sort and to prescribe a native form of treatment? It is difficult at this stage to give a clear answer to this question, although one can be anticipated: the more the depression reflects changes we interpret as psychotic, the more likely it is to be judged as illness, since psychotic disturbances are typically found among the illnesses recognized by nonliterates. It certainly is true that all behavioral changes that informed observers would judge as psychotic are not necessarily seen as illness by members of the cultural group [26]. One should remark on the difficult problems that a mythical observer might face when attempting to find or diagnose depression cross-culturally. Besides the problem of establishing relevant norms against which deviations are to be marked (a problem the psychiatrist shares with other epidemiologists who may rely on purely biological indicators), the observer will need to know something about the language and behavioral rules prevalent in the cultural group in order to make meaningful references to changes in mood, activity, self-conception, etc. (This will be elaborated upon later.) Last, it should be emphasized that although an occurrence of depressive disease may be judged as an illness in a particular group, the meaning given to that illness (its name, etiology, mechanism, significance, etc.) will be highly variable and characteristically will draw on the important cultural symbols and premises.

Some Biocultural Aspects of Cross-Cultural Studies

A preoccupation of persons who work in the field of cross-cultural psychiatry has been whether psychiatric diseases are in fact universal— whether one can find among nonliterate peoples, persons who show evidence of the psychiatric diseases that we have identified and recognize in our Western culture. Perhaps it would be useful to turn the argument around and ask what the implications would be of the hypothetical finding that depression does *not* exist in a given culture. Investigations in the anthropological tradition and many psychiatrically based studies have been addressed to this issue in the past, and a purely social-psychological model has been used. Consequently, little attention has been paid to the possible biological (genetic, neurochemical, physiological) causes or correlates of this category of illness. The result has been a bifurcation in the literature and a failure to address the complex interactions that may be occurring between sociocultural, neurological, and other biological systems in depressive illness [24]. There is now a strong trend in both psychiatry and anthropology for this mode of analysis to be related to biological matters, and we will try to emphasize these aspects here in a general way.

Let us assume that on the bases of empirical research findings derived from studies of Western societies we had postulated that certain distinctive neurochemical factors constitute necessary and sufficient conditions for an individual to develop depression. If depression as a category of illness were not discovered in a certain cultural group, one would conclude that previously postulated neurochemical factors were not present. A variety of inferences are possible from this finding: (1) that the group's genome differed, e.g., that particular alleles were absent in the group; (2) that the physical environment of the group differed or that the group stood in a substantially different relationship to the environment in which they lived (e.g., ingested differing concentrations of minerals and elements). Chemical, physiological, and in a limited way even structural features of the human body are not fixed and invariant but rather can be modified by environmental differences, as any physical anthropologist knows. We can then be led to hypothesize that persons living in distinctive ecological niches may show gross differences of a quantitative (if not qualitative) sort in cerebral functioning. In short, one assumes that the human brain, considered structurally, neurophysiologically, and chemically, is an entity that is common to all members of the human species; but since homeostasis allows for a variety of connected ranges in function, differences in environmental pressures can constrain and modify this functioning in diverse ways. I have discussed elsewhere the complex relations that obtain between disease (considered both as a biological and behavioral form) and the social and physical environment of man [25, 123]. Such environmental differences or differences in social-psychological adaptations (since these may also be presumed to affect brain function by altering levels of hormones and minerals [52]), could be the bases of the observed absence of depression and the hypothesized neurochemical factors.

We may in this context entertain the following theoretical question: Could it be that members of a group do show such neurochemical factors but that somehow they nevertheless do not show depression? A logical possibility, in other words, is that the previously mentioned neurochemical factors might constitute necessary and sufficient conditions for depression in *Western* man but not in all persons. In short, in spite of our conviction that depression and neurochemical factors of a distinctive sort are invariably associated, cross-cultural studies could leave us with either of two possibilities: (1) depressive disease can occur in the absence of such neurochemical factors, or (2) our assumed distinctive neurochemical factors can be demonstrated in the absence of depressive disease. The first possibility points to obvious differences in the entity depression and constitutes evidence that diverse types of changes or mechanisms can presumably produce depression. Regarding the second possibility, one might be led to postulate that the neurochemical factors were part of an altered chemical milieu made possible by environmental variables and that together these biological considerations served as the matrix for influences implied by our notions of personality configurations or behavioral dispositions.

The general point needing emphasis is that the finding that depressions do not exist in a particular culture, together with the assumption that neurochemical factors are invariant features of depression, allows the researcher to examine hypotheses about the comparative importance of genetic, environmental, and social-psychological influences in this disease. In the present context, establishing that environmental differences are critical, for example, does not necessarily exclude genetic influences, for knowledge that the heritability of depression was high in Western societies would merely indicate that genetic and environmental influences interacted to produce depression. I assume that a disease such as depression is an outcome of the interplay of genetic, physical environmental, and psychosocial influences, each of which acts at various levels in the causal network [7]. Differences in one or all three types of influences can account for the alleged absence of depression in a given group, and the extent of accessible information about the groups involved will determine how understanding of depression is furthered by comparative studies.

Certainly it is true that if neurochemical factors were not assumed to constitute a necessary and sufficient condition for the occurrence of depression, then the finding that no depression exists in a given culture has narrower implications. Such a finding leads directly to the examination of how personality and behavioral dispositions contribute to depression in Western cultures but apparently fail to do so in the particular culture. It is in the light of these psychosocial considerations that psychiatrists and social scientists have approached the study of the distribution of psychiatric disease cross-culturally [65].

A tenet of comparative psychology draws central attention to the heterogeneity of child-rearing practices across cultures. Indeed, a central assumption in the field of psychological anthropology is that these practices, together with the myriad of other behavior-organizing rules and practices that are subsumed by the term culture, play a determining role in shaping adult personality. Anthropologists have long been aware of intracultural individual differences in personality structure and functioning, but a guiding heuristic nevertheless has been that culture-wide patterns and dispositions can be discerned and that these contrast across cultures. Adult personalities, in short, are believed to reflect the requirements of living in a distinctive social and cultural world. It is the linkage (or lack thereof) that exists between personality dispositions on the one hand, and sociocultural rules and norms regarding behavior on the other, that lead personality theorists to speak of psychosocial adaptation. In this regard, cultures are expected to differ in terms of how they influence personality formation, the expectations and demands that they place on adults, and, by extension, how they provide for the psychological well-being of their members. It is the assumed relative plasticity of the human organism and its shaping by culture, as it were, that contribute to the explanation of cross-cultural personality differences and to the assumption that cultures will differ in terms of type and quantity of psychiatric disturbances.

The conceptual and methodological problems associated with any attempt to define, evaluate, and measure psychiatric disturbances cross-culturally have heretofore been so encompassing that they have not allowed precise answers to questions posed by psychiatric epidemiologists of a comparative bent. As we shall see, the evidence suggests that the more carefully one probes the psychosocial adjustment of non-Western peoples, the more one is likely to encounter Western nosological entities such as depression. This poses another set of question involving the universality of depressive disease, for example: How can the claim be substantiated that no instances of depression have been recorded in culture X? Clearly, the claim would have to be made following empirical studies of the sort that successfully met those anthropological conditions for accurate descriptions and interpretations of behavior that were briefly touched on earlier [23]. At the same time, such empirical studies would have to be guided by definitional criteria that were unproblematic, that competent psychiatric nosologists and epidemiologists would judge as appropriate and valid. Given the difficulty of evaluating behavior in other cultural groups and the controversy surrounding the meaning and definition of depression that one sees in psychiatry today, a conservative person would say that the claim that depressive disease does not exist in a particular culture cannot be made and that it is in fact nonsensical to assume such a possibility.

One is left with the conclusion that the question of the possible universality of depression (or that of any Western defined psychiatric entity) as ordinarily stated is rather simplistic and not particularly productive. On the one hand, given the bases of definition and diagnosis in psychiatry, it would be difficult to claim that certain cultures do in fact lack a given disease. However, if empirical data did allow the making of such a claim, then obviously our understanding of the disease would afford a basis for testing key hypotheses or premises about the disease. Earlier some of these considerations were entertained in a preliminary way, in particular the line of inquiry that might be followed if highly specific neurochemical factors were found to be invariably associated with depression in Western culture.

A Case Illustration

The prevalence of depression in Africa may be used as an illustration of the problems just discussed. Although there are exceptions [92], the literature indicates that during the Colonial Era (1890-1956) instances of depression (of a psychotic nature) were absent, rare, or less intense and shorter in duration if present, rarely included self-castigation, and rarely involved suicide. These generalizations are based on data drawn from mental hospitals. Various reasons have been offered for these alleged findings: One set involves the validity of the findings; for example, that hospitalized patients constitute a statistically poor and biased sample, or that what an external observer would judge depression is not differentiated medically by Africans and hence cannot be brought to the attention of medical personnel. Another set of reasons assumes the validity of the reports and involves psychosocial factors believed to play a role in the etiology of depression; for example, that the extended family and funerary rules "protect" persons who are mourning over object loss; that Africans make extensive use of the defense mechanism projection and consequently cannot develop guilt; that among Africans a clan as opposed to a personal superego prevails and that such a form of psychosocial control also eliminates the need for depressive symptoms.

Reports suggest that during the era of independence (1957 to present) instances of depression were not only not rare but actually common. The reasons for the increased prevalence of depression are believed to be that the newer observations took place in so-called open hospital settings as well as in indigenous treatment centers, and that researchers were now relying on newer concepts of depression that included somatic preoccupations as indicators of the disease. As stated earlier, persons showing evidence of depression are often not judged as ill by their co-equals, but if they are, they are more likely to be treated in indigenous centers where psychiatrists are now available. Furthermore, researchers were now using the label depression for states that earlier would have been classified as neurasthenia or hypochondriasis. Given these considerations (equivocal findings and conflicting methods of procedure) and the absence of suitable field epidemiological studies, one is forced to conclude that we do not know whether in fact depression is as prevalent in Africa as it is in Western nations.

An exception to the preceding assertion may be found in the comparative studies undertaken by Leighton and his colleagues. In the study by Leighton et al. [63] in Nigeria, evidence of depression was found in up to 60 percent of the hospitalized patients; interestingly, 35 to 262 village respondents classified as having certain or probable psychiatric disease showed "prominent depressive symptoms, and a further 25 had depressive in addition to other prominent symptoms. The remaining depressive symptoms (24) came from persons who [were classified as questionably psychiatrically ill] . . . or whose depressive symptoms were noted with only medium or low confidence" [p. 140]. These figures further illustrate the general point mentioned earlier. As careful and more refined comparative psychiatric epidemiological studies are performed, there is a tendency for depression to be found in greater and greater numbers. In fact, so-called neurotic depressive symptoms were more common in Nigerian villagers than they were in community respondents from Stirling County. Nevertheless, one needs to reemphasize here the general limitations of studies, such as Leighton's, that rely on symptom questionnaires [17].

Differences between United States and United Kingdom

Even when depression is studied in settings that share a common language and a set of traditions the problem of a comparative epidemiology is a perplexing one, one that involves a number of theoretical issues. Thus, a long-standing finding in studies that compare rates of hospitalization for psychiatric disease in England and in the United States has been the differential rates observed for manic-depressive psychosis and schizophrenia. Consistently, investigators have uncovered higher rates for manic-depressive psychosis and lower ones for schizophrenia in England [58]. For reasons to be outlined later, hospital rate differentials are difficult to interpret. One way of explaining them is in terms of differences in the behavior of psychiatrists as opposed to that of the patients. The rate differential, in other words, could be due to differences in the way U.K. and U.S. psychiatrists construe and use concepts such as schizophrenia and manic-depressive. The U.S./U.K. Diagnostic Project was designed in part to answer just this type of question [131]. It involved the training of a small group of project psychiatrists in the use of a standard interview—the present State Examination developed by John Wing [128] and his colleagues in London—and the evaluation and diagnosis by these psychiatrists of one group of recently hospitalized patients in New York and another in London. In each locality, the diagnoses rendered by the project psychiatrists on a group of patients were systematically compared with the diagnoses rendered by the regular hospital psychiatrists on the same group of patients. Hospital diagnostic profiles conformed to expectations, with British personnel rendering a higher frequency of manic-depressive and a lower frequency of schizophrenia compared to the Americans. The project psychiatrists, on the other hand, produced diagnostic profiles in each of the two settings that were in closer agreement, although across-nation differences of a smaller sort still prevailed, suggesting to the researchers that actual patient differences may have existed. At any rate, the elimination of significant amounts of across-nation variation indicates that much of the difference one observes in international comparisons may stem from differences in the way diagnostic concepts are used or, stated differently, from differences in the way the corresponding diseases are construed by the psychiatrists. Thus, when relatively standard instruments are used by a homogeneously and rigorously trained group of psychiatrists, the actual diagnoses rendered on patients from allegedly contrasting populations tend to resemble each other more closely [14, 35].

Another approach to evaluating this same possibility that cross-national differences in rates of hospitalized patients stem from behavioral differences in psychiatrists involved the audiovisual taping of patient interviews and the subsequent use of the tapes as data by psychiatrists in the U.S. and U.K. to render diagnoses. In one of these studies, examining psychiatrists were furnished with additional back ground data on the patients. Despite the fact that U.S. and U.K. psychiatrists were evaluating the same patients, as it were, across-nation differences in proportion of depression still prevailed and conformed to expectations [101]. The other study, which used only the audiovisual tapes and did not furnish psychiatrists background information, also produced significant across-nation differences in use of psychotic diagnostic categories, as anticipated. This again indicated basic differences in concept meaning and suggested to the investigators that serious restraint be placed on the interpretation of cross-cultural differences in psychiatric disease rates [54]. Katz [48] conducted a similar series of studies and concluded that perhaps basic differences in the way psychiatrists perceive and interpret behavior itself (in addition to differences in the way psychiatric concepts are used) may be a factor explaining cross-national differences in psychiatric disease rates. It goes without saying, of course, that rate differences such as these must ultimately be traced to social-cultural differences in the way the psychiatrists are socialized, both as members of their respective social units and as professionals.

New Approaches to the Study of Psychiatric Disease

The recent program of studies undertaken by the Clinical Research Branch of the National Institute of Mental Health promises to reveal a great deal about the social and cultural correlates of depression and to meet some of the objections raised in this section and in the earlier part of the chapter [46]. In an early study conducted in Maryland these researchers compared community respondents who showed prominent evidence of depression with hospitalized depressives [39]. It was reported that the behavior and not the mood factor per se differentiated the groups, with the hospitalized depressives distinguished by their level of self-accusation, helplessness (as reflected in decision making) and by differences in the tempo of their behavior. These findings in a sense point to indices of hospitalization, a factor that must be taken into account in evaluating epidemiological findings (see Chapter 5). (In a logical sense, Hogarty and Katz's study is similar to those that point to striking differences in the behaviors and symptoms of depressives diagnosed in different types of hospital settings. It has been shown that the standards of the groups that use certain types of facilities importantly influence the kinds of symptoms that persons bring to these facilities [55].) Later work by Katz and his group was carried out in a multiethnic setting, namely Hawaii, and involved studying psychiatric in-patients from various ethnic groups [51]. The behavior of these patients at two points in time was compared. Psychiatric personnel in the hospital applied Western clinical criteria dealing with the phenomenology of illness while lay persons in the community (significant others) who had had contact with the patient prior to admission completed questionnaires about the patient's social behavior. These questionnaires inquired about a variety of clinically relevant social behaviors, and the behaviors were described in everyday language [50].

Unfortunately, few results of this program of study are available. Although these results do not focus exclusively on persons with depressive disease, they do touch on gross symptom patterns, and depression-related behaviors form a part of these patterns. Caucasian patients showed very high indices of depression-anxiety (an affective symptom factor) compared to Japanese patients. In evaluating the community behavior of these patients as perceived by significant others, the researchers attempted to rely on the behavioral norms in the respective ethnic groups. The behavioral expectations of community residents and the earlier behavior of the patients themselves as perceived by significant others served as the baseline against which clinically relevant behavior was judged. In short, the researchers attempted to uncover behaviors perceived by co-equals as most problematic, and hence justifying hospitalization. The researchers discovered that components of the affective symptom factor (e.g., helplessness) were most prominently singled out by lay Caucasians, whereas this type of behavior did not appear problematic to lay Japanese-Hawaiians.

The preliminary nature of these results and the informal way in which they have thus far been presented prohibits us from going into greater detail about this study. It is significant, however, that the researchers are aware that community norms and standards vis-à-vis deviant behaviors must be used as a background against which to evaluate the clinical behavior of hospitalized patients. It is these norms that force or prompt hospitalization. Let us elaborate upon this point. We will assume that members of Culture X judge a particular set of behaviors as normal, expected, or appropriate and another set as deviant (X_n vs. X_d). A similar formulation applied to another group Y would yield behaviors Y_n and Y_d respectively. Now, it is behaviors X_d and Y_d that lead the patient or those responsible for him to seek medical care or hospitalization. Why this is the case requires explanation and involves probing the traditions, values, and behavioral rules of the respective group. Explaining the presence of the behaviors in the first place involves sociocultural, genetic, and other biological factors. The behaviors X_d and Y_d may not, of course, be parallel and in fact may include segments that the contrasting group judges as normal. If such socially defined normal behaviors include clinically relevant symptoms (defined biomedically), we are again forced to inquire about cultural traditions for an explanation of this community tolerance. In brief, we are led to visualize behaviors of a particular type as distributed in some fashion in a social group. Members of the group partition or grade such behaviors in terms of their appropriateness. Explaining the reasons why behavior is inappropriate in this sense requires going into social-cultural considerations, although the basis for the behavior itself may rest heavily on genetic factors. Distributions of certain behaviors along the continuum of appropriateness need to be compared across social groups, and it is implicit in the researcher's formulation that the judgments and labels placed on such behaviors (e.g., vis-à-vis deviance) will be substantially different and will require a social-cultural explanation. Given these considerations, it should be clear why the comparative study of symptom patterns of hospitalized patients is of limited value in understanding generic questions about disease entities. Such comparisons merely yield data on a certain subset of patients with a given disease, namely those judged (for whatever reason) as problematic in their respective social groups.

In addition to offering insights about the processes that lead to hospitalization, studies of this type also offer the potential for clarifying how cultural patterns affect behavioral organization, maintenance, change, and deviation. They are consequently addressed to rather basic social-behavioral issues. Why are certain forms of behavior judged abnormal or aberrant by members of an ethnic group while others (perhaps equally pathological from the observer's standpoint) are viewed as appropriate? Similarly, why do ethnic or cultural groups differ radically on these parameters, and what can we learn about behavior dynamics from these issues? These questions highlight the fact that the behavioral expressions of psychiatric disease (assuming for the moment that such diseases are what biological psychiatrists claim they are, namely, truly psychobiological entities) must be evaluated in the light of the cultural rules that organize what passes as normal behavior among members of the ethnic group. Such questions, often bypassed, are going to have to be answered before we can answer others, such as what and how social variables cause psychiatric disease. Studies in this vein, although ostensibly epidemiological and psychiatric, must be seen as contributing to our understanding of far more fundamental questions that are of concern to people in medicine and social science.

Psychological Implications of Cross-Cultural Studies

It should be emphasized that evaluating how a Western disease type such as depression is manifested at the psychological level in contrasting cultural settings offers the researcher a rich opportunity to clarify fundamental aspects of human behavior. Traditional approaches to this problem have involved studying socialization patterns in relation to processes of personality functioning, the latter construed in motivational and dynamic terms. Perceptual-cognitive aspects of this same issue, namely that of the form and expression of psychiatric disease in contrasting cultures, have been relatively underemphasized. Yet it is precisely the careful evaluation of such processes that is currently receiving a great deal of attention in anthropology [28, 33]. If properly applied to the study of psychiatric disorders, such evaluations would offer an opportunity for the testing of prevailing assumptions about both psychiatric disease and the influence of culture on psychological functioning.

Culture, in this light, may be defined as the shared cognitive processes of a people; these, to be sure, encompass ordinary rules of conduct; however, such rules need to be seen as grafted onto basic perceptual-cognitive constancies that grow out of how people represent the physical and nonphysical worlds. Let us posit that persons, in relating to their physical and social environments, employ a finite number of perceptual categories to order sensory input. Perceptual categories are an outgrowth of both biological attributes and culturally programmed learning experiences and can be seen as furnishing the raw units of experience. These categories may be described as ordered into various classes, which in turn are ordered to form a cognitive map of the world. The learned meanings of a group or culture can be seen as represented by such a map. Through the execution of various rules that are culture-specific, individuals are believed to process in a meaningful and consistent way the data of experience (the meanings furnished by the cognitive map of the world) [123, 124].

A group's language acts as a similar kind of filter for experience. Although there is controversy as to whether thought actually derives from language, as some have suggested, there is little doubt that language influences cognition through memory and guides perception under conditions of ambiguity [13, 68].

Let us now see how this formulation may be used to understand the way culture and depression might be related. It is the positing of such relations, their articulation in the form of hypotheses, and the subsequent testing of these in the field that may help to clarify basic aspects of behavior and disease. I will, in this discussion, adopt for heuristic purposes a purely psychological approach, and will compare depression with schizophrenia. Depression, I will posit, is a bonafide disease entity that primarily affects the individual's coloring of experience and level of activity; and in particular, that a feeling tone, sadness, is a component of this entity depression. According to many, sadness constitutes one of the primary emotions of man—a biological verity, if you will. Cultures may differ with regard to what produces sadness, but that such an emotional tone is realized by all people is accepted. Following the registration of the emotions in the central nervous system, there is an activitation of distinctive facial muscle groups by what is termed a facial affect program; however, situational factors and cultural conventions are believed to influence the possible activation of such muscles [20]. In brief, the consequences of emotions, their meanings, their elaboration into behavior, and the way they are expressed are affected by culturally specific display rules, although all people everywhere are believed to share and recognize to some extent the workings of the facial affect program.

Given the complex way in which the primary emotions get reworked and channeled by culture, an altered psychobiological organismic state that is long-lasting and includes sadness and diminished activity can be expected to assume various appearances across cultures. I will assume, nevertheless, that changes brought about during an instance of depression do not alter the basic ordering or form of the individual's cognitive apparatus. The model reviewed above, in short, is not seen as structurally altered during an instance of depression;

perceptual categories, the orderings of these into a cognitive map, the rules of operation, etc., are judged as structurally intact in depression, at least in its early stages. The manifestations of the disease are believed instead to reflect quantitative alterations in the functioning of the cognitive apparatus. Thus, a slowing of bodily processes and information processing together with changes in the coloring of an individual's experiencing of his world, I anticipate, will be expressed in habitually ordered ways. In other words, when viewed against the prevailing cultural norms, the form of behavior during depression is preserved, though exaggerations or deviations in content are to be expected. The investigator wishing to find and understand depression is thus required first to construct a model of the culture by means of an analysis of the prevailing language and then to use both the model and the language to infer how behavior is ordered in the culture, since it is in terms of such habitual behavioral patterns that the changes of the disease processes are likely to be channeled and expressed. Alternatively, by analyzing the behavior of disturbed or deviant individuals, he is expected to infer the meanings of various actions and verbalizations using the understanding of the culture generated by his model and his command of the language. Once this is accomplished, he is in a position to see which of these behaviors might correspond to behaviors ordinarily taken to indicate depression. The investigator, for example, is required to study the culture and learn the various emotional terms, the meanings and interpretations given to these, how emotions are likely to be expressed behaviorally in the light of such meanings, the ways in which sensory information about the body and the physical world are ordered and represented cognitively, the interpretations placed on fundamental physical and biological processes, etc., since it is in terms of these culturally shared perceptions, cognitions, and culturally based theories of the world (i.e., existential premises) that the individual will experience and express the changes associated with a profound organismic change such as depression. Using this paradigm, then, we would say that cross-cultural differences in the manifestations of depression are a direct expression of and, consequently, are deducible from differences in the prevailing cultures (as represented in our models or maps of these cultures). For this reason, the manifestations of depression could be hypothesized to be derived, in a systematic and direct way, from fundamental perceptual-cognitive categories and rules of operation that differ cross-culturally but that retain their form and order during the disease process.

For purposes of contrast, let me posit that schizophrenia is also a bonafide disease entity, that it affects the way in which the individual regulates attention (specifically, that the disorder involves the stimulus-response process), and that failure to regulate and inhibit attention selectively brings about a breakdown in perceptual constancies or, stated differently, a change in the individual's perceptual categories [73, 108]. In schizophrenia, thus, I ancticipate a loosening or outright alteration in the ordering and form in which experience is cast. Thought, mood, and behavioral changes in schizophrenia are seen as consequences of, or responses to, these fundamental perceptual-cognitive alterations. Now, the pattern of a culture or a cognitive map can also be expected to influence the way schizophrenia is expressed, but not in the way it influences depression. Since such a map is judged as formally unaltered during depression, its structure and central organizing themes will bear a direct, almost isomorphic relation to the structure and organization of behavior during an instance of disease. In schizophrenia, on the other hand, key concepts in the map that determine how the individual defines his position vis-à-vis the world become differentially important since it is in terms of these that attention is regulated and these that in turn determine the overall meaning given to the information furnished by the perceptual categories as a result of the channeling of attention.

In other words, I assume that man, like other animals, attends to the world and processes sensory data by means of perceptual categories that are biologically constrained. However, the information furnished by these categories is interpreted on the basis of fundamental conceptions of who he is, where he is, and what he is. These fundamental explanations implicitly guide and give significance to any experience that is sustained by the activation of the perceptual categories, and these explanations, furthermore, are part of what culture is all about. In our culture, for example, a central concept is that of the person who is articulated as though somehow separated from the world and as though composed of different sorts of elements and processes, e.g., mind as opposed to body. Attention is regulated and perceptual categories are formed on the basis of a cognitive map that isolates the individual from his world and even his body, and this gives him a separated, controlling, almost superordinate position in the web of experience. Failures in the regulation of attention and the consequent breakdown in perceptual constancies, which are assumed here to be hallmarks of the schizophrenic process, are interpreted in the light of what they portend for the person who in our culture is defined as someone who is supposed to be centrally and autonomously placed in a world of space and time, and who judges himself a master or controller of sorts.

We must assume that other cognitive maps and linguistic systems do not articulate such a view of self or person and that, therefore, attentional regulation and perceptual constancies are not predicated on this view of personhood. Consequently, processes that disrupt the regulation of attention and the function of perceptual categories (i.e., an instance of schizophrenia) will be expressed differently—partially in terms of the substance or content of the categories, partially in terms of the organization and form they take on in the cognitive map, and partially in terms of the central assumptions and premises that furnish symbolic and structural significance. I anticipate, then, that manifestations of schizophrenia in a particular culture will represent a complex function of the group's cognitive map, that such manifestations will not preserve in a systematic way the form and orderings of the perceptual categories observed. Behavior changes traced to schizophrenia, when compared cross-culturally, would not necessarily be deducible from propositions that directly express the form and content of a culture's perceptual categories and cognitive map (as in the case of depression), but instead would indirectly and complexly reflect fundamental changes in the orderings and form of these and, in particular, in terms of those basic notions of self that articulate experience. The task of the investigator studying schizophrenic disease cross-culturally can for this reason be expected to be far more complex, since in addition to obtaining an accurate cognitive map of the culture he must uncover and specify those underlying and fundamental premises about self in terms of which he channels attention and which give meaning to any information furnished by the perceptual categories.

The psychological study of neuropsychiatric entities such as depression and schizophrenia in various cultures thus presents the researcher with an opportunity to probe the very essence of how culture articulates and rationalizes for man his unique position in the world. The one disease disturbs his basic level of activity and his degree of satisfaction with himself and his position; whatever emotional quality attaches to the experience of being a participating member of culture (and we must assume that this quality is a product of the unique cultural map that the individual draws on to explain his position in the world), this quality is hedonically despoiled and undermined in depression. On the other hand, the other disease shatters or at least alters the fundamental constancies that the individual draws on in order to sustain the unique position and role in the world that his culture endows him with; whatever structure, organization, and meaning the individual is provided with or draws from culture, they all require perceptual regularities for their articulation, and it is precisely these regularities that schizophrenia disturbs. It should be clear, then, that when studying these neuropsychiatric entities, the researcher is placed in a strategic position to uncover elemental aspects about man's conception of his place in the world. Indeed, it is because these matters are so elementally tied to notions of self, identity, and meaning vis-à-vis the world that they require very rigorous methods of procedure for their elucidation.

COMMENT

The preceding discussion has two limitations that need to be made explicit. In the first place, the view of the two psychoses is an overly simplified one. Thus, in psychotic depressions one obviously finds associated perceptual and cognitive difficulties and, on the other hand, persons classified as schizophrenic manifest perceptual cognitive changes in an emotionally charged context. I do not mean to imply either that thought and emotion can be easily separated or that one is reflected in the absence of the other. I dealt with the early changes in the psychoses (as we have come to understand them), analytically treating thought and cognition as though they were separate, and adopting a descriptive (as opposed to dynamic, etiological) approach. Second, the discussion proceeded on the a priori assumption that the entities we term depression and schizophrenia are universal and that the fundamental processes they disturb are those that *we* have identified as significant. As I have tried to emphasize in this chapter, such assumptions are either erroneous or fraught with difficulties; they also essentially beg the very questions that need examination cross-culturally, i.e., elucidating the influences of culture and social systems generally on human disease. Assumptions such as these, which involve the nature of depression and schizophrenia, thus cannot be more than mere *working assumptions*. Indeed, the task of the researcher is that of *refining* his understanding of depression or schizophrenia by cross-cultural analyses. A strategy that is often adopted is that of working with a model or a picture of the disease in question and of exploring various elements of the model by systematic comparisons with related phenomena. To the extent that the researcher's model is open to modification, then to that extent he can profit from his observations and be in a position to modify ethnocentric assumptions. Viewed in this light, examining the psychological manifestations of neuropsychiatric entities in contrasting cultures allows the researcher to test fundamental relations between disease, self, and social system.

ACKNOWLEDGMENTS

I am grateful to Mark Charles for help in the preparation of this manuscript, to Peter K. Manning, who read an early draft and provided helpful comments, and to Susan De Horn for secretarial assistance.

REFERENCES

All references for Chapter 4 appear at the end of Chapter 5.

5

Social Factors in Depression

HORACIO FÁBREGA, JR.

Theoretical and Methodological Considerations

In studying the amount and distribution of a psychiatric disease such as depression, statistics from hospitals and other mental health facilities have limited utility. Figures based on hospital statistics can be taken to reveal little more than clinical-administrative policies of the facility in question—their diagnostic habits, as it were. Such figures have been used to make general and essentially imprecise inferences about the attitudes, habits, and social conditions of the respective population groups—e.g., that certain groups do or do not use hospitals or are more likely to use hospitals; that one group is more tolerant of deviant behaviors than another (hospitalization rates being taken as a measure of the exclusion of deviants); or that one group has a different level or amount of psychiatric problems than another. These inferences, and no doubt others, can be drawn from epidemological studies that rely on hospital statistics. When combined with data from various sources collected under different conditions, hospitalization rates can help to answer limited questions, as Kramer [58] has already indicated.

It may seem that field studies offer the solution to the problem of establishing meaningful expressions of the prevalence or incidence of a disease such as depression. However, very little in the way of cogent generalizations can be drawn from field studies purporting to measure the prevalence and incidence of psychiatric disease. Not only are there fundamental conceptual problems regarding the definition and meaning of normality, psychopathology, and disease, but current methodologies for establishing "caseness" in such field studies—untreated instances of the disease, as it were—can be faulted on so many accounts that results of these studies give only limited insight. Furthermore, conceptions of depression are currently in such a fluid state that little can be gained by reviewing in detail early studies that employed differing and overlapping definitions of depression. In spite of these reservations, I will include some material on the incidence and prevalence of depression.

Ideally, a social epidemiological inquiry should begin with a clear analytic definition of a particular disease entity. This definition should in turn be operationalized by the development of *indicator tests* of the disease. In practice this means that demonstrating a particular set of indicators can be said to constitute necessary and sufficient conditions for inferring (i.e., diagnosing) the disease. The measurement of the indicators of such a disease should be easily accomplished and subject to unambiguous interpretation. Studies employing such operational definitions of disease should be conducted by using a well-defined social group as a reference population. Field methods and survey analyses are called for, and a probability sample drawn from the community is evaluated so that both treated and non-treated instances of the disease can be unambiguously marked. Concomitant with this there should be a survey of the rosters of all in-patient and out-patient facilities that service the group, so that treated instances of the disease can be verified and discovered. Private psychiatric and other medical practitioners should also be consulted. Questioning the latter is critically important in the case of depressive disease, since patients so diagnosed, it has been established, are frequently seen by general practitioners and internists [105, 106].

In general, social epidemiological studies that meet these standards are not common, and conceptual and methodological problems involving how disease is to be marked contribute importantly to this state of affairs. As one might anticipate, social *psychiatric* epidemiological studies that meet these standards are rare. A number of field investigators have used as their definition of psychiatric caseness, scores derived from symptom questionnaires. Although useful for certain purposes [79, 115], such data are of little value in evaluating a particular nosological entity. In these studies, subjects (i.e., potential cases) are not interviewed by psychiatrists. Rather, protocols of interviews conducted by lay persons and social scientists are subsequently rated by psychiatrists. In the Leighton studies [63, 64], symptoms were classified into syndromes by reference to the *Diagnostic and Statistical Manual of the American Psychiatric Association;* consequently, a degree of nosological specificity was sustained. Still, rather general questions were used as the basis of generating clinical data.

More recent studies by Dohrenwend [16] have brought to light some of the biases and deficiencies of these types of studies and have raised questions about the validity of conclusions drawn from them. Dohrenwend points to differences in the way ethnic groups respond to symptom questionnaires (modes of expressing stress), to the neglect of contextual factors in the evaluation of responses, and to the fluctuating nature and predictive inaccuracy of such responses. There are, to be sure, a number of rather basic problems associated with the use of such scores. These will be discussed here briefly.

Symptom questionnaires used in psychiatric epidemiological field studies typically include psychological and psychophysiological referents. Persons are asked whether they experience sweaty palms, sadness, tiredness, and the like. What is obtained in such a study is a distribution of scores representing number of symptoms, though in some instances information about the person's social adjustment is included. By setting cutoff points using similar data obtained from *known* psychiatric patients, the investigator infers how many potential cases are likely to prevail in his sample. The comparison group "patients" is usually heterogeneous and includes various diagnostic types. Use of this procedure would seem to be based on the following assumptions: that since psychiatric disorders are handled in terms of symptoms, they must all be of a similar behavioral, psychological, or biological type; that all diseases can be graded comparably as to severity; that each instance of a disease can be placed unequivocally on a continuum of severity for that disease; and that any disease-symptom relation holds unvaryingly both across the continuum of disease types and across the continuum of disease severity. It hardly seems necessary to emphasize here that these assumptions are very questionable. These criticisms are directed not at the epidemiological approach per se but rather at the tendency to generalize uncautiously about matters of psychiatric nosology using results from field epidemiological studies in which responses to symptom questionnaires constitute the major data.

Substantive Findings

Recently, several review studies of the social epidemiology of depression have appeared [61, 94, 110, 129]. The conclusions of these reviews and some of the more recent literature can be summarized as follows:

PREVALENCE

Annual first admissions to psychiatric hospitals for affective disorder range from 2.2 per 100,000 in New York state (1949) to 28.8

per 100,000 in England and Wales (1960), for males; the corresponding figures for females are 3.8 and 49.3 per 100,000. Naturally, if outpatient facilities are also included, such rates tend to rise (to a figure about three times as high, according to Lehmann [61]), but the sex difference is maintained. The prevalence of depression in the general population based on information that includes the patients treated by general practitioners is higher still—according to Rawnsley [94], ten times that of the first-admission rates for depression in England and Wales. It is generally acknowledged that the prevalence of depression is positively correlated with age. As we have just seen, females have a higher prevalence of depression.

LIFETIME MORBID RISK

An estimate of lifetime morbid risk is obtained by drawing a large sample from birth registers of a period of time long enough removed so that those persons have passed the age of risk and determining the prevalence of disease in that sample. Records of hospitals and other mental health facilities are searched and, whenever possible, probands or significant others are interviewed regarding possible psychiatric disorder. For males, estimates of lifetime morbid risk range from 4.2 per 1000 to 18 per 1000; corresponding figures for females are 6 to 28 [94]. Lehmann [61] believes that the lifetime expectancy of being treated for depression, for anyone in the general population, is about 10 percent.

OCCUPATIONAL CLASS AND DEPRESSION

Bagley [3], while acknowledging the problems associated with the diagnosis of depression, has concluded that there is some support for the view that depression (some types) and upper-class economic position are related [3]. This generalization, based on a survey of the literature, appears to apply principally to psychotic as opposed to neurotic depressions. The class difference appears to be an outcome of diagnostic biases, underlying personality traits that favor upward social mobility and depression, and the kinds of stresses that upper-class (and socially mobile) persons are subjected to.

DEPRESSION IN AMERICAN BLACKS

Comparisons of depression in blacks and whites in the United States have had two main thrusts: (1) Jaco [44], Malzberg [71], and Simon [111] all reported that depressive disease is much rarer in blacks than in whites. These were demographic studies relying on formal contacts with treatment agencies. (The methodological limitations of this mode of analysis were discussed earlier in this chapter and in Chapter 4.) (2) Other researchers (e.g., Frank [29], Miller, Knapp, and Daniels [75], and Pettigrew [89]) have asserted that depression manifests itself differently in blacks than in whites. These studies suggest that guilt and suicidal feelings, for example, are comparatively rare among blacks and that somatic complaints are more frequent. While these ideas have gained widespread acceptance, empirical evidence based on careful clinical comparisons is mixed.

Tonks, Paykel, and Klerman [119] found that presumed ethnic or racial differences in severity ratings on some 40 symptoms were largely eliminated when they controlled for social class; when they controlled for *both* social class and severity of illness, these differences virtually disappeared. The investigators interviewed 220 depressed persons who were sampled from the in-patient case loads of four psychiatric facilities in an urban area: a mental health center, the psychiatric ward in a general hospital and in a Veterans Administration hospital, and a state mental hospital. These findings should be viewed with caution, for two reasons. First, the procedure used to control for severity (matched subsamples) resulted in a very small sample: only 31 persons in each group. Such a small sample could have resulted in a failure to detect substantial differences if they did exist. Second, virtually all the blacks in the subsample were patients at the mental health center and were only mildly ill. The finding of no apparent difference in symptom pattern cannot be extended to other psychiatric patients who are more seriously ill.

Simon et al. [112] provide evidence that black-white differences in symptom manifestation among psychiatric in-patients do, in fact, exist. Using the methods of the Cross-National Study of Diagnosis of Mental Disorders, they examined 192 first admissions to state mental hospitals in an urban area. They found that blacks and whites show similar distributions of two diagnostic categories (depression and schizophrenia) and seven categories of psychopathology. Among those patients diagnosed as depressed, a number of ethnic differences on mood disturbance scales were observed: black depressive patients showed significantly more worry, general anxiety, muscle tension, irritability, and somatic complaints. This seems to support the assertion that depression may be reflected differently in blacks, at least in those who become hospitalized.

COURSE OF DEPRESSION

Most of the studies on the course of depression have been conducted in the hope of clarifying the nature of manic-depressive disease [120]. It is commonly held that depressive disease is episodic. Periods of incapacitation are separated by periods of apparently normal functioning. Episodes of mania may punctuate the course of depression, and the relationship between depression and mania is complex. Numerous attempts have been made to relate these seemingly different courses to nosological and etiological schemas. Perris [87], for example, argues for a distinction between diseases having only depressive attacks, which he calls unipolar and those having both manic and depressive episodes, called bipolar. Winokur [130] suggests further that unipolar depressive disease be divided into pure depressive disease and depressive spectrum disease. These terms are not widely accepted at present. Later researchers vary in their usage: some separate unipolar depressives into a distinct group (usually called depressive psychosis); others include them with bipolar depressives under the general terms manic-depressive psychosis. These studies, then, provide only a rough indication of what may be found by studies that pay more attention to diagnostic homogeneity.

Despite the usual conception of depression as an episodic disease, it has been repeatedly observed that a substantial number of persons suffer only one attack. Pederson [86], for example, found that fully one-half of the patients in his study had not suffered a second attack in the four to five years following the first attack. In Robins and Guze's summary [96] of 11 studies of depressive psychosis, manic-depressive psychosis, involutional depression, or endogenous depression, the number suffering from only one attack varies from 21 to 93 percent. As might be expected, the studies with longer follow-up periods found fewer single-attack patients. Nevertheless, two studies with extended follow-up periods (20 and 30 years) found that 40 to 60 percent of the subjects had not had a second attack.

Six studies reviewed by Robins and Guze found that the median duration of the first attack (of depressive disease or manic-depressive disease) varied from 4 to 13 months. The first attack was generally followed by a remission period of 5 to 8 years. Second and subsequent attacks were generally found to be somewhat shorter: 3 months [80], 4 to 6 months [69], or 6 months [95]. Intervals between attacks after the first also tended to be shorter: 1 to 3 years [69] or 5 years [80]. Shobe and Brion's [109] estimates from a series of manic-depressive patients of a psychiatrist in private practice are similar in magnitude, although these authors do not distinguish between first and subsequent attacks. Similarly, Angst and Weiss [1] found that the average interval between attacks was 2 to 3 years and the average duration, 2 to 3 months. Due to mortality and the relative infrequency of attacks, few patients were found in any study who had had more than four attacks.

OUTCOME

Due to the episodic nature of depression, and the fairly long period between attacks, it is often hard to assess the effects of treatment on the course of the disease. Some general observations can, however, be made. (1) *Death:* It is generally recognized that depressives are at much greater risk of suicide than the general population (see below). It is less well recognized that they are also apparently at greater risk of death by all causes. Babigian [2], in one of the best studies available, found that persons with a history of depression in a psychiatric case register in Monroe County, New York, had an age-adjusted death rate twice that of the general population. Norris [78] reports a similar finding among patients hospitalized for depression. (2) *Chronic impairment:* A second readily identifiable group are those who are chronically impaired by depressive illness: those unable to function in their usual social roles over an extended period because of depressive symptoms. Six studies summarized by Robins and Guze found that 5 to 28 percent of the patients studied were chronically impaired. Unfortunately, the nature of such impairment is not often specified (see Depression and Social Performance p. 104). (3) *Remission and recovery:* When a person who has suffered one or more attacks of depressive disease is functioning normally, it is difficult to distinguish between remission (and high risk of another attack) and recovery (low or absent risk). With these states considered together, Robins and Guze report 46 to 92 percent "improved" in studies with followup after 3 to 20 years. Shobe and Brion [99] classed 60 percent of their series "recovered" and 20 percent "improved" at an 18-year followup. They noted that patients who had suffered their first attack at a fairly early age had a much poorer prognosis than the others. None of the studies cited here compared treated patients with untreated controls, so it is difficult or impossible to establish how much of this improvement is in response to treatment and how much is spontaneous recovery.

DEPRESSION AND SUICIDE

Depression, as is well known, is an important contributing factor in suicide. In several studies approximately half of all suicides were judged to be suffering from depressive disease on the basis of data gathered from coroner's records, from medical and mental health agency records, from survivors, or a combination of these [10, 18, 97, 100, 107]. Further, as stated earlier, depressed persons are more at risk of suicide. Pokorny [91] found that the suicide rate in his series of persons formerly hospitalized for depressive psychosis was 25 times that of the general population. Temoche, Pugh, and MacMahon [117] report a similar finding: the suicide rate among persons formerly hospitalized for depressive psychosis was 36 times that of the general population. It is a common clinical impression that most suicides among depressives take place soon after discharge. Epidemiological data support this. Pokorny found that 66 percent of all suicides in his series of formerly hospitalized depressives took place within 9 months of discharge. Perris and d'Elia [88] report, in a follow-up study of persons discharged after treatment in a mental hospital for psychotic depression, that 74 percent of all suicides took place within one year of discharge. Paykel and Dienelt [82] followed 189 depressed patients for 10 months after discharge from a variety of psychiatric treatment facilities. They found that 13 (6 percent) attempted to commit suicide, and one was successful. Further, they noted that the attemptors were younger, had a previous history of suicide attempts, and had a clinical pattern of neurotic rather than endogenous depression. Their observations led them to conclude that better after-care was needed, a conclusion also reached by Sainsbury [100a].

SOCIAL FACTORS AND ONSET OF DEPRESSION

At every point during the evolution of depressive disease, social-cultural events and processes must be assumed to play an influential role. Rules dictated by the culture affect mating practices, what foods people eat, when they eat, how and when energy is expended, the course of pregnancy and parturition, and the practices surrounding the care and feeding of the newborn, among other things. Thus, genetic, constitutional, and physiological factors and the eventual health status of the human organism are affected and constrained by social-cultural factors. Further, the educational and economic level, the values espoused, and the physiological and psychological well-being of parents must be assumed to influence the development of the child, his behavioral adjustment, and the likelihood of his developing psychiatric problems. Family influences in depression have not been studied with the intensity that they have in other disturbances, though psychological studies of depressives inevitably refer to such influences [12]. In general, these and other social-psychological factors discussed elsewhere in this volume constrain and shape adult adjustment. In conjunction with later, more proximal circumstances, which themselves are of a social-cultural nature, such factors significantly affect the likelihood that a psychiatric disease such as depression will develop.

A number of issues need to be discussed in relation to the question of whether social factors play a role in the onset of depressive disease. One of these involves the definition of what has come to be referred to as stress or social stress. Sociomedical researchers use the term stress in a variety of ways [42, 66]. In this formulation I shall use the term *situation, precipitant,* or even *stressor* to refer to environmental events or circumstances that are potentially problematic to the individual and the term *stress* to signify the internal organismic changes that may result from such situations and that may interfere with the person's adjustment and adaptation. A reading of the social-psychiatric literature will show that researchers do not ordinarily distinguish these two categories conceptually, let alone empirically. Stressors are usually assumed, a priori, to produce stress. Often, the mere presence of depression is taken to indicate that stress has occurred. What is actually demonstrated then is simply an association between the clustering of stressors in persons classified as showing a depression. The association is inferred to be a causal one, though this cannot be proved except by psychological analyses.

It should be appreciated that the problem of evaluating empirically the influence of social stressors in depressive disease is confounded with the problem of what depression is and how it should be defined. For example, it has been shown that in so-called grief reactions one observes many of the phenomenological features of the depressive state [11]. Now, deciding when a grief reaction merges into depression as opposed to remaining a temporary crisis reaction is difficult to ascertain. At the least, one might anticipate that the association between stressors and depression will differ depending on the extent to which purely behavioral descriptions (to the exclusion of situational ones) are used as criteria to diagnose depression. Along these lines, it is a clinical truism that strong affective reactions of a depressive sort occur as stages in preexisting psychiatric disturbances such as alcoholism, anxiety neurosis, and drug intoxication. Despite the fact that these "depressions" include behavioral features included as diagnostic of depressive disease, arguments have been marshalled that such secondary depressions should be excluded from studies aimed at careful evaluation of social influences on the onset and course of a presumably separate entity, the so-called primary depressions. Certainly the line between primary and secondary depressions is not an unambiguous one; for example, drug abuse can often be seen as a way of coping with depressive feelings. One must grant that brief reactions and most so-called secondary depressions are tied *logically* to social circumstances; however, if both are totally excluded from a category depression, then empirical inquiries into the influence of social stressors on depression are somewhat suspect. At the same time, one cannot allow the concept of endogenous depression to depend exclusively on the inability of a clinician to uncover a clear precipitating factor. We observe, then, that the way one defines depression will have an important influence on empirical attempts to measure the role of social stressors.

Events and situations that we call stressors and that are related to the social placement of the person may precede the onset of depression, in which case they could be given a causal role. However, deciding *when* a disease begins is a very difficult matter. Since a person who is developing a depression can be expected to be somewhat compromised in the social sphere, one must assume that interpersonal difficulties of various sorts are more likely (e.g., loss of job, marital discord). So what in a study appears to be a potential cause of depression may in fact be a consequence. Deciding between these alternatives, again, involves matters of definition and reflects directly a central problem of social-psychiatric inquiries: the attempt to distinguish between, on the one hand, social events that both affect and reflect a person's psychological status and, on the other, psychological status or psychiatric disease. A related problem is deciding on the length of the time interval preceding the onset of disease in which one will define events as stressors. This interval will depend on the investigator's model of how the disease develops. Ultimately this question of etiology brings in once again the issue of the definition of depression.

Two specific questions involving the possible influence of situations and stress on the development of depression can be entertained. The first is quantitative: are such situations and their attendant stresses *more frequent* than in the life experiences of nondepressives or non-psychiatrically ill persons? The second question is qualitative: Are such situations, when independently rated (e.g., by nonpatients), found to be stressful; are they in fact more or less stressful than situations involving persons who do not develop illness or persons who develop a nondepressive illness? With regard to the first question, some studies do tend to show that depressives, compared to normals, more frequently report antecedent situations of a stressful sort [83]. Other studies also indicate in general that primary depressions frequently are preceded by a variety of events and changes that can be described objectively as stressful [9, 60, 118]: losses, threats, and a variety of other undesirable or negative events have been singled out. Indeed, in some of these studies, findings indicate that such stressors are equally frequent in *various types* of depression; specifically, patients receiving a diagnosis of endogenous depression [60] and those with a positive family history for depression (where genetic factors may be especially relevant [118] were not distinguished from other depressives in terms of prevalence of stress preceding the onset of illness. The alleged differences between endogenous and reactive depression are brought into question by these findings.

An intriguing set of issues arises when an attempt is made to answer the second question raised above, namely, evaluating and quantifying the magnitude or significance of situations believed to produce stress and determining whether depressives are differentially vulnerable. From one standpoint, of course, the attempt to quantify objectively the stress potential of environmental situations misses the mark. It is a generally held assumption of psychodynamically oriented psychiatrists that the significance of situations is highly idiosyncratic; such situations have relevance precisely because they are enveloped or framed in symbols that have significance only to the actor. From this particular vantage point, then, the alleged objective weighing of the situation is irrelevant. However, to those who espouse an epidemiological orientation and who wish to understand human adaptation generally and the so-called depression-prone individual in particular, the question of the magnitude of presumed stress-producing situations is an important one. The theoretical problem at stake here is also a central one to investigators who hold an ecological and psychosomatic orientation and who aim to understand the general nature of disease and stress [38, 40, 41].

The most careful attempts to measure the stress potential of various social events have been made by persons interested in evaluating the onset and cause of various types of diseases, not just those termed psychiatric. These investigators have used the Social Readjustment Rating Scale to quantify the presumed magnitude of readjustment to the individual entailed by a variety of events and have related these scores to disease onset and to hospitalization in a variety of retrospective and prospective studies [93]. The magnitude of readjustment or life change score has also been related to seriousness of illness. To the extent that one adopts a priori a unified or unitary perspective vis-à-vis disease—namely that all diseases are caused in part by stress and in fact represent the organism's attempt at adaptation in the face of this stress—then general medical studies that involve social stressors are relevant to the specific question dealing with the social precipitants of depression [21]. It should be emphasized that researchers exploring relations between social environmental factors and disease onset and disease severity have, by and large, been interested in obtaining empirical support for the proposition that these events qualitatively and quantitatively influence disease causation generally.

One concludes that the question as to the comparative vulnerability to social situations of persons showing different diagnoses was not salient in earlier studies. A refined understanding of the way disease is affected by environmental factors obviously requires focusing on diseases of various types and on a variety of social precipitants. A recent study by Beck and Worthen [6] was addressed in part to the ways schizophrenics and depressives differed in their responses to precipitating stressors. The authors abstracted from case records the relevant data bearing on antecedent social events and changes in depressives (neurotic depression) and schizophrenics, and had persons in the waiting room of the hospital (of a social background similar to that of the patients) rate these data in terms of how upsetting it would be to them. The authors, first of all, showed that there was a striking relation between clarity of precipitant and diagnosis, with clear precipitants more often associated with depression. Second, and more germane to this discussion, the mean "hazard score" (the "upsettingness" of the social circumstances of the patient) of depressives was significantly higher than that of schizophrenics. "Schizophrenics' life situations prior to hospitalization are rated as less hazardous than are those of depressives" [p. 127]. The investigation was directed to the general question of the validity and relevance of crisis theory for explaining hospitalization and psychiatric problems. The authors concluded that the term "crisis-oriented" poorly described their service, since they saw themselves as essentially treating sick persons who "broke down" easily as opposed to healthy ones who were coping with clear-cut crises. Nevertheless, within these constraints, depressives seemed to fit the crisis model more appropriately. It should be emphasized that the authors' principal focus was hospitalization and that their results can be generalized to the question of overall susceptibility to disease only with caution.

The role of hospitalization in complicating the evaluation of social stressors in the onset of depression cannot be overestimated. We shall see that the complication produced by hospitalization in this evaluation is similar to the role played by hospitalization in the interpretation of social epidemiological findings that was touched on in the previous section. Since patients who are classified as depressive ordinarily are selected and interviewed in hospitals, so-called stressors tend to be evaluated in relation to depression and often only inadvertently in relation to the issue of hospitalization itself. Obviously, few psychiatric diseases begin with hospitalization, and furthermore, those stressors that antedate (and precipitate) hospitalization might not be the same as those that antedate (and precipitate) the onset of depressive disease. The question of the timing of the stress, as already emphasized, is all-important.

The issue of hospitalization is problematic in still another way. Even though investigators may be careful to interview about stressful situations using onset of depression and not hospitalization as the point of focus, the fact that the sample of depressives is usually formed in the hospital probably means that some bias was operating. Persons who seek (or are brought in for) formal care may be more pliable and characterized by greater responsiveness to and trust in the social system. These factors, in turn, may mean that hospitalized persons show a *differential vulnerability* to so-called social precipitants. The findings of Morrison and of Hudgens [43, 76], who evaluated the influence of a number of life events in affective disorders using hospitalized medical and surgical patients as controls are noteworthy precisely because these investigators failed to turn up any striking differences. Compared to the controls, patients classified as having an affective disorder showed more frequent changes of residence and reported interpersonal discord during the year prior to admission, but this was usually after the disease had become manifest. It is possible that hospitalization, which all patients including controls shared, obscured the differential role of stresses in the onset of affective disorder. In other words, it is possible that all patients were selected in terms of their general responsiveness to social influences, symbolized in this instance by their readiness to turn to the hospital. In addition, of course, the fact that the control group was composed of persons showing disease of various types further complicates matters. I have stated that a large body of research points to the importance of social stressors in the onset of a number of diseases, not just the so-called psychiatric ones. Since both the depressive and control groups may have shown an association with social stressors, any unique influences relating to affective disorder would have been obscured.

In summary, a clear and unambiguous answer to the question of the influence of environmental factors on the onset of depression would seem to require, first, uncovering by means of field studies persons showing *untreated* as well as treated depression. These persons must then be systematically compared in terms of frequency of antecedent social stressors with subjects (both nondepressives who are ill and persons who are not ill) who are also drawn from the roster of community residents, some of whom are under treatment and some not. In short, to determine whether social precipitants play a unique role in the onset of depression, one must establish that any association that exists between depression and the clustering of such precipitants does not result from (1) random factors that also affect normals, (2) selective factors associated with treatment, and (3) effects attributable to illness in general.

Insofar as the indicators of the various types of depressive disease refer to social behaviors (i.e., changes in activity, expression of life satisfaction, verbalizations about mood, etc.), an evaluation of how depression is related to social performance naturally involves dealing with matters of definition that have been touched on earlier. Theoretical questions about the ontology of depression and empirical ones regarding its distribution in social space can for this reason be seen as inextricably linked to the question to be discussed here, namely that of the relation that exists between showing a disease and showing some interference in social performance. We saw, for example, that the question of the comparative prevalence of depression involves not only methodological problems of measurement but also, to some extent, the matter of how depression might be expressed in contrasting cultural and linguistic communities. This of course involves the appraisal of normal and abnormal social behavior. Even if one assumes that an instance of depression is associated with specific neurochemical changes, the onset of these changes is affected by culturally programmed experiences that are tied to the performance of social roles [7]. It is often the evaluation of such performance that allows the investigator or clinician to diagnose depression in the first place. Similarly, how the individual socially copes with or expresses these brain changes will be largely governed by social demands that are articulated by cultural rules of behavior. Regardless of the relevance of neurochemical changes in depression, in marking and tracing an instance of this disease the researcher is involved in evaluating social behavior in terms of notions such as performance or competence. Attempts at isolating the possible forms of depression (e.g., unipolar vs. bipolar, endogenous vs. reactive) have in fact involved careful scrutiny of alternative behaviors that differentially reflect the performance of social roles [4, 81].

When one discusses depression and social performance, then, one implicates definitional as well as epidemiological matters. We shall not go into these matters here. Rather we shall assume for analytic convenience that there is a logical independence between the disease depression and social behaviors. We shall thus discuss the question of how the presence of depression may affect a person's social adjustment and shall overlook the likelihood that the very existence of the entity depression is to some extent predicated on the identification of social maladjustment. Our position, in short, is: Given that a person shows depression, how does his having this disease affect the performance of his social duties? Later we shall discuss the logically opposed position of seeing in depression nothing but changed social behaviors —a position that altogether eschews the notion of mental illness or psychiatric disease.

The relevance for medicine and psychiatry of considering a diseased individual's altered performance of social roles (termed social maladjustment or disability) has been lucidly set forth by Ruesch and his associates [98, 99], although, to be sure, such a notion has always been implicit in social epidemiology and social medicine generally [25, 30, 62, 74]. As Ruesch and Brodsky state: "Disability may be brought about by bodily impediments resulting in physical impairment, by mental difficulties leading to psychological impairment, and by cultural, economic and social conditions such as unemployment, old age, imprisonment, inadequate education, and cultural deprivation leading to social impairment" [99, p. 397]. The broad context of disability and impairment are clearly set forth. Obviously, situational demands that vary and fluctuate, as Ruesch and Brodsky point out, are critically important, although, quite often, important insights can be gained by dealing generically with social environmental factors and focusing exclusively on individual characteristics. In psychiatry, the utility of such an orientation has been demonstrated most convincingly with schizophrenia, where the concept of a continuum, termed the process-reactive continuum, has been used as a way of organizing data and thinking. The rationale of this continuum, which leads to the view that the onset, symptoms, and prognosis of the schizophrenic disorder are related to the social developmental milestones reached by the person (e.g., educational, occupational, heterosexual), can be traced to the definitive writings of Leslie Phillips [90].

Only recently have researchers addressed themselves to social performance with regard to the disease depression. The social performance of women was evaluated by Schaeffer [103] by means of factor-analytically derived scores based on a large number of social variables. Depressives, compared to schizophrenics, scored significantly higher on a factor believed to measure marital adjustment, although as a group the depressives married later and tended to have children later in life. Depressives scored significantly lower on a factor termed withdrawal, which was allegedly based on adult and childhood social behaviors, although these were not discussed. In general, this study reported that schizophrenics demonstrated lower levels of social performance than did depressives, although these social behaviors were not probed in any elaborate manner.

The work of Paykel and his associates [84, 85, 115] has been directly concerned with the evaluation of social performance (termed by them social adjustment) and is notable for the degree of care taken and the detail that it reflects. Drawing on items from earlier scales, these workers developed a Social Adjustment Scale (SAS). The items of this scale could be ordered into either of two sets of social behaviors, termed role areas (e.g., work, parental) and qualitative (e.g., behavior performance, feelings, and satisfactions). It should be emphasized that these two classifications of social behavior were not independent; for example, items reflecting leisure role behavior could also be distributed into the various qualitative groupings. Using the SAS, three patterns of social performance scores were obtained—the two already described (role area and qualitative) and an empirical one derived from factor analysis. The SAS was administered to 40 women showing a primary depressive disorder; 40 other women living in the same area as the patients served as controls. Interesting differences were reported. As one might anticipate, depressed women generally tended to score lower in most role areas and in most aspects of role behaviors. Depressed homemakers, particularly, scored lower in instrumental role behaviors. Depressed women who worked outside the home, on the other hand, were only slightly impaired in the role area "work," although they did report considerable distress, friction, and disinterest associated with social demands. Interestingly, although depressed women reported less interest in sex, the groups did not differ markedly in frequency of sexual relations with spouse. It should be emphasized that it was in the expressive home role activities that depressed women showed greatest impairment.

The design of this study, as the authors correctly point out, does not permit establishing causal priorities, so one cannot judge whether depression led to role difficulties or vice versa. The study does point to a dilemma confronting such social studies of psychiatric disease: persons classified as depressed (and in general in any psychiatric disease category) more frequently offer discrediting reports about social performance. Persons that are hurting and experiencing distress and dissatisfaction can be expected to solicit care more frequently and can be counted in such studies as patients; consequently, any appraisals of their behavior that they themselves volunteer will naturally reflect this phenomenological feature. Their actual behavior (if indeed this could be determined) might not indicate the impairment that the subjective report suggests. Evaluating the social behavior of a person as observed by significant others may avoid this personal bias, although this approach introduces the additional problem of the observer's own view of and feelings toward the patient [39]. Indeed, one may question the meaning and usefulness of diagnostic impressions or behavior evaluations based on reports proffered by others who are, so to speak, parties to any disturbed behaviors that may prevail. It should be clear that this dilemma is inevitable, given the epistemological basis of data about psychiatric disease and human behavior. The data of psychiatry are embedded in social relations and partake of their logic and rationale, and the attempt to measure or evaluate such behavior independently raises epistemological questions [127].

In a subsequent paper, Paykel and Weissman [85] reported on the social adjustment of the same 40 depressed women during the ensuing eight-month interval. On most of the original SAS items, depressed patients reflected significant improvement at eight months when compared with their initial levels of performance. Although this improvement was in the direction of the normal controls, it did not actually reach the level of performance shown by the control group. A definite residual deficit remained. Most striking improvement occurred in the area of work performance, and the least improvement occurred in the factor termed inhibited communication. In general, dysfunctions in the interpersonal area showed little change and the greatest residual impairment. Interestingly, when improvement in social adjustment occurred, it occurred more slowly than did improvement in symptoms; relapses in symptoms tended to be associated with rapid worsening of social adjustment. When the researchers plotted changes in each social adjustment area in relation to changes in symptom levels, interesting observations were made.

The studies just reviewed relied on the assumption that depressive disease produced or at least is associated with impaired social adjustment. Furthermore, if one accepts at face value the empirical findings reported, the pattern of relations demonstrated between stage of illness, symptom level, and changes in social adjustment offers a form of support for the theoretical model employed. Such a model first posits an entity such as psychiatric disease and then assumes its logical independence from social performance. Ultimately, such a model prescribes the search for norms of social adjustment in various population groups and leads to the evaluation of how the various psychiatric diseases differentially affect social performance in different populations when relevant performance norms are used as baselines [50]. The development and evaluation of such baselines or norms raise a number of complex theoretical questions, as persons who work directly on such matters have indicated [39].

To balance this discussion involving depression and social performance, we should draw attention to an alternative view of depression, one that may be termed social labeling and that has been vigorously and insightfully articulated by social scientists [32, 102, 104] and some psychiatrists [59, 116]. This view altogether eschews the existence of psychiatric disease. Persons classified as ill by the psychiatric profession are described merely as deviating or perhaps failing in role performance; that is, they violate norms of social behavior. Given the political realities of our social institutions, persons showing such deviant behaviors are labeled with symbols or metaphors *inappropriately* drawn from medical science, with the result that they end up being socially penalized (stigmatized) and subjected to unwarranted control by others. Such a view of mental illness ascribes critical importance to the effects produced by the application of social symbols (e.g., exclusion, ostracism, behavior shaping), argues for the social embeddedness and symbolic basis of all behavior, even that inappropriately abstracted out of context and termed psychopathological, and ultimately minimizes the value of employing abstractions such as emotional state, mind, and personality (see LeVine [65] for a critical review of this tradition).

An illustration of this orientation is provided by the work of Sarbin [102], who has argued that the word "anxiety," referring to an alleged mental trait or state somehow "in" the person and thus separated from ongoing activities, can obscure consideration of current ecological conditions that need to be evaluated. These conditions are correlated imperfectly with behavioral changes and are imprecisely labeled by such trait words. Sarbin sees the present meanings of such mental state words as resulting from historical social-linguistic processes that led to the reification of metaphors. Words with specifiable public referents or words signifying behavioral dispositions, when influenced by religious mandates involving the eschatological soul, eventually are applied to alleged mental states, and these are accepted thereafter as (reified) entities that in turn become the focus of exploration. Sarbin's argument, if extended to the entity depression, would presumably draw attention to the humoral, cosmological, and social-behavioral basis of the term melancholia (literally "black bile") as used by the Greeks. The proto-personality implication of such terms involving the humors would have to be acknowledged. Such terms, in short, signified a composite of items that we now may view as separate and independent, including mood, personality, bodily function, and behavioral forms and activities. They were used at the time both to *describe* and to *explain* regularities and changes in the way people behaved socially. Medieval and Renaissance influences might then be seen as transforming the meaning of such behavior disposition terms as mel-

ancholia, depression, dejection, and despondency into words signifying states of the soul, spirit, or eventually mind or mood. Under the
influence of writers such as Robert Burton [8] these mood states,
when persistent, were in fact judged as diseases of the soul [121]. The
chain of "disease making" would be seen as completed by Kraeplin.

The artificial bases of psychiatric disease, this time involving nothing but changes in social behavior brought about by situational factors that involve the mediation and manipulation of symbols, has
been postulated by others. Goffman [32], for example, has recently
given a behavioral interpretation of an episode of mania, very much
tying the sequence of behavioral changes of such episodes to circumstances and motivations that involve the person in his family and
work situation. An important element of this formulation is that psychiatric readings of the behavior of a given person affect the behaviors of all participants, and in turn shape the course and meaning
given to the episode. No comparable analyses of depressive episodes
have been put forth, though the general formulation of Scheff [104]
naturally applies to depression. Scheff asserts that the various mental
illness terms are used to label persons who violate special types of social norms, "those norms which are so taken for granted that they are
not explicitly verbalized" [p. 38]. He terms such norms *residual rules*.
Thus, Scheff feels that most symptoms of mental illness are classifiable as violations of culturally particular normative networks. Presumably he might see the depressive as failing to meet certain basic social
requirements of self-sufficiency and as verbalizing statements about
social and personal failures in areas that most persons find unproblematic and simply overlook or take for granted. The articulations of
such deviant views in distinctive types of social situations might then
bring into question the person's capacity, competence, and commitment to ordinary rules of social order and propriety. Eventually, the
question of mental illness might be raised in an attempt to resolve
dilemmas set in motion by such types of social behavior.

The view of Liberman and Raskin [67] is in certain ways similar in
orientation to the position being discussed here. These writers present
a behavioral interpretation of depression. They state that a critical application of a behavioral perspective requires the clinician to uncover
critical depressive behaviors, to measure the frequency of these, and
to determine what environmental and or interpersonal contingencies
originally precipitated and now maintain such behavior. Liberman
and Raskin then go on to review the clinical descriptive literature on
depression and to present a reformulation of it in a learning theory
framework. Classic writings of Freud, for example, are taken by them
as examples of the social reinforcement of behavior, including physi-

cal symptoms. Similarly, the fact that infantile helplessness may be thought of as a frequent predisposing factor in depression is explained by them this way: particular types of respondents are evoked by the loss of reinforcement, which happens to replicate the earlier history of the person. Depressive equivalents—behaviors that substitute for and or mask depression—are seen as providing needed reinforcements for the individual. It is important to emphasize that Liberman and Raskin do not directly broach the theoretical question of the ontology of disease, and more than likely they would uphold the medical model, i.e., that depression is an entity of sorts, having a psychobiological basis and identity. They are, instead, principally concerned with recasting the *descriptive* psychoanalytic writings into behavioral terms and see much support for the view that behaviors subsumed by the term depression can be analyzed functionally using the principles of reinforcement contingencies. Nevertheless, here also, just as with Sarbin [102], Goffman [32], and Scheff [104], the entity depression as a disease sui generis, having its own natural history as it were, seems to fade away and leave one with a pattern (deviant and altered, to be sure) of social behaviors that have meaning only when viewed with reference to the social field of the person.

How is one to respond to the challenges posed by this perspective toward psychiatric disease, in this instance depression? What are the implications that can be drawn from this labeling and essentially behavioristic view of the psychiatric domain, a domain powerfully influenced by the notion of disease and of the differences between mind and body? First, it needs to be emphasized that psychiatrists, like other physicians, unquestionably aim to identify diseases precisely because it is assumed that only in the light of such a refined understanding can the effective control of disease be achieved. Robins and Guze [96] have briefly but cogently summarized the rationale and value of pursuing a rigorous nosological approach vis-à-vis depression (see also the book by Katz, Cole, and Barton [47]). Similarly, working within a dualistic framework that acknowledges the unity and interconnectedness of mind and body, psychiatrists espousing a psychophysiological position have succeeded in bringing about a better understanding of human disease generally, not just the so-called psychiatric diseases.

An approach, and let us term it *the medical approach*, that has been successful in general medicine and that stems from sound biological principles should not be discredited a priori on epistemological grounds without a careful evaluation of its accomplishments. Thus, to the extent that one acknowledges some success in the effort to control and treat various psychiatric diseases—and modest success has unquestionably been achieved [126]—to that extent one must grant a measure of validation to the approach in question. The strong claim of the labeling theorists (that psychiatric diseases are myths, falsely created entities, and *"nothing but"* changed social relations powerfully embedded in and responsive to the social system) has to be dismissed in the light of the successes so far achieved. (The reader wishing a critique of the labeling perspective that focuses primarily on theoretical matters is urged to read LeVine's analysis [65].) The weaker claim of labeling theorists remains, and it is a cogent one. Unquestionably, some misguided and injudicious use is made of psychiatric terms and paradigms, and such misuse raises perplexing social and political questions. At the same time, it must be granted that symbols and labels generally, especially those termed medical and psychiatric, powerfully shape behavior and can mark in important ways persons associated with them. In this light, persons espousing a labeling perspective have performed a service to the profession by underscoring the social embeddedness of behavior generally and psychiatric practice specifically, and by sensitizing practitioners to the fact that their terms and paradigms also function as social symbols. As a result, such critics have probably succeeded in bringing about a more rational *medical* application of behavioral science principles and knowledge.

REFERENCES

1. Angst, J., and Weiss, P.   *Periodicity of Depressive Psychoses, Neuropsychopharmacology.* In H. Brill et al. (Eds.), *Proceedings, Fifth International Congress of the Collegium Internationale Neuropsychopharmacologicum.* Amsterdam: Elsevier-Excerpta Medica, 1967.
2. Babigian, H. M., and Odoroff, C. L.   The mortality experience of a population with psychiatric illness. *Am. J. Psychiatry* 126:470, 1969.
3. Bagley, C.   Occupational class and symptoms of depression. *Soc. Sci. Med.* 7:327, 1973.
4. Baker, M., Dorzab, J., Winokur, G., and Cadoret, R. J.   Depressive disease: Classification and clinical characteristics. *Compr. Psychiatry* 12:354, 1971.
5. Beck, A. T.   *Depression.* New York: Harper & Row, 1967.
6. Beck, J. C., and Worthen, K.   Precipitating stress, crisis theory, and hospitalization in schizophrenia and depression. *Arch. Gen. Psychiatry* 26:123, 1972.
7. Blumenthal, M. D.   Heterogeneity and research on depressive disorders. *Arch. Gen. Psychiatry* 24:524, 1971.
8. Burton, R.   *The Anatomy of Melancholy.* Edited by F. Dell and P. Jordan-Smith. New York: Tudor, 1938.
9. Cadoret, R. J., Winokur, G., Dorzab, J., and Baker, M.   Depressive

disease: Life events and onset of illness. *Arch. Gen. Psychiatry* 26: 133, 1972.

10. Capstick, A.   Recognition of emotional disturbance and the prevention of suicide. *Br. Med. J.* 1:1179, 1960.

11. Clayton, P. J., Desmarais, L., and Winokur, G.   A study of normal bereavement. *Am. J. Psychiatry* 125:168, 1968.

12. Cohen, M. B., Baker, G., Cohen, R. A., Fromm-Reichmann, F., and Weigert, E. V.   An intensive study of twelve cases of manic-depressive psychosis. *Psychiatry* 17:103, 1954.

13. Cole, M., Gay, J., Glick, J. A., and Sharp, W.   *The Cultural Context of Learning and Thinking: An Exploration in Experimental Anthropology.* New York: Basic Books, 1971.

14. Cooper, J. E., Kendell, R. E., Gurland, B. J., Sartorius, N., and Farkas, T.   Cross-national study of diagnosis of the mental disorders: Some results from the first comparative investigation. *Am. J. Psychiatry* 125:21, 1969.

15. Dobzhansky, T.   *Mankind Evolving: The Evolution of the Human Species.* New Haven: Yale University Press, 1962.

16. Dohrenwend, B. P.   Some Issues in the Definition and Measurement of Psychiatric Disorders in General Populations. Paper presented at the annual meeting of the National Conference on Mental Health Statistics, 1972.

17. Dohrenwend, B. P., and Dohrenwend, B. S.   *Social Status and Psychological Disorder: A Causal Inquiry.* New York: Wiley-Interscience, 1969.

18. Dorpat, T. L., and Ripley, H. S.   A study of suicide in the Seattle area. *Compr. Psychiatry* 1:349, 1960.

19. Durell, J.   Introduction. In J. Mendels (Ed.), *Biological Psychiatry.* New York: Wiley, 1973. P. 1.

20. Ekman, P.   Universals and Cultural Differences in Facial Expressions of Emotions. In J. Coleman (Ed.), *Nebraska Symposium on Motivation.* Omaha: University of Nebraska Press, 1972.

21. Engel, G. L.   A Unified Concept of Health and Disease. In D. J. Ingle (Ed.), *Perspectives in Biology and Medicine.* Chicago: University of Chicago Press, 1960. Vol. 3, p. 459.

22. Eysenck, H. J.   The classification of depressive illness. *J. Psychiatry* 117:241, 1970.

23. Fábrega, H., Jr.   The study of disease in relation to culture. *Behav. Sci.* 17:183, 1973.

24. Fábrega, H., Jr.   Medical Anthroplogy. In B. J. Siegel (Ed.), *Biennial Review of Anthropology.* Stanford: Stanford University Press, 1972. P. 167.

25. Fábrega, H., Jr.   *Disease and Social Behavior: An Interdisciplinary Perspective.* Cambridge, Mass.: M.I.T. Press, 1974.

26. Fábrega, H., Jr., Metzger, D., and Williams, G.   Psychiatric implications of health and illness in a Maya Indian group: A preliminary statement. *Soc. Sci. Med.* 3:609, 1970.

27. Fábrega, H., Jr., and Silver, D.   *Illness and Shamanistic Curing in Zinacantan.* Stanford: Stanford University Press, 1973.

28. Frake, C. O.   The Ethnographic Study of Cognitive Systems. In *Anthropology and Human Behavior.* Washington, D.C.: The Anthropological Society of Washington, 1962. P. 72.

29. Frank, J. D.   Adjustment problems of selected Negro soldiers. *Nerv. Ment. Dis.* 105:647, 1947.
30. Freidson, E.   *Profession of Medicine: A Study of the Sociology of Applied Knowledge.* New York: Dodd, Mead, 1970.
31. Gajdusek, D. C.   Physiological and psychological characteristics of Stone Age man. *Eng. Sci.* 33:26, 56, 1970.
32. Goffman, E.   *Stigma: Notes on the Management of Spoiled Identity.* Englewood Cliffs: Prentice-Hall, 1963.
33. Goodenough, W. H.   Cultural Anthropology and Linguistics. In P. L. Garvin (Ed.), *Report of the Seventh Annual Round Table Meeting on Linguistics and Language Study.* Monograph Series on Language and Linguistics, no. 9. Washington, D.C.: Georgetown University Press, 1957.
34. Grinker, R. R., et al.   *The Phenomena of Depression.* New York: Hoeber Med. Div., Harper & Row, 1961.
35. Gurland, B. J., Fleiss, J. L., Cooper, J. E., Kendell, R. E., and Simon, R.   Cross-national study of diagnosis of the mental disorders: Some comparisons of diagnostic criteria from the first investigation. *Am. J. Psychiatry* 125 (Suppl. 10), 1969.
36. Hage, J.   *Techniques and Problems of Theory Construction in Sociology.* New York: Wiley-Interscience, 1972.
37. Hill, D.   Depression: Disease, reaction or posture? *Am. J. Psychiatry* 125:4, 1968.
38. Hinkle, L. E.   Ecological observations of the relation of physical illness, mental illness, and the social environment. *Psychosom. Med.* 23:289, 1961.
39. Hogarty, G. E., and Katz, M. M.   Norms of adjustment and social behavior. *Arch. Gen. Psychiatry* 25:470, 1971.
40. Holmes, T. H., and Masuda, M.   Life Change and Illness Susceptibility. Paper presented at the annual meeting of the American Association for the Advancement of Science, Chicago, December 1970.
41. Holmes, T. H., and Rahe, R. H.   The social readjustment rating scale. *J. Psychosom. Res.* 11:213, 1967.
42. Howard, A., and Scott, R. A.   Proposed framework for the analysis of stress in the human organism. *Behav. Sci.* 10:141, 1965.
43. Hudgens, R. W., Morrison, J. R., and Barchha, R. G.   Life events and onset of primary affective disorders. *Arch. Gen. Psychiatry* 16:134, 1967.
44. Jaco, G.   *Social Epidemiology of Mental Disorders.* New York: Russell Sage Foundation, 1960.
45. Katz, M. M.   Discussion of Previous Three Papers. In E. H. Hare and J. K. Wing (Eds.), *Psychiatric Epidemiology.* Proceedings of the International Symposium held at Aberdeen University, July 1969. London: Oxford University Press, 1970.
46. Katz, M. M.   The Classification of Depression: Normal, Clinical and Ethnocultural Variations. In R. R. Fieve (Ed.), *Depression in the 1970's.* Amsterdam: Elsevier-Excerpta Medica, 1971. P. 31.
47. Katz, M. M., Cole, J. O., and Barton, W. E.   *The Role and Methodology of Classification in Psychiatry and Psychopathology.* Washington, D.C.: Department of Health, Education, and Welfare pub. no. (HSM) 72-9015, 1968.
48. Katz, M. M., Cole, J. O., and Lowery, H. A.   Studies of the diag-

nostic process: The influence of symptom perception, past experience, and ethnic background on diagnostic decision. *Am. J. Psychiatry* 125:109, 1969.

49. Katz, M. M., Gudeman, H., and Sanborn, K.   Characterizing Differences in Psychopathology Among Ethnic Groups: A Preliminary Report on Hawaii-Japanese and Mainland-American Schizophrenics. In W. Caudill, and T.-Y. Lin (Eds.), *Mental Health Research in Asia and the Pacific*. Honolulu: East-West Center Press, 1969.

50. Katz, M. M., and Lyerly, S. B.   Methods for measuring adjustment and social behavior in the community: 1. Rationale, description, discriminative validity and scale development. *Psychol. Rep. Monogr.* (Suppl. 4) 13:503, 1963.

51. Katz, M. M., Sanborn, K. O., and Gudeman, H.   Characterizing Differences in Psychopathology Among Ethnic Groups in Hawaii. Paper presented at the annual meeting of the Association for Research on Mental and Nervous Diseases, New York, December 1967.

52. Katz, S. H., and Foulks, E. E.   Mineral metabolism and behavior: Abnormalities of calcium homeostasis. *Am. J. Phys. Anthropol.* 32: 299, 1970.

53. Kendell, R. E.   *The Classification of Depressive Illnesses*. London: Oxford University Press, 1968.

54. Kendell, R. E., Cooper, J. E., Gourlay, A. J., and Copeland, J. R. M. Diagnostic criteria of American and British psychiatrists. *Arch. Gen. Psychiatry* 25:123, 1971.

54a. Klerman, G. L.   Clinical research in depression. *Arch. Gen. Psychiatry* 24:305, 1971.

55. Klerman, G. L., and Paykel, E. S.   Depressive pattern, social background, and hospitalization. *J. Nerv. and Ment. Dis.* 150:466, 1970.

56. Klibansky, R., Panofsky, E., and Saxl, F.   *Saturn and Melancholy*. London: Nelson, 1964.

57. Kraepelin, E.   *Manic-Depressive Insanity and Paranoia*. Translated by M. Barclay. Edinburgh: Livingstone, 1921.

58. Kramer, M.   Cross-national study of diagnosis of the mental disorders: Origin of the problem. *Am. J. Psychiatry* 125:10, 1969.

59. Laing, R. D.   *Self and Others*, ed. R. R. Fieve. London: Tavistock, 1969.

60. Leff, J., Roatch, J. F., and Bunney, W. E., Jr.   Environmental factors preceding the onset of severe depressions. *Psychiatry* 33:293, 1970.

61. Lehmann, H. E.   Epidemiology of Depressive Disorders. In *Depression in the 1970's*. Amsterdam: Elsevier-Excerpta Medica, 1971. p. 21.

62. Leighton, A. H.   *My Name Is Legion: Foundations for a Theory of Man in Relation to Culture*. New York: Basic Books, 1959.

63. Leighton, A. H., Lambo, T. A., Hughes, C. C., Leighton, D. C., Murphy, J., and Macklin, D. B.   *Psychiatric Disorder Among the Yoruba*. Ithaca: Cornell University Press, 1963.

64. Leighton, D. C., Harding, J. S., Macklin, D. B., MacMillan, A. M., and Leighton, A. H.   *The Character of Danger: Psychiatric Symptoms in Selected Communities*. New York: Basic Books, 1963.

65. LeVine, R. A.   *Culture, Behavior, and Personality: An Introduction*

to the Comparative Study of Psychosocial Adaptation.* Chicago: Aldine, 1973.
66. Levine, S., and Scotch, N. A.   *Social Stress.* Chicago: Aldine, 1970.
67. Liberman, R. P., and Raskin, D. E.   Depression: A behavioral formulation. *Arch. Gen. Psychiatry* 24:515, 1971.
68. Lloyd, B.   *Perception and Cognition: A Cross-Cultural Perspective.* Middlesex, England: Penguin Books, 1972.
69. Lundquist, G.   Prognosis and course in manic depressive psychoses: A follow-up study of 319 first admissions. *Acta Psychiatr. Neurol. Scand.* (Suppl.) 35:1, 1945. (Cited in Robins and Guze [96], p. 289.)
70. Madden, J. S.   Melancholy in medicine and literature: Some historical considerations. *Br. J. Med. Psychol.* 39:125, 1966.
71. Malzberg, B.   Mental Disorders in the U.S. In A. Deutsch, and H. Fishman (Eds.), *Encyclopedia of Mental Health.* New York: Franklin Watts, 1963. Vol. 3, p. 1051.
72. Mayr, E.   *Populations, Species, and Evolution.* Cambridge, Mass.: Belknap Press of Harvard University Press, 1970.
73. McGhie, A., and Chapman, J.   Disorders of attention and perception in early schizophrenia. *Br. J. Med. Psychol.* 34:103, 1961.
74. Mechanic, D.   *Medical Sociology: A Selective View.* New York: Free Press, 1968.
75. Miller, C., Knapp, S. C., and Daniels, C. W.   MMPI study of Negro mental hygiene clinic patients. *J. Abnorm. Psychol.* 73:168, 1968.
76. Morrison, J. R., Hudgens, R. W., and Barchha, R. G.   Life events and psychiatric illness. *Br. J. Psychiatry* 114:423, 1968.
77. Neel, J. W.   Lessons from a "primitive" people. *Science* 170:815, 1970.
78. Norris, V.   *Mental Illness in London.* Maudsley Monographs, no. 6. London: Chapman and Hall, 1959.
79. Parker, S., and Kleiner, R. J.   *Mental Illness in the Urban Negro Community.* New York: Free Press, 1966.
80. Paskind, H. A.   Manic depressive psychosis in private practice, length of the attack and length of the interval. *Arch. Neurol. Psychiatry* 23:789, 1930. (Cited in Robins and Guze [96], p. 289.)
81. Paykel, E. S.   Correlates of a depressive typology. *Arch. Gen. Psychiatry* 27:203, 1972.
82. Paykel, E. S., and Dienelt, M. N.   Suicide attempts following acute depression. *J. Nerv. Ment. Dis.* 153:234, 1971.
83. Paykel, E. S., Myers, J. K., Dienelt, M. N., Klerman, G. L., Lindenthal, J. J., and Pepper, M.   Life events and depression. *Arch. Gen. Psychiatry* 21:753, 1969.
84. Paykel, E. S., Weissman, M. M., Prusoff, B. A., and Tonks, C. M.   Dimensions of social adjustment in depressed women. *J. Nerv. Ment. Dis.* 152:158, 1971.
85. Paykel, E. S., and Weissman, M. M.   Social adjustment and depression. *Arch. Gen. Psychiatry* 28:659, 1973.
86. Pederson, A. M., Berry, D. J., and Babigian, H. M.   Epidemiological considerations of psychotic depression. *Arch. Gen. Psychiatry* 27:193, 1972.

87. Perris, C. (Ed.)   A study of bipolar (manic-depressive) and uni-polar recurrent depressive psychoses. *Acta Psychiatr. Scand.* (Suppl. 194), 1966.
88. Perris, C., and d'Elia, G.   A study of bipolar (manic-depressive) and unipolar recurrent depressive psychoses: S. mortality, suicide, and life-cycles. *Acta Psychiatr. Scand.* (Suppl. 194), 1966. P. 172.
89. Pettigrew, T. J.   *A Profile of the American Negro.* Princeton: Van Nostrand, 1964. P. 72.
90. Phillips, L.   *Human Adaptation and Its Failures.* New York and London: Academic, 1968.
91. Pokorney, A. D.   Suicide rates in various psychiatric disorders. *J. Nerv. Ment. Dis.* 139:499, 1964.
92. Prince, R.   The changing picture of depressive syndromes in Africa. *Can. J. African Studies* 1:177, 1968.
93. Rahe, R. H.   Psychosocial Determinants of Illness Onset. In S. J. Lipowski (Ed.), *Advances in Psychosomatic Medicine: Psychosocial Aspects of Physical Illness.* New York: Karger, 1972.
94. Rawnsley, K.   Epidemiology of Affective Disorders. In *Recent Developments in Affective Disorders. Br. J. Psychiatry* Special Publications, no, 2, 1968.
95. Rennie, T. A. C.   Prognosis in manic depressive psychoses. *Am. J. Psychiatry* 98:801, 1942. (Cited in Robins and Guze [96], p. 289.)
96. Robins, E., and Guze, S. B.   Classification of Affective Disorders: The Primary-Secondary, the Endogenous-Reactive and the Neurotic-Psychotic Concepts. In T. A. Wiliams, M. M. Katz, and J. A. Shields, Jr. (Eds.), *Recent Advances in the Psychobiology of the Depressive Illnesses.* Bethesda, Md.: Department of Health, Education, and Welfare pub. no. (HSM) 70-9053, 1972. P. 283.
97. Robins, E., Murphy, G., Wilkinson, R. H., Jr., Gassner, S., and Kayes, J.   Some clinical considerations in the prevention of suicide based on a study of 134 successful suicides. *Am. Journal of Public Health.* 49:888, 1959.
98. Ruesch, J.   The assessment of social disability, *Arch. Gen. Psychiatry* 21:655, 1969.
99. Ruesch, J. and Brodsky, C. M.   The concept of social disability, *Arch. Gen. Psychiatry* 19:394, 1968.
100. Sainsbury, P.   Suicide in London. London: Chapman and Hall, 1955.
100a. Sainsbury, P.   Suicide and depression. In *Recent Developments in Affective Disorders,* no. 2, *Br. J. Psychiatry* 1968.
101. Sandifer, M. G., Hordern, A., Timburg, G. C., and Green, L. M.   Psychiatric diagnosis: A comparative study in North Carolina, *Br. J. Psychiatry,* 114:1, 1968.
102. Sarbin, T. R.   Ontology recapitulates philology: The mythic nature of anxiety, *Am. Psychol.* 23:411, 1968.
103. Schaeffer, D. L.   Patterns of premorbid and symptom behaviors in schizophrenic and depressed women, *J. Nerv. Ment. Dis.* 150:449, 1970.
104. Scheff, T. J.   *Being Mentally Ill: A Sociological Theory.* Chicago: Aldine, 1966.
105. Schwab, J. J., et al.   The affective symptomatology of depression in medical inpatients, *Psychosomatics* 7:214-217, 1966.

106. Schwab, J. J., McGinnis, N. A., Warheit, G. J. The differential perception of anxiety in medical patients: Sociodemographic aspects, *Psychiatry Med.* 1:151, 1970.
107. Seager, C. P. and Flood, R. A. Suicide and Bristol, *Br. J. Psychiatry* 3:919, 1965.
108. Shakow, D. Some observations on the psychology (and some fewer on the biology) of schizophrenia. *J. Nerv. Ment. Dis.* 153:300, 1971.
109. Shobe, F. O., and Brion, P. Long-term prognosis in manic depressive illness. *Arch. Gen. Psychiatry* 24:334, 1971.
110. Silverman, C. *The Epidemiology of Depression*. Baltimore: Johns Hopkins Press, 1968.
111. Simon, R. J. Involutional psychosis in Negroes. *Arch. Gen. Psychiatry* 13:148, 1963.
112. Simon, R. J., Fleiss, J. L., Gurland, B. J., Stiller, P. R., and Sharpe, L. Depression and schizophrenia in hospitalized black and white mental patients. *Arch. Gen. Psychiatry* 28:509, 1973.
113. Simpson, G. G. *Principles of Animal Taxonomy*. New York: Columbia University Press, 1961.
114. Snell, B. *The Discovery of the Mind*. New York: Harper Torchbooks, 1960. (Originally published in 1953 by Harvard University Press.)
115. Srole, L., Langner, T. S., Michael, S. T., Opler, M. K., and Rennie, T. A. C. *Mental Health in the Metropolis: The Midtown Manhattan Study*, vol. 1. New York: McGraw-Hill, 1962.
116. Szasz, T. S. *The Myth of Mental Illness; Foundations of a Theory of Personal Conduct*. New York: Hoeber Med. Div., Harper & Row, 1961.
117. Temoche, A., Pugh, T. F., and MacMahon, B. Suicide rates among current and former mental institution patients. *J. Nerv. Ment. Dis.* 138:124, 1964.
118. Thompson, K. C., and Hendrie, H. C. Environmental stress in primary depressive illness. *Arch. Gen. Psychiatry* 26:130, 1972.
119. Tonks, C. M., Paykel, E. S., and Klerman, G. L. Clinical depression among Negroes. *Am. J. Psychiatry* 127:329, 1970.
120. Veith, I. English melancholy and American nervousness. *Bull. Menninger Clin.* 32:301, 1968.
121. Veith, I. Elizabethans on melancholia. *J.A.M.A.* 212:127, 1970.
122. Veith, I. Diseases steal both day and night. *Mod. Med.* 39:188, 1971.
123. Wallace, A. F. C. Mental Illness, Biology and Culture. In F. L. K. Hsu (Ed.), *Psychological Anthropology: Approaches to Culture*. Homewood, Ill.: Dorsey, 1961. p. 255.
124. Wallace, F. C. *Culture and Personality*. New York: Random House, 1962.
125. Weissman, M., Paykel, E. S., Siegel, R., and Klerman, G. L. The social role performance of depressed women: Comparisons with a normal group. *Am. J. Orthopsychiatry* 41:390, 1971.
126. Williams, T. A., Katz, M. M., and Shield, J. A., Jr. (Eds.). *Recent Advances in the Psychobiology of the Depressive Illnesses*. Proceedings of workshop sponsored by the National Institute of Mental Health. Washington, D.C.: Department of Health, Education, and Welfare pub. no. (HSM) 70-9053, 1972.

127. Winch, P.   *The Idea of Social Science*. London: Routledge & Kegan Paul, 1958.
128. Wing, J. K.   A Standard Form of Psychiatric Present State Examination." In E. H. Hare and J. K. Wing (Eds.), *Psychiatric Epidemiology*. Proceedings of the International Symposium held at Aberdeen University, July 1969. London: Oxford University Press, 1970.
129. Winokur, G.   *Manic Depressive Illness*. St. Louis: Mosby, 1969.
130. Winokur, G.   The types of depressive disorders. *J. Nerv. Men. Dis.* 156:82, 1973.
131. Zubin, J.   Cross-national study of diagnosis of the mental disorders: Methodology and planning. *Am. J. Psychiatry* 125:10, 1969.

II

The Genesis of Psychoanalytic Concepts Relating to Depression

It is often said of psychoanalysts (perhaps because they are popularly regarded as historians of the psyche) that they never seem to tire of recounting their history. If Santayana is correct, they should be, among behavioral scientists at least, the least likely to repeat history. Santayana's aphorism does appear to hold with regard to the psychoanalytic history of depression. Unlike so many other areas of psychoanalysis, the efforts of psychoanalysts in the study of depression are not dwarfed by the gigantic contributions of Freud. Here, he is a concept-builder like other analytic concept-builders, adding his important section to the imposing edifice that psychoanalytic theorists have constructed. The psychoanalytic house of depression is imposing when considered in its entirety. Unlike the tower of Babel, the total structure is surprisingly consistent, comprehensive, and coherent. Clearly the builders have communicated surprisingly well over the years; some may have stressed one aspect and some another, but the consensus has been more notable than in other parts of psychoanalysis.

The pioneers of psychoanalysis, such as Freud and Abraham in the first generation and Rado in the second, were not trying to formulate a general theory of a disease entity. Their investigations represented cornerstones in the structure of psychoanalytic theory. In reviewing the large literature on depression that has accrued over the past fifty to sixty years, one sees "phase-specific" developments corresponding to periods in the evolution of psychoanalysis, at times illuminating a particular psychodynamic factor, and at other times giving support to general theory. For example, when libido theory was in the forefront, the role of the oral phase in depression received considerable attention; when structural theory was introduced, the superego problems of guilt and punishment were added to the picture; and still later, as the concept of the self was delineated, the concept of self-esteem came to have crucial significance.

These psychoanalytic concepts of depression, arising from different chronological periods, have begun to coalesce to form an overall conceptual picture, conforming to the general pattern of concept formation described by Cassirer:

> *Each newly acquired concept is an attempt, a beginning, a problem; its value lies not in its copying of definite objects but in its opening up of new logical perspectives, so permitting a new penetration and survey of an entire problem complex. . . . One of its essential tasks is not to let the problems of knowledge come prematurely to rest but to keep them in a steady flux by guiding them toward new goals which it must first anticipate hypothetically. Here again we find that the concept is far less abstractive than prospective; it not only fixes what is already known, establishing its general outlines, but also maintains a persistent outlook for new and unknown connections [1].*

Psychoanalytic investigators today, as in earlier times, study the problems of individuals, but their generalizations often encompass more than just a specific disorder. For instance, the conceptualization of primary structures in the self and the process of sublimation that results in character trends of a high order refer only tangentially to the psychology of depression, yet they illustrate the ways in which changes in self-esteem, so characteristic of the affective disorders, are brought about.

The idea of specific phases of investigation, as described in this commentary, is very much in keeping with Kuhn's description of the history of science as essentially discontinuous [2]. According to Kuhn, the impetus for scientific work may reside in the discrepancy between the observations of a science and its theory, since the fit between the two is always imperfect. When there is a tacit agreement among the practitioners that the fit is good enough, the central paradigm remains unchallenged, and this corresponds to a period of well-being, optimism, and confidence. Eventually there is less certainty regarding the ability of the central paradigm to account for the observations or to organize them. This sense of disquietude may precipitate something of a crisis, in the resolution of which the central paradigm either is modified in accordance with new observations or is replaced by a more workable theory. In the case of the psychoanalytic theory of depression, these steps have followed one another slowly, and the problem has mainly consisted of fitting the developing concepts into a coherent central paradigm.

The bridge-building activities between disciplines are well recog-

nized by the contributors. Goldberg feels, with ample justification, that psychoanalysis has made "unique, lasting, and essential contributions to understanding depression" (see Chapter 6), but he emphasizes that while psychoanalytic theory must conform to biochemical, physiological, and sociological theories, the converse must also be true. The historical evolution, as he sees it, is one in which the disciplines mutually influence one another in an "epigenetic process" striving toward a theory of depression, and he reflects a cautious optimism about "getting there." In the same context Benedek raises the critical question for the book as well as for the understanding of depression: "Why is it that some individuals overcome the universal, innate predisposition to depression and are able to master its transient manifestations in moods and affects while others succumb to illness?" (see Chapter 7). She points out that psychoanalysts must concede that there are factors present that cannot be elucidated by psychoanalysis alone.

As the concept of the self was gradually elaborated in psychoanalysis, various attributes of the self came into prominence including the important one of self-esteem. Current psychology has studied this particular self concept, with academic thoroughness, as a function of well-being; but psychoanalysts, such as Jacobson, have explored its roots and its dynamic regulation in health and illness.

The two remaining papers in this section connect psychoanalytic investigation directly with biological theory. One might consider them as suggesting possible routes by which the memory traces of the oral phase influence the genesis of factors conducive to depression, although their authors themselves are not overtly subscribing to this view. Schmale and Engel have attempted to show that a biological defense, namely "conservation-withdrawal," becomes the basis on which other somatic and psychological influences lead to depression. The feeling states of helplessness and hopelessness are the psychological correlates of biological conservation-withdrawal, both representing a slowing down of the body to conserve energy in the face of an actual or threatened deficiency. The bridging elements here are self-evident, since the authors repeatedly call attention to the relationship between the biological and psychological adaptive feedback mechanisms; they also make passing reference to the biochemical and genetic factors that may predispose individuals to develop initially depressive characteristics and after depressive neuroses. The "mysterious leap" between soma and psyche, between neurochemistry and Kierkegaard, is handled with surprising smoothness: "Those who have genetic predispositions and associated neural transmission abnormalities may in fact have the greatest difficulty in achieving trusting relationships and

realistic self-goals because of the early failure of such biological mech-
anisms during the periods of giving up that regularly occur in the
course of growing up," (see Chapter 9). Here, conservation-withdrawal
functions as an intervening mechanism between the genetic and bio-
chemical factors and later psychological disturbances.

Wolpert's contribution combines the energy factors with the devel-
opmental problems that account for oral fixation and attempts to con-
ceptualize manic-depressive illness as a "genetically determined actual
neurosis in which the typical psychological symptoms are the outcome
of alternation of periodic excess and lack of physiological energy,"
(see Chapter 10). Wolpert rightly calls attention to his theory's ex-
planatory power with regard to the wide range of disparate clinical
and experimental facts, uncontaminated by any prior knowledge of
the work of Engel and Schmale; he lends support to their view of the
depressive state as an outcome of energy deficiency in the affective
system. It is also relevant to note that one form of chemotherapy of
depression is based on the same assumption (see Chapter 20).

REFERENCES

1. Cassirer, E.   *Philosophy of Symbolic Forms.* New Haven: Yale University Press, 1955.
2. Kuhn, T. S.   *The Structure of Scientific Revolutions.* Chicago: University of Chicago Press, 1962.

6

The Evolution of
Psychoanalytic Concepts of Depression

ARNOLD I. GOLDBERG

The famous biologist and geneticist Waddington [34] states that evolution is no longer seen in terms of the simple development of a genotype but rather in the sense of a total "epigenetic system" in which genes react to a whole set of regulations throughout the entire process of embryogenetic growth in interaction with the environment. Perhaps this more vital and dynamic concept of evolution can be applied to that of ideas or concepts which can change, be modified or altered, accelerate or slow down as our knowledge accumulates and becomes organized. The concept of depression is a dynamic one that had its psychoanalytic underpinnings in Freud's seminal work, *Mourning and Melancholia* [13], but that has grown and is still developing today.

Throughout the history of psychoanalysis there has been a struggle over how to organize thinking about affects, feelings, and emotions. Affects may, for the sake of this presentation, be considered as processes or physiological states that make an impression, perhaps as potentials. We must therefore delineate their relation to instinctual drives, which are at the border of biology, and to feelings, which are in the realm of consciousness. The myriad of physiological and psychological processes at times coordinate and reach a level of awareness that we call feeling. A host of related terms and concepts, such as perception, sensation, and mood lie within this broad category of feeling and feeling states. Whether one considers depression as mood or emotion or affective state or something else, it is a feeling that we know. The goal of psychoanalysis is to explain and understand the unconscious psychological contributions to this feeling state. For this, psychoanalytic theory offers data relating to developmental consid erations, clinical phenomena both within and outside the analytic setting, and introspective material. Even so, a total theory of depression can no more evolve from psychoanalysis alone than from any other single field. The host of clinical and theoretical data derived from psychoanalytic investigation is the contribution that should become part of, and integrated by, a future theory of depression (see Chapter 21). This chapter will direct itself to an examination of the evolution of our conceptual thinking about depression.

HISTORY

Since the history of the psychoanalytic concept of depression is that of significant names and associated contributions, modification and growth of the concept is an ongoing process.

Freud [10] first wrote of periodic depression as a third form of anxiety neuroses. He felt that although every case of neurasthenia is marked by a lowering of self-confidence, the emergence of anxiety as a separate factor should be detached. Anxiety relating to the body was designated as hypochondria, and lasting anxiety was termed periodic depression. He separated the latter from melancholia, which was a more elaborate phenomenon related to loss and which initially he thought was mourning over loss of libido. Freud described three forms of melancholia relating to masturbation, severe anxiety, and heredity. His thinking at this time was primarily neurological. The problem of hypochondria remained somehow linked to depression, and later Freud explained hypochondria as an "actual" neurosis, based, again, on damming up of the libido when it returns to the body or self or ego. This was a variation of narcissism, which we will describe below. Later works by Freud and others help to clarify whether depression and melancholia are equivalent and to elucidate the brooding associated with hypochondriacal preoccupation.

Freud's original neurological explanation of depression in 1897 became a psychological one involving a wish in conflict: a crucial ingredient to all psychoanalytic phenomena. In *Mourning and Melancholia* Freud compared the two states in the phenomenological picture of dejection following the external precipitating factor of a loss. In mourning, there was a real loss, with detachment from the lost object occurring over time, and this in most circumstances resulted in the mourning work. Mourning lacked a disturbance of self-regard (today we might call this self-esteem). In melancholia, the loss was different; it was more of a withdrawal of connection or cathexis. There was, however, a characteristic and significant drop in self-regard, and the loss was experienced as a loss to one's ego. We might call this a loss to one's self; indeed, this article was written before *The Ego and the Id*

[14] and before the more elaborate concept of ego was developed. The fundamental feature of self-reproach directed to one's own ego (or self) disclosed that the old love object had taken up residence within the psyche of the melancholic: everything said about oneself was really said about someone else. Freud clearly separated and compared these two states, the one (mourning) normal and the other (melancholia) pathological, although they shared the picture of depression. Depression was equated primarily with sadness and dejection and not with the self-accusation of melancholia. For better or worse, depression did not keep its pure form and has come to be considered a blanket term that encompasses mourning, melancholia, and other states.

A clarification of a term that has plagued contributors to psychoanalytic theory is in order. The term is narcissistic or narcissistic object. Freud said that the object choice in the melancholic is narcissistic and that the object cathexis regresses to narcissism. Later psychoanalytic contributions enlarge and clarify this concept, for now let it suffice to underline the definition of narcissism as "psychologic investment in the self" [21]. Therefore, the narcissistic object is one that either is like the self (looks like the self) or is an extension of the self (is experienced as a part of the self). Thus the narcissistic object can be separate from *or* a functional part of the self. The "regression of object cathexis to narcissism" indicates an increase of feeling or interest in the self: what we would call a heightened self-centeredness. This follows upon object loss and may result in the object being internalized. Therefore, the lost object can be replaced by another one or replaced through an identification. Depending on how such a loss is handled, one may experience depression or merely a shift in object interest.

One cannot help but notice that Freud's *Mourning and Melancholia* [13] followed *On Narcissism* [12] and was a clinical elaboration of the theory of that paper. The "ego" of this effort is not that of the later *The Ego and the Id* [14]; perhaps more appropriately, *Mourning and Melancholia* [13] is a study of the psychopathology of the self. Freud also noted that the oral libidinal phase seems to predominate in melancholia, but he credits this concept to Abraham [2]. In obsessives the ambivalence may give a pathological cast to mourning, which as noted is usually in itself not pathological.

The theory developed here explains other phenomena of depression. Suicide, for example, is explained by the model of the object dwelling inside the ego; the ego kills itself by treating itself as an object. Freud felt that a somatic factor was probably involved here. It bears repeating that the loss in the ego in melancholia is a purely narcissistic blow quite apart from the physical presence or absence of the object. A psychoanalytic concept of loss is restricted to the intrapsychic experience and may be at odds with the observable facts; i.e., parent loss may or may not be a narcissistic blow followed by melancholia, and true melancholia may result from an injury such as an insult.

In his discussion of mania Freud expanded on the idea of detachment of libido. This disengagement was from the unconscious cathexis and occurred in both mourning and melancholia. The latter is complicated by ambivalence and is occasioned by other than real losses. Mania differs from pathological mourning in that the libido that has returned to the ego is now available to triumph over inhibitions and thereby can be employed for new object cathexes. The explanation is not an adequate one, and one cannot help but feel that Freud felt so as well. The availability of libido does not explain its unwarranted use in mania. Other authors have elaborated on this point, some stressing especially the somatic factor involved in mania.

In summary, mourning is a normal reaction to a real loss in which one works to detach the libido invested in the lost object. The process involves the return of the libido to one's ego (or self) and a reinvestment of it in other objects. Dejection or sadness is the predominant feeling. To the degree that one has or had ambivalent feelings toward the lost object, there may occur a pathological cast to the mourning when one's sadism is expressed via the process of identification with the object (temporarily) while new objects are sought. Melancholia is a pathological state involving narcissistic blows to the ego experienced as losses and involving more wholesale or traumatic internalization of the offending object. The depressed state adds the striking phenomenon of self-reproach that is really directed to the inner object and that may culminate in suicide. Since the writing of *Mourning and Melancholia* preceded the dual-drive theory, aggression was not singled out, although sadism was emphasized. Oral libido has been considered another important factor.

Before proceeding to other significant contributions it may serve well to emphasize that different ideas and words grow independently in the evolution of the understanding of depression. One such combination is narcissism and orality. These are separate ideas; they may coexist in depression, as some authors maintain, but they refer to different areas of psychological processes. Much confusion can be avoided by emphasizing that orality is a stage in libido development whereas narcissism may occur in any of the various stages of libido.

Abraham [2] gave the fullest emphasis of any psychoanalytic writer to the role of orality in depression. He felt that certain individuals become fixated at the oral level and have inordinate oral needs, manifested by eating, talking, and sucking or by insatiable demands for orally expressed affection. Likewise these fixated persons are extremely sensitive to oral frustrations. Initially in 1911 Abraham [2] felt that obsessives and depressives were similar. He connected anal fixation and its ambivalence to the attitudes of depressives toward their object. In his later [1] papers of 1924 he emphasized oral characteristics. The picture was further complicated by his postulating a primal depression, which followed an injury to one's infantile narcissism through a combination of disappointments in love. The aggression of melancholics was attributed to the newly formulated oral-aggressive stage. One must keep in mind that Abraham wrote at a time when psychoanalysis and libido theory were almost synonymous; therefore psychopathology was connected in a sort of parallel fashion to disturbances in libidinal stages. His classic papers constitute a study of libido via mental disorders.

Later authors, such as Rado [26] and Fenichel [8], have expanded on the issue of orality and depression. Rado discussed the influence of the nursing situation on the infantile ego and thus extended the concept of orality to include all the pleasurable sensations the infant experiences at the mother's breast, such as general feelings of warmth, security, and nourishment. Fenichel further broadened the interpretation of orality and described the "narcissistic" oral character of the depressive as "a person who is fixated on the state where his self-esteem is regulated by external supplies." He emphasized the dependency of the orally fixated character and his need to be loved and nurtured by his love object. As Chodoff has stated, "for many psychoanalysts, the oral character has come to have lost its moorings in psychosexual and constitutional orality and to have become synonymous with exaggerated affectional and supportive needs and with traits expressing an excessive dependency" [7]. However healthy a sign that may be in the growth and development of the clinical status of psychoanalytic science, it is less salutary for the clinical theory. If depression is everything, then it is nothing.

Edward Bibring [5] proposed a model of depression based on conflict involving an emotional expression of a state of helplessness and powerlessness of the ego. He thereby advanced psychoanalytic thinking about depression from a preoccupation with the instinctual drives to one involving ego psychology. To summarize, Bibring presented the following goals and objects as characteristic of all persons: (1) a wish to be worthy, loved, and appreciated, (2) a wish to be strong and secure, and (3) a wish to be good and loving. He felt that it is the tension between one's charged narcissistic aspirations and the ego's awareness of its helplessness that leads to depression. He differentiated depression from depersonalization, in which the feeling or anxiety is blocked, and from boredom, in which action is blocked. Depression, boredom, and depersonalization are all states of mental inhibition, but in depression self-esteem is broken down. Anxiety is the ego's desire to survive; depression is the wish to die.

Bibring clarified several basic ego states: (1) balanced narcissism, (2) excited self-esteem, (3) threatened narcissism—the anxious ego, and (4) broken down self-regard—the ego in depression. He felt that the ego's awareness of helplessness is the core of depression. Bibring distinguished this basic mechanism from predisposing conditions, from attempts at restitution, from complicating conditions, and from the secondary use of depression. Aggressions and orality are conditions that complicate depression. Self-hatred is secondary to a breakdown of self-esteem. Self-esteem is regained via attaining the goals mentioned above (being loved, being strong, and being good). Elation, for Bibring, is a manifestation of an actual or imaginary fulfillment of narcissistic configurations. To repeat, Bibring's theory states that depression is an affective state of the ego that resonates with fixation to an infantile state of helplessness. This state is revived when there is a blow to the one's self-esteem and results in depression when tension between charged narcissistic aspirations and the ego's awareness of helplessness and weakness ensues.

The question of the concept of the ego as a person within the person is not to be construed as a criticism of Bibring. Much of ego psychology utilizes the concept of ego as a supreme intelligence that does superior things such as integrate, synthesize, fractionate, and organize as well as less desirable activities such as submit, endure, suffer, and revolt. The ego's being aware of itself is, however, a philosophical problem. The substitution of self for ego does not remove this problem [31]. Only a redefining of ego as activities or processes instead of agent leads to a solution of sorts.

For a while, Bibring's position was considered to be the definitive statement on depression, but it soon came under criticism for ignoring the drives. Rubinfine [28] feels that Bibring makes a generalization about the limitations of the ego without any explanation as to why some people master the depressive affect and others succumb to it. He insists that the role of aggression needs to be incorporated into the explanatory theory of depression, and he does so by introducing the concept of a narcissistic unit of the mother and infant. When this is disrupted, the event leads to helplessness, narcissistic disillusionment, and resulting rage. Aggression is placed in a developmental sequence of psychosis, psychosomatic disorders, and depression. Depression occurs in an infant who experiences narcissistic unity with the mother but becomes fixated on this state because of premature and abrupt reversal to prolonged tension states. This leads to premature awareness of the object as separate from the child and to premature differentiation of the aggressive drive. Depressive affect is a signal that an aim is unattainable because of ego weakness and helplessness. Parallel to the ego's mastery of anxiety signals there is an increasing ability to master depression. In a sense Rubinfine expands the theory by insisting on developmental factors and including the aggressive drive. He (and also Klein) does "adultomorphize" infancy, however, and perhaps the argument is less significant because of this.

No historical sketch of psychoanalytic concepts of depression can neglect the work of Melanie Klein [20], who introduced the concept of the depressive position, defined as that phase of development in which the infant recognizes a whole object and relates himself to this object. In this depressive position, anxieties spring from ambivalence. The child's anxiety is that his own destructive impulses have destroyed or will destroy the object he loves and depends on. In the depressive position, introjective processes are intensified. This position is believed to begin in the oral phase, and its working through is accompanied by a radical alteration in the child's view of reality. The infant becomes aware of himself by perceiving his dependence and the ambivalence of his own instincts and aims. (Such early *recognition* is unlikely in infancy, based on present-day neurophysiology, but this does not invalidate the concepts entirely.) The early phases of the depressive position are said to portray the superego as severe and persecuting, but it loses some harshness as the whole object relation is established. The pain of mourning experienced in the depressive position and the reparative drives developed to restore the loved internal and external objects are believed to be the basis of later creativity and sublimation. The depressive position is never fully worked through; and anxieties pertaining to ambivalence and guilt as well as situations of loss, which reawaken depressive experiences, are always with us. Thus depression, for Klein, is a state of mind in which painful feelings of the depressive position are partly or fully experienced. Each psychoanalyst seems to make an individual decision as to how much of Klein's thinking is useful and how much is to be disregarded. The usual criticisms are attributing sophisticated thinking to an infant who is without the capacity for elaborate cognition. However, the problem is not only one of timing, since some of the processes such as introjection and projection may be inexact or erroneous renderings of mental processes.

CONCEPTS

Certain key concepts or aggregates of ideas seem to occur over and over in a historical survey of depression. There is the persistent connection of depression with orality or the oral phase of development, the mother-child unit, or the nursing situation. There is always a connection with narcissistic issues in the description of object relations, identification, and, in particular, the regulation of self-esteem. And finally, there is the regular association of aggression or hostility, superego, and resultant guilt. To be sure, other issues present themselves in an overall survey of depression, such as the nature of the defenses, the capacity to neutralize, the fate of the autonomous ego functions, and the role of masochism, but these key concepts are more or less the cornerstones for a psychoanalytic theory of depression.

Orality

Therese Benedek [3] demonstrated that the universal nature of a depressive constellation lies in the psychobiology of the female procreative function, in motherhood and motherliness itself, and is to be understood in terms of reciprocal interactions between mother and child. Though the article was not about depression per se, it attempted to lay the groundwork for an organizational principle of depression based on the feeding experience, which establishes the relationship between mother and child. Stressful situations or disruptions in the mother-child unit lead to regressions to a phase of separation for both mother and child and thus to the resultant ambivalence inherent in the union. Benedek felt that transactions involving alimentation are the basic processes of human development and that, through reciprocal introjection and identification, both mother and child develop personality structure. The mother and child are conceived of as a transactional unit. The aggressive charge involved in disruptions of the unit, with the ambivalent core of the personality, leads to "the depressive constellation," which is conceptualized as a universal core organization. The universality of this concept implies a generalization about depression that is in keeping with many clinical and theoretical ideas on the subject: that everyone, after a certain modicum of sufficient mothering, reaches a developmental stage in which depression can be considered as normal.

The work of Spitz and Wolf [33] on anaclitic depression in infants may seem to be at odds with the concept of a normal stage of depression. They observed children (a total of 170) in institutions and noted that they undergo a marked behavioral change in the second six months: they become weepy, withdrawn, and finally apathetic, and seem retarded. All of these children were said to suffer from emotional deprivation in that they had been deprived of their mothers for periods of about three months. They felt that the infants' "incomplete psychic apparatus did not allow for a diagnosis of depression" and so called the syndrome anaclitic depression. Bowlby [6] has made similar observations on early separations of infants from others. The problem of determining the feelings of others from observation always hampers the accuracy of work on infant observation, although it *is* subject to some corroboration by retrospective psychoanalytic studies.

As an aside let me emphasize a point made earlier, that the accumulation of data from various disciplines toward a unitary theory of depression will necessarily have varying degrees of relevance for each discipline. There is a point in early development when psychological material becomes relevant to the understanding of behavior, but we are still unsure when this transition from physiological to psychological processes (summarized as "mind") occurs. Data gathered from observations made during a prepsychological period are colored by empathic guesses of the investigator. Depression is a disorder that overrides disciplinary divisions, and can occur *with* and *without* an associated psychological problem. Perhaps the depressions of animals are equivalent to disorders of function that do not elaborate the psychological issues noted above, such as struggling with an internalized object. Psychoanalysis must confine itself to the psychology of depression while recognizing the contributions of these earlier states to the phenomenological picture. Whether Spitz's infants had a "true" depression, however that may be defined, or whether their tension states were experienced by the adult observer as depression, is unanswered. But a stage of normal depression in infants apart from possible pathologic states is accepted by most observers.

Melanie Klein postulated such a stage, and recently Margaret Mahler [24] has presented clinical evidence for such a stage. Mahler defines the depressive response as a basic affect and notes its occurrence during the separation-individuation era. For some children it becomes the habitual negative reaction. Mahler feels that the depletion of confident expectation (the "confidence" of Benedek) and the diminution of self-esteem with a concomitant deficit in neutralized aggression creates the basis for the depressive mood. For the children she studied (ages 4 to 36 months) the main problem was severe separation anxiety in the second 18 months of life.

In a clinical paper that seems to substantiate these theoretical and developmental considerations, Zetzel [35] introduces a developmental evaluation of depression parallel to that of anxiety constructed by Max

Schur. After defining depression as an ego state characterized by loss of self-esteem, she differentiates the reactive symptom, the illness, and the character structure. The decisive areas involved are the development of object relations, the acceptance of the limitations of reality, and the capacity to renounce an omnipotent self-image. The critical period for depression parallels the "intermediate area" of anxiety, in which responses are externally directed rather than intrapsychic. The dual developmental task of this time is to tolerate the passive experience of one's inability to modify a painful existing reality and to adapt to mobilize appropriate responses for gratification and achievement. For Zetzel, each individual must achieve a state of capacity for depression. Genuine sadness or depression marks the final decisive step toward achieving the passive component of psychic maturity. Once achieved, this must be followed by active mastery.

Thus among concepts of depression there is a universal psychobiological core related to early transactions between mother and child in the feeding situation, thereby involving the oral zone or phase. This is also a crucial developmental moment that carries with it the seeds of ambivalence and aggression that must be mastered or adequately endured for continued development. The signposts for this stage of development are the behavior in separation or the experience of disruption and the concomitant basic mood of depression, which is perhaps more nicely expressed as genuine sadness. The correlation of this concatenation of biology, behavioral manifestations, and subjective experience to adult pathology is emphasized.

Narcissism

Freud and Bibring have already been cited as fundamental contributors to the psychoanalytic concept of depression in the area of self-regard or self-esteem. Few psychoanalytic authors (with some exceptions as noted below) have failed to emphasize this factor. The clarifying step of separating the self as a psychic entity in opposition to objects from the ego as an organization of functions was taken by Hartman [18]. For him, the self was a construct of the ego; it was important in some investigations (i.e., schizophrenia) and less significant in others (i.e., autonomous ego functions such as thinking and memory). A further clinical step in analyzing the development and construction of this psychic entity was taken by Kohut [21], who simultaneously considered the self as a "content" of the ego closer to experience.* The contributions of Kohut pertain to the development

---

* This may or may not answer the philosophical muddle of the ego experiencing itself, which unfortunately evokes an image of a person within the person or the "ghost in the machine" of Koestler and Ryle [20a, 29]. However, feeling or experienc-

of a self from separate nuclei to a cohesive and enduring psychological construct. He notes separate but parallel forms, the "grandiose self" and the "idealized parental imago," in narcissistic development. He also postulates transformations of narcissism to creativity, empathy, humor, and wisdom. The clinical elaboration of these concepts in the analysis of narcissistic personality disorders and the transference-like phenomena that buttress and confirm these developmental considerations will not be touched on here. However, the subdivisions of narcissism, especially the crucial elaboration of the drives that are peculiarly attached to narcissistic development—the exhibitionistic, grandiose, and omnipotent cohort—need to be emphasized.

An in depth psychological investigation must concern itself with the instinctual wish, the stage of development, and the total organismic response (concerning both the individual and the environment). Self-esteem regulation is now placed within the province of the self, which balances the exhibitionistic drives. Development proceeds via these two narcissistic forms in interaction with either an empathic or an insensitive environment. Internalization is achieved through phase-specific experiences of near optimal gratification of the narcissistic drives. The proper or relatively nonpathological result of such internalization leads to the grandiose self being tamed to healthy pride and enjoyment of performance, and the idealized parental imago being modified into the idealizing aspect of the superego. Disruptions of such narcissistic equilibrium may lead to depression, which is manifest as deadness of the self or as massive inhibition of an otherwise disruptive grandiose, exhibitionistic drive. However, the regulation of self-esteem is a complex task with multiple channels of interaction with the psyche. One other corollary to the concept of *depression* is that of narcissistic injury [17], whereas the image of a damaged self may be transformed into a mood of sadness preceded or followed by aggression. This can be related to the earlier discussion of melancholia and injury.

Hypochondriacal preoccupation might be considered here. It was first reckoned with in a discussion of neurasthenia and thought of as chronic anxiety over one's body. Fifteen years later, Freud [11], writing on masturbation, said his ideas were unchanged and that the "actual" neuroses provide the psychoneurosis with the necessary "somatic compliance." The damming up of the libido in organic illness or hypochondria gave a physiological component to the psychological

---

ing is something we all do, and it is the backbone of psychoanalysis. The danger is in anthropormorphizing the concept and not understanding it as metaphor. Thus "content" is as real and valid as "ego," but in more refined language both refer to organizational patterns rather than to entities as such.

disturbance. The mood associated with hypochondria was often depression, worry, or brooding. In severe melancholia there is a far-reaching hypochondria, and Fenichel, for one, explains this as distorted recognition of the process of introjection. Kohut places hypochondriacal preoccupation as a phase of narcissistic development, one of the forms of the "grandiose self." He feels the phenomena are manifest during regressive movements from cohesion to fragmentation and can be studied in analyses of narcissistic personality disorders. The connection of the psychological and the physiological at this way station remains an open question, but depression and hypochondriasis are often seen together.

The investigation of narcissism in this context also allows a new perspective on certain forms of suicide. Kohut [22] discusses such suicides as based on the loss of the libidinal cathexis of the self. These suicides do not come from structural conflicts such as unmanageable guilt. Characteristically such suicides are preceded by feelings of unbearable emptiness or by intense shame, i.e., by signs of profound disturbance in the realm of the libidinal cathexis of the self.

The issue of narcissistic development and regulation of self-esteem is on a different plane from the issue of libidinal development, such as orality, but it is a parallel developmental consideration in the mother-child relationship, where *these* drives are recognized, accepted, modified, and responded to. Parallel lines of development likewise may proceed at equal or unequal rates, and thus correlation is not always to be expected [16]. Anna Freud emphasizes our need to concentrate on developmental lines in assessing pathology.

Aggression

The other key concept in our overview of depression is aggression. Although this separate instinctual drive was introduced late to psychoanalytic theory as a co-equal with libido, it was not long neglected. Unfortunately, as Anna Freud [9] has pointed out, too much effort was directed to making it parallel to libido, hence a satisfactory developmental history of aggression has not been articulated. However, there is no theory or clinical study of depression that has not emphasized the role of aggression. For some it is a primary factor; for others it is reactive or secondary.

David Beres [4] is a most staunch and articulate spokesman for the view of depression as a superego conflict that arouses and evokes guilt. Although Beres describes the problem of depression in familiar terms and delineates the phenomena of depression with the usual descriptions such as masochism, identification, disturbance in self-esteem, and helplessness, he feels all these are secondary to the problem of the superego. Beres summarizes his work by noting that depressive individuals are more narcissistic and dependent and therefore have aggressive fantasies with accompanying superego responses. The aggression mobilizes guilt, and guilt plus sexualization leads to masochism. The regression of the individual patient determines whether the issue will be a psychotic or neurotic one. The loss of self-esteem is not seen as a cause of depression. The underlying guilt is or may be more primary than ego helplessness. Object loss leads to depression when accompanied by ambivalence and guilt. Therefore this concept of aggression brings the problem of depression up to date in that it utilizes the model of the mind involving id, ego, and superego, and constructs pathology as typical of that of neurosis formation. For Beres, depression is a continuum. Unfortunately he does not explain depressions that occur before superego formation, although he would probably fall back on ideas such as superego precursors.

A word may be necessary here in order to clarify the problem involving the role of the superego in depression. An epigenetic view of growth and development underscores the idea that structures are not preformed but emerge in a viable interaction with the environment. Now Freud clearly felt, and most non-Kleinians agree, that superego formation is an oedipal event. Attempts to determine what structure regulates the drives before the superego is formed usually fall back on the precursor concept. But Hartmann and Loewenstein [19] have carefully explained that this is inaccurate, that we do not employ a small superego when we are small and enlarge it as we grow. The problem cannot be solved here, but it seems to negate the explanation of non-neurotic depression as one that involves the superego. Indeed it remains uncertain whether guilt exists before oedipal issues are confronted. Clearly, aggression as a line of development undergoes a crucial transformation at the oedipal period, after which it serves at the superego's behest. But just as clearly, the role of aggression in depression is not the same as or equivalent to the role of the superego.

Such a brief overview of the key concepts of depression begs for a final conclusion to "clear it all up." However, our evolutionary progress has not reached that point as yet; psychoanalysis has made unique and fundamental contributions to our understanding of depression, but it has not explained it; yet without the concepts of psychoanalysis there will be no explanation of depression. No one discipline today seems capable of carrying the burden alone. One of the problems is the search for causes or even primacy. Whether self-hatred follows breakdown of self-esteem or the reverse may be an empty pursuit. Fractionation of the observing field may be another problem; we notice the child's aggression and depression while we are unaware of the mother's feelings and reactions and totally oblivious to the social factors that may be operating. This is not a call for a holistic approach but rather a reminder that observation per se is an artifact in scientific investigations. Another difficulty in our psychoanalytic explanation of depression lies within psychoanalysis itself, since present-day theory has not caught up with present-day clinical comprehension. There is no adequate psychoanalytic theory of psychosis. The one that is often employed, that deals with quantitative factors (more severe regression, malignant superego), often is at odds with clinical observation and ends up explaining things in terms of absences (e.g., lack of ego capacity, missing integrative functions). Clearly, psychotic patients have structures that are to be explained in terms other than what they do not have.

Likewise, psychoanalysis has a theory of affects that parallels the theory of anxiety in Freud's *Inhibitions, Symptoms, and Anxiety* [15] but it has never adequately handled the problem in a comprehensive way. David Rapaport's [27] work on affects integrates three components: (1) inborn affect-discharge channels and discharge thresholds of drive cathexes; (2) the use of these inborn channels as safety valves and indicators of drive tension and the modification of these thresholds by the drives, the derivative motivations prevented from drive action thereby leading to the formation of drive representation called affect charge; and (3) the progressive taming and advancing of ego control, in the course of structure formation of affects, which are now turned into affect signals and released by the ego. To some extent this is where psychoanalysis is now in regard to affects, but it is a hydrostatic model and probably is not consistent with neurophysiological findings on pleasure centers or the contributions of other disciplines. The voluminous literature on affects produced by psychoanalysts does not always differentiate drive from affect and only sometimes differentiates affect from feeling and emotion [30]. No doubt depression must be ultimately defined within an affect theory, perhaps the comprehensive theory that psychoanalysis still needs. No attempt will be made to review all of the work on affects, but as yet no satisfactory theory has been articulated. This is not to condemn psychoanalysis as such, because the entire problem of experiencing is something we have yet to work out.

Perhaps the attempt by Langer [23] to present us with a comprehensive theory of feeling will be fruitful. This is a problem that involves basic philosophical concepts such as the ego doing the feeling, neurophysiological problems such as how the brain operates (are there centers of feeling or a totality of responses?), and psychoanalytic concepts concerning the role of the unconscious in the feeling experience. Depression is a symptom of existence, but it is also a symptom of the immaturity of our science.

Because of the fact that depression is used to signify a mood, feeling, affect, disorder, or symptom, it is difficult to organize a consideration of the psychoanalytic treatment of depression. Freud considered melancholia to be a category of psychopathology, but he did not have a separate category of depression as one of the neuroses alongside hysterias, phobias, and the obsessive-compulsive disorders. Melancholia was one of the narcissistic neuroses, and these were not considered objects of psychoanalytic treatment. Narcissistic disorders did not allow for the proper development of the transference, and without a transference there could be no analysis. Depressive feelings that arose during analysis could be analyzed primarily on the basis of the conflicts over the drives, which led to guilt and thereby to depression. This was conceptualized as a struggle between the superego and the ego that was resolved not in the usual neurotic configuration of conversion, phobia, or an obsessive-compulsive symptomatology but rather in an experience of guilt and a feeling of depression. This follows from the struggle of an aggressive superego and a submissive ego. From this conceptualization one can derive a diagnostic category of neurotic depression and a natural analytic treatment of such. This is a legitimate consideration of a classic psychoneurotic disorder of depression but not one that Freud entertained specifically.

Most psychoanalytic concepts dealing with depression, as we have noted, have confronted issues outside of the usual neurotic disorders, i.e., libidinal fixations are preoedipal; object relations are narcissistic and diadic; and the main features ascribed to the ego are weakness and helplessness. The emphasis on oral fixations, regressions, the focus on the mother-child unit, and the new prominence of the disordered self-esteem redirect one's attention to the narcissistic neuroses or disorders. In consideration of the emphasis on narcissistic disorders, there must be a differentiation of this overbroad group into the true psychoses, which are considered not analyzable, the psychosomatic disorders, which may be analyzable, and the primarily analyzable narcissistic personality disorders. Psychotic depression can be distinguished from other depressions by the usual criteria for psychoses, and, although the above-mentioned attributes of depression are relevant, an analytic treatment is not usually considered. The reasons for this are manifold but can be best explained by considering the criteria for analyzability of certain narcissistic disorders.

The work of Kohut, in particular *The Analysis of the Self* [21], describes the crucial developmental step related to analyzability, the formation of a cohesive self. To this one can add the usual criteria for analyzability (age, capacity for insight, etc.) to derive an assessment of the psychoanalytic treatment of depressive disorders. No attempt is made here to delineate the transference and countertransference issues described by Kohut in the analysis of narcissistic personality disorders. But to the degree that depression falls into this category, these considerations of such analyses apply. As stated earlier, depression may fall outside this area into the arena of classic neuroses or the psychoses, and this basic conceptual schema of a cohesive self may not be overriding. The analyst's attention to issues of self-esteem regulation are significant in any analysis, perhaps of prime importance in analyses of all depressive disorders, but it is primarily directed to the elaboration of the vicissitudes of the formation of the cohesive self in analyses of narcissistic personality disorders involving depression.

Other analytic investigators have conducted analyses of moderate or severe depressive disorders either as primarily neurotic conflicts with preoedipal regressions or fixations or as nonneurotic conflicts in which parameters of treatment are introduced. It is beyond the scope of the present paper to discuss such endeavors. Suffice it to say that depression is usually considered treatable, providing the general assessment of the patient as to potential for analysis is positive.

CONCLUSION

Psychoanalysis has made unique, lasting, and essential contributions to understanding depression. Someday scientists will have a theory of feeling with which psychoanalytic findings will interdigitate, and we will be closer to a conceptual understanding of what depression is and how to treat its pathology. The source of data of psychoanalysis or the nature of the investigating tool (introspection and observation) of course determines that analytic findings are psychological images or the familiar fantasies, dreams, and free associations of psychoanalysis. From this we must derive a theory that has validity, i.e., that meets criteria for scientific theory formation and that works to explain things. Such a theory must conform to biochemical, physiological, and sociological theories. The converse is also true; for example, no biochemical theory that cannot at some level articulate with lowered self-esteem will endure. The evolution of many disciplines which grow independently as they influence one another is really epigenetic development toward a theory of depression. We may be getting there.

REFERENCES

1. Abraham, K. The First Pregenital Stage of the Libido (1916). In *Selected Papers on Psychoanalysis.* London: Hogarth Press, 1948. P. 248.
2. Abraham, K. A Short Study of the Development of the Libido, Viewed in the Light of Mental Disorders (1924). In *Selected Papers on Psychoanalysis.* London: Hogarth, 1948, P. 418.
3. Benedek, T. Toward the biology of the depressive constellation. *J. Am. Psychoanal. Assoc.* 6:389, 1956.
4. Beres, D. Superego and Depression. In R. M. Loewenstein et al. (Eds.), *Psychoanalysis—A General Psychology.* New York: International Universities Press, 1966.
5. Bibring, E. The Mechanism of Depression. In P. Greenacre (Ed.), *Affective Disorders.* New York: International Universities Press, 1953.
6. Bowlby, J. Grief and mourning in infancy and early childhood. *Psychoanal. Study Child* 15:9, 1960.
7. Chodoff, P. The Depressive Personality: A Critical Review. *Arch. Gen. Psychiatry* 27:666, 1972.
8. Fenichel, O. Depression and Mania. In W. Gaylin (Ed.), *The Meaning of Despair.* New York: Science House, 1968.
9. Freud, A. *Normality and Pathology in Childhood.* New York: International Universities Press, 1965.
10. Freud, S. Draft B. The Aetiology of the Neuroses (1893). In *The Standard Edition of the Complete Psychological Works of Sigmund Freud,* transl. and ed. by J. Strachey with others. London: Hogarth and Institute of Psycho-Analysis, 1950. Vol. 1, p. 175.
11. Freud, S. A Discussion on Masturbation (1912). *Standard Edition.* 1958. Vol. 12, p. 239.
12. Freud, S. On Narcissism: An Introduction (1914). *Standard Edition.* 1957. Vol. 14, p. 67.
13. Freud, S. Mourning and Melancholia (1917). *Standard Edition.* 1957. Vol. 14, p. 237.
14. Freud, S. The Ego and the Id (1923). *Standard Edition.* 1961. Vol. 19, p. 19.
15. Freud, S. Inhibitions, Symptoms, and Anxiety (1926 [1925]). *Standard Edition.* 1959. Vol. 20, p. 77.
16. Gedo, J., and Goldberg, A. *Models of the Mind: A Psychoanalytic Theory.* Chicago: University of Chicago Press, 1973.
17. Goldberg, A. Psychotherapy of narcissistic injuries. *Arch. Gen. Psychiatry* 28:722, 1973.
18. Hartmann, H. Contributions to the Metapsychology of Schizophrenia. In *Essays on Ego Psychology.* New York: International Universities Press, 1965.

19. Hartmann, H., and Loewenstein, R. M. Notes on the superego. *Psychoanal. Study Child*, vol. 17. 1962.
20. Klein, M. *The Psychoanalysis of Children*. London: Hogarth Press, 1932.
20a. Koestler, A. *The Ghost in the Machine*. London: Hutchison, 1967.
21. Kohut, H. *The Analysis of the Self*. New York: International Universities Press, 1971.
22. Kohut, H. Thoughts on narcissism and narcissistic rage. *Psychoanal. Study Child*, vol. 27. 1972.
23. Langer, S. *Mind: A Theory of Feeling*, vols. 1 and 2. Baltimore: Johns Hopkins Press, 1973.
24. Mahler, M. Notes on the Development of Basic Moods:—The Depressive Affect. In R. M. Loewenstein, et al. (Eds.), *Psychoanalysis—A General Psychology*. New York: International Universities Press, 1966.
25. Moore, B., and Fine, B. *A Glossary of Psychoanalytic Terms and Concepts*. New York: American Psychoanalytic Association, 1967.
26. Rado, S. The Problem of Melancholia. In W. Gaylin (Ed.), *The Meaning of Despair*. New York: Science House, 1968.
27. Rapaport, D. *The Structure of Psychoanalytic Theory*. Psychological Issues Monographs, no. 6. New York: International Universities Press, 1960.
28. Rubinfine, D. Notes on a theory of depression. *Psychoanal. Q.* 37: 400, 1968.
29. Ryle, G. *The Concept of Mind*. London: Hutchison, 1949.
30. Schafer, R. The Clinical Analysis of Affects. *J. Am. Psychoanal. Assoc.* 12:275, 1964.
31. Schafer, R. Internalization: Process or fantasy? *Psychoanal. Study Child*, 27:411, 1972.
32. Segal, H. *Introduction to the Work of Melanie Klein*. New York: Basic Books, 1964.
33. Spitz, R., and Wolf, K. M. Anaclitic depression: An inquiry into the genesis of psychiatric conditions in early childhood, II. *Psychoanal. Study Child*, 2:313, 1946.
34. Waddington, C. H. The Theory of Evolution Today. In A. Koestler and J. R. Smythies (Eds.), *Beyond Reductionism*. Boston: Beacon, 1969.
35. Zetzel, E. Depression and the Incapacity to Bear It. In M. Schur (Ed.), *Drives, Affects, Behavior*. New York: International Universities Press, 1965.

7

Ambivalence and the Depressive Constellation in the Self

THERESE BENEDEK

When I first formulated the concept of a depressive constellation, I meant it to represent a primeval psychic construct that evolves from memory traces of hunger and its satiation. Since the sensation of hunger implies sensory perceptions of frustration, the concept indicates that positive and negative energy charges are components of the psychic precipitate that evolves during the undifferentiated state of the neonate [4]. The problem of ambivalence, however, was not discussed in the context of the mental development that takes place during the symbiotic phase, i.e., before the infant perceives the mother as being outside his body.*

Psychic representations evolve under the influence of the repeated course of physiological events: hunger–feeding–satiation; bowel tension–evacuation–relief. Memory traces of sensory, kinesthetic, and auditory sensations stimulated by percepts from outside the infant are part of the psychic representation of the physiological processes that become "mental factors" [22]. In my first publication dealing with adaptation of infants to variations in feeding situations, I described the positive outcome of the mother-infant interaction and conceptualized it as leading to a primary construct, "confidence" [3]. Confidence functions like an emotional shelter, thus becoming a factor in the infant's ability to learn to wait. It was many years later that I conceptualized the negatively charged representation evolving during the symbiotic phase as a "depressive constellation."

Confidence and depressive constellation are not equivalent terms.

* Rubinfine [34] refers to the same period of postnatal development as "the state of narcissistic unity with the mother," which expresses the dynamics of the balanced symbiotic phase.

The term *confidence* expresses object relationship, even if it refers to a preobject state of development. The meaning of confidence is understood by empathy. The term *depressive constellation* is an abstraction for which an experiential background cannot easily be formulated.

The crying fit of the hungry infant, his global anger, is the paradigm of the discharge of aggressive energy. Since survival is only possible if vital needs are satisfied, aggression does not form structures without the participation of libido. Depressive constellation is a construct based on the assumption that in the memory traces of feeding experience, the negative charge may outweigh the positive charges in labile equilibrium. In the evolution of primary object representations, the precipitate of aggression takes part.

It is easy to assume that the primary processes of alimentation influence dispositions that are usually considered as constitutional givens. Investigation of the conditions in which confidence evolves reveals the libidinal core of a disposition that increases the ego's capacity to delay gratification, i.e., it increases the tolerance for frustration. The manifestation of angry disposition in a newborn indicates low tolerance of frustration, a constitutional factor that regulates the psychophysiological economy before ego develops. These fundamental manifestations of psychic economy serve as a model of the influence of the primary constructs within the self.

ON AMBIVALENCE

It is the tradition of psychoanalysis, a genetic psychology, to attempt to clarify a concept (whether it refers to structure or to process) by giving a historical view of our knowledge of it. Although the history of the concept is not the aim of this presentation, it is tempting to show the cross-currents in our concept formation.

Freud [10] gave credit several times to Bleuler for the "happily chosen term" ambivalence. Bleuler described ambivalence in a clinical context and referred to it as a characteristic of emotional situations. "He distinguished three kinds of ambivalence: (1) emotional, i.e., oscillation between love and hate, (2) voluntary, i.e., inability to decide on an action, and (3) intellectual, i.e., belief in contradictory propositions. Freud generally uses the term in the first of these senses" [13 p. 131n]. According to the broad relevance of the term, it is often used as an adjective—ambivalent attitude, ambivalent behavior, ambivalent feelings.

Freud struggled with the concept of ambivalence. At times he used it as manifestation of ambiguity; at other times he attributed the characteristics of instinct to it. In *Totem and Taboo* Freud spoke of ambivalence as a pervasive psychological factor, ". . . the origin of which we know nothing. One possible assumption is that it is a fundamental phenomenon of our emotional life" [12]. This would mean that it is innate, i.e., instinctual. But he continues in the opposite vein: "But it seems to me quite worth considering another possibility, namely, that originally it formed no part of our emotional life but was acquired by the human race in connection with their father complex . . ." [p. 157].

A few years later in *Instincts and Their Vicissitudes*, Freud [13] proposed the hypothesis that instincts undergo their own development and that on the basis of this, an instinct that originally had an active aim might acquire a passive aim. Thus two contrasting aims of the same instinct are directed to or invested in the same object. This constellation (my term) ". . . deserves to be marked by the very apt term introduced by Bleuler: 'ambivalence'" [p. 131]. It is not necessary to review here the propositions that show what great significance Freud attributed to the concept of ambivalence; yet he maintained his hypothesis that ambivalence is a secondary development, a change of the instinct itself, which under the pressure of pleasure-unpleasure relation changes its aim. In *Beyond the Pleasure Principle* Freud stated:

Our views have from the very first been *dualistic* and today they are even more definitely dualistic than before—now that we describe the opposition as being, not between ego instincts and sexual instincts but between life instincts and death instincts . . . now object-love itself presents us with a second example of a similar polarity—that between love (or affection) and hate (or aggressiveness). If only we could succeed in relating these two polarities to each other and in deriving one from the other! [15, p. 53].

Indeed, Freud struggled with the idea that ambivalence is a quality of instinct.

The theory of death instinct was not generally accepted by psychoanalysts, but psychoanalysts investigating the early stages of psychic organization observed the role of aggression in primary structure formations. Otto Fenichel [9] anchors the phenomenon of ambivalence in that early stage of postnatal existence in which the organism cannot "bind" tensions by anticathexis, when pleasure and unpleasure sensations correspond to "release and increase of tension" [p. 27], respectively, and accounts for a primary model of oscillation of antithetical energy positions that may be expressed later as ambivalent feelings, ambivalent drives, etc. According to Fenichel, the first object representation "must arise in the state of hunger" [p. 29]. Consequently, he assumes that the "arising of the ego" and arising of "reality" are simultaneous, one inside and the other outside the organism. Assimilation of the external world by oral incorporation is a "primitive coming to terms with the environment" [p. 30] in which Fenichel finds the basis of ambivalence. Freud's quest regarding the relation of the polarities had not been achieved.

The zeitgeist of science in general had to change before psychoanalysts were encouraged to look to biology for clarification of psychoanalytic theory. Though it was not the problem of ambivalence that I set out to study, its solution appeared evident to me while I was reading about the thermodynamic processes in open systems.

In lay terms, entropy is a characteristic of open systems, a measure of the state of order necessary to the normal function of the system —increasing entropy means increasing disorder or chaos, or decline in the organization and functional capacity of the system. Phenomena of life can occur only in open systems. How can open systems maintain their level of entropy, or their labile stability? It seems a contradiction of the second law of thermodynamics, which states that the outcome of every physical and chemical process that takes place in nature is an increase in the total entropy of the system (negative entropy). This would mean increasing randomness, a step toward disintegration of the system.

This paradox of organismic life was elucidated by Schrödinger, a physicist. Every living system receives a flood of energy from the environment; sunshine, air, water, and food are assimilated. The more highly organized the organism, the more complex the chemical compounds that constitute its nourishment. Yet the entropy of the system is maintained. The digestion and assimilation of energy necessary to life require work. The resulting negative entropy balances the surplus caused by metabolism—thus organization is maintained. Schrödinger [36] condensed the meaning of his investigation in a famous statement: "What the organism feeds upon is negative entropy." In a more complete statement he says, "The device by which the organism maintains itself stationary at a fairly high level of orderliness (fairly low level of entropy) really consists in continually sucking orderliness from its environment [p. 32]. Szasz concludes that the ability of living matter to suck orderliness (or negative entropy) from the environment ". . . must be regarded as the primary manifestation of life instinct" [37, p. 32]. But this does not explain the concept of instinctual ambivalence, since metabolism occurs between the organism and its environment; instinctual ambivalence means the bipolarity of the instinctual process toward the same object and aim within the organism itself.*

A simple experiment shows dramatically that the biochemical process that maintains entropy on a low level is the source of what we call ambivalence. Monod [31] reports the following: One bacterium (*Escherichia coli*) was set in a simple medium; 36 hours later the medium contained several billion of the same bacteria. The bacteria converted 40 percent of the sugar content of the medium into its cellular constituents; the rest had been oxidized into carbon dioxide and water. The entropy of the system as a whole (bacteria and medium) increased just a little more than the minimum prescribed by the second law. But, says Monod, "something unfailingly upsets our physical intuition as we watch this phenomenon. Why? Because we see very clearly that this process is bent or oriented in one exclusive direction: the multiplication of cells" [p. 20]. This process does not violate but utilizes the laws of thermodynamics to carry out "the project" and to bring about (as Francois Jacob put it) "the dream of every cell, i.e., to become two cells" [31, p. 20].

The poetic insight or anthropomorphic analogy of the experimenter should not deflect our interest from the topic. The experiment shows that the invariant multiplication of a monocellular organism occurs in order to maintain entropy, to keep the organism (in this case the species) alive.† Why did this experiment appear to me to be a model of ambivalence? That which occurs in the culture bent on survival at the cost of splitting the existing unit in two impressed me as an illustration of Freud's concept of "fusion and defusion of energies." We may interpret the process as the manifestation of the bipolarity of the life instinct. The positive and negative poles are not antagonistic; they are partners in living [32]. Freud's concept of "fusion and defusion" refers to such a partnership, which apparently functions even on the level of microbiology.

In this essay the term aggression is used in this sense exclusively: on the level of physiology, the positive and negative energy charges are regulated to become species-specific physiological processes that allow for a more or less limited adaptational range. In psychological

---

* Ambivalence is an attribute of animals as well as humans. Ethologists describe the manifestations of ambivalence in a great variety of animals. Two activated instinct systems may exert their influence simultaneously—simultaneous ambivalence —or alternately—successive ambivalence. Interestingly, these ambivalent "attitudes" are ritualized in the courtship behavior of many species; fright, aggressiveness and sexual approach are integrated in stable "fixed action patterns" [35].
† On the level of organization at which entropy is maintained by cell division, individual death does not occur. But it is known that cultures die when the medium is exhausted as a result of the "slight death" owed to the laws of thermodynamics.

processes, a wider range of adaptation is feasible and necessary. On this level, one can speak of aggressive drives. The concept of fusion and defusion refers to energy charges, not motivation. Drives, aggressive or libidinal drives, refer to the organization of motivational energy. Drives, the channels of motivational energy, are derivatives of instinctual energy, with its potential for ambivalence. The behavioral manifestations of drives, feelings, moods, emotions, and behavior can often be characterized by the adjective "ambivalent," since they reflect the polarity between the active and passive, integrating and destructive energy.

The concept of psychic energy is in focus in the thinking of psychoanalytic theorists; some argue against and others for the concept. In Freud's time the concept did not create a problem. On the basis that libido is felt as force, he formulated the thesis that libido is the psychic representation of sexual energy. In this sense, physiological activating factors—hormones—appear to support his theory. The problem arose with Freud's second instinct theory (1920), in which libido came to mean "integrating energy," and "aggression," the manifestation of disintegrating factors in the process of living. Psychic energy is inherent in the manifestation of instinct; it is governed by the laws of thermodynamics that maintain entropy, i.e., organization, or order, in every living system.

One may look upon instinct as an organizer that can be conceptualized only in its manifestations. Thorpe [38], a leading ethologist, considers directedness and purposiveness the primary manifestations of instincts. Ruwet [35] adds to this "the capacity for orientation." Ethologists talk about conflict and instinctual energy in the same sense as psychoanalysts do; they know that instinctual force is not even remotely related to the physical concept of force. "Those who view the concept of psychic energy and libido as real phenomena have to search for its physical basis in the communication process of the neural network"* [30, p. 142]. At the present level of our knowledge we may say that ambivalence is the manifestation of a disequilibrium perceived by the nervous system, assuming that "such equilibrium oscillates between active and passive aims and libidinal and aggressive poles of an instinct" [20]. The bold analogy that says the model of ambivalence is in the thermodynamic laws of open systems would mean that ambivalence is innate; it is the characteristic of the life instinct.

* Traces of such a view can be seen in Freud's hypothesis of communication within the systems of the mind, between unconscious, preconscious, and conscious [14].

If we consider ambivalence innate, we have to ask: when does ambivalence become an observable phenomenon in the human infant?
(Crying is a signal of need; in itself it is not ambivalent.) An investigation undertaken by the Tavistock Child Development Unit places
the manifestation of ambivalence in the fourth month of life; its behavioral expression is the laughing of the infant. Ambrose [2] considers
these expressions to be manifestations of contrasting motivational
systems. He found that an infant's laugh is a response to a stimulus
that elicits two contrasting tendencies simultaneously. His investigation shows that the prerequisite for laughing is the physiological
maturity of the respiratory apparatus sufficient to maintain the respiratory mechanism necessary for the vocalization of laughter. It is
well known that laughing is the result of a change in the combination
of the two respiratory components, inspiration and expiration. Either
part of the respiratory mechanism—deep inspiration or deep expiration—may express emotion in young infants, but audible laughing
does not occur before the fourth month. The stimulus-maintaining
tendency is stronger in the beginning, and the terminating tendency is
stronger at the end of the laughing response. The tendency to terminate, however, may occur not because the stimulus is decreased but
because the respiratory mechanism necessary for laughter cannot be
continued. The ambivalent motivation of laughter is especially obvious in shy, adult individuals who often cannot suppress the tendency
to laugh when they are embarrassed or fear embarrassment. The analysis of the structure of the infant's laughter exposes the demand that
ambivalent motivation represents for the organism. It calls attention
to the role of "unconscious ambivalence" in the mental life and its
somatic correlates.

To summarize: ambivalence is innate, and it is a universal characteristic of instinctual processes.

In formulating his structural theory, Freud adhered to his concept
of "the two classes of instincts": libidinal (integrating) life instincts,
and aggressive (destructive) death instincts. He speculated whether
ambivalence was a result of fusion or defusion.

. . . The question also arises whether ordinary ambivalence which is so
often unusually strong in the constitutional disposition to neurosis should
not be regarded as the product of a defusion; ambivalence, however, is
such a fundamental phenomenon that it more probably represents an instinctual fusion that has not been completed [16, p. 42].

Indeed, the problem could not be solved as long as one considered
the "two forms of energies" as separate entities.

THE DEPRESSIVE CONSTELLATION

This concept was derived from two areas of investigation. One was the ontology of the ego during infancy, the other the psychobiology of woman's procreative function. These investigations revealed that the roots of the procreative drive organization are in the postpartum symbiosis, in the mother-infant unity, which in turn repeats the oral phase of the mother's development. This statement implies the concatenation of generations and indicates that one of the many links in that chain relates to a concept for which, so far, no other term has been found than that which is partially preempted for an illness, namely, depressive constellation, which can easily be mistaken for depression.

The term depressive constellation refers to the primary object representation evolving (in the infant) from the percepts of the negative pole of experiences connected with alimentation. Alimentation is the term that takes the place of "oral" in my terminology; it indicates that manifold stimuli, coming from inside and outside the body, are involved in the earliest experience of the infant. Karl Abraham [1] recognized in 1911 that melancholia, the term that at that time was also used to designate depression, is motivated by regression to the oral state, i.e., to the earliest phase of postnatal development. This is recalled here to show, first, that later investigations did not contradict but only elaborated on this early hypothesis and, second, that the concept of depressive constellation has no direct connection with depression.

Here it seems necessary to defend the term itself. Winnicott [40], in a paper in which he elaborates Melanie Klein's concept "depressive position," criticized the term. According to Klein's and others' observations, this condition occurs normally in children around the age of three months or more. Winnicott finds it misleading to designate a normal developmental event with a term that refers to a pathological condition. I agree. Indeed, "depressive constellation" appears worse in this light. According to two illustrious followers of Klein, Winnicott and Riviere [33], the depressive position refers to a mood change or an observable reaction to weaning, to dentition, to mother's leaving the room, etc. Klein's term refers to a mood that presupposes some level of object relationship and ego development. All we know about depression and mourning seems to justify the term depressive position on this basis. The two terms—depressive constellation and depressive position—refer to different propositions and express different levels of abstraction.

Depressive constellation does not refer to any mood, symptom, or clinical entity. It is assumed to be rooted in ambivalence, which is a characteristic of instinctual processes. Fenichel [9] stated that ambivalence is the manifestation of antithetical energy positions involved in hunger and its satiation. The mother, the object of the infant's need, is a constituent of the instinctual system of the child. Object relationship evolves slowly as the ever-oscillating balance of active-passive energy cathects the object and forms primordial structures: confidence and depressive constellation.

Depressive constellation is a construct representing the negative pole of the mother-infant interaction from the moment when the sensation of hunger activates the signal of crying and continues until the baby feels close to the breast. Rooting for the nipple indicates a negative charge still in the system. Then rhythmic sucking sets in, followed by satiation. As the positive cathexis outweighs the negative, the infant falls asleep.

With the hunger cry of the newborn begins the process by which the infant introjects the memory traces of frustrated hunger associated with frustrating mother. These negative memory traces lead to the structuring of feelings of badness: bad self = bad mother. When satiation has soothed the infant, with the libidinous state of well-being, the images become feeding-soothing, good mother = satiated, good self. Some weeks later, the infant's crying fit appears to be a diffuse, aggressive discharge. In the process of calming down, the intense grasping, unrhythmic, hasty sucking of the still excited child indicates that the motor excitement of the infant is projected onto the mother. Thus it appears that the infant has developed hatred for the object of his instinctual gratification, for the mother whom he needs. "At the same time he develops a precursory hatred of the subject he needs" [21]. This brief statement explains a third, the active, dangerous factor in the depressive constellation. The anger arising in the infant affects not only the mother but also the infant's "self." As this experience is repeated, the needful, helpless self, dependent on the mother for survival, becomes a nucleus for the self-image of the infant.

How do primary constructs effect the frustration tolerance? An excess of libidinal cathexis arising from satiation and other sensory gratifications associated with the image of good mother = good self builds confidence and thus increases the tolerance of frustration. An excess of negative cathexis from the infant's experience decreases tolerance; by activating anger and negativistic behavior, it brings about a negative spiral in the reciprocal processes between mother and infant. Clinical observation shows that individually characteristic variations in tolerance of frustration are not direct corollaries of depressive constellation. This construct may be viewed as a continually interacting stress factor that exerts influence in the organization of the personality and its idiosyncrasies.

Whether the dissociation of affects later in life becomes manifest in anxiety or depressive affects depends on many factors, constitutional as well as experiential. Constitutional factors are responsible for that third factor in the depressive constellation, which, by maintaining dissatisfaction with oneself, brings about deficiency in self-esteem, an important factor in the dynamics of depression.

Congruent with what we know about the reciprocal processes during the symbiotic phase [4], we conclude that the depressive position [Klein, 25], and the basic depressive mood [Mahler, 29], refer to mood changes, the disposition for which develops under the influence of the depressive constellation. The mood changes may occur in some infants spontaneously; more often they are brought about by the mother's leaving the room or other, similarly disappointing events.

The concept of depressive constellation is based on the interaction of instinctual ambivalence with the instinctual process of feeding and its instrument, mother. The primary constructs—confidence and depressive constellation—represent the two interwoven roots of object representations. I assume that these constructs border on problems of constitution.

The hypothesis that the depressive constellation evolves as a universal attribute of mental life necessitates pointing out that it originates in the direct connection with the organization of woman's procreative drive.

Reviewing my own publication, *Toward the Biology of the Depressive Constellation* [4], twenty years later, I realize that the two "the's" in the title are not substantiated by my findings.* The presentation rested on observations supporting the hypothesis that the psychic structure, ego, evolves from reciprocal communications that influence both mother and infant. The psychodynamically significant discoveries concerning the sexual cycle and the psychology of pregnancy, briefly reported in that study, now appear shortchanged. The linkage of ambivalence and depressive constellation with procreative physiology was not in focus.

I do not intend to repeat what has been published before, but I must sum up the factors that show that ambivalence and the depressive constellation are transmitted from one generation to the next.†

---

* Twenty years ago psychoanalysts took hypotheses for facts more easily than today.
† I speak of transmission through interpersonal processes of communication. My

Growth, neurophysiological maturation, and psychosexual development are interwoven processes. The master gland, the anterior lobe of the pituitary, secretes the hormones that regulate metabolism, growth, and the procreative functions, including lactation. I have often repeated this general statement, and I do so again because I would like to convey the excitement I felt when I discovered that the psychodynamic processes that accompany ovulation were the same as those that characterize the oral phase of development.

Psychoanalytic investigation suggested the correlation between the hormonal and emotional cycles of women [7]. When the mature ovum ruptures the follicle, the ovum is emptied into the Fallopian tube and ovulation has occurred; oscillations in body temperature and other physiological reactions indicate that ovulation is a systemic event. On the instinctual level, a change in the direction of the psychodynamic tendencies occurs: the active, extraverted sexual energy, characteristic of the follicle-ripening (estrogen) phase of the cycle, is turned inward toward the woman's body. This narcissistic emotional state, the result of heightened hormone production, represents the "hidden estrus" of woman. Ovulation is the link that connects the receptive-retentive tendencies of metabolism with procreative physiology. Ovulation is a real and, at the same time, symbolic turning point in the life cycle of the individual. With her ovaries producing ripe ova, the young woman reaches her procreative maturity. From then on to menopause, each ovulation represents the actual possibility of being impregnated, of becoming a mother.

After ovulation the walls of the ruptured follicle function like a gland of internal secretion; they turn into a yellow substance, the corpus luteum, which produces lutein hormone, "the hormone of maturity," better known as progesterone.* The four to six days following ovulation, the progesterone phase of the cycle, represent a plateau in hormone level; both hormones, estrogen and progesterone, are produced. In the psychodynamic manifestations, however, the estrogens seem to be masked. While progesterone prepares the lining of the uterus for the nidation of the fertilized ovum, the emotions also reveal the preparation for motherhood. This is expressed by intensified receptive and retentive tendencies in dreams, in fantasies, in behavior, and in symptoms. Thus one can say that regression to the oral phase

---

clinical observations include in some instances three generations in which I observed the quantitative and qualitative variations of these processes and their influence on personality structure. Such observations may stimulate genetic research in the field of psychology.

* So named by George Corner [8], who first synthesized the hormone and defined its function in procreation. He also characterized the estrogens as hormones of preparation, since they are produced from infancy on.

is the psychodynamic correlate of progesterone. It seems paradoxical. The hormone of maturity activates the psychodynamic characteristic of the early postnatal development. This paradox is inherent in the physiology of procreation. On the mature level, sexual development stimulates the wish for pregnancy, or the defense against that wish, fear of pregnancy. At the same time it stimulates regression by intensifying receptive-retentive tendencies. If fertilization does not occur, the corpus luteum degenerates, the hormone level decreases, and a sudden hormone withdrawal ushers in menstruation. From puberty to menopause, the cyclically returning progesterone phase affords a repetition of the oral phase of development and with it a working-through of the developmental conflicts with the mother.

The psychodynamic processes of pregnancy can be viewed as an immense intensification of the progesterone phase. The dominance of the receptive-retentive tendencies is obvious during pregnancy. They are the psychological representations of the physiological need for fuel to supply energy for growth. The hormonal and metabolic processes that maintain the normal growth of the fetus augment the vital energies of the mother. This is a manifestation of the biological symbiosis. The pregnant woman in her calmness enjoys her body, which is replenished with libidinous feelings, enhancing her general well-being. This is the instinctual source of motherliness. Supplied by the freshly produced psychic energy (primary narcissism), it increases her pleasure in bearing the child and her patience with the discomforts of pregnancy. The generally optimistic emotional state of normal pregnancy, however, should not let us forget that it is a result of receptive and retentive tendencies that activate ambivalent instinctual processes. Pregnancy, the very condition for the survival of the species, harbors dangers for those women whose personality organization cannot withstand the regressive pull inherent in the metabolic requirement of procreative physiology.

Just as during the progesterone phase of the cycle, often during the first trimester of pregnancy the inclination of depression becomes manifest in moods and in symptoms that spring from oral receptive and eliminative tendencies. Just as girls gradually adapt themselves to the discomforts of menstruation, pregnant women in the second trimester usually lose their sense of vulnerability, giving way to self-confidence and a feeling of strength, free energy, and optimism. Toward the end of pregnancy this positive mood becomes contaminated by the fear of parturition, which often drains away the feeling of optimism. After parturition the mother has to face a new phase of adaptation. One aspect of this task comes from the change in her hormonal physiology; the other is caused by the reality of motherhood itself. Until then, motherhood is more or less a fantasy, not only with primiparas but also with women who have borne several children. During pregnancy, women fantasize about the unborn child. After parturition the infant and the tasks of mothering become real, and the task has to be met with an emotional economy fueled by intensified receptive-retentive tendencies.

Lactation, the postpartum symbiosis of mother and infant, is usually the happiest and most gratifying period in a mother's life. Yet her contentment is often disturbed by sundry external events; since her self is submerged in her infant, she is in a vulnerable ego state. She is even more likely to respond with a deep sense of frustration if she is disappointed in her child. On the other hand, mothers often blame themselves for any disturbance in the infant's routine. Whether in her regressed emotional state she blames herself or her child for her frustration, the intensification of receptive-retentive tendencies is in the service of the propagative function, implanting in the infant the depressive constellation from the time the mother functions as surrogate-instinct, i.e., from birth, regardless of the sex of the infant.

Since this discussion shows that the roots of the depressive constellation are in the psychophysiology of woman's procreative function, the question arises: are men constitutionally less disposed to acquire what we have termed depressive constellation? Only future research holds the answer. Man's function in procreation does not involve tissue changes and does not require intensification of regressive psychodynamic tendencies. However, during the symbiotic phase and throughout infancy the reciprocal interaction between mother and infant conveys to the male infant, just as to the female, the introjects of experiences charged with the negative component of instinctual energy.

The male child, growing up under the care of both parents, introjects the memory traces of his father's attitude and behavior into his self-image. These, in interaction with the introjects of the mother, influence the development of fatherliness, which will become manifest in his behavior toward his child. The difference in the effect of parental behavior on the infant is primarily determined by the calendar.

The primary drive organization, the oral phase, has no gender differentiation; it is asexual. As prerequisite and consequences of metabolic needs that sustain growth and maturation, it leads to differentiation of the procreative functions, including parental tendencies: motherliness and fatherliness. Ambivalence influences mothering behavior negatively and so affects the infant; the infant's frustration, his crying, reverts back to the mother, activating a spiral of negative transactions through which the depressive constellation is implanted in the child, male or female. The ambivalence in mothering behavior affects the child at a younger age, probably soon after his birth; the father's ambivalence or negativistic attitude will affect the child somewhat later. However, one may say that motherliness and fatherliness as experienced by parents toward their infant is a mutual experience between that father and mother. Helping each other in loving and caring for the child, they neutralize negative components in their behavior toward each other and toward the child. In such a tolerant atmosphere, the interaction between parents and children makes confidence prevail over the depressive constellation.

THE PRIMARY STRUCTURES IN THE SELF

From the foregoing discussion of the biological roots of the depressive constellation, we are not surprised that its influence on the mind has more generalized manifestations than that which establishes it as precursor of depressive illness. The origin of depressive constellation indicates that the term depression in itself does not signify an illness but is a characteristic of human existence. The significance of the depressive constellation should stimulate further investigation of its role in development.

When elaborating primary constructs, be it confidence or the depressive constellation, we deal with instincts—"on the frontier between mental and somatic [14, p. 122]. Primary constructs are primarily unconscious; they reach the penetrable level of the unconscious, i.e., the system of the "dynamic unconscious" through interaction with other systems of the mind. The construct confidence can be easily visualized. To trace the negative cathexis of the depressive constellation, which I shall attempt, does not appear to be a difficult task, since the experiential verification of psychoanalytic theory makes the problem accessible.

A study of Freud's writings from this point of view makes it appear that he consciously avoided generalization of his awareness of a force that makes life "real and earnest." Yet his concept of conflict represented a struggle between contrasting needs and wishes from the beginnings of his theory formation. However, conflicts, viewed in whatever frame of reference, were under the sway of the pleasure principle, the regulator of psychic economy. Pleasure and pain, those experiential regulators of psychic economy, did not satisfy Freud for long.*

* For psychoanalysts today it is difficult to imagine that between the essay *Formulations on the Two Principles of Mental Functioning* in 1911 [11] and *Beyond the Pleasure Principle* in 1920 [15] only nine years passed.

In *Beyond the Pleasure Principle*, he formulated his second instinct theory, according to which "libido and aggression" are universal manifestations of instinctual or life energy. This condensation refers not only to Freud's hypothesis but also to elaborations made by other psychoanalysts. It may therefore misrepresent Freud's use of his hypothesis, but not the meaning of the dual instinct theory. Freud himself was not at ease with his new theory. He conceived of fusion and defusion of instinctual energy in the sense of metapsychology; he did not like to see "aggression" as a factor in normal psychological processes, although he soon conceptualized it in the structure superego.

Accumulated clinical investigations illustrated that the memory traces of the controlling punitive attitudes of parents, incorporated in the child's image of the parent, participate in the unconscious process by which internalization of instinctual controls evolve; thus the role of aggression became part of the developmental theory before *The Ego and the Id* [16]. In this work Freud spoke of "desexualized libido which may also be described as sublimated energy." But he did not discuss the introjection of the aggressive component of psychic energy as "deaggressivized energy," as Hartmann [22] referred to it. Freud probably did not consider the strictness of the superego as manifestation of displaced, deaggressivized aggression. He equated aggression, incorporated in the structure of the superego, with "dangerous death instincts," which ". . . to a large extent undoubtedly continue their internal work unhindered" [16, p. 54]. In the same publication, Freud wrote, "The more a man controls the aggressiveness, the more intense becomes his ideal's inclination to aggressiveness against his ego [p. 54]. This statement refers not only to the psychopathology of compulsion neurosis and depression but also to that mental attitude which is termed—moral masochism. According to Freud, moral masochism is a derivative of death instinct. Its psychic representation is conscience.

What is conscience? According to Freud's definition, conscience is "the superego at work in the ego which may then become harsh, cruel and inexorable against the ego which is in its charge" [17, p. 16]. Conscience is a relentless reminder of wrongdoing, but we also speak of "good conscience," which often has to assert itself as true. A phenomenology of conscience written by a psychoanalyst still does not exist. Its psychodynamics have never been more precisely formulated than "it is the superego at work in the ego. . . ." It functions as a warning signal that sets in motion feelings of remorse and makes one aware of responsibilities and of guilt. Guilt, however, is not necessarily the consequence of actual wrongdoing, but more often than not it originates in the conscience itself, which may be so sensitive that it responds with guilty feelings to repressed instinctual conflicts.

In his large-scale investigation of the influence of human emotions on cultural processes, *Totem and Taboo,* Freud [12] related the origin of civilization to the guilt that originates in "emotional ambivalence," in the love and hate that led to killing the Ur-father. The inhibition and repression of the impulse to kill led to the identification with the father as the model, the ego-ideal. Since then:

Through the forming of the ideal, what biology and the vicissitudes of the human species have created in the id and left behind in it is taken over by the ego and re-experienced in relation to itself as an individual. . . . What has belonged to the lowest part of mental life in each of us is changed through the formation of the ideal into what is highest in the human mind by our scale of values [16, p. 36].

The span between instinct and ego, between the instinctual being and the ideal self, is the topic of the genetic theory of development and psychoanalytic psychopathology. In each psychological problem we can analyze and evaluate the interaction of libidinal and aggressive factors. In Freud's social theory, elaborated in *Civilization and Its Discontents* [18], it seems that the death instinct overshadows the constructive factors that guide the survival of the species. Thinking about this, I have to ask again, what is conscience? Would it have been possible to form the "ideal" after the killing of the Ur-father if the murder had activated only fear of retaliation? Or was there also regret, a remnant of the need for the object that was destroyed? I realize that I have expressed my question in words used in discussing the psychic response of infants to feeding, the "introjection of the object." This helps to make my point. I assume that conscience is the psychic representation of the memory traces of ambivalence, the instinctual constituent of the process of sublimation. Of course, conscience is a highly refined psychic quality that takes time to develop; it may be observed as early as in a 12- to 14-month-old child. We consider it a result of sublimation brought about by precursors of the superego. It does not seem too farfetched to assume that it is rooted in the sublimation of ambivalence.

SUBLIMATION AND CHARACTER TRENDS

Sublimation is an almost neglected concept of psychoanalysis today. Since the structural theory incorporated the instinct theory in the conceptualization of psychobiological processes, the older hypotheses did not suffice. In an excellent paper, Kaywin [24] investigates the concept and puts it in the perspective of modern psychoanalytic theory. He shows that our observations do not deal with sublimation as an instinctual process but as behavior distant from the primary aim and object of instincts. For this reason, he argues, Hartmann's concept of "desexualization, deaggressivization," or neutralization, of psychic energy does not add to the clarification of the theory of sublimation. Considering sublimation as a result of displacement of particular instincts, Freud's hypothesis is too specific. Hartmann's hypothesis is too general since it is applicable to any psychological process [24]. In this context Kaywin cites an investigation by Kris [28], who observed toddlers learning to paint; he illustrated the points by which the impulse to smear is overcome by fantasy and by the perception of form that becomes attached to the use of paint; Kris observed a learning process in the frame of age-adequate development and concluded that what is called sublimation is not a process and that the term progression would better encompass the intrapsychic event involved in sublimated behavior. Since behavior is necessarily a manifestation of changes in objects of drives, normal behavior is always sublimated. Is there a process of sublimation per se? Normal behavior implies drive organization and efficiency of functioning—these are ego functions. Thus the term sublimation may refer to all processes that add up to adaptability to social norms. This is the goal of that complex of interpersonal and intrapsychic processes that we call development of the personality. Yet in the web of all these processes, one can recognize trends that show sublimation as a process.

Closer investigation of developmental processes may reveal in children, and even more in adults, differences in the degree to which a conflict or a process is remote from its original impulse. Glover [19] saw in this a key to the understanding of the process of sublimation and he added, "We are, however, unable to estimate precisely [the remoteness] owing to the elements of symbolism present" [p. 144]. Kaywin explains the remoteness by emphasizing what connects the sublimated psychic content with its instinctual origin: "It is the degree of ideational associativeness at a certain hierarchic level that determines the sexualization ("sexual meaning") or the aggressivization of any reaction pattern" [24, p. 331]. Sublimation is a part of any psychological process that implies progression.

It is easier to understand and trace the breakdown of a sublimated pattern than to see it as progression to intrapsychic accomplishment. In discussions a few years ago of my early clinical papers [6] I investigated the breakdowns and reintegrations of defense systems in the disease process during psychoanalytic treatment. Of course, those defense structures do not represent sublimations, although some of them may be viewed as such in the progress of the therapy. But the analogy is justifiable. Just as during normal development the instinctual conflict becomes "deinstinctualized" (Hartmann [22]) and becomes integrated in the processes of development, so conflicts of pathological intensity, through therapeutic working-through, become more remote from their instinctual origin; they become, so to speak, more tractable.

The word tractable comes to mind as an association to some difficult (intractable) patients. What made them so? The answer lies in the deficiency in tolerance of frustration, which, activating aggressive energy, breaks down the normal and intensifies the pathological defenses, thus exposing unguarded instinctual impulses. The deficient tolerance of frustration was discussed earlier as a manifestation of the depressive constellation. Here it is pointed out as a factor that, in motivating regression, impedes sublimation.

In spite of the foregoing discussion of sublimation as part and parcel of each step in development and learning, I can take a long look backward in psychoanalytic theory and recall the libido theory before object relations were included. Freud, and especially Abraham [1], conceptualized each phase of pregenital development as a stage in the development of the libido and assumed that the phasically changed libido, deflected from its primary object, becomes sublimated as a character trend in adults. It is known that envy and greed as well as generosity, indulgence, and other attributes that appear to express the wish to receive and hold (or the opposite) were considered transformations of oral libido; parsimony, miserliness, obstinacy, meticulousness, and fastidiousness were assumed to be reaction formation to anal libido and its transformation. This certainly would not need to be recapitulated here if the investigation of the sexual cycle in women [7] had not corroborated these long outdated assumptions. In analyzing the record of women in psychoanalytic treatment, each time the material revealed (in dreams, fantasies, emotions, and behavior) motivations referable to oral libido, I defined the unconscious motivating factor as a "receptive-incorporative" or "giving" tendency; if the material appeared motivated by anal libido, the motivating factor was defined as "retentive-eliminative tendency." The psychodynamic tendencies, unconscious correlates of the physiological components of the sexual drive, corresponded to the phases of the hormonal cycle [7].

On this basis I differentiated two groups of character trends. In the first group belong those in which the instinctual root is recognizable by psychoanalysis. The character trends pertaining to the second group are a result of higher organization; their origin cannot be related to any one phase of development. Progression through several interacting processes leads to the evolution of such character trends. The simplest example is conscientiousness, which appears to be on the border between the two groups.

Conscience is a psychic phenomenon. Conscientiousness is a character trend; as such, however, conscientiousness is not remote from its instinctual origin. The affinity of conscience to anxiety is well known. Conscience and the anxiety activated by it are in the service of the superego. The ontological development of the superego reveals individual differences in the severity of conscientiousness. From these, the influence of the depressive constellation may be inferred.*

It is not surprising that Lionel Trilling's essay, *Sincerity and Authenticity* [39], is a fitting illustration of the hypothese formulated in this paper. Trilling, a literary historian and essayist, well versed in Freud's writings, investigates the cognate ideals of sincerity and authenticity from a historical perspective.

Although long recognized as a characteristic of certain people, sincerity was not always an integral part of moral life. It has become so during the last three hundred years. Trilling traces the origin of sincerity to man's search for his "true self" rather than society, which, more with its opportunities than its requirements, distorts "natural man," his "true self." Trilling gives many captivating examples of the efforts of poets and philosophers to find the "locus of the self" within. While these reveal deep insights of individuals, they reflect the slowly evolving changes in society through which sincerity arose as an ethical requirement in Western man.

Although sincerity is not a psychoanalytic concept, it is certainly a prerequisite for the profession of psychoanalysis. But we take this requirement to be such a self-evident characteristic of maturity that only if it is lacking do we investigate its absence and the developmental factors that impeded the integration of this superego function.†

What is sincerity from the psychoanalytic point of view? It would be difficult, if not impossible, to formulate a phenomenology or psychodynamics of sincerity. We know by intuition what it is, but we cannot describe it. We know how it feels. Sometimes it is like a well-fitting shirt, easy to wear; at other times it feels heavy on the shoul-

---

* Conscience is felt; yet it is experienced only if it is troubled, if it activates some degree of anxiety. The more sensitive the conscience, the more easily it activates anxiety. Conscience and anxiety are essentially different phenomena. The physio-chemical (hormonal) mechanisms of anxiety are known; it is universal throughout organismic life and is primarily in the service of survival. Conscience is a specifically human attribute. Since it is an intrapsychic "measure" of behavior, it prompts defenses such as repression and sublimation; thus conscience promotes integrative processes, or progression of the mind.

† For Freud, sincerity was such an ever-present expression of his whole being that it escaped his self-observation. Lack of sincerity in a person represented for him such a basic character defect that he avoided dealing with that person. He considered psychoanalysis such a sincere approach to a human being that he would not have liked to see psychoanalysis wasted on a less than sincere situation.

ders, or even in the heart. In comparison, consider serenity, also a character attribute, but accessible to phenomenological description since it is expressed in a mood. Sincerity is revealed in action, although the action may be just a choice. Choices, even in dreams, are indicators of sincerity. But the wish to seem sincere is just the opposite of sincerity. It is not necessary to elaborate further to show that sincerity is not a direct derivative of the superego. It does not originate in a conflict. Probably because sincerity cannot be described as a phenomenon but only as a character trait, Trilling connects it with authenticity. Authenticity is not a character trait. Authenticity is a result of sincerity. Acting according to the "true self" makes an "authentic" personality.

Sincerity is a characteristic; as such it is remote from instincts and their unconscious representations; sincerity implies a personality in active interaction with its "surround."* Yet we can observe unmistakable sincerity in a 2-year-old girl playing with her doll or a 3-year-old boy putting together a toy he has just taken apart. Some observers conclude that children are more sincere than adults. This is correct; the child's interest, as long as it lasts, is totally involved. The child's authenticity reveals his closeness to his instincts, to his unconscious. It seems paradoxical that the child, close to his instincts, reveals an attribute that we consider a result of sublimation, which, in the adult, indicates remoteness from instincts. Indeed, the whole development of personality, with its unpredictable vicissitudes, lies between the play of the child and the sincerity of the adult.

At this point, sincerity appears as a transformation of instinctual energy. Where in the instinctual system is sincerity anchored? The seriousness of the sincere individual's approach to life originates, let us hypothesize, in the excess of the depressive constellation during the early stages of development. This does not contradict the premise that the primary constructs, confidence and depressive constellation, interact in every representation of instinctual processes and influence sublimation and integration of all systems of the psyche. In the healthy, normal process of life, libidinal components are always in the ascendancy. Difficulties, hardships, and conflicts arise in life from infancy on, but every solution of a conflict, every victory over an impediment, is an achievement leading to progression, to integration, to development toward the life the individual intuitively pursues. Sincere individuals, probably more than others, are directed by their conscience to follow the path. It may be "straight and narrow" from some points of view, but sincere individuals are usually successful in

---

* René Spitz's favorite expression for the environment of the child, who takes in what the eyes see.

achieving their goals. The achievement may involve productivity and creativity of high ethical and emotional value, yet the feeling that life is "real and earnest" accompanies the sincere individual, even while at play. In sincerity, we can trace the influence of the depressive constellation in the sensitivity of conscience, in the highly attuned superego that tends to turn the aggression against the self, but in the sincere individual this rarely reaches such a deep dissatisfaction with the self that it would result in depressive illness. Usually other character traits counteract the severity of the superego in the sincere individual.

Looking for developmental factors accounting for sincerity, one turns readily to the concept of identification and assumes that the child's identification with the sincere parent is responsible for this characteristic. This of course plays a role, but not on that primary level of instinctual processes that this essay is attempting to elucidate. A child can take his father's spectacles and newspaper and imitate his reading. When he peers over the glasses and imitates his father's frowning, he is not sincere; he does not even intend to be; he feels that he is comical, and he is. Sincere means to be true to oneself. It cannot be comical, although it may be humorous.

The deepest sense of humor is expressed in the insight which is so true to the self that it can be remote and smile about the predicament in which the self finds itself. This concept of humor brings us close to defining sincerity as originating in a fortunate balance of the primary constructs, confidence, and depressive constellation. Both sincerity and the sense of humor reveal the ego's distance from intrapsychic conflicts. We recognize in sincerity and also in the genuine sense of humor the contributions of libidinal factors such as indulgence, tolerance, and empathic understanding, originating in the primary construct confidence. These factors protect sincerity from becoming severity, humor from becoming sarcasm.

This leads involuntarily to tolerance. It is, indeed, fitting to include in this essay a brief definition of tolerance as a character trend, since we have relied so much on the lack of tolerance to explain "free" aggression. Tolerance, a mental attitude, is not the opposite of lack of tolerance, which is expressed in the psychophysiological signal, anger. Tolerance is a manifestation of libido. One would not normally expect tolerance in children.* Tolerance as an integrated part of the personality is a sign of maturity in the most humane sense of the word. The

---

* Older children who suffer from chronic illness acquire endurance of pain and frequently show indulgence toward the doctor who "causes" pain. Although tolerance implies reconciliation with pain suffered, one should not generalize. A person less endowed with empathy, with libido, may become bitterly intolerant, especially if he is frustrated in some of his ambitions.

French proverb says it simply: "*Tout comprendre c'est tout pardonner* [to understand everything is to forgive everything]." What kind of understanding will forgive without resentment? "Empathic understanding" would be the easy answer of a psychoanalyst. A more complex answer is: the understanding of the other is rooted in the understanding of oneself. Tolerance is a result of a development that achieves the resolution of one's conflicts with one's aggression and one's anxiety. Is tolerance then a transformation of aggression or of libido? Tolerance is probably the result of the transformation of that libidinal energy that neutralizes aggression and thus wards off anxiety. No doubt, tolerance is a virtue (at least in our culture) and has a great share in constituting ". . . that highly esteemed human attitude to which we refer as wisdom" [27, p. 40].

In his early investigation of narcissistic processes, Heinz Kohut [26] describes manifestations and transformations of primary narcissism. He discusses these processes in relation to the general theory of development and assumes that primary narcissism, i.e., libido that is not unduly invested in the ego, is the source of humor and wisdom.

SUMMARY

This chapter, investigating the influence of primary constructs in the personality, adds to humor and wisdom two other character trends, sincerity and tolerance. Humor, tolerance, sincerity, and wisdom seem to be found in close proximity, confirming each other in the mature personality. They have a common denominator: from the point of view of psychodynamics these characteristics are far remote from an instinctual source; their psychodynamic origin is not recognizable. The active-passive, positive-negative poles of emotional life seem reconciled, are in stable equilibrium in these sublime attainments of the mind.

The broad scope of this essay reflects the growth of ideas gained from observation with the ever-enlarging body of psychoanalytic experience and theory. The primary constructs confidence and depressive constellation took shape as a result of experience with the transactional processes in the symbiotic mother-infant unit and in the transference relationships of the psychoanalytic situation. Expressed in terms of psychoanalytic theory of ego development, the basis of these constructs is the bipolarity, the ambivalence of experiences of drive frustration and gratification, gradually organized in relation to the object. When the concept of the unity of energy in the universe and the theory of entropy penetrated my theorizing, their similarity to concepts of the bipolarity of psychic energy in relation to instinctual drives stimulated an effort to conceptualize further the concept of ambivalence in relation to my earlier concept of a depressive constellation.

Ambivalence, since it is just energy, can be recognized in connection with its object. The primary object of ambivalence is the mother, the instrument of the process of alimentation. Both the positive and negative poles of the infant's experience cathect the mother. The libidinal, positive result in the infant is recognizable in his sleep, in his thriving, his smiling response, etc.; his negative condition is observable in the signal of his instinctual need and its frustration.

The development of the mind, like the growth of the body, is a result of the organization of the primary processes and their derivatives. With each turn in the spiral of interaction, new vistas, new fields, new problems arise. It seems a long jump from psychic representations of primary processes to sublimation and the sublimated characteristic of the mind, but the aim of this excursion was to show that both poles of instinctual energy participate in all psychic processes, including sublimation.

If that seems to go beyond the limits implied in the title of this chapter, it does not reach the bounds of the psychodynamic processes that interact in the evolution of the depressive *anlage*. The psychology of normal development reveals the microscopic stresses and critical phases in which culture and individuals interact in increasing the disposition to depressive illness. Sincerity and authenticity, for example, have become required characteristics of the moral individual. As sincerity increased the responsibility of the individual for the morality of his actions, the differentiations of intrapsychic controls increased and ramified the unconscious stress accompanying decisions and actions. Thus depression itself has become a characteristic of our culture.

The pervasive effect of the depressive *anlage* urges upon us the question: why is it that some individuals overcome the universal, innate predisposition to depression and are able to master its transient manifestations in moods and affects while others succumb to illness? Here we have to concede that there may be factors that cannot be elucidated by psychoanalysis but that play a major role in depressive illness.

REFERENCES

1. Abraham, K. Notes on the Psycho-Analytical Investigation and Treatment of Manic-Depressive Insanity and Allied Conditions (1911). In *Selected Papers*. London: Hogarth Press, 1927. P. 137.

2. Ambrose, A.   The age of onset of ambivalence in early infancy. Indications from the study of laughing. *J. Child Psychol. Psychiatry* 4: 167, 1963.
3. Benedek, T.   Adaptation to reality in early infancy. *Psychoanal. Q.* 7:200, 1938. (Reprinted in *Psychoanalytic Investigations; Selected Papers.* New York: Quadrangle, 1973.)
4. Benedek, T.   Toward the biology of the depressive constellation. *J. Am. Psychoanal. Assoc.* 4:389, 1956. (Reprinted in *Psychoanalytic Investigations; Selected Papers.* New York: Quadrangle, 1973.)
5. Benedek, T.   On the organization of the reproductive drive. *Int. J. Psychoanal.* 41:1, 1960. (Reprinted in *Psychoanalytic Investigations; Selected Papers.* New York: Quadrangle, 1973.)
6. Benedek, T.   Discussions: Mental Processes in Thyrotoxic States; Dominant Ideas and Their Relation to Morbid Cravings; Some Factors Determining Fixation at the Deutero-Phallic Phase. In *Psychoanalytic Investigations; Selected Papers.* New York: Quadrangle, 1973. Pp. 43, 84, 107.
7. Benedek, T., and Rubenstein, B. B.   *The Sexual Cycle in Women.* Washington, D.C.: National Research Council, 1942.
8. Corner, G. W.   *Ourselves Unborn; An Embryologist's Essay on Man.* New Haven: Yale University Press, 1944.
9. Fenichel, O.   Early Stages of Ego Development. In *Collected Papers,* second series. New York: Norton, 1954. P. 25.
10. Freud, S.   Three Essays on the Theory of Sexuality (1905). In *The Standard Edition of the Complete Psychological Works of Sigmund Freud,* transl. and ed. by J. Strachey with others. London: Hogarth and Institute of Psycho-Analysis, 1953. Vol. 7, p. 135.
11. Freud, S.   Formulations on the Two Principles of Mental Functioning (1911). *Standard Edition.* 1958. Vol. 12, p. 218.
12. Freud, S.   Totem and Taboo (1913). *Standard Edition.* 1958. Vol. 13, p. 1.
13. Freud, S.   Instincts and Their Vicissitudes (1915). *Standard Edition.* 1957. Vol. 14, p. 117.
14. Freud, S.   The Unconscious (1915). *Standard Edition.* 1957. Vol. 14, p. 161.
15. Freud, S.   Beyond the Pleasure Principle (1920). *Standard Edition.* 1955. Vol. 18, p. 7.
16. Freud, S.   The Ego and the Id (1923). *Standard Edition.* 1963. Vol. 19, p. 157.
17. Freud, S.   The Economic Problem of Masochism (1924). *Standard Edition.* 1961. Vol. 19, p. 157.
18. Freud, S.   Civilization and Its Discontents (1930). *Standard Edition.* 1961. Vol. 21, p. 64.
19. Glover, E.   Sublimation, Substitution and Social Anxiety. In *On the Early Development of the Mind.* New York: International Universities Press, 1956. P. 130.
20. Graubert, D. N., and Miller, J. S. A.   On ambivalence. *Psychiatr. Q.* 31:458, 1957.
21. Grinker, R. R., Sr.   Discussion of "Toward the Biology of the Depressive Constellation" [4], paper read at a meeting of the Chicago Psychoanalytical Society, February 1953, Chicago.

22. Hartmann, H.   Notes on the theory of sublimation. *Psychoanal. Study Child* 10:9, 1955.
23. Hartmann, H.   Concept formation in psychoanalysis. *Psychoanal. Study Child* 19:11, 1964.
24. Kaywin, L.   Problems of sublimation. *J. Am. Psychoanal. Assoc.* 14: 313, 1966.
25. Klein, M.   *The Psycho-Analysis of Children.* London: Hogarth Press, 1932.
26. Kohut, H.   Forms and transformations of narcissism. *J. Am. Psychoanal. Assoc.* 14:243, 1966.
27. Kohut, H.   *The Analysis of the Self.* New York: International Universities Press, 1971.
28. Kris, E.   Neutralization and sublimation. Observations on a young child. *Psychoanal. Study Child* 10:30, 1955.
29. Mahler, M. S.   Notes on the Development of Basic Moods: The Depressive Affect in Psychoanalysis. In R. M. Loewenstein et al. (Eds.), *Psychoanalysis: A General Psychology.* New York: International Universities Press, 1966. P. 152.
30. Marcus, R. L.   The nature of instinct and the physical basis of libido. *Yearbook of the Society for General Systems Research* 7:134, 1962.
31. Monod, J.   *Chance and Necessity.* New York: Knopf, 1971.
32. Rangell, L.   A further attempt to resolve the problem of anxiety. *J. Am. Psychoanal. Assoc.* 16:371, 1968.
33. Riviere, A-P.   Dentition, walking and speech in relation to the depressive position. *Int. J. Psychoanal.* 37:167, 1958.
34. Rubinfine, D. L.   Note on a theory of depression. *Psychoanal. Q.* 37:402, 1968.
35. Ruwet, J-C.   *Introduction to Ethology: The Biology of Behavior.* New York: International Universities Press, 1972.
36. Schrödinger, E.   *What Is Life?* New York: Macmillan, 1940.
37. Szasz, T.   On the psychoanalytic theory of instincts. *Psychoanal. Q.* 21:25, 1952.
38. Thorpe, W. H.   *Learning and Instinct in Animals.* Cambridge, Mass.: Harvard University Press, 1950.
39. Trilling, L.   *Sincerity and Authenticity.* Cambridge, Mass.: Harvard University Press, 1972.
40. Winnicott, D. W.   Depressive position of normal development. *Br. J. Psychol.* 56:89, 1955-1956.

8

The Regulation of Self-Esteem

EDITH JACOBSON

Since a pathological lack of self-esteem commonly plays an outstanding role in depressive states, the problem of self-esteem regulation certainly deserves special consideration in the context of this book. To be sure, all our patients, neurotic, borderline psychotic, or psychotic, suffer from disturbances in the regulation of self-esteem. They may suffer from feelings of shame and inferiority and from conscious or unconscious feelings of guilt. In narcissistic and psychotic disorders these disturbances may assume particular significance and, in the case of psychosis, may even lead to delusional ideas of sinfulness or grandeur.

What I have said does not imply that self-esteem in normal people is always in an even balance. Within certain limits, it too may show similar fluctuations, mostly in accordance with mood changes. Normally, however, the rise or fall of self-esteem develops in response to actual experiences, such as success or failure, and the intensity and direction correspond to the nature and extent of the provocation. The more irrational factors and unconscious conflicts come into play, the more abnormally will self-esteem be altered in its level of intensity and its affective and ideational expression.

We should not forget to mention the operation of hereditary factors nor the effects of physiological changes that may decisively influence self-esteem and mood, as in the premenstrual period [1], involutional depression, and certain psychotic disorders, especially manic-depressive. Since the genetic and neurochemical aspects of depression have been discussed in other parts of this book, only the influence of psychological factors on the normal and pathological regulation of self-esteem will be considered in this chapter.

Before dealing with the details of this process, it is important to define what is meant by this term. Although the testing of external and internal reality is of great significance for the maintenance of a comparatively even level of self-esteem, one cannot explain the regulation of self-esteem simply in terms of a regulatory principle such as the reality principle. One has to consider a series of rather complex problems the understanding of which might help to throw light on this.

One may begin with the statement that a comparatively normal level of self-esteem reflects a state of narcissistic balance, while a conspicuous and lasting elevation or fall indicates the presence of an intrapsychic narcissistic conflict provoked by either external or internal (unconsciously motivated) factors.

Such a statement presupposes a clear understanding of what precisely one means by the terms narcissistic balance and narcissistic conflict. The term narcissism was first introduced into psychoanalysis by Freud in 1914 [5], but it has undergone further elaboration since then. Today, it refers to the intrapsychic cathexis of the self-representations with more or less neutralized or deneutralized libidinous or aggressive drive energy [8, 9]. This drive investment finds ideational and affective expression in the extent to which one likes, respects, and accepts, or dislikes and deprecates his or her own bodily and mental self. This defines what is meant by sufficient, high, or low self-esteem, but it fails to throw light on the regulatory mechanism. In order to do this it will first be necessary to clarify the relation of self-directed to object-directed drives, the concepts of narcissism and object relations, the vicissitudes they undergo, and their mutual influence on each other during normal and pathological development.

In his first postulation, Freud spoke of narcissism in a way that compared and contrasted the self-directed and the object-directed drives. Although he discussed the infantile stages of primary and secondary narcissism, and the development of the ego-ideal from the original narcissism and omnipotent feelings of the child, it was in the context of the narcissistic withdrawal that occurs in psychosis, where narcissism develops at the expense of object libido. This is as true as the statement that the child's attachment to the parents is initially highly narcissistic in nature and only gradually develops into a truly loving object relationship. Both these views, nevertheless, oversimplify the situations.

Next we come to the early development and nature of the child's object relations. In the first, the relationship is symbiotic in nature in that the infant desires to be one with the mother and perceives her as a need-satisfying object [14]. Object constancy is gradually built up, signifying that inner mother and father images are formed and remain with the child even when he is separated from his parents. The development of a self-image proceeds more slowly, beginning with the child's discovery of his own body parts, and only in the second year of life is the child able to speak of himself as "I." Yet the boundaries between intrapsychic object-images and self-images remain indistinct and the child very easily projects his own impulses and attitudes onto the mother and introjects her impulses and attitudes onto himself. This is referred to as projective or introjective identification. In those cases in which the mother cultivates the symbiotic tie for needs of her own, the child may either fail to develop adequate boundaries between mother and self or, later in life, may regress somewhat easily to this stage of object relations. This has an important bearing on the psychology of borderline psychotic and psychotic patients, who tend to establish narcissistic relations and to develop narcissistic identifications, introjective or projective, with them. This leads to severe pathology in the development of narcissism and the regulation of self-esteem.

In contrast, the normal child sets up firm boundaries between object and self, which enable him to relate normally to parents and others as to objects different from himself. This does not mean that normal children invest their psychic forces in objects and object representations at the expense of their own selves—that would lead to masochism. Normal object relations, on the contrary, presuppose sufficient self-love and self-regard to permit the individual an active approach to his objects and a healthy self-assertion on the part of his ego.

What must be emphasized and has been emphasized by Kohut [11] and Kernberg [10] is that narcissism is a normal phenomenon and plays a significant and enduring role in mental life. It may undergo either normal or pathological development, and in the latter case it may interfere with normal self-esteem regulation, with instinctual and affective life, with object relationships, and with ego and superego functions.

To further our understanding of how self-esteem is regulated, how this regulation may undergo normal or abnormal development, and what effects these various outcomes may have on mental life and function, some instinctual, structural, economic, and genetic problems need to be discussed.

If self-esteem is reflective of the drive investment in self-representations, the sources of the self-directed drives must be explored from the structural point of view. Object- and self-representations are both certainly part of the conscious and unconscious ego, but self-esteem should not be equated with self-love or self-hate. It presupposes self-judgment and the involvement of a self-critical institution that must not only observe but also evaluate the self.

As far as moral and ethical standards are concerned, it is the superego, a separate and special part of the ego, that either accepts and praises or rejects and condemns one's thoughts, feelings, impulses, and behavior. Therefore, the superego, which is deeply rooted in the unconscious, can be regarded at least in part as a source of the energy invested in self-representations. Self-critical attitudes, however, are not limited to moral behavior. The conflicts involved in low self-esteem are not only between the superego, the ego, and self-representations; self-judgment may also extend to such general assets as physical, practical, vocational, professional, artistic, and intellectual accomplishments as well as various aspects of love life and personal relationships. These self-critical evaluations are functions not of the superego but of the ego. This can be clarified as follows.

Measured against one's inner standards and those of the external world, the ability or inability to achieve what is desired may result in experiences of success or failure, that is, of narcissistic gratification or injury. Whereas good moral behavior may lead to a "good conscience" or even to feelings of moral superiority, moral failures find expression in guilt feelings. One's general assets and accomplishments, on the other hand, may bring about feelings of pride and superiority in successful situations and shame and inferiority when unsuccessful. Where there is a marked narcissistic vulnerability, the experience of moral failure or deficits in other areas may be conducive to depression.

The standards by which the individual measures his moral attitudes and behavior or his general assets and defects stem from the structure of the superego and the identifications that contribute to it. During the preoedipal stage of development the child already begins to develop a wishful image of the self, of what he wants to be or to become. These wishes have their source partly in the child's envy of his parents and older siblings, but partly also in his own instinctual and narcissistic needs, his oral greed, his anal wishes for possessions, his aggressive wishes for phallic power, or, to put it generally, in his own ambitions and wishes for growth and accomplishment. Mahler [13] has described the child's feelings as parents observe junior toddlers taking their first steps alone, with pride and elation very visible on their faces.

The child who needs and depends on parental love, help, and approval wants, in turn, to live up to his parents' expectations. These extend from the need of the parents to have a "good," clean, obedient child to their desire, expressive of their narcissism, for a healthy, good-looking, intelligent, capable offspring. These wishes and ambitions, demands and prohibitions, approvals and disapprovals, are expressed to the child in a wide variety of ways, gently and tactfully or rudely and strictly. Through the process of identification, rooted in the child's own wishes to become like the parents and to gain their love and approval, the parents' standards are gradually internalized within the child. The earliest identifications originate in imitations of the mother and symbiotic wishes to be one with her. In many borderline psychotic and schizophrenic adult patients, one can observe that this wish for symbiotic union either was never relinquished or is regressively revived. Such wishes are expressive of weak inner boundaries between self- and object-representations. Normal children go through the separation-individuation phase (described by Mahler [13]) and develop partial rather than total identification with the parents; these identifications undergo further development in the early oedipal stage, leading to superego formation and definite alterations in the ego. Normal children are able to replace the fantasy of being one with mother or father with wishes of acquiring the admired attributes and traits in the parents and later in other authoritative figures. Such selective identifications presuppose the development of the firm boundaries between object- and self-images, which make the child realize that it has a self of its own that is different from the external objects. These feelings of self-identity should not be confused with self-esteem. Severe psychotically depressed patients, whose self-esteem is profoundly lowered, do not show any evidence of the fearing or feeling a loss of identity that is so characteristic of borderline psychotic or schizophrenic patients.

As the child enters the oedipal period, he builds up from the various forerunners of the superego a consistent structure. This consists of the ego-ideal, representation of the internalized moral standards and demands of the parents, and the self-critical part of the superego that praises, accepts or condemns the ego's thoughts, feelings and actions.

When Freud [6] called the superego the "heir of the Oedipus complex" and the "motor of repression," he meant that it is a psychic institution intended to help the child to ward off his forbidden sexual (incestuous) wishes and his hostile impulses toward the parents. With respect to the regulation of self-esteem, the defenses against hostility appear to be even more important, at least nowadays, than the warding off of forbidden heterosexual and homosexual impulses. The superego also lends general support to the taming of the affects and the neutralization of the drives.

Inasmuch as the ego-ideal encompasses not only the child's moral standards but also his material goals and his physical and intellectual ambitions, it could be said that the ego-ideal straddles the line between superego and ego. Clinically one frequently sees that an individual's business or professional ambitions are quasi-idealized or actually ideal in nature. Of course it happens just as often, or even more often, that an individual's ambitious, aggressive wishes for money, status, and power—goals indicating perhaps an arrest at an earlier developmental stage—interfere with ethical standards and lead to moral conflicts. To be good and decent and to be big and powerful are two quite different goals. We can observe the conflict between power goals and moral aims particularly well in the field of politics, whether in government or in minor conflicts arising in business, professional, or sporting groups.

Whereas some psychoanalysts assume that the ego-ideal straddles the border between superego and ego, or even regard it as not being part of the superego, it is not the ego-ideal but the superego that evaluates one's ethical activity, and where there are morally reprehensible attitudes and behavior, feelings of guilt or remorse are provoked. On the other hand, self-evaluation with regard to assets or deficits in material aspirations appears to be a self-critical ego function that may induce feelings of shame and inferiority. In many patients, guilt is coupled with feelings of shame and inferiority, but more frequently they mask each other. For example, patients may suffer feelings of shame and inferiority over their passive-masochistic attitudes but then display intense guilt feelings as soon as their sadistic impulses come to the surface.

It can be inferred, therefore, that self-esteem depends on the extent to which the individual can live up to the goals and standards of his ego-ideal. The statement, however, fails to take into account the qualities of the ego-ideal, in the broadest sense of the term, of the self-critical functions and state of the ego, that is, of the essential factors that determine the regulation of self-esteem. This leads directly to a consideration of the prominent role that the drives and drive qualities play in this regulation, whether normal or pathological. The fact that the terms ego-ideal and superego are used indicates that these structures must be vested with both positive (libidinous) and negative (aggressive) drive energy.

Since the ego-ideal represents the system of values and is the site of moral and ethical standards, it must certainly be cathected with libido. If it is included in worldly goals and ambitions, these may be loved but need not be "moral" and "good." Vanity and wishes for power and possessions certainly do not represent moral values. For this reason, it would be preferable not to include such worldly objectives in the term ego-ideal.

The higher or lower level of moral standards depends, at least in part, on aspects of infantile development: the parental standards and expectations conveyed to the child, the parental behavior, and the child's identifications with its parents. This is true for the superego structure in general. However, since the superego exercises critical functions, it must be the source of the libidinous or aggressive forces that are invested in the "good" or "bad" self-representations and are involved in praising or depreciating the self. The same is true for the self-critical functions of the ego. As in the case of the ego-ideal, the severity or mildness of the superego depends mainly on infantile development. With normal self-esteem, the drives vested in the self become at least to some extent neutralized, a fact emphasized by Hartmann [7]. Being self-critical does not mean that one hates himself, and self-approval does not imply self-love. Moreover, both self-approval and self-reproach usually refer to specific impulses, attitudes, and behavior that one finds either acceptable or unacceptable. One does not regard his whole self as either wonderful or despicable when he has had a good or bad impulse or has commited a good or bad action. For this reason a normal person does not react to failure or narcissistic hurt with a lasting depression nor to success and narcissistic gratifications with a long period of elation, whereas individuals who are prone to depression and are unable to tolerate injuries to their narcissism are apt to react to failures with a hostile rejection of the entire self, which may induce a prolonged and severe depressed state. The intensity of this self-rejection depends on the strictness, hostility, or even cruelty of the superego and the self-critical functions of the ego. The self-directed sadism of a potentially suicidal psychotic depressive can hardly be overrated. In such cases, as with all psychotics, the drives have become regressively deneutralized and sadomasochistic tendencies then dominate the clinical picture.

THE ROLE OF AMBIVALENCE IN THE REGULATION OF SELF-ESTEEM

Bibring [2], in his paper on depression, paid no attention at all to the hostility conflicts in depression. He spoke of anxiety, depression, and elation as primary ego states. It is true, as reported by Mahler [14], that very small children display such states, but their elation and depression are affective responses to corresponding experiences of achievement or failure.

It is difficult to evaluate the development of self-esteem during the first years of life. Spitz and Wolf [16] described what they termed anaclitic depression in institutionalized children. To be sure, children who are deprived of maternal love and care may easily turn into depressed adults, but one can also observe the transformation of hostility into self-destructive drives in apparently normal small children.

A charming, gay little girl of 1½ years begins to hit her head on the wall when she becomes angry at being put to bed when she does not want to go. The head banging is enough to raise a bump but she does not seem to notice this. Her mother has to slap her hand to stop the action. The little girl already shows very definite signs of ambivalence. She can be very affectionate with another little girl, but at any moment may grab the friend's top and pull at her hair should she want to have them back. Since she has very loving, affectionate parents, she gives the impression of possessing innate strong aggressive impulses, even though she appeared to be in general an easygoing, happy child with good frustration-tolerance.

It therefore seems that the aggressiveness of children does not depend only on the parents' love and ability to teach the child to tolerate frustration. Some children manifest a tendency to strong aggressive or self-destructive reactions from birth, and this may, later on, result in self-derogatory attitudes. One sees adult patients with very early memories of guilt feelings, mostly in reaction to derogatory, angry, or punitive attitudes or to overly strict demands and prohibitions on the part of the mother. The parents of such patients are generally very narcissistic, aggressive individuals who expect too much too early from their children. Such attitudes may result in either excessively high moral and worldly standards or excessively strict self-critical functions, that lead to pathological development of narcissism and regulation of self-esteem. In the most severe cases there are usually unloving, hostile, punitive parents whose own behavior does not correspond to the standards they set for the child and whose marital relationship is poor. One may then observe the development of such intense hostility toward and derogation of the parents that it prevents the normal identification that is necessary for the development of a normal superego and ego-ideal. Surprisingly, such a patient may develop a reactive ego-ideal of his own that is in striking contrast to the parental personality. Whenever his own behavior shows any similarity to that of the parents, he reacts with severe anxiety, guilt, and inferiority feelings, which are often warded off by reactions of anger.

EGO FUNCTIONS AND OBJECT RELATIONS IN NARCISSISTICALLY VULNERABLE INDIVIDUALS

Narcissistically vulnerable individuals respond to narcissistic injuries with feelings of guilt, shame, and inferiority. It would not be correct to call all such patients narcissistic or to state that they suffer from narcissistic disorders. The fact is that many are able to relate very well to other people, to get married, to love their partners and their children, and to function adequately in their jobs or professions. In psychoanalytic treatment, which they may need because they suffer from anxiety and depressive states with feelings of guilt and inferiority, they may develop a classical transference neurosis, although their analysis may bring to light their narcissistic disturbances. In view of this, one certainly cannot speak of a weakness of the ego in such patients—a term that anyway should be used with utmost caution. Of course, there are some persons with a pathological regulation of self-esteem whose object relations and ego functions are severely disturbed by their narcissistic disturbances. Reich [15] has described different types of persons who show a pathological regulation of self-esteem, while Kernberg [10] and Kohut [12] have also discussed it in relation to narcissistic personalities.

It should be emphasized that among our "common neurotics" one may find many patients who, for unconscious reasons, tend to develop overly intense feelings of guilt and inferiority and sometimes states of depression. Their transference may show a narcissistic coloring that otherwise is not different from what is commonly seen in neurotics.

There is a tendency to believe that the aggressiveness of the superego is always caused by the turning of hostility toward others back to the self, and even that self-derogation always reflects the accusations of objects, especially the love object. This happens in the case of psychotic depressives and has been described by Freud [5]. However, in common neurotics who suffer from feelings of guilt and inferiority, it may not occur at all. It would be more correct to say that people who suffer from intense conscious conflicts over ambivalence tend to have severe guilt feelings because of their intense hostility. It is also true that individuals who have set too high a standard for their physical appearance and achievements may develop feelings of inferiority because of being unable to live up to their goals. Sometimes their conflicts may be justified inasmuch as their looks, body appearance, intelligence, and abilities are actually not as good as they want them to be. The problem with such persons lies in their inability to give up their immoderate ambitions and accept themselves as they are, including their failings—not an easy task.

CLINICAL ILLUSTRATIONS OF PATHOLOGICAL
REGULATION OF SELF-ESTEEM

A few clinical vignettes may help us to understand the problem of pathological self-esteem regulation. The patients suffered from anxieties, anger, guilt, and inferiority feelings that originated in childhood experiences and were brought about by emotionally disturbed, unstable, angry parents who constantly fought with each other and derogated their children (and in one case even beat them up).

Case 1.   Dr. A., a gifted young surgeon, was brought up in a miserable environment. His father was a professional man but a gambler and waster, and his mother a very angry woman who despised, derogated and fought with the father. She fluctuated in her moods, "screamed" at everybody and would alternately caress and physically attack her children so that they never knew what to expect from her. Dr. A., who during his childhood called his mother "the enemy," became a very angry young man who was terrified of women and hated them. After some years of treatment with another psychiatrist he developed a strong relationship with a girl who unfortunately fell severely ill and was separated from him. Professionally he was gifted and capable, but personally he was easily hurt and disappointed by women. On the surface he seemed self-assertive and self-assured, and his angry reactions appeared to be an effective defense against underlying feelings of guilt and inferiority. However, he himself felt that he had a "paranoid core" that showed in his distrust and defensiveness, his suspiciousness and his attacks of anger. Nevertheless, he hardly ever distorted the reality of what he reported. Yet he always managed to get into conflicts with certain colleagues, especially his "superiors," and liked to "fight for causes" in the hospital and elsewhere.

It did not take long to discover that this handsome, intelligent, efficient young man regarded himself as ugly, ignorant, unattractive to women and morally "bad" because of his violent temper, only too reminiscent of his "enemy," the mother. He was horrified by the idea that he might have identified with someone whom he despised. He was also antagonistic to and contemptuous of his father, whom he regarded as a sociopath and who had never given him any attention or any money for his education.

This case is interesting because on the surface the man showed no signs of low self-esteem and was almost unaware of being frequently in a state of depression. He said in the first interview that he was an "angry young man," and a skillful surgeon, but that he had been unable to establish a happy, lasting relationship with a woman. He had been throughout his childhood and adolescence an unhappy, depressed, lonely child. After leaving home, he made a good adjustment in college and developed lasting friendships with other young men. His ability to relate to men had its origin in his relationship to a brother 10 years older than him, whom he had admired and who had been very kind to him. But this brother, too, had turned into an "angry man." Only during his first course of treatment did the patient begin to relate to women and to develop a lasting relationship (on his part)—to the girl who fell sick and left him. These were the "only happy years" in his life.

This case is presented to demonstrate the peculiarity of self-esteem regulation and the role of hostility in it. This patient only gradually became aware of his depressiveness and lack of self-esteem in areas other than his professional work. His analysis revealed that he had rather successfully built up reactive counteridentifications in his superego. His ideal was to become the opposite of his parents, that is, a competent professional man who held on to his money, who had friends (in contrast with his parents), who was kind and loving and could rescue his patients, and who would found a family and become a warm, loving father. His main reason for going into treatment was his wish to get rid of his violent temper, which reminded him of his mother. Actually he had achieved much of what he had wanted to be. When he began to understand that his aggressiveness was actually a defensive device that helped him to ward off depression and raise self-esteem, he changed to a surprising degree. He began to feel compassion for his poor, disturbed parents and to call them regularly; he was surprised to hear his mother say over the phone, "You know that we love you, don't you?" With the decrease in hostility toward his parents, his self-esteem rose and his depressiveness and attacks of anger were greatly reduced.

The case illustrates the ability of a patient to build up a reactive ego-ideal in opposition to his parents and to develop into a normal human except for his identification with the angry mother. Although this anger helped him to ward off his underlying depression and guilt feelings, it did not succeed in reducing his feelings of inferiority, which revolved mainly around his conviction that he was the unworthy child of worthless parents.

Case 2.   A female patient is the happily married wife of a husband whom she adores and the loving mother of two very intelligent and happy children. Her father was a competent but paranoid, sociopathic man, and her mother was a very disturbed woman whose inability to keep house forced the patient and her sister even as small children to take over the housework and prepare the meals for the family. The parents constantly fought with each other, and the mother frequently expressed her wish to run away from home. The patient was an excellent student and planned to go to college and to have professional training, but her father declined to support her because she was "only a girl." He wanted her either to help him in his grocery store or to get married to a wealthy man. She managed, despite the father's opposition, to find jobs that enabled her to go to college. It was then that she began to develop severe anxieties and depression, with loss of self-esteem that revolved only around her supposed inability to learn and her fears of authorities and examinations. Her symptoms have continued up to the present, even when she worked to support her husband during his years of professional training. She made some futile efforts to train in several fields that attracted her, but her anxieties and depression soon put a stop to the training. She is currently obtaining professional training in a field for which she has a definite gift.

So far this woman's analytic treatment has not helped her enough to rid herself of her anxious and depressive reactions, but at least she is able to continue her training and to be a good student. The analysis has raised her self-esteem sufficiently so she can master her work. This patient, too, had occasional attacks of rage and displayed marked hostility toward both parents. Since she was deeply attached to her siblings, she was able to develop the ability to love her husband and children and to have close, intimate friends. Her symptoms related only to her professional activities. The analysis showed that she was unable to permit herself to study successfully because her father was opposed to it. She punished herself for her ambitiousness, her hostility, and her derogation of her parents by showing that she could not accomplish this "superior" type of work. She had a strong, conscious oedipal attachment to her father (who used to kiss her on the mouth), but at the same time she despised him.

In this case, too, the hostility to the parents has been reduced, although her contempt for them remains intense, and her guilt feelings about her own "selfishness" and her inner detachment from them are still not resolved. The attacks of rage have almost disappeared. Here, too, the patient was able to build up an ego-ideal that was in definite opposition to the parental standards and behavior, and to form reactive counteridentifications. This helped her to become a decent human being and a competent, loving wife and mother. Her guilt feelings did not allow her until now, despite her superior intelligence, to have a professional career, and thus interfered quite severely with her ego functions.

What is of particular interest is that this patient, who never had a mother on whom she could depend and who very early became quasi-independent, developed a strong wish to be as dependent on her analyst as she had wanted to be on her mother. Yet she is very much afraid of these passive-dependent trends, which remind her of her mother's attitudes and might, she fears, represent an identification with her.

REFERENCES

1. Benedek, T.   Parenthood as a developmental phase. *J. Am. Psychoanal. Assoc.* 7:389, 1959.
2. Bibring, E.   The Mechanism of Depression. In P. Greenacre (Ed.), *Affective Disorders.* New York: International Universities Press, 1953. P. 13.
3. Fenichel, O.   *The Psychoanalytic Theory of Neurosis.* New York: Norton, 1945.

4. Fenichel, O. Identification (1926). In *Collected Papers*. New York: Norton, 1953. P. 97.
5. Freud, S. On Narcissism: An Introduction (1914). In *The Standard Edition of the Complete Psychological Works of Sigmund Freud*, transl. and ed. by J. Strachey with others. London: Hogarth and Institute of Psycho-Analysis, 1957. Vol. 14, p. 73.
6. Freud, S. The Ego and the Id (1923). *Standard Edition*. 1963. Vol. 19, p. 13.
7. Hartmann, H. Comments on the psychoanalytic theory of instinctual drives. *Psychoanal. Q.* 17:368, 1945.
8. Hartmann, H. The application of psychoanalytic concepts to social science. *Psychoanal. Q.* 19:385, 1950.
9. Jacobson, E. *The Self and the Object World*. New York: International Universities Press, 1964. Pp. 136, 194.
10. Kernberg, O. F. Factors in the psychoanalytic treatment of narcissistic personalities. *J. Am. Psychoanal. Assoc.* 18:51, 1970.
11. Kohut, H. Forms and transformations of narcissism. *J. Am. Psychoanal. Assoc.* 14:243, 1966.
12. Kohut, H. *The Analysis of the Self*. New York: International Universities Press, 1971.
13. Mahler, M. Thoughts about development and individuation. *Psychoanal. Study Child* 18:307, 1963.
14. Mahler, M. Notes on the Development of Basic Moods: The Depressive Affect. In R. M. Loewenstein et al. (Eds.), *Psychoanalysis— A General Psychology*. New York: International Universities Press, 1966. P. 152.
15. Reich, A. Pathological Forms of Self-Esteem Regulation (1960). In G. Gero (Ed.), *Psychoanalytic Contributions*. New York: International Universities Press, 1973. P. 288.
16. Spitz, R., and Wolf, K. Anaclitic Depression: An Inquiry into the Genesis of Psychiatric Conditions in Early Childhood. *Psychoanal. Study Child* 2:313, 1946.

9

The Role of
Conservation-Withdrawal
in Depressive Reactions*

ARTHUR H. SCHMALE
GEORGE L. ENGEL†

Although it is said that depressive reactions are among the easiest to diagnose clinically, there is disagreement as to the genetic, constitutional, developmental, cultural, social class, age, family history of depression, and psychosocial setting of onset characteristics, all of which may be important to how the class of depressive reactions is subdivided, particularly for treatment purposes. From our own work and study of depressive reactions, we feel there is one basic biological fact upon which all the other somatic and psychological influences and characteristics are superimposed. This fact has to do with the somatic regulatory processes that produce what we call the conservation-withdrawal reaction. Conservation-withdrawal and its counterpart, active-engaging, reflect the extreme states of biological functioning inherited by man to interact with and cope with fluctuations in his environment. Although these rhythmically experienced reciprocal states are probably a property of all organisms, in man they find their highest level of integrated functioning through the central nervous system.

The hallmark of the conservation-withdrawal state is relative immobility, quiescence, and unresponsiveness to external environment input. A number of psychological patterns may be expressive of and derivative from or reactive to the conservation-withdrawal response. Thus, our approach to understanding depressive reactions involves a basic understanding of the individual's conservation-withdrawal experiences, which, as the individual grows and develops, become more

* This study was supported by U.S. Public Health Service Grants MH 14151 and MH 11668 and the San Francisco Foundation.
† Dr. Engel is a Career Research Awardee of the Public Health Service.

and more related to his psychological needs and to his experiences in fulfilling such needs. It is our belief that an individual's psychic awareness of and reaction to the somatic response of conservation-withdrawal, which occurs at varying points in time developmentally, will have a specific influence on the individual's potential for depression and the type of depression or alternate behavior and reaction that may be subsequently experienced. A detailed consideration of the phylogenetic and ontogenetic characteristics of the conservation-withdrawal response can be found elsewhere [11].

In general, while active-engaging serves to enable the organism to find external sources of nutriment, security, and comfort, inactivation and disengagement may occur when the environment is perceived as no longer providing needed nutriment, security, or comfort or when the organism's attention is turned to internal needs such as repair, renewal, and growth. All organisms, including man, go through cycles of relative activity-inactivity that are related both to external or environmental influences (amount of light, temperature, barometric pressure, etc.) and to internal influences (states of metabolism, cell division, and the more obviously rhythmically functioning systems such as the cardiac, respiratory, autonomic nervous, and endocrine systems, etc.) [22]. The human, even in its infant state, also has the capacity to become inactive and disengaged, periodically as well as aperiodically, from his external environment when his own efforts to interact with the environment become unrewarding because the external environment becomes either overstimulating or nonstimulating. As a threshold reaction, this conservation-withdrawal state may have its set points of responding, based on genetic as well as prenatal, perinatal, and postnatal experiences. In this regard, then, one might postulate that the earlier and more profound the experiences of organismic deprivation or excessive stimulation, the more significant or influential their effect on the developing organism and its subsequent propensity to invoke inactivity and disengagement and the conservation-withdrawal state.

Schur [34] has linked Freud's pleasure-unpleasure principle to the underlying biphasic biological processes of active approach and active avoidance or withdrawal. Further, Schur thinks Freud's ideas about the principle of inertia proposed in 1895 and the death instinct proposed in 1920 are attempts to deal with withdrawal phenomena. We distinguish the passively experienced withdrawal that we call conservation-withdrawal from what Schur, Schneirla [33], and others have referred to as active withdrawal or avoidance and regard it as closer to what Freud referred to as inertia and the death instinct.

One of the earliest and easiest to identify forms of evidence of the conservation-withdrawal process is sleep. Greenacre [17] thinks withdrawal may be the most primitive defense reaction. Spitz [36] also regards the sleep of the newborn as the prototype of all ego defenses. But it would be premature to equate all forms of sleep with conservation-withdrawal. Perhaps only those forms that occur suddenly after very intense stimulation or sudden exhaustion should be so identified and thus differentiated from the sleep that comes on gradually and is preceded by a number of presleep manifestations, such as yawning and stretching. Engel and Reichsman [8] noted this distinction between the withdrawal sleep and spontaneous sleep of the infant Monica [9]. Also since sleep is not a single state, we are inclined to think that it is the non-rapid eye movement (NREM), stage 4, high voltage, slow wave, or delta sleep that is most closely related to the conservation-withdrawal reaction. Support for this proposal has come recently from the demonstration of a marked decrease in REM sleep with a proportionate increase in NREM sleep in infant monkeys exhibiting a profound "depression" experimentally induced by separation from the mother [26]. The NREM sleep also seems to be the phase in which many bodily repair and growth processes are accelerated. It is of interest that blood serum levels of growth hormone are highest during the early sleep cycles, when there is a predominance of NREM sleep. This also is the time of rest for those neural structures involved in slow or plastic activities, such as learning and memory.

The inactive-disengaged awake state may be associated with a drop in metabolic rate, sometimes with hypothermia, and reduced sympathetic activity, with slowing of heart and respiratory rates [26]. It is currently popular to undergo specific exercises or training to enable one to extend such periods of relaxation and tranquility which include making one's mind a blank (e.g., alpha wave training, yoga, transcendental meditation).

Our group's first awareness of the importance of the conservation-withdrawal phenomenon goes back to 1953 and the gastric secretion study of the infant Monica, who had a gastric fistula because of a congenital esophageal atresia and was admitted to the hospital at age 15 months in a profoundly withdrawn state [8]. When observed in a laboratory setting between the sixteenth and twenty-first months of life, after recovery from this initial withdrawn reaction, she revealed a stereotyped behavior that was reproduced each time a stranger came into her view. If alone when the stranger came into view, she instantly ceased all movement and within the next half minute became limp, her eyes no longer focused, and she stared off into space. The lids then began to fall and within 10 to 15 minutes she went into what seemed to be a sleep state. During this period gastric secretion ceased and remained unresponsive even to histamine stimulation [10].

It was thought that several factors probably contributed to this reaction. One was the limitation of mobility imposed by her physical underdevelopment. But more important was the impact of a five-month period between 6 and 11 months of age during which her depressed mother failed to interact with her and particularly to respond to her crying. Since feeding was by fistula, it was possible for the mother to feed her whenever it was convenient for the mother and not necessarily when it was most desired by the infant. Thus, by the end of her first year of life, she had given up the active crying response, which she had learned would not bring relief, and had become a severely withdrawn and unresponsive baby, markedly retarded in both physical and psychological development. It was our interpretation that by bypassing the crying response and going immediately to the conservation-withdrawal response she was saving energy. The loss of muscle tone and cessation of gastric secretion were part of this general withdrawal from the environment.

Such overuse by Monica of the conservation-withdrawal reaction from an early age as an adaptive response to a depriving environment has led to a number of interesting personality characteristics in this individual (who is now 21 years old). These will be mentioned later in the chapter. This withdrawal reaction of Monica's in infancy, although more profound in intensity and extent, is otherwise not different from a response pattern in infancy commonly observable even in the first days of life [14, 24, 35].

As already indicated, as one looks around nature and observes organisms from the very simplest to those as complex as man, one sees many patterns of inactivity and disengagement. These may take the form of encystment, hibernation, or, as it is frequently called in animals, "hypnosis," sham death, or tonic immobility. Examples of such patterns are described in more detail elsewhere [11]. All of these are adaptive devices that reflect the organism's turning away from the excessive or insufficient stimulation characterizing the external environment at the time. The biological slowing down, which includes a decrease in metabolic requirements, allows the organism to carry on through a period of nonrewarding external conditions with as little involvement, cost, or risk as possible. In effect then, there are biological feedback controls that can decrease as well as increase the organism's activity and engagement with its external environment. We suggest that the adaptive processes producing and maintaining inactivity and disengagement, which we refer to as conservation-withdrawal, make up the biological substrate that in the case of man will be perceived and integrated in the mind as feelings or states of depression.

NEURAL FEEDBACK SYSTEMS FOR CONSERVATION-WITHDRAWAL

In man the feedback regulatory mechanisms for maintaining homeostasis reach their highest level of integration through the central nervous system. There are many levels within the nervous system in which an incoming awareness and outgoing action can be either facilitated or inhibited. The diencephalon area of the brain is where the final integration of the homeostatic mechanisms is provided. Hess [18] and Gellhorn [15, 16] have independently developed elaborate concepts based on animal work that indicate the importance of reciprocal systems that activate and inactivate the organism in relation to fluctuations in the external environment and to the organism's internal needs for growth and replenishment. Hess introduced the terms ergotropic and trophotropic to designate these contrasting neural patterns. The biogenic amines may be involved in the neural transmission that either facilitates or inhibits the ergotropic or trophotropic systems in a reciprocal feedback way and thus influences activity, appetite, sex drive, sleep, and the many biochemical activities that are associated with these functions. Akiskal and McKinney [2] postulate that chemical, genetic, developmental, and interpersonal-experiential factors all converge on midbrain reward centers and can create reversible, functional derangements in the diencephalic mechanisms of reinforcement. They propose that the clinical syndromes of depression occur as a consequence of such functional disengagement.

PSYCHIC AWARENESS OF CONSERVATION-WITHDRAWAL

Although we at one time supported the idea that the first psychic awareness of somatic discomfort was experienced as anxiety and that anxiety was the undifferentiated prototype from which all the other negative affects were derived, more recently others, beginning with Bibring [3], have come to recognize the equal importance of depression, which has built-in biological antecedents that we are calling the conservation-withdrawal processes [6, 8].

The experiencing of conservation-withdrawal is of special importance at two particular times of intrapsychic developmental differentiation of self and other, and because of these phase-specific experiences, we suggest that two distinct, separate types of affects of depression result.

During the first year of life the child becomes increasingly aware that somatic tension and the relief of such tension are associated with specific interactions with the external world that he can perceive visually, auditorily, tactually, and kinesthetically. By the end of the first year of life, the child is increasingly able to recognize from his experiences that he is dependent upon an external object that has acquired readily identifiable characteristics. The child can now perceive that in the absence of this object, usually called the mothering object, feelings of discomfort may occur. If no adequate replacement object becomes available, these feelings will continue until the somatic threshold has been reached at which the conservation-withdrawal processes are brought into play. With the accompanying reduction in interest to engage with the environment, there is an awareness of a feeling that we have come to call *helplessness*. This feeling is defined as an awareness of discomfort that can be overcome only by a change in the external environment while at the same time the individual feels unable to do anything to bring about this needed change in the environment. Thus, he has to wait for a change in the external environment before he can again feel gratified and comfortable. After a period of sleep or withdrawal there may be a renewed interest in searching the external environment for the missing mothering object. If needs are not met (and tension reduced), a period of withdrawal will again ensue, and the cycle repeats itself. Thus, when Monica awakened from her withdrawal sleep to find the stranger still present, she would remain inactive and even relapse into sleep again. If the stranger was gone, she would gradually resume her usual pattern of activity or—if the mothering object appeared—would display joyful welcoming behavior—smiling, vocalizing, and reaching—while her stomach produced large amounts of gastric juice.

During this phase of development, mainly the first two years or so, the child learns through repeated experiences that differing levels of comfort and discomfort are associated with specific activities involving external objects. He experiences these objects as having control over his feelings of comfort and discomfort. Through the repeated experience of having his feelings of helplessness overcome by virtue of the return of a gratifying object, he develops what we call trust, in Erikson's terms, or confidence, in Benedek's terms. Such trust or confidence in specific objects gives rise to specific object representations in the mental apparatus, which are retained as memory traces. Thus, it is in relation to the infantile trauma of separation that we identify the first of the two affects of depression. Subsequently, feelings of helplessness will be reexperienced at various times in life when expected gratification is not forthcoming from specific objects, when activities associated with an active attempt to pursue the object are unrewarding, and when efforts to avoid an object known to produce discomfort are unsuccessful.

The other primary affect of depression is first experienced somewhere between the ages of 3 and 6 years and evolves as the child more and more is obliged to accept the reality that he cannot have or achieve what he desires because of his own inadequacies of physical size, family role, intellectual understanding, etc. This development revolves around the infantile oedipal conflict and involves the shattering of the fantasy of being all-powerful, all-giving, and an all-satisfying object for the opposite-sex parent. This follows the infantile period Erikson called the crisis of the will to the autonomous versus doubt and shame. Thus, as the child perceives his goals and interests as unachievable, he may become inactive and withdrawn, and with the experience of the somatic manifestations of conservation-withdrawal he will have his first awareness of the feelings of *hopelessness*. The feeling of hopelessness is defined as an inability to achieve a desired gratification that is perceived as being directly and solely related to the individual's own inadequacies. The period of latency is usually ushered in by what appears to be the child's rather sudden loss of interest in achieving gratification through a close parental relationship. The exclusive need for the parents as external objects is replaced by identifications that permit the focusing of attention on the internalized representations of objects which become part of the self [13]. Various defensive and adaptive mechanisms help to block out the feelings of defeat and facilitate the intellectual and physical growth that takes place during this period [31].

Any requirement to return to an almost complete dependence on parental objects may place the child in the position of reexperiencing feelings of helplessness when he is unable to achieve gratification or to avoid extremes of discomfort. As the child is able to achieve partial gratification through his own intellectual and physical achievements, he may then postpone the reexperiencing of hopelessness until adolescence, when the desire for the parental type object relationship again becomes evident. The hopelessness experienced in adolescence with the inability to achieve the desired reawakened love relationship can be worked through if the individual can tolerate the feelings of hopelessness and gradually give up the single-minded desire for a particular object and select alternate or substitute objects available for relating. Indeed, such a change in goals is essential for achieving a sense of self and reality. This break with the past, which comes gradually over a period of several years and involves the sexual identity formation and the turning from the self to heterosexual love objects, is greatly compressed in this overview presentation. Needless to say, the type of intrapsychic self and object representations and the specific experiences with parental and peer objects during this period may facilitate or inhibit the giving up of old objects and goals. Painful though it is, this must occur in order to go from the world of childhood privileges and to the prerogatives of adulthood [4]. The characteristic psychological mechanism utilized and acquired for tolerating object loss and self-defeat become a part of the personality.

These affects of depression, helplessness and hopelessness, and their signal functions, which help to anticipate the danger of specific traumas once experienced, are available to defend the individual against the complete reexperiencing of the earliest forms of deprivation and defeat, which include the conservation-withdrawal process. The perception of these signals helps to defend the individual against the conscious idea of possible deprivation or failure. However, if the defense mechanisms employed or the actions taken are ineffective, feelings of helplessness or hopelessness reoccur. Such experiences of losing gratification provided by others' or by one's own efforts occur repeatedly during life as a part of the process of growing up, relating, and aging. As stated elsewhere [30], there are a number of regularly occurring milestones in life that require shifts in one's expectations of others and his goals for himself. These include leaving home for school, graduation from school, going into military service, undertaking a career, getting married, becoming pregnant, having a child, buying a home, cessation of menstrual functioning, beginning retirement, losing a parent, sibling, or spouse, and others. Even though many of these events can be anticipated, and their immediate impact is lessened when they can be anticipated, they nevertheless require a period of taking leave or letting go, which involves grieving, and which we have come to call "giving up." Such a process has to take place before new goals and new relationships are undertaken; the total complex is designated "giving up–given up."

GIVING UP–GIVEN UP COMPLEX

The giving up–given up complex refers to the combination of psychic processes specifically associated with the affects of helplessness and hopelessness [32]. These include a loss of ego autonomy or capacity to cope psychologically; a feeling of disruption in all of one's object relationships; and a loss of motivation to pursue a relationship or a goal, commonly with the idea that things are never going to change and thus there is no reason to make any effort to try to make things different. In addition there are memories of past occasions when similar reactions were experienced. Indeed, the feelings associated with recollection of such symbolically similar and significant experiences reinforce and even prolong current feelings of helplessness or hopelessness. These all characterize the *giving up* phase of the complex.

Once the individual can recognize the feelings of giving up, can begin to understand what is responsible for them, and can tolerate the idea of having to find substitutes and replacements, the *given up* phase of the complex will begin. The given up portion is the resolution phase. Here there is finally an acknowledgment that the preexisting conditions, including the old gratifications and goals, are no longer attainable and that new ideas, approaches, and relationships must be found [30].

The feelings characterizing the giving up phase, helplessness and hopelessness, commonly are experienced and reported as depression, and the individual typically struggles to remain active while at the same time becoming more inactive and disengaged. Thus feelings of giving up wax and wane as prospects for help or resolution rise, only to dissipate again. It is during this phase that the individual's predisposition for somatic malfunctioning and vulnerability to external pathogens appear to be greatly increased, as reflected in the high incidence of illness onset under such conditions. In a series of studies with hospitalized medical [27] and psychiatric [1] patients, we reported that the first symptoms of disease occurred for 80 percent of such patients in a psychosocial setting in which feelings of helplessness or hopelessness were reported or were interpreted as having been experienced. These findings, expressed in terms of life crisis units or inability to cope, have been confirmed by a number of other investigators [19, 20, 21, 23].

When the giving up–given up complex is evoked by the loss of a highly valued object or the failure to achieve a self-set goal, the working through involves the grieving process and the work of mourning. It has long been part of folklore that people are more prone to fall ill during periods of grieving. We have identified phases in which feelings of helplessness or hopelessness were associated with the clinical onset of disease in 10 of 14 women whose husbands had cancer, who were studied from three months before the death of the spouse to a year and one month after the loss [29]. Others have reported increased morbidity and mortality after the death of a spouse [25]. Thus, such a period of vulnerability associated with giving up provides an openness for change both psychologically and somatically that in some instances contributes to somatic or psychological breakdown and illness and in others facilitates progression to a new level of functioning that is more appropriate to the new reality. This is a commonplace sequence in everyday life—infrequent, fleeting, and mild in some; frequent, prolonged, and pronounced in others. The former more readily move on to new objects, goals, and developmental levels and for the most part remain well; the latter increasingly contribute to the pool of those distressed, disturbed, or disabled with somatic and psychiatric illness, including the clinical syndromes of depression.

DEPRESSIVE CHARACTER STYLES

As a result of genic, constitutional, and early relationship experiences, some individuals may be extremely sensitive to what they assume is the ever-present possibility of reexperiencing loss or failure and the associated affects of helplessness or hopelessness. Thus, they may develop character styles that attempt to defend against the repeated reexperiencing of such feelings. Those who have difficulty in placing trust or confidence in their environmental objects and consequently reexperience feelings of helplessness may develop a dependent, clinging type of demanding relationship with a few key objects. Such individuals remain or become attached to parental type objects who are willing to give without demanding much in return. Such was the case with Monica. Over the first 14 years of her life she went from an active disengaging response to deprivation, marked by blatant feelings of helplessness during infancy and early childhood, to active control over her object world by means of an attractive facade of helplessness and hopelessness (pseudohelplessness and pseudohopelessness) which rallied her family, her rural community, and her school around her [9]. Ultimately, at age 19 she married a very stable, reliable, hard-working man, the oldest of several siblings, orphaned at 12 years of age, who was strongly motivated to care for his younger siblings and who transferred this highly developed caretaking mode to Monica. Under these conditions she successfully moved from the parental home without experiencing depression, though she did become transiently depressed, with self-depreciation and recrimination, when she failed in her goal to become pregnant before her younger sisters [9].

Individuals who are defending themselves against the repeated reexperiencing of feelings of hopelessness constantly try to provide all the things they would like and feel they need for themselves by providing these things for others, often to the exclusion or fulfillment of their own realistic needs. Their goals are unrealistically high and unreachable, which forces them to be constantly at work trying to do more and better. They never have the satisfaction of a job well done because no job or accomplishment is enough. These individuals are frequently referred to as masochistic, obsessive, and pseudoindependent. These are selfless individuals who often devote themselves to family and community causes.

THE CLINICAL SYNDROMES OF DEPRESSION

Psychologically, the syndromes of depression have frequently been classified into two varieties, neurotic and psychotic, exogenous and endogenous, or, more recently, unipolar and bipolar. From our own clinical experience and treatment of individuals with the clinical depressive states, we think we can identify two specific types of clinical depression that fit with the ways in which adult individuals develop a neurosis to defend themselves against the reexperiencing of the somatic conservation-withdrawal reaction and its associated affective reactions. These two forms of depression utilize a neurotic symptom formation to protect the individual against feelings of either helplessness or hopelessness. We see these forms of neurosis as not unlike that of the individual who cannot tolerate feelings of anxiety in relationship to conflict and who defends against the feelings of anxiety by the formation of a phobic reaction. These forms of neurosis, with case examples, are presented elsewhere [31].

"NEED TO PROVE NEGLECT" DEPRESSION

A type of depression related to what others have described as exogenous, reactive, or unipolar occurs in individuals who have attempted to avoid the reawakening of memories of the disruptions caused by the absence of mothering type gratification when they are unable to avoid the conscious realization that they are about to lose an object to whom they have a dependent attachment. With this comes a threatened reawakening of the memory of the unresolved loss of the mothering object. Here, as with all neurotic symptom formation, a splitting occurs—two contrary and independent ideas are fantasied. On the one hand objects are deemed available for such desired mothering gratification, but on the other hand such objects are seen as unwilling, rather than unable, to provide the desired gratification. When the first of these ideas is prominent, there is a oneness with the external world that, in its most intense form, can be identified as a form of mania, an unrealistic feeling of being loved, cared for, blissful. When the second idea takes precedence, the individual fantasies that external objects and the world are against him, that they do not care for or love him. These ideas may reach psychotic proportions and may even take on some qualities of a paranoid reaction.

Some individuals have recourse to a neurotic compromise to the two ideas. They utilize a "need to prove neglect" as a means of actively trying to undo the passively experienced infantile events of abandonment. Such persons are constantly trying to get what they want with no regard for the needs or interests of the object. When their demands are rejected, the rejection is taken as a confirmation of their belief that they are neglected, and they are then able to derive some gratification from knowing they have correctly predicted what was going to happen even though the outcome is not what they originally wanted and needed. Thus, they succeed in proving to themselves that they are unloved and unwanted. When environmental objects are not available, such individuals may retreat to more primitive forms of self-administered immediate gratification, such as the excessive intake of food, alcohol, drugs, etc. Should the neurotic mechanism of the "need to prove neglect" become ineffective in protecting the individual in his relationship to his environment, the feelings of helplessness as well as the underlying biological conservation-withdrawal reaction may break through. Thus, to the picture of the symptom compromise may be added a number of adaptive and defensive adjustments, resulting in a mixed picture of somatic inactivity and disengagement, with transient bursts of excessive misuse of external sources of nutriment (e.g., drugs) and clinging behaviors or impulsive delinquent or other antisocial behavior.

It is interesting to note that such individuals rarely if ever express any guilt or shame. Recovery involves many phases of acting out, both in and out of therapy, during which the individual comes to develop a relationship of trust and confidence with the therapist. With successful treatment he gradually develops a sense of separate identity after a prolonged period of utilizing the therapist and the therapist's ego as a surrogate ego [5]. Such therapy is usually extended over many years, with numerous interruptions and discontinuations as a result of the patient having to break off treatment whenever experiences of helplessness occur and are too threatening for him to tolerate for more than a brief period. Thus, the major effort in therapy is to get the individual to recognize situations in which feelings of helplessness can be anticipated and then to help him to tolerate such feelings while learning how to find ways in which they may be overcome through meaningful accomplishments and relationships with others.

"NEED TO PROVE SELF-NEGLECT" DEPRESSION

A form of depression close to what is usually called endogenous or bipolar (manic-depressive) depression occurs in individuals who have repressed unresolved and unfulfilled desires for the oedipal love object and thus are vulnerable to the loss or forced realization that they have failed to achieve a highly desired goal. Associated with the current failure is a recurrence of the feelings of hopelessness and a vague awareness of the underlying unresolved infantile conflict. In order to prevent the full reexperiencing of the earlier conflict, a symptom compromise may ensue. It is in such a setting that a depressive neurosis called "need to prove self-neglect" has its origins. Again, a disavowal of the painful reality results in the "splitting of the ego." There are two contrary fantasied ideas that come into the individual's mind. First, he thinks he has the capacity to satisfy everyone, including himself, and second, he thinks of himself as shameful because of not accomplishing such satisfaction for others, a failure he attributes to his unwillingness rather than his inability to fulfill such goals. If the first idea becomes predominant, there is an acceleration of thoughts and desire for action that may reach proportions of mania. When the individual feels himself unwilling to make the effort to accomplish what he considers important, he considers himself subject to punishment for his bad performance. Such punishment may take the form of self-destructive behavior, including suicide. Such persons, therefore, go to great lengths to prove to themselves and others that they are neglectful and despicable and that they deserve to be ostracized and done away with. When the compromise symptom is unable to protect the individual from the feelings of hopelessness, the biological attributes of the conservation-withdrawal process will become evident as part of the picture described as the "need to prove self-neglect" depression.

The therapeutic task in this type of depression involves helping the patient to reexperience the feelings of inadequacy and hopelessness repeatedly with an increasing awareness of the early determinants of the associated unresolved fantasies that occurred in association with these feelings. To recognize these feelings of hopelessness through a transference relationship and to be able to tolerate such feelings when they are experienced in the therapeutic setting will finally lead to new attitudes, ideas, and feelings of worthiness. Zetzel [37] has described the details of the therapeutic task for significantly depressed individuals.

SUMMARY

Depression can take many forms and one must understand which form he is observing to make the appropriate intervention. Utilizing a developmental model, we can see the feelings of depression as having their biological antecedent in the adaptive feedback mechanisms that we have come to call conservation-withdrawal. These mechanisms act as a counterpart to the biological arousal processes that may be associated in their more intense forms with the affect of anxiety. Some of the biochemical and genetic factors that are postulated to be important in some forms of depression may augment or facilitate the experiences of some individuals so that they are unable to tolerate feelings of helplessness or hopelessness and the conflicts associated with their feelings. Such individuals are those most predisposed to developing depressive character styles or, at a later time in life, a depressive neurosis. Those who have genetic predispositions and associated neural transmission abnormalities may in fact have the greatest difficulty in achieving trusting relationships and realistic self-goals because of the early failure of such biological mechanisms during the periods of giving up that regularly occur in the course of growing up. Such individuals may therefore, later in life, run the greatest risk of developing one of the two neurotic syndromes of depression with their associated symptom complexes.

REFERENCES

1. Adamson, J. D., and Schmale, A. H.   Object loss, giving up and the onset of psychiatric disease. *Psychosom. Med.* 27:557, 1965.
2. Akiskal, H. S., and McKinney, W. T.   Depressive disorders: Toward a unified hypothesis. *Science* 182:20, 1973.
3. Bibring, E.   The Mechanism of Depression. In P. Greenacre (Ed.), *Affective Disorders: Psychoanalytic Contributions to Their Study.* New York: International Universities Press, 1953.
4. Blos, P.   On Adolescence: A Psychoanalytic Interpretation. New York: Free Press of Glencoe, 1962.
5. Engel, G. L.   The Surrogate Ego Role of the Physician in the Management of Physically Sick Patients. Paper presented at the midwinter meeting of the American Psychoanalytic Association, December 1951.

6. Engel, G. L. Anxiety and depression withdrawal: The primary affects of unpleasure. *Int. J. Psychoanal.* 113:89, 1962.
7. Engel, G. L. Ego development following severe trauma in infancy: A 14-year study of a girl with gastric fistula and depression in infancy. *Bull. Assoc. Psychoanal. Med.* 6:57, 1967.
8. Engel, G. L., and Reichsman, F. Spontaneous and experimentally induced depressions in an infant with a gastric fistula. *J. Am. Psychoanal. Assoc.* 4:428, 1956.
9. Engel, G. L., et al. Unpublished data, 1973.
10. Engel, G. L., Reichsman, F., and Segal, H. A study of an infant with a gastric fistula. I. Behavior and the rate of total hydrochloric acid secretion. *Psychosom. Med.* 18:374, 1956.
11. Engel, G. L., and Schmale, A. H. Conservation-Withdrawal: A Primary Regulatory Process for Organismic Homeostasis. In R. Porter and J. Knight (Eds.), *Physiology, Emotion and Psychosomatic Illness*, Ciba Foundation Symposium 8 (N.S.). Amsterdam: Elsevier-Excerpta Medica, 1972.
12. Erikson, E. H. *Identity: Youth and Crises.* New York: Norton, 1968. P. 91.
13. Freud, S. The Dissolution of the Oedipus Complex (1924). In *The Standard Edition of the Complete Psychological Works of Sigmund Freud*, transl. and ed. by J. Strachey with others. London: Hogarth and Institute of Psycho-Analysis, 1961. Vol. 19, p. 173.
14. Fries, M. E., and Woolf, P. J. Some hypotheses on the role of the congenital activity type in personality development. *Psychoanal. Study Child* 8:48, 1953.
15. Gellhorn, E. The neurophysiological basis of anxiety: A hypothesis. *Perspect. Biol. Med.* 8:488, 1965.
16. Gellhorn, E. *Principles of Autonomic-Somatic Integrations.* Minneapolis: University of Minnesota Press, 1967. Pp. 173, 182.
17. Greenacre, P. Toward an understanding of the physical nucleus of some defense reactions. In *Emotional Growth*, vol. 1. New York: International Universities Press, 1971. P. 132.
18. Hess, W. P. *The Functional Organization of the Diencephalon.* New York: Grune and Stratton, 1957.
19. Hinkle, L. E., and Wolff, H. G. The nature of man's adaptation to his total environment and the relation of this to illness. *Arch. Intern. Med.* 99:442, 1957.
20. Holmes, T. H., and Rahe, R. H. The Social Readjustment Rating Scale. *J. Psychosom. Res.* 11:213, 1968.
21. Jacobs, M. A., Spilken, A., and Norman, M. Relationship of life change, maladaptive aggression and upper respiratory infection in male college students. *Psychosom. Med.* 31:31, 1969.
22. Luce, G. G. *Biological Rhythms in Psychiatry and Medicine*, Public Health Publication No. 2088. Washington, D.C.: U.S. Government Printing Office, 1970.
23. Parens, H., McConville, B. J., and Kaplan, S. M. The prediction of frequency of illness from the responses to separation. *Psychosom. Med.* 28:162, 1966.
24. Peiper, A. *Cerebral Function in Infancy and Childhood.* New York: Plenum Pub., 1964.

25. Rees, W. D., and Lutkins, S. G.   Mortality of bereavement. *Br. Med. J.* 4:13, 1967.
26. Reite, M., Kaufman, I. C., Pauly, J. D., and Stynes, A. J.   Depression in infant monkeys; physiological correlates. *Science*, in press.
27. Schmale, A. H.   Relationship of separation and depression to disease. *Psychosom. Med.* 20:259, 1958.
28. Schmale, A. H.   Importance of life setting for disease onset. *Mod. Treat.* 6:643, 1969.
29. Schmale, A. H.   Psychic trauma during bereavement. *Int. Psychiatry Clin.* 8:147, 1971.
30. Schmale, A. H.   Giving up as a final common pathway to changes in health. *Adv. Psychosom. Med.* 8:20, 1972.
31. Schmale, A. H.   Depression as affect, character style and symptom formation. In R. Holt and E. Peterfreund (Eds.), *Psychoanalysis and Contemporary Science*, vol. 1. New York: Macmillan, 1972. P. 327.
32. Schmale, A. H., and Engel, G. L.   The giving up–given up complex illustrated on film. *Arch. Gen. Psychiatr.* 17:135, 1967.
33. Schneirla, T. C.   Aspects of stimulation and organization in approach/withdrawal processes underlying vertebrate behavioral development. In R. Hinde and E. Shaw (Eds.) *Advances and the Study of Behavior.* New York: Academic Press, 1965. P. 2.
34. Schur, M.   A principle of evolutionary biology for psychoanalysis. *J. Am. Psychoanal.* 18:442, 1970.
35. Spitz, R. A.   Anaclitic depression. An inquiry into the genesis of psychiatric conditions in early childhood. *Psychoanal. Study Child* 2:313, 1946.
36. Spitz, R. A.   Some early prototypes of ego defenses. *J. Amer. Psychoanal. Assoc.* 9:626, 1961.
37. Zetzel, E.   The predisposition to depression. *Can. Psychiatr. Assoc. J.*, 11 (special supplement):S236, 1966.

10

Manic-Depressive Illness as an Actual Neurosis

EDWARD A. WOLPERT

Bellak, writing in 1952, stated that "if a definition is a 'delimitation of the species or kind of thing named, by specifying the genus which includes it and the specific difference or distinguishing property, of the species,' a definition of manic depressive psychosis is an achievement yet to be attained" [8, p. 16]. While such a statement was valid 20 years ago, today we have data from varying vantage points that allow us to define the illness more specifically and more rationally than was possible earlier.

It is the purpose of this chapter to present the hypothesis that manic-depressive illness represents an actual neurosis, that it is basically a physiological illness with psychological consequences. The symptomatology of the illness is a manifestation in the psychological sphere of physiological phenomena. Precipitants of the untreated illness may be either exogenous, in that an external loss is noted, or endogenous, representing a spontaneous physiological change in the *milieu interior*. When the underlying physicochemical abnormality is treated, the person may no longer be subject to wide mood swings despite experiencing psychologically significant losses if his psychological development is otherwise adequate. In some cases in which psychological development was not adequate, treating the physicochemical abnormality is not enough and psychological treatment is also necessary.

We are presenting an hypothesis foreshadowed by Freud, Fenichel, Jacobson, and Freeman in particular, but it applies only to patients who evidence both a manic and a depressive phase to their illness. It is our contention that patients with recurring depressions, melancholias without hypomanic sequelae, and neurotic or psychotic depressive reactions are basically different from manic-depressive patients. The diagnosis of manic-depressive illness will be reserved for those patients who display a bipolar phasic illness in which one phase contains some or all of the cardinal symptoms of mania: exaggerated self-esteem, self-confidence, and well-being; grandiose conceptions of their physical, mental, and moral powers; exaggerated motor activity in every sphere; exaggerated libidinal activities and desires; fragmentation of thought processes by intrusions of external stimuli. Secondary symptoms that sometimes occur include delusional and magical thinking, identification with others, and paranoid thought processes. Patients with episodes of mania usually also demonstrate periods of depression, but not all patients with severe depression show even mild states of hypomania.

BACKGROUND OF THE HYPOTHESIS

Psychological Considerations

In the first two decades of this century Kraepelin [39, 40] described in detail a number of syndromes differing in surface symptomatology and in clinical course but appearing identical in certain fundamental features, in mutual replaceability, and in favorable prognosis. To these syndromes, including simple mania, most cases of melancholia, periodic and circular insanities, and mild affective mood swings, he gave the name manic-depressive illness. Abraham [1], who in 1911 gave us our first understanding of the psychology of melancholia, accepted the Kraepelin nosology. From his clinical work Abraham felt that in the depressive phase of the manic-depressive illness the patient is weighed down by his complexes. When repression fails in the manic phase, he is indifferent to his complexes and is, as it were, swept off his feet by the upsurge of the no longer repressed instinct. Of critical importance to our present understanding is the fact that Abraham came to this conceptualization by studying "light manic depressive patients" and patients with rapidly recurring states of depression or unitary melancholias as if dynamically they were identical.

Freud [26] by 1915 was not so sure. "Melancholia," he wrote, "whose definition fluctuates even in descriptive psychiatry, takes on various clinical forms the grouping together of which into a single unity does not seem to be established with certainty; and some of these forms suggest somatic rather than psychogenic affections" [p. 243]. Again:

The most remarkable characteristic of melancholia, and the one in need most of explanation, is the tendency to change round into mania—a state which is the opposite of it in its symptoms. As we know this does not happen to every melancholic, some cases run their course in periodic relapses, during the intervals between which signs of mania may be entirely absent or only very slight. Others show the regular alternation of melancholic and manic phases which has led to the hypothesis of a circular insanity" [p. 253].

Nevertheless, Freud explained melancholia as a response to the loss of the love object, with attendant impoverishment of the ego, and mania as the resolution of the loss of the object, with an attendant release of previously bound energy.

In 1921 Freud [28] elaborated on the mechanism involved in mania, describing a psychogenic and a spontaneous type of cyclical illness. In the psychogenic type the loss of an object precipitates a melancholia in which the object is set up inside the ego by identification and is condemned by the ego-ideal; if the ego and ego-ideal fuse because of rebellion of the ego, then a mania supervenes. In the spontaneous type of cyclical illness, on the other hand, "external precipitating causes do not seem to play a decisive part; as regards internal motives, nothing more or nothing less is to be found in these patients than in all others. It has consequently become the custom to consider these cases as not being psychogenic" [p. 132]. Freud speculates on the origin of these spontaneous oscillations of mood. He is attracted to the hypothesis that the ego reacts in an automatic way with a change in mood if the ego-ideal is too strict. He had no evidence to support this hypothesis and stated that these oscillations of mood may be due to other causes.

By 1923 Freud [29] elaborated his most far-reaching view of manic-depressive illness, stating that in melancholia "the excessively strong superego which has obtained a hold upon consciousness rages against the ego with merciless violence. . . . What is now holding sway in the superego is, as it were, a pure culture of the death instinct, and in fact it often succeeds in driving the ego into death, if the latter does not fend off its tyrant in time by the change round into mania" [p. 53].

Abraham [2] accepted Freud's emendation to his previous work and in 1924 listed five etiological factors, which all together were necessary to cause the occurrence of a melancholic depression: (1) A constitutional accentuation of oral erotism; (2) a special fixation of the libido at the oral level (these were considered necessary, predisposing factors for the development of the illness); (3) a severe injury to infantile narcissism; (4) occurrence of the injury before oedipal wishes were overcome; and (5) a repetition of primary disappointments later in life. In addition Abraham tentatively explains manias that arise without antecedent depression. "In 'pure' mania, which is frequently of periodic occurrence, the patient seems to me to be shaking off that primal parathymia [a feeling of hopelessness the child has when his oedipal wishes are thwarted] without having any attack of melancholia [in the present] in the clinical sense" [p. 124].

Thus by 1924 psychoanalytic thinking had conceptualized manic-depressive illness as being of two types—spontaneous and psychogenic. In the spontaneous type, a change in psychic structure periodically occurs for unknown reasons; this leads to the same psychological symptoms as are found in the psychogenic type of illness. In the psychogenic type, an object loss is followed by identification with and incorporation of the object into the ego. The superego, reproaching the incorporated object in the ego, is responsible for the generalized impoverishment of the ego manifested in melancholic symptomatology. By unknown mechanisms the ego can dethrone the superego (or fuse with it), and the previously bound energy is released in the typical symptoms of a manic excitement. Constitutional and development factors were postulated that would predispose the individual to develop the illness. Presumably a complimentary series would hold so that in some cases the constitutional, and in other cases the developmental factors would predominate in importance in the genesis of the disease. Hints exist that the spontaneous form of the illness is linked to somatic or physiological factors. Various syndromes fall under the diagnosis manic-depressive illness—circular and periodic bipolar affective swings, recurring depressions, and unitary depressive reactions, among others.

Most later analytic discussions of manic-depressive illness elaborate still further the work of Abraham and Freud without either differentiating bipolar from unipolar illness or following up on Freud's distinction of spontaneous and psychogenic episodes.

Helene Deutsch [14], writing in 1933, stressed the role of denial and felt it underlies all mania: "It is an attempt to resolve an inner conflict, an attempt which should serve, in its complicated fashion, to deny the aggression of the id and thus forestall the harshness of the superego" [p. 212]. In this state the mania represents a "form of activity undertaken by the now unburdened ego in which the potential of the melancholic process, instead of remaining anchored in the inner world is transformed into kinetic energy in the outer world" [p. 213].

Fenichel [16], in his 1945 summary, accepts Freud's and Abraham's conceptualization of manic-depressive illness. It is orally tinged. A loss precipitates a depression in which the superego reproaches the ego and which is reversed in the manic triumph. He traces the manic-depressive cycle back to the cycle of satiety and hunger. Like Freud,

Fenichel notes that some patients demonstrate periodicity in their illness connected to external circumstances while others do not. He implies that although analysis may demonstrate psychogenic factors to be operative, "yet it is impossible to get rid of the impression that additional purely biological factors are involved" [p. 411].

Jacobson [36], in her 1953 discussion of cyclothymic personalities, felt that physiology plays an important factor in the illness: "The assumption that psychosis, in contradistinction to psychoneurosis, represents not only a mental but an unknown psychosomatic process is well founded. . . . True cyclothymics will experience their slowing up quite differently from the way depressive neurotics experience their inhibitions. Cyclothymics seem to be aware that there is a somatic quality to this phenomenon" [pp. 50–51].

Katan [37], also writing in 1953, viewed the manic episode as a restitutional phenomenon—believing the aggression demonstrated to be an attempt to control the external object, not to destroy it—and the mania as an attempt to restore normal relationships. Freeman [19] in 1971 elaborates on Katan's view. In a formal discussion of symptom formation, Freeman considers the reaction to certain danger situations in neurotics, schizophrenics, and manics:

In the neuroses the danger situation is allayed by the formation of symptoms which are also the vehicle for the expression of the repudiated drives. . . . In schizophrenia repression fails entirely and the whole pressure of the drive derivatives becomes an even greater threat to psychic stability. The attempt to deal with this by decathexis of real object representations and a libidinal regression to pathological narcissism still finds the drive derivatives obtaining expression through the products of restitution, the delusions and hallucinations. . . . The reaction in mania is different. In the face of the danger situation . . . there is a regression to the state of the "purified pleasure ego." This narcissistic organization as it occurs in mania has one other accompaniment, namely over-activity. This psychomotor over-activity is the direct outcome of the free expression of the drive derivatives, the ultimate cause of which must be sought for in the sphere of neurochemistry (p. 486).

In 1973 Feinstein and Wolpert [15] presented a case of juvenile manic-depressive illness in which the first symptoms were noted by the mother by age 2 and bipolar mood swings were clearly observable by age 5½. Under close observation, lithium carbonate therapy quickly relieved a manic episode that psychotherapy had not affected. At that time we presented the hypothesis that

the affective systems of patients with manic depressive illness may have a basic vulnerability which, when overstimulated, begins a discharge pattern which does not easily lend itself to autonomous emotional control. . . .

Some biochemical variation, possibly on a genetic basis, leaves the affective system with a specific vulnerability to affective stress. The occurrence of a depressive reaction to some loss experience may trigger off an affective crisis [p. 134].

This hypothesis, with its obvious question of energy systems—psychological or physiological—leads us to a consideration of what Freud called the "actual" neuroses.

Physiological Considerations

The concept of the actual neurosis has an interesting history. In 1896 Freud [20] differentiated between simple neuroses (the direct effects of sexual noxae) and the neuro-psychoses of defense (the consequences of memory traces of the sexual noxae). In 1898 he used the term "actual neuroses" for the first time. The actual neuroses were considered to be the result of current sexual noxae while the psychoneuroses were considered to be the mental consequences of past sexual noxae [21].

In a 1910 paper on visual disturbance Freud [22] stated:

Psychoanalysts never forget that the mental is based on the organic, although their work can only carry them as far as this basis and not beyond it. . . . Generally speaking, the neurotic disturbances of vision stand in the same relation to the psychogenic ones as the actual neuroses do to psychoneuroses. Psychogenic visual disturbances can no doubt hardly ever appear without neurotic ones, but the latter can appear without the former. These neurotic symptoms are unfortunately little appreciated and understood even today; for they are not directly accessible to psychoanalysis and other methods of research have left the standpoint of sexuality out of account [pp. 217-218].

In the same year Freud [23] listed neurasthenia and pure anxiety neurosis as two examples of actual neuroses.

In 1912 Freud [24] added hypochondria to his list of the actual neuroses and pointed out that at the center of each psychoneurotic symptom was a "small fragment of undischarged excitation connected with coitus which emerges as an anxiety symptom or provides the nucleus for the formation of hysteroid symptoms" [p. 248]. Thus the actual neuroses take on a physiological cast—the "sexual noxae" of the 1890s became the "undischarged excitation of coitus" by 1912. In 1914 Freud [25] related each of the actual neuroses to a psychological illness—hypochondria is related to paraphrenia (schizophrenia) as neurasthenia is to obsessive neurosis as anxiety neurosis is to hysteria. Each psychological illness has at its core a physiological state that achieves psychological representation as a symptom.

In 1917 Freud [27] discussed the actual neuroses in the most complete exposition he was ever to give. The actual neurotic symptoms have no psychical meaning but "are also themselves entirely somatic processes" [p. 387]. Further, the actual neuroses, "in details of their symptoms and also in their characteristic of influencing every organ system and every function exhibit an unmistakable resemblance to the pathological states which arise from the chronic influence of external toxic substances and from a sudden withdrawal of them—to intoxications and conditions of abstinence. . . ." But what these toxins might be, "the vehicle of all the stimulant effects of the libido" we do not know. "The theoretical structure of psychoanalysis that we have created is in truth a super structure, which will one day have to be set upon its organic foundation. But we are still ignorant of this" [pp. 388–389].

Thus Freud conceptualizes the actual neuroses as illnesses of a physiological nature caused by toxin-like substances released by a damming up of excitation or the sudden withdrawal of such damming up. After the creation of the tripartite structural theory and the signal anxiety theory, Freud [30] stated in 1925 that he continued to maintain his original view of the actual neuroses despite the changes in details the new theories would necessitate. In 1926 Freud [31] described the psychoneuroses as being caused by a psychical danger in the id activating the ego's danger signal and the actual neuroses as caused by a somatic danger in the id causing an automatic reaction.

Fenichel [16] discusses the actual neuroses under the subtitle "Actual neuroses: Symptoms of unspecific inhibitions," pointing out that "any defensive mechanism using a countercathexis necessarily creates a certain impoverishment of the personality" [p. 185]. Some of the symptoms noted are inhibitions, a direct and automatic experience of the state of being dammed up; other symptoms represent floods of uncontrolled excitement and involuntary emergency discharge.

Thus the actual neuroses present symptoms appearing in the psychic sphere caused by either a lack of or an excess of physiological factors leading to symptoms of poverty or overabundance of psychological functioning. The symptoms in such an illness do not have a primary psychogenic meaning, since they are the result of inhibitions or excess of discharge. While it is true that the symptoms may secondarily become invested with a psychogenic meaning, such investment is usually quite rare.

Manic-depressive illness may thus be added to the list of actual neuroses. It is an illness characterized by periodic excesses and retardations in function in the psychic sphere as a consequence of physiological changes in the nervous system. As such it is a bipolar process and must be differentiated from unipolar processes. Manic symptomatology results when the psyche is acted upon by a sudden burst of increased physiological energy; depressive symptomatology results when there is a decrease in physiological energy available. The content of the illness, oral in nature, as so well described by Abraham and all who followed him, depends on the relation of the overabundance of or lack of physiological energy to the psychological process. (See Benedek [9], who feels that the origin of the depressive constellation lies in the psychophysiological state of nursing.)

In the spontaneous cyclic episode described by Freud, the cycles of behavior depend on a basic fault in the physiological affective system being triggered off internally, while in the psychogenic type they depend on external loss reactions triggering off the same mechanism. If biochemical treatment can be devised, the internally triggered attacks cease to exist, but the externally triggered attacks must be handled by a different mode of treatment. This is exactly what has occurred with the use of lithium carbonate in the treatment of manic-depressive illness: the chemical treatment aborts the spontaneous episodes, and psychotherapy teaches the patient to handle losses in a way that sidesteps the fault in the physiological affective system. Some manic patients are treated successfully with lithium carbonate alone; others need psychotherapeutic intervention as well.

Other depressive symptomatology included by Freud and Abraham as manic-depressive illness but not demonstrating manic episodes would not be dependent on internal triggering of the basic fault in the physiological affective system; hence they belong to nosological categories other than manic-depressive illness.

EVIDENCE

What evidence can be brought to support this conceptualization? At best the hypothesis is able to embrace a variety of data and to make a coherent story out of interesting but disparate facts. By no means can it be said to be proven. The evidence to be discussed includes electroencephalographic (EEG) findings, the phenomena of prodromal symptoms, the results of treatment with lithium, genetic studies, and the norepinephrine or catecholamine theory of transmission of the nerve impulse. Objections to the theory to be discussed include the work of those who view the illness as an interpersonal illness rather than as an intrapsychic or physiological illness and the uncertainty of the biochemical theories themselves.

EEG Findings

Bellak [8], in his 1952 review of the literature, reports contradictory findings concerning the clinical daytime EEG in manic-depressive patients. While Davis and Davis [13] found the clinical EEG of manic-depressive patients, both manic and depressed, to be little changed from the normal, Greenblatt et al. observed the pattern to be very different in both manic and depressed groups as compared to normals. In more recent work Platman and Fieve [48] found no difference in the number of abnormal EEG patterns recorded in manic, depressive, or normal episodes from manic-depressive patients during working states.

The usual clinical EEG recording includes not only a waking record but also a record taken during drug-induced sleep. In such a record abnormalities of wave form, not pattern abnormalities, are reported. If, on the other hand, one continuously records sleeping human subjects, one observes throughout the night a regular cyclic replacement of one EEG pattern by another. This pattern replacement is relatively constant for a normal subject over time under resting conditions, but it will not be observed unless continuous recording is done throughout the night. Because of the great significance of the findings in manic-depressive patients when continuous nocturnal EEGs are recorded, the procedure will be described in detail.

The pattern seen in nocturnal EEG recordings consists of the following four stages, which replace each other over the night:

Stage 1. Modified alpha, preceded by sawtooth waves in occipital leads, in which the sleeping alpha is typically 2 to 3 cycles per second lower than waking alpha, superimposed on a low-voltage, fast-activity background (often called REM sleep or D sleep).

Stage 2. Sleep spindles of 12 to 14 cycles per second superimposed on the low-voltage, fast-activity background.

Stage 3. Low-voltage delta activity—3 to 6 cycles per second activity —of less than 50 μv amplitudes with or without sleep spindles.

Stage 4. Delta activity greater than 50 μv in amplitude without sleep spindles.

These patterns replace each other regularly so that over a given night the depth of each successive cycle tends to decrease, the length of the cycle tends to increase, and the time spent in the higher-numbered stage of the cycle tends to decrease. Just before awakening the subject spends most of the time in the lowest-numbered stage of sleep. In studies of various species of mammals it has been found that there is an inverse relationship between metabolic rate and length of the cycle. The ontogeny of the cycle is such that premature infants spend most of their sleeping time, both in terms of percentage of sleep and in absolute terms, in the lowest-numbered stage, and this value decreases through the neonatal period, the infantile period, the childhood and adolescent period, until it rises slightly in young adulthood, to decrease further in older adulthood and the senium.

In the course of studying these cycles of activity, which are relatively constant for a given individual and quite similar from one normal individual to another, it was found that if the subject was awakened during stage 1, dream reports were elicited in 75 to 90 percent of all cases, but that the percentage of dream reports elicited in other stages dropped precipitously as a decreasing logarithm of the time interval between the end of the preceding stage 1 and the awakening of the subject. This seems to indicate that dreaming was a psychological concomitant of the stage 1 pattern. This stage was then subjected to intensive investigation along many parameters. In quantitative studies stage 1 may appear as "D time %" or "REM time %," and the time from sleep onset to the first REM period (alternatively, stage 1 sleep) is called "REM latency" or "D latency." A summary of some of these findings can be found in Fisher [18] and Wolpert [58].

Longitudinal studies by Hartmann [34, 35] of sleep in manic-depressive patients have yielded very interesting differences in the sleep cycle seen in the manic-depressive patient in the manic, the depressed, and the intervening normal state. Significantly, the nocturnal pattern of manic-depressive patients in the depressed phase differs from the pattern of psychotic depressed patients. Because the manic-depressive patients were studied for periods of 10 to 26 months, each could act as his or her own control along various physiological dimensions in each of the three states—manic, depressed, and intervening normal. "Overall, manic periods were found to be characterized by low total sleep, low D-time and D-time % and slightly low stage 4 time. Depressed periods showed normal total sleep time, high D-time and D-time %, low D-latency, and slightly low stage 4. These results differ from those found in other (nosological categories of) depressed patients" [34, p. 328]. Other depressed patients usually "have less total sleep than normal subjects . . . [but] the results on D-time . . . are equivocal" [p. 312]. Hartmann concludes:

depression may be characterized by an increased need for D . . . while mania is characterized by a decreased need for D . . . [and that] on a neurochemical level changes in monoamine, especially norepinephrine, metabolism underlie both the changes in . . . [types of sleep] during the night, and the changes between mania and depression. The fact noted here that when a sudden shift from depression to mania occurs it occurs during the night, is probably related to these monoamine changes [p. 328].

Prodromal Symptom Phenomena

It has often been noted anecdotally that episodes of mania are ushered in by prodromal symptoms that can be said to be pathognomonic of the episode for the given individual. According to Lange [43]:

. . . there are manic depressive patients who become confused and hallucinated for a day, and only on the next day display a well defined mania. Occasionally, during this time, the patients seems to have undergone a rich experience strongly reminiscent of an oneiroid subjective state but fugitive in character. Manifestations such as these take place in sleepless or dreamy nocturnal episodes and they may be repeated on several nights in succession [quoted in Lewin, 45].

Levitan [44] presents two dreams in which a dangerous situation is replaced by a magical solution to the problem accompanied by hilarity. In each case a hypomanic episode resulted. In our study of manic patients [47, 54, 59], we noted several patients who were normothymic or depressed who had dreams in which an external authority (police, government authorities, university authorities) was overwhelmed either by the patient in disguise or by id elements in disguise (barbarians, rioters). A manic episode followed each of these dreams.

Hartmann [34], in his longitudinal study of manic-depressive EEGs observed one patient who was very depressed switch into a manic episode during sleep. After seeing this, he began to collect cases of a switch into mania, and he noted that all such switches occurred during sleep. Unfortunately dreams were not available.

One of our lithium-treated manic-depressive patients [Case 33]* is able to recognize the beginnings of the manic episode by typical prodromal symptoms. The first indication of the mania soon to develop is a typical nocturnal dream experience in which he sees swirling vortices of multicolored lights and experiences equilibratory and somesthetic sensations without any ideational content or story line. If lithium is not increased, he will within a day develop racing thoughts and a high degree of distractability, and his sleep the second night will be much decreased in total length and accompanied by an exaggeration of the previous night's visual dream experience. The second day is a frank manic episode. If lithium is increased after the visual dream of swirling vortices is reported, no episode of mania develops. Similar experi-

---

* Numbered cases refer to patients participating in the Michael Reese Hospital study of lithium carbonate treatment in manic-depressive illness [49, 54, 59].

ences have been reported by many of our manic patients. Now we try to teach manic patients to recognize those prodromal symptoms that signal for them the beginnings of a manic episode so they can abort the episode with increased lithium.

In those patients who have recognizable prodromal symptoms of a manic episode, the prodromal symptoms never occur after a loss experience, whether real or fantasied, but always without observable external loss. The prodromal experience may occur in dreams and may consist of raw sensory experience of any type without dream content or may consist of typical dreams of authority figures or institutions being overwhelmed. Such prodromal experiences may also occur during the day and may consist of typical daydreams or vague feelings of dread, or of strong sensations in any modality.

It does not seem to do violence to the facts to interpret these dream patterns or other prodromal experiences as being the psychological results of physiological changes in the affective structure. Somehow there is a physiological change in which energy becomes hyper-available to the nervous system and is discharged psychologically either by the symbolic representation of an overthrow of a psychological controlling structure or by a pure sensory experience of extreme intensity. Once these phenomena appear, and if they are untreated, the whole train of manic symptomatology appears, and a manic episode supervenes. This, then, is the spontaneous manic episode.

The externally triggered psychogenic manic episode does not, in our experience, show such prodromal symptoms. For example, in Case 1, the initial depression occurred after the patient shook hands with an admired older teacher. She had been having an affair and felt no guilt until, while shaking her mentor's hand at a party, she suddenly was overwhelmed with concern about how he would think of her if he knew of her infidelity. She developed an acute, full-blown retarded depression with suicidal ideation and for a few minutes contemplated jumping out a window. Just as suddenly as she had become acutely depressed, she "realized," in a restitutive movement (according to Katan's formulation), that he would agree with her, and she entered into a period of manic excitement characterized by progressively greater hyperactivity and ultimate hospitalization. During the next nine years of her illness, the first three without lithium treatment, one could see manic episodes triggered either psychogenically, as above, or spontaneously as in the previous cited case. In each psychogenic attack there was a clear loss that could be noted; in the spontaneous attack no loss could be discerned, but prodromal symptoms, consisting of dread and a skin sensation akin to pinpricks, were noted during the day before a frank mania began. After she was on lithium, external losses, real or fantasied, could not initiate a depression or a mania in this patient.

Results of Lithium Treatment

Since its modern introduction into psychiatric treatment by Cade [11] in 1949, lithium has excited in the researcher the hope that not only has a psychiatric illness been conquered on a physiological basis but also that a major breakthrough has been made in understanding the physiological basis of the mind. In 1959 Schou [52] presented the results of ten years' experience with lithium in the treatment of manic-depressive illness, and in 1968 [53] he reviewed the limits of our knowledge of the clinical use of lithium and the biochemical action of the drug. Kline and Kistner [38] in 1969 reviewed the history of the use of lithium. By 1971 Kupfer [41] presented a 424-page collection of 51 published articles related to the clinical application of lithium under the imprimatur of the Medical Examination Publishing Company, Inc., testifying to the importance the examiners of the American Board of Psychiatry and Neurology placed on knowledge of the drug.

In 1970 Gershon [33] reported a composite of 50 studies indicating that lithium was effective in relieving acute manias in 60 to 100 percent of patients treated. The Michael Reese Hospital study of lithium in manic-depressive illness was begun in 1966. Reports of our results were published in 1969 [59] and in 1974 [47] (the first also includes a description of the clinical use of lithium). Our most recent statistics [54] show that of 35 acutely manic patients started on lithium, 29 showed a resolution of the mania within four to seven days after initiation of the therapy, and 6 failed to respond. This 86 percent response of acutely ill patients to lithium is well within the limits noted by Gershon.

While these findings are striking—and would surprise psychiatrists practicing in the first half of the twentieth century, who saw manic episodes last for months on end, unaffected by hydrotherapy, sleep therapy, and rarely by electroshock therapy—the most striking use of lithium is in preventing episodes of the illness from occurring. In 1967 Baastrup and Schou [5] reported the "relapse frequency" and "psychosis rate" before and after the institution of lithium treatment in 88 female manic-depressives. The findings were striking: "Without lithium treatment relapses occurred on the average every eight months, during lithium treatment only every 60 to 85 months. Without lithium treatment the patients spent on the average of 13 weeks a year in a psychotic state, during lithium treatment less than two weeks" [p. 166].

In our own study, closed on July 1, 1972, when the Federal Drug Administration released lithium for general use, 29 patients were given prophylactic lithium for periods ranging from two months to five years nine months. Of these patients, 6 discontinued lithium, 2 because of serious physical side effects and 4 because of the patient's failure to continue treatment. Of the 23 patients who took lithium prophylactically only 3 had to be rehospitalized. Considering that the frequency of psychotic episode (either depressed or manic) had ranged from one every two years to six per year prior to the institution of lithium therapy, our results appear quite good and suggest that whatever the specific mechanism, lithium is operating at a physiological level.

Case 2.   This 41-year-old woman became depressed when the last of her children left home for college. In order to ameliorate the depression she went back to the professional work she had given up just before her first child was born. Feeling she had undertaken too much, she again became depressed and consulted a psychiatrist. The patient presented a relatively benign personal, family, and childhood history. No unusual traumata or earlier depressions could be isolated. Object relations and self-image development appeared within normal limits. There was no obvious past history of gross object loss.

For the next five years the patient underwent psychotherapy in which she was seen two or three times a week in an attempt to uncover the causes of this illness and to support her through difficult times. Although the patient felt better periodically, and frequently terminated treatment unilaterally only to return more depressed, the overall picture was of a progressively downward course. The psychiatrist diagnosed recurring depression and noted that while some recurrences seemed to be triggered by external events, e.g., an argument with her 76-year-old mother, an unpleasant visit by the youngest daughter, a family business reversal, other recurrences seemed independent of the outside world. The progressive deterioration did not seem to be explained by the past history.

In August five years later, following the engagement of her youngest daughter, the patient became even more depressed than usual, sought a consultation, and was hospitalized. At the time of admission she was observed to be a frail but well-groomed woman of slight stature who showed evidence of recent weight loss and who appeared ten years older than her stated age (46). There were no signs of a thought disorder. Speech was slow and halting, and while recent and distant memory were intact, conceptualization seemed overly concrete and difficult to form. There was a constant affect of sadness, but hypochondriasis and somatic delusions were absent. On psychological testing it was noted that she displayed extreme circumstantiality of speech and thinking, occasional tangential rambling, evasion and displacement to the irrelevant, and attempts to simultaneously express and disguise anger. During the two months the patient was hospitalized, supportive psychotherapy led to a marked decrease in the depth of the depression. As the depression diminished, migraine, absent for the past five years, returned. The patient was discharged in October of the same year, diagnosed as depressive reaction.

Following discharge from the hospital the patient was unreliable in psychotherapy. Business and pleasure trips interfered with continuous treatment, and the woman again became depressed and was rehospitalized about two weeks later. Once in the hospital the patient became hypomanic, with grandiosity, flight of ideas, and pressure of speech, and the true nature of her illness was recognized. She refused to participate in the lithium research then being carried out under an FDA-approved research protocol. In early December, with her husband's consent, she signed out of the hospital against medical advice.

The woman was not seen again until late March the following year. In the interval, she took an overdose of Cafergot in New Mexico in February and was hospitalized medically in Santa Fe for seven days. Psychiatric consultation was refused at that time.

Early in April, after a week of urging, the patient again agreed to a psychiatric hospitalization. At the time of admission the patient appeared cachectic and disheveled. Her speech was markedly slowed, sentence formation was absent, and the intake of foods and fluids was low. No thought disorder could be demonstrated directly or by inference. The impression was of marked deterioration since the previous hospitalization. Lifesaving supportive measures were instituted. Seventeen electroshock treatments were given, and the depression was clinically relieved. Following the electroshock treatment lithium carbonate was started (300 mgm twice a day); blood levels ranged between 0.6 and 0.8 mEq per liter. The patient was discharged improved in mid-June of the same year.

In the six years following discharge the patient has been maintained on lithium carbonate (300 mgm twice a day); the frequency of her psychotherapy sessions has decreased from twice a week to once a month. She has been taught to recognize her unique prodromal symptoms of depression ("sinus" aches above the eyes, "migraine" headaches) and to increase her lithium from two capsules a day to three capsules a day if she feels either a decrease or an increase of "psychological energy." Interpretive work of an uncovering nature has not been done.

Under this regimen the patient has not needed hospitalization nor has she had either a clinical depression or a clinical hypomanic episode. She has successfully returned to the professional work she did earlier in her life and has been able to surmount difficulties in her life that earlier would certainly have caused a depression—the marriage and divorce of both her daughters, the discovery of Hodgkin's disease in her oldest daughter (who herself is the mother of twins aged 3), the failing health of her father with several CVAs, and other, less significant events.

In summary, this patient appears to have been psychologically a relatively sound person in her first four decades and for unknown reasons expressed her manic-depressive potential at age 41. The illness was not recognized at first—what in retrospect appear to have been hypomanic episodes were misinterpreted at the time as remissions of the depression. As the illness got progressively worse, increasingly severe measures had to be taken until, at one point, just before ECT was given and lithium was started, the possibility of a fatal outcome was present. With the patient on lithium, the illness quickly came under control. Psychotherapy sessions became brief, more like those an internist would have with a diabetic than the psychotherapy sessions of a psychiatrist with a patient. Having learned how to use lithium, the patient could control her disease and has been able to meet the vicissitudes of her life with greater resilience than would have been predicted from her course prior to lithium.

Not all studies show such favorable results [55], and the statistical approaches to the problem have been questioned severely [10] and defended equally strongly [6, 7], leading some investigators [17] to take the position that a methodological impasse has been reached in evaluating these data. Newer double-blind studies [56] confirm the utility of lithium prophylaxis. Today it would almost be considered negligence if a manic-depressive patient were not evaluated for and offered lithium treatment when no medical contraindication was present.

Studies of the Effect of Lithium on the Manic-Depressive EEG

Mayfield and Brown [46] reported in 1966 that "profound changes in the form of diffuse slowing, widening of the frequency spectrum, potentiation and disorganization of the background rhythm, sensitivity to hyperventilation" [p. 219] could be noted in the EEGs of each lithium-treated patient. Platman and Fieve [48], using lower lithium dosages, found abnormalities in only 15 of 28 patients.

Kupfer et al. [42] studied the effect of lithium carbonate in manic-depressive patients. Confirming Hartmann's findings, prelithium manic patients demonstrated, compared to control groups, reduction in total sleep time with a corresponding decrease in REM sleep, shortened REM latencies, and almost no delta or stage 4 sleep. Lithium administration, on the other hand, caused a sustained decrease in REM sleep, prolonged REM latencies without compensation for the lost REM sleep upon cessation of the drug, and increased delta or stage 4 sleep. Interestingly, delta sleep is most often absent or decreased in depressed patients. While lithium may lead to quick resolution of the mania, its nocturnal EEG effects include both a decrease in REM sleep and an increase in stage 4 sleep; the normothymic individual shows the latter but not the former. Thus, the administration of lithium leads to a partial but not complete return to a normal nocturnal EEG.

These findings—that nocturnal EEG patterns differ between manic-depressive and other depressed patients and normals, that nocturnal EEG patterns differ in manic and depressive episodes in the same patient, and that treatment with lithium can quickly aid the resolution of acute manic episodes, serve as prophylaxis against recurrences of either mania or depression, and aid in normalizing the nocturnal EEG—support of our contention that the illness is physiological in nature and that lithium is somehow involved in the metabolic structure of the affective system.

Genetic Studies

Bellak [8] reviewed the literature to 1952 on heritability of manic-depressive illness. He found evidence both for and against a genetic factor in manic-depressive illness and concluded "the question of the significance of hereditary factors in mental disease is part of the problem of the relative significance of nature and nurture, one of the oldest and most bitterly embattled problems of science" [p. 77]. Winokur, Clayton, and Reich [57] in a careful review of the more recent literature and after careful genetic studies of their own, concluded the disease is heritable. By studying patients with both manic-depressive illness and color blindness, using the color blindness as a genetic tracer, they concluded that the "affective disorder in which mania occurs (manic depressive disease, bipolar psychosis) is quite probably linked on the X-chromosome with the locus for color blindness. This finding adds to the evidence in favor of X-linkage for manic depressive disease. Perhaps more important, it provides further proof of a genetic factor in manic depressive disease" [p. 125]. Further, the genetic defect shows partial, not complete penetrance, making manifestation of the disease a function of both genetic background and psychological development.

According to our conceptualization, manic-depressive illness represents a genetic fault in the affective system. If the fault becomes manifest, and it is only of incomplete penetrance genetically, spontaneous manic episodes occur, ushered in by prodromal symptomatology (as previously described), representing the psychological consequences of the increased physiological energy now available. If a patient with the genetic fault sustains an external loss, and his psychological development does not allow for a psychological resolution, then manic symptomatology will follow, either immediately, or after a period of depression, as the affective system fault is triggered. If, on the other hand, a patient without the affective fault sustains a loss, either a depression or a normal period of mourning will occur, depending on the level of psychological development of the patient.

Biochemical Evidence

In 1967 Schildkraut and Kety summarized the catecholamine hypothesis of affective disorders, which states that "some, if not all, depressions may be associated with a relative deficiency of norepinephrine at functionally important adrenergic receptor sites in the brain, whereas elations may be associated with an excess of such amines" [51, p. 28]. Lithium was thought to both increase intracellular deamination of norepinephrine and decrease available norepinephrine at receptor sites and hence to have an antielation effect. Its antidepressant effect would be due to its participation in other reactions in the transmission sequence [49]. Recent work [50] indicates that in manic patients excretion of the norepinephrine metabolite MHPG in the urine is higher and D time is lower during hypomanic episodes than during depressive episodes. All of this suggests that manic episodes are accompanied by an increased turnover of norepinephrine at the CNS synapse and a decreased need to dream while depressed episodes are accompanied by a decreased turnover of norepinephrine at the synapse and an increased need to dream.

While the catecholamine hypothesis is attractive, it is itself far from proven and is mentioned only as one of many biochemical theories offered to explain what we have postulated as the physiological affective system. Alternate theories are discussed in the recent interesting multifactorial conceptualization of the etiology of depression presented by Akiskal and McKinney [3]. Fieve has recently reviewed the literature and concludes that "because of the complex interrelationship among these various biochemical, electrical, and ionic events following lithium administration it is difficult, if not impossible to synthesize all the findings into any single unifying hypothesis with regard to lithium's mode of action" [17, p. 143].

OBJECTIONS

We have presented the hypothesis that manic-depressive illness is an intrapsychic phenomenon, based on physiological processes perhaps genetically determined, that may be activated either spontaneously at times for unknown reasons or activated psychogenically if psychological development is not completely adequate to deal with external object loss. A very different view has been offered by Fromm-Reichmann and her associates [12, 32] supported by Arieti [4]. In this view, manic-depressive illness is a disease of interpersonal relations. Cohen et al. [32] give an example:

Each [of 12 manic-depressive] family(s) was set apart from the surrounding milieu by some factor which singled it out as "different." In every case the patient's family had felt the social difference keenly and had reacted to it with intense concern and with an effort, first to improve its acceptability in the community by fitting it with "what the neighbors think" and, second, to improve its social prestige by raising the economic level of the family. . . . The children of the family played important roles; they were expected to conform to a high standard of good behavior . . . based largely on what the parents . . . [thought] the neighbors expected [p. 241].

The way this behavior was effected in the children led to a "depersonalization of authority," and the children were used as instruments for improving the family's social position. The mother was seen as the ultimate authority in such a family, although cold and nonloving, and the father was seen as faceless and powerless against the attacks of the mother. In such a family a child faces the dilemma of finding the unreliable and more or less contemptible parent the lovable one and the reliable, strong parent the disliked one.

Arieti [4] gives a similar social formulation, which differs only in detail. For him, the future manic patient was traumatized in childhood by a sudden change from a giving, duty-bound mother to a mother giving less and expecting a great deal from the child. The result is resentment on the part of the child, who cannot form normal parental introjects. Such a child incorporates other objects in the environment and, having no stable parental introject, is particularly vulnerable to losses.

Theoretically, such formulations could be tested by double-blind techniques in which anamneses of manic-depressive patients were checked against these formulations. Although this has not been done in a formal manner, we have seen too many manic-depressives in which these typical constellations did not occur to believe that these hypothesized interpersonal constellations are the necessary or sufficient cause for the development of the illness. In our experience, no one family constellation is associated with the disease. Even if such a constellation is found in some manic-depressive families, are there not also families in which such constellations occur but in which the outcome is not manic-depressive illness?

CONCLUSION

We have conceptualized manic-depressive illness as a genetically determined *actual* neurosis in which the typical psychological symptoms are the outcome of an alternation of periodic excess and lack of physiological energy. Individual manic episodes may be spontaneous, due to shifts of physiological energy in the central nervous system, or psychogenic, in which an external loss cannot be handled in a psychologically adequate manner and triggers the same reaction as would be caused by a spontaneous shift in energy. The manic state differs from the normal state not only in the classic psychological symptoms (hyperactivity, pressure of speech, exaggerated self-esteem, grandiosity, exaggerated libidinal activities, fragmentation of thought processes by intrusion of external stimuli) but also in physiological changes (need for less total sleep, need for less dream sleep) only recently discovered.

Although we did not discuss the differentiation in detail, purely depressive illnesses differ from manic-depressive illness in that the physiological affective system does not show shifts of energy as in manic-depressive illness. While unitary psychotic depressions are usually associated with external losses, and hence are psychogenic, recurring depressive illness, like manic-depressive illness, is associated with both psychogenic and spontaneous episodes.

Lithium carbonate normalizes the physiological affective system of manic-depressives so that the periodic excess and lack of physiological energy no longer occur. In this aspect the treatment of manic-depressive illness with lithium is reminiscent of the treatment of diabetes mellitus with insulin: it is as if an absent physiological substance is replaced by the treatment. The exact mechanism by which lithium does this is not known, but the probability is that it is able to both increase and decrease the speed of transmission of the nerve impulse across the CNS synapse by affecting the kinetics of two different reactions in the release-acceptance norepinephrine cycle at the synaptic junction.

Whether future work will support or deny this conceptualization in each of its details, it stands now as a consistent whole that explains disparate clinical and experimental facts. Such a conceptualization does define a disease entity and separates it from similar, yet different phenomena.

REFERENCES

1. Abraham, K. Notes on the Psycho-Analytical Investigation and Treatment of Manic-Depressive Insanity and Allied Conditions. In B. D. Lewin (Ed.), *On Character and Libido Development*. New York: Norton, 1966. P. 15.
2. Abraham, K. A Short Study of the Development of the Libido, Viewed in the Light of Mental Disorders. In B. D. Lewin (Ed.), *On Character and Libido Development*. New York: Norton, 1966. P. 67.
3. Akiskal, H. S., and McKinney, W. T. Depressive Disorders: Toward a Unified Hypothesis. *Science* 182:20, 1973.
4. Arieti, S. Manic-Depressive Psychosis. In S. Arieti (Ed.), *American Handbook of Psychiatry*, vol. 1. New York: Basic Books, 1959. P. 419.

5. Baastrup, P. C., and Schou, M. Lithium as a prophylactic agent: Its effect against recurrent depressions and manic-depressive psychoses. *Arch. Gen. Psychiatry* 16:162, 1967.
6. Baastrup, P. C., and Schou, M. Prophylactic lithium. *Lancet* 1: 1419, 1968.
7. Baastrup, P. C., and Schou, M. Prophylactic lithium. *Lancet* 2:349, 1968.
8. Bellak, L. *Manic-Depressive Psychosis and Allied Conditions*. New York: Grune and Stratton, 1952.
9. Benedek, T. Toward the biology of the depressive constellation. *J. Am. Psychoanal. Assoc.* 4:389, 1956.
10. Blackwell, B., and Shepherd, M. Prophylactic lithium: Another prophylactic myth? *Lancet* 1:968, 1968.
11. Cade, J. F. J. Lithium salts in the treatment of psychotic excitement. *Med. J. Aust.* 36:349, 1949.
12. Cohen, M. B., et al. An Intensive Study of Twelve Cases of Manic-Depressive Psychosis. In D. Bullard (Ed.), *Psychoanalysis and Psychotherapy: Selected papers of Freida Fromm-Reichmann*. Chicago: University of Chicago Press, 1954. P. 227.
13. Davis, H., and Davis, P. A. The electrical activity of the brain: Its relations to physiological states and to states of impaired consciousness. *Res. Publ. Assoc. Nerv. Ment. Dis.* 19:50, 1939.
14. Deutsch, H. The Psychology of Manic-Depressive States, with Particular Reference to Chronic Hypomania. In H. Deutsch (Ed.), *Neuroses and Character Types: Clinical Psychoanalytic Studies*. New York: International Universities Press, 1965. P. 203.
15. Feinstein, S., and Wolpert, E. Juvenile manic-depressive illness: Clinical and theoretical considerations. *J. Am. Acad. Child Psychiatry* 12:123, 1973.
16. Fenichel, O. *The Psychoanalytic Theory of Neurosis*. New York: Norton, 1945.
17. Fieve, R. Lithium studies and manic depressive illness. *Proc. Amer. Psychopathol. Assoc.* 60:135, 1972.
18. Fisher, C. Psychoanalytic implications of recent research on sleep and dreaming. *J. Am. Psychoanal. Assoc.* 13:197, 1965.
19. Freeman, T. Observations on mania. *Int. J. Psychoanal.* 52:479, 1971.
20. Freud, S. Further remarks on the neuro-psychoses of defense (1896). In *The Standard Edition of the Complete Psychological Works of Sigmund Freud*, transl. and ed. by J. Stachey with others. London: Hogarth and Institute of Psycho-Analysis, 1962. Vol. 3, p. 159.
21. Freud, S. Sexuality in the Etiology of the Neuroses (1898). *Standard Edition*. 1962. Vol. 3, p. 261.
22. Freud, S. The Psycho-Analytic View of Psychogenic Disturbance of Vision (1910). *Standard Edition*. 1957. Vol. 11, p. 209.
23. Freud, S. "Wild" Psychoanalysis (1910). *Standard Edition*. 1957. Vol. 11, p. 220.
24. Freud, S. Contributions to a Discussion on Masturbation (1912). *Standard Edition*. 1958. Vol. 12, p. 241.
25. Freud, S. On Narcissism: An Introduction (1914). *Standard Edition*. 1957. Vol. 14, p. 69.

26. Freud, S.   Mourning and Melancholia (1915). *Standard Edition.* 1957. Vol. 14, p. 243.
27. Freud, S.   Introductory Lectures on Psychoanalysis. Part III. General Theory of the Neuroses. Lecture XXIV (1917). *Standard Edition.* 1963. Vol. 16, p. 378.
28. Freud, S.   Group Psychology and the Analysis of the Ego (1921). *Standard Edition.* 1955. Vol. 18, p. 69.
29. Freud, S.   The Ego and the Id (1923). *Standard Edition.* 1961. Vol. 19, p. 12.
30. Freud, S.   An Autobiographical Study (1925). *Standard Edition.* 1959. Vol. 20, p. 3.
31. Freud, S.   Inhibitions, Symptoms and Anxiety (1926). *Standard Edition.* 1959. Vol. 20, p. 77.
32. Fromm-Reichmann, F.   Intensive Psychotherapy of Manic-Depressives. In D. Bullard (Ed.), *Psychoanalysis and Psychotherapy: Selected Papers of Freida Fromm-Reichmann.* Chicago: University of Chicago Press, 1959. P. 221.
33. Gershon, S.   Lithium in mania. *Clin. Pharmacol. Ther.* 11:168, 1970.
34. Hartmann, E.   Longitudinal studies of sleep and dream patterns in manic-depressive patients. *Arch. Gen. Psychiatry* 19:312, 1968.
35. Hartmann, E.   Mania, Depression, and Sleep. In A. Kales (Ed.), *Sleep, Physiology and Pathology.* Philadelphia: Lippincott, 1972. P. 182.
36. Jacobson, E.   Metapsychology of Cyclothymic Depression. In P. Greenacre (Ed.), *Affective Disorders.* New York: International Universities Press, 1953. P. 49.
37. Katan, M.   Mania and the Pleasure Principle: Primary and Secondary Symptoms. In P. Greenacre (Ed.), *Affective Disorders.* New York: International Universities Press, 1953. P. 140.
38. Kline, W., and Kistner, G.   Lithium: The History of its Use in Psychiatry. *Modern Problems of Pharmacopsychiatry,* Vol. III. New York, Basel: Karger, 1969. P. 75.
39. Kraepelin, E.   *Lectures on Clinical Psychiatry,* translated by T. Johnstone. London: Ballière, Tindall & Cox, 1904.
40. Kraepelin, E.   *Manic-Depressive Insanity and Paranoia.* Edinburgh: Livingstone, 1921.
41. Kupfer, D. J.   *Lithium and Psychiatry Journal Articles.* New York: Medical Examination Publishing, 1971.
42. Kupfer, D. J., et al.   Lithium carbonate and sleep in affective illness. *Arch. Gen. Psychiatry* 23:35, 1970.
43. Lange, J.   Die endogenen und reaktiven Germutserkrank Heiten und die manisch-depressive Konstitution. II. In O. Bumke (Ed.) *Handbuch Der Geisteskrank Heiten* (VI spez. Teil 2). Berlin: Springer, 1928. Cited in Lewin [45].
44. Levitan, H.   Dreams preceding hypomania. *Int. J. Psychoanal. Psychother.* 1:50, 1973.
45. Lewin, B. D.   *The Psychoanalysis of Elation.* New York: Norton, 1950.
46. Mayfield, D., and Brown, A. G.   The clinical laboratory and electroencephalographic effects of lithium. *J. Psychiatr. Res.* 4:207, 1966.

47. Mueller, P., and Wolpert, E.   Lithium carbonate in the treatment of manic depressive disorders: A follow-up study. *Ill. Med. J.* 145:505, 1974.

48. Platman, S. R., and Fieve, R. R.   The effect of lithium carbonate on the electroencephologram of patients with affective disorders. *Br. J. Psychiatry* 115:1185, 1969.

49. Schildkraut, J. J.   *Neuropsychopharmacology*. Boston: Little, Brown, 1970.

50. Schildkraut, J. J., et al.   MHPG excretion in depressive disorders: Relation to clinical subtypes and desynchronized sleep. *Science* 181: 762, 1973.

51. Schildkraut, J. J., and Kety, S. S.   Biogenic amines and emotion. *Science,* 166:21, 1967.

52. Schou, M.   Lithium in psychiatric therapy: Stock-taking after ten years. *Psychopharmacologia,* 1:66, 1959.

53. Schou, M.   Special review: Lithium in psychiatric therapy and prophylaxis. *J. Psychiatr. Res.* 6:67, 1968.

54. Silverman, R., and Wolpert, E.   The use of lithium carbonate in manic-depressive illnesses. Unpublished paper, 1973.

55. Spring, G. K., et al.   Prophylactic use of lithium carbonate. *J.A.M.A.* 208:1901, 1969.

56. Stallone, F., et al.   The use of lithium in affective disorders. III. A double-blind study of prophylaxis in bipolar illness. *Am. J. Psychiatry,* 130:1006, 1973.

57. Winokur, G., Clayton, P. J., and Reich, T.   *Manic Depressive Illness*. St. Louis: Mosby, 1969.

58. Wolpert, E. A.   Psychophysiological Parallelism in the Dream. In L. E. Abt and B. F. Riess (Eds.) *Progress in Clinical Psychology*. Vol. VIII. *Dreams and Dreaming*. New York: Grune & Stratton, 1968. P. 76.

59. Wolpert, E. A., and Mueller, P.   Lithium carbonate in the treatment of manic depressive disorders. *Arch. Gen. Psychiatry* 21:155, 1969.

The Life Cycle

III

This part of the book deals with the clinical manifestations of depression, yet it makes no attempt to provide a systematic description of syndromes in the Kraepelinian sense. Nor will the reader find in it the characteristic comprehensiveness of earlier psychoanalytic papers, in which the treatment data were used to try to confirm the "phase-specific" assumptions motivating the study. As our knowledge has increased, the approach has become more complex. Observations are seen to be multifaceted: not only do they appear to fit more than one theory, but several theories may serve to explain a single observation. The interplay of theory and observation adds constantly to our understanding, hence a psychoanalytic investigation can never be regarded as completed; both data and meaning remain open-ended.

The skill of the investigator lies in recognizing the thread of his experience, and this leads him eventually, through many detours, to the discovery of the etiological factors underlying his initial hunches. If that is his objective, then the delineation of depression as a clinical entity will not emerge. An example of this current trend will be found in the chapter by Anthony dealing with a manic-depressive environment. Its focus is on the emotional atmosphere generated by a parental pathology that distorts the parent-child interaction and at the same time transmits to the offspring a modified version of the disturbance. Whatever modification there is permits us to hope that some independent growth potential in the child will make it possible for him to "outgrow" his parents. The dynamics of the interaction processes involved are fairly clear, and their influence on normal and pathological development can be easily inferred. The metapsychology behind the interactions is beyond the immediate interest of the clinician.

Clinical presentations of this type have one shortcoming. Their aim is to depict the kaleidoscope effect of human relationships, and since this is an ever-changing process, the amount of detail required to convey this effect obviously cannot be presented within the scope of one chapter. But it does demonstrate the fact that the self develops not in isolation but in continuous interaction with objects in real life. In the somewhat rarified atmosphere of the therapeutic environment, the patient's self and the therapist's self are similarly engaged in more or less interminable interaction.

The emergence of depression as a predominant affect and mood during childhood, as well as a disorder occurring with increasing frequency, has been related somewhat daringly to changes in the human condition in the chapter on childhood depression by Anthony. Evidence is brought forward from psychohistory to support the view that whereas open hostility toward the child is no longer as widespread or as well tolerated as it may have been in the past, an increasing covert ambivalence may be providing a nucleus for the depressive constellation. The chapter also suggests that the reported rise in adult depression may be having repercussions on family life and through it on the child's early development. Both these contributions (Chapters 11 and 12), therefore, place a special significance on the developmental environment as a joint construction by the child and his family. Whether a growing awareness of children, coupled with a greater understanding of the depressive reaction, has helped to create a new clinical entity for our time is still debatable and in need of further study.

If existing parental depression is pathogenic to the child, then why, one may ask, does the general theory of depression attribute such causal importance to "parent loss"? Is there a contradiction here? Can presence and absence have the same predisposing and precipitating effect? In either case, the parents, as "primary objects," represent a unique influence during the child's development. Nevertheless, there is a profound difference between the parent's being present and not present. Interaction with the living parent is an ongoing process in which the demands on the adaptive capacity of the parent are minutely and incessantly balanced against the demands on the developmental potential of the child. Thus every conflict is fought out on both the intrapsychic and interpersonal levels and has its own outcome. When the parent dies or otherwise disappears irrevocably from the everyday life of the child, this ongoing give and take is brought to a standstill, and a new type of process, termed mourning, enters the picture. Mourning is the intrapsychic means by which the lost object is made an integral part of the self of the mourner by being incorporated into the ego-ideal or superego institutions.

Feinstein looks at adolescent depression within the framework of object loss, using the term in an extended sense to include both real and psychic loss, as when love is withdrawn and is imagined to be gone forever. The process of mourning, according to Feinstein, occurs with every stage of genetic development, each with its own loss and reactions to loss. Adolescent depression is described in accordance with this paradigm, and case histories are presented to illustrate the point.

The phenomenon of mourning has played an important role in the evolution of psychoanalysis. It allowed Freud to conceptualize not only the metapsychology of the affective experience of depression but also the fundamental role of the ego in personality development. He was not able, however, to correlate these two spheres. As in neurophysiology, there appears to be in psychology a wide gap between the theory of the developing ego and our understanding of a depressive disorder. Nevertheless there is clearly some affinity between the two processes, as is evident in the repeated phase-specific connections during the course of development, but until recently there has not been a theoretical umbrella to cover them both.

Psychoanalysts and ethologists have used the term phase-specific to describe a characteristic aspect of a maturational or developmental stage. If one were to select a construct from psychoanalytic theory that would bring together in the same context the concepts of phase-specificity and phasic psychodynamic processes conducive to depression, the best choice at the present time seems to lie in Erikson's schema of the life cycle. His chart (see Chapter 14, Figure 1) defines the developmental stage of the ego in terms of the dominant interpersonal conflict in which it is adaptively engaged. This is fully discussed by Benedek in Chapter 14. The conflict may repeat itself daily, as does the hunger of the infant, and not necessarily lead to a crisis in the usual sense. In the Eriksonian framework, "crisis" simply expresses the emotional manifestation of the conflict and the necessity for its resolution. Although based on the interpersonal conflicts of ego psychology, this epigenetic approach does not contradict the genetic and instinctual approach of psychoanalysis. Rather, it reminds us of the unity of general psychoanalytic theory. Freud repeatedly emphasized the fact that nothing would be known about instincts if they were not attached to the affects generated by them.

Human emotions have, presumably, individual meanings that change during the life of the individual as a result of interpersonal experiences that may or may not lead to intrapsychic crises. One can make the assumption that suicides are motivated by such intrapsychic crises stemming from past or present interpersonal conflicts. A common opinion is that suicide represents the end point of severe and chronic depression, but a large number of suicides do not fit that view. Suicidal behavior is best understood as an existential phenomenon for which the motivations are many and arise from a variety of sources— interpersonal, impersonal, social, and cultural. Not infrequently, it is simply expected behavior "at the end of the road." Yet, with every type of motivation one still needs to consider the role of the self-directed aggression apparent in so many suicide notes.*

The chapter by Pollock points to the fact that suicide often results from an acute depressive reaction to a significant anniversary. Even a wedding anniversary may prompt a suicide (or an attempt) if the meaning connected with the date implies that one has failed unalterably. As a consequence of the guilt, shame, or regret, life becomes meaningless and unlivable. Anniversaries, therefore, may trigger either happiness or sorrow. Institutionalized anniversaries, such as Christmas or New Year's, traditionally regarded as times of cheer, have recently gained prominence as potent periods for psychotic and suicidal developments. The phenomenon is so familiar that psychiatrists have given it a name: the holiday paradox. The holiday season inexorably stirs up early childhood and family associations and may bring into focus one's failure to meet youthful expectations. The past is put into vivid contrast with a present that is unable to live up to the past or to live down the past. It has been said that holidays are organized to guarantee disappointment. Suicides tend to peak sharply just after Christmas Day and New Year's Day. The first week of the year is notorious at all suicide prevention centers as the worst week of the year.

Of an estimated fifty thousand to seventy thousand suicides in the United States annually, about half occur among persons suffering from depression. In terms of mortality, this makes depression as serious a problem as diabetes and leukemia; in terms of morbidity, the toll is equally alarming. According to figures provided by the National Institute of Mental Health, one in eight Americans will suffer a bout of depression serious enough to need psychiatric help during his lifetime; one hundred twenty-five thousand Americans are hospitalized each year with depression, while another two hundred thousand are treated in the offices of psychiatrists and psychoanalysts. It has been estimated that between four and eight million depressives go unrecognized as chronic underachievers, tired housewives, and hypochondriacs. There is some evidence that depression is spreading most rapidly among the nation's young people. The suicide rate for persons

---

* A good example of this was furnished by the well-known novelist Virginia Woolf, whose suicide note stated that she was killing herself in order to save her husband from the suffering that her depression and anhedonia were causing him.

in their twenties has more than doubled, while the rate for older persons has dropped steadily. The use of "mood" drugs as self-medication for depression by the young is another sign of the spreading epidemic of a disorder that has become the leading mental illness.

The association of suicide with active physical illness has been found to be very high. About 70 percent of people who commit suicide have one or more active illnesses, and in 50 percent of these cases the illnesses were considered to have contributed to the suicide. Rheumatoid arthritis, peptic ulcer, and hypertension were found to have the highest absolute rates, while the highest ratio of suicide to the prevalance of the illness occurs in those with malignancies. Among the contributors to this book, Fawcett [3] has found urological surgery to be one of the more common precipitants of severe depressive episodes and suicide attempts in men; and Winokur in Chapter 1 of this book has shown a correlation between alcoholism, affective disorder, and suicide. It has been suggested that the self-isolation of the depressive that comes from living in an interpersonal vacuum greatly increases the danger of suicide. Among those at high risk for suicide are the independent, noncomplaining, achievement-oriented individuals who are unable to share their feelings of dependency and hopelessness with others and who cannot, therefore, cope with the overwhelming sense of isolation that accompanies a severe depressive state. Unable to tolerate the "weakness" in themselves, such persons often successfully prevent even their associates from recognizing their depression and proceed quietly to a well-planned suicide that stuns their "close" colleagues.

It would seem, therefore, that, as Anthony notes in Chapter 11, an apparent paradox exists, in that two antithetical types of childhood experiences may both predispose to later depression and suicide: one characterized by serious loss or deprivation and the other by a great deal of success, love, and attention. The latter is an interesting group in that, as Beck [2] has put it, they seem not to have learned "the taste of defeat" and are unable to cope with it.

What of childhood suicide, if adult depression is on the increase and childhood depression has made its appearance? Successful suicide among children continues to remain rare, although there are reports from children's clinics in both Europe and the United States that suicide threats and attempts are becoming more common. The systematic study of nonlethal suicidal behavior in childhood may help to shed light on the phenomenology of depressive states in childhood.

Ostow, in Chapter 16, describes the transactional processes involved in preserving psychic equilibrium. At the same time, he emphasizes what is implicit in Erikson's chart of the life cycle: that the principle of psychic equilibrium is invested in the self-concept and that this structure, built up from infancy, must be preserved at all cost.

The disposition to depressive illness appears to be universal. Its instinctual components, such as ambivalence and low frustration tolerance, also seem to be innate, and these influence both the course of object relationships and their psychic representations. The consistency of the self-concept may be disturbed and even disrupted by hostility turned against the self. This is the core of anxiety that precedes all severe depressions, even those of short duration. It is therefore somewhat paradoxical that the mental functions remain relatively intact during a depressive illness as compared with schizophrenia. Yet the slowly encroaching emptiness and the inability to feel may be as threatening as death itself. The wish to forestall the depressive process and to overcompensate for the oncoming deficiency with over activity brings out the latent pathology in the guise of defense. Alcoholism and drug addiction have been considered as depressive equivalents ever since Abraham [1] formulated his theory: both of these dangerous alternatives are experienced as less damaging to the self. Not all defenses, however, are noxious; positive, constructive activities may also be useful in preventing depression. Together, these positive and negative defensive activities may become gradually structured into a character trend serving the unconscious purpose of mitigating the threat. They range from the comparatively simple, such as a change in the usual pattern of behavior, to a complex chain of intrapsychic reactions. In their mode of operation, they reflect both the individuality of the person and the unity of his psychic apparatus.

For the most part, the integrity of the self-concept is preserved during a depressive illness, but if the ego is unusually weak and the weight of depression too burdensome, the individual can lose himself in alcoholic euphoria or drug-induced fantasies. But when he emerges from these, fortunately he can again count on his wholeness.

The unity of the psychic apparatus is also well demonstrated by Grinker in Chapter 17. Anhedonia can be a painful symptom in both schizophrenia and depression. It is one of the characteristics shared by the two conditions, which are so markedly different in their clinical manifestations and yet so close together in their psychobiological depths. The symptom is the same in both conditions and is equally painful, and the discomfort comes from the feeling of not being able to feel. It may seem contradictory to describe a nonfeeling as painful, but patients often refer to it in terms of hurt— "a stone in my chest," etc. It is probably not an affect but a sensation, and different from sadness. It is as if affect had become a dehydrated end product in the natural history of depression from succulence to aridity. But surpris-

ingly, it is found in children. In fact, the first case of anhedonia was reported in a child. Ribot [4], the French psychopathologist who coined the term (as an analogue to analgesia), described it as follows:

A young girl, suffering from congestion of the liver and spleen, ceased to feel any affection for father or mother, showed no delight in her doll and could not be drawn out of her apathetic sadness. Things which previously had made her shriek with laughter now left her uninterested.

In another case quoted by Ribot, a man, also suffering from liver disease, showed a complete absence of emotional reaction. All affection seemed to be dead in him, and he could feel no pleasure at all. "Thoughts of his home, his wife, his children affected him no more, he said, than a theorem of Euclid."

In the absence of more solid evidence, anhedonia might be regarded as a manifestation of energy deficiency, the end phase of conservation-withdrawal. However, it could also be described as a defense against an impending disorganization of the self, or in the last resort, against death.

REFERENCES

1. Abraham, K.   A Short Study of the Development of the Libido, Viewed in the Light of Mental Disorders (1924). In *Selected Papers of Karl Abraham, M.D.* London: Hogarth Press, 1948. P. 418.
2. Beck, A. T.   *Depression.* New York: Harper & Row, 1967.
3. Fawcett, J.   Suicidal depression and physical illness. *J. A. M. A.* 219: 1303, 1972.
4. Ribot, T.   *The Psychology of Emotions.* New York: Scribners, 1914.

11

Childhood Depression

E. JAMES ANTHONY

SOME GENERAL CONSIDERATIONS

Childhood Depression as a Matter of Definition and Usage

When two variable terms are brought together in a single diagnostic label, the complexity can be impressive. Both "childhood" and "depression" are conceptions that are rapidly outgrowing their original meanings, so specific connotations associated with either of them are continually compounded over time. For example, in the light of current knowledge, it is no longer adequate to subsume the various stages of psychological growth, each with its own complex subsystem of developmental events and environments, under the single rubric "childhood." Depression is also an expanding notion that defies definition. "Many of the previous formulations of depression and of the depressive character structure," according to Mendelson, "are simply not comprehensive enough to do justice to the variety of clinical types" [59]. Time seems to have stood still. Three-hundred fifty years ago, Burton [18] called attention to the same fact:

The four and twenty letters make no more variety of words in diverse languages, than melancholy conceits produce diversity of symptoms in several persons. They are irregular, obscure, various, so infinite, Proteus himself is not so diverse . . . as a true character of a melancholy man . . . who can distinguish these melancholy symptoms so intermixed with others, or apply them to their several kinds, confine them into method? . . . Not that they are all to be found in one man . . . but some in one, some in another, and that successively or at several times.

Both statements remain valid. If depression is protean in the adult, one would expect it to be equally multifarious in the child, and all descriptive data point in this direction. Burton referred to depression as "the most universal of human afflictions" and doubted whether any individual could go through life without experiencing it to some degree in one of its many changeable forms. If it is indeed as universal as he suggests, one might wonder in what way or for what reason children could remain immune from it, since they are as much affected by anxiety as adults are. Children at different stages of development might experience it differently and might manifest it differently, and these experiences and manifestations might also differ from those that occur at later phases of the human life cycle. Therefore, universality should logically comprehend childhood.

A number of questions arise: How does the child come to understand and to communicate a feeling of depression? To what extent is this understanding and communication a function of his cognitive, affective, and linguistic development?

Childhood Depression as a Function of Language and Relationship

The communication of a feeling to someone else is a complex task at which the individual child becomes more adept with every year of experience. Three differentiating processes occur more or less simultaneously: the observer (mother) differentiates the child's affects and by labeling them helps him to become aware of them; the child differentiates the observer's feelings and relates them to specific circumstances; and the child differentiates his own feelings for himself and begins to categorize them and compare them with those of others. Each affective event represents a corrective experience for the child and renders him more competent in identifying and classifying his increasing range and complexity of feelings. His developing skill depends on the construction of affective chains of response in which a particular situation is perceived in a certain setting, understood in a certain context, felt in a certain way, expressed in certain body gestures, and communicated verbally in certain terms. As the chain becomes more elaborate and subtle, increasing demands are made upon the functions of apperception, cognition, expressiveness, and verbal ability. During the early part of childhood, communication is dominated by nursery usage. Feelings are labeled "sad," "bad," and "glad" but not as yet "depressed." Depending on individual circumstances, many years may elapse before the term depression becomes part of the regular interchange between parent and child. Both are so trapped within the Whorfian confines of linguistic habit that neither the family, the class, the society, nor the culture may possess an appropriate label for a particular feeling at a particular age. In accordance with social and cultural prescriptions, it may be incongruous for a child to be depressed until he reaches a certain level of maturation. As Wittgenstein summed it up: "the limits of language mean the limits of the world" [84].

Only Wittgenstein has attempted to analyze the problem of connecting language to inner experience and of "attaching" words to feelings and sensations that supposedly belong to our purest privacy. In his revolutionary approach, he discards the idea that naming is nothing more than baptizing something by giving it a label. For him, it involves a far more intimate relationship between language and experience in which language is not simply the mirror of experience but a kind of experience itself:

The child has hurt himself and he cries; and then adults talk to him and teach him exclamations and, later, sentences. They teach the child new pain-behavior. "So you are saying that the word pain really means crying?"—On the contrary: the verbal expression of pain replaces crying and does not describe it.

What Wittgenstein is arguing here is that feelings cannot be completely private since they follow a whole set of linguistic rules governing memory, identity, and similarity that belong to everyone. Furthermore, there is not one language but many languages, and one develops "language games" for different purposes, such as describing the physiognomy of the depressed individual, his outward behavior, or his mode of interaction and communication. All these "games" bear a family resemblance and together make up a complicated network of similarities. We therefore have to consider the structure and the texture of the whole, including tone of voice, expression, symptom, and context. Unless one becomes aware of the total language that involves the feeling, one may overlook its depth, its intensity, its meaning, and its nature.

To find words to describe his feelings, the child, especially the small child, requires much help from his parents. They may hear but not understand what he is trying to say to them, or they may be sidetracked by other issues that they consider more important. An illustration of an unhelpful way of clarifying feelings for a child is provided by McNeill [58]. The following exchange occurs between a mother and her child:

Child: Nobody don't like me.
Mother: No, say, "Nobody likes me."
Child: Nobody don't like me.

*

*

(eight repetitions of this dialogue)

*

*

Mother: No, now listen carefully; say,
    "Nobody likes me."
Child: Oh! Nobody don't likes me.

The operative word here for the child is "don't," and he cannot get away from it because it sums up the negativity of his situation. He appears to be trying desperately hard to communicate to his mother the sad condition of his life—he regards himself as unloved and perhaps unlovable. She, on her side, is engrossed with teaching him to express himself correctly. The child's condition may be transient, but he is beginning to learn the lesson that adults (and this includes clinicians) are sometimes less concerned with how he feels than with how he communicates his feelings.

The problem for the child of having his feelings understood is further complicated by the fact that certain words may be forbidden because of undesirable associations. For example, there are many ways to describe low-spiritedness, such as sadness, mournfulness, depression, melancholy, unhappiness, grief, gloom, and despondency, some of which are available to the child's vocabulary and some not. Unknown to him, common everyday words like depression, melancholy, and grief are surreptitiously promoted to clinical status and cannot be used without subjecting the individual to the charge of being "sick." In this way, clinical usage constantly appropriates terms in common usage and contaminates them permanently in the eyes of the user.

Childhood Depression as a Function of Cognition

It is important for the child to explain and verbalize his feelings in order to get the required feedback from his surroundings. If he depends too much on the naive language of expression and gesture, the signals may be insufficient to call attention to his total predicament. He must learn to express himself through as many channels as possible.

To feel what others feel is a function of empathy, and the lesson begins with the mother. To understand what another feels in a particular situation is a more complicated task and demands an appraisal of the situation, a recognition of expressive clues, an association with similar past experiences, and an understanding of the verbal communication. If cognitive-affective development is represented by the split halves of an inverted pyramid, cognition and affect would each expand within the parallel relationship so that as affects became more elaborate, there would be an enlarged cognitive apparatus to deal with it. This is in keeping with Piaget's proposition [61] that intellectual and affective schemas are two aspects of the same indissociable reality. The affective schemas are less susceptible to generalization and abstraction than intellectual schemata, but both are integrated into "person" and "object" structures. As intelligence grows from sensory-motor and intuitive preoperational stages to those of concrete and abstract operations, the affective schemata evolve from the elementary regulations of pain and pleasure, sympathy and antipathy, to complete sentiments. For example, a feeling in the representational phase may be intuitively understood while the rationale of the feeling is far from clear. At this stage, the egocentricism of the child makes it impossible for him to put himself into the thinking, feeling, and perceiving role of the other person, so his capacity to understand his own experience is limited by his incapacity to understand the experience of anyone else. When he reaches the concrete stage, he may be able to categorize feelings and even to provide a simple and naive classification of emotions, but once again the total cognitive-affective experience is curtailed by the relatively simple "groupings" possible at this time. It is only when the child attains an abstract level of intellectual operation that he can analyze his feelings and "attach" them to complex modes of thought expressed with all the clarity of a logical proposition. The child is then clearer not only in how he thinks but in how he feels, and he may attempt to explore systematically why he thinks and feels in a certain way about something. The language ability grows in association with these other progressions.

If one accepts this close relationship between cognitive and affective development, as advocated by Piaget, it would stand to reason that the experience of depression in late childhood will be radically different from the earlier experience. It is possible to go further and suggest that depression itself undergoes development throughout the child's development and that its characteristics are determined by parallel developments in symbolism, representation, language, and logical operations. The question whether depression does or does not occur during childhood, therefore, can no longer stand by itself.

Childhood Depression and the Culture of Bereavement

Every phase of the human life cycle is associated with experiences of loss. Some of these are built into the structure of development and are therefore inevitable, while others can be regarded as accidental or external; some are psychic, others actual and material. Man has therefore become accustomed to loss and has developed many different styles of mourning that vary with the culture to cope with loss to themselves and to others. For maximum efficiency, they have even ritualized it. Depression, in its more normal aspects of grief and sadness, has been equated with mourning, and clinical depression with abnormal or pathological mourning. From early life children are witnesses to the ways in which their parents and relatives handle loss and frustration, and the child's capacity to deal actively with the same situations may reflect the nature of these passive experiences.

He must be considered, therefore, an integral part of the recurrent mourning cycles that beset human existence. To what extent he himself displays typical mourning reactions will depend on the actual circumstances that surround him. In some cultures children participate fully in the ritual mourning and are encouraged to appreciate the loss and to display an appropriate measure of grief. In general, if the environment is emotionally "open" and feelings are expected to be expressed, the child will participate fully in the bereavement process from the time he can share in other collective experiences. When adults are confused about mourning and the child's role in it, or embarrassed about the display of grief, they may hide both the event and their feelings from the children and thus expose them to incongruous and mystifying behavior. In such circumstances, as in so many others, the children enter into the adult conspiracy and conform to the expectation of seeing no sorrow, hearing no grief, and expressing no sense of loss. Families of this type cause an early closure of emotional outlets and thereby predispose individuals to withdrawal reactions. Although no systematic work has yet been done in this area, there is some evidence to suggest that in cases where normal grief is blocked in childhood, depression and suicide in the adult are more likely to occur. There is also evidence, although it is far from solid, to suggest that in "good" families, in which the child's psyche is constantly overprotected from loss, depression may be the sequela in adult life, whereas in "bad" families, in which neglect and rejection are the order of the day, the child may turn out to be an "affectionless psychopathic adult" [14]. Obviously the latent forms of these remote effects will be operating during childhood.

Childhood Depression as an Emergent Phenomenon of Our Time

Depression, for some time the leading mental illness in the United States, is reaching almost epidemic proportions, and the spread is more rapid among younger people. The use of mood drugs, regarded as "self-medication for depression," is extending from the high school into the upper reaches of the grade school. Recent reports from child psychiatry clinics both in the United States and in Britain have been consistently reporting incidences between 7 and 10 percent of all referrals of threatened or attempted suicide and an even higher percentage of cases seen as psychiatric emergencies [73].

If childhood depression, either normal or clinical, is an emergent phenomenon of our time, it might be attributed to one or both of two sets of factors: (1) an increasing recognition of childhood as an essential component of human existence and of the child's psychological potential for perceiving, thinking, and feeling; and (2) recent changes in the "human condition" of the child as reflected in child rearing practices, parental attitudes, and the load of adult depression in the immediate orbit of the child. In other words, we are asking ourselves whether childhood depression is something old that has always been with us of which we have become conscious quite suddenly, or something new and disturbing that has entered the human situation. These are questions for historians who can cast a clinical eye on history and diagnose its psychosocial ailments.

These psychohistorians, with their new historical perspectives, have attempted to chart the elusive dimensions of social consciousness through the centuries and have marshalled their evidence from such humble sources as diaries, children's games and toys, photographs, letters, etc. The pioneer in this field of the systematic documentation of the commonplaces of human existence has been Aries [7], who has brought sufficient evidence, taken from these indexes of daily life, to argue that the modern idea of childhood as a distinct phase of life did not develop, at least in Western society, until the seventeenth century. This is surprising, because although the concept of the human life cycle seems like a contemporary invention, it actually dates back to the writings of the Ionian philosophers of the sixth century B.C. However, the fact that childhood has been allocated a place in human existence for a long time in no way presupposes that it has always carried the status of a developmental phase as this is conceived today. In fact, it is very evident that childhood has had to struggle for existence.

During the Middle Ages, there seemed to be no place for children as we know them. The child was virtually a nonperson. "The idea of childhood did not exist" [7] in the sense that there was no awareness of the particular nature of childhood as distinguished from adulthood. The child was defined mainly in negative terms as someone who was not adult and whose only significance lay in the very uncertain chance (because of the high infant and child mortality rates) that he would one day become an adult.*

Following the Renaissance, childhood began to impinge on the contemporary consciousness. The new concept of the child professed by the upper class (the old concept continued unchanged among the peasants) tended to regard him as a toy whose simplicity and drollery were sources of amusement for the adult. Montaigne described chil-

---

* A thirteenth century poem confirms that the child of this era was valued only as a potential adult:

> Thus the child six summers old
> Is not worth much when all is told.
> But one must take every care
> To see that he is fed good fare,
> For he who does not start life well
> Will finish badly, one can tell.

dren as being treated "like monkeys." The contemptuousness implicit in many of the comments found more direct expression in a treatise on education by Gratien, published in 1646, in which this judgment is made: "Every man must be conscious of that insipidity of childhood which disgusts the sane mind, that coarseness of youth which finds pleasure in scarcely anything but material objects. . . . *Only time can cure a person of childhood*" [38].

Things began to change radically with the appearance of Rousseau, with his strong insistence that the child must be considered a child and not a miniature adult in both his thinking and his feeling, and by the nineteenth century parents were becoming so intrigued by their offspring that "baby biographies" began to appear with increasing frequency. The child became an object of avid study, and following the turn of the century, he began to acquire a psychology of his own although not yet a psychopathology. Only organic deficiencies and disorders of the brain were possible. By the mid-twentieth century, both neurosis and psychosis had become part of the expanding psychopathology of childhood disorders and new illnesses were added to the list with almost every decade. As Aries remarked wryly, Western civilization had become "obsessed by the physical, moral and sexual problems of children" [7].

Not only were children being better considered but they were also better treated; not only were they becoming people but they were also becoming individuals capable of subtle and sophisticated psychological reactions; and not only were they treated as though they had minds of their own but their bodies were no longer subjected to gross abuse, at least not to the degree that had been prevalent earlier.

DeMause sums up this latest improvement by saying that "the history of childhood is a nightmare from which we have only recently begun to awaken. The further back in history one goes, the lower the level of child care, and the more likely the children are to be killed, abandoned, beaten, terrorized, and sexually abused" [21]. Murder and abandonment of children prevailed throughout antiquity to about the fourth century A.D., and from the fourth to the fourteenth century parents gave their children over to wet nurses, not to suckle but to "lie upon," expose to the elements, and sell into servitude. The battering and gross abuse of children continued into the nineteenth century, when European governments for the first time attempted to legislate against infanticide, child abuse, and child labor. DeMause has put forward a psychogenetic theory of history in which he postulates that history changes because personality changes and personality changes because of changing parent-child interactions. In reviewing the sequential developments in the family over the centuries, he has observed that parents have slowly overcome their anxieties and aggressions and have moved into a closer, more gratifying, and more understanding type of relationship. From murdering, abandoning, molding, and dominating their children, they have reached the stage of working cooperatively with them.

This psychohistorical view that everything has been getting better for the child is unfortunately valid only on the macroscopic level. Rexford [65] has helped us to see that while it is true we are less openly murderous toward our children than were our predecessors in history, we are far more ambivalent and hypocritical. She has documented for us the sad fact that contemporary adults, parents or professionals, are constantly of two minds in their dealings with the young. The ambivalence takes many different forms. For example, there is a growing resistance among young adults in our society to child rearing and a decided trend toward the postponement of child bearing. Fewer children are being produced, and these are often turned over to the care of others. The manifest reason given for not wanting them or not wanting to take care of them is the desire for self-fulfillment, but a deeper analysis often reveals an unresolved ambivalence originating from the would-be parents' earliest experiences.

Therefore, there is much to suggest that a "core of ambivalence" is fairly widespread in the adult-child relationship of our time and culture. It is perhaps too speculative to consider this the historical evolution of Benedek's "depressive constellation," but some such proposition may help to explain the emergence of childhood depression.

SOME PSYCHOANALYTIC CONSIDERATIONS

From the psychoanalytic point of view, there are six crucial questions that need to be answered with regard to childhood depression:

1. Is there such an entity as a "basic depressive affect" or "depressive mood," comparable to anxiety and operating throughout the human life cycle *including childhood?*
2. Is there such an entity as a "depressive tendency," comparable to anxiety proneness, that predisposes the individual to depressive responses and reactions throughout the human life cycle *including childhood?*
3. Is there such an entity as a "primary depression" or "nuclear depressive conflict," comparable to the nuclear anxiety complex, occurring during the first five years of life?
4. Is there such an entity as a "depressive reaction" or "clinical depression" during childhood? And if there is, is this a new disorder of childhood or an old disorder previously overlooked but now better analytically recognized and understood?

5. Is childhood depressive reaction or clinical depression the same as or different in degree or kind from the clinical depression of adults?
6. Can both child and adult clinical states be considered within the same theoretical framework, or does each require its own specific theory?

Is There Such an Entity as a Basic Depressive Affect or Depressive Mood?

Zetzel [85] has claimed that many psychoanalytic discussions of depression are obscured because of the failure to distinguish clearly between depression as a basic affective experience of general psychological significance and depressive illness as a regressive clinical syndrome. There seems to be little doubt among most observers that transient depressions and moods similar to those that occur in the adult can be observed during childhood following the infantile period. Whether the low-spirited responses during normal infancy can be regarded as depressions or "depressive positions" is more debatable, especially if one is looking for a comparable emotional picture. Once it is allowed that the presentation can range from somatic to psychosomatic to psychological modes of expression, the objections to a depressive response at any age seem to be less valid.

Rapaport [64] speaks of "the universal experiences of grief and sadness ranging from passing sadness to profound depression" and implies that "such an ego state exists in all men." Here he agrees with Bibring that depression is "*a human way* of reacting to frustration and misery whenever the ego finds itself in a state of (real or imaginary) helplessness against 'overwhelming odds'" [12]. Both these statements reiterate the existential viewpoint within the framework of psychoanalytic ego psychology. Neither specifically excludes children as participants in this universal experience.*

Joffe and Sandler [47] are careful to distinguish the basic depressive response from the more clinical "depressive reaction" and from "unhappiness." Unhappy children, according to them, are still manifesting the presumably healthier response of protest and fight, whereas depressed children are seen to have capitulated and retreated, at least for a while, from pain-producing situations. The pain to which they refer may be either physical or psychological; in either case, a discrepancy occurs between the actual state of the self and an ideal state of well-being or primary narcissism. The ideal state is linked

---

* It is frequently observed that adult analysts, when speaking of incidence or prevalence, seldom refer directly to childhood as part of the human spectrum. For instance, Hartmann observed that "a healthy person must have the capacity to suffer and be depressed" [41]; would he have agreed that this remark applied equally to the child?

with feelings of security, satiation, and contentment, in contrast with the opposite pole of chronic discomfort, unrelieved hunger, and frustration. Certain individuals or individuals under certain conditions respond to the latter situation with the development of a primary psychobiological state, which may occur at any time in the individual's life span and represents the ultimate reaction to the experience of helplessness in the face of unremitting pain.

Interestingly, Bibring, Joffe and Sandler, and Engel and Schmale [25] have all focused their attention on the element of helplessness. Bibring sees it as a narcissistic shock, Joffe and Sandler as a painful capitulation, while Engel and Schmale regard it as part of a conservation-withdrawal response in which it represents the psychological concomitant of "giving up." Conservation-withdrawal is a universal mechanism comprising the behavioral triad of immobility, quiescence, and unresponsiveness "that occurs periodically and aperiodically among virtually every species of animal" and that is "a primary regulatory process for organismic homeostasis" [25]. On the somatic side, the individual experiences lassitude, weakness, fatigue, and loss of energy; psychologically, he feels "down in the dumps," discouraged, helpless, and hopeless. Like Joffe and Sandler, Engel and Schmale also distinguish between this nonspecific manifestation of defeat from clinical depressive reactions, which they consider "psychologically more complex disorders of adaptation" involving neurobiological abnormalities and specific neurochemical processes. They are unclear as to how and when the basic response becomes transformed into the clinical syndromes of depression.

The depressive mood, according to Mahler [55], originates during the separation-individuation process and is an exaggeration of the basic depressive response, similar to anxiety, that evolves at this time. During the "practising" phase, junior toddlers show evidence of a phase-specific elation (as if they were "intoxicated with their own faculties" and with "the greatness of their own world"), but with the next phase, depression enters the developmental picture, as the older toddler becomes gradually aware of himself and of his parents as separate people and of his mother no longer administering immediately and magically to all his needs. Since she is still the Omnipotent One in his eyes, he feels that she is deliberately withholding her power on his behalf. The more understanding and accepting she actually is, the less upset he becomes about this, but when her mothering is in reality deficient, his self-esteem suffers and he becomes susceptible to depressive moods.

When this tendency develops in the toddler, there is an observable change in his behavior. He is clinging, demanding, coercing, and angry with his mother while at the same time reacting to any hint of separation with tempestuous grief. The ambivalence is striking on both sides. Curiously, the picture is commoner in girls, which Mahler attributes to the additional discontentment of not having a penis.

When the depressive mood has set in as a consistent and constant pattern of response, both allocentric and autocentric senses, to use Schachtel's terminology [72], are affected. As he puts it, "the world loses its valences to the degree that the person loses his interest and does not turn toward the world. Usually he is at the same time angry at the world because he feels that it fails him in some respect, but his anger need not necessarily be conscious." The child, in such a mood, seems less of a self, less alive, less receptive, and certainly far removed from conducting "a love affair with the world." In fact, he may complain bitterly that everything is boring, uninteresting, and "dumb," and that he has nothing to do. Yet, he in no way appreciates any helpful suggestions that are made. Such periods of depressed boredom can be understood in terms of conservation-withdrawal theory or of Fenichel's [29] principle of "heterostasis," which he put forward as a supplement to Cannon's principle of homeostasis. According to this, equilibrium generates a certain monotony of its own and eventually drives the dissatisfied organism into pursuit of novel stimuli. As a result of the working of these two principles, a natural alternation between monotony and excitement ensues.

The answer to the question posed earlier is that a basic depressive affect comparable to anxiety does appear to exist and that in many individuals it becomes almost the "affect of choice" and may, under certain circumstances, consolidate into a periodic or persistent mood. Like anxiety, it has a signal-scanning function related to the possibilities of object loss. It is different in certain important respects, being more inner-directed and less object-related. Childhood is no stranger to this affect, and certain children are undoubtedly more depression-prone than others.

Is There a "Depressive Tendency" Predisposing to Depressive Responses and Reactions?

There has not been any definitive work done on the predisposition to depressive reactions, either constitutional or acquired, or on the stage at which predisposition can be said to become clinical depression. The field is still nebulous in these respects and investigators understandably vague. This is especially the case with constitutional factors. Joffe and Sandler remark that they can recognize the influence of constitutional factors, and then they proceed briefly to summarize these factors as "the predisposition to use particular defenses, frustration and discharge thresholds, differences in the apparatuses of primary autonomy, and variations in drive endowment" [47]. Most of these are unresearchable with the techniques currently available and in general amount to no more than clinical "hunches." Engel and Schmale [25] find themselves confronted with an awkward gap between the somatic and the psychological: "How and whether the neurochemical processes alleged to be involved in the syndromes of depression . . . are related to the conservation-withdrawal system remains to be seen, especially if individual vulnerability to depression proves to have a biochemical determinant." Engel has observed that some babies respond to frustration with inhibition-withdrawal and then with depression-withdrawal, while others become predominantly anxious. The differences are more evident later on, when some react to frustration with anger, protest, and resentment, while others become manifestly depressed and helpless [24]. It is difficult at this point to say whether the differences are a function of constitution, of the mother-infant relationship, of the total situation of frustration, or, as Bowlby [16] has suggested, steps in a regular sequence of response to separation and less.

In this presentation, for the purpose of clarification, the predispositional phase will be taken to include the first five years of life, during which genetic-constitutional factors and factors within the early environment are compounded in epigenetic fashion to generate the depressive tendency (see Table 1).

It is difficult to assess the factor of inheritance in any psychiatric disorder, but the difficulty is even greater when the disorder itself is still far from being accepted as a definable entity. In several clinical investigations of childhood depression, a high incidence of depressive illness in the parents has been reported, but to what extent the association is predominantly genetic or environmental is not at all clear. Cytryn and McKnew [19], for example, found parental depression only in child cases that were labeled chronic depression, but whether this entity exists during middle childhood is open to question unless the term chronic is redefined to mean something less intractable.

The neurochemical evidence for a genetic or acquired proclivity is equally scarce and sketchy. The investigation of catecholamine metabolism has failed to throw much light on etiology, diagnosis, or predisposition to childhood depression. The findings so far suggest that the patterns of biochemical changes are not consistent, a phenomenon already reported in adults with affective disorders [20].

With regard to a possible constitutional tendency toward inhibition-withdrawal, the position is somewhat different, and this appears to be a more promising avenue of research. From the evidence amassed

Table 1. Reactivation Theory of Depression

Genesis of Depressive Predisposition during First Five Years			
		Predisposing Factors	
Developmental Phases	Primal Depression	Genetic-Constitutional	Environmental
Prenatal	—		
Infantile (oral)	Anaclitic depression Depressive position Depressive constellation Conservation-withdrawal Frustration-helplessness	Family history of affective disorder Excessive tendency to conservation-withdrawal Inhibition Orality Narcissism	Parental loss Separation Hospitalization Maternal rejection Parental depression Emotionally closed families Divorce
Toddler (anal)	Basic depressive mood Preoedipal disappointment	Neurochemical-neuropsycho-logical anlage	Broken homes Chronic illness
Preschool (oedipal)	Primal parathymia Oedipal disappointment		

Reactivation of Primal Depression through the Life Cycle			
	Clinical Depression		
Stage of Life Cycle	Egopsychological Theory	Classical Theory	Precipitating Factors
Midchildhood (latency)	Failure of regulation of self-esteem Failure of separation-individuation processes	—	School failures Loss of self-esteem Identity conflicts Onset of menstruation Childbirth Miscarriage
Adolescence	Real-ideal ego state discrepancy	—	
Adulthood Old age	— —	Pathological mourning Internalization of lost object Aggression turned against self, narcissistic injury Libidinal regression to level of oral fixation	Menopause Anniversary reactions Failing powers Unemployment Loss of loved ones Failure to achieve life's objectives

by Benjamin,* the "stimulus barrier" (originally conceptualized by Freud) underwent "changes" during the first year of life (probably related to neurophysiological developments), toward the end of which a shift in inhibition occurs from passive to active. In the transition, there is a vulnerable period during which the infant is in special need of outside protection; where this has been insufficient, it is possible to speculate on the development of an excessive tendency to inhibition and withdrawal. Ribble [66] described infants with inadequate mothering who developed patterns of prolonged sleep withdrawal under any conditions of frustration. Engel [24] interpreted this behavior as essentially energy-conserving, since the infant raised the barrier against stimulation and reduced his activity, rather like a hibernating animal. Heider [42] described a group of vulnerable infants who, from the very beginning of life, manifested a poor physique, a badly functioning autonomic system, a low level of energy, a lack of interest, a disinclination to move much, a narrow range of curiosity, and a singular absence of trust and confidence. Any discomfort tended to drive the child further into itself, until gradually a withdrawal tendency, associated with low energy resources, evolved. Thomas et al. [80] also found that certain "primary activity patterns" in the areas of activity level, approach-withdrawal, intensity of reaction, threshold of response, and mood quality convey a general picture of unresponsiveness and retreat and that the tendencies remain fairly stable over time. Fries and Woolf [36] also described congenitally underactive babies and demonstrated that this inhibition-withdrawal "constitutional complex" remains relatively unchanged through normal and clinical developments; an apathetic, anergic baby may show at adolescence or even later a pronounced tendency to inhibition and depression under stress.

Psychoanalytic investigators have considered a vulnerability to depression in terms of an "instinctual constitution" involving the nature and intensity of the drive endowment and the presence of early "fixation points," coupled with certain environmental experiences in early life. Abraham [2], for instance, postulated a constitutional excess of oral erotism as a fixating factor at this level of development, to which was added a serious injury to infantile narcissism following disappointment in oedipal love. This was further elaborated by Jacobson [44]. The only connection, however, of this "primal parathymia" to childhood depression was made by Anthony [6], who related it to the occurrence of "discontentment" during latency. For Freud [34], the predisposing factors included the constitutional increase in both am-

* Benjamin's fascinating work in this area was unfortunately mostly unpublished except for a few short reports [e.g., 10].

bivalence and orality, the experience of object loss, and a regression to narcissism. Rado [63] focused on the orality and the sequence of rage-guilt-atonement-forgiveness in the context of hunger followed by orgastic satisfaction at the breast; the repetition of this sequence eventually creates the predisposition. Decades later, psychoanalytic theorists still have found it necessary to specify a constitutional factor in addition to depressive mechanisms. Klein [49] spoke of a constitutional excess of oral sadistic envy, and Benedek [9], of the congenital inability of some infants to be satisfied in conjunction with a hormonal factor.

Is There Such an Entity as a Primary Depression or a Nuclear Depressive Complex during the First Five Years?

When does the hypothesized primary depression occur? Some have placed it during the infantile phase, some during the toddler period, and some as late as the oedipal conflict (see Table 1). Probably none of these formulations based on sound observations and experience is altogether wrong or right, and each point of view represents some facet of the phenomenon that occurs. From all the data available, there appears to be good support for the thesis that the depressive personality is already predisposed by genetic-constitutional factors and by certain primary experiences during the first five years of life, and that this predisposition grows steadily during this period with each step in development. The retrospective view from the adult end tends to confirm this. "Whenever it is possible to observe [the reactive depressions] analytically, it becomes clear over and over again that they only arise in individuals who have already gone through inconspicuous depressive changes of mood. The latter can be tracked down regularly into early childhood" [51].

This raises a number of questions regarding the infantile antecedents of depressive illnesses in later life. In the first place, is it necessary to have experienced a primary depression in the first five years of life in order to develop a childhood, adolescent, or adult depressive disorder? Is such a primary depression a normal, inevitable developmental occurrence, or does it need to be generated by abnormal constitutional or environmental factors? Is this primary depression predominantly a preoedipal or an oedipal phenomenon? These questions are of special pertinence and interest in that they suggest a close correspondence with the developmental and clinical transformations undergone by anxiety during the life cycle. It may stretch the parallelism too much to suggest that a depressive "complex" emerges normally during the first five years, that it is "nuclear" for the development of the normal personality, and that a failure to resolve the complex leads to the subsequent development of clinical disorders. Although tempting, such extrapolations must be resisted in the light of our current ignorance.

There have been several important theoretical suggestions put forward as to the nature of this primary depression, but whatever its precise nature might be, it is likely that some sort of structured state is set up that can be reactivated subsequently (as Bibring [12] has suggested), the ease and intensity of the reactivation depending on constitutional factors, early life experiences, the strength of the ego during its development, and the kind and severity of precipitating events. The theories relevant to this are summarized in Table 1.

Table 1 suggests that the predisposition comprises genetic-constitutional factors and a series of prototypical depressions affecting the infant, the toddler, and the preschooler. As a result of some precipitating event or circumstance, a reactivation of the prototypical depression takes place in childhood, adolescence, and adult life with increasing degrees of complexity; that is, the primary manifestations of the prototypical depression are added to first by ego psychology reactions and later, with the development of psychosis, by the "classical" elaborations.

Is the prototypical episode diagnosable on observation? Or is it part of a heuristic attempt to explain a presumed connection between infantile experience and adult disorder? The primitive dismay manifested by the baby frustrated at the breast has long been recognized. Even the philosopher Descartes spoke of *"La première tristesse de l'enfant—la faute de nourriture,"* and every mother is well aware of the way the pains of teething can transform their happy, smiling babies into fretful, peevish, demanding, somber, miserable tyrants almost overnight. Separation from the mother can bring about a similar change. The joyousness of the 8-month infant, according to Spitz and Wolf [78], soon gives way to an anaclitic depression characterized by apprehension, sadness, weepiness, lack of contact, rejection of environment, withdrawal, retardation of reaction to stimuli, slowness of movement, dejection, stupor, loss of appetite, refusal to eat, loss of weight, and insomnia. The infant's facial expression, he says, if seen in an adult would be described as depressed. Sandler and Joffe [71] have pointed out that the same reactions and the same physiognomy can be observed in cases of pellagra. One would expect a change in the picture as the child moves through the quinquennium, and as the tie to the mother shifts from the biological to the psychological, from the anaclitic to the object-related, what began as a biological discharge phenomenon progresses to the level of a psychological experience in which self and nonself have been differentiated.

PRIMARY DEPRESSION DURING INFANCY

Neither Spitz and Wolf [78] nor Bowlby [15] have made any constructions as to what was taking place in an infant manifesting anaclitic depression or separation reaction following loss. Spitz did insist on certain prerequisites for infantile depression: (1) that a concept of the object must be attained before it can be cathected and that the object must first exist for the infant before it can be lost; (2) that the depression cannot appear before the 8-month anxiety (the "second organizer"); and (3) that a hostile environment, functioning like a superego, or an absence of cathectable objects is needed to bring about a turning inward of aggression. Anaclitic depression is not mourning but "beyond mourning" since the prognosis is so serious. The infant either dies of cachexia or settles into a catatonic stupor or an agitated idiocy. Such a terminal clinical picture does not suggest a linkage between anaclitic and adult depression, but perhaps, in less advanced cases, in which object substitution has eventually occurred, the groundwork for a depressive development is laid down. Bowlby has suggested that both the immediate and the remote outcome are functions of the preseparation tie to the mother and her use of separation, illnesses, and deaths within the family [16].

In strong contrast to Spitz and Bowlby, Benedek [9] and Klein [49] both offer a rich theoretical reconstruction of the primary infantile depressive experience, relating it meaningfully to all subsequent depressive experiences. Benedek's account seems "nearer to life," closer to what can be observed, and psychobiologically more probable. She offers an empathic picture of the transactional processes operating within the mother-infant symbiosis and bases it on the bipolarity of the alimentary phase of development. In this system, orally significant for both partners, the infant is the object of the mother's receptive needs, and, with the increased demands upon her, the mother responds with an increased wish to receive. Through the repetition of hunger and satiation, the biological unity is gradually replaced by a psychological one. With the failure of gratification, a number of sequences develop:

In the child: sudden total regression—projection of aggression onto the nongratifying object—introjection of aggressive impulses—equation of bad mother and bad self—development of the ambivalent core—emergence of the depressive constellation.

In the mother: frustration of her receptive needs—regression to the oral phase—reactivation of her ambivalent core—intensification of her aggression toward the infant—revival of preverbal memories of her own aggression and dependency toward her mother and of the equation of bad mother and bad self again.

In the child: intensification of ambivalent charge of the depressive constellation—setting up of a predisposition to later psychopathology, including depressive illness.

This complex but satisfying explanatory model satisfies a number of theoretical needs: it is psychobiologically well grounded; it is rooted in observable experience; it encompasses not only the transactions of the present but also the transactions of the past; it is intrapsychically meaningful within general psychoanalytic theory; and it contains a structural state that can be reactivated later by evocative experiences.

Although Klein's "depressive position" has some resemblances to the "depressive constellation," such as the frustrating alimentary experience, the use of introjection-projection mechanisms, the conflict based on ambivalence, and, when there is a failure at working through, the persistence of a proclivity toward depressive illness, it has none of the advantages cited for Benedek's theory. Most handicapping of all, it cannot be incorporated successfully into general psychoanalytic theory. Nevertheless, one can be grateful to both authors for formulating the thesis of a crucial and fundamental core experience in the child's development and linking it with later psychopathology.

PRIMARY DEPRESSION IN THE TODDLER PHASE

Reference has already been made to Mahler's description, based on careful, systematic observation, of the transformation of the basic depressive response, which is a normal part of separation-individuation, into a depressive mood. She is impressed with the occurrence of depressive-like reactions with mental content in the latter part of the second year of life and considers these the first affective reactions that can be said to be related to later depressions. (She rejects earlier "depressions," considering anaclitic depression to be simply a "marasmic reaction" and infantile depressive positions and constellations to be untenable for want of structure.) Her criteria for diagnosing a pre-oedipal depressive reaction (which may or may not be forerunners of later depressive illness) are the following: a readiness for sadness and grief interspersed in the matrix of a somewhat flattened mood, lacking spontaneity and joyousness, and a feeling of not being loved and of not being lovable (which, she says, is not a superego phenomenon). According to Mahler [54], it is only after separation-individuation is well under way that the necessary ego structures and functions are present for the occurrence of anything resembling the depression of adult life. Repeated grief reactions when a mother is physically present but emotionally unavailable forces the child into direct conflict with her, with the result that the integration and objective evaluation of the multiplicity of good and bad maternal images is impaired *and an ambitendant attitude develops.* When the mother is depressed, the child may identify with her and become depressed.

PRIMARY DEPRESSION IN THE OEDIPAL CHILD

Abraham [1] was the first to suggest the possibility of an infantile prototype of later melancholia originating in severe disappointments of the oedipal period that reinforce and regressively revive unresolved pregenital conflicts and eventually lead to repetitive depressive responses to all subsequent disappointments in life. This "primal parathymia" (*Urverstimmung*) is similar in nature to that described much later by Bowlby and is characterized by the same rage, resentment, and resignation to feelings of loss and abandonment. All subsequent depressive episodes "brought with (them) . . . a state of mind that was an exact replica of . . . (the) primal parathymia."

Jacobson [45] accepted this thesis with some qualifications. She recognized disappointment as the forerunner of depression and defined it as an experience arising from unfulfilled promises and expectations of gratification. Although oral frustrations were the earliest disappointments, "the primary childhood depression," she said, was "precipitated by coinciding severe disappointments *in both parents* in the beginning of the Oedipal period." The collapse of the love relationship was the primary factor, and guilt was secondary. In support of this, she pointed out that many mild adult depressions show little or no guilt and appear to stem not from a powerful superego but from the weakness of an ego disillusioned by the loss of belief in the magical omnipotence of the parents. As a result, the child is set on a pessimistic course and begins "to live on its superego rather than on its ego, with a further impoverishment of the latter."

The primary depression manifests itself through disillusionment, pessimism, joylessness, apathy, and a sense of emptiness, and represents a denial of anything worthwhile in the self and in the world around him. This remains the core experience of all later depressions. After recovery from this "primal parathymia," the vulnerable individual tends to maintain fragile object relations based on oral dependency and to reproject inflated superego and ego-ideal images onto the outside environment. The history of such a person is characteristic: frustrations during the preoedipal period, "spoiling" followed by de-

ficient mothering, a precocious onset of the father relationship, oedipal disappointments in both parents leading to a hateful turning away
from one to the other and the playing of one against the other, an escape from both into a resentful, narcissistic retreat, and, finally, a
breakdown into depressive illness.

The concept of disappointment is clearly an important one in the
general evolution of the depressive personality, but whether it should
be given a nuclear role is debatable. The disillusionment experienced
by the child in the early oedipal period may be doubly severe because
of the increased awareness of sexual wishes and prohibitions at this
time and because of the feelings of hopelessness that first emerge during the phallic phase [74]. Nevertheless, there are many disappointments and frustrations prior to this, and earlier theories do account
for the genesis of the depressive proclivity—in fact, there is almost a
surfeit of causal explanations, each of which appears singularly valid
within its own frame of reference. In reviewing them all, one cannot
help but feel that the differences are due to the focusing on different
phases of early development and that each explanation evolves logically from the previous ones. There is no doubt that the theory of the
depressive constellation affords the fullest and most meaningful picture of the infantile phase, especially when it is coupled with the
conservation-withdrawal hypothesis. At the next phase, Mahler's description of the emergence of the depressive mood during separation-
individuation can be taken in conjunction with Jacobson's delineation
of preoedipal disappointments. The final phase is best understood
within the context of the Abraham-Jacobson concept of disillusionment, although, once again, the explanation can be enhanced by the
Bibring-Sandler thesis of a narcissistically hurtful discrepancy arising
between actual and ideal ego states (see Table 1).

We should add that the transmission of depression may have both
a hereditary and a psychic basis. The intergenerational psychic transmission is fully implied in Benedek's theory, but it is also at work in
the account given by Mahler. For example, the toddler's problem with
a depressed mother may be that he identifies too closely with her or
that she cannot let go of him and allow him to individuate in spite of
his protests. The situation may become a symbiotic unit, one part of
which constitutes the depressed mother with her poor self-concept
and the other, the elated omnipotent child, whose self-esteem is constantly being fed by her and whose vulnerability away from her is consequently great.

This curious mixture of theories has been derived in part from the
direct observation of the child's development investigated prospec-

tively and from the genetic reconstruction of depressed adults in analysis. It is therefore not altogether surprising that the two approaches to primary depression should illuminate different viewpoints.

Is There Such an Entity as Clinical Depression Occurring during Childhood?

There is an old clinical truism that diagnoses are made after a diagnosis has been made, meaning that once a clinical state has been recognized and described, the less perceptive begin to see it. This was true of "hospitalism" as described by Spitz [77], which had passed unnoticed in children's wards, even when grossly displayed, until he first drew attention to it. There are, of course, many reasons for not seeing what is abundantly manifest, and clinical depression in childhood could be one of those conditions for which adults (even analytically trained ones) develop a surprising blind spot.

The controversy surrounding the existence of a depressive neurosis in childhood has repeated much of the earlier argument affecting anxiety neurosis. Before Freud, children could be naughty or physically ill but not neurotic. Their emotional disturbances, as Freud put it, were "shouted down in the nursery." With the publication of the analysis of the phobic 5-year-old boy, the "age of the neurotic child" set in to the extent that Hartmann complained that the pendulum had swung too far in the opposite direction—from a point of no recognizable neurosis of childhood to the point where "every naughtiness, actually every behavior of the child that does not conform to the textbook model, every developmental step that is not according to plan is considered as neurotic" [41]. He agreed that anxiety neurosis did occur during childhood but believed it differed from adult neurosis in being usually limited to a single functional disturbance. In this sense it was simpler and less convoluted: "The way from conflict to symptom seems often to be shorter than in adult neurosis."

We are now retracing this same historical course with regard to clinical depression as seen from the psychoanalytic point of view. From not being recognized at all, it is reaching the point that whenever the child is "out of sorts," disappointed with some lack of success, chagrined by a loss of prestige among his peers, or saddened by the loss of a pet, he is very likely to be regarded as clinically depressed and in need of treatment. Contemporary parents have been alerted to depression as they once were to anxiety, and there is the same risk, referred to by Hartmann, that the concept of a depressive illness during childhood may be lost in the new diagnostic cult.

It seems important, once again, to preserve a balance and to exercise a special clinical vigilance. At the present stage, when the new disorder is being reviewed for clinical acceptance, every case in which the diagnosis is made should be scrutinized in detail and carefully followed up. In accordance with the guidelines suggested by Hartmann, one would anticipate a diagnostic profile that is different in many respects from that of the adult and yet sufficiently similar in its antecedents and subsequent developments to be included within the same class. Furthermore, one would expect that each developmental stage would add its own overtones to the product. In general, the way into the disorder and the way out of the disorder would tend to be shorter and more frequently limited to a few functional disturbances.

As mentioned earlier in a general context, the question of how much children think, feel, and suffer depends on the concepts of childhood prevailing at the time. These may be contradictory, and opposing views on psychology and psychopathology may exist. This is equally true of psychoanalysis, which initially exposed the surprisingly complex inner life of the small child. When Freud said "I am aware that I am attributing a great deal to the mental capacity of a child between four and five years of age" [33], he was well aware that he was taking a new and radically different clinical look at childhood; but this did not deter him: "I have let myself be guided by what we have recently learned, and I do not consider myself bound by the prejudices of our ignorance" [33]. Unhappily, later psychoanalysts have not always followed this precept, and some have allowed their conceptual biases regarding the nature of the child to determine their understanding of his clinical productions.

This is especially true with regard to current analytic attitudes on childhood mourning and depression. There are psychoanalysts who state that for structural reasons these phenomena cannot occur during childhood. Clinical depression, according to Rochlin [70], for example, is a superego phenomenon involving aggression directed against the self with a certain intensity and duration. Neither of these is possible with children, and they therefore conclude *ipso facto* that there is no such entity as clinical depression in children. When confronted by apparent examples of mourning and depression, these analysts counter it with two arguments: first, that simple grief reactions or moodiness are being erroneously amplified into full-blown depressive illnesses; and second, that this is an example of the usual adultomorphic tendency to assume that since adults and children share a common humanity, they also share a common psychology. The child's immaturity, they insist, precludes such psychological intricacies: his ego and superego are still underdeveloped; he has still to establish object constancy in the face of ambivalence and conflict; he has still to establish mature identifications with the object; he is as yet unable to respond to object loss without immediate surrogation; and he has yet to develop a biological idea of death. For all these reasons, he is unable to be depressed and will not be able to mourn or to complete the act of mourning until the termination of adolescence. Freud described the work of mourning as characterized by the gradual decathexis of the internal mental representative of the lost object accomplished through recurrent remembering, the painful acceptance of permanent absence, and identification with the lost object [35].

The alternative view is that the child, irrespective of what he shows externally, can be depressed and can mourn inwardly. To undertake the work of mourning, the child must understand the irreversibility of death, must have developed a sufficient degree of object constancy, and must have sufficient feelings available for new objects. *The same is true for clinical depression*, which is why it is rarely if ever seen in the prelatency child. When mourning fails, the feelings remain invested in the lost object and cannot be used for further growth and maturation. This may lead to developmental arrest at the stage of loss, a tendency to ward off feelings, and, in about 30 percent of the cases, puts the child at risk for adult depression. Although a "loss complex" [69] may be associated with adult depression, it is theoretically important to keep it clinically separate from childhood depression.

The either-or argument of Rochlin [70] is based on the classic analytic view of depression, and it is certainly true that the childhood depressive reaction does not measure up to this. This does not mean, however, that the child's reaction cannot be a special variant of the human depressive reaction, in developmental continuity with the classic adult form. In a later section, an attempt will be made to find an analytic framework for the childhood disorder so that it need not be disbarred solely on theoretical grounds.

*Is the Clinical Depression of Childhood the Same as
or Different from Adult Depressive Illness?*

It is undoubtedly true that the fully developed picture of melancholia is never seen during childhood; the position has been categorically stated by Mahler: "We know that the systematized affective disorders are unknown in childhood. It has been conclusively established that the immature personality structure of the infant or older child is not capable of producing a state of depression such as that seen in the adult" [54]. She attributed this to the fact that the child's ego is unable to survive in an objectless state for any length of time. However, she does not say that unsystematized affective disorders do not exist in children, and the implication of her statement is that states of depression in keeping with the immature personality structure can and do exist.

It seems clear that clinical depression has many faces and that some of these are seen only in adult life while others may show themselves at any stage of the life cycle. To clarify the issue, even at the risk of simplification, we might try to classify depressive reactions into compounds of primary, secondary, and tertiary manifestations, the mixture varying with the stage of development, the psychosocial setting, and the severity of the condition. The primary manifestations include the core of the depressive disorder—the ambivalence (Benedek [9]), the feelings of decreased strength, energy, and interest in the outside world (Engel and Schmale [25]), disillusionment, anhedonia, pessimism, apathy, joylessness, emptiness, and worthlessness (Jacobson [45]), ego inhibition and lowered self-esteem (Freud [35]), helplessness, diminished self-esteem, and inhibition of functions (Bibring [12]), and, in metapsychological terms, less than normal libidinal investment in the self-representation, aggression not sufficiently fused with libido, and a lack of adequate neutralized energy for ego development (Mahler [55]).

The secondary manifestations occur in response to defense and restitution and include the search for new objects, the clinging to people, obsessive attempts to control the self and the environment, reversals of affect, affect-equivalent psychosomatic states, antisocial behavior (as a denial of helplessness), and an apparently endless series of self responses representing a crucial lowering of self-esteem— self-abnegation, self-shame, self-hate, self-abasement, self-sacrifice, and self-doubt.

The tertiary manifestations imply a more total involvement of the personality, a more complete regression, and a profound reduction in the sense of reality. The melancholic experiences an enormous loss in himself through anal expulsion and tries to compensate for this by a devouring cannibalistic activity that seeks to introject the lost object (primarily the mother), which is then treated with intense sadism and ambivalence. What ensues is guilt and remorse, and a delusional expectation of punishment and death that may become suicidal. The critical mechanism involved seems to be the narcissistic identification with the hated object and the turning of the aggression against the self.

As a general rule, one can say (although exceptions are inevitable) that the primary manifestations occur by themselves in the infantile period; that both primary and secondary manifestations are evident during childhood; and that the primary, secondary, and tertiary manifestations can be observed sometimes together and sometimes alone during adult life. Childhood and adult depressions are therefore clinically fairly distinct from one another, and the differences are based on both descriptive and dynamic aspects.

The manifestations represent a sequence of changes from the predominantly biological to the psychobiological, the psychosomatic, and the psychodynamic. In old age, the manifestations tend to move back toward the biological. Psychologically, the manifestations reflect a lack of self-consciousness and later on ideational richness and variety. This succulence of expression eventually gives place to senile aridity. Thus depression faithfully mirrors the stages of life.

Can Child and Adult Clinical Depressions Be Considered within the Same Theoretical Framework or Does Each Require Its Separate Theory?

There is a tendency on the part of analysts working at the adult end of the continuum to construct adult models of illness in their more or less final forms (e.g., melancholia) and then to use the presence or absence of these as confirming or disconfirming the diagnosis in any given case. Childhood cases have understandably failed this test in most instances, and child analysts have generally accepted the verdict and searched for innocuous labels that do not provocatively suggest developmental continuity with the adult illnesses.

In psychoanalysis, two syndromes have been vying for some time for the title of depression. The classic Abraham-Freud syndrome was rooted in instinct theory, primary narcissism, and narcissistic injury suffered in childhood. From Freud [35] came the following components: loss of the love object, introjection of the lost object, attacks on the internalized object with resulting self-reproach, and libidinal regression to the oral-cannibalistic stage. From Abraham [1] we have: the ambivalence of simultaneous love and hate, repressed and projected sadism and its associated guilt, and inhibition and loss through anal expulsion. The love object is taken in orally and ejected anally. Narcissism is represented in both positive (delusional self-esteem) and negative (delusional self-hatred) forms. In the second syndrome, the ego psychology view, there is a marked shift of emphasis from guilt and the repression of sadistic instincts to the problems of frustrated ego development, in which the roles of orality and aggression inwardly directed at the self are largely underplayed.

Only melancholia can be understood in terms of the classic theory. Most other depressions, and these constitute the majority, are milder in form, occur in both adults and children (in whom they are diagnosed as reactive or neurotic), and require an explanatory theory other than the classic one. They can be easily understood in terms of the second syndrome, the best theoretical statement of which is Bibring's [12].

There has been more or less general agreement that the classic theory, with its demand for a high development of structure, can have little bearing on the clinical depressions of childhood. Sandler and Joffe "legitimately doubt whether theories which are heavily influenced by the study of melancholia in adults provide the most suitable starting-off point for the investigation of depression in children" [71], and Rochlin has repeatedly insisted that "no real theory of childhood depression has evolved, perhaps because theories of depression in adults have been applied too generously" [68].

The position of Bibring [12] is not too dissimilar from that of Joffe and Sandler described earlier, but it does have the advantage of keeping the concept of a structured infantile ego state of helplessness separate from its reactivations in later life. According to this theory, the early experience, resulting from frequent frustrations of the infant's oral needs, consists at first of anger and protest and subsequently, as the "signals" are disregarded, of exhaustion and helplessness.

Rapaport [64] points out that Bibring's formulation of the epigenesis of narcissistic aspirations "is an important step toward specifying the conception of autonomous ego development . . . introduced by Hartmann." The formulation is summarized in Table 2.

One has here a structural theory that treats depression as the reactivation of a structured state and maintains that though the persisting aspirations are threefold, "the mechanism of the resulting depression appears to be essentially the same."

Bibring insists that depression is determined not by intersystemic conflicts between ego, id, superego, and environment but by tensions within the ego itself, *an intrasystemic conflict* in accordance with Hartmann's theory. He therefore defines depression as "everything that lowers or paralyzes the ego's self-esteem without changing the narcissistically important aims."

This ego psychology theory has a number of advantages that seem especially pertinent to the childhood situation. First of all, there is nothing in the theory that would preclude the consideration of clinical depression on the grounds of immaturity. The regression in Bibring's schema is not a regression of libido to an oral fixation point but primarily an ego regression to an ego state, with the implication that the depressive condition is a *reactivation* of a primary infantile state. This reactivation could well occur during latency. Second, ego inhibition, self-esteem, and helplessness are all within the child's psycholog-

Table 2.   An Epigenetic Ego Psychology Theory of Depression
(Bibring [12])

Psychosexual Level	Narcissistic Aspiration	Defensive Need	Depression Follows Discovery of:	Central Conflict Is over:
Oral	To be loved To get supplies To be cared for	To be independent To be self-supporting	Not being loved Not being independent	Dependency needs
Anal	To be good To be loving To be clean	Not to be bad and defiant Not to be hostile Not to be dirty	Lack of control over impulses and objects Feeling of helplessness Guilt	Controls
Phallic	To be admired To be center of attention To be strong and triumphant	To be modest To be inconspicuous To be submissive	Fear of being defeated Fear of being ridiculed Fear of retaliation	Competition

ical grasp. Third, the fact that Engel and Schmale also put helplessness in the forefront of their conservation-withdrawal theory lends further support to Bibring's position, since their views are based on intensive, systematic clinical investigation. Furthermore, helplessness is the bread and butter of childhood, a constant existential experience coupled with humiliation, and any theory that concentrates on it is speaking very much to the condition of childhood. Fourth, all the metapsychological difficulties associated with the operation of classic theory—oral fixation and incorporation, aggression against the self—are here given merely a peripheral or complicating role. The child's depression can assimilate them later when he becomes an adult. Fifth, the fact that depression is an intra-ego conflict and undergoes an epigenetic devolopment in a manner corresponding to Erikson's epigenesis, particularly with regard to such psychosocial conflicts as trust versus mistrust, autonomy versus shame and doubt, and initiative versus guilt, links Bibring's theory very effectively to childhood. Sixth, the concept of narcissism is considered, in ego psychology terms, related to the psychosexual level and correlated with the defensive need, the precipitating factor, and the central conflict (see Table 2). For all these reasons, the ego psychology theory of depression becomes the theory of choice for the classic depressions of childhood, with the added possibility that the child can "qualify" for the classic theory when he later succumbs to adult melancholia.

Self-esteem is at the heart of Bibring's theory (as it is with Jacobson's), and the regulation of self-esteem is therefore a crucial issue in the life of the depressive individual. In childhood, love and self-esteem are never far apart. As Fenichel puts it, "The small child loses self-esteem when he loses love, and attains it when he regains love" [28]. The ego psychology cycle described by Bibring, in which high aspirations give rise to feelings of helplessness and hopelessness and finally to depression, is more conceivable as a psychological event in the child than are the complex sequences demanded by classic theory (see Table 3).

Within the context of self-esteem and also pertinent to the child's experience, Jacobson also makes a significant additional contribution relating to the factor of shame in the cycle of depression. According to her, a lowered self-esteem is not necessarily based on a superego conflict; hence depression can occur in the absence of guilt—a point about which there has been much controversy—and in the presence of inferiority feelings or shame, which are also intrasystemic conflicts. Quite often, the two exist together, the shame covering up the guilt. A further relevant point about the shame system is that it can develop in small children before the establishment of the superego system; children can experience "shame depression" as a primitive narcissistic conflict before they are capable of feeling "guilt depression." The cycle of lowered self-esteem, culminating in depression, should therefore also include inferiority feelings, shame, and self-consciousness [46].

It should be added, before we leave this section, that although a number of viewpoints have been put forward from psychoanalysis, the field is still beset by uncertainty. We are still not sure what kinds of "constitutional complex" initiate the predisposition nor whether the primal depression invariably antedates all subsequent depressions. There is no firm prospective or retrospective evidence on such a linkage. From the point of view of life experiences, a number of factors, such as object loss and contact with rejecting or depressed mothers, have been cited, but more longitudinal data are needed. If one picks his theory carefully, there may appear to be a reasonable case for assuming that clinical depression can occur during childhood. To support this assertion we must turn to the clinical evidence.

Table 3. Cycles of Depression

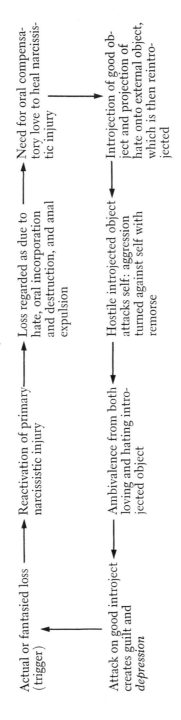

Classic Cycle

Actual or fantasied loss (trigger) ⟶ Reactivation of primary narcissistic injury ⟶ Loss regarded as due to hate, oral incorporation and destruction, and anal expulsion ⟶ Need for oral compensatory love to heal narcissistic injury

Attack on good introject creates guilt and *depression* ⟶ Ambivalence from both loving and hating introjected object ⟶ Hostile introjected object attacks self: aggression turned against self with remorse ⟶ Introjection of good object and projection of hate onto external object, which is then reintrojected

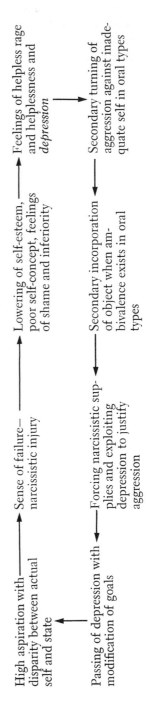

Egopsychology Cycle

High aspiration with disparity between actual self and state ⟶ Sense of failure—narcissistic injury ⟶ Lowering of self-esteem, poor self-concept, feelings of shame and inferiority ⟶ Feelings of helpless rage and helplessness and *depression*

Passing of depression with modification of goals ⟶ Forcing narcissistic supplies and exploiting depression to justify aggression ⟶ Secondary incorporation of object when ambivalence exists in oral types ⟶ Secondary turning of aggression against inadequate self in oral types

CHILDHOOD DEPRESSION: CLINICAL
MANIFESTATIONS

In his review of depression in childhood, Rie [67] pointed out that none of the leading textbooks in child psychiatry made any mention of depressive disorders and that symposia on depression conducted by leading psychiatrists and psychoanalysts have made only passing reference to childhood depression and none to depressive illness. It is understandable that those working in the adult field might consider it nonexistent, but until recently child psychiatrists also questioned its existence. It is only very recently that this early occurrence of clinical depression has been "discovered" and described, and there is resistance to the idea. Rochlin, for instance, has stated firmly that "clinical depression as we psychoanalytically understand the disorder, *does not occur in childhood*" [68]. What does occur, according to him, is a reaction to loss that produces "a highly organized galaxy of sequential psychic phenomena," at the center of which is the dread of abandonment. Rochlin sums up the opposition very clearly and conclusively:

It is misleading and confusing to regard the children who suffer severely and react by withdrawal from living objects as clinically depressed or suffering melancholia. The ego seems not to have differentiated sufficiently at a young age to suggest that the highly complex mechanisms of depression are present. Object loss in the young child finds expression in withdrawal, often with regression and disorder in the process of identification. Instead of looking for signs of pathological depression, it appears more fruitful to follow the process of identification in relation to the loss.

Furthermore, he feels that the clinical data to support the concept of a depressive disorder are not convincing. His emphasis on withdrawal would fit in with the conservation-withdrawal theory. The rest of his argument, based on an either-or premise, has already been considered earlier in this chapter and was dismissed as too monolithic to fit with the flexible developmental picture being presented. Yet, he is correct on one count: the evidence offered to substantiate the claim is far from convincing, is mostly based on inadequate clinical observations and unwarranted extrapolations from the adult position, and is backed by very tenuous theory.

The combined clinical wisdom and experience of the Group for the Advancement of Psychiatry's Committee on Child Psychiatry [39] comes down on the side of clinical depression in childhood, but their statement has an *ex cathedra* quality for which no evidence is provided:

Psychoneurotic depressive disorders of a more chronic nature, involving internalized conflicts in relation to deeply ambivalent feelings *are only rarely seen in children at peak intensity*, as they and their equivalents are characteristically modified by the child's stage of development. When they occur, they are to be distinguished from more acute reactive disorders in which depression may be involved as in the anaclitic type. Such disorders should also be separated from fleeting feelings of depression in healthy children undergoing developmental or situational crises.

The report also mentions a clinical depression manifested by eating and sleeping disturbances, hyperactivity, and other patterns precipitated by actual, threatened, or symbolic loss of a parent or parent substitute. Loss of self-esteem, feelings of self-depreciation, guilt, and ambivalence toward the loved person *"may be present in older children."*

It would appear that clinical depression in childhood has all the protean qualities cited by Burton: at times it shows an infantile, anaclitic picture, at other times a psychosomatic, acting out, inhibitory, or neurotic characteristic. It may also oscillate between internalized and externalized modes of expression. Beres [11], for example, describes the case of a child who showed depressive reactions associated with superego introjection, identification with a dead mother, masochistic trends, and guilt feelings at one time, and impulsive, aggressive attacks on others at another time.

An intolerance for prolonged depression has been mentioned by several authors to account for the child's lapse into psychosomatic illness or aggressive, hyperactive, or acting out behavior. Many have remarked on the alternation between brief periods of depression and "depressive equivalents." The latter construction has run the gamut through every conceivable symptomatic expression in child psychiatry, making depression in this covert form the bedrock of all clinical disorders. Sperling [76], who believed strongly in the equivalents, concluded very logically that there is a high incidence of depression in children and that this is mainly manifested by an acting out through bodily channels, giving rise to sleep disturbances, anorexia, pruritus, migraine, and ulcerative colitis. Toolan [81] carried this idea of depression without depressive affect to such an extreme that the whole concept of equivalents ceased to be clinically credible. His approach has been rightfully criticized by Rie [67] as atheoretical, uncritical, circular, semantically complacent, and devoid of any real evidence. It outlines a development but completely lacks a developmental frame of reference. The symptomatic "stages" shift from eating and sleeping disturbances, colic, crying, and head banging in infancy to behavior problems such as temper tantrums, disobedience, truancy, running away, and accident proneness. The lowered self-esteem of the children is stressed, but what this has to do with the condition etiologically, developmentally, or dynamically is never discussed. If one had to rely solely on the concept of depressive equivalents to illuminate the field of clinical child depression, one would remain very much in the dark, since it both explains too much and explains nothing at all. One would not, however, deny it a place in the classification, provided it is used with greater discretion than hitherto.

Progress on the overt forms of depression encountered clinically continues, and in recent years papers on clinical depression in childhood have been multiplying at a rate typical for a new clinical "discovery."*

A recent view of depressive states in childhood and adolescence published in Europe [4] reveals the extent to which a clinical depression of childhood has become a disease entity constructed in the medical model and treated with a host of antidepressant drugs. Apparently the Europeans take it for granted that the childhood variety includes both exogenous and endogenous types; nevertheless, they are generally in agreement that the reaction tends to be episodic, relatively brief, clinically different from the reaction in adults, and symptomatically changeful not only during the course of development but also during the illness.

The American clinical literature in recent years has taken a more dynamic course, and important position papers by (in order of merit) Malmquist [56, 57], Poznanski and Zrull [62], and Cytryn and McKnew [19, 20] have helped considerably in clarifying the current state of knowledge. It is of some interest that although the difficult authors continue to have doubts about the existence of this particular clinical entity, and express them at times with vague discomfort, they write their papers as if the question were a foregone conclusion.

The diagnosis of clinical depression in children is generally based on various combinations of signs and symptoms that have been found empirically to cluster together. Sandler and Joffe [71] found nine pathognomonic items characterizing the depressed child. He is sad, unhappy looking, and depressed; withdrawn, bored, and disinterested; discontented, not readily satisfied, and with little capacity for pleasure; moved by feelings of being unloved and rejected, and ready to turn away disappointing objects; unable to accept help or comfort;

---

* It seems that references to childhood depression in the older literature may also have been "masked"; Stutte [17] has recently pointed out that nearly all the old literature on child psychiatry contained accounts of it but that it then underwent submergence until its present rediscovery.

prone to regress to oral passivity; suffering from insomnia and other sleep disturbances; given to autoerotic and various repetitive activities; and having difficulties making sustained contact with his therapist. These items were reviewed by Poznanski and Zrull [62] in their series of depressed children, and five of them were found valid for a sample selected by quite different means. Those validated included the sad and unhappy appearance, the withdrawal, the feeling of being unloved and rejected, insomnia, and regression to oral passivity. Cytryn and McKnew [19] distinguished between the symptomatologies of acute and chronic depressive illnesses. The acute cluster contained a sadness of affect, social withdrawal, hopelessness and helplessness, psychomotor retardation, anxiety, scholastic and social failure, sleeping and feeding disturbances, and suicidal ideas and threats (but rarely attempts). The chronic cluster (present for several months) comprised severe impairment of scholastic and social adjustment, sleeping and feeding disturbances, and, in serious cases, feelings of despair, general retardation, and self-destructive ideation.

If these clinical reports are even partly correct, that does give strong support to the view that children can present a diagnostic picture fairly similar to the ones encountered in adults with depressive illness. The prevalence and incidence may be less, and the disorders not so severe and protracted, but there seems to be little doubt that the childhood condition belongs within the same class of disturbance. Anthony attributed the difference between the child and the adult clinical pictures to "the inability of the child to verbalize his affective state, to the incomplete development of the superego, and to the absence of consistent self-representation" [5]. His symptomatic picture included "weeping bouts, some flatness of affect, fear of death for self or parents, irritability, somatic complaints, loss of appetite and energy, various degrees of difficulty in school adjustment, and vacillations between clinging to and unreasonable hostility toward . . . parents."

There seems to be good agreement that the depressive reactions seen in children are highly intermittent, coming and going frequently in relation to the environmental conditions. Depressive reactions in children appear to be more exogenous than the adult states and more susceptible to external influences. While the underlying psychopathology persists, the depressive affect is a temporary phenomenon. Poznanski and Zrull [62] also regarded the depression as "part of an ongoing process where its appearance was episodic," and they compared it to the characterological depression seen in adults, "where depression occurs as a character defense."

Another aspect of the childhood condition is its close relationship to the family situation. Cytryn and McKnew [19] have called attention to the frequency of parental loss by separation, divorce, or death, to rejection and depreciation by parents, to loss of interest in and involvement with the child on the part of a parent, and to parental depression (with the child frequently identifying with the depressed parent). Malmquist [56] puts emphasis on the family's demand for conformity and dedication to duty and on the requirement of earning parental approval. Such "superego families" constantly force the children into patterns of "goodness." Like Cytryn and McKnew, Poznanski and Zrull discovered a high incidence of parental depression in which the depression was used ostensibly to control outbursts of rage. These families had special difficulty in handling aggression and hostility, and the child inevitably became a scapegoat in the process. He was traumatized in a variety of ways, from being battered and belittled to being rejected and neglected. Other characteristics of these families were absence of anxiety and oscillation between aggression and depression. The children experienced the most depression when they were not discharging it through aggressive play. Poznanski and Zrull considered aggressive behavior to be a means of avoiding depression and the difficulties in controlling aggression part of the cause of the poor self-concept. They shared the opinion of Fast [27] that the child who is prone to depression is one who must keep the "good" inside and the "bad" outside and who has failed to integrate "good" and "bad" within his own body limits. This was part of a primitive projection-introjection defense system that was very likely to break down under stress.

Other defense mechanisms vary in the effectiveness with which they can keep depression at bay. Aggressive behavior has already been mentioned as a counteraction to it, but there are many other, less disturbing ways of preventing the arousal of depressive affect and its emergence into consciousness. When depression is signaled, obsessive magical controls may be invoked to compensate for feelings of helplessness, hypomanic excitement to overcome lack of energy, reversal of affect to master sadness, denial to avoid all unpleasant affects, withdrawal to put distance between the self and an overwhelming emotional experience, antisocial behavior to distract the person's attention from internal pressures, and somatization to obscure the psychic realities.

Although there seems to be a certain amount of concordance with regard to the components of the depressive symptomatology and its familial ambience, this is little agreement about classification. Cytryn and McKnew [19] have constructed a tidy system, empirically derived from their clinical investigations, that affords a baseline for further work (see Table 4).

Table 4.   Classification of Midchildhood Depressive Reactions (Data from Cytryn and McKnew [19])

Type	Frequency	Precipitation	Premorbid Adjustment	Family Pathology
Acute	Not uncommon	Recent loss	Well adjusted	Mild
Masked	Most frequent	None	Severe, varied acting out	Serious psychopathy
Chronic	Rare	None	Marginal adjustment	Depressed parent; frequent early separations

Malmquist [56] has produced an even more elaborate nosology with a theoretical underpinning that stems from a thorough critical review of the field rather than from empirical research (see Table 5).

Whether any of these types and subtypes exist clinically with any appreciable frequency outside the theoretical formulation is a moot point, but the classification has a heuristic value and may direct clinicians toward certain possibilities. It is, as Malmquist has said, a "tentative classification" based on age, etiology, and description. The common principle is "the predominance of depressive affect."

Malmquist sees depression proneness in Adlerian terms, that is, as "a set of characterologic maneuvers" by such prototypes as "the discouraged child" who tyrannizes with tears, "the passive-aggressive child" who gets his way by whining, the future manic-depressive who begins enthusiastically but is soon defeated, and "the hostile, manipulative child" who is out to get to the top. All these individuals are candidates for depression when they come up against circumstances that leave them helpless.

Eisen [23] reviewed the depressive symptoms of 50 children and found three typical symptom patterns that are interesting in that they overlap items in the two other classifications. The type 1 child is *withdrawn* and feels empty and alone. He is born after an anxious pregnancy, the birth is difficult, and his mother has a postpartum depression. The infantile phase is stormy. The family is covertly aggressive. The type 2 child acts out with hyperactivity, aggressiveness, and destructiveness. Again, pregnancy and birth are physically and psychologically traumatic for the mother, and the infantile period is stormy. The families deal with the central problem of aggression either by aggressive acting out or overcontrol and conformity. The type 3 child is prone to *psychosomatic* disorder and is characteristically passive. There were significant separations in the first two years of life, and the child is constantly threatened by the loss of his mother or her love. As a result, he suppresses his own angry feelings from fear of retaliation. The families also tend to suppress aggression.

Table 5.   Classification of Childhood Depression (Data from Malmquist [56])

Type	Subtypes	Description
Physically based syndromes	Part of physical process Resulting from physical process	Seen in neoplastic, degenerative, infectious, metabolic, and nutritional disorders
Deprivational syndromes	Anaclitic type Affectionless type	Reality-based reactions to impoverished environments
Separation-individuation syndromes	Subphase disturbances Depressive school phobias Antecedents of moral masochism	Related to problems of "hatching" from symbiosis
Latency syndromes	Associated with object loss or failure to attain ideals Depressive equivalents Manic-depressive status, anhedonia, and obsessive character reactions	Traumatic reactions Covering somatization, hypermobility, "acting out," delayed grief reactions, obesity Seen at this stage?

The "school phobia subtype" has received more than its share of study, since the symptom is an arresting one and demands immediate attention and action of some sort. Agras reviewed seven such children and found six of them to be depressed in a way that was "close phenomenologically to the depressive disorders of adults" [3]. There were also two school phobias and five potential school phobias with difficult school adjustments among seven depressed latency girls described by Harrington and Hassan [40]. The seven girls were all model children aspiring to be good, clean, and clever but so self-depreciatory that their self-esteem was constantly eroded. As predisposing factors, the authors point to a splitting of the mothering function during the first two years of life and faulty identifications conducive to ego weakness and consequent difficulties in separation-individuation.

The role of specific traumatic events in the genesis of depression has been much debated. However, there have been cases described in which the earliest years were so uneventful and benign that the children seemed unprepared for the expectable crises of life. Hunter [43] has referred to such traumatized individuals as "root-damaged" and differentiates them from the deprived by the fact that they retain their capacity for relationship. Nevertheless, they are sensitive, easily hurt, insecure, profoundly dependent, and very prone to depression, because of which in adolescence they commonly resort to drugs. They also tend to depress the adults with whom they come in contact. But the prognosis is good because the "roots" are basically good.

The "physically based syndromes" with accompanying depression are relatively common but are often overlooked. They tend to occur not in the hospital, where anxiety is the predominant affect, but during the period of convalescence, when a particular personality reaction may occur that renders the child "unforthcoming" or inhibited. Bierman, Silverstein, and Finesinger reported the case of a 6-year-old boy who, while recovering from acute poliomyelitis, became "a weakened depressed child who had lost all hope," as if he had had "all his energy drained out of him" [13]. His self-concept was low, his symptoms were markedly oral, and it was clear that the paralysis was experienced as a narcissistic injury. The mother's orality was believed to be an additional transactional factor in the emergence of his depression.

CLINICAL DEPRESSION OF CHILDHOOD
IN THE CONTEXT OF A REACTIVATION HYPOTHESIS

In 1914, Freud wrote that the analytic experience had convinced him "of the complete truth of the common assertion that the child was psychologically father of the man" [34]. Today's psychoanalyst, with his perspective on both oedipal and preoedipal development, would no doubt extend the truism to include the concept of the child as mother to his later self and the significance of the early mothering experience, through reciprocal identification, in the subsequent emergence of psychopathology. In this respect, anxiety syndromes tend generally to show a predominance of oedipal influences, while the clinical depressions give stronger indications of shaping by preoedipal factors. Yet, even in the latter, the preoedipal-oedipal ratio may vary with the extent to which privation or conflict is the basic cause of the disturbance.

The depressive tendency can be understood within Hartmann's theory of the "sign systems" [41] as the latent set of signs, fed continuously during the earliest phase by preoedipal and oedipal predispositions (see Table 1). During the middle years of childhood, this resulting sign system may have only a "low probability of direct manifestations"; hence depressive reactions may be relatively infrequent, mild, and expressed in terms of ego functioning. The different syndromes would represent reactivations from different predispositional levels. The main sign systems would then be as follows:

1. *The anaclitic syndrome* would derive its signs from the latent elements provided by the Benedek-Engel constructions. There is an early history of failure and frustration within the "nursing couple," marked ambivalence on both sides, and negative transactions during which trust and confident expectation are constantly eroded. The partners become more and more irritated by each other and by the child's tensions. The onset of schooling generates a separation crisis for both of them, culminating in a depression in the mother and a depressive type of school phobia in the child. Both express a longingness to be loved coupled with strong feelings of not being lovable. Both real life and dream life are haunted by the threat of abandonment, of being alone and empty. One 9-year old girl spoke of a "hole" inside her, of "dark feelings" that overcame her upon separation, and of the intensification of her sadness and panic whenever she was in any way immobilized. Psychosomatic symptoms multiply, and the general picture is one of withdrawal, weakness, tiredness, loss of energy and drive, and helplessness.

2. *The inhibition syndrome.* Inhibition has sometimes been called the depression of childhood. The level of reactivation of this system is anal—the time when the child is undergoing the stresses of training and individuation. He aspires to be "good," clean, and obedient, and fights hard not to allow his "dirty" thoughts and impulses to get the better of him. At times he loses control and then feels thoroughly ashamed and depressed. His overcontrol alternates with disinhibition, and there are times when his aggression leaks out in vicarious ways and he becomes afraid of retaliation. Depressive moods often dominate the picture, especially when anger is suppressed. The family

tendency is to demand conformity and thus reinforce the inhibition. In severe cases, various forms of learning disability may occur.

3. *The disillusionment syndrome.* The main reactivation is from the early oedipal phase, when the child is exposed to disappointment with both parents. He very much wants to be admired, praised, and successful, and he tries to occupy center stage. After the initial struggle, he "gives up," often quite suddenly, shies away from competition, and avoids any situation in which he might be defeated or shown up as inferior. Gradually, these changes become a chronic pattern, and an attitude is expressed that is pessimistic, cynical, disillusioned, and lacking in any expectation of success. The discrepancy between real and ideal is increasingly widened. The parents have high aspirations and foster overidealization.

With each of these sign systems, depression may be latent or manifest, depending on the phase of the transactional cycle (see Table 3), the regulation of self-esteem, and the process of intenalization with the development of guilt. Anhedonia may occur in any of the systems but is more likely in severe cases with reactivation of all three levels of response.

SUICIDE AND SUICIDE ATTEMPTS DURING CHILDHOOD

Although childhood depression, as a normal or a clinical entity, may be emerging with greater frequency and intensity, the suicide rate among children remains fairly low, which may to some extent reflect the lack of technical ability on the part of the child to accomplish his own self-destruction. However, suicide threats, as mentioned earlier, seem to be on the increase, both in general child psychiatric practice and in emergency referrals.

Suicide

Except as noted, the following facts and figures (obviously subject to a great deal of distortion) relate to the suicide rate in children (5 to 14 years) in the United States. Bakwin [8] and Despert [22] have both given an annual estimate of between 35 and 60. There were no recorded cases under the age of 5 years, and only 10 percent of cases occurred among children 5 to 10 years of age. *In none of the cases was any mention made of depression.* However, in a group of 26 children who had expressed realistic suicide threats, Despert found *mani-*

festations of a depressive mood combined with suicidal preoccupation.
Five had gone on to make the attempt. Among the motivations discovered were retaliation for deprivation of love and identification with
a lost love object. Shaw and Schelkun [75] found a slow rise in frequency through the latency period. There was again *no mention of
depression*, but the emotional correlates included impulsiveness, aggressiveness, sadomasochism, and magical thinking, which suggested
a profile of childhood suicidal personality. Toolan [82] reported a
finding for children that is true for the whole human life cycle: more
males commit suicide, but more females attempt suicide. Schaffer
[73], reporting from Britain, found no suicides under the age of 12
years, but thereafter the frequency increased with age. The most frequent precipitating factor was a disciplinary crisis relating to acting
out behavior at school; the notes left were markedly hostile. The children, who were described as intellectually superior and impulsive,
belonged to *families with a high incidence of clinical depression.*
Gould [37] felt that although only three cases of suicide in children
under 10 years of age were reported in 1958, many more went unrecognized, were listed as accidents, or were covered up. He was sure
that the actual statistics are quite unreliable for both suicide and
attempted suicide. According to him, the underlying psychodynamic
mechanisms are a function of physical, intellectual, and psychological
levels of development, together with the child's concept of death. He
concluded that depression, in either its "pure" or "disguised" forms,
is much commoner than was previously thought and that the underlying motivations for suicidal behavior involve such *typical depressive
content* as the wish for reunion with a lost love object, retaliation for
abandonment, atonement for sins, and a last cry for help.

Suicide Attempts

Lawler [52] has discussed 22 suicide attempts in children, all save
one of superior intelligence, who were characterized by long-standing
and unrecognized intrapsychic and interpersonal conflicts in the setting of disturbed family relationships. Toolan [82] attributed the
smaller number of suicide attempts in children as compared with
adults to the fact that the parents, however bad, are still the child's
real external parents, upon whom he is dependent for love and support. In fact, the more neglected he is by them, the greater is his need
for them. Consequently, he has to deny their badness and assume
the burden of evil himself. As reality testing improves with age, it becomes increasingly difficult for him to preserve this myth. His hostility toward his parents reaches consciousness and provokes guilt feelings. With the maturing of the superego in adolescence, much of

this hostility is then redirected toward the introjects, and with the inward-turning of aggression a depressive suicide attempt becomes more likely. Lourie [53] pointed to the multiple determinants of the suicide attempt in childhood, many of which originate in the first few years. The majority of cases have problems of impulse control and come from environments that encourage and stimulate impulsiveness. The step between suicidal ideation and suicide attempt in these children is a short one, and when the act is carried out, very frequently no parents are around to control it. *The depression seen is a situational and not a superego phenomenon.*

The conclusion to all this is that childhood suicide is not a truly depressive phenomenon, although it may make its appearance in a familial depressive setting. The close connection of suicide with depression begins in adolescence, when the superego enters the picture. Prior to that suicide appears to be symptomatic of a weak ego. Attempted or threatened suicide, on the other hand, does have more evident links with depression of the ego psychology type, and thus it can be incorporated into the reactivation paradigm suggested for the clinical depressions of childhood.

CONCLUSION

This chapter represents a tentative, suggestive, and perhaps premature effort to find a place for childhood depression in the wider perspective of the human existence and human condition. In studying the phenomenon, we have attempted to take several observational positions to enhance the breadth and depth of view. First, we have located ourselves at different points of development and looked at the impact of the developmental process on the manifestation of depression. We found that as the ego functions were slowly perfected in the direction of becoming, as Anna Freud put it, "accurate and reliable as a mechanical apparatus" [32], the depressive affect and reaction underwent increasing elaboration.

Our second vantage point was, to quote Anna Freud again, "equidistant from the id, the ego, and the superego" [31], which enabled us to evaluate the varying roles of these three institutions in the genesis of depression during different periods of development. At different times, depression may appear as predominantly an ego or predominantly a superego phenomenon.

Our third position was derived from Erikson [26] and encouraged us not only to look more closely at the ego (to which Bibring had already led us) but also to examine the relation of the ego to the social prototypes of the day and to the pool of images, both good and bad, that are brought together in any historical era and that reflect, with infinite variety, the illusive nature of historical change.

Finally, we took, with some presumption, a position *sub specie aeternitatis* and focused our attention on the entire spectrum interrelating history with psychobiology and psychoanalysis in an attempt to discover lawful connections between the generalities of the human existence and the accidents of the human condition.

Childhood depression is still, as Kuhn would say, an underdeveloped field on the way to becoming scientifically conceived but still in a protoscientific state [50]. A multitude of ideas are scattered throughout it, none of which has yet quite got "off the ground." There is not much consensus about "findings," and formulations still have to be constructed from the beginning. We are still at the stage of "problem solving" rather than "puzzle solving." But interest in the field is great, and there is evidence of maturation. Our prediction is that the diagnosis of clinical depression of childhood will be made with increasing frequency in the future.

REFERENCES

1. Abraham, K. Notes on the Psycho-Analytical Investigation and Treatment of Manic-Depressive Insanity and Allied Conditions. In *Selected Papers of Karl Abraham, M.D.* London: Hogarth Press, 1948.
2. Abraham, K. A Short Study of the Development of the Libido, Viewed in the Light of Mental Disorders. In *Selected Papers of Karl Abraham, M.D.* London: Hogarth Press, 1948.
3. Agras, S. The relationship of school phobia to childhood depression. *Am. J. Psychiatry* 116:533, 1959.
4. Annell, A-L. *Depressive States in Childhood and Adolescence.* Stockholm: Almqvist and Wiksell, 1972.
5. Anthony, E. J. Psychoneurotic Disorders. In A. M. Freedman and H. I. Kaplan (Eds.), *Comprehensive Textbook of Psychiatry.* Baltimore: Williams & Wilkins, 1967.
6. Anthony, E. J. The Reactions of Parents to the Oedipal Child. In E. J. Anthony and T. Benedek (Eds.), *Parenthood—Its Psychology and Psychopathology.* Boston: Little, Brown, 1970.
7. Aries, P. *Centuries of Childhood.* New York: Knopf, 1962.
8. Bakwin, H. Suicide in children and adults. *J. Am. Med. Wom. Assoc.* 19:489, 1964.
9. Benedek, T. Toward the biology of the depressive constellation. *J. Am. Psychoanal. Assoc.* 4:389, 1956.
10. Benjamin, J. D. Further Comments on Some Developmental Aspects of Anxiety. In H. S. Gaskill (Ed.), *Counterpoint.* New York: International Universities Press, 1963.

11. Beres, D.   Clinical notes on aggression in children. *Psychoanal. Study Child* 7:241, 1952.
12. Bibring, E.   The Mechanism of Depression. In P. Greenacre (Ed.), *Affective Disorders*. New York: International Universities Press, 1953.
13. Bierman, J., Silverstein, A., and Finesinger, J.   A depression in a six-year-old boy with acute poliomyelitis. *Psychoanal. Study Child* 13:430, 1958.
14. Bowlby, J.   Some pathological processes set in train by early mother-child separation. *J. Ment. Sci.* 99:265, 1953.
15. Bowlby, J.   *Attachment and Loss*. Vol. 1. *Attachment and Loss*. New York: Basic Books, 1969.
16. Bowlby, J.   *Attachment and Loss*. Vol. 2. *Separation*. New York: Basic Books, 1973.
17. Burks, H. L., and Harrison, S. I.   Aggressive behavior as a means of avoiding depression. *Am. J. Orthopsychiatry* 32:416, 1962.
18. Burton, R.   *The Anatomy of Melancholy*. New York: Farras and Rinehart, 1927.
19. Cytryn, L., and McKnew, D. H., Jr.   Proposed classification of childhood depression. *Am. J. Psychiatry* 129:149, 1972.
20. Cytryn, L., and McKnew, D. H., Jr.   Biochemical correlates of affective disorders in children. *Arch. Gen. Psychiatry*, in press.
21. DeMause, L.   The evolution of childhood. *History of Childhood Q.* 1:503, 1974.
22. Despert, J. L.   Suicide and depression in children. *Nervous Child* 9:378, 1952.
23. Eisen, P.   *Depression in Childhood*, unpublished.
24. Engel, G.   Anxiety and depression-withdrawal: The primary affects of unpleasure. *Int. J. Psychoanal.* 43:89, 1962.
25. Engel, G., and Schmale, A.   Conservation-Withdrawal: A Primary Regulatory Process for Organismic Homeostasis. In *Physiology, Emotion and Psychosomatic Illness*, Ciba Foundation Symposium 8. Amsterdam: Elsevier, 1972.
26. Erikson, E.   Ego development and historical change. *Psychoanal. Study Child* 2:359, 1946.
27. Fast, I.   Some relationships of infantile self-boundary due to depression. *Int. J. Psychoanal.* 48:259, 1967.
28. Fenichel, O.   *The Psychoanalytic Theory of Neurosis*. New York: Norton, 1945.
29. Fenichel, O.   The Psychology of Boredom. In D. Rapaport (Ed.), *Organization and Pathology of Thought*. New York: Columbia University Press, 1951.
30. Ferenczi, S.   The unwelcome child and his death instinct. *Int. J. Psychoanal.* 10:125, 1929.
31. Freud, A.   *The Ego and the Mechanisms of Defence*. London: Hogarth Press, 1942.
32. Freud, A.   Indications for child analysis. *Psychoanal. Study Child* 1:127, 1945.
33. Freud, S.   Analysis of a Phobia in a Five-Year-Old Boy (1909). In *The Standard Edition of the Complete Psychological Works of Sigmund Freud*, transl. and ed. by J. Strachey with others. London: Hogarth and Institute of Psycho-Analysis, 1957. Vol. 10, p. 1.

34. Freud, S. On the History of the Psycho-Analytic Movement (1914). In *The Standard Edition*. 1957. Vol. 14, p. 1.
35. Freud, S. Mourning and Melancholia (1917 [1915]). *Standard Edition*. 1957. Vol. 14, p. 237.
36. Fries, M., and Woolf, P. The Influence of Constitutional Complex on Developmental Phases. In J. McDevitt and C. Settlage (Eds.), *Separation-Individuation: Essays in Honor of Margaret S. Mahler*. New York: International Universities Press, 1971.
37. Gould, R. Suicidal problems in children and adolescents. *Am. J. Psychother.* 19:228, 1965.
38. Gratien, B. *El Discreto*. Madrid: Huesca, 1646.
39. Group for the Advancement of Psychiatry. *Psychopathological Disorders in Childhood*. Report No. 62. New York: Group for the Advancement of Psychiatry, 1966. Vol. 6.
40. Harrington, M., and Hassan, J. Depression in girls during latency. *Br. J. Med. Psychol.* 31:43, 1958.
41. Hartmann, H. Problems of Infantile Neurosis. In *Essays on Ego Psychology*. New York: International Universities Press, 1964.
42. Heider, G. M. Vulnerability in infants and young children. *Genet. Psychol. Monogr.* 73:1, 1966.
43. Hunter, H. D. Depression in Root-Damaged Children. Paper presented at the meeting of the Association for Child Psychology and Psychiatry, January 1969.
44. Jacobson, E. The Oedipus conflict in the development of depressive mechanisms. *Psychoanal. Q.* 12:541, 1943.
45. Jacobson, E. The effect of disappointment on ego and superego formation in normal and depressive development. *Psychoanal. Rev.* 33:129, 1946.
46. Jacobson, E. *Depression—Comparative Studies of Normal, Neurotic, and Psychotic Conditions*. New York: International Universities Press, 1971.
47. Joffe, W. G., and Sandler, J. Notes on pain, depression, and individuation. *Psychoanal. Study Child* 20:394, 1965.
48. Keeler, W. R. Children's Reactions to the Death of a Parent. In P. Hoch and J. Zubin (Eds.), *Depression*. New York: Grune & Stratton, 1954.
49. Klein, M. A Contribution to the Psychogenesis of Manic-Depressive States. In *Contributions to Psycho-Analysis*. London: Hogarth Press, 1948.
50. Kuhn, T. *The Structure of Scientific Revolutions*. Chicago: University of Chicago Press, 1970.
51. Lampl-De Groot, J. Depression and Aggression. In R. Loewenstein (Ed.), *Drive, Affects, Behavior*. New York: International Universities Press, 1953.
52. Lawler, R., et al. Suicidal attempts in children. *J. Canad. Med. Assoc.* 89:751, 1963.
53. Lourie, R. Clinical studies of attempted suicide in childhood. *Clin. Proc. Children's Hospital of D.C.* 22:163, 1966.
54. Mahler, M. On sadness and grief in infancy and childhood. *Psychoanal. Study Child* 16:332, 1961.
55. Mahler, M. Notes on the Development of Basic Moods: The Depressive Affect in Psychoanalysis. In R. Loewenstein, (Ed.), *Psycho-*

analysis—A General Psychology. New York: International Universities Press, 1966.

56. Malmquist, C.   Depressions in childhood and adolescence. Part I. *N. Engl. J. Med.* 284:887, 1971.

57. Malmquist, C.   Depressions in childhood and adolescence. Part II. *N. Engl. J. Med.* 284:955, 1971.

58. McNeill, D.   Developmental Psycholinguistics. In F. Smith and G. Miller (Eds.), *The Genesis of Language.* Cambridge, Mass.: M.I.T. Press, 1966.

59. Mendelson, M.   *Psychoanalytic Concepts of Depression.* Springfield, Ill.: Charles C Thomas, 1960.

60. Piaget, J.   *The Child's Conception of the World.* New York: Humanities Press, 1960.

61. Piaget, J.   *Play, Dreams and Imitation in Childhood.* New York: Norton, 1962.

62. Poznanski, E., and Zrull, J.   Childhood depression. *Arch. Gen. Psychiatry* 23:8, 1970.

63. Rado, S.   The problem of melancholia. *Int. J. Psychoanal.* 9:420, 1928.

64. Rapaport, D.   *The Collected Papers of David Rapaport*, ed. by M. Gill. New York: Basic Books, 1967.

65. Rexford, E.   Children, child psychiatry, and our brave new world. *Arch. Gen. Psychiatry* 20:25, 1969.

66. Ribble, M.   *The Rights of Infants—Early Psychological Needs and Their Satisfaction.* New York: Columbia University Press, 1943.

67. Rie, H.   Depression in childhood: A survey of some pertinent contributions. *J. Am. Acad. Child Psychiatry* 5:653, 1966.

68. Rochlin, G.   Loss and Restitution. *Psychoanal. Study Child* 8:288, 1953.

69. Rochlin, G.   The loss complex. *J. Am. Psychoanal. Assoc.* 7:299, 1959.

70. Rochlin, G.   *Griefs and Discontents.* Boston: Little, Brown, 1965.

71. Sandler, J., and Joffe, W. G.   Notes on childhood depression. *Int. J. Psychoanal.* 46:88, 1965.

72. Schachtel, E.   *Metamorphosis.* New York: Basic Books, 1959.

73. Schaffer, D.   Suicide in Childhood and Early Adolescence. In *Proceedings of the Eighth International Congress of Child Psychiatry and Allied Professions*, 1974, Philadelphia, 1974.

74. Schmale, A. H., Jr.   A genetic view of affects: With special reference to the genesis of helplessness and hopelessness. *Psychoanal. Study Child* 19:287, 1964.

75. Shaw, C., and Schelkun, R.   Suicidal behavior in children. *Psychiatry* 28:157, 1965.

76. Sperling, M.   Equivalents of depression in children. *J. Hillside Hospital* 8:138, 1959.

77. Spitz, R.   Hospitalism. *Psychoanal. Study Child* 2:113, 1946.

78. Spitz, R., and Wolf, K.   Anaclitic depression. *Psychoanal. Study Child* 2:313, 1946.

79. Stutte, H.   Epochal Changes in the Classification and Symptomatology of Depressions in Childhood. In A-L. Annell (Ed.), *Depressive States in Childhood and Adolescence.* Stockholm: Almqvist and Wiksell, 1972.

80. Thomas, A., et al. A longitudinal study of primary reaction patterns in children. *Compr. Psychiatry* 1:103, 1960.
81. Toolan, J. M. Depression in children and adolescents. *Am. J. Orthopsychiatry* 32:404, 1962.
82. Toolan, J. M. Suicide and suicidal attempts in children and adolescents. *Am. J. Psychiatry* 118:719, 1962.
83. Winnicott, D. W. The Depressive Position in Normal Emotional Development. In *Collected Papers*. London: Tavistock, 1958.
84. Wittgenstein, L. *Philosophical Investigation*. New York: Macmillan, 1968.
85. Zetzel, E. Symposium on depressive illness. *Int. J. Psychoanal.* 41: 476, 1961.

12

The Influence of a Manic-Depressive
Environment on the Developing Child *

E. JAMES ANTHONY

A PRELIMINARY NOTE ON ENVIRONMENT

The Philosopher's Environment

Common sense has always postulated a real, external environment that was shared with others "under a common sky," and common man has always lived his life taking for granted the hard reality of things that he regarded as coexisting with him. As philosophical thinking developed, the shortcomings of common sense in offering only a partial view of reality were increasingly appreciated, and a new environment, within the mind, was brought into consideration. Thereafter, the world of philosophy was split between those for whom the internal environment became the only environment (the idealists) and those for whom the observable universe existed outside the mind and endured after mind was extinguished (the empiricists).

The idealists have sometimes carried subjectivism to a point that seemed to common sense almost psychotic, implying, as it did, that the world existed only because it was posited by the self and consequently had a subordinate reality. It was nothing more than a wonderful mirage, a figment of thought. On the opposite side, the empiricists found this grandiosity not only repugnant but devious; Locke referred to it contemptuously as a "kind of fiddling." A mind was a product of things operating on it "in a natural way," and, in the words of Hume, there could be "no idea without an antecedent impression." An intermediate approach, the philosophy of naturalism, postulated that the environment was indeed "out there" but that it consisted, as Russell put it, "of events, short, small, and haphazard." If there were order, unity, and continuity, these were human inventions just as truly as were catalogues and encyclopedias.

With a clinical reading of history, there seem to be elements of

* This study forms part of an ongoing investigation, "The Influence of Parental Psychosis on the Development of Children" supported by MH12043, MH14052, MH24819.

depression bound up with these various philosophical positions. Behind the omnipotence and narcissism of idealism one can detect a disquieting concern at being entirely on one's own, deprived of the familiar furnishings of environment. To the radical empiricists, the universe extended endlessly into space and minutely into things so that man appears to be suspended at the midpoint of a vast environment with infinity looming on both sides. It is not difficult for the clinician to perceive here a sense of helplessness, which occasioned so much dread in sensitive observers like Pascal. The same can be said of the naturalistic position. It seems to be difficult for man to endure existence with a fragmentary vision of environment without compulsively setting about to repair the discontinuities in the fabric. It has even been suggested that the hedonistic philosophies represented elaborate devices or "manic defenses" to combat the melancholy produced by such depressing considerations.

Toward the end of the last century, the empirically oriented William James [17] pointed out that when the world of physical things, as conceived by the popular mind, was discounted as an anthropomorphic fiction, a number of subuniverses based on science, religion, beliefs, prejudices, and idiosyncrasies, all of which were less "real," came into view and dominated the human perspective until discarded for something more satisfying. In this sense, one invented the environment in which one felt most at home. One of the subuniverses that lay behind the face of reality he referred to ominously as the "world of sheer madness and vagary," as if to indicate that psychosis of some kind was constantly lying in wait for the too-intrepid philosophical explorer.

The inference to be drawn from these speculations, which have haunted men from the beginning of time, is that a sturdy sense of reality and a confidence in the experienced environment are the only safeguards against the encroachments of the non–common sense viewpoint, and more recent evidence suggests that these safeguards are built up in childhood.

The empirical and idealistic perspectives are not altogether stable, in spite of the history extending back into early life. Every now and then a shift in perspective may occur, and the philosophical structure that has been erected with such care begins to look more tenuous. With characteristic perceptiveness James describes this transient upheaval: "The world now looks remote, strange, sinister, uncanny," and behind it is an "all-encompassing blackness." It is as if everything has suddenly given place to nothingness and as if, without any prior philosophical preparation, the empiricist is given a glimpse of an existential or idealistic perspective. It results, says James, in an indescribable feeling of melancholy associated "with a horrible dread at the pit of my stomach, and with a sense of the insecurity of life that I never knew before. . . . It was like a revelation and after this the universe was changed for me altogether. . . . I dreaded to be left alone." Following these attacks, James arrived at his vision of an unfinished pluralistic environment that is still in a state of development. One could look at this environment both objectively and subjectively. The room in which one sits may have occupied the same geographic place for thirty years, but its mental representation could be destroyed in an instant by closing one's eyes or shifting one's attention. Furthermore, one could think of the room when one was somewhere else, and it still possessed the same reality, although, as James pointed out humorously, you could live in it rent-free! He denied that there was any chasm between the mind thing and the physical thing that had to be bridged and insisted that the whole procedure of apprehension occurred within the experienced world, where subjective and objective points of view coexisted. Developmentally, the objective preceded the subjective, and this was essentially the child's point of view.

The Psychoanalyst's Environment

Like philosophy, psychoanalysis has oscillated between several positions with regard to the environment during the course of its historical evolution. In his earliest formulations, Freud was much preoccupied with the causal efficacy of environmental factors such as syphilis and seduction, but, after being seemingly let down by the facts, he turned the microscope of his attention from the physical to the psychological and from the interpersonal to the intrapsychic. Psychoanalysis, as a growing body of knowledge, followed faithfully in his footsteps as he became exclusively engaged with psychic reality as the only reality that mattered to the patient. "Real" reality was considered only as it had been filtered through the individual mind 'and had become a transmuted version of the outside world.

This reorientation in favor of a more inward reality was repeatedly referred to by Freud throughout his life as a turning point in his thinking, and there can be no doubt of its importance, in conjunction with his self-analysis, for the discovery of the oedipus complex, which subsequently shaped and organized all experience. According to Benjamin, it had another effect as well: "It led him for a long time to an underestimation of the importance of reality experiences. . . . External reality only slowly regained the place in Freud's ego-psychological thinking that he gave to it originally; and it never did approach Hartmann's, and Anna Freud's in generality" [5].

This downgrading of environment remained a conspicuous feature of psychoanalysis for the first thirty years of the century, but already by the mid-1930s the importance of external reality was again realized. At a meeting of the British Psychoanalytical Society during this period, a speaker suggested that the mother of an adult patient had exerted a baneful influence on her son's development and hence on the formation of his symptoms. Many of the analysts present disagreed profoundly with this conclusion, maintaining that the mother's "badness," as recalled by the patient, was in itself a product of his neurosis and therefore subject to defensive distortions. They pointed out that such mother-hatred was often salient at different stages of treatment and was the cover for deeper love attitudes that were intolerable to consciousness at the time. The patient's need to portray a "bad" maternal image was related to his inability to love and thus served to preserve a "good" internal representation. Glover, who reported the matter, happened to know the mother and judged her to be in every sense "a perfectly dreadful woman" [15]. Nevertheless, he argued that this evidence of an actually bad environment did not in any way absolve the analyst from exploring the part played by the patient's own impulses in creating his pathological anxieties. It did, however, suggest to him that such endogenous anxieties were readily reinforced by external factors. At this period, classically oriented analysts were especially concerned with not weakening the central psychoanalytic paradigm of intrapsychic conflict by diluting it with environmental factors, and they were reluctant to leave this important matter to the judgment of individual practitioners, who might be inclined, as Strachey suggested (cited in Glover [15]), to favor the operation of environmental factors when they felt hostile to the parents and the influence of intrapsychic factors when they considered the child a nuisance!

The direct observations of the developmental environment during early infancy and the emergence of a psychoanalytic ego psychology, coupled with attempts to treat serious narcissistic disorders, led to a new consideration of environment and its relationship to ongoing intrapsychic events. Rapaport [14] insisted on the equal causal status of drive and environment and repeatedly pointed to the ever-present danger in psychoanalysis of deemphasizing environment. In his view, a comprehensive psychoanalytic psychology needed to take account of external reality without losing sight of the drives, and he vigorously opposed those who accentuated one at the expense of the other. The individual's world was *not* shaped by his drives alone or solely by environmental counters. For the past thirty years, Erikson has attempted to study the interplay of psychosocial and psychosexual factors during development, but he has experienced difficulty in bringing his work into line with ego psychology, chiefly because the environmental influence could not be satisfactorily explained in terms acceptable to the psychoanalyst. Erikson has a disparaging comment to make on the psychoanalyst's environment:

The so-called basic biological orientation of psychoanalysis has, it seems, gradually become (out of mere habituation) a kind of pseudobiology, and especially is the conceptualization of man's "environment." In psychoanalytic writings the terms "outer world" or "environment" are often used to designate an uncharted area which is said to be outside merely because it fails to be inside—inside the individual's somatic skin, or inside his psychic systems, or inside his self in the widest sense. Such a vague and yet omnipresent "outerness" by necessity assumes a number of ideological and certainly unbiological connotations, such as an antagonism beween organism and environment. Sometimes "the outer world" is conceived of as "reality's" conspiracy against the infantile organism's instinctual wish world and sometimes as the indifferent or annoying fact of the existence of other people. But even in the recent admission of the at least partially benevolent presence of maternal care, a stubborn tendency persists to treat the "mother-child relationship" as a "biological" entity more or less isolated from its cultural surroundings which then again becomes an "environment" of vague supports or of blind pressures and mere "conventions." . . . Not even the very best of mother-child relationships could, by themselves, account for that subtle and complex "milieu" which permits a human baby not only to survive but also to develop his potentialities for growth and uniqueness [9].

Erikson clearly feels that the psychoanalyst's usual environment is a dim ancillary to the organism and leaves much to be desired. The same criticism had been applied by the "cultural" school of psychoanalysts to Freud's conception of culture. Erikson extends Hartmann's, conception of the infant's preadaptedness to an "average expectable environment" to a whole integrated sequence of "expectable" environments, each containing its own life tasks and psychosocial crises.

Winnicott [23] has had a little more success in this regard. He prepared the way for environment by first postulating an intermediate area of experience from which the infant slowly constructs his representation of the mothering person and begins to differentiate what is inside from what is outside. These developments depend upon the actual quality and quantity of the mothering offered to the child; if the mothering was "good enough," it led to the ego's control of the id and the formation of the self. If, on the other hand, it was not adequate, the identification with the "good" mother failed to take place, and the capacity to sublimate instinctual drives remained defective.

Winnicott was certain that the maturational processes could not be understood without taking into account the environment that facilitated them and that was, in the first place, synonymous with the mother. According to him, there were two mothers for every infant: the "environment mother," whom the child experienced as a caring person and to whom he responded with affection, and the "object mother," who was the target of his drives and to whom he responded with excitement. It was the "environment mother" that helped the child to make amends for the ruthless way in which he sometimes used the "object mother." When the "environment mother" failed or proved inadequate, the child began to require a great deal of "management" before he could continue in a developing relationship with the object. When the "environment mother" was erratic or markedly inconsistent, it could result in a failure of the development of object constancy, the establishment of which presupposed some degree of neutralization of both libidinal and aggressive energy.

In recent years, the penetrating and pervasive nature of environment in the genesis of borderline psychotic disturbances has raised some question as to whether the psychoanalytic structure of the mind can account for the psychology and psychopathology of object relations. While the classic neuroses can be well understood in the context of fixation and regression of instinctual development, it has been suggested that the narcissistic neuroses are explicable only in terms of an *actual* failure of the human environment, principally its maternal component. For example, when the "environment mother" becomes psychotically ill, a number of consequences inevitably follow: object constancy fails to develop, a high degree of narcissism persists, and the sense of reality remains deficient. When the mother becomes mentally ill during the early life of the child, there is a strong chance that development will become disordered. It is not sufficient to explain the resulting *folie à deux* simply as a product of contagion, imitation, incorporation, identification, or empathy. It is more complicated than that. What takes place inside the child in response to what is happening outside the child has a development of its own somewhat akin to the interplay of a traumatic and an infantile neurosis. In speaking of the effect produced by the mentally ill mother, Winnicott had this to say: "It must be remembered, however, that *the child's illness belongs to the child. . . .* The child may find some means of healthy growth in spite of environmental factors, or may be ill in spite of good care" [24]. The exact mechanisms by which parental illness manifested in the child's environment brings about disturbances in the psychosexual disorders in the child remains a mystery, but that it occurs can no longer be doubted.

THE INTERPLAY OF INTERNAL AND EXTERNAL
ENVIRONMENT IN THE CAUSATION OF
CHILDHOOD DISORDERS

The interplay of internal and external environments in the genesis of childhood disorders is not at all easy to understand or to explain psychoanalytically. First of all, a preoedipal disturbance originating in the environment may gradually become internalized and have repercussions on the developing infantile neurosis, causing it to become clinically manifest. On the other hand, a psychoneurosis is thought to arise sui generis or with only minimal provocation from the environment. An internal disorder may invade the external environment and transact with it, as do the acting out and behavior disorders. In contrast, a disturbance in the external environment may invade the internal environment for a while and affect intrapsychic developments, as do reactive or traumatic disorders. Very frequently, the strength of the disturbance in the external environment is not sufficient to interfere significantly with intrapsychic development, so there is only a mild situational reaction.

The constitutional elements may exert a powerful influence on the interaction between the internal and external environments. Furthermore, it would appear that once the child has taken in selective elements of the environment, his own view of it begins to change. Thus, a traumatized child may become oversensitive to the multitude of frightening things that actually do exist in his environment but were previously disregarded, and the phobic child may become fertile in creating fearful objects out of his object world.

Cimbal [6] referred to children showing many features of general immaturity, who were literally afraid of everything. This reaction was a permanent one, and there appeared to be no history of any frightening event. These children grew up to become timid, undecided, withdrawn adults, who retreated from even the most benign environments. Cimbal referred to this reaction as *Lebensfeigheit,* or a cowardice with respect to living. Freud himself was never too sure in what way this type of constitution is inherited. In 1923 [13] he declared categorically that it is not possible to speak of direct inheritance in the ego, and a little later [12], he stated that the id contains everything that is inherited. However, he reconciled these two statements by remarking that "the question whether it was the ego or the id that experienced and acquired these things soon comes to nothing," since "the ego is a specially differentiated part of the id" [12]. It is becoming increasingly commonplace to assume that endowment and environment are constantly in interaction throughout the life cycle of the individual and that no one lives his life in an intrapsychic vacuum.

There is much evidence to suggest that the predisposed individual reacts to the environment from almost the beginning of life as if it were abnormal or threatening. A good example of this comes from Kafka [18] who, throughout his life, was unable to rid himself of the "affliction" that transformed benign into malignant environments. He felt certain that benign environments did exist but that as soon as they were exposed to him they underwent a change. Many times in his life he remembered a childhood experience in which he heard two women calling to each other across the garden:

When I was a child, I opened my eyes after a short sleep in the middle of the day, and while still quite drowsy, I heard my mother calling down from the balcony, in a quite natural tone, "What are you doing, my dear? It's so hot." A woman answered from the garden, "I'm having tea outside." They spoke without reflection and not particularly clearly, as though it were only what anyone would expect.

It seemed unbelievable to Kafka, with all his inherent sensitivities and suspicions, that there was "an average, expectable environment" in which people transacted their ordinary human business in an ordinary human way without being menaced by a myriad hidden considerations. He felt that as soon as he arrived on any scene, fear invaded the situation. "I always have a desire to see things as they may be before they show themselves to me. That's when they are beautiful and quiet no doubt, because I often hear people speaking of them in this way."

The developmental environment changes constantly throughout development. The setting is phase-determined and is fashioned to the specifications of the transacting parent and child. The child is responding both to the realities of the situation and to the fantasies that he fabricates from that reality. In the present state of our knowledge, it is by no means easy to distinguish precisely between what was already part of the internal milieu and what has been internalized from the environment. In the manic-depressive environment, the responses of the children who populate it undoubtedly stem from inherited, acquired, and environmental factors. The question that is being raised in this chapter is whether the succession of developmental environments through which the child passes differs in any significant way from the developmental environments experienced by normal and neurotic children.

THE DEVELOPMENTAL ENVIRONMENTS
GENERATED BY MANIC DEPRESSION

In the ensuing discussion, Winnicott's dictum, already quoted, must be kept in mind: irrespective of the illness present in the parent, "the child's illness belongs to the child" and is part of the child. *Folies à deux,* or the so-called contact disorders, are by no means simple echoes or reflections of the disturbance in the child's environment. What is taken in undergoes a complex transformation in the new "host." In physiological terms, not only must it be digested and assimilated, it must also find a place for itself in a new metabolism. The notions of imitation or modeling convey no indication of the complexity involved. Outside psychoanalysis, two developmental principles help us to realize that taking in from the environment is much more than just a passive experience. To quote Piaget, environmental influences "are not imprinted on the child as on a photographic plate: they are "assimilated," that is to say, deformed by the living being subjected to them and become implanted in his own substance" [21]. This principle of assimilation can be paired with the unassailable methodological principle of convergence, postulating that development must be studied as a process determined by the interaction of organism and environment. It is through such mechanisms that environment becomes child; even though they are not yet fully or clearly understood even through psychoanalytic psychology, the clinical literature is replete with illustrations of this event. What determines the elements to be selected for assimilation is still a mystery, although various modes of identification and identity formation furnish hints as to the factors involved. Looked at from the outside, it would seem that the parallel processes evolving in the child and the parent during certain phases become closely enmeshed, so exchanges are facilitated and assimilation enhanced [3].

In considering the impact of manic-depression on the developing child, one must, to paraphrase Rapaport [14], give equal consideration to drive and environment, as well as to the interplay between them. As pointed out earlier, despite the work of Hartmann and Erikson in recent decades, we still lack an operationally and theoretically valid psychoanalytic psychology to synchronize and orchestrate the internal and external movements into a unified and comprehensive schema. Even to begin to accomplish this, one must be able to correlate what is unfolding within the child and what is simultaneously taking place in his immediate ambience. However, another factor complicates this relationship and makes it difficult for the observer to disentangle: the child perceives and conceives the external reality in a fashion that is not only idiosyncratic to him but idiomatic to his stage of development. He is therefore inclined to be very selectively responsive to the different ingredients of a situation that is presented to him. The term developmental environment is meant to indicate the consortium of influences at work in the environment that are consciously and unconsciously selected for response by the child at any given developmental stage. The principal implication underlying the concept is that infantile elements persisting abnormally in the parent are taken up empathically by the child as he passes through periods of development in which such elements would normally be phase-specific. This could lead, hypothetically at least, to a reinforcement of the elements in the children, causing them to become exaggerated and persistent as they are incorporated into the personality. These negative identifications would then contribute, in Erikson's parlance, to negative components of identity. At the same time, the child may also react traumatically to psychotic inconsistencies and incongruities of thought, affect, and behavior in the parent that reverberate for some time.

For these reasons, it takes two sets of facts to describe the developmental environment generated by a manic-depressive parent: the ingredients of manic-depression as manifested in the environment and the child's experience of it. Subsequently, an attempt will be made to delineate the successive developmental environments codetermined by the stage of psychosexual development and the manic-depressive environment. The instinctual interplay may at times involve the manic-depressive psychopathology (when the patient is in a state of remission) and at times the manic-depressive psychosis (when the patient is in a state of relapse). Since different types of environment are produced by male and female parents, it is important to consider the impact of psychosis in fathers as well as mothers.

THE INGREDIENTS OF MANIC-DEPRESSION
AS MANIFESTED DURING REMISSION AND RELAPSE

The main ingredients manifest in the bipolar manic-depressive environment are the cycles of omnipotence and impotence, of high and low self-esteem, of surplus and depleted energy, of adequate and defective reality testing, and of optimism and pessimism, and, above all, the surprising variations in mood. During periods of relapse, the ups and downs in the cycle are grossly exaggerated, and the patient's behavior becomes unreasonable and irrational. His capacity to control the extreme manifestations is quite deficient. At the times of remission, careful observation reveals that subclinical cycles continue to persist and that variations in day-to-day and week-to-week behavior are apparent to those living within the orbit of the patient. These minor cycles are often no more conspicuous than the emotional variations that occur during the normal menstrual cycle.*

During the manic phase, the patient appears to recreate the urgent and insistent environment of a narcissistically hungry infant, lacking the necessary external care and vehemently demanding the much-needed supplies. The evident hunger for objects relates not to the objects themselves but to the vehicle they provide for the expression of impulses. The patient feels "gloriously free" as his inhibitions are shed and his energies flow out in search of activities. There is a sense of triumph and victory rooted in rebelliousness, and obligations, liabilities, and responsibilities are thrown overboard with grandiose unconcern. Life appears abundant, and the cornucopia of objects and activities are run through rapidly and as rapidly discarded. As Abraham [1] described it, it seems as if the entire "mental metabolism" had been shifted to a higher level rendering the patient hyperactive, hyperaffective, hyperconfident, and exaggerated in all his pronouncements during this "festival of the ego."

This, at least, is how it looks to the nonparticipant observer for whom the patient may be putting on a show. Within the family, the story is somewhat different. The individual still appears as large as life and more than natural, but the defensiveness, based on a massive denial of opposite attitudes and feelings, is more readily discerned. The self-sufficiency and air of liberation are exposed as pretenses and as, in Fenichel's words, "a cramped denial of dependencies" [10]. The projections that are used insist that the patient is loved and admired by everybody, but again, in the family circle, paranoid elements emerge. He is mistreated, misunderstood, and misesteemed; therefore, why should he treat anybody with any show of consideration. Every now and then, the upsurging depression emerges, and the deep fearfulness in which the manic-depressive patient lives becomes apparent.

When the "festival" is over and the cycle reverses, the patient enters a veritable slough of despondency. A cloud descends not only upon him but on the family, who are now exposed to his sense of worthlessness, emptiness, impotence, and black pessimism. His hopelessness and helplessness and his utter despair hound the members of the family through the day, and they may struggle to avoid becoming suffused with depression in themselves.

* "Patients often exhibit mild parathymias in their free interval, which, slight as they are, bear all the essential marks of true melancholia or mania" [Abraham, 1].

THE CHILD'S EYE VIEW OF THE
MANIC-DEPRESSIVE PARENT

Understandably, a child, whether he likes it or not, is caught up in the maelstrom created by the manic parent and is sucked in, like all other objects within the parent's circle; nor can he avoid being enveloped in the depression when it settles on the household. During a mania, the parent needs to be pacified, protected, fed, and taken care of, and the children are very susceptible to becoming "magic helpers" who wait vainly upon the omnipotent one and in turn hope to share in his omnipotence. The parent, in turn, basks in the feeling of being loved. What the child in this environment quickly learns is the extreme vulnerability of the psychotic parent to even minimal narcissistic injuries, and he will develop extraordinary diplomatic skills to avoid inflicting any of these. In the early stages of the psychosis, he may find it difficult to adjust to the biphasic disturbance; no sooner does he come to terms with the manic manifestations than he is suddenly asked to cope with the depressive withdrawal.

The children in this type of milieu are frequently left with the feeling that all the objects within it are being manipulated for the private and personal gratification of the manic parent and that they themselves are involved in these transactions. In time they come to appreciate that the parent has a defective reality sense and that his megalomania or extreme self-depreciation is not guided by any realistic appraisal. They themselves may begin to live out narcissistic daydreams involving games of omnipotence that are unconsciously equated with "killing off the father," "playing God," "creating the world," and controlling parental intimacies. It is often surprising how aware they are of the delusional fantasies, especially those involving them, and how they gradually learn to develop a system of cues enabling them to anticipate developments in the cycle.

One child described home life under these conditions as a "fun fair"; everything seemed exciting, and one could see and do things that could not be seen or done in the outside world. "Everything goes up with Father like a balloon, and then all of a sudden the balloon is punctured and we all come down to the ground." He had once visited a fun fair on the morning after and had been surprised to find how dismal, tawdry, and empty it all seemed as compared with the night before. This is what it was like at home from one phase of the cycle to the next.

The child's eye view of the manic-depressive environment can be conveyed in two ways, the retrospective and the prospective. Although the former is contaminated by secondary elaborations, it offers the additional perspective of the adult as seen through the child's eyes. Let us look at reports of two individuals who grew up in manic-depressive environments. The first commentary (retrospective) is by a woman in her 30s looking back on the environment and recalling its more memorable aspects.

Case 1. My mother went numerous times to a private mental hospital. She was 21 years old when she started, some months after my brother was born. Dr. A. says it is sometimes easier for children to adjust to parents who are psychotic all the time than only part of the time. This is so true —we kids never knew what to believe. Mother was so completely different when she was well. She listened, she was kind, she was generous, she was fun to be with, she never criticized Dad, and she was always at home. But the big problem was the inconsistency, hearing one thing at one period and something quite different at the next. This is what I am fretting over now with my own children: how is a mother to act? I really had no consistent model; I don't know what the image of a good mother is supposed to be. Perhaps that is why I'm having problems with my own children.

The inconsistency also does funny things with one's feelings. For instance, when my father got seriously ill and I thought he was going to die, I could not stop laughing. All the time when I was a little girl I would laugh when somebody would get hurt, but what I was really doing was crying on the inside. We seemed to have two sets of everything at that time: two sets of feelings and two sets of thoughts that did not really fit what was actually happening. Life was like a big pretense. We gradually got to recognize the signs that meant she was going to have another attack: she would start cleaning the home and never finish the job, buying things that were just junk and never needed, talking about relatives in the wildest sort of way, and chatting constantly about nothing. We gradually began to learn how to live in our own worlds. Both I and my sister were always looking around for homes outside our own to "adopt" us, and we tried to spend as much time as possible with these families. This helped a great deal, but it also made us realize how differently normal families lived. There was no inconsistency. You could get up in the morning and almost know inside you what was going to happen for the rest of the day. We never knew how any day was going to turn out.

The thing that she did when she was sick that bugged me the most was never finishing a job, and even while I was still a child it became an obsession for me that I had to finish what I started. At that time, I felt it was my special duty to clean up after her, collect after her, and finish what she left unfinished. It was like being a slave, and you never questioned it.

Because of Mother being in and out of our world, we had a very close relationship with my father. Other children might have resented his authoritarian attitude, but it made us feel secure and confident, because when he was around everything was steady. He demanded obedience, and we gave it without thinking because he made us feel so much safer. The three of us, my sister, my brother, and myself, were never able to talk freely about what was happening—we were supposed not to mention it anywhere—but I can remember us crying in each other's arms at night when Mother would be becoming sick again and attacking Dad. I can remember wrapping my head in a pillow and putting cotton in my ears and earmuffs over my ears and still not being able to drown out what was happening, because at the same time I was straining to hear if something was going to be said about Dad leaving, because he was our one link to sanity. He never did because they were so dependent on each other, and she treated him like one of her babies and even talked to him like that.

When Mother became ill, I always thought that some terrible show was being put on, but she was never ashamed of what she did and what she said. She always felt that she was the greatest and could not be wrong. My brother was so much like her that today he is extremely difficult to live with, and his wife has frequently threatened to leave him. I can remember that as a boy he always had to be the best and right. He would never admit that he could not handle something and would always put on a big act. But when we were teenagers, I remember him once saying to me: "Well, Sis, there's one thing about us—we have to be the best, and we are the best, and there is nobody who is better than we are." It seems funny when I think about it now: we were in such a crazy business, and yet here we were, certain that we were the greatest, and certain that we could do anything that we wanted to do, and never feeling that we had any weaknesses at all. It seemed natural for me to become a cheerleader and homecoming queen. As a cheerleader, I wanted to scream louder than anybody in the whole school, and my sister was the same. We had to be tops. Our parents were very proud of us, and our trophies and photographs lined the wall. What we seemed to lack, all of us, was self-control. I can remember my brother when he was only 4, facing the maid with a kitchen knife and completely demolishing her room because he was mad with her. Yet his parents and his sisters could forgive him everything then, as they could later because he was captain of the football team and could do no wrong. Today I realize how self-centered he really is.

What effect did all this have on us children? I have already mentioned how fussy I became about tidiness and the need to have everything "just so." But there was also a special danger in my case. Ever since I was small, I have been told that I was just like my mother. I was named after her, and very soon I took to thinking that I was going to be committed when I was 21, like she was. In college, as I neared this age, I took all the psychology courses to try to find out about it. As if it was predetermined, I found myself getting extremely impatient, nervous, muddleheaded, and unable to concentrate. I was sure that they were going to come and haul me away. I felt that I was destined to become exactly like her. When I reached puberty, this fear had grown stronger and stronger because of the usual female cycle, when one goes up and down. I had to be put on tranquilizers. I felt that the only way I could separate my thoughts and feelings from her would be for her to die, and I often hated her and wished for her death, especially when she was manic and treating Dad so badly. During the menstrual cycle, I really felt I was becoming her: everything seemed to be getting on top of me—the children, the finances, the house, the cooking, etc., and at such times, I didn't seem to say anything to anybody. I felt as if I were reliving her life. I could not separate her from me inside me. We seemed to be one person inside. I have forgotten to mention one important thing: when she was manic, she acquired every illness around her—sinus trouble, indigestion, kidney disease, etc., and of course it was inevitable that I began to have the same round of imaginary illnesses. It sounds funny now, but it was never funny when I was growing up.

Here we have a description of a child's reaction to the alternating psychosis and the way she and her siblings were sucked into the maternal vortex until they were unable to tell whether they were inside or outside her and whether, in fact, they were being transmogrified into her. She reports the constant wish to escape from the symbiosis, and, even to this day, she is not at all sure whether she is living her mother's life or her own and whether her children are going to repeat the same pattern. The two opposing forces have continued to tug at her: becoming like mother and struggling not to become like mother. Becoming like mother meant becoming unstable, "up and down," narcissistic, omnipotent, hypochondriacal, and ready to take flight into unreality under pressure. Not becoming like mother meant being extremely compulsive, realistic about the future, and neither too optimistic nor too pessimistic.

The prospective accounts of the manic-depressive environment have, understandably, a more childlike quality that is less leavened by wisdom gained after the event. The following is a report by a 14-year-old girl whose mother had recurrent bipolar attacks of manic-depression with sometimes prolonged hypomanic periods in the interval between the psychotic episodes.

Case 2. Ever since I was little, I've had tornado dreams, and they're always the same. First, everything is fine, and the sun is shining and the sky is blue, and then, all of a sudden, without warning, this great wind starts up and comes tearing along, breaking up everything in the way, and then it's on top of us and I feel we're all going to die. Then it stops suddenly and everything is quiet and dark, and you feel just as scared because you don't know what is happening, you only know it's very quiet and dark. I had these dreams long before my mother had her first attack. This is why I think dreams are real. They tell you what's going to happen.

When I was 9, it suddenly happened just like in the dream. She was talking and getting around as if she couldn't stop, and she would be very angry if we even got in her way. Yet she wanted me around all the time, she would scream for me if I wasn't there. I had to keep running around getting her things. She was like a queen, and we all had to do her bidding. I used to be very scared, especially when I heard Dad and her arguing at night, and I would cover my head with a pillow so I wouldn't hear. I thought that they would kill each other, and we'd be left all alone. I still feel like that even though I'm getting more used to it.

When she has little attacks, it's not so bad. She would be talking big, and we'd go into the stores and buy things and order all sorts of clothes, and I'd feel like a princess. She made me feel like a princess. She'd say: "You don't have to think small." I'd sometimes go to school feeling grand and pretending I was some sort of princess and that all the children would know about it and stare at me and think I was great. Sometimes I began to feel so great that I got on everybody's nerves, and the kids soon started to tease me for putting on airs. I hate myself now when I think of it. But when Mother was like that, she'd dress me up and do my hair. We'd sit for hours in front of the mirror, and she'd say that we were both beauties and that you couldn't find a pair like us in all the world. You know, I really believed it, and I began to think that I might become a film star or go on the stage. She always said: "You've got to think big because you are big." When she talked and talked and talked, I also talked and talked and talked, and my friends at school thought that I talked too much, that I was too bossy, and that I wanted everything my way. If it weren't for the kids, I think I would have believed everything my mother told me. She made me feel special, and they just made me feel ordinary.

When she became depressed the first time, it was just like the dream coming true. Everything went quiet. I almost felt as if she'd gone away. I also became sad, but not because she was sad. I was sad because she didn't seem to take any notice of me anymore. She just wasn't interested in me. She only wanted to be by herself, and it seemed as if I bothered her just being around. I would try to get over my sadness by going over to my friends. I would try to find anybody who would have me so I wouldn't be sad. Once I remember I followed a woman all the way to her home, and I was thinking all the time that I was her daughter, pretending you know, and how when I walked into the house there would be a big welcome for me, and she would give me a hug and cook me a big dinner. You know, when she got depressed there would often be no dinner, and we'd have to get something for ourselves. It felt as if I was all empty inside, with no food or anything. My grades began to go down in school because I couldn't think of anything, and I would only be worrying about her. Sometimes I wished that she would die, then that made me feel bad. When my periods started, I began to get depressed, and I felt I was becoming just like her. I would be fidgety and bite my nails and shake my foot, like she would before she had an attack. Now I just feel exhausted, as if I had no energy for anything, but when my period is over, I'm able to go dancing again, and then my Dad thinks I have too much energy. I'm on the go all the time.

Here again we have a vivid picture, not too dissimilar from the retrospective one, of the struggle against being taken in by the mother at one phase of the cycle and thrust out "into the darkness" at another. The circular tendency in the mother was already present during the child's early life and was reflected in the recurrent dream sequence. The narcissism and omnipotence were so gratifying that she found herself identifying with these exaggerated attributes in the mother and behaving in a miniature manic way at school, bringing about the disapprobation of her peers. She realizes that the sadness, anger, and death wishes are not simply contagiously derived from the mother but are reactions to loss. Her thoughts, as she revealed later, were often loaded with guilt, since she felt it was her badness that upset her mother. In a masochistic way, she prayed that she might get some injury or disease and that this would be considered enough suffering to relieve her mother of all illness. She wondered if she would ever get married because she always felt afraid of getting close to someone only to be left "high and dry." She was aware that she had already become a very dependent person, who found it difficult to do without people but always ended up losing them for some reason. All her friends got fed up with her after a while because she was always clinging and demanding and jealous. She never knew what to feel about herself because sometimes she thought of herself as worthwhile and other times as worthless; she was never sure which it was going to be at any time. She knew that she had no confidence and that this was only one of the many things that she lacked. She later began to understand the tornado dreams as oscillations in her own anger and destructiveness. When she felt thwarted by her mother in any way, she felt she could blow up and destroy everybody and everything. This was so different from the times when her mother was just "ordinary," like anybody else but still believing she could be "great." At such moments, she could imagine becoming someone famous, such as a painter or a writer or even a saint (the family was Roman Catholic). As a saint she could save dozens of people through her prayers and miracles.

THE SUCCESSIVE DEVELOPMENTAL ENVIRONMENTS GENERATED BY MANIC-DEPRESSION

Every individual, throughout his life, suffers from "the almost incurable megalomania of mankind" and returns to it from time to time in wishful thinking, daydreams, fairy tales, and narcissistic illness. After the period of complete infantile omnipotence, followed by a period of magic and hallucinatory wish fulfillment, the child naturally begins to distinguish between inner and outer, subjective and objective, and things that respond obediently and immediately to him and things that do not. In an environment of loving care and concern he can retain his illusion of omnipotence longer, since intuitive mothering anticipates his needs and brings him what he wants at the time he wants it. A satisfying feeding relationship with the mother, according to Winnicott [23], furthers a positive omnipotence, leaving the infant with a strong feeling that there is something powerfully good inside; this is a necessary precondition for his later creativity. The absence of intuitive mothering, on the other hand, may reinforce his negative omnipotence, leading to the belief that he possesses unlimited powers for destruction. When the environment fails him, the child may either fall back on destructive fantasies or resort to magical ideas that may become the nucleus of a "God complex" in which the belief is nurtured that every person is essentially self-sufficient and that what one obtains in life is due entirely to his own efforts. This type of autistic omnipotence protects the individual magically from the realities of the environment, but if it is suddenly dissipated, he may show himself to be critically helpless and vulnerable. Autistic omnipotence believes in the magical power of excreta, of looking, of gestures and acts, and of thoughts and words. Symbiotic omnipotence is part of the merging with the parents and is accompanied by oceanic feelings. In the process of separation-individuation, the toddler, while relinquishing belief in his own omnipotence, internalizes the parental omnipotence along with the parents, and the omnipotence becomes part of the superego and ego-ideal, which then takes over the regulation of self-esteem from the parents. Even after he has de-idealized the parents, he may continue to believe in someone or something besides himself that is omnipotent, such as a religion or a political system, and by merging with it try to recapture some of the old omnipotent feeling.

During the preoedipal stage, the oral and anal areas are what Jacobson [16] refers to as "the fantasy playground" of the child. He is intensely preoccupied with omnipotent ideas as part of the power struggle between his mother and himself. He attempts to control her by soiling or withholding his feces, and she to control him by giving or withholding food and love. It is only at the oedipal stage that the child begins to develop more realistic notions about the limits of his own power and strength.

Two important and apparently antithetical developments begin to take place. The child begins to devalue his parents as objects that are at times weak and empty, dirty and disgusting, destroyed and castrated, at the same time he is idealizing them as part of his libidinal strivings. If disillusionment and disappointment are experienced by the child before he is ready for them, the counterbalancing idealization may prove inadequate and may lead to an arrest of ego-ideal and superego formation. A disturbing cynicism results, and, since ego boundaries are still indistinct, this may be experienced as a self-devaluation.

At the same time, the parents are attempting to disillusion the child about his own omnipotence and to bring him down to reality. Again, if this is done too vigorously, it can lead to loss of self-esteem and the development of conspicuous shame and inferiority, whereas, if it is done inadequately or not at all, the child may be left with a permanently grandiose self.

During normal development, the child's self-esteem remains within normal limits and so does his self-confidence. The parallel to this, his esteem for his parents, remains within normal limits, as does his confidence in them. Neither the omnipotent self nor the omnipotent parent on the road toward normal potency suddenly turns impotent, leaving the child in a developmental crisis of extreme insecurity. The parents need to handle the child's situation with themselves empathically. As Winnicott [23] points out, they need to disillusion the child gently and tactfully, and at the same time they need to accept graciously the "glory" thrust upon them by the child and not frustrate his search for some semblance of infantile omnipotence by behaving with "unempathic modesty." There is an appropriate time for them to glorify the child and for the child subsequently to glorify them.

As development proceeds, there is a decrease in omnipotence, a succession of displacements into parents and parental surrogates, a decreasing idealization of the parents, an increasing sensitivity to disillusionment, and a diminution in optimism, all in relation to the growth of the reality sense. From time to time, the child oscillates between omnipotence and impotence, as he is dominated in turn by the pleasure principle and the reality principle. The same is true with regard to the parents, who may at one time seem all-powerful and at another weak and ignorant.

When the environment is abnormal in the sense of containing pathological amounts of narcissism and omnipotence, the regulation of self-esteem, of confidence and security, of pleasure versus reality principle dominance, and of the proportion of optimism to pessimism may be seriously unbalanced. The manic-depressive ingredients may then enter into the psychosexual development of the child and affect the normal resolution of the nuclear complex. The upsurge of manic-depression is attended prepsychotically by an upsurge in the basic ingredients, but during periods of remission these elements may be quantitatively within the ordinary range. In assessing the impact of this type of environment, therefore, one needs to bear in mind the prepsychotic exaggeration of the ingredients.

Two types of disturbance have been observed in the children of manic-depressive parents: (1) a preoedipal megalomanic disorder, most distinctly seen in a case of manic-depressive mothers and their daughters, and (2) an oedipal megalomanic disorder, mostly involving manic-depressive fathers and their sons.

The preoedipal developmental environment with respect to depression has been most fully described for the mother-infant relationship by Benedek [4] and for the mother-toddler relationship by Mahler [20]. Benedek's singular and significant contribution lies in her description of the basic symbiotic unit of mother and infant in terms of a circular "feedback" process. If the mother can establish self-confidence in her own motherliness, and if symbiosis proves predominantly satisfying for both members of the pair, the child will develop confidence in the organization of his satisfactions and will respond positively to the pacifications exercised by the mother. Where pacification fails because the mother is unable to produce the right response to the child's needs from her "instinctual reservoir of motherliness," the confidence of the infant is gradually sapped and he begins to hate the object of his needs. In her subtle analysis of the feedback mechanism, Benedek [4] explains how the regressive response to frustration leads to certain reciprocal developments in the child and the mother. With good management, the child responds to frustration with a partial regression that can be handled by the intrapsychic processes alone; with bad management, the regression becomes massive and demands a full restitution of symbiosis. The regression induced in the mother by the frustrated infant stirs up the oral-dependent phase of her own development and, depending on the outcome of that relationship, she will have sufficient or inadequate confidence in her own motherliness to take care of her infant's disappointment. Through the process of introjection, a good mother–bad mother: good self–bad self representation is established within the infant and becomes the "core of ambivalence." Through identifications with her mother and her child, the mother becomes both the delivering and the receiving parts of the symbiosis. In failing to give successfully, she becomes the bad mother of her child and the bad child of her mother; as the frustrated receiver, the infant becomes her bad self as well as her own bad mother. Thus, in this two-way process, the ambivalent core is created in the infant and reactivated in the mother. This leads to the defusion of aggressive energy and the establishment of what Benedek [4] refers to as the *depressive constellation. Klein's depressive position* [19], based on the continuous operation of projective-introjective mechanisms, has a superficial resemblance to the depressive constellation, but there are a number of important differences. Klein is referring here to a system of psychotic anxieties in which the depressive anxieties are genetically derived from an earlier paranoid anxiety; at no time does

Benedek suggest that the infant's part in the constellation is psychotically based. Second, Klein believes that the depressive position is directly linked to the depressions of adult life, whether normal, neurotic, psychotic, or mixed, whereas Benedek's term does not imply a pathogenesis in relation to any particular clinical entity in adult life but only "a significant variation in the primary psychic organization which, in transaction with all other psychic processes, participates in the future developmental organization of the personality and its adaptive reactions, and represents one of its primary (basic) determinants" [4]. Thus, the depressive process for Klein is intrapsychic to the infant, whereas the depressive constellation is related to the life cycle of the mother and to her transactions with the infant. Not only is Benedek's construct altogether clearer and more comprehensive, but it is also, to use Glover's expression, far less "psychobiologically improbable." The interplay that Benedek describes between the generations is a crucial (and clinically ascertainable) fact in the genesis of inadequate mothering.

Elation is not included per se in this framework, but it appears in the one provided by Mahler [20] based on her observations of mood swings in the toddler. She describes the occurrence of both intermittent and continuous elation during the second phase of separation-individuation and regards it as a phase-specific mood. In the next phase of *rapprochement*, the toddler becomes aware of his separateness from the mother, who further lets him down by withholding her omnipotence from him.

The preoedipal developmental environment that is generated by the manic-depressive mother would involve a deteriorating mother-child symbiosis, with the baby gradually regressing toward an undifferentiated state and having no surplus energy available for play and pleasure. Instead of responding to frustration with characteristic anxiety, the child's response becomes depressive, indicating that he is now in a vulnerable state and is, depending upon future environmental factors, predisposed to depressive disorders. One would therefore expect the developmental environment to contain an inadequate mothering person, a nuclear psychodynamic constellation that is "potentially depressogenic" (to use the term employed by Engel and Reichsman [8]), a tendency to marked orality, and an intensification of free, defused aggression.

In the oedipal type of developmental environment, in which mothering is not woefully inadequate although the depressive constellation is established, it is the father's manic-depressive influence that deprives the mother of needed support during the neonatal period and affects in a powerful and troubling way the subsequent oedipal configuration. The narcissistic and omnipotent daydreams associated with this type of environment would involve the "primal" depressions associated with exclusion from the parental dyad, a killing off of the father, the carrying off of the mother, and the unconscious controlling of parental intimacies. The children become elated or depressed participants on a larger stage than the preoedipal one.

EXAMPLES OF THE MANIC-DEPRESSIVE INFLUENCE
DURING THE PREOEDIPAL AND OEDIPAL
PERIODS OF DEVELOPMENT

Major Influence during the Preoedipal Phase

The symbiotic unit is the vulnerable institution during the preoedipal period of development. A complete transactional glossary has gradually evolved, categorizing the different elements believed to be involved. Subtle differences between the metonyms reflect the theoretical approach. Curiously, they also reflect the basic interpersonal virtues of faith, hope, and charity that lie at the heart of religious experience. Faith is defined generally as complete trust, confidence, reliance, or unquestioning belief in someone or something; hope as the feeling that what is wished for will happen and that expectations will be fulfilled; confidence as trust, reliance, belief, or certainty in the capacity of oneself and others; trust as faith, belief, or confidence in the reliability of others; mutuality as sharing of feelings or being interdependent, or being on a level of intimacy; preoccupation as total engrossment with, concern with, or absorption in someone or something, to the virtual exclusion of everyone and everything else.

All these terms have their genesis in the feeding situation, the agape or love feast in which mother and infant assimilate elements from each other: the mother gives to the child and is identified with the child, and the child gives to the mother. The quintessence of the relationship depends on their meeting each other's needs in a way that is mutually satisfying and does not leave one partner frustrated. The mother has at her command mothering techniques that can mitigate the crises of frustration in the infant, and these are extended to techniques for dealing with separation and loss. The techniques are often transmitted from one generation to the next almost unaltered. The following case illustrates many of the features that have been discussed.

Case 3. The family is composed of a father (at a middle management level of employment), the mother (hospitalized on three occasions with depression and once with hypomania), a daughter age 13, a son 8, and a baby boy 12 months. The parents had a trial separation for seven months and came together again. During the trial separation, the mother was somewhat depressed but not seriously enough for hospitalization. The mother was interviewed first with her husband, a quiet, compulsive man trying very hard to keep everything under control. He was very much concerned, and had been for many years, for the safety of his children and was constantly checking to see if they were in any danger with respect to electrical and gas equipment, ladders, tools, and medicines. His own mother had abandoned her children and her husband when he was about 12, and he had taken over the responsibility of the younger ones. There was a very strong maternal quality about him, mostly in the areas of protection and succorance. He was openly critical of his wife's maternal behavior, stating that when she was depressed she neglected her children, when she was "normal" she worried excessively about them, and when she was manic she attacked them, often irrationally. He said that in his opinion she had no idea how to behave like a mother, that she had not received a good example from her own mother, who treated her, he said, in a very shabby manner. He saw them as having very much the same problem, since the maternal grandmother had also been hospitalized on one occasion for depression. He could not see how she could function as a mother when she remained for the most part tense and anxious. He was not an expert in these matters, he said, but in his view it was fundamental that a good mother know how to feed her children so that they learn to enjoy their food and thrive.

When asked for her opinion, the woman agreed with every word her husband had said; she realized that she was not a good mother, that she should not have had children, and that she often had very angry and aggressive thoughts toward them. She sometimes wondered how she kept from killing them, especially when they cried excessively and would not stop. She felt she did not know how to give to her children or to make them feel happier when she felt so empty and inadequate herself. She did not feel, deep down inside her, that they were *her* children: in fact, with each one of them, she had wondered whether the hospital had not mixed them up in the nursery and had given her the wrong child. She had suffered from "baby blues" with every pregnancy and birth. She acknowledged her husband was right when he said she lacked the maternal instinct. Other mothers, when their babies cried, would rush to feed them: in her case, she often rushed off to feed herself because she felt so anxious and helpless. She was sure that her husband would have made a much better mother than she was, had he been a woman, and, even as a man, he seemed to know better than she exactly what to do when the children were upset. When her babies screamed, she first felt afraid of them and then wanted to attack them. She was constantly guilty for these angry ideas and ashamed at being such an inadequate mother. Her husband said that she often upbraided herself for being a bad daughter to her mother and a bad mother to her children, and he regarded this as her way of punishing herself. When she acted inappropriately toward the children, he often felt that it was not because she did not know what to do in the circumstance but because she was so preoccupied with her own thoughts that she could not think about the situation. He cited a recent example in which the household pet, a kitten, had been run over. The children had been extremely upset. Without a word of explanation, she had bundled them all up in her car and had taken them to a fun fair and encouraged them to take as many rides as possible. This was the way her own mother had dealt with family crises during her childhood, and she was repeating the same pattern. Both children had vomited, and the baby also had been sick. When they had arrived home, they all looked very ill and depressed. His own parents would have allowed him to have a good cry and thus work the sadness out of his system. He thought that getting the children excited was not the way to deal with their grief.

The second interview was with mother and infant and was extremely low-key. The baby seemed apathetic and lacking in energy. At no time did he smile or reach out for objects that were placed within arm's length. He did, however, begin to whimper when the interviewer attempted to get too close to him. His mother said that he had become "somber" when the father had left home during the trial separation. Later during the interview, he did make a feeble attempt to retrieve some hidden objects but quickly gave up the first time he failed. His response to defeat was not to cry but to whine. The mother remarked that in earlier months he had screamed a great deal, and when she found herself unable to pacify him, she would cover her ears, run out of the house, and stay away until she thought the storm was over. She always felt very bad about this, especially when she thought what a terrible picture he was getting of her; but at such times she could not stand him and she could not stand herself, and all she wanted to do was get away to some dance hall and dance until she got tired. While she talked, the infant remained listless and did not turn on a single occasion to look at his mother.

The third interview was with the daughter, Mary, a restless, angry child who seemed to be looking for a fight with the interviewer. She complained continuously throughout the session about everything, since nothing seemed to be right in her world. She felt that her mother did not care what happened to her, that if she walked off the top of a building, her mother would still continue to read the newspaper or watch TV. Her teacher and classmates did not like her, and she, in turn, hated them all without exception. Her mother, she said, treated her "like shit" and at times, she felt, she would like to smash her mother into pieces. But then she thought that each little piece would come back and poison her. She hated taking anything from her mother and she hated giving her anything. She tried to avoid doing things for her or helping her in any way. She especially hated her when she became crazy and left the whole house in a mess and never cleaned up anything. Her father had to do it all when he came home in the evenings. "She calls herself a mother, but she's a real big baby. Even my baby brother is better than her in some things." Asked about herself, she said that she was dumb and stupid and could never do anything right; she had no confidence in herself in the way that other kids had. She always thought that things would turn out badly, and she could not look forward to anything good happening to her. She had no friends because she did not trust any of them; they had all let her down in the past. She did not believe anybody could help her. Her father was away from home so much that he really did not count. When asked why she had no friends, she said that she did not know how to make them or keep them. She always expected them to be bad, and they always turned out bad. She thought that they must get fed up with her because she was so jealous, she hated it when they spoke to anybody other than her. Then she felt that she wanted to kill them. When asked whether she ever got depressed, she replied that she did when she was not mad: "When I'm not mad, then I'm sad." The teacher's report referred to her hyperaggressiveness, her garrulousness ("she is forever talking in class and listens to nobody"), her gluttony ("she would often steal food from other children and stuff herself in an offensive manner"), her messy habits, her excremental vocabulary ("she is the only child I've ever known where the thought has occurred to me that she should have her mouth washed out with soap!"). Toward the end of the third session, Mary's rage and vitriolic commentary seemed to dry up for a few minutes, and the interviewer remarked that listening to her had made him realize how unhappy she was with herself and with everyone else and how sorry he felt for her: "It must hurt so much to be so miserable and to feel so unloved." Surprisingly, the defiance all seemed to melt away and the years to fall away from her, and she suddenly became like a very little and vulnerable girl; she came over and put her arm around the interviewer and her cheek against his face while she wept quietly. It was a striking transformation from a tough, provocative harridan to a soft, needy, dependent, depressed little child. It was following this interview that the observer rated her vulnerability to future depressive disorder as high.

The interview with the son, Richard, was altogether different. He more or less took control of the session and gave a rapid account of his everyday world at school, limiting himself almost entirely to activities that called for very little affect or conflict. However, in the middle of these "bread and butter" associations, he unexpectedly remarked that how he felt at school on any particular day depended on how his mother was feeling at home: 'If she's sad, it gets me down, and I have sort of dark feelings inside me. I keep seeing pictures of her sitting in a chair at home with her head bowed down. I try to do a thousand things to get away from it, but it keeps being in my head. I wonder if she's getting enough to eat when we're not there. If I think of her drinking a big glass of milk it makes me feel better!" His eyes looked bright, as if he had thought of something troubling, and the observer asked him about this. He said that it did not happen very often but that sometimes at school he thought of her eating something that might make her die and he would not be there to help her. "Sometimes I get angry that she's not taking care of us properly, as my father says, but sometimes I know she's my mother and that she really loves us even if she doesn't show it. Sometimes she gets very fed up and hollers at us and tells us to get out and stay away from her and that she doesn't want to see us again and that we are the cause of all her trouble. When she talks like that, I almost hate her. She can be so mean. Mary hates her a lot when she's like that, but I can't say things against her. When she's okay, she makes us fine hamburgers and lets us eat as much as we like. She says it's to make up for when she doesn't have enough for us to eat and Dad has to get something from the corner shop." When asked about his relationships at school, he said that he had one or two friends and that kids did not like him because he was so moody. "It's like what I said—sometimes I'm thinking about my mother, and then I feel all dark inside." He went on to say that no one could really like him because there was nothing to like. He had nothing to say because he could not talk about home or take anyone home. He didn't think he was good at anything, and when he was asked to do anything in class, he always looked so dumb. When asked about a vocation, he replied that he never thought of things like that. He always expected things to turn out bad, and he felt sure he would fail if he tried to become anything good. He was silent for a little while and then said, "I don't suppose I'll live very long." When asked to amplify this, he said that he just thought that he would get some kind of sickness. "I think I've got an open door to my body—any germ that wants to get in just has to walk in. If any kid gets a cold, I know I'll get one, too, because the germ just has to walk through my door. There's nothing to stop him."

Here we have what appears to be a devastating impact on the internal and external lives of three children. The "core of ambivalence" is very evident, as is the lack of self-confidence, the hopelessness, the insecurity, and the low self-esteem. The self, in fact, for all of them, is a very poor thing, unnourished by maternal concern and preoccupation. The father functions as an ancillary mother, but he is not around enough to make his presence felt psychologically. The major impact of the manic-depression appears to have been on the symbiotic unit in each case.

The Main Influence on the Oedipal and Postoedipal Phase

The object choice of the manic-depressive individual, judging from our sample, has less flexibility and scope than that of the normal person. An obsessive-compulsive partner is chosen quite frequently, and in such situations one can observe chaotic, undisciplined, and unpredictable behavior in the manic-depressive responded to by increased rigidity, carefulness, orderliness, and "safety measures" in the partner. During the manic attack, such espousals create a reassuring background for the children; the more psychotic the individual becomes, the more compulsive, controlled, restrictive, cautious, and altogether rigid the partner is. At times it almost seems as if the psychosis is being supervised and curtained off by the neurosis.

Case 4. The family consists of the father with manic-depression, his wife, and their son 15 and daughter 13. The father is one of the leading authorities in the world in his particular specialty. His capacity for work is remarkable when he is elated and almost negligible when he is depressed. His mother also suffered from manic-depression, and he recalled the periodic onslaught of her illness on family life until she died quite suddenly of a heart attack at the age of 50. His own heart attacks began as an anniversary reaction at his mother's age of onset, and he expected to die at the age she died. He was overwhelmed not only by her psychosis but also by her personality, which completely swamped him at times, and by her somatic complaints. Recently it was found that he did, in fact, have severe occluding coronary disease, and he was invited to undergo a new and revolutionary type of cardiac surgery. Characteristically, he and his wife read all the available literature and discussed the odds seriously with the children. Even more characteristically, and in line with his usual arrogant nature and sarcastic approach to all human problems, he pointed out that the outcome of the decision depended on the phase of his cycle in which it was made: When he was on the upswing, he felt like Superman and could manage everything, accomplish everything, and survive everything; nobody could kill him. On the other hand, if it was made on the downswing, when he was vulnerable, weak, pessimistic, despairing, and ready to destroy himself, the opportunity to die would be too good to refuse. His manic-depressive attacks were superimposed on his "normal" cyclothymia, which was as regular as clockwork. His wife would say, with a certain amount of humor, "Let's see, it's Tuesday, which means we can go out, because you're not due for depression until Wednesday morning!" His own comment on the cycle was: "What can you say about a life in which at one point you're the king of the world and ready to challenge God or any of his prophets, and at another point you're just a helpless baby, completely dependent on women to look after you. In my life, I simply exchanged an intensely dependent relationship with my mother for an equally dependent relationship with my wife. They both took over the job of feeding me, medicating me, looking after me, and in general keeping me alive. Were it not for both of them, I would have died a long time ago, and the world would have been rid of one splendid neurotic. I often compare myself to those intriguing little fish found in some tropical seas, where the males live their entire lives safely within the vaginas of the female fish. When I am paranoid, I hate all women, who carry us all inside them and keep us infantile. What they do not realize, however, is that my weakness is my strength and that I can dominate them through my helplessness. I can make them do anything I want simply by wanting it, and they scurry around like mother hens trying to make wonderful things come true for me. I used to think that I had fulfilled my mission in life when I pushed my weakling father completely out of the picture. I made such psychological mincemeat out of him that he was never able to raise his head or penis in our house again. That's the sort of damnable kid I was!"

His wife also had a mild father who was "sweet and giving" but could never be relied upon to stand up against her dominant mother. In the battle with her mother, she always felt trapped and helpless and to this day complains that her mother puts her "identity imprint" on everything she does. She had married her husband because he was the most brilliant person she had ever known and the greatest figure in his area of work. After marriage, she found that not only was he sexually impotent most of the time but he found intimacy repellent: he said he did not want to be eaten up by women. On the only occasion that she was ever unfaithful to him, he found out, and he has never forgiven her. The marriage has been almost constantly stormy, "a perpetual hell," and she was constantly bombarded, especially during his manic phases, with his sadism, sarcasm, and even physical brutality. At no time during the affective cycle does there seem to be any place for normal sexuality. "He cannot live with me, and he cannot live without me; at times he wants to get inside me, and at other times he hates to come near and touch me." He is so demanding and time-consuming that she has hardly had a life of her own to live.

However, the more ill he becomes physically, the better she finds herself feeling. She can eventually see herself becoming independent of him even without him dying. She regards herself as the family integrator, keeping peace among her three children. She has only to turn her back on them and she immediately imagines that something catastrophic will happen.

The daughter, Joan, is quiet, compulsive, and inhibited, taking refuge in her room when the recurrent emotional storms hit the household. She has never been introspective: "I don't really look at myself closely, so I can't really tell you anything about myself." She was sure of only two things: she was never going to get married or have any children, and she was going to become an archeologist. Archeologists lived solitary, calm lives, and, like real scientists, they were never upset if things happened unexpectedly. She saw herself living in a little hut not far from the digging site with only the essentials to keep her alive, perfectly self-sufficient. She did not need anybody and could manage everything on her own. She had something like that little hut in her home at present. She was surrounded by all the artifacts that she collected daily in the neighborhood; she sorted them out and classified them without interference from anybody. She described her family as very different from other families. Something wild was always happening, and you could never tell what would take place next. At times she became very frightened when her father and brother got into a squabble, and she was always afraid they might kill each other without meaning to do so. When she and her mother went out shopping, it seemed almost impossible to realize that other people lived such normal lives and did such normal things. But she wondered if it would remain like that if she went to stay with one of those families. Maybe everyone in her family had gotten so used to trouble that they would take trouble with them wherever they went.* She felt best and safest with things, because they always remained the same, never had tantrums, never got depressed, and never got aggressive (she smiled as she made this comment). One of the reasons she wanted to be an archeologist and go far away to strange lands (mainly South America) was that she hoped never to meet anyone like her father. She knew that he was the greatest person in the world, and she loved him very dearly, but she was also very afraid of him, afraid that he might hurt her without meaning to do so. She was always apprehensive when she was alone in the house with him, because she was never sure what he would do next.

Jim, the son, could only be described as a phenomenon. He had seen the interviewer at different stages of his development and enjoyed the sense of being understood and remembered. "You've seen me 'up' and you've seen me 'down,' so you know every side of me—the killer and the dope fiend!" Both parents reported on his "extraordinary babyhood," and some of the stories that sounded exaggerated turned out to be close to the facts. There were stories of his "insight" as an infant, his inventiveness as a toddler, and his industry and accomplishments after he got to school. He had always been a superconfident child with a strong belief that nothing was beyond his powers. His mother had sighed when she said that it was rough for a mere woman to live with two geniuses in the

---

* Compare this with Kafka's reaction, cited earlier (p. 286).

same household. She had married a genius, and they had produced a genius, and what more could a woman ask for in her life? His energy during childhood matched these other attributes. "He seemed to be on the go everywhere all the time." Even today there were parts of the wall, the ceiling, the stairway, and the furniture that were almost worn down by his need to match his strength constantly against the world. His mother remarked (with a certain amount of complacency) that what was so disturbing about her son was that he had always to show that he was the greatest. "Now, I do think that he is great, but not all that great, and certainly not as great as his father. He wants to be and do every-thing. He has to be the strongest, the cleverest, and the brightest." It was clear that Jim had been nourished on many myths and legends that had grown up around his infancy and childhood. He knew that as a baby his thirst had been so insatiable that his mother alone had not been able to satisfy it and that they had had to send out to the hospital for milk from other mothers to supplement his own. He knew that he had been trained overnight, his parents having pointed out the many and manifest advantages of urinating and defecating in the bathroom. He knew that he had awakened one night as a toddler and had repainted the walls of the living room in a magnificent potpourri of color to the height that he could reach after his father had done the job during the day. Both parents had been flabbergasted and dismayed at first but subsequently were excited and admiring; years later they recognized this as his earliest aspiration to outstrip his father. Jim was very conscious of his father's being a great man, but, in his opinion, he was not great enough; in his "family romance" he included fathers at the presidential and senatorial level. His current aspirations were quite discrepant with his achievements. At school he was constantly in trouble with the authorities for his arro-gant and abrasive behavior, his outrageous opinions, his contempt for the staff, and his readiness to experiment with drugs. In spite of a fairly me diocre performance at school, he was certain that he had something to contribute to the world in the area of constitutional law. In fact, he felt that his knowledge of law put him in an unassailable position to deal with difficult authority figures. At times he felt uncomfortable with his mother, and he complained that she was always trying to get inside him to find out what his secrets were. He wished that she would keep out, since his mind was no place for a woman! His mother always thought she could feel his feelings and anticipate his wishes. When would she realize that his feelings were his own and separate from her feelings? For her part, mother felt that she had a ringside seat and in fact was promoter, producer, and director of one of the great dramas of history—the struggle between her husband and her son, which often took the form of a knock-down fight with both of them slinging at each other. "Jim wants to kill his father, but he would be the saddest child in the world if he were really to succeed." She added, with a giggle, that it was just like the Sophoclean drama: these two tremendous figures meeting at the cross-roads and never giving ground. "If my husband keels over with a heart attack, it will be a disaster for Jim and will make him guilty for the rest of his life." The slightest hint of criticism generated a whirlwind in either of them. "They are equally sensitive, and I try to bring a sense of reality to the proceedings. I tell them: 'You are not all-powerful; there are bigger things in life than you.'" She tries not to choose between them or to make either feel jealous of the other, but she says "My primary loyalty must be the man I married and not to the child I bore." When she married her husband, he had meant more to her than anyone else in the world, and even now she went every night to tuck him in bed and kiss him goodnight. She realized the danger of this. "I would hate for him to confuse me with his crazy mother. She overwhelmed him, but I just try to support him. I would hate to overwhelm Jim in the same way, but I am sure that he cannot do without me." Each night her husband says to her: "I hope that you are prepared for the fact that one of these mornings you will come in and find me dead." She says of this, "I remain terribly calm. If I don't hold up, nobody else in the family will. I love this man very much even though I hate him more than I can say." Her ambivalence toward Jim was equally profound. When he had been born, she said, she had been very disappointed: the night before she had had a dream about a girl with male sex organs. With the birth of Joan two years later, she felt a great sense of exhilaration, almost amounting to ecstasy.

[The interview with Jim gives some of the flavor of this type of child, where the developmental environment has been heavily impregnated with an overload of typical manic-depressive ingredients of both manic and depressive varieties. The exaggeration of these elements in the father's personality did not occur, to the mother's knowledge, until Jim had started to kindergarten. The conflicts between the mother and son appeared to have their onset around this time.]

Jim came in dressed eccentrically even for the youth of today, with all sorts of strange medallions hanging from his neck and his waist. He very clearly wanted admiration and blatantly "fished" for it. He again remarked that he had read something in *Time* magazine about the interviewer and expressed pleasure that he was seeing somebody of some consequence. "I might have ended up with some petty little shrink!" He said that he had been practicing forging signatures while waiting for me. He pointed to a signed portrait of Freud on the wall with the comment: "He was so educated and yet his signature is so childish. And you're no better." He boasted that he could copy any signature, and this set off a wild fantasy in which he was the brains behind a huge criminal outfit. "If ever I get into crime, I'll be going over the top of Al Capone." He seemed quite uncritical of his rather clumsy efforts to forge signatures. All the while, he talked ceaselessly about making big money forging tax returns. "It would be something in the millions." He said that since last seeing the interviewer he had been able to do "a lot more living and loving" with his current girlfriend. His only problem was his father. "If I wasn't afraid that his heart would explode, I'd bite his ass." He said that he had been thinking of six good ways of killing his father and demonstrated various karate attacks that would rapidly put an end to him. He said that if the interviewer did not believe in his power, he had only to get up and Jim would show him how easy it was to throw him bodily out the window. "There are ways in which I could kill you and it would pass for an accident, but I would always get away with it. Whenever I run into any trouble, my luck always holds up." He touched a large medallion on his chest. "As long as I have this around my neck, I cannot be hurt." This reminded him that when he was very small, he used to fancy that he could fly and would occasionally take off from trees and buildings. He never got hurt, because something always seemed to be protecting him. Some people, like the Kennedys, did not have his luck. This led him to talk about the assassinations. He thought he was probably the only person in the country who knew exactly how President Kennedy had been killed. "If people knew the details I know and deduced everything from first principles, they would come to the same conclusion, but everyone is so stupid." For the first time during the session, he sat quietly and stared at the interviewer. After a short pause, in tones that sounded genuine, he said: "You are the first person I have ever met who believes that I have any good inside me—everyone thinks I am crummy, or crazy, or ready to blow up the world." In an almost shy manner for him, he offered me one of his medallions, Taurus, illustrating the 69th sexual position. "It will bring you luck like it's brought me luck, and I want you to be lucky." For a brief moment, behind the narcissism, the omnipotence, the superconfidence, the apparently undeflatable optimism, the prodigious energy, and the fluent associations, one could sense a latent depression that was constantly being suppressed. When asked about his sadness, he at first looked surprised and then admitted it. "I'm not usually aware of it, but when I am not doing something, I can get very bored and down. It's as if the world had suddenly come to an end and there was nothing but a black pit in front of you. My father has the same trouble, and I think he must have inherited it from me." He asked whether the interviewer had taken his threats about killing his father seriously. "It's both true and not true. It's true deep inside me but not true in my everyday mind. I can think of killing him, but I can't bring myself to face the fact that he could die any day from a heart attack if I get him too worked up. That's where the true and not true business comes from. I tell myself, 'You mustn't work him up, because then he'll die,' and then without thinking about it, I find myself working him up. I also don't like the idea of you dying. Just think of that great brain going underground. That's why I believe in life after death. There must be a place for clever people like you, my father, and myself."

DISCUSSION

An attempt has been made in this chapter to correlate the ongoing conditions in the environment with the interpersonal and intrapsychic development of the child. The concept of the developmental environment seems especially pertinent in this context. The lines of development are contaminated as they pass through each developmental environment.

Children of manic-depressive parents are considered to be genetically at risk, that is, they are more likely to develop manic-depression than children of parents who did not suffer from this psychosis. The childhood of psychotic patients has so far been studied only retrospectively, but a study of children at risk for manic-depression currently being conducted in St. Louis [2], is attempting to disentangle the influences of the genetic endowment of the child. Since the psychosis itself rarely begins before young adulthood, a close investigation of these children is likely to reveal at least some of the antecedents of the disorder. In this chapter we have been looking for early evidence of the psychodynamic elements found in the full-blown state. What is inherited, if this is the major factor, is not manic-depression itself but the manic-depressive tendency, and the cases presented would seem to offer support for the existence of this tendency during childhood. The tendency itself probably has physical, psychological, and environmental components, but here we have limited our exploration to the psychodynamic component. The so-called ingredients of omnipotence, narcissism, grandiosity, unreal thinking, and false optimism—together with the reverse components—are found during normal development but are corrected by normal parental management. Under conditions of abnormal parenting or parenting that manifests the ingredients to an exaggerated degree, the components present in the children are amplified to a subclinical or clinical level. At what point of intensity the manic-depressive tendency becomes a manic-depressive psychosis is still unknown, although there is reason to believe that new elements are added to the picture with the psychobiological developments of puberty and adolescence that facilitate the emergence of the psychosis in its alternating form.

From the psychodynamic point of view, it seems feasible to assume that the overload of narcissism and omnipotence in the developmental environment would interfere with the normal subsidence of these elements during development. The mechanism by which these ingredients are maintained and increased is still something of a mystery, but the process of identification might account for some of it. What seems to happen is that the susceptible individual in such an environment does not easily relinquish his infantile omnipotence and does not de-idealize the omnipotent parent or test his attitudes and behavior against reality. The parents, from their side, appear to foster the megalomania of the child without undue concern for his reality sense.

It was especially interesting to observe the interlocking of two affective cycles under the same roof, the clinical periodicities of the parent meshing with the subclinical periodicities of the child. Occasionally, the cycles become synchronous, and parent and child are driven to confront each other from respective peaks of omnipotence and arrogance or from respective depths of helplessness and misery. This could sometimes lead to constructive attitudes and behavior but also has led to destructive omnipotent fantasies that are eventually acted out in the environment. It often seemed that after they had exhausted their potential for constructive omnipotence, they turned to sadistic fantasies and activities.

In Case 3, the symbiotic unit is constantly under attack from the defused aggression of the pair, and every now and then one of them seemed to provoke aggression to the oral-dependent phase and reactivate the depressive constellation.

The impact of the manic-depressive ingredients on the triangle in Case 4 brings about a fierce struggle between father and son and the intense involvement of the mother. It sometimes ended with one or the other triumphing. For example, when Jim was overcome, his omnipotence would often rise to a new height and take on a very destructive turn. The game of "killing the father" could at times become realistically ugly. When this happened, depression sooner or later set in, whereupon the mother would move into action, reconcile Jim to his father, restore his self-confidence by her own display of confidence in him, and help him to make amends by undertaking work around the house.

One of the most disturbing experiences for the child in the manic-depressive environment is to realize suddenly that the omnipotent object has become powerless. As Jim explained it in the context of his father's heart attack: "It's as if you were fighting someone for the world championship, and suddenly he becomes a bag of jelly and completely at your mercy. You don't know what to do. You can't hit him when he's down, and yet you still want to hit him. What's worse, you begin to feel sorry for him and wish that he would stand up and fight as he always did. It can get you very mixed up in your feelings." The recurrent phenomenon in this milieu is "death and resurrection" —the omnipotent one is down, but he will certainly be up again, and omnipotence will prevail in the end. The same is true of depression. It descends like a black cloud on the household, but sooner or later the atmosphere lifts, and elation gradually asserts itself. A narcissistic hurt or a narcissistic boost is enough to reverse the apparently implacable conditions.

The failure of the environment to modulate the forces at work during development is particularly striking in these children. Reality comes but slowly into their lives, resisted by each and every member of the household in their different ways; grandiosity is often encouraged and confused with masculinity; and the most immoderate affects in the human emotional repertoire become the plain facts of existence. Whether in Pumpian-Mindlin's [22] schema these children will respond to the acid test of omnipotentiality by a shift to unreality remains to be seen. Even if Mary and Jim do not become manic-depressive patients, they will both undoubtedly remain crippled individuals who are constantly at variance with their environments. Both will inevitably wreck the relationships that form around them.

Mary will seek out symbiotic partners, but these, she will find, are hard come by and difficult to maintain outside the ambience of the nursery. Jim may well make a creative contribution to his environment, but his bitter and almost relentless pursuit of the father will compel him to destroy the oedipal units into which he gets drawn. Nevertheless, unless he becomes psychotic, he will remain sufficiently engaging and delightful and charming to draw the unwary object into his narcissistic net.

CONCLUSIONS

In this chapter, the study of the developmental environment created by the manic-depressive parent, father as well as mother, for their children from birth onward and its epigenetic interplay with constitutional and intrapsychic factors differs significantly from previous studies in the following ways:

1. It was designed as a multifaceted psychobiological investigation in which a selected group of children and parents would be studied more intensively through the closer scrutinies offered by the therapeutic approach.
2. It was based on the *prospective* observation of the actual environment as experienced by the child.
3. It focused on the evolution of potential manic-depressives in the making.
4. Its sample was much larger than those obtained in other studies concentrating on the same area.
5. Its ongoing records were kept in considerable detail so that earlier and later comparisons could be made directly from the raw content of interviews.

It says much for a theoretical framework when retrospective and prospective findings show a significant degree of concordance, although even then one would hope that the direct approach would furnish us with a more microscopic analysis than that afforded by anamnestic reconstructions. In comparing the prospective and retrospective approaches in the case of Little Hans, Freud had this to say: "Strictly speaking, I learned nothing new from this analysis, nothing that I had not been able to discover (though less distinctly and more indirectly) from other patients analyzed at a more advanced age" [11].

There is no doubt that the direct findings of prospective study are more distinct, detailed, and vivid, and there is also no doubt that the multiplicity of phenomena observed later in life tend to converge, as we trace them developmentally backward "from a very limited number of processes concerned with identical ideational complexes," to quote Freud [11]. This is in keeping with the differentiation principle of development. Nevertheless there are other important services offered by the prospective method. It allows not only for the expansion, modification, and revision of existing theory but also for the elaboration of new theory, as has been amply demonstrated in much of the current work dealing with direct mother-child observations. New theory from Benedek, Mahler, Klein, Anna Freud, and others has extended our knowledge to the extent that future analysts might feel tempted to paraphrase Freud and to say that, strictly speaking, one learns nothing new from adult analysis that was not already discovered for patients analyzed and observed at earlier ages, and always more distinctly!

Yet it is reassuring to find areas of concordance with retrospective work and with conclusions drawn from the *transference* data of adult patients. A good example of such concordance is offered by Cohen and her colleagues [7]. They found that their manic-depressive patients were brought up in families that were set apart from their social milieu by some differentiating factor that gave them the status (and reactivity) of a minority group. The families attempted to rectify this by aspiring constantly to better themselves, a situation that put a good deal of pressure on the children, since they were often regarded as instruments to bring this about. The constitutions of the families were such that the *crucial dilemma* for the children consisted of finding the unreliable parent lovable and the reliable parent unlovable. The *critical period* for this development seemed to be up to about the end of the first year, when the "hatching" of the separating-individuating individual is about to occur and the child is beginning to experience difficulties in integrating the earlier "good" with the later "bad" mother into a whole person who is sometimes "good" and sometimes "bad," a contradiction that lays the groundwork for the quintessential ambivalence in these individuals. As a result, the child feels cut off and alone and may initiate a pattern of self-destruction to gain love and approval, and, at all costs, to avoid the incitement of envy.

The authors point out that the manic-depressive character in adult life has one or two extremely dependent relationships within which he repeats the childhood demands for unconditional love and attention, but at the same time *not giving anything of himself*. His self-depreciation is his way of informing others that he has nothing to give. This causes them to feel badly that it is they who have been unable to give, so that they afford him a reason for hating them for making him what he is. (This is reminiscent of the earliest transactions of the depressive constellation, and we can confirm that similar circularities exist in the children that have been directly observed.)

Another feature to emerge from both prospective and retrospective approaches is the fear of abandonment; both depressive and manic attacks are often triggered by any separation from the source of supplies. Behind this lies the constant unconscious hope in these patients that all needs will be unconditionally and completely met. The manic attack, by its very nature, provokes rejection and separation, and makes the vicious cycle inevitable.

As a parent, the manic-depressive is loaded with damaging deficiencies: he takes but refuses to give; he has little or no awareness of others as people but only as stereotypes and consequently has little capacity to empathize with them; he shows a minimal respect for reality and is always ready to substitute magical manipulation for realistic reaction and interaction. The combination of infantile dependency, manipulativeness, exploitation, shallowness, insensibility to give anything of himself, and the very extraverted approach to reality renders the manic-depressive unfit for the complex tasks of parenthood and puts his children at risk for some form of depression at all stages of their development.

REFERENCES

1. Abraham, K.   *Selected Papers of Karl Abraham M.D.* London: Hogarth Press, 1948.
2. Anthony, E. J.   The impact of mental and physical illness on family life. *Am. J. Psychiatry* 127:2, 1970.
3. Anthony, E. J., and Benedek, T.   *Parenthood—Its Psychology and Psychopathology.* Boston: Little, Brown, 1970.
4. Benedek, T.   Toward the Biology of the Depressive Constellation. In *Psychoanalytic Investigations: Selected Papers.* Chicago: Quadrangle Books, 1973.
5. Benjamin, J. D.   Discussion of Hartmann's Ego Psychology and the Problem of Adaptation. In R. M. Loewenstein et al. (Eds.), *Psychoanalysis—A General Psychology.* New York: International Universities Press, 1966.
6. Cimbal, W. J. O.   *The Neuroses of Childhood in Relation to Bedwetting* [Die Neurosen des Kindesalters] Berlin: Urban and Schwartzenberg, 1927.

7. Cohen, M. B., et al. An intensive study of twelve cases of manic-depressive psychosis. *Psychiatry* 17:103, 1954.
8. Engel, G. L., and Reichsman, F. Spontaneous and experimentally induced depressions in an infant with a gastric fistula. *J. Am. Psychoanal. Assoc.* 4:428, 1956.
9. Erikson, E. H. *Identity, Youth and Crisis.* New York: Norton, 1968.
10. Fenichel, O. *The Psychoanalytic Theory of Neurosis.* New York: Norton, 1945.
11. Freud, S. Analysis of a Phobia in a Five-Year-Old Boy (1909). In *The Standard Edition of the Complete Psychological Works of Sigmund Freud,* transl. and ed. by J. Strachey with others. London: Hogarth and Institute of Psycho-Analysis, 1955. Vol. 10, p. 1.
12. Freud, S. Inhibitions, Symptoms and Anxiety (1925). *Standard Edition.* 1959. Vol. 20, p. 77.
13. Freud, S. The Ego and the Id (1923). *Standard Edition.* 1961. Vol. 19, p. 1.
14. Gill, M. (Ed.) *The Collected Papers of David Rapaport.* New York: Basic Books, 1967.
15. Glover, E. *The Technique of Psycho-Analysis.* New York: International Universities Press, 1955.
16. Jacobson, E. *The Self and the Object World.* New York: International Universities Press, 1964.
17. James, W. *The Principles of Psychology.* Chicago: Benton, 1952.
18. Kafka, F. *Beschreibung eines Kamfes.* Berlin: Der Heizer, 1906. P. 183.
19. Klein, M. *Contributions to Psycho-Analysis.* London: Hogarth Press, 1948.
20. Mahler, M. Notes on the Development of Basic Moods: The Depressive Affect. In R. M. Loewenstein et al. (Eds.), *Psychoanalysis: A General Psychology.* New York: International Universities Press, 1966.
21. Piaget, J. *The Child's Conception of the World.* New York: Harcourt, 1929.
22. Pumpian-Mindlin, E. Vicissitudes of infantile Omnipotence. *Psychoanal. Study Child* 24:213, 1969.
23. Winnicott, D. W. The theory of the parent-infant relationship. *Int. J. Psychoanal.* 41:585, 1960.
24. Winnicott, D. W. The Effect of Psychotic Parents on the Emotional Development of the Child. In *The Family and Individual Development.* London: Tavistock, 1965.

13

Adolescent Depression

SHERMAN C. FEINSTEIN

Depression remains one of the most common, but still not clearly defined, emotional reactions in childhood and adolescence. Depressive reactions are manifestations of conflicts in object relationships and, when they occur during adolescence, are indicative of and contribute to difficulties in psychic development. Object loss is particularly traumatic to the adolescent and makes a deep impact on the still developing psychic structure. The longitudinal, observational approach has confirmed the etiological importance of early infantile development, the oedipal period, and latency to psychic growth; adolescence as a developmental stage may achieve the same degree of significance as an etiological precursor of later development as has been assigned to these earlier periods [9]. This developmental work, which has been described by Blos [6] as a recapitulation of the separation-individuation tasks, makes the adolescent vulnerable not only to normal everyday losses but also to unresolved conflicts from infancy and childhood. From these present and past reactions various depressive manifestations emerge, which tend to confuse the observer and make the true diagnosis of depression difficult because of the ubiquitousness of its expressions.

This chapter will focus on a developmental cognitive-affective model of depression based on a synthesis of previous models that have been found useful. Depressive reaction is viewed as the usual method for integrating the cognitive and affective recognition of loss. The ego's perception of loss demands an immediate reintegration of ego structures, since the affective elements that accompany the recognition of an object loss render the ego helplessly vulnerable to feelings of abandonment and fears of annihilation. The capacity to experience object loss and the accompanying depressive affect is a normal complication of the establishment of lasting emotional relationships.

If we postulate the capacity to form an object relationship during infancy, early developmental studies indicate that the neonate has an immature nervous system and little or no object relationship development during the first few weeks of life. At 12 weeks, assuming adequate mothering, the infant shows some recognition of the mothering object and on prolonged separation may manifest irritability and crying. From the age of 4 to 6 months, a dramatic change in object relationships occurs. The child now has achieved a rather distinct bond to the mothering person, described by Mahler [20] and Benedek [5] as a symbiotic relationship. The earliest development of the self is now manifested in ego structures that include a narcissistic grandiosity and an idealization of the symbiotic mothering object. These cognitive operations allow the infant to proceed further with the development of object relationships.

The developmental position at 6 months of age is what Melanie Klein has called the depressive position [26]. The mother's absence is often experienced as her death. The infant, still in the oral stage of development, links the affects of love and hate with incorporation. In states of depressive anxiety, the infant feels not only that he has lost the ideal mothering object in the external world but also that the internal self is in danger of being destroyed, a feeling sometimes described as emotional surrender. This state of affairs is the prototype for later reactions in which one experiences the loss or *fear of loss* of an object or of self-esteem in childhood, adolescence, and adulthood.

The concept of what the child views as a loss during such primitive developmental stages must be considered. Any action, either external or internal, that in any way disrupts the early ego balance, which still must rely exclusively on an external object (the mother) as its main source of energy, can be interpreted by the child as a loss and may set off a primary loss reaction, which Bowlby [7] describes as separation anxiety. Therefore, the concept of loss may be expanded to include any dramatic change in the delicate narcissistic balance in attachment bonds. Separations, changes in the mothering object because of emotional or physical illness, sensory deprivations, parental loss, physical moves, and at times even minor disruptions in the child or the environment can be experienced as a loss.

Beck [4], in describing a cognition-affect chain, states that there is an intimate connection between cognition and affect. A particular cognitive content produces affects that are congruent with it. Therefore, ideation arising from a fantasied or symbolic loss produces the same affect as an actual loss. The converse is also true—affects can act as stimuli in the same fashion as an external stimulus. Affects can be subjected to the cognitive processes of monitoring, labeling, and interpretation, with the result that, to a patient, dysphoric affects can suggest a loss or produce the fear that a loss may occur. If the patient feels badly when getting up in the morning, it is as though something bad has happened or will happen. This cognitive error is crucial to the understanding of depressive ideation and also suggests some possibilities for therapeutic interventions.

The impact of these cognitive perceptions (either realistic or in error) is to bring about partial regression to the stage of growth that exists at the symbiotic level of interpersonal development [13, 18]. The developmental achievements of the ego determine whether the resolution of the depressive reaction is immediate or delayed, or whether it results in a clinical depressive state. The efficient resolution of a depressive reaction is essentially nonsymptomatic, although definite variations of mood, sadness, and anger can be recognized by both the individual and his close associates. Symptoms of clinical depression, with its affective, cognitive, motivational, vegetative, and motor components, result from a lack of adequate resolution and indicate conflict and fixation in the mourning processes.

THE MOURNING PROCESS

Possibly one of the difficulties in understanding the depressive reaction has been the tendency not to see the components of the reaction to loss or fantasied loss and the reconstitutive reactions by the ego mechanisms available to resolve the reaction as part of the same process [7]. While perception of loss sets off particular affective reactions, such as feelings of abandonment and fears of annihilation, it also sets into immediate motion restitutive mechanisms that restore the ego's homeostatic equilibrium. These mechanisms are the products of successful growth and development of the psychic apparatus and find their clearest expression in mourning. When the loss can be handled by mourning, there is a rapid restoration of equilibrium, and the person's response is considered a normal depressive reaction. When the mourning mechanisms are quantitatively or qualitatively deficient, various states of incomplete mourning and clinically manifested depressions develop.

To clarify this point, let us briefly review the author's concepts of the stages of mourning and compare these stages to the developmental phases responsible for their production. There are five stages of mourning, which follow their corollary stages of development: denial (presymbiotic); depression (symbiotic); separation-individuation (separation-individuation); rage at lost object (oedipal-latency); reconstitution (adolescence).

Stage 1. *Denial.* Normally the first perception of a loss is delayed by attempts to deny its recognition. "I can't believe it," "I saw him just yesterday," "I'm sure she will pull through," are typical reactions to the news of a loss. In pathological reactions, the denial is persistent and varies from delays in perceiving the loss to a delusional repudiation of reality. The denial that is characterized by inappropriate perceptions and affects is an attempt to ward off what are seen as frightening emotional consequences following from a loss. The ego state here is the equivalent of the presymbiotic level of development. In the regression to those early months of infancy, when the child had not yet developed the intense human bond that eventually leads to a higher level of object relationship capacity, there is either a lack of recognition or discomfort in the anticipation of the pain involved in the next or depressive stage of mourning, and an attempt is made to delay or neutralize this stage by denial.

Stage 2. *Depression.* The cognitive perception of or affective reaction to a loss will precipitate a feeling of sadness with a sense of vulnerability described as feelings of loneliness, fears of abandonment, and a certainty of annihilation. Characteristic of the symbiotic child's response to even a momentary perception of the absence of the mother, this is the most treacherous reaction the ego experiences, since an inability to institute a rapid restitution of the symbiotic tie, once these vulnerabilities are felt, leads to the fear of emotional surrender. The whole scheme of child development is devoted to the resolution of the dilemma of insecurity that Bowlby [7] describes as separation anxiety. The serious consequences of early anaclitic depression relate to the dangers of overstimulating and disrupting the ego mechanisms without the immediate availability of resolution defenses.

If this phase of depressive shock is not quickly resolved by ego mechanisms developed through maturation or provided by the "mothering" figures involved in the caretaking of the infant (who must supply the ego defenses until adequate growth has occurred), secondary symptoms will result as a consequence of the now affected ego's attempts to relieve the depression through other, more pathological defenses. These defenses during adolescence may include acting out, aggression against the self, guilt reactions, agitated states, suicide attempts, affective sadomasochistic reactions, and repression and displacement to depressive equivalents. In the anaclitic child, after the phases of protest, despair, and detachment, death is a possible out-come of the unrelieved depressive state.

Stage 3. *Separation and individuation.* The resolution of symbiosis leads to the development of the self, a narcissistically oriented self that has achieved certain defenses. These defenses allow the depressed ego to experience relief from the frightening possiblity of dissolution by providing memory traces sufficient to reassure the temporarily de-pressed ego of survival. Moving from Stage 2 to Stage 3 is the most crucial aspect of the mourning work and, from a clinical viewpoint, indicates whether the depressive stage is to be efficiently resolved or delayed, with subsequent secondary symptom formation.

The early stages of object relationship development, first described by Freud [12] and subsequently clarified by Erikson [8] and Benedek [5], were finally brought to the current level of understanding by Mahler [19]. The ego defenses and character states erected by these developmental steps provide a mechanism for the resolution of the normal regression effected by the perception of an object loss. The forward movement provided by defenses away from the depressive po-sition is a recapitulation of early developmental vicissitudes experi-enced in the first three to four years in a child's life. Ego damage caused by interference with early development leads to incomplete resolution of this stage of mourning, with subsequent secondary symp-toms of depression characteristic of fixations at this early developmen-tal period. In adolescents these symptoms are manifested as remark-able fluctuations in mood, intense dependency conflicts, insatiable seeking of affection, confusion in identification, and identity diffusion.

Stage 4. *Rage toward the Lost Object.* The oedipal resolutions and the subsequent latency operations involving superego formation allow the developing psychic structure to deal with the ego restitution neces-sary during mourning to successfully reestablish homeostasis. By the age of 9 to 12, the ego, now increasing in strength, with a firm sexual identification, an ego-ideal, and superego introjects, is able to differen-tiate itself more clearly from the lost object. This may result in rage at the lost object and can occur for two important reasons: First, the loss is a great inconvenience because it results in interruption of an important relationship and forces the ego to experience the subse-quent mourning with its concomitant depression. Eventually the su-perego will recognize the validity of this rage as a normal aspect of the mourning process and will effect its resolution. However, with incom-plete superego development, guilt and shame may develop because of the fear of having unacceptable impulses. Second, the ego is forced to face the more general truth of death and loss as part of life. The developmental efforts at this period of life are actively dealing with concrete operations that allow for the grasping of this perception [24]. The rage toward the lost object is related to being forced to perceive the fact that loss and death are present and must be dealt with. It is this aspect of the mourning process that results in mourning reactions when no actual loss has occurred but one is reminded of the possibility of loss by the occurrence of a casual event.

Stage 5. *Reconstitution.* The final stage of mourning is related to structures eventually completed during adolescence. The reworking of sexual and aggressive impulses, the recapitulation of identifications, resolution of dependency, and synthesizing an independent character structure are normal tasks of adolescence. Once available as ego mechanisms, these same defenses are utilized to complete the goals of dealing with object loss and converting the external object to an introject, with the eventual achievement of homeostasis and a reassurance that the energies exist to continue survival operations.

In my opinion the mourning process cannot be completed until all the stages of psychosexual growth and development through adolescence are resolved. This helps explain why the adolescent ego, with early defense mechanisms but without reconstitutive defenses, is frequently thrown into a state of vulnerability. The mechanisms needed to deal with loss are injured by the demand for their premature utilization. Overwhelmed by these demands, the adolescent ego regresses and may become fixated at an early stage of the mourning process. The adolescent then begins to use immature and ineffectual mechanisms, such as acting out, withdrawal, and ascetic and sadomasochistic defenses, which can lead to clinical depressive states and identity diffusion.

TYPES OF ADOLESCENT DEPRESSION

Normal Adolescent Depression

The adolescent, with his multiple developmental tasks, is subjected to a wide range of experiences, both intrapsychic and interpersonal. Partial regressions, in the service of mastering ego stresses related to the necessary loosening of ego structures, subject the adolescent to frequent loss experiences. Since adolescence contains a renegotiation of both the original separation-individuation efforts and previous oedipal resolutions, it can be considered that the mourning mechanisms are in a state of relative incompleteness. As discussed, the final stage of mourning depends on the successful resolution of adolescence.

It is because of this state of affairs that Anna Freud [11] believed that all adolescents could be thought of as being in a state of mourning and, in fact, longing for the periods of childhood when solutions were relatively simple. Denial, depression, separation, and rage at the lost object may be mobilized when the teenager perceives an object loss. However, the final stage of reconstitution can be only partially resolved, leaving the adolescent confused, ambivalent, and at times fearful of diffusion of the ego. It is during these states that the adolescent frequently reaches out for help. Unfortunately, at times the plea is not a direct attempt to secure counsel but is expressed in aggression, suicidal gestures, wandering, and various action fads or religious explorations.

The adolescent is capable of resolving a normal depressive reaction by self-therapy, by support received from peers or meaningful adults, and particularly by intelligent counseling. The realization that the feelings of the depressive reaction are normal responses to a loss or the fear of a loss is reassuring and can provide the support needed for ego mastery.

Case 1. Chuck was seen after he requested psychiatric consultation. He reported that he felt fatigued all the time, found it difficult to concentrate, and was worried that he was ruining his excellent high school record. This state started after an episode of infectious mononucleosis, which resulted in the loss of several weeks of school. On his return to school he noticed a lack of interest in his numerous extracurricular activities and an increasing panic that he might get poor grades for the semester. He had elected to take incomplete grades in several courses in order to gain time to bring up his average, but he found himself unable to function and growing increasingly depressed.

An attractive, bright, verbal 16-year-old, he was able to discuss his shock about his current feelings since, until the onset of the current episode, he had felt strong and sure of his ideas and directions. The oldest of three boys, his parents had divorced when he was 10. He believed he had come to terms with the divorce, although he and his father still had many differences. He needed good grades in order to attend a top school; otherwise, his father would insist on his going to a state university, which he felt was degrading. He had worked through his use of psychosomatic symptoms as a way of avoiding responsibility in the past and was angry about his current depression, which might render him helpless and interfere with his plans.

We were able in three sessions to trace his current depression to his regression to earlier periods of helplessness and particularly to the depression from the loss of his father at the time of the divorce. Pointing out to him that certain illnesses in adolescence, particularly infectious mononucleosis, frequently resulted in normal depressions was helpful. This led him to rework the still unresolved mourning for the loss of his intact family and deal, for the first time, with his rage at his father. Interestingly, Chuck did not appear for his fourth and last session. He called to tell me he had gotten a job, was completing his courses satisfactorily, and would come to see me if he felt the need.

Adolescent Depression with Oedipal and Latency Fixations

Depressive reactions in adolescents are frequently characterized by a notable absence of phase-appropriate behavior, and a remarkable immaturity of the mourning capacity. Anthony has described a type of adolescent depression that has marked oedipal characteristics and manifests significant guilt and moral masochism derived from a punitive superego. "Hostility, intended for the parents, is deflected back on the self, and the self-depreciating trends are ultimately related to the wish to destroy the idealized image of the parents by whom the child feels betrayed" [1]. During the mourning process, this hostility, which normally is directed toward the lost object, may be misdirected because of the guilt involved in the unacceptable direction of the rage. The hostility may then be directed toward a surviving parent or the self, resulting in provocative, argumentative behavior, or masochistic or suicidal attempts at handling depressive affects.

The difficulties involved in the treatment of these depressions are many. The adolescent is already struggling with oedipal fixations that he is using to defend himself against the fear of loss of controls inherent in the preadolescent and adolescent process. On the other hand, the adolescent is developmentally able to move out of the depressive phase of mourning into the phase of separation-individuation. This allows him to make a powerful treatment alliance and to attempt to deal with depressive elements with some confidence in his own survival capacities. The difficulties involved relate to the narcissistic defenses the adolescent is forced to use, which include omnipotence in evaluating his own efforts and a shattered idealism in the adults with whom he is involved. An early interpretation of the normal aspects of rage toward the lost object can be most helpful in providing a structure for the adolescent struggling with still unresolved oedipal-latency development.

Case 2.   Ralph entered treatment after making a rather serious suicide attempt in his third year of college. He had become unable to concentrate and had developed obsessive ambivalence about course selection. He readily accepted the suggestion to leave school and seek psychotherapeutic help. Ralph was very interested in therapy and developed a very positive relationship, but he attempted to compete intellectually on every point.

He traced his current depression to the previous year, when he was selected for a special tutorial program. He had become ambivalent and worried about whether he deserved the honor and whether it was a good curriculum for him. It became clear that he was struggling with deep feelings of inadequacy; he recalled that these were feelings he had struggled with all through his early school years. He commented that he had reached his peak by the age of 10 years, being recognized as a child prodigy, and that it had been "downhill" from that time on.

His parents were intelligent, interested people who reported a rather uneventful childhood. Ralph was bright and responsive, and related well to peers and adults. He enjoyed school but became somewhat isolated starting in his junior high school years. This was a period of serious financial reverses for his father, who became very depressed and eventually had to make important business adjustments, becoming an employee rather than the owner of his own concern.

Ralph was very content to be at home and working while undergoing therapy. He had never been happy at school; he had felt alienated, and unable to participate in college life. He had never found a satisfactory roommate and had drifted from suite to suite in the dormitories. He had joined an athletic team but quit on several occasions, returning only because his parents persuaded him to. The only happiness he had had was a brief summer relationship with a girl, who seemed uninterested in continuing the friendship when school resumed. Since then he had had repetitive dreams about this girl, usually characterized by their getting together after enormous vicissitudes that kept them apart.

As mentioned, the therapy frequently became rather intellectual, as Ralph would gleefully point out an error the therapist had made in some fact. At times he had a sneering, hostile attitude, but he always denied any feelings of anger or disappointment. Gradually he began to deal with his deep feelings of emptiness and discussed his fears of masculine inadequacy and his concern that something was missing within him.

A rather dramatic occurrence put Ralph in touch with his anger. After a semester furlough, he returned to school and suffered a recurrence of symptoms. He had suicidal thoughts and, after much long-distance consultation, returned home. He was furious with the therapist during his first hour, accusing him of being overprotective. He eventually realized that he himself was responsible for his coming home and that he was hoping to receive something from the therapist that would allow him to cope with his separation anxieties. He has become aware of his intense rage at his father for not being available during his oedipal years and now seems to be slowly developing a more autonomous self-concept.

Adolescent Depression with Defective
Separation-Individuation Resolution

From a clinical point of view, adolescent depression in which pre-oedipal features predominate manifests itself in highly volatile fluctuations of mood and dependency. Early interferences with separation-individuation are characterized in adolescence as immaturity, lack of consistency, and a shallowness of character structure. Such adolescents show a remarkable degree of unresolved dependency that places the demand for dealing realistically with loss phenomena on their parents and surrogates. The lack of firm, constant introjects prevents them from completing that stage of mourning that reaffirms their own intactness.

Frequently, an intense dyadic relationship exists with the mother, resulting in a dependent, symbiotic type bond manifested by clinging, or sometimes in sadomasochistic relationship replete with hostile attacks on the family and external authorities. Malmquist [21] describes these children as being aware of their needs to become emancipated as they struggle with despair over their incapability. They are frequently hypochondriacal or manifest psychosomatic disorders. Acting out behavior, with verbal as well as physical violence, is seen; it has a symbiotic quality and alternates with clinging demands for reassurance and protection.

Fluctuations of mood, which are mentioned by Malmquist [21] and Anthony [1] as important in adolescent depression, are a frequent component of depressions with early developmental fixations. Phenomena of mood are critical during early child development. Most children demonstrate major periods of exhilaration or relative elation. This mood alternates with low-key periods when they become aware that mother is absent from the room [19]. Fixations during this period of mood-control development leave the adolescent with defective controls that reappear during adolescent depressions as marked rapid fluctuations of mood between despair and elation.

Case 3.   Nancy, age 18, was struggling to remain in college, severely depressed by the loss of a boyfriend. She was a tall, plain-looking girl, inappropriately well dressed compared to the typical student. Having graduated at the top of her high school class, she had chosen to attend a small, unsophisticated college near home with the goal of becoming a teacher. It was clear that she had few defenses to deal with the depression and was anxious about being alone as she struggled with suicidal thoughts.

Nancy, the older of two children, was obsessively concerned with her relationship with her mother, whom she felt she needed desperately. She worried about her friends rejecting her and complained of her father's and brother's better relationship with her mother. She demanded evidences that the therapist "cared" for her and was irritated by his generally neutral attitude. She asked for additional hours frequently and wanted double appointments so that she could deal more deeply with her problems.

Nancy's first year of life was difficult because of frequent infections. The mother was under great tension because of a depression related to the stress of moving and some difficulties with her husband. However, Nancy was a bright, well-behaved child who developed normally. The mother was separated from Nancy when she was 2½ for surgery, and subsequently several deaths occurred in the family. These incidents deeply affected the mother, who believes that she had limited resources available for her daughter.

Nancy was a very serious child; she was usually unhappy and was easily frustrated. She reacted to the birth of her brother when she was 5 with an obsessive possessiveness. The mother describes her as being "too good to him." Later she demonstrated enormous jealousy toward her brother or her mother's friends or relatives, and resented any plans her mother would make with them.

Psychotherapy with Nancy was difficult because of the concretistic thinking that predominated. She saw every separation and every interpretation as a battle that she begrudgingly gave in to rather than feeling emancipated. There was a continuous gloom in the office as she whined and complained over every aspect of her miserable existence. She was constantly concerned about how she could explain this or that to her friends and needed and demanded reassurance about every trivial issue. She fantasied ideal situations, usually time alone with her mother, which when they did not work out resulted in depressive reactions, as though something had been lost. She also reacted to any uncomfortable affect, convinced that something was wrong even if she had no realistic reason.

Her life had become dominated by obsessive and compulsive rituals. Her attempts to control her anxiety by ritual resulted in long, complicated efforts to reduce the anxiety around going to sleep, awakening, going to school, and taking care of her general functions. In addition, her mother had been subtly woven into these rituals. Although she claimed great reluctance to participate, the mother had guiltily acquiesced to Nancy's demands and had gone along, ambivalently complementing the compulsive operations. It was at this point that the mother entered treatment in an attempt to resolve some of the symbiotic relations that were interfering with Nancy's progress.

Nancy's mother, an attractive, intelligent woman, was currently pursuing a master's degree in education. She felt that she had done an adequate job with her son and that she had a relatively good marriage. She was generally angry at Nancy, who seemed to be deteriorating and who she felt had always been a demanding, clinging child. She was locked in a continuous biting, argumentative struggle with her daughter and felt that hospitalization was becoming a necessity. However, when it was pointed out that Nancy seemed to be depressed and that another approach was possible, she agreed to work in a collaborative therapeutic program.

A crucial maneuver at this point was to attempt to reduce Nancy's anxiety by giving her trifluoperazine. This seemed to give both Nancy and her mother a new lease on life and allowed for some important shifts. Nancy was able to return to a normal sleep pattern after struggling with a day-night reversal for several years. She was now able to attend classes and gradually was more able to concentrate and do her homework without needing her mother's continuous presence. The mother was able, through her therapy, to recognize the remarkable immaturity in Nancy's development and began to avoid getting caught in dependency demands. She encouraged her daughter to slowly make decisions and allowed her to use regressive techniques if they seemed to be at the service of mastery. For example, the mother was able to let Nancy and a friend go "trick-or-treating" on Halloween even though it was completely inappropriate. They had a good time and were able to talk about their wishes for "reliving the old times."

With a more supportive, less hostile relationship with her mother, Nancy was able to make a positive commitment to treatment. The mother continued to complain that too much affectively charged material was directed toward her, but this gradually decreased. An area of improvement that was most remarkable was Nancy's growing ability to concentrate and complete her work. She was more able to make plans. She began to enjoy school and became more involved in campus activities. She handled several disappointments very positively, showing the beginning of strength in using separation-individuation solutions to deal with loss reactions.

Early evidence of manic-depressive illness may appear during adolescence. While the illness can appear in childhood, most cases show alternating mood patterns developing early in adolescence. The diagnosis may be difficult, but an emerging pattern of longer, alternating mood swings are seen in those adolescents finally diagnosed as manic-depressive [10].

Case 4.   Bert, at the age of 15 years, had been in treatment for five years because of emotional outbursts that became intense, almost psychotic. He was the source of derision by his peers because of his grandiose boasting about his athletic prowess and his compulsive, bet-on-anything form of gambling. Although he had been described as depressed for the nine months before referral, the history revealed that there had been alternating moods of depression with sudden, abrupt periods of elation during which he was described as continuously talking, euphoric, restless, and hypomanic in mood.

The oldest of six children, Bert was close to his father until the age of 10 years, when he began manifesting his emotional problems. The father, a psychologist, was described as being a depressive character who spent a great deal of time in bed. He had refused to seek treatment for his own depressions or to participate in Bert's treatment program. The mother was seen as an adequate but exhausted woman who had, in recent years, been close to Bert. She felt ready to divorce her husband because of his withdrawal. Bert was an active child who had cried a great deal in infancy and had resisted cuddling. His gross motor development was advanced, and he showed great skill and interest in athletics. However, his athletic potentials had been compromised because of his erratic moods and conflicts with his teammates. Fine motor coordination was poor, with some learning disability. His attention span was short, concentration was poor, and he was extremely disorganized in work habits. He had an insatiable appetite, and his parents had to put a lock on the refrigerator to stop his early morning food excursions. He was relatively insensitive to pain and weather and had an almost unbelievable history of accident proneness.

Bert's therapist noted that there were two predominant moods, either of which might last for some months. During periods of depression Bert was insistent that he was hated by everyone and was capable of nothing good. He was particularly expressive of his father's rejection. During upswings, he was grandiose, was convinced that he could do anything, and especially was confident that he would become a basketball superstar.

During the evaluation, Bert, tall and immature, started a breathless conversation about his discovery of another man in the psychiatric unit who had similar complaints of anxiety. His pressure of speech was punctuated with requests for reassurance about the future as he related his current low level of self-esteem. A recent episode of manic behavior had been precipitated by the death of his dog. He related how sad and desperate he felt and how, being preoccupied by his thoughts, he had run in front of a bus, narrowly escaping injury.

Observation of the patient over the next several weeks indicated the absence of any thought disorder, but a remarkable affective lability was present that was most sensitive to interpersonal relationships among the staff and patients. The evaluation was that Bert manifested a manic-depressive illness and that his depression was an endogenous, cyclic affair but that it was deeply influenced by exogenous, interpersonal factors. Psychotherapy was continued, but a course of lithium was also instituted. Initial reports, after 6 months, were very positive; Bert has been described as radically changed in mood and behavior.

The therapeutic course with adolescents with early defects in the separation-individuation resolutions is frequently a difficult one. The difficulties with object relationships and the mercurial quality of the adolescent process makes progress slow. Residential treatment is often required, and special techniques often are needed to deal with narcissistic transferences [17, 23, 25].

Adolescent Depression with Anaclitic Depression in Childhood

Although the preoedipal type of depression has been described, there are qualitative differences among certain early fixations that require separate discussion. The child who has suffered an anaclitic depression [27] struggles from a lack of even those defenses normally developed during the separation-individuation process. These children struggle with reality armed only with symbiotic ego structures, which makes them completely vulnerable to all loss experiences.

The mother-child dyad may be an intense continuation of the symbiotic ties, with subsequent depression in both during the adolescence of the child, or the mother, unable to satisfy her child's cravings for a symbiotic relationship, becomes depressed and hostile toward the child. The adolescent hangs on with alternating dependent clinging and rejecting sadomasochistic provocativeness. Masterson [22] describes these children as borderline psychotic characters and recommends intensive residential care since he believes that they do not "grow out" of their difficulties. Psychotherapy with these symbiotic adolescents is usually very intense because of the large element of affective acting out present in the therapeutic relationship. Regressions are rapid, since the capacity to maintain self-esteem at a stable level is deeply influenced by the perceptive distortions related to loss and by the reliance on affective signals as indicators of the state of reality. Essentially, these adolescents are fixated at the depressive level of development. With the development of only minimal defenses to ward off noxious stimuli, they have little capacity to deal with narcissistic breakdown and the accompanying feelings of vulnerability, abandonment, and fears of annihilation emerge.

It is in these two forms of separation-individuation fixation that collaborative treatment of the dyadic partner is most important. The mother must be able to slowly rework the intense aspects of the early relationship and attempt to reestablish a positive tie, resolutely devoted to slow but certain separation from the child with a definite goal of establishing individuation both in the mother and in the child. It is usually discovered that adequate development of the symbiosis had not occurred at the time of the original trauma and that there was an interference with object relationship development that then resulted in a sadomasochistic relationship. The reestablishment and working through of this original symbiotic relationship in a therapeutic setting has led several authors to think of adolescence as a second chance for the reworking of structures not adequately developed in childhood.

Case 5.   Sally, adopted at birth, was described as a pretty baby who was loved at first sight. Difficult at first because of eating problems, she later settled down and seemed content. She rarely cried and slept a great deal, and had to be awakened for meals. Development was reported as normal. When she was 11 months of age, Sally was separated from her mother for 10 days while the mother had surgery. Although the maternal grandmother took care of her, Sally was described as a changed child on her mother's return. She had cried during the entire separation and had begun to rock on her hands and knees, a symptom that persisted until she was 13 years old. From that time on, she resented being touched, and reportedly her first sentence was "Leave me alone." On moving, at age 1½, she cried for a week. She completely ignored her brother, adopted when she was 2 years old. Later she was jealous and rather sadistic toward him. She disliked school and frequently refused to attend. She had severe eating difficulties and refused most foods; the mother fed her meat with applesauce to cover the taste until Sally was 10 years of age.

An average student in the elementary grades, she had a few good friends, but she never enjoyed herself in school or in the various activities in which she participated. Gradually she became a behavior problem. She was never happy or comfortable in the company of adults, and when asked why she would not talk to family or relatives she would answer, "I have nothing to say." She seemed uninterested in what was going on in the world. She had little interest in television but listened to the radio and rock music. Her mother reported that Sally would rock until her legs ached.

Sally was well liked by the boys and started developing relationships with some in the seventh grade. These affairs were very difficult, however, since she was jealous and breaking up with a boy led to intense feelings of remorse.

Sally was referred after she became depressed and made a suicidal gesture at 13. This followed her being placed in a body cast for a severe scoliosis, secondary to her rocking activities. She fought the cast and the body brace she was later asked to wear and began to act out with rather dramatic sexual and aggressive behavior.

Sally was a thin, fragile but pretty girl who, looking like Alice in Wonderland, with her long, blond hair, was sullen and angry. At the first interview she was accompanied by her parents, whom she treated with disdain and indifference, making it clear that they were impotent to alter her behavior. Her attitude was cold and uninvolved, her voice distant and flat. Her mother, an attractive, young-looking, emotionally bland woman, seemed completely at a loss and tended to back down each time Sally confronted her. The father, also young and attractive, attempted to cajole and tease his daughter into a better humor; he was rather flirtatious and seemed able to communicate with Sally by a glance or a wink. At times the father and daughter joined together against the mother, insisting that she yelled too much, was too demanding, or simply did not understand.

The therapeutic course has been a long and frustrating one, punctuated by placement for a period of several years in a residential treatment center. Sally forms intense but superficial relationships. She has developed some intellectual insight into her difficulties, but her capacity to deal with any frustration or narcissistic loss is minimal. She is aware of her difficulties in dealing with loss and is compliant and agreeable in discussing the dynamics. However, she can't tolerate the discomfort of being alone and the paralyzing effects of feelings of aloneness. No amount of support and investment seem to become introjected. Elaborate plans and preparations fragment into nothingness under the stress of minimal anxiety or frustration. So far she can function only in a highly structured environment. On one occasion, after leaving her residential center, she began making compulsive suicidal attempts. These started after she became depressed following the loss of a boyfriend, several years her junior, who she, at least consciously, understood was most inappropriate for her to relate to. She pleads to be allowed to die, explaining that she is empty and cannot tolerate her existence.

Therapeutic efforts with the mother have not been successful because of her total inability to relate to Sally except on a symbiotic level. Once, while talking to her daughter on the phone, while Sally was in residential treatment, the mother said she couldn't stand Sally being away. (This was at a time when plans were being formulated to keep Sally at the center.) Sally immediately ran away from the institution, experiencing a serious rape episode on her way home. It is likely that continued long-term separation from the mother and analytic restructuring in a therapeutic milieu will be necessary.

TREATMENT

The treatment of depression during adolescence can be very effective, since the adolescent patient is continuously struggling with regressive phenomena and depressive reactions are only an exaggeration of the normally dealt with vicissitudes. On the other hand, serious clinical depressive reactions in those cases where there is early ego damage can be very difficult, and the danger of suicide is always a critical issue.

Phase-appropriate depressive reactions are dealt with by a variety of therapeutic techniques; they usually respond well to reassurance or short-term psychotherapy. The depth of the mourning varies with the stimuli. Parent loss through death or divorce calls forth deep mourning, which may result in temporary incapacitation. The adolescent, however, can be helped to resolve the mourning by making him aware of the stages of the process and reassuring him of the normality of his reactions. Of particular importance are comments about the stage of rage toward the lost object. Since this stage depends on the resolution of the oedipal complex and the superego negotiations of latency, the adolescent may still be actively struggling with these issues. Helping him to deal with the rage directly and to prevent the frequent projection or displacement will help in the resolution.

Self-therapy has been described as a very common phenomenon during adolescence by Anthony [2]. He concludes that it can be included among the classic therapeutic processes and that it may result in expansion of the ego and a moderation of the superego. However, the dangers may be great because of possible incompleteness of resolution. Josselyn [15] believes that the relatively normal adolescent who is able to verbalize his turmoil is a legitimate treatment prospect because of the advantages in minimizing the energy investment in resolving adolescent reactions.

The treatment of adolescent depressions with fixations at oedipal and preoedipal stages of development calls for intervention and requires a total approach to the individual, including the family or milieu that is interacting with the adolescent. There are essentially two phases to the treatment. First, the depression must be relieved so that the ego defenses can become operative. Second, an attempt must be made to locate the early fixations and conflicts and to attempt the resolution and working through of these developmental defects.

The establishment of a therapeutic alliance and overcoming of normal resistances is at times very difficult with the adolescent. However, it has been found helpful to approach the adolescent as though one were responding to a plea for help. Aggressive and sadomasochistic defenses are used for mastery and become destructive only when the fear of emotional surrender becomes overwhelming. Accepting the manifest behavior as an attempt at adaptation and proceeding directly to the depressive core with an interpretation of the depression frequently will relieve the despair and communicate to the adolescent that you have received his message.

With the child struggling with an anaclitic depression, the role of the therapist is to serve as a facilitator of the mourning reaction. The therapist's support and analysis of the interfering conflict will help the patient to proceed with the mourning process and, in those patients in whom early defects are present, will serve as a surrogate ego. Since the complete range of mourning defenses is not available until adulthood, the therapist working with an adolescent must always be prepared to use supportive treatment parameters along with the gradual development of insight gained through analysis. This careful balance of support and insight therapy is one of the most crucial characteristics of therapy with adolescents and demands flexibility and resourcefulness on the part of the therapist.

The relief of acute depression is only the first step in dealing with the depressive character structure. This is a dangerous stage in the therapy since the removal of the surface conflict leaves the still-undeveloped underlying structures vulnerable to further loss reactions, and the patient has little to support him except the newly established therapeutic relationship. It is at these times that a suicidal gesture, acting out, or impulsive termination of treatment is likely to occur. Active intervention—such as mobilizing the family into a therapeutic team or hospitalization, which serves as an artificial stimulus barrier until the character defenses can deal with sensitive conflict issues—may be required.

Once it is demonstrated that he in fact has the capacity to deal with loss, the adolescent's capacities to neutralize affects and utilize ego observation grow. The question of whether loss has actually occurred becomes a crucial issue. The possibility of a cognitive-affective distortion has to be considered, particularly during adolescence, when unfulfilled wishes frequently are interpreted as losses, with the precipitation of subsequent depression.

The working through and modification of depression proneness and depressive character structures is a difficult procedure and requires insight techniques. The recapitulation of earlier relationships in the transference and the careful analysis of the preoedipal and oedipal elements slowly relieves the use of depressive defenses. The patient begins to become aware of the deep infiltrations made into his character defenses by the depressive process. He sees how the fear of loss colors his everyday dealings.

Treatment of the adolescent requires modification of the techniques used in child and adult therapy. Gitelson [14] observed that while the

role of the therapist with the child or the adult is clearly defined as
the adult helper or parent, the adolescent allows no such definition.
He reacts frequently to the current situation (vis-à-vis the therapist)
and arouses much anxiety. The emotional attitudes of the patient are
not merely a repetition of the past, they also deal with the here-and-
now. The therapeutic role with adolescents requires dependability,
controls through the intelligent use of authority, and the providing of
an ego-ideal. Gitelson saw the goal of therapy with adolescents as fa-
cilitating a character synthesis rather than analysis, and the special
therapeutic skills required were the ability to tolerate mistrust, the
capacity to develop empathy, and the making of narcissistic contact,
especially in crisis situations. The adolescent's establishment of identification and reformation of the ego-ideal leading to final consolida-
tion of the superego is crucial and allows the adolescent to begin to
interact with his peer group. This therapeutic process must be carried
out at an optimum ego distance, which allows the therapist to support
and encourage the patient during his explorations.

CONCLUSIONS

The depressive reaction is among the unsolved chemical problems
in medicine. It is becoming clear that neurophysiological and biochemical components are intimately involved with emotional ones as
cognitive and affective elements set off reactions that deeply affect
the individual. Still the psyche is struggling for synthesis, and some
of the emerging brain research is beginning to explain reasons for the
enormous difficulties the human has in processing loss experiences.
One clue is the complicated manner in which object relationship development occurs. The very long, sensitive process leading to the development of object relationship capacity takes the developing ego
structures through all the stages of childhood and adolescent development before achieving maturation and the capacity to deal with loss
experience. Another possibility, reviewed by Koestler [16], is that the
brain, as it exists, is inadequate to process the stress of human interaction without pathological processes developing.

Depression in adolescence is described as constituting a major
problem, and the failure to resolve normal depression results in psychopathological reactions. The form of depression depends on the
level of psychosexual growth and development, provides a diagnostic
opportunity to review the ego defenses available, and consequently
provides some outline for the psychotherapy that must be provided.
The foundations of the psychotherapy depend on the enhancement

of the mourning that is inherent in every new step of independent function, since, as Mahler [19] points out, all growth and development is first perceived by the individual as a minimal threat of object loss.

REFERENCES

1. Anthony, E. J.   Two contrasting types of adolescent depression and their treatment. *J. Am. Psychoanal. Assoc.* 18:4, 1970.
2. Anthony, E. J.   Self-therapy in Adolescence. In S. C. Feinstein and P. L. Giovacchini (Eds.), *Adolescent Psychiatry*, vol. 3. New York: Basic Books, 1974.
3. Beck, A. T. *Depression*. Philadelphia: University of Pennsylvania Press, 1967.
4. Beck, A. T.   The Phenomena of Depression. In D. Offer and D. X. Freedman (Eds.), *Modern Psychiatry and Clinical Research*. New York: Basic Books, 1972.
5. Benedek, T.   The psychosomatic implications of the primary unit mother-child. *Am. J. Orthopsychiatry* 19:642, 1949.
6. Blos, P.   The second individuation process of adolescence. *Psychoanal. Study Child* 22:162, 1967.
7. Bowlby, J.   Separation anxiety: A critical review of the literature. *J. Child Psychol. and Psych.*, 1:251, 1961.
8. Erikson, E. H.   *Childhood and Society*. New York: W. W. Norton, 1950.
9. Feinstein, S., Giovacchini, P., and Miller, A.   Preface. In *Adolescent Psychiatry*, vol. 1. New York: Basic Books, 1971.
10. Feinstein, S., and Wolpert, E. A.   Juvenile manic-depressive illness. *J. Am. Acad. Child Psychiatry*, 12:123, 1973.
11. Freud, A.   Adolescence. *Psychoanal. Study Child* 13:255, 1958.
12. Freud, S.   Three Essays on the Theory of Sexuality (1905). In *The Standard Edition of the Complete Psychological Works of Sigmund Freud*, transl. and ed. by J. Strachey with others. London: Hogarth and Institute of Psycho-Analysis, 1953. Vol. 7, p. 135.
13. Geleerd, E.   Some aspects of ego vicissitudes in adolescence. *J. Am. Psychoanal. Assoc.* 9:394, 1961.
14. Gitelson, M.   Character synthesis: Psychotherapeutic problems of adolescence. *J. Am. Orthopsychiat. Assoc.* 14:422, 1948.
15. Josselyn, J.   *Adolescence*. New York: Harper & Row, 1971.
16. Koestler, A.   *The Ghost in the Machine*. New York: Macmillan, 1968.
17. Kohut, H.   The psychoanalytic treatment of narcissistic personality disorders. *Psychoanal. Study Child* 23:86, 1968.
18. Kris, E.   *Psychoanalytic Explorations in Art*. New York: International Universities Press, 1952.
19. Mahler, M. S.   On the first three subphases of the separation-individuation process. *Int. J. Psychoanal.* 53:333, 1972.
20. Mahler, M. S., and Gosliner, B. J.   On symbiotic child psychosis: Genetic, dynamic and restitutive aspects. *Psychoanal. Study Child* 10:195, 1955.

21. Malmquist, C. P.   Depressions in childhood and adolescence. N. *Engl. J. Med.* 284:887, 1971.
22. Masterson, J. F.   *The Psychiatric Dilemma of Adolescence.* Boston: Little, Brown, 1967.
23. Masterson, J. F.   The Borderline Adolescent. In S. C. Feinstein and P. L. Giovacchini (Eds.), *Adolescent Psychiatry*, vol. 2. New York: Basic Books, 1973. P. 240.
24. Piaget, J., and Inhelder, B.   *The Psychology of the Child.* New York: Basic Books, 1969.
25. Rinsley, D. B.   Theory and Practice of Intensive Residential Treatment of Adolescents. In S. C. Feinstein and P. L. Giovacchini (Eds.), *Adolescent Psychiatry*, vol. 1. New York: Basic Books, 1971. P. 479.
26. Segal, H.   Melanie Klein's technique. *Psychoanal. Forum*, 2:198, 1967.
27. Spitz, R. A.   Anaclitic depression: An inquiry into the genesis of psychiatric conditions in early childhood. *Psychoanal. Study Child* 2:313, 1946.

14

Depression during the Life Cycle

THERESE BENEDEK

"Life cycle" is a relatively recent term in the conceptual equipment of psychoanalysts. It was introduced by Erik H. Erikson's [16] publication of a series of his former papers under the title "Identity and the Life Cycle." The developmental theory of psychoanalysis covers personality as it evolves from birth to maturity on a basis of inborn genetic patterns. The concept of "life cycle" refers to a broader developmental field, one that takes in the infant with his genetic makeup and considers his development as the effect of phase- and age-specific interactions with the environment. The immediate environment reflects the sociocultural milieu in which the child grows up to become active when adult. Such a broad field is the source of the experience of all analysts, but it had not previously been conceptualized with such consistency as a continuum.

The teaching of psychological phenomena and processes has to be reductionistic to be accomplished. This was my belief when, at the end of a long lecture course on personality development that included maturity, the procreative phase, and aging and senescence, I [8] summarized the psychobiological course of life in terms of Alexander's vector concept. He states, "If we deprive . . . emotional sequences of their ideational content and only pay attention to the dynamic quality (direction) of the tendencies, we come to simple dynamic relations . . ." [3, p. 120]. The vectors refer to receptive, retentive, and eliminative tendencies, which include the tendency to give. It may seem questionable to stress reductionism in the extreme and attribute each major phase of an individual's life to one dominant vector tendency. Yet I did this at the end of the course, summing up life as a concatenation of generations: Beginning at birth, the organism is a link between his parents and his children to be born after he or she reaches maturity. The first phase of the life cycle is in the service of growth and maturation. This proceeds normally on the basis of the overall positive balance of metabolic and psychobiological processes afforded by the dominant receptive tendency. The procreative phase of life uses the stores accumulated by maturation in the biological task of the species—procreation and parenthood. These psychobiological processes and the sundry productive and creative functions of adulthood are supplied by the dominant tendency of giving-sharing. During the first phase of growth and development, the vector is self-directed; during the procreative phase the dominant vector is object-directed. The third phase, old age, which approaches slowly, is characterized by gradual change in the vector of psychic and somatic processes. The expansive, giving attitudes of the procreative period in time become outweighed by the receptive-retentive, self-centered tendencies characteristic of old age. Meaningful old age provides an integrated heritage, the fruit of experience, which prepares for the regressive processes of aging. But as the exhaustion of vital energies proceeds, expenditure of psychic energies lessens; in time, even the receptive needs diminish, since abundance can no longer be enjoyed. When life has only enough strength to maintain itself at a low metabolic rate, mental functioning is reduced to a minimum, and one can no longer speak of a structured personality. (Every year that I gave that course, I was impressed by the impact of this final lecture on the students.)

As long as psychoanalysis conceptualized the personality in terms of the evolution of an innate anlage, the instinctual model in its structuralized form was satisfactory. The environment remained outside the individual, even after Freud [21] conceptualized the process by which traditional attitudes are transmitted to and become incorporated in the child's psychic system. As closer observation of infancy turned attention to ego development and substituted for the "oral phase" the mother-child unity [6], the awareness of the psychodynamic significance of the interaction between the individual and his immediate and wider environment became central in the conceptualization of personality organization. It led Erikson [14] to his formulation of the concept "identity."

Psychoanalytic psychology expanded its frontiers in several directions. It is not within the scope of this chapter to elaborate why, speaking of the human life cycle today, it is not enough to consider it as an arc, although as we view the individual alone it is just that—a curve from birth to death. But the individual includes within himself the genetic and acquired consequences of his parents' life as well as those he transmits to his children. The term life cycle implies the idea that the individual's life is rounded out by the coherent experience of parents with each of their children [10]. In the course of events, the cycle of each individual intersects the life cycle of others, not only in his own family and social milieu (school, friends, colleagues, collaborators) but also the wider society and the whole cultural scene.

How does all this relate to depression, a systemic dysfunction (see Chapter 21) that affects man from infancy to old age? The question will be considered further, but here suffice it to say that the condition defined as climacteric depression offers the best illustration of how the widest circles of the life cycle, the cultural and social influences, modify the manifest emotional and psychosomatic reactions to aging.

At this point, let us look at Erikson's elaboration of the life cycle. He defines eight stages in the life cycle and considers each as dominated by a give-and-take between two contrasting manifestations of the stage of ego development (see Figure 1). This is not a contradiction to the genetic theory of development since each phase can be defined by the underlying phase-characteristic, instinctual conflict. Each stage of conflicting ego-manifestation originates in a psychosocial crisis evoked within the psychobiological system (e.g., the mother-infant unit in infancy). The crisis is overcome by the drives and capacities that the crisis activates. The favorable outcome of such processes is the source of adaptation; unfavorable outcome accounts for maladjustment. The balance between the factors of adaptation and maladjustment forms the "epigenetic pattern" that directs the development; in the depth of the unconscious mind, it elaborates, constructs, and reconstructs strengths and weaknesses to form the personality or the identity of the individual.

To use this concept as a framework in which to show the potential for depressive illness through the life cycle, I shall elaborate briefly Stages I, II, III, and IV. The psychological stage of Stage I is defined by the balance of the interaction between mother and infant during the symbiotic phase of infancy. I [5] describe the ego quality that originates in a positive outcome of these interactions as confidence; Erikson defines it as basic trust, opposed by basic mistrust. In any case, we assume that repetition of experiences in which need is satisfied leads to hope in the epigenetic pattern of the individual. Hope is "the first source of psychosocial strength" [17, p. 288] since it alleviates crises and thus furthers the processes of adaptation. Basic mistrust is a source of maladjustment.

In Stage II, Erikson subsumes those processes that, on the positive side of development, lead to autonomy and, on the negative side, lead

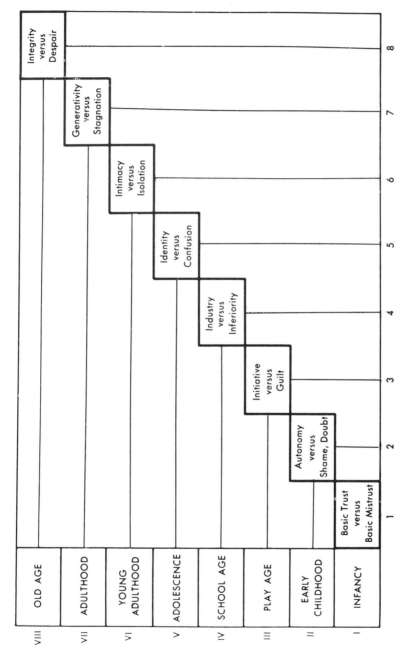

Figure 1. *Psychosocial crises in the life cycle. Adapted from* Childhood and Society *by Erik H. Erikson, copyright 1950, © 1963 by W. W. Norton & Company. Reproduced with permission of W. W. Norton & Company, Inc., and Hogarth Press, Ltd. Reprinted from the International Encyclopedia of the Social Sciences by David Sills, with permission of the author and Macmillan Publishing Company, Inc.*

to shame and doubt, characteristics that, if not alleviated, lead to low self-esteem. In the second year of life, one often observes the influence of the negative aspects of the first stage. Shame and doubt, the results of insecure autonomy, plus insufficient trust often lead to "negativism," or exaggerated willfulness. This is an expression of ambivalence that complicates the object relationship with both mother and father. Stage II includes chronologically the beginning of the oedipal phase, which is full-blown and even partially overcome during Stage III, defined by Erikson as "play age." The positive outcome of this developmental level is expressed in "initiative" (curiosity and fantasy); the negative outcome is characterized by guilt. Guilt may motivate regression to earlier phases of development. Play age harbors the core of neurotic conflict and thus the regression to the sources of depression. Stage IV encompasses "latency," when the social environment is the neighborhood and school, with their tasks and challenges. The positive outcome of this development is expressed in the child's responsiveness to the environment, industry in pursuing accomplishment in school work, and competence in social situations with classmates and teachers. The negative outcome of this stage is characterized by an inhibition of the expected normal behavior, resulting in inferiority feelings.

This interpretation of the lower half of Figure 1 [16] refers to those phases for which we have a valid image of the social environment and of the nature of the normally expectable psychosocial crises that children usually overcome and thus derive benefit from. We also have general knowledge about conditions that produce undue stress from without and that account for greater vulnerability within the child. On such experiential knowledge and on the combination of many other, unknown factors we base our prediction of the course of development and our diagnosis of an emotional disturbance and its probable source and significance.

The upper half of Figure 1 summarizes the positive and negative effects of psychosocial crises characteristic of the four stages of life from adolescence through old age. Each of these generalizations refers to complex psychological and social interactions. These interactions are motivated by the developmental past of the individual as well as by the current situation; the outcome of each crisis depends on the strength and weakness of the individual facing the crisis; his hopes and fears color his anticipations and influence the future course of his experience.

This construction is disturbingly vague, but it cannot be otherwise. However, I want to emphasize Erikson's implied optimistic philosophy. In this discussion, which is based on the assumption that depression is universal and may occur as illness in any phase of life, it is necessary to emphasize the curative potential of any crisis. This is not an attribute of Homo sapiens alone but is innate in all organisms; if survival is threatened, the reaction to danger (fear) activates the forces that support survival. It is a condition of the human species exclusively to experience crisis (danger) from within (anxiety), but man is equipped with drives, capacities, and psychological defenses that enable him to anticipate danger and, by anticipating it, to overcome it.

The survival reaction is such a natural attribute of our existence that my emphatic restatement of Erikson's principle may appear superfluous. The idea is not new to psychoanalysis. Freud [20], in his study *Mourning and Melancholia*, elaborated both aspects of the crisis activated by the loss of a needed and loved object. Here he described for the first time the metapsychological factors that contribute to the formation of the ego—introjection and identification—as functions of the mourning process. Mourning activates regression to primary narcissism, which allows for shifts in cathexes leading to termination of the mourning. In the "closed system" of the psychic apparatus, this means that the lost object, decathected, becomes elevated as ego-ideal [21]. The trauma of loss is overcome by the growth of the ego.

PSYCHODYNAMIC FACTORS IN DEPRESSION

In his study of the mourning process, Freud [20] discovered the factors in ego formation (introjection and identification) at the same time that he described the feeling of guilt as a contributor to the affect of mourning. In the structural theory, guilt as a psychic manifestation of the superego was established as a basic motivation of depressive states. It was Abraham [1] who discovered the significance of the oral phase of development in depression and related conditions. In describing clinical phenomena, both Freud and Abraham were implying the significance of ambivalence in instinctual processes and its influence on the evolution of object relationships. I [9] have elaborated the concept of ambivalence in the symbiotic phase. In Chapter 7 of this book, I elaborate ambivalence as a genetic characteristic of all instinctual, psychodynamic processes, thus making it a factor in depression. We now believe there are four fundamental factors in depressive illness—ambivalence, guilt, mourning (i.e., loss of an object), and loss of self-esteem.

Observation of infants and their mothers during the symbiotic phase makes all observers, both parents and researchers, realize that some degree of discomfort and frustration is unavoidable, even if the mother is in the best emotional and physical condition. Infants respond to nursing according to their innate anlage. Thus there are differences in the infants' reactions to the normal frustrations of the symbiotic phase. Ambivalence and the resulting frustration influence the emotional climate of the symbiotic interaction, leaving its precipitate as mistrust in the not-yet-developed mind of the infant. Yet depressive illness is not a condition that one can attribute to the child in the first stage of life.

The concept of depressive constellation does not refer to depressive illness or to depressive moods but refers to the negative pole of the primary object-representation of the infant. It evolves through the ambivalent processes of alimentation—hunger, frustration, need, and gratification. The percepts of the negative aspect of the ambivalent experience are introjected as the negative representation of mother, or nursing object. If the negative introjects outweigh the positive introject of the primary objects, tolerance for frustration cannot develop satisfactorily. The deficiency in frustration tolerance intensifies the negative impact of the transactional processes, thus intensifying the disposition to depression. The term depressive constellation refers to the phase of incipient ego development during which the object of instinctual needs appears to the infant as a part of himself. It should not be confused with the mood change defined by Melanie Klein [23] as depressive position nor with one of the basic moods described by Margaret Mahler [24]. Both authors refer to an observable mood change occurring at the maturational level (5 to 6 months) at which the infant perceives the object of his instinctual needs as outside and separate or separable from himself. Neither of these moods justifies the assumption of depression at that stage. (One might define these moods as incipient reactions to separation, before object relationship reaches the level at which separation activates anxiety.)

Observation of abandoned infants in the Hospital for Foundlings in Budapest (1916–1918) gave me [5] an opportunity to study the emaciated, unresponsive infants who were given the diagnostic label marasmus. The same kind of observations led René Spitz [30] (and others before him) to describe the syndrome as hospitalism. Later Spitz defined the condition as anaclitic depression. Hospitalism, however, is not a depressive illness; it only appears so. Hospitalism, especially if the infant is abandoned soon after birth, deprives the newborn of that intimate contact with the body of the mother that conveys to the child the principle of primary ordering (see Chapter 21) that is necessary for instinctual learning such as sucking, swallowing, and even breathing. Even if hospitalism does not lead to marasmus and death, it causes severe sensory deprivation and metabolic disorder.

Anaclitic depression is a condition of severe apathy. The condition manifests the extreme need of the infant to the observer, but the infant does not respond to the need of his body. Children suffering hospitalism do not cry. They do not have the energy to cry. They are not angry. Their perceptions of their own bodies and, even more, of the objects who care for them, are not sufficient to develop object relationships in any meaningful way. Thus, what is termed hospitalism is not a mental condition, and is not a depression.

In this context I refer to the concept of conservation-withdrawal (see Chapter 9). Engel and Reichman [13], in their publication on observations of the severely damaged baby, Monica, referred to the marasmus-like condition as withdrawal-depression. As in hospitalized children, so in this case of esophagus atresia the symptoms were like those of depression, but it could be demonstrated that they were caused by an instinctual, self-preserving defense against expenditure of energy. Long after the corrective operation, when Monica's physical and psychological condition were considered recovered from the illness, she responded to any stress with a reflex-like withdrawal, i.e., she fell asleep. Her behavior was in the service of conservation of energy. The same physiological defense can be observed in cases of Simmond's disease or in the terminal stages of anorexia nervosa. This may be a factor in senescence and in the recovery states after a serious illness.

Much has been written about anaclitic depression in infants and young children growing up in normal families, cared for by loving parents. The depression is attributed to separation or object loss, be it weaning, or actual loss of the mother by death or long illness, or partial loss as by having to share her with a new sibling. These are all significant events in a child's life, and healthy children will respond to them. The age-adequate responses, especially in the first and second stages of the life cycle, will depend on the balance between trust and mistrust. Ambivalence in object relationship is evident long before the child is one year old. Any loss, any trauma, increases ambivalence; the child responds with very mixed feelings and, consequently, with a lessened tolerance for frustration. Increased clinging to the mother is a characteristic reaction to trauma, if the mother is available, but even if the loss is permanent, the young child does not mourn; at that age, the trauma activates insecurity. In the first stages of the life cycle, trauma intensifies the infantile modes of object relationship, which are receptive and incorporative. Thus the child needs and accepts a substitute for the mother if she is not traumatizing. In summary, the primary root of depression is the instinctual ambivalence, which enhances, via the primary object relationship (the depressive constellation), a disposition to depression. Fleeting moods of depressive affects occur during infancy, especially during the second half of the first year. But one can speak of depression as an affective disorder or as "narcissistic disorder" only when the development has reached a level of ego autonomy, the loss of which may be feared. This is expressed in shame and doubt during the second stage of the life cycle and later.

Stage III is characterized as play age; it includes the oedipal phase. During this stage, the child establishes the primary self-concept and ego-ideal, which set the goal for his pursuits; failure, even in play, brings about loss of self-esteem and doubts of autonomy. To reestablish what he fears he has lost, the angry child fights, sometimes with success, sometimes with failure; it depends on the reservoir of hope and strength which will dominate the epigenetic pattern.

If development proceeds without a hitch, the child enters Stage IV, the latency period, with optimism and enjoying his competence in play and learning. But the contest of positive and negative developmental factors is burdened by guilt accrued from crises in earlier phases of development. The feeling of guilt is the pulley by which the psychodynamic processes turn and reactivate the past. Conscious memories and unconscious memory traces of developmental experiences compound the motivations and symptoms of depressive illness that may develop later in life.

SEX DIFFERENCES AND THE LIFE CYCLE

Stage V of the life cycle is the developmental phase of adolescence, characterized by identity or its opposite, confusion. At a time when the social structure was more coherent, adolescence was characterized as the period of creativity and Weltschmerz, a kind of "oceanic feeling" in which adolescents, boys more than girls, used to be submerged; then they emerged, ready to take the next step. Now we would define it as depressive mood, easily explained by the adolescent struggle that Anna Freud [18] conceptualized as polarization of affects. In earlier times, identity grew with the self; it was not problematical. Confusion was rarely observed; if it was obvious, it was taken as weakness or badness, rarely as illness. Today, confusion is a regrettable consequence of the condition in which adolescents have to try to become adults. Confusion may also, however, be a narcissistic neurosis, a defense against depressive illness, or the result of loss of confidence in a culture in which nothing is safe any more. One cannot be certain even about his own sex and certainly not about the role function, which, not so long ago, was considered an attribute of one's sex.

Deeper than the psychosocial factors are the psychodynamic (instinctual) motivations. Abraham [2] formulated the process by which the early genital phase (implied in Stages II and III), being overcome, reaches the final genital stage (implied in sexual identity, Stage V). According to Abraham, this means that the boy has "attained a point in his development where he no longer has an ambivalent attitude toward the genital organ of his heterosexual object, but recognizes it as a part of that object whom he loves as an entire person" [p. 410]. Not only the male but the female also has to overcome the fear of the other sex "in order . . . to reconcile with love the existence and function of her own sexual organ and that of the heterosexual love object" [10, p. 96]. With adolescence, one's sex determines his psychosexual responsiveness and role. Not so long ago, Abraham's idea corresponded to psychosocial reality—that is, psychosexual maturity was achieved by overcoming the alienation of the sexes that the culture implanted and required as a rule. Now the rule has been suspended or abolished. This is a serious problem of our age. It is implied in Erikson's conceptualization of the life cycle. He gives to adolescents (Stage V) an extension during young adulthood (Stage VI) during which to reach psychosexual maturity and consolidate sexual and social identity.

Until puberty, the sexes could be viewed as moving on parallel routes toward their goal, psychosexual maturity. This changes during adolescence. Puberty refers to physiological maturation. In girls it is heralded by menarche, the first menstruation. Not so long ago this was considered a trauma in Western civilization.* Girls' reactions to menstruation have changed under sociocultural influence. Young girls now try to deny or minimize the discomforts related to or caused by the menses. Yet with the monthly returning menstruation, the womb enters the body schema, and the future role of motherhood comes closer to reality and mobilizes the conflicts that accrued during and after the symbiotic phase of her development.

Concurrent with the time during which the girl adjusts to the "unfairness of nature," the boy's reaction to puberty is free from denial and shyness. The center of his body narcissism is his penis; its growth and the accompanying secondary sex characteristics he accepts with pride. Normal reaction to puberty in boys is expressed by exhibitionistic tendencies and increased autoeroticism. Yet if Stage II of his development was burdened with shame and doubt, he might now feel

---

* It would be worth investigating, if it were still possible, whether women considered menstruation a trauma and reacted accordingly in tribal civilizations in which menstruation made the woman taboo and excluded her from contact with men and from women who were not menstruating.

his autonomy threatened; this increases his insecurity, which may lead to withdrawal. Thus his self-involvement, a narcissistic state with negative feeling tone, might account for transient depressions. This is one aspect of the intrapsychic struggle that Anna Freud [18] conceptualized as polarization of affect. The adolescent self has many sources of compensation, so that the self, when reassured, feels competent until it is again defeated by the sexual need for which he has no adequate means of gratification. For this he has to be accepted by a girl of the same psychosocial class and maturity. One has to know boys of age 12 to 16 to know how many suffer, in spite of all the sex education (or because of it), from the "healthy" depression of adolescence. The polarization of affects, even with its moderate oscillations of elation and depression, is the process by which the fear of the other sex is overcome and mature adulthood is reached. If there is fixation to pregenital conflicts caused by dispositional bisexuality and consequent doubt in sexual identity, puberty activates manifold defenses against sexual anxiety. In such individuals, the adolescent process may lead to identity confusion, with a variety of symptoms that may represent defenses against the underlying depression. If the narcissistic conflict of the adolescent struggle is met by an unforgiving superego that does not tolerate self-indulgence and is punitive toward the defenses also, the adolescent may be driven to desperation (or to drugs, nowadays).

The difference in the psychosexual processes of male and female adolescents is rooted in the fact that boys prepare for sexual activity that is exposed in its performance while the female's sexual performance is, by its nature, hidden [26]. The girl's puberty may activate depressive moods also, but since her narcissism is invested in her total appearance, her genital sexuality may not enter into normal adolescence. That depression activated by the puberty of girls may become intensified during adolescence is the result of the girl's regressive identification with her mother. Ambivalence toward the mother, accrued during infancy and reinforced during the phase of separation-individuation, is reactivated by the maturational processes of puberty; it is acted out in hostility toward the mother. Ambivalent fantasies and open hostility create guilt feelings. The regressively intensified dependence on the mother in the ongoing interaction with the mother increases the guilt feelings, thus bringing about clinical forms of anaclitic depression.*

Independent of any developmental fixation are the depressive mani-

* The most severe forms of this condition are expressed in psychosomatic illness, such as anorexia nervosa [4], and in other manifestations of extreme ambivalence toward mother-self.

festations that originate in the female procreative physiology (see Chapter 7). In this context, only the premenstrual phase is relevant. In the last two to three days before the flow begins, the hormone level is rather low and the mood changes. Girls complain of fatigue, headache, sleepiness, and a tendency to cry; a vulnerability that creates conflict with peers and especially with siblings characterizes the premenstrual mood. More significant is another type of premenstrual depression characterized by increased tension, decreased tolerance of frustration, and a high degree of irritability, which leads to overt anger; the mood resembles agitated depression and often forecasts difficulties at climacteric.

The potential for clinical depression is innate in the procreative function of women. The fear of being a woman, the woman's rejection of and defense against her sexual role, is an ingrained concept in the clinical literature of psychoanalysis, yet I dare say the psychosocial crisis of adolescence is not as serious as it is for boys in our civilization. Erikson [15] developed his concept of identity from observation of the processes by which boys learn and accept their role function within the social structure in which they grow up. Girls' role function and social identity are implicit in their sex.

If one took a poll and asked adolescents, girls and boys ages 10 to 14, "What do you want to be when you are an adult?" I assume that more than 80 percent of the girls would answer, "I want to be married and be a mother." Probably the same percentage of boys would reply, "I don't know."* Having outgrown the age of wanting to be a fireman or policeman or being certain that they want to continue in their father's work, boys become more insecure as they become aware of choices. For girls, the first choice (voiced by the hypothetical 80 percent) is paramount; they begin to think of work outside the home if economic necessity prompts them and of career only in later adolescence or during young adulthood. Even then, the motivation often is to find the right husband.

Civilization has brought about a shift in the emotional structure of the family, creating psychological conditions in which the male child may develop greater self-awareness but less self-confidence. By the age of adolescence, he may doubt his sexual power and certainly does not feel his "right" to dominance in sexuality. The doubt is in the self. The denial of the doubt and the need for overcompensation are the sources of the neurotic disturbances of young men in our society. This

---

*This seems to be valid in our urban society, especially for the middle class. It should be noted that the same stratum produces the boys who suffer from identity confusion.

leads to the identity confusion, which activates depressive moods far beyond what was once described as Weltschmerz.

Adolescent depression (see Chapter 13) has many sources. Here, viewing it in the perspective of the life cycle, it should be stated that just as the premenstrual depression may indicate the course of climacteric depression, so the sense of sexual inadequacy and adolescent confusion forecast the syndrome of the 50-year-old man who has achieved his social and sexual goals but at a cost of expending his energy to overcompensate for his narcissistic vulnerability.

Adolescence is extended in our civilization by sociological conditions that prolong the time required for a young man to establish his identity through his work. It takes several years of young adulthood (Stage VI) for a man and woman to develop the particular strength that enables him or her to fulfill his personal potentialities in a manner that is true to himself and true to the significant other, the partner in parenthood, the spouse for life.*

Young adulthood is that phase of the life cycle during which the ability to "love and work" (Freud's characterization of normality in adulthood) is attained. Looking for the modality of depressive reactions characteristic of this stage of the life cycle, one has to think of the psychodynamic state of "being in love." Freud [19] described this process in "Narcissism: An Introduction," written after the *Sturm und Drang* of his seven-year engagement. According to him, a person who is in love invests his "ego libido," his narcissism, in the object of his love. Thus the object of love is idealized while the subject, the lover, impoverished in self-love, feels depressed and dependent on the beloved for recovery of his self-esteem. Waiting and suspense cause painful tension and preoccupation. If the love is returned, the tension is relieved, and the gratification reestablishes the self-esteem; each of the lovers feels a better person than before, as if the self-love of each was refilled through their reciprocal identification. These are, of course, not the exact words of Freud, but they explain what everyone who has ever loved knows from experience: the vulnerable ego state that being in love brings about. The repetition of normal frustrations are part and parcel of maturation. Their memory becomes the source of fidelity, the ego strength that warrants commitment and sacrifice in the mutuality of marriage.

If earlier developmental fixations interact with the normal fear of

* In our culture many young men and women marry as adolescents or quasi-adolescents; experiencing their young adulthood in the partnership of marriage, they hope to develop together through the often complicated give and take of marriage. In many instances, it works out well and leads to lasting marriages.

disappointment, the actual experience of rejection may activate severe depression, withdrawal that may lead to isolation. While the depression characteristic of puberty and adolescence appears to differ in motivation in the sexes, the "normal depression" of being in love is characteristic of both sexes but affects women more often than men.

DEPRESSION IN ADULTHOOD

The biological and psychosocial routes of the sexes toward adulthood are separated at puberty, to intertwine again in adulthood in the common biological task of parenthood. In the generative phase of adulthood, psychobiology unites and differentiates the sexes. In Chapter 7 of this book there is discussion concerning the predisposition for depression that is built into the female procreative function. It bears repeating here that each phase of the female procreative function —the progesterone phase, pregnancy, and lactation—activates certain metabolic processes; the psychological representation of these is a manifold increase in receptive tendencies. In some instances this is manifest in a regression to the oral phase of development, which Abraham [1] recognized as the instinctual motivation of depression. The psychological regression caused by physiological need is a primary source of depressive emotional states. Therefore, the physiological condition that is the prerequisite for the survival of the species can harbor dangers for those women whose personality organization cannot withstand the regressive pull inherent in the procreative physiology. The sources of acquired factors motivating the psychopathology of pregnancy are many. Closest to psychobiology is the infant girl's relation to the mother and its sequence, the developmental identification of the child with the mother. The mother's attitude toward her pregnancy is influenced by the culture in which she grew up. Some cultural influences increase the woman's fear of pregnancy, some alleviate it.* The total personality of the mother, her instinctual wish for pregnancy, her hopes and fears for herself, her unborn child, and for family—are all involved in every pregnancy. Besides psychological factors, the reality situation may activate apprehension and depression, since the integrative task of pregnancy, and even more, that of motherhood, is a task much greater, biologically, psy-

---

* In our fast-moving civilization, communication in general speeds up cultural influences. An example of this is the currently favored preparation for parturition for wife and husband; this increases the narcissistic gratification of pregnancy, decreases anxiety, etc. It seems that the young husband relishes the experience and feels gratified by not being an outsider, alien to the great experience of his wife.

chologically, and realistically, than the woman has faced before. The challenge may reactivate conflicts and anxiety, and may revive the other factors significant in bringing about severe depression. Most important among these is the ambivalence toward the state of pregnancy and therefore against the content of the womb. Women may panic at any fantasy that indicates they harbor hostility toward the unborn child. The hostility toward the fetus also means hostility toward the self, a rejection of the self. Anorexia, vomiting, and resulting severe metabolic disturbance, such as eclampsia, may express the self-destructive tendency of the woman.

The physiology of pregnancy normally brings about a narcissistic ego state. The fetus is a part of the woman's body, a token of the loved self if the woman loves herself in her pregnancy. If not, if the fear of pregnancy reactivates the infantile ambivalence toward the mother-self, the fetus comes to represent the "bad, aggressive, devouring self," engendering the fear that she is harboring a monster. If the fantasy that is projected onto the fetus is highly ambivalent, the fetus becomes the representation of a hated and feared person, as once the woman's own mother was, and motherhood is anticipated as an overwhelming menace. Such an experience during pregnancy may forecast serious postpartum depression, but this is not always the case. It may happen that after the child is born, the mother overcomes the fear of dying in childbirth, looks with triumph and relief at her baby, and feels secure in her motherliness.

Parturition is a trauma for the mother. The hormonal changes that induce labor pains and the excitement of delivery, even without the use of narcotics, interrupt the symbiotic unity of pregnancy. After delivery, when the organism is preparing for the next function of motherhood, lactation, but is not yet ready for it, mothers, especially primiparas, may experience an emotional lag. For nine months of pregnancy they prepared to love the baby. After delivery, they are often surprised by a lack of feeling for the newborn. Fortunate are the mothers whose love for the child wells up as she first hears the cry of the child. The sensation of love reassures the mother about her motherliness, and she can relax and wait serenely to receive the child on her breast. If it is different, if instead of love the mother feels a sensation of emptiness, loss, and distance, views the infant as an outsider, an object, and asks herself with estrangement, "Is this what I had in me?"—this is a disquieting experience. Many young women cry in this state, filled with fear that they will never be able to love the child. Disappointed in themselves, such mothers feel guilty and become anxious, and, with this, insecurity toward the child begins. Such incipient postpartum depression is probably a more frequent event than anyone knows. Fortunately, the wife is reassured by the love of the husband, her mother, and others, and when her breasts fill up and the infant begins to suck, the incipient postpartum depression passes. But if the course of pregnancy earlier revealed basic ambivalence toward the child, the mother may develop phobic reactions such as fear of harming the child, making her feel compelled to avoid the baby, or she may turn against it. This is the full-fledged depression that often necessitates hospitalization to avoid catastrophe.

Lactation is the final stage of the procreative physiology. It is the continuation of the mother's biological symbiosis with the infant. Whether the mother breastfeeds or nurses the baby on the bottle, the close body contact permits her to feel united with her infant, to "regress" and so repeat and satisfy (on the unconscious level) her own receptive, incorporating wishes. This is the axis around which the activities of mothering revolve. The transactions of the postpartum (emotional) symbiosis permit a slow, step-by-step integration of motherliness, a new developmental achievement in the mother's personality.

Motherliness is a quality of woman's personality that, in its behavioral manifestation, is influenced by psychodynamic factors. Primary among these, we assume, is the mother's identification with her child. Her child is a major source of narcissistic gratification for her, but the newborn might also be a persistent, wounding disappointment. This generalization does not explain the variations by which we characterize motherliness. We talk of oversolicitous, overprotective, perfectionistic mothers and of rejecting, hostile mothers. The characteristic attitudes of motherliness originate in the mother's personality organization. The types of mothering, however, do not explain the interacting factor that motivates her behavior. The anxious, insecure mother may be oversolicitous; when the oversolicitous, overprotective mother is also hypochondriacal, in her anxiety she may be negligent when the child is ill. This, of course, evokes guilt feelings in her, which may increase solicitude and thus induce a pathogenic spiral in the transactional processes. The same is true for the perfectionistic mother who loves the child with the narcissistic overevaluation of herself and thus expects more of him than he is capable of fulfilling. If disappointment activates the mother's ambivalence, her anger and the child's reaction to it activate a depressive spiral in the mother-child relationship. Normally, the same mothers have enough love to counteract the adverse reactions and reassure the child, so serious pathology does not develop as often as this brief presentation might suggest. Here it serves to show that even loving mothers' interactions with normal children may activate depressive reactions in both participants. It is superfluous to add that depressed, withdrawn mothers, whether they voluntarily reject the child or just neglect him, increase their own pathology as they inflict it on the child. But sometimes a miracle happens and a satisfactory, smiling baby cures the mother.

In motherhood lies the origin of depression (see Chapter 7). The foregoing discussion outlines how depression can be activated by each phase of the procreative process and raises the question whether fatherhood, becoming and being a father, has a similar role in the emotional life of men. The answer is no. Since man's procreative function depends on a single act, tissue changes and metabolic processes are not involved in the male procreative function beyond the production and discharge of semen. Fatherhood, the survival of self in the offspring, and evidence of his virility is an experience of gratification and joy. According to tradition, fathers used to be more distant from their infants than they are now. In general, one would say that fathers were then and are now also more active and work more efficiently and with more pleasure during the postpartum period, especially if mother and child are doing well. Yet we often see young fathers who are anxious and depressed during that time, whose duodenal ulcer or other psychosomatic symptoms appear as a reaction to the birth of a child. There is no need to elaborate further that the "trauma" of the birth of a child (not necessarily the first child) may activate conflicts at all levels and, along with them, ambivalence toward the child; the ensuing guilt feeling activates depression. Often the defense against depression is manifest in the father's behavior. Avoidance of the home and even alcoholism may cover up the ambivalence; often egosyntonic reactions such as overwork may serve the same purpose in fathers and mothers alike.

Biology distributed the task of the preservation of the species between the sexes. The male, as an adult, becomes the father and provider. This "sociological" role is not only a human task. In many animal species, fatherliness, like motherliness, is under hormonal regulation. The male defends the territory or the home, and he provides or helps to provide for the offspring and often also for the mate as long as the female is bound by her procreative task. When the procreative process is terminated, the male is free from his obligation. Does he recognize his own offspring? Only the human species has the privilege and burden of rearing children beyond infancy, through their long period of dependence, often lasting even after the children have reached procreative maturity. In this complex and arduous task, man's intrapsychic help comes from his identification with his child and from the fatherliness which is a developmental attainment originating in the father's early identifications with his own mother and father.

Fatherliness is a character trend, a mental attitude that enables the father to have empathy for his children. It in turn wins the children's attachment and love for him. Fatherliness supports not only the children but the father also, since his gratification in his children's love and their development is the feedback that compensates for the psychic and physical energy needed to provide for them.

This task has had to be accomplished since time immemorial, in different cultures, in differing family structures, and under more or less pressure from existing social and economic conditions. The external conditions mold the individual and influence the course of his life.

In this discourse, the focus is on depression. It should be reiterated that men, genetically or via infantile experiences, incorporate the seeds of depression; these, however, come to symptom manifestation under the pressure of the psychosocial crises during the life cycle. Depression in men, even during the generative, productive phase of their lives, is mainly the result of conflicts and problems related to their identity. Earlier phases of doubt and inferiority feelings are activated by interpersonal conflicts within the family or in his work situation; his goals and ambitions, his success and failure are tested by every experience. Among these, most critical is a failure of his children or his failure with the children. One might generalize to say that depression of women in the procreative phase is a psychosomatic condition; depression in men can be classified as narcissistic neurosis.

THE CLIMACTERIC

The term *climacteric* is relatively new in medical dictionaries. It is derived from the Greek word *klimakter*, which means the rung of the ladder; after this critical point has been reached, there can only be a turn downward. When I first used the concept in a publication [7], I considered the term relevant only to women, indicating the termination of the procreative period. Because men's procreative capacity does not end definitely with obvious signs, I assumed that the term was applicable only to the female sex. Since that time, my own observations as well as the publications of others have convinced me that the term climacteric is justifiably applied to both sexes. The unique manifestation of the cessation of the procreative capacity in women is menopause. The terms menopause and climacteric are not interchangeable. Just as the term puberty refers to a physiological process and adolescence to psychological development, so menopause refers to the physiology, and climacteric to the psychology of the processes that accompany and follow the termination of the procreative phase.

The title of that first paper was "Climacterium: A Developmental Phase" [7]. The concept implied in this title can hardly be defended from a biological point of view. The time passed when "overflow of surplus energy" nourished the procreative functions of the woman and the ebb and flow of ovarian hormones brought about her menstruation with regularity. Now the flow has abated, indicating that the biologically most significant part of her life is over. Helene Deutsch summarized the hormonal changes of menopause as follows: "With the cessation of ovarian activity, the remainder of the endocrine system is deranged in functioning" [12, p. 456]. This is an overstatement, as is her assumption that the woman in climacteric is mortified because she has to give up everything she received at puberty. This could be true only if women attained sexual maturity with puberty in one parcel as the promise and guarantee of fulfillment and kept it as such until it disappeared at climacteric as traumatically as it presumably had come. Actually, many writers have this attitude. Alberta B. Szalita writes: "Menopause is invariably perceived as trauma" [31, p. 67]. She describes it a "staggering shock" and writes as if involutional melancholia were an immediate consequence of menopause, a condition she characterizes as a "form of surrender to fear."

The fact is that after menopause, or even before it occurs, the developing deficiency in gonadal hormones brings about a hormone imbalance, which is usually accompanied by systemic disturbances of the sympathetic nervous system. Insomnia, restlessness, and vasomotor symptoms such as hot flashes and palpitations are the most common. These symptoms respond very well to small doses of ovarian hormones, relieving in women the often embarrassing exposure of the menopausal state. Other physiological signs of aging develop slowly, often decades after menopause—the fat distribution changes, the breasts may atrophy, hair appears where before there was none. Aging is an involutional process, but menopause is not an illness. The typical symptoms of menopause disappear after different time periods and are not in themselves incapacitating. In surveys of large groups of women, it has been shown that 85 percent pass through climacteric without interrupting their daily routine, and in the remaining 15 percent it could not be established that menopause was the sole cause of the complaints [22]. There is no need to emphasize that the number of women in the work force has grown tremendously in every field since the above survey was published (in 1946). But the productivity of postclimacteric women is not a result of technological civilization's having relieved her of heavy chores. O'Higgins and Reede [28], in their book, *The American Mind in Action*, discuss the role of women in American society. With fine psychological insight, they describe types of women in various levels of early American society and attribute the greatest significance to the Puritan woman, who used to be, and still is, the "home and mother type." I can see many women shaking their heads at this idea, but those authors ascribe to the Puritan woman the "emotional and ideological education of the nation." On the other hand, I have asserted that "Much of the work was done, and is being done, through the almost inexhaustible idealism and educational ambition of women, outside the family, in communal and cultural activities, and much of it is accomplished after they reach and pass the climacterium" [7].

Development in general is a process in which physiological change and psychological processes stimulated by it are integrated in a way that enables the individual to master new environmental stimulations. It would lead us far afield from our focus on depression to discuss the integrative processes that account for the postclimacteric development. In Erikson's schema Stage VII, adulthood, should be taken to include postclimacteric adulthood. Procreativity in the biological sense (generativity) is definitely terminated in women and markedly declines in men also, while creativity may continue undisturbed for many years up to mature old age (Stage VIII).

Considering the climacteric as the characteristic experience of middle age for both sexes, I dare to emphasize the biological advantage of the female over the male. The cessation of the procreative function in women releases psychic and physical energy for other tasks. Their sexual capacity is retained for an unforeseeable period, for some better, for others worse than it was, depending on many factors. Women may have depressive reactions during this phase of their life, but they are not activated by the menopause, although they may be aggravated by it. Climacteric is not a "critical phase" as is pregnancy, since in itself it does not provoke existential anxiety; it is not a threat to life. For many women, it is a new beginning.

In observing the course of the sexual cycle in the same individual before marriage and after giving birth to a child, one is impressed by the fact that the conflicts that are inherent in the procreative function appear to be absorbed.* I used the term "developmental absorption" [8, p. 344] to refer to the adaptational processes motivated by the cyclical changes of the ovarian hormones and menstruation, and even

---

* This refers only to women who had no serious emotional disturbances during pregnancy or postpartum. Probably it cannot be clearly observed now, when the pill interferes with the cycle; yet I had an opportunity to observe the same in primiparas recently.

more by the stress of pregnancy and motherhood, which gradually lead to diminishing tension in the area of conflicts connected with procreative physiology. These processes prepare the woman for menopause in the unconscious depths of her physiology. Thus the event of menopause does not have such intense emotional impact as it once had, and to some degree still does.*

The stages of the life cycle represent profiles (outlines) of the characteristics a culture attributes to each developmental stage. Women's climacteric is no exception. Climacteric women are characterized in novels, dramas, even fairy tales as being of two types: One is the weak, anxious, insecure person, driven by the idea that she has not lived and has not fulfilled her aim, and she is urged from within to start life anew; therefore, her stirred up pseudosexuality may expose her to greater risks than she dared to take before. Clinically, this is rather the opposite of depression, but obviously it may lead to depression, frequently of the melancholic type (not to be confused with cyclical manic-depressive psychosis).

The other type is the strong woman who has lived with self-confidence in her ability to work, to dominate her family, to achieve. In climacteric she cannot bear up under the sense of internal frustration. Of course, every frustration is internal, a psychic experience. But I differentiate as "internal" the frustration that appears in climacteric and causes the sense of inability to feel love. Every little frustration, such as waiting for service in a department store, may be taken seriously, since it is not tolerance but anger that is activated, a negative affect of interpersonal reactions. Individuals of this type are overactive and even overproductive before and during climacteric, but later they suffer from "arid depression." This kind of depression is characterized by a painful sensation of dryness (some place in the chest), an inability to feel pleasure (anhedonia) even if the woman knows that what she is experiencing is really good or is meant well and should be pleasurable. This might develop into severe agitated depression in women in their 60s.

A third form of postclimacteric depression can be defined as the breakdown of the narcissistic structure of the personality. (Compare the two cases described in some detail in "Climacterium: A Developmental Phase" [7].) This form of postclimacteric depression occurs in

---

* It would require cross-cultural investigations in historical perspective to find an answer to the question why men in the upper strata of society accept without question that menopause is traumatic for women, that the mourning for her youth, sexual capacity, and power makes her emotionally unstable and probably organically ill. Men and women of the lower strata of the same social structure seem to accept menopause as relief from the fear of pregnancy and as a result expect increased sexual freedom.

women whose ego is concentrated on being an achiever, whether as mothers or professionals or both. The menopause itself hardly disturbs these women; even if they have some of the usual symptoms, they shrug them off as normal, expectable, and therefore accepted. But slowly the disappointments mount. They may be familial, such as a conflict with a married daughter or son or with the husband; even a disappointment in a friend or neighbor may seem a betrayal. But worse is the disappointment in the self, which does not respond in its accustomed way. The insightful woman's response to this may be, "This is not me," but any alienation from the self activates a depressive mood. If the loss of self-esteem is reinforced by the increasing decline of sensory systems—hearing, sight, or other organic dysfunction—anxiety is added to the loss of self-esteem. Defensive anger felt toward the self—"this cannot happen to me"—may herald a variety of psychopathology motivated by the psychodynamic structure and past experiences of the individual. These feed the regressive pull of the underlying depression, which may lead to suicide. Loss of self-esteem is involved in every form of depression and also in menopause, which is a physiological turning point if not a crisis. Schmale and Engel (Chapter 9) describe climacteric depression as a process of two phases: the first is motivated by the necessity of giving up narcissistically charged aspects of the personality; the second is a state of "given up" that follows the resolution of the conflicts involved. Generally, one may assume there is a struggle of "separation from the past" accompanying menopause, but the resolution is usually not preceded by clinical forms of depression—these occur later. The connection with involution can be assumed in cases where postpartum depression or other indications of pathology substantiate the diagnosis.

To summarize: menopause itself is not a cause of depression; normal climacteric is a phase of psychological reorganization in women. This, however, does not exclude the possibility that severe depressions may develop in women later, with approaching old age.

Do men have climacterium? Does "the syndrome of the 50-year-old man" justify the assumption that there is, in general, a male climacteric? Currently, it seems to me that the assumption may have a prophylactic value since the psychosocial crises of middle-aged men appears quite general in our society.

Men do not have a climacteric comparable on physiological grounds to the menopause of women. There is general agreement that "for men, there is no evidence of . . . a state secondary to diminished secretory action of the sexual glands consequent of aging" [27, p. 472]. It is, indeed, questionable whether the prolonged, gradual decline in sexual appetite in men parallels the regression of gonadal hormone production in women. Yet the term male climacteric (or male menopause) persists; even the term andropause was coined, unjustifiably I think. Gregory Marañon, a renowned Spanish pathologist, spoke in 1929 of "the existence of the critical age in the male," defined as follows:

Climacterium or the critical age should be understood not as a genital episode, not as an incident of the sexual life more or less accompanied by reactional [sic] symptoms on the part of the other apparatus of the economy, but as a stage of organic evolution, perfectly characterized anatomically and physiologically, in whose center the extinction of active genital life stands out prominently, yet not limited to this genital extinction [25, p. 244].

Marañon views climacteric as a normal developmental phase in men and women leading toward mature, normal old age. On this we can agree.

Investigators of the syndrome of the 50-year-old man did not base their generalizations on the psychosexual crises of middle-aged men. Cultural characteristics of the Spanish Marañon and his patients, and those of American investigators and their patients, may explain some of the factors that have distracted psychoanalysts from studying and conceptualizing the problems of climacteric in men.

After World War II, attention was focused on young middle-aged men who suffered from psychosomatic symptoms, duodenal ulcers and high blood pressure being the most common, leading all too often to disease of the coronary arteries and early death. Most of the men so affected are high-powered, hard-driving achievers who at that age level often do not show signs of declining sexual appetite; rather, the opposite—they overcompensate for what they do not want to acknowledge and often use extramarital affairs to try to prove their sexual potency and keep it in balance with their ability to work and achieve. The tremendous acceleration of technology, and with it all aspects of life, offer unlimited opportunities and therefore the obligation to live up to them. If one considers the frequency of psychosomatic symptoms in middle-aged men, the syndrome of the 50-year-old man appears to be a cultural phenomenon, a side effect of technological civilization.

Work is a psychic organizer. Age-adequate achievement plays a role in the evolution of the self-esteem from infancy on. Every observer of infants recognizes the differences in their pleasure activity. Every parent responds to the glow of satisfaction when a 6- to 8-month-old reaches the spoon or toy that he wanted. Even more obviously, the child's ego registers satisfaction if he achieves a self-set goal, if he puts one more block on the tower today than he did before. The effective experience of achievement becomes incorporated in the self-image as the "achieving self." Self-esteem originates in the minute experiences of play, the exercise of mastery. This leads to the self-concept "I am a good, lovable, capable, achieving self."*

From infancy on, each person learns to expect of himself what is expected of him. The variation in expectations and their fulfillment in the individual can be visualized as interaction between ego, superego, and ego-ideal. The ego-ideal sets the standard and the anticipation; the superego requires that the work be done; the ego does the work. If the work is well done, the ego-ideal is satisfied and the superego and the ego-ideal are in harmony.

Work is a biological necessity. Every organism works for survival of the self and, beyond this, for the survival of the species. Only the human species works beyond the need for survival, for "surplus." The achieving self, so charming in the playing child, so productive in young individuals, may become dangerously distorted and aggrandized when it is geared toward more and more "surplus" for the sake of achievement alone. The expectations of an aggrandized ego-ideal increase the wear and tear of life, the more so if the achievement serves as defense against the fear of aging and the fear of losing sexual potency. Psychic *and* somatic is the "stress of life" causing the syndrome of the 50-year-old-man [29].

Obviously, the male of the species has no menopause and does not experience a definite termination of sexual potency or procreative capacity; both may be rekindled after many years of dormancy. But men do experience decreased sexual appetite and diminution of sexual potency. A man's sexual physiology does not prepare him for these signs of aging, which come earlier in some individuals, later in others. Fantasies and perversions may deceive those who want to be deceived. Since a man's narcissism is so highly invested in his phallic nature and the nature of his sexual performance, one can say that men in general respond to the decline of sexual capacity more often with marked regression than do women. Psychoanalysis of such men reveals the role of the castration complex in the psychosocial life of the individual. Indeed, it convinced Marañon that the sexual decline of middle-aged men is a universal source of psychosocial problems, which if not outgrown will interfere with normal old age.

The psychopathology of middle-aged men originates in two areas

---

* In this brief presentation, the role of the smiling, approving parent in the evolution of the self-esteem is omitted for two reasons: (1) here only the innate potentials for achievement are pertinent; (2) the parent's role is usually one-sidedly overestimated and very often overdone. The latter, however, may lead to pathology in the regulation of self-esteem, the activating factor of narcissistic neurosis and depression.

of the psychic economy, both intricately interwoven with the regulation of self-esteem, at least from puberty on. One is the psychosexual organization of the personality invested with primary libido, which energizes object relationships; the other is self-directed work achievement invested by secondary narcissism. The two areas of gratification, the interpersonal and the object and self-directed, complement each other. Work and what one can buy with it (e.g., status and money) are not for the achieving self alone; usually it turns into giving—its first aim is to provide for the family. One kind of man does not begrudge the giving since it is the main goal of his achieving. Another man, consciously or unconsciously, cannot give even the result of his work because he cannot give himself; he has become identified with his work. Fortunate is the man whose primary object relationships supply emotional gratification and keep in balance the spending of energy necessary to sustain his ambitions and his relationships with others in his work situation. Otherwise, the expenditure of energy needed to provide the success he desires becomes a steady drain on his emotional resources. This is one but not the only cause of chronic attrition of libido. Man's self-esteem is derived not only from his work achievement but primarily from his sexual potency, his dominance. The two sources of gratification are complementary. One functional capacity may be used to overcompensate for the other. In young men, or in a happy marriage, the intrapsychic result of such processes is usually positive in the long run; in middle-aged men, it may be the opposite. Whatever fires the work ambition of the man in later middle age intensifies the strain, especially if it involves financial and other risks; combined with interpersonal pressures, it may drain the psychic resources to a degree that adversely affects his sexual potency. The emotional reaction to sexual failure, or the fear of it, may activate depression, which impedes work capacity.

To summarize: men's depressive reaction to the problem of middle age originates in the crisis of the regulation of self-esteem. Whether the burden of the failure is in sexual performance or in work achievement, a balance may be maintained at a cost to the more successful component. Sooner or later the sources of gratification dissipate, leading to depression. The symptoms and the course of the depression are preformed in the life history of the individual.

DEPRESSION IN OLD AGE

The foregoing discussion of the climacteric emphasizes the significance of developmental integrations in individuals of both sexes during that phase of the life cycle that precedes actual old age. If physical or mental illness does not interfere, the prolonged middle age may continue well into the 60s. Figure 1 defines the contrasting characteristics of old age as integration and despair. But no single word can account for the variety and complexity of phenomena that characterize a personality in old age. The integration of experiences of a lifetime in proper perspective to the past and the future may be characterized as "wisdom"; its extreme contrast is "despair," which is a consequence of a life-long, bitter, hopeless fight against anxiety and frustration.

In meaningful old age, the first and most intimate area of judgment is the self; this implies the acceptance of one's aging, the finality of life with as much maturity and self-knowledge as physical and mental health permit. In this framework, we shall briefly consider those factors that characterize and influence the course of depression in old age, indeed the psychology of old age, since all psychological changes caused by aging have a depressive tone.

It is generally known that chronological age is not the most significant variable of aging. The wear and tear of life affects individuals differently, not only because of the nature of their situation in life but mainly because of their genetic anlage as this is expressed in their physical and emotional resilience. Of the factors that accelerate aging, only the trauma of life-endangering illness will be mentioned here. It does not need much proof or testimony that any form of cancer represents such trauma; it activates fear of death as reality. After the acute anxiety abates, depression may set in as a defense against acute anxiety and its somatization, hypochondriasis. But even in the reactive depression to acute trauma, one can recognize the factors motivated by the premorbid personality structure. The depression may be "melancholic," quasi giving in to fate, or it may be agitated, blaming fate and often the closest of the family members who are healthy and could not prevent the illness. Such depressions (usually mixed regarding symptoms) are usually diagnosed as psychoneurotic reactive depressions.

Depressive illness occurring many years after menopause in women and in late middle age in men are considered to be *involutional depressions*. In women the hormone imbalance and in men the fear of or actual loss of potency are considered primary activating factors. In most cases these are reactive psychoneurotic depressions, which are differentiated from involutional psychoses. They are rare since, to be exact, the diagnosis has to be based on the fact that no serious psychopathology had occurred earlier in the same individual. The differential diagnosis from the viewpoint of psychoneurotic depression is tenuous and is based mainly on the degree of loss of self-esteem, the intensity of the feeling of worthlessness, and the inability to accept the idea that one is not the cause of that for which he feels responsible and guilty. Delusional ideas may occur later in the process, or they may be avoided by therapy. A manic-depressive, cyclical condition is differentiated from reactive depression on the basis of genetic factors. In the state of depression, the history of manic episodes clarifies the diagnosis, but this condition may appear at any age and is described in children also (see Chapter 10). The reactive depression of the involutional phase may remain and continue into the psychopathology of old age, but this is not generally the case. Surprisingly, one hears frequently about permanent recovery, that men and women in their 70s feel better and are more even-tempered, more satisfied, and more satisfiable than when they were younger.

Slowly, with the passing of years, the depressive tone pervades the structure of the personality. There is no doubt of the enhanced narcissism of the elderly, which is often expressed in egocentric behavior. The aged person's gratification comes from maintaining his ability to do, to feel, to be aware of the self in the details of his everyday life. This is helped by rekindling his memories of past achievements and gratifications; in his tendency to identify with the young, he expects the younger members of the family to listen to him, to reassure him by their love and admiration. This is a benign manifestation of the narcissism of the old person, but the same process becomes more tension-producing in those who feel they have heard the reminiscences too often. His enforced self-awareness increases his watchfulness and hypersensitivity toward the people in his environment who might perceive and respond to his shortcomings with criticism or just with a sigh of realization that he does not function as he did before. Consequently, he may withdraw, harboring his pain, or he may fantasy his paranoid reactions or may have angry outbursts. In any case, a painful spiral of interactions follows.

Every individual has an area in which his executive faculty, his ability to decide and act is not functioning with the same security in his old age as it did previously. Thus indecisiveness and reluctance to function appear in these areas much before the usual apprehensiveness of senescence sets in. Attempts to overcompensate for the weak area with activity in the area of greater competence and self-assurance may work for a time, but if they fail, the ensuing shame increases the tendency to withdraw in depression.

Another general symptom is the rigidity of the senescent person. It is difficult to describe this phenomenon better than the term itself reveals. It is a diffuse result of the slowing down of mental processes.

The elderly person is not "frozen" in his mental attitudes, but the ingrained patterns of behavior lose their flexibility and appear mechanically repeated (because of the retardation of the neurological processes). This explains the truth in the popular characterization of the old person, usually by his own children, "He is as he used to be, only more so." An example of this is the compulsive neurotic individual who was known as a parsimonious person; in his old age he becomes miserly, and his fear of being impoverished makes him hoard, while at the same time he denies himself the necessities of life.

As cerebral arteriosclerosis gradually develops, the rigidity increases [11]. One reserves the diagnosis for individuals 66 years and older. It affects males more frequently than females. One assumes that in men, physical and mental stress bring about the frequency of the pathology; in women, on the other hand, estrogens and other hormones may have a protective effect. The incipient symptoms of the condition can hardly be differentiated from diffuse background anxiety, which activates worries, hypochondriasis, etc. These are not necessarily symptoms of cerebral arteriosclerosis, but sooner or later other typical symptoms of aging appear, such as loss of memory of intentions for action or for recent events, and a retardation in switching attention from one topic to another. Individuals accustomed to self-observation suffer increasingly from the mental signs of aging since each one represents a narcissistic injury. The fear of such exposure in itself may activate anxiety and phobic reactions. These, in turn, limit the area of activity and mobility, thus causing more loss of self-esteem. It is futile to try to determine how much of the agitated depression or the paranoid behavior of the arteriosclerotic individual is secondary reaction to the existing tissue changes in the brain wrought by aging and how much is caused by the narcissistic injuries caused by the process. (There are known instances in which the emotional reaction accelerated the organic pathology.)

Cerebral accidents may be caused by circulatory disturbances in the brain and also by pathology leading to tissue damage without gross circulatory damage. This can occur in younger persons also. Whether the cerebral accident is caused by circulatory pathology (thrombosis or hemorrhage) or by other pathology, in any case, it is a severe trauma. If the damage is not too extensive, one can differentiate the reactive depression from the later reaction to the pathology. The patient's capacity for recovery is influenced by his age, physical and psychic capacity to tolerate invalidism, and the degree of helplessness caused by the illness. If it is the result of extensive cerebral arteriosclerosis, minimal but multiple thromboses accelerate the senile process and may activate a senile psychosis. In senile psychotic cases, only a thorough knowledge of the premorbid personality can separate what is emotional and what is organically determined in this final state of mental pathology. One thing is clear: whatever the particular motivation, the emotional processes are increasingly dominated by the depression of senescence.

Does this sketch of senescence belong in a discussion of depression during the life cycle? Depression in old age is a somato-psychic process. The onset and course of senescence bear the traces of what the individual was before. His capacity for adaptation molds his ego to face the decline of the self with relative equanimity. The depression of old age, so far as it is still motivated by affect, is as it was from childhood throughout his life: fear of separation, reaction to object loss, mourning, even more, mourning for the self that does not function as the efficient "organ" that it once was. It has lost control of the ego, which now cannot direct its experiences. Viewing depression as part of the total course of the life cycle, we can but realize a basic similarity between what is diagnosed as anaclitic depression in infants and the depression of the senescent individual. In infancy, the deficiency in metabolic ingredients or processes impedes the evolution of brain function; in old age, the somatic deterioration brings about involution of psychic processes, which is felt as and appears as depression.

REFERENCES

1. Abraham, K. Notes on the Psycho-Analytical Investigation and Treatment of Manic-Depressive Insanity and Allied Conditions (1911). In *Selected Papers of Karl Abraham, M.D.* London: Hogarth Press, 1942. P. 137.
2. Abraham, K. Character-Formation on the Genital Level of Libido-Development (1925). In *Selected Papers of Karl Abraham, M.D.* London: Hogarth Press, 1942. P. 407.
3. Alexander, F. *The Scope of Psychoanalysis, 1921-1961: Selected Papers of Franz Alexander.* New York: Basic Books, 1961.
4. Benedek, T. Dominant ideas and their relation to morbid cravings. *Int. J. Psychoanal.* 17:40, 1936. Reprinted in T. Benedek, *Psychoanalytic Investigations: Selected Papers.* New York: Quadrangle/New York Times Book Co., 1973. P. 71.
5. Benedek, T. Adaptation to reality in early infancy. *Psychoanal. Q.* 7:200, 1938. Reprinted in T. Benedek, *Psychoanalytic Investigations: Selected Papers.* New York: Quadrangle/New York Times Book Co., 1973. P. 113.
6. Benedek, T. Psychosomatic implications of the primary unit: mother-child. *Am. J. Orthopsychiatry* 19:16, 1949. Reprinted in T. Benedek, *Psychoanalytic Investigations: Selected Papers.* New York: Quadrangle/New York Times Book Co., 1973.

7. Benedek, T.   Climacterium: A developmental phase. *Psychoanal. Q.* 19:1, 1950. Reprinted in T. Benedek, *Psychoanalytic Investigations: Selected Papers.* New York: Quadrangle/New York Times Book Co. P. 322.
8. Benedek, T.   Personality Development. In F. Alexander and H. Ross (Eds.), *Dynamic Psychiatry.* Chicago: University of Chicago Press, 1952.
9. Benedek, T.   Toward the biology of the depressive constellation. *J. Am. Psychoanal. Assoc.* 4:389, 1956. Reprinted in T. Benedek, *Psychoanalytic Investigations: Selected Papers.* New York: Quadrangle/New York Times Book Co. P. 356.
10. Benedek, T.   Parenthood as a developmental phase. *J. Am. Psychoanal. Assoc.* 7:389, 1959. Reprinted in T. Benedek, *Psychoanalytic Investigations: Selected Papers.* Chap. 14. Pp. 377-407.
11. Busse, E. W.   Psychopathology. In J. E. Burren (Ed.), *The Handbook of Aging and the Individual.* Chicago: University of Chicago Press, 1959. P. 383.
12. Deutsch, H.   The Climacterium. In *The Psychology of Women*, vol. 2. New York: Grune & Stratton, 1945.
13. Engel, G. L., and Reichman, F.   Spontaneous and experimentally induced depressions in an infant with a gastric fistula: A contribution to the problem of depression. *J. Am. Psychoanal. Assoc.* 4:428, 1956.
14. Erikson, E.   *Childhood and Society.* New York: Norton, 1950.
15. Erikson, E.   The problem of ego identity. *J. Am. Psychoanal. Assoc.* 4:56, 1956.
16. Erikson, E.   Identity and the life cycle. *Psychol. Issues*, 1:1, 1959.
17. Erikson, E.   Psychosocial Crises in the Life Cycle. In *International Encyclopedia of the Social Sciences.* 1968. Vol. 9.
18. Freud, A.   *The Ego and the Mechanism of Defense* (1936), transl. by C. Baines. London: Hogarth Press, 1937.
19. Freud, S.   On Narcissism: An Introduction (1914). In *The Standard Edition of the Complete Psychological Works of Sigmund Freud*, transl. and ed. by J. Strachey with others. London: Hogarth and Institute of Psycho-Analysis, 1957. Vol. 14, p. 67.
20. Freud, S.   Mourning and Melancholia (1917). *Standard Edition.* 1957. Vol. 14, p. 243.
21. Freud, S.   The Ego and the Id (1923). *Standard Edition.* 1963. Vol. 19, p. 13.
22. Greenhill, M. E.   A psychosomatic evaluation of the psychiatric and endocrinological factors in menopause. *South. Med. J.* 39:786, 1946.
23. Klein, M.   *The Psycho-Analysis of Children.* London: Hogarth Press, 1932.
24. Mahler, M.   Notes on the Development of Basic Moods; the Depressive Affect. In R. M. Loewenstein et al. (Eds.), *Psychoanalysis—A General Psychology.* New York: International Universities Press, 1966. P. 152.
25. Marañon, G.   The Climacteric. In A. M. Krich (Ed.), *Men; the Variety and Meaning of the Sexual Experience.* New York: Dell, 1954. P. 244.
26. Masters, W. H., and Johnson, V. E.   *Human Sexual Response.* Boston: Little, Brown, 1966.

27. Noyes, A. P., and Kolb, L. C.   Psychophysiological Autonomic and Visceral Disorders. In *Modern Clinical Psychiatry*. Philadelphia & London: Saunders, 1958.
28. O'Higgins, H., and Reede, E. H.   *The American Mind in Action*. New York: Harper, 1924.
29. Selye, H.   *The Stress of Life*. New York: McGraw Hill, 1956.
30. Spitz, R.   Hospitalism; An Inquiry into the Genesis of Psychiatric Conditions in Early Childhood. *Psychoanal. Study Child*, 2:313, 1947.
31. Szalita, A. B.   The Psychodynamics of Disorders of the Involutional Age. In S. Arieti (Ed.), *The American Handbook of Psychiatry*. New York: Basic Books, 1966. Vol. 3, p. 66.

15

On Anniversary Suicide and Mourning*

GEORGE H. POLLOCK

Stimulated by J. Hilgard's [10] recognition and description of the importance of anniversary reactions in parents precipitated by their children's ages, I have investigated various aspects of anniversary phenomena and their relationship to trauma, mourning, time, and psychopathology [18, 19, 20, 21, 22, 23, 26, 27]. In this chapter I present some of my findings and theoretical considerations of a specific aspect of the anniversary situation, namely, anniversary suicide.

It is generally accepted that living creatures are involved in two general concerns: the first is to preserve their own existence, and the second is to reproduce themselves. These concerns formed the basis of Freud's [5] first instinct theory. The relationship between fertility, contraception, and immortality has been previously considered [24] and is connected with the task of species preservation. The first concern, preserving the existence of the individual, has been discussed by many and from various points of view. Since life is precarious, a number of biological and psychological responses have evolved that serve as protections against dangers that threaten us with injury or death. One function of our sense organs and memory is to protect us from danger. Once we are alerted, protective mechanisms, designed to help us either avoid danger or deal with the effects of trauma, are set in motion. If successful, danger is avoided, coped with, or reacted to in such a fashion as to restitute—as quickly as possible and with a minimum of aftereffect—the so-called homeostatic state of well-being. Emotions and emotional conflict also play their role in this adaptive struggle.

* This research has been assisted by the support of National Institute of Mental Health Research Grant MH20562 and the Anne Pollock Lederer Research Fund.

One particular state of feeling about which much has been written but which is still incompletely understood or treated is the state of depression. One might approach the study of depression from the premise that it is a state of alerting and defending, thereby maintaining a state of psychic equilibrium, or in which withdrawal occurs defensively. Because of its discomfort, questions can be raised about the normality of depression. When one considers pain or anxiety, however, it is not difficult to appreciate the so-called normal defensive aspects of these states of feeling, even if such feelings are uncomfortable. If we can visualize depression as an indication or a symptom of altered equilibrium, we can approach depression as a manifestation of normality, albeit one that may have pathological significance under certain circumstances. Bibring [3] considered depression an ego affective state in normal, neurotic, and psychotic depression states.

In psychiatry depression is usually considered a disease. A more fruitful approach to our understanding of this reaction may be to examine depression as an indicator or manifestation of disequilibrium and not as a disease per se. Bibring, a pioneer in this approach, notes that depression may occur when one feels helpless, hateful, destructive, lonely, isolated, unloved, weak, inferior, or a failure. These feelings may lead to a diminution of self-esteem and a state of narcissistic imbalance. Bibring writes that the tension between highly charged narcissistic aspirations on the one hand, and the ego's acute awareness of its real or imagined helplessness and inability to fulfill these aims on the other hand, gives rise to depression. Thus, according to Bibring's view, depression is a manifestation of an intrasystemic conflict in the ego and is not primarily determined by a conflict between the ego and the id, superego, or environment. Even in uncomplicated mourning, when there is an actual loss, the resulting tension from the longing and love of the lost object and the awareness that the object is realistically gone and cannot be resurrected reflects intrasystemic disequilibrium. An exacerbation of the grief response, whenever certain perceptions acutely bring the loss and the inability of its retrieval into awareness, can be seen as intrasystemic disruptions. Where there has been an uncompleted or an abnormal mourning process, the ego is vulnerable, and depressive affects may appear.

Depression, as a symptom, may have different precipitating factors; it may have varied antecedent personality configurations; and it may have different outcomes and resolutions, ranging from complete, rapid, and relatively nonrecurrent resolutions without sequelae to conditions of total despair ending in suicide. Depression cannot be viewed as a single pathological entity, and perhaps it does not have a single unitary explanation for its occurrence. Suicide also need not be considered solely as the manifestation of disease. Just as is true of depression, suicide may be precipitated by many situations in a variety of personality organizations and may have different meanings to the victims.

Karl Abraham [1, 2] and Sigmund Freud [7] very early distinguished between normal and abnormal states of depression and mourning. Their still-valid classic contributions can be summarized in the following way: in melancholia, the great ambivalence toward the introjected object does not allow for the normal instinctual decathexis when the object is lost, and frustration results, as is seen in mourning. To effect some form of resolution, the melancholic person partially regresses to an identification with the object, but a strong sadistic core still remains. In this way, the object may not be lost, and some level of equilibrium may result. In some instances melancholia spontaneously resolves itself; however, the vulnerability to recurrence still exists, and when specific precipitating circumstances reappear, the pathological state may again become manifest. In the earlier ideas of Abraham and Freud we find the suggestion that the latent sadism can become manifest. When this sadism is directed against the internalized object- and self-representations, which previously were identified with the lost or frustrating object, the outcome may be suicide. In such cases suicide may be viewed as one outcome of pathological mourning. I have previously discussed the adaptive significance of mourning [16] and have indicated that if the mourning process does not go on to completion, the arrest at an intermediate stage resembles pathological mourning. I have also suggested that anniversary reactions are manifestations of either uncompleted or deviant mourning processes. This distinction is important with regard to therapeutic management and outcome but will not be discussed further at this time.

The identification inside the ego with the internalized representation of the lost or abandoning object makes the ego-self the target for the aggressive discharge, with resulting self-destruction, in the form of suicide, psychotic disintegration, or somatic dysfunction and change. The hostility and rage toward the internal object-representation and the earlier self-representations may be manifested in the feeling of self-depreciation, self-degradation, and depression. The classic explanation of suicide is the murder of the ego-self–contained object-representation. Abraham, studying the self-accusations of his patients, noted their similarity to feelings that earlier had been directed against the object that the patient had internalized. One might say that the internalization that had occurred much earlier was later re-externalized and that only late in the pathological process did the feelings return to the ego-self. Freud pointed out that the actual death of a meaningful figure was not a prerequisite for melancholia, although such an event could act as the trigger of the melancholic state in the vulnerable victim. Thus the precipitating factor could set in motion a state of disequilibrium during which the underlying predisposing pathological state, stemming from childhood, emerges. Menninger [13] described this process as a three-fold wish: (1) the wish to kill the introjected object; (2) the wish to be killed as the death penalty for the murderous wish; and, (3) the wish to die. More current theoretical considerations modify this formulation to reflect our understanding of regression of the ego to early fragmented states with defective reality testing and the expression of early unneutralized aggressive impulses.

Sandler and Joffe [28] call attention to the lack of emphasis on aggression or (I would say) hostility in Bibring's ideas and seek to link his explanations with the earlier inter-systemic conflict formulations. They believe that

the experiencing of mental pain mobilizes aggression which is then directed against what is felt to be the source of the pain. This aggression can be used to alter either the . . . self or . . . circumstances, so that the degree of mental pain which is being suffered is diminished . . . if the child feels impotent in the face of the pain, and cannot discharge his aggression, the accumulation of undischarged aggression may reinforce the painful state so that he is forced into a state of helpless resignation.

These authors indicate that impotent and ineffectual rage that has not been expressed is frequently observed in depressive reactions. "It is an over-simplification to say, however, that this aggression has simply been turned against the self via identification with the hated object." More frequently observed in children is either the direct inhibition of aggression or the direction of anger against the actual self, which is disliked or hated because it is unsatisfactory. Anger with the frustrating object (or introject) and displacement of aggression from self to object and vice versa may occur. Hostility directed against the self is still consonant with the intrasystemic conflict postulated for suicide.

Friedlander [8], classified suicidal patients into the melancholic type described by Abraham and Freud and the addictive type in whom the wish to die seems more pleasurable than tolerating the tension and despair of living. This tension, characteristic of early states of ego integration and following the pleasure principle, demands immediate discharge and gratification. Death is viewed as the pleasurable release from an unsubsiding craving and tension. Friedlander [8] asserts that addictive suicides do not have the hostile conflicts of the melancholics but are more severely regressed in their reality operations as they relate to actions taken to secure release and gratification. Self-destruction does not appear to be the primary goal of the self-destructive action. These patients are more involved in fantasied reunions with early lost objects and not with the direct and reactive aspects of the ambivalent hostile oral aggressiveness characteristic of the melancholic suicidal patient. The particular means of suicide, as well as the presuicide communication, may give us a clue to the intensity of the desire for reunion or of the hostile destructive wish. Friedlander's addictive suicides long for symbiosis, not destruction. Instead of revenge and retaliation, they seek rejoining through retreat and regression.

Freud, in his essay "Thoughts for the Times on War and Death," written in 1915, two years before *Mourning and Melancholia* [7], pointed out that "no one believes in his own death" and that "in the unconscious everyone of us is convinced of his own immortality." Thus the act of suicide may be one not of total final destruction of the self but an act manifesting early narcissistic rage and revenge vented on the internalized object- and self-representations, an act symbolizing the wish for reunion in an afterlife in which one lives on in a blissful tension-free existence, or a combination of these motives.

When a normal mourning process occurs, there is either an identification of the mourner with the deceased or, under the traumatic impact of the final separation, earlier identifications that had become quiescent or integrated into the self emerge in more unassimilated and destructive form. Freud noted

when a death has fallen on some person whom we love—a parent or a partner in marriage, a brother or sister, a child, a dear friend . . . our hopes, our pride, our happiness, lie in the grave with him, we will not be consoled, we will not fill the loved one's place. We behave then as if we belonged to the Asra, who must die too when those die whom they love [6, p. 290].

This reunion with the deceased or continuation of existence after his death has been discussed in "Manifestations of Abnormal Mourning: Homicide and Suicide Following the Death of Another" [27]. Friedman [9], in his foreword to *On Suicide: Discussions of the Vienna Psychoanalytic Society, 1910*, refers to Freud's discussion of the cavalry officer who became depressed following his mother's death and suffered a fatal accident shortly thereafter: "The mechanisms of grief, guilt and identification are clearly evident here."

Death is primarily perceived as a separation and an instinctual and narcissistic frustration. It can reawaken old concerns dealing with need gratification, rage, guilt, unfulfillment, or idealization. These concerns vary from individual to individual, and obviously will depend upon the psychic maturity, integration, and cohesion of the mourner. However, the identification of the mourner with the mourned may be in evidence, and I believe that even without overt behavioral manifestations there is a bilateral identification. On the one hand, the mourner survives and remains, but internally something has left and is dying. Various mourning rituals and reactions seen as manifestations of this duality of identifications have been previously described [23].

When the ego and superego structures are functioning well, the self is relatively cohesive, and reality testing is operating in close accord with reality, the mourning process is completed without difficulty. The process of decathexis takes place, and the reality and finality of the event is eventually accepted. When ego-superego integration has been faulty prior to the death or when the self is partially cohesive and in danger of fragmentation, the mourning process cannot progress, and the identification with the lost object remains as a distinct unassimilated intrapsychic representation moving in tandem with the faulty self-representation. If there is hostile tension inside and between these psychic structures, melancholic symptomatology can appear. If narcissistic and libidinal tension predominates, the wish for regression to the earlier pleasurable symbiotic state may be sought. Either of these situations can result in suicide. When external events occur in a particular temporal-spatial-object contextual relationship that symbolically recapitulates or repeats the earlier unsuccessfully resolved traumatic state, an economic imbalance may result in the unleashing of previously bound sadistic and regressive impulses (related of course to a state of psychic disorganization). The psyche attempts to defend itself against these primitive states, and symptoms occurring at this point are due to the expression of the primitive psychic forces as well as the attempts to defend against these strivings. If these defense maneuvers fail, further regression occurs, and symptoms reflecting concern over self-destruction or actual self-destruction occur. In other words, the intrapsychic consequences of pathological or incomplete mourning precipitate states of disequilibrium that may lead to self-destruction.

CLINICAL DATA

In an attempt to obtain clinical data that might enable me to test some of my ideas about anniversary reactions, I wrote in November 1971 to every member of the American Psychoanalytic Association and to 12 selected institutions specializing in suicide studies, asking them to send me whatever clinical data they had in their records on instances of successful or unsuccessful anniversary suicides, and on situations in which there had been suicidal symptomatology in connection with an anniversary. I was very pleased to obtain 140 clinical protocols from all sections of the country. A detailed analysis of the material will be presented later. In the sample clinical reports presented below, minor changes have been made to protect the individuals' identity.

Before turning to the clinical material, I wish to mention Hilgard's [11] case of the suicide of a 43-year-old man the day after his son reached his 12th birthday. The anniversary suicide coincided with the victim's childhood trauma: the day after his 12th birthday, his older brother had died suddenly and unexpectedly of encephalitis. The victim, who had become successful after his brother's death, felt guilty and, as an adult, said his success came only as a result of a death. Hilgard points out that he had been aware of his intense jealousy and death wishes against his brilliant, conforming, and scholastically successful brother before his death. The victim himself became a successful criminal lawyer. At his son's birth, the suicide said to a friend, "I probably have less than 15 years to live." This strange predictive reference to time, I believe, was an indication that the fuse of self-destruction had been lit, to explode fatally on the exact day coinciding with the anniversary repetition of the victim's childhood trauma. Because there are no further data, I cannot speculate about the internal mechanisms underlying the victim's self-destructive act. However, the bipolar identification of the victim is clear. On the one side, he was his brother, who died one day after his brother reached his 12th birthday. On the other side, he was his son, who became 12 the day before the suicide. As has been found in other anniversary reactions, it might be suggested that the victim had a latent uncompleted and abnormal mourning process that ended with his anniversary suicide.

Sadger notes that "in one family the father shot himself at a certain age; his sons grew up and at the same age, all turned to the same weapon. In such cases I always suspect . . . an identification with the father. . . . Love, or the unsatisfied need for love, remains fundamental" [9, pp. 75-76]. Even the psychoses yield an illustration. No psychotic commits suicide without some subjectively compelling reason, which we rarely discover. It is not without reason that the suicidal psychosis, melancholia, is found frequently in the aged—people who observe their declining capacity to love and can no longer hope for love from others. When such melancholics typically complain that although they are rich they are impoverished, we know today that it is they who are right, and not the healthy people who in their arrogant incomprehension are unable to understand them. It is not money of which they are deprived but love. At this point I should like to formulate a principle based on my own experience: the only person who puts an end to his life is one who has been compelled to give up all hope of love in this life. The hope of reunion in an afterlife may still be a deep motive for self-destruction and hence tension release.

Case 1.   A woman seen following her release from a sanatorium, where she had been admitted because of an ever-increasing consumption of barbiturate sleeping pills, gave her age as 43 in the initial interview. In correspondence from the hospital, this also was her stated age. In a later interview, she confided that she actually was 46 but told people she was younger because she was concerned about "getting older." She expressed the wish to look youthful to herself and others. The patient was the middle child and only daughter in the family; she had two older and two younger brothers. The home situation was described as a most unpleasant one because of her father's very rigid and strict moral attitudes. His suspiciousness at times seemed to take on overt paranoid qualities. As a result of this tension, the patient stated, her mother left the home when the patient was 12, and abandoning the entire family.

The patient spoke of the mother's actions in connection with this event only in such a way as to try to justify them. She had longed to see her mother but continued to live with her father out of economic necessity. At 15, when she could no longer tolerate the situation with her father, she ran off to find her mother, whom she located about eight months later; an older brother supported her while she searched for her mother. Even after she found her mother she could not live with her, since her mother was involved in a common law relationship with a man and could not care for her. When the patient's mother subsequently was murdered by her lover, the patient was very shocked and upset. The great publicity that followed caused her additional anxiety. Very soon after her mother's murder, the patient (then aged 16) married a man three years older than herself and immediately had two children in a short period of time. The marriage ended in divorce after a few years.

Significantly, after her mother's death and after her own marriage, but the same calendar year, her father died of a chronic disease. She recalled no mourning for her father but spoke with great emotion about her mother's murder, and this was still in evidence at the time of the interview. When asked about the ages of her parents at their deaths, she stated that the mother was 46 at the time of her death and the father was 49. The coincidence of the mother's age at death and the patient's true age was noted by the interviewer, as was the correspondence in age between the patient and her first husband, and between her mother and father.

About four or five years after divorcing her first husband, the patient had married an inadequate chronic alcoholic man. The patient masochistically tolerated this individual's demands upon her for over six years but finally separated when the situation became impossible. She did not sue for divorce and was somewhat relieved when the man died as a result of a fight that occurred while he was drunk. Although she had no contact with him and was uninvolved in this matter, she felt sorry when she heard of his death.

The year following her second husband's death, she married a much younger man, with whom she had a "fine relationship." Despite this, the patient had noticed that she was getting quite upset in the six months prior to the interview and had begun to use barbiturates very heavily, which she had started during her "horrible" second marriage. After several additional interviews, the patient's anxiety markedly increased, and hospitalization was suggested; but before hospitalization was arranged, the patient managed to obtain a sizable quantity of sedatives and killed herself. Although she was not seen in the period immediately before the suicide, it was reported to the interviewer that the patient constantly spoke about her mother and about how she had been praying to return to her even though mother was dead. Her religious beliefs reinforced this idea of reunion in an afterlife.

The temporal correspondence of this woman's age at suicide with her mother's age at death is more than a coincidence. The particular mode of orally ingesting the lethal agent seems to correspond with the regression wish to effect reunion with her mother, which she expressed overtly. The possibility that other components (e.g., rage at the mother for abandoning her and subsequent guilt) contributed to her action must be considered; however, the need to "stay young," and thus deny the fateful anniversary year, seemed strongly to indicate the importance of her unresolved mourning for her mother and her father. The identification with the mother in her unsuccessful marriages and in the time-age parameter is clear.

Case 2. A man who initially stated he was 52 years old, and who later corrected himself to say that he was 53 years old, was seen on consultation because he had developed a fear of a catastrophic lawsuit in which he would be morally degraded and lose all his money and so be responsible for depriving his family of all support. In attempts to elicit details about this possible litigation, it became apparent that these fears were unrealistic and delusional. The patient had had surgery about one month earlier and in the postoperative period became amnesic and amblyopic. He felt that during a subsequent amnesic period he may have acted in such a way as to precipitate the feared litigation, although this was without foundation. Because of complaints suggesting possible organic cerebral involvement, a neurological examination was requested; no organic pathology was discovered. The neurological consultation was obtained on a Wednesday afternoon, and the following morning the patient killed himself. His son reported that he had slashed his wrists and chest and had actually opened his abdominal cavity with the razor blades he had used. Before he died he muttered that he did not want his son to see him this way but that he felt he had to die as there was no other way out of what he knew was going to destroy him and perhaps all who were dear to him.

As indicated, his manifest reason for this behavior was the delusional fear that he had done something that had hurt or angered a particular man, who now was going to :"get him." He felt, however, that he might have "imagined" all of this, since he could not recall having such thoughts before the operation. Approximately ten years earlier he had had a "nervous breakdown," from which he recovered while receiving psychotherapy. At that time, he felt he had taken undue advantage of an older man who was a business competitor. This man committed suicide, and the patient felt completely responsible. At the time of his earlier disturbance, he had felt he had to be punished, becoming depressed, self-accusatory, and suicidal. He was able to recover with psychotherapeutic assistance and returned to his activities. He had been married for 24 years and had three children, the oldest 19 and the youngest 13. His marital relationship had always been a good one, and there were no major financial problems.

The patient had two older brothers, one older sister, and one younger brother. His mother never remarried but supported the entire family and saw to it that they all had a "good education." He spoke of his closeness to his mother and of how he had missed her after her death, from "heart trouble," about 18 years earlier. In talking of his parents, he mentioned casually, "My father died when I was 6 years old. He was 53, the age I am now, when he died. Although I don't remember him and don't know what he died of, I have frequently visited his grave and have said memorial prayers for him every year." He knew his father had been ill and had died at home. The patient unknowingly spontaneously associated to the older man who committed suicide ten years earlier, after talking of his father. He then spoke of his guilt about this man, but added that he had worked things out so that he could "recover." He could not understand why these guilty and self-recriminatory feelings had now returned.

In this patient, the hostile identification with the dead father, whom he feels he killed, actually came out in his associations to the event of ten years earlier, when he had experienced an acute melancholic episode. The confusion about his age and his inability to remember his father and present actions about which he felt frightened also seem to be related to his impending anniversary suicide. After his suicide, his wife was contacted, and she stated that his father did die at age 53, which was the patient's age at the time of the suicide. The cause of his father's death on the operating table was peritonitis secondary to a ruptured appendix. Without consciously being aware of it, the patient had chosen the blade as his mode of suicide. The anatomical locale (abdomen), the perforation, and extravasation mechanisms may have been associated in his mind with his father's death. Once again, the anniversary correlation between the age of the father at his death, and of the age of the patient at the time of suicide is clear. The patient's concern with his own son just prior to his death may well have reflected the preoccupation he had about problems with his own father. The confusion about his age in the initial consultation closely resembled that of the patient in Case 1.

Case 3.   A 24-year-old married woman was seen after she attempted to destroy herself by ingesting "sleeping pills." She felt very guilty over an extramarital affair she had had with her husband's friend. She had been married for three years and had been trying to become pregnant without success. She had been examined and told that she was not responsible, that perhaps her husband was partially sterile. The patient secretly hoped she might be pregnant as a result of her extramarital activity but became very depressed after she found she actually was pregnant and then felt that she could only "atone for her guilt" through death.

The patient was the youngest of six children, all of whom are living. When the patient was 4½, her mother died of tuberculosis. She could not recall her mother, except that her mother was "very wonderful." After her mother's death, the patient lived with her father until age 8, then with an aunt until age 14, then with her father again until she was 17. She never liked and actually feared her father, who had an "awful temper and was brutal," and who had incestuously attacked her older sister, although he had never touched her. Despite her attempt to portray her father negatively, it was apparent that she was his favorite.

Prior to the patient's marriage, her husband had impregnated her, but the pregnancy was terminated by miscarriage. She believed this was a punishment for premarital sexual activity, and she viewed her infertility as further punishment for her guilt. When asked why she should be punished, she could not answer but stated that during her adolescence she had been quite promiscuous. For a long period in her teens she had carried on an illicit affair with her older sister's husband. She felt very guilty about these affairs and felt especially reprehensible when seen about her latest infidelity because her husband was such a kind, considerate, faithful man. Psychotherapy was recommended to this patient, but she preferred to return to her home in another part of the country where there were no therapists.

The patient's mother was 25 when she died. Although it is impossible to relate her unsuccessful suicide attempt directly to the anniversary age of her mother at death, the oedipal guilt toward her mother can clearly be inferred. The subsequent acting out of this situation in later life with her brother-in-law and the friend of her husband, plus the exposure to a seductive father, undoubtedly contributed to her guilt. The guilt based on ambivalent feelings toward her mother, reinforced by her mother's actual death, seemed insufficient to restrain the patient's sexual acting out. However, the approaching anniversary date might well have been the harbinger of the reawakened melancholic process following her mother's death. This ambivalent identification with the mother may have been the psychological determinant of her suicide attempt.

These three patients were seen for comparatively short periods of time. Any greater discussion of their situations would have to be based in large part on inference and speculation. The identification with the deceased parent seemed clear in two of the patients. Data relating to ambivalent feelings prior to the significant parent's death were unavailable, although in each instance the parent that died during the childhood of the patient was of the same sex as the patient; the event occurred during the oedipal developmental period in two patients, and during adolescence in the third.

In the next three cases suicidal and self-destructive impulses were present but were handled, during the course of psychoanalysis or dynamically oriented psychotherapy, with successful resolutions.

Case 4. A 23-year-old unmarried woman consulted an analyst because she was fearful of becoming an alcoholic. She began to drink at the age of 17, while still a student in high school, and had found her alcohol ingestion increasingly difficult to control. Her mother, with whom she had strained relations, had always depreciated and severely controlled her. This pattern was still present at the time she was initially seen. Her father had committed suicide when he was 55, by running his car over a cliff. The patient was 16 at the time. As subsequent information became available in the therapeutic relationship, it was clear that he too restricted the patient in regard to dating, sexual activity of any sort, smoking, cleanliness, and practically all other instinctual gratifications.

After the father's death it was revealed that he had been secretly gambling away the family resources for some time. This information came as a great shock to the family, and resulted in a severe downgrading and reorganization of their scale of living. The mother was forced to work, and the family properties had to be sold to pay the father's debts. It was in this period (after the father's death) that the patient began to drink heavily and to be depressed for prolonged periods of time. It was also at this time that the patient first began to be preoccupied with self-destructive fantasies. In all of these she characteristically destroyed herself by jumping off a tall building. These suicidal preoccupations were revealed only after four years of continuous psychotherapeutic contact. She feared talking of these ideas because she felt her therapist would disapprove of her ideas and might reject her. The transference aspects of these preoccupations emerged in various ways and clearly indicated the relationship to her father. She sometimes became deeply depressed when an appointment had to be changed. Only gradually did she permit her anger toward the therapist to emerge when such events occurred. Her destructive fantasies toward men were also slowly revealed, but on each occasion with such caution and anxiety that she would literally shake as she spoke. Vacations and other separations were very traumatic for her, even with months of discussion before their occurrence. After these events, the self-destructive fantasies increased in frequency and intensity.

On one occasion, when she was called by the analyst's secretary about a sudden cancellation of an hour, she became exceedingly frightened and anxious. She was very angry with the analyst for the cancellation but was terrified because she thought that the analyst's death was the reason for the omitted session. She feared calling the office lest she hear the "terrible news," and she approached the office for the next appointment with great trepidation. When she heard the office air-conditioner working and saw that the secretary looked cheerful, her anxiety diminished. But only when she saw the analyst did she feel relief. Her first comment to the analyst was an enraged outburst about why he had worried her so. She quickly went on to tell of her tremendous fear that he was dead and how she had been certain this accounted for the cancellation by the secretary. When asked about her feelings of anxiety, she reluctantly talked of how her suicidal preoccupations had reached their greatest intensity after the cancellation. She felt that if the analyst had died, she would also have to kill herself.

In later sessions the transference implications of this dramatic experience became clear. Her anger with her punitive and at times sadistic father actually were accompanied by conscious death wishes directed toward him. The appearance of her suicidal preoccupations after his death and the news of his clandestine gambling related to her guilt about his death and the magical fear that she was responsible for it. At a deeper level she was terrified at being left alone—a punishment meted out to her as a child. The idea of death as a punishment, as an escape, as the ultimate in isolation became clearer. Several months after the canceled appointment episode, the patient came in with great excitement and revealed that the day of the cancellation by the secretary was the same as the date on which her father had died. She had forgotten all about it until shortly before seeing her analyst at this later time.

In this patient, utilizing the transference neurosis facilitated the working out of the traumatic events relating to this patient's suicidal preoccupations. The regression to oral gratification, coupled with the depressive self-destructive fantasies, indicated a melancholic type of mourning response to her father's death, which was chronically acted out and yet avoided through the acting out behavior. The identification with the dead parent was observed in the fantasied mode of suicide.

Case 5. A 37-year-old married woman who had been seen previously for limited psychotherapy with a successful result suddenly called for an appointment after an absence of contact for many months. When asked why she decided to come in at the particular time she chose, she said that she had heard of a 37-year-old woman who had died of cancer of the breast that day and that this greatly upset her. She wondered whether she should go to the funeral and could not understand the reason for or intensity of her feeling. When asked about this situation, she immediately associated to her mother's death from carcinoma of the breast. The mother was in her early 50s at the time, and the patient had wished for her mother's death because the mother had suffered so with her disease.

One month after her mother's death the patient married and soon began to have marital difficulties. Significantly, at that time she developed the fear that she would get breast cancer and die shortly. Although very anxious, she found her concerns diminished with time. In childhood the patient depreciated her mother and admired her handsome, enthusiastic, active, seductive father, who had died suddenly of a heart attack when she was in her late teens, five years before her mother's death. Although she was very shocked at her father's death, it was only after her mother's death that she felt very guilty and depressed. Her cancer phobia started at that time.

The precipitating event that stimulated the sudden appointment request was discussed with the patient. As she talked of it, she noted the identification of herself with the dead 37-year-old woman and how this related to her previous fear of cancer and its connection with her mother's death from breast carcinoma. Several additional interviews were sufficient to aid her in understanding more fully what had given rise to the recurrence of the sudden anxiety. The anxiety about dying of cancer as her friend had exacerbated her fear of being left. The need to have a temporary contact with the analyst was in the service of denying separation, i.e., the analyst still lived. In other words, her identification with the departed friend-mother existed along with the feelings of being left alone that occurred after her mother (and father) died. The mother's death served as an actual catapult into marriage for her.

In this situation the guilt toward and identification with the dead mother was clear. The fear that she would have a fate similar to that of her mother seemed to indicate the presence of an unconscious self-destructive impulse and her conscious reactive fear and phobia about this possible fate. There were no thoughts or attempts of suicide, but the fear of destruction through the process of internal malignancy indicated the internal self-destructive wish and fear.

The basis of the anniversary phenomenon for this patient seemed to trigger the identification processes that had been repressed. The more closely the patient's life pattern or time relationship coincides with that of the unassimilated ego-self representation of the object toward whom ambivalences are felt, the greater the possibility of the emergence of the self-destructive impulses.

Case 6.   This patient, in analysis for over seven years, when first seen was extremely anxious and fearful that she had cancer that would "eat her up inside" and that she was going to die. This phobic concern so frightened her that she had been continuously involved in a process of repeated medical examinations to reassure her that she was still healthy. Initially she indicated that her fear of dying from cancer started when her child was 6 months of age. However, as the analysis progressed, it became evident that her fear of dying actually emerged as a conscious preoccupation very shortly after she was married. When she was first seen she was 27 years old, married, and had a daughter 3 years old. This fear of death, which started immediately after her marriage, had been getting progressively worse and was the reason she sought help. Her constant concerns undermined her marriage to the point where her husband was contemplating divorce. He felt that for the five and a half years of their marriage, her active resistance to intercourse because of her fear of pregnancy, her constant preoccupation with her health, and the resulting excessive medical expenses involved in her search for reassurance added up to a situation he could no longer tolerate.

Her history as she gave it initially was that her mother had died in childbirth, when the patient was 4½ years old. Her only sibling was a sister born at the time of the mother's death. Her father remarried when she was 6 years old, and he had no other children. The patient and her sister lived with the maternal grandmother from the time of the mother's death until after the father remarried, when they rejoined him. In talking about her sister, the patient felt that her own fear of childbirth related in some vague fashion to the birth of her own sister, although this was very unclear to her. After marriage she never intended to have a child, but her husband tricked her into the pregnancy. Her husband, wishing a child, had secretly perforated a condom, and she had conceived. Her anxiety at the time of conception and throughout the pregnancy was most intense. Her concern at the time of her child's birth was that she would die in childbirth, and she was uncomfortably surprised to find that she had survived. Her fantasy about her mother's death had been that her mother died as the result of hemorrhage in the postpartum period. Shortly after her daughter's birth, when she herself had a slight postpartum hemorrhage, she became so panicky that it required emergency sedation to calm her down.

The first part of the analysis was concerned mainly with the great resentment that she had toward her stepmother, with whom she had never established a relationship and about whom she had many competitive feelings and hostile fantasies. She had always idealized her father and could not understand his great love for her stepmother. At 21 the patient met her husband-to-be and married him. Her husband, like her father, was a traveling salesman for a clothing company. On her honeymoon she felt so miserable that she cried constantly and wanted to return home to "Daddy." She found sexual relationships unsatisfactory. Although a virgin at marriage, she managed to adjust so that she was able to have an orgasm practically every time she had intercourse. However, her constant fear was that if she became pregnant she would die in childbirth. She resented her husband for tricking her into pregnancy. In a somewhat magical fashion she stated that she knew she would have a daughter and felt that her death from childbirth would be from extravasation, as she had fantasied her mother's death. Despite the panic and anxiety, she managed to go through the pregnancy and give birth to a daughter, as she had predicted. After the birth the patient became increasingly anxious and depressed about pregnancy, and there gradually evolved marked restrictions as to the times that she would allow intercourse to occur. These prohibitions were specifically related to certain months, which turned out to be the months in which her mother had conceived. Intercourse was always accompanied by great caution and ritual.

The anniversary features of her difficulties were even more strikingly brought out by the fact that she was married on the day that she had established as the death date of her mother. In talking about this coincidence she stated that she set the wedding date without conscious awareness of the significance of the date. While applying for the marriage license, when asked for her mother's name she unconsciously gave her real mother's name even though she had intended to follow the practice she had established of always listing only her stepmother's name. It was only after a long period of analysis that the facts about her mother's death became clarified. Her mother did not die in childbirth of extravasation, but apparently died two weeks after giving birth to the patient's sister, from what sounded like a pulmonary embolus set off by delayed postpartum ambulation. Her sister's birthday (which the patient always knew) actually was two weeks before the date of her mother's death. The patient's daughter was born on March 25; the patient was born on March 22. The bipolar identification with daughter and mother became clearer as the significance of this coincidence emerged. On the one hand the patient was her own mother giving birth to her, and on the other she was the daughter who was born again.

As mentioned above, the patient came to see the analyst when her daughter was 3½ years old. In retrospect she may already have been unconsciously anticipating a serious anniversary reaction when her daughter would reach the age that she was at the time of her mother's pregnancy and death. Analysis continued, and it was apparent that her resistance reflected the attitude of her father, which had always been to avoid talking about or recognizing the death of the patient's mother. The reconstructed anamnestic material that is presented here is a compilation and condensation resulting from the many analytic hours filled with resistance, silence, and anxiety. When the patient's daughter was born, she wanted to name her after her real mother, but feared doing this as it would infuriate her father and stepmother; furthermore, she felt that she might be condemning her daughter to die at age 32, the age of her mother at the time of her death. As a compromise, she gave her daughter the middle name Hope, using the first initial of her real mother's name. The patient herself had changed her own given name about the time that she met her husband. Her mother had named her Norma, but she changed it to Helene. When asked why this change occurred, she said that it related to a movie she saw at that time. In this movie the heroine's boyfriend had gone off to war, and she waited for him. The scene she recalled most vividly was one in which Helene was "waiting for her man to return." All of the soldiers came back, with the hero at the end of the procession, blinded by the war. Helene, while crying, professes her love for him, and reunion is accomplished. Shortly after seeing this movie, the patient decided to adopt the name Helene, and she did so. She is still called Helene by everyone but her parents and old friends. She further indicated that she did not wish to have the name of Norma because she wanted to completely divest herself of her mother's influence and believed that changing her name could do this. In addition to the name change, she also tried to alter her physiognomy, hair style and coloring, because she felt unhappy about her unattractive appearance. However, she felt more secure in that she now physically resembled her father and not, as before, her deceased mother. As the analysis proceeded, many aspects of this patient's life emerged and were worked through and clarified. A complete account of these is not germane to this presentation, but significant features and developments can be highlighted.

While in analysis the patient voluntarily became pregnant again. Significantly, her second child, whom she predicted would be a girl, was born when her older daughter was 4½ years old. This child, a girl, was born several weeks before her sister's birthday. The patient stated that again she knew she would have a girl. The time interval between her daughters' births was four and a half years, the same as the interval between her and her sister. Much later in the analysis, when talking about her unconscious magical activity, she stated: "I knew both times it would be a girl. I did it to test the Gods to see if I was mother. I got married on the day that I thought she died. Mother was 32 when she died, and I felt certain that I would never survive this age. Father was the same age as mother, and my husband is the same age as I am. It is amazing how I never realized, until we have worked this out in the analysis, how I did everything the same way as mother. I got married and tried to get away from being like mother. I changed my name, I changed my appearance, but inwardly I always felt that my fate would be exactly as mother's. I am now 34 years old. I passed the critical year in which I was to die only because I could work on these feelings here with you. I tried unconsciously to repeat the pattern but found that I was different and not my mother. I fought you for three years of the analysis. Nothing happened. I wouldn't let myself feel or depend on anyone as I had with my mother."

After the birth of her second daughter she again believed that she was going to die. However, even though she had some understanding, her amazement at surviving the pregnancy was remarkable. Her anxiety about death, though still present, was markedly diminished, and she could accept this child with far less ambivalence than her first.

The patient, throughout the analysis, frequently made allusion to suicidal ideas. Her marked fear of malignancy became understood as a manifestation of the fear of the wish to atone for guilt feelings through a self-destructive process, though her death would occur as the result of an internal cellular malignancy instead of an actual suicidal gesture. As her fear of malignancy lessened, her suicidal wishes increased. In the course of the working through some particularly frightening material in the maternal transference neurosis, she did on several occasions make pseudo-attempts at self-destruction. These were interpreted directly, and she understood them in the context of her need to identify with mother, and her guilt and need to punish herself for her own destructive fantasies at the time of her mother's pregnancy when she was 4½ years old. The oedipal aspects of these fantasies clearly emerged.

Particularly trying periods throughout the analysis occurred when there were vacations or interruptions by the analyst. Initially, the patient began to experience a feeling of complete emptiness within her body, then became exceedingly depressed, and then various self-destructive fantasies began to preoccupy her. At first she would have symptoms that she believed indicated the presence of a malignancy. Later these changed to thoughts of suicide through the ingestion of barbiturates or by throwing herself out a window of a high building. She always associated a vacation with the time when her mother left her to have her sister and never returned. Some of her material before one of the analyst's vacations illustrates this association: "You are leaving again and will be gone on the anniversary of my mother's death. This is a bad time for me every year. Always something comes up. One year I feared that I had a brain tumor. The next year I thought that I had cancer of the stomach. Another year I feared cancer of the uterus. It is connected with your leaving. I fear your going away in summer. This morning I thought of your dying. I know that you won't. You are not my mother. You are not going away to have a baby. Maybe your wife will. If your wife dies, I will die. This will be the punishment, but I can also in this way be your wife. In times past I used to think of death as peace. No more feelings, turmoil, no more hurting, and also if I were to die, I might be able to be with her again if there is an afterlife."

Although she was aware of the fact that her mother had died, throughout her childhood she refrained from talking about this matter to her parents. Nonetheless, throughout her childhood, and even during the first half of the analysis, she secretly maintained the fantasy that her mother existed in heaven and that she could communicate with her mother by talking to her silently in her mind. Gradually this fantasy changed and she substituted the analyst for mother. This paralleled the decrease in anxiety about her own death, which disappeared, but her concerns about the analyst's death markedly increased.

As the maternal transference evolved, she became increasingly angry with the analyst, and there followed great anxiety as she associated her anger with the magical destruction of the object against whom these feelings were directed. Then her guilt markedly increased, and she would resurrect fantasies of self-destruction. Slowly she recognized that she had wished her mother dead when the pregnancy occurred. When she herself was pregnant, she was overwhelmed by her own anxiety, guilt, and death concerns. Two dreams illustrate the therapeutic reactivations of this conflict: "I tried to come and see you. The elevator was self-service. It took me to the fourth floor but would go no higher. I wanted desperately to see you and so I walked up all of the stairs to nine. I waited to see you, but then had to go to a hospital and take an old lady there. It began to rain heavily. The old lady was a plastic bag full of bones and flesh. It moved and was alive. She was dead when I got to the hospital." The second dream, occurring the same night, was: "I was on a golf course—a man tried to show me how to play. Suddenly it was flooded. Like Noah's ark. A boat was there, and so was father." Her associations to the fourth floor related to her fourth year. If she could stay at age four she could avoid her mother's death, but she had to work in the analysis and finally recognize that her "old lady" was dead and all that remained was skin and bones. She felt that the analyst was teaching her how to play. The water in both dreams referred to her crying. She had never cried prior to analysis, and even now could only cry when she had an analytic session. She felt that all of her crying started as light rain, but gradually as her feelings about mother emerged, the tears were like the flood associated with Noah's ark. They threatened her: all might be destroyed. She went on to say that she felt as though she were in a plastic bag at times. She thought that a plastic bag was a quick way of killing oneself, and she felt that she would have had to do this if she could not realize that she did not kill her mother. The evening following her discussion of these dreams, and shortly before a separation from the analyst, she wrote the following note: "This too shall pass—as night follows day. How long do I have to keep paying? I've paid for 30 years and am still paying for my crime; I've paid with anxiety, tension, and depression. I've paid with my stomach, throat, ears, and eyes. I've paid with unhappiness and never enjoyed anything. I am in my own plastic bag and I can't get out. Is death the only and final payment? Who am I writing this to—my own mind? The one that is so strict and doesn't bend? The one that says 'an eye for an eye and a tooth for a tooth'? I've made this little Hell all for myself and now I am entangled in and can't get out. I am enclosed in my fears, anxieties, and angers. I wake up in the morning with this horrible anxiety—like something awful is going to happen. The only thing that happens throughout the day is punishment. I am drained of any real human feelings as I am just aware of the terrific struggle going on within me. There must be another part which is rational and knows I committed no crime —or else I would have killed myself long ago. I think of death as the final payment, yet a part of me keeps fighting to stay alive. What are my crimes? I killed my mother by wishing her dead, I wanted my father and the baby he gave to my mother. I am so angry with her for leaving me with no one to love me. But this anger doesn't come out in pure anger—it is turned inward at me. Everything is turned inward right now. All I am aware of is my hurting body and my unhappy mind. All I want is some measure of peace within myself. You are going away from me like my mother did. The one person that I love. I know it is just a vacation, but I react to it like I did 30 years ago. Only 30 years ago I didn't know she wasn't coming back. Now I know she isn't coming back. I am deserted and alone, and even now my father might leave me. I am not reacting to all this as a grown-up woman over 30, but as a child of 4. I know all this and yet I don't know it or I wouldn't feel like I do now. How long do I have to keep this up? I've paid enough—it is about time I start acting to things as they are now. It is so easy to say this but inside of me is still that 4-year-old who lost everything in one day and never again was a whole person."

The reaction to the vacation of the analyst paralleled that which occurred at mother's death, but now she could write and dream of it and so could work out more feelings about the "greatest blow" she ever had. The bipolar identification of the patient with the dead mother and the surviving little girl once more was apparent.

This revealing analysis presents many features that could be discussed in greater detail than is possible here; however, we can note the close bipolar identification that she had made with her dead mother. The patient was the mother who was going to die at a particular time, under specific circumstances, and whose life had to be patterned as closely as possible after her mother's. However, this was not completely desired by her, and she did make attempts magically to alter this fate. Because of her oedipal guilt and certain aspects of pregenital conflicts not described here, she concomitantly was the object (archaic self included) who was persecuted by a punitive unintegrated maternal superego. Her suicidal preoccupations manifested themselves through active self-destructive fantasies with partial acting out, as well as anxiety about death-dealing physical malignancies. The anniversary components are clearly seen but also brought about by the patient in her need to repeat the pattern.

Psychoanalysis allowed her to understand that which was unclear for her. Each anniversary was reacted to and worked on after it occurred. The process of living through the event seemed to be essential. Her 32nd birthday came and went, and only later did she say, with much surprise, that she was over the hurdle. The actual acceptance of reality, in addition to the experiencing and understanding of the transference neurosis, facilitated the differentiation of herself from mother as well as from other significant, though less meaningful, objects in her life.

DISCUSSION

Zilboorg [30], on the basis of investigation of the differential diagnostic types of suicide, concluded that

a history of the death of a person close to the child or circumstances bringing the theme of death into the actual life of the child at one of the two turning-points of the psychosexual development of the child (oedipus period which reaches its height at about the age of six, and the period of puberty, at which time all the conflicts of the oedipal period are revived under the pressure of physiologic maturity) makes suicide a highly probable outcome.

In one of his cases, that of a woman aged 28, whose mother died when the patient was 13, the deep-seated sense of guilt resulting from hatred of her mother, with whom she identified, seemed to relate to her suicide attempt by gas poisoning. Unfortunately, the age of the mother at the time of death is not mentioned, but it is inferred that the mother at death was older than the patient's age at the time of the suicide attempt. In the course of the analysis of this patient Zilboorg was able to recognize the "severe unconscious mourning" this girl went through after her mother died. It was at this time that the identification with the dead mother was experienced. In the suicide act, she acted out this identification with the dead mother. The similarity of these data to several of the clinical examples cited earlier is striking. In another publication, Zilboorg [31] points out that

the actively suicidal individual . . . appears to be in mourning, but his is not a sublimated gratification of the need to identify himself with the dead; instead he reverts to the primitive pattern of mourning. A regression to the primitive impulses invades his motor system so that in acting out his neurotic mourning he actually joins the fantasied dead by killing himself.

Zilboorg believes that in nonneurotic mourning, the identification with the dead is transitory and self-limiting. Rituals such as dressing in black (covered with earth) and withdrawing from life action are the indicators of this normal mourning identification with the dead. I have discussed these rituals in detail elsewhere [23]. In the melancholia suicidal case, there is regression to a level of ego integration at which reality awareness is so impaired that the acting out of hostile aggressive impulses occurs toward the introjected object, which is not differentiated from the self.

Identification is the basic process by which the ego and superego structures are differentiated. This process may more directly involve parents than siblings during the childhood developmental periods; hence childhood parental loss may play a more significant role than childhood sibling loss, unless, of course, the sibling has symbolically become a parental transference figure or, in instances of severe sibling rivalry, the object of destructive wishes.

The normal mourning process is a process of undoing some aspects of past identifications as well as beginning autonomous differentiation, which includes decathexis. In some ways the analytic process is predicated on reestablishing the normal mourning process with its decathectic aspects of the transference object, even when there has been no real object loss in the patient's childhood. Hence anniversary reactions are responses that are indicative of mourning abnormality and faulty identification processes, and they may be more prevalent than we realize. External indicators of this pathology occur when the temporal or life situations parallel the much earlier and identifiable traumatic experience with an object that is deceased.

Only one patient of Palmer's [15] 25 cases of consecutive suicide was a sibling loss in childhood. Hilgard's case report, cited earlier, involved a childhood sibling loss. One of Zilboorg's patients lost an 8-month-old brother when the patient was 4 years old. In general, however, the incidence of childhood sibling loss as opposed to childhood parent loss in psychiatric patients seems to be much less; this was also seen in my comparative study of childhood parent-sibling loss patients [17, 25].

Wall [29], in studying 33 patients who actually did destroy themselves, found a family history of suicide in 11 families, and the suicide of a near relative as the precipitant in 4 cases. He observed that the tendency to identify with relatives who killed themselves was noteworthy. Moss and Hamilton [14], evaluating 50 patients who were seriously suicidal, reported that they found a "death trend" in 95 percent of all of their cases. They state: "this involves the death or loss under dramatic and often tragic circumstances of individuals closely related to the patient, generally parents, siblings, and mates." In 75 percent of their cases, the death occurred "before the patient had completed adolescence." In the remaining 25 percent, the "death trend" occurred later and precipitated the illness. Sixty percent had lost one or both parents in early life, the majority during puberty or early adolescence, and others in childhood or infancy. Forty percent lost their fathers and twenty percent their mothers during this period. In every case of paternal loss, however, the patient felt a removal of the mother's usual love and support brought about by a disruption of the home after the father's death. Later deaths of persons close to the patients served to reactivate suicidal preoccupations in these individuals, of whom 11 died by suicide. Wall's study in many ways confirms the earlier observations of Palmer about the significant correlation of suicide with loss of a parent in childhood. The Wall report stresses the importance of identification with the deceased relatives but does not focus on the mourning processes of the survivors who later destroyed themselves or on the significance internally of these early losses.

In accordance with these observations—but in addition to them—in these childhood parent-loss patients, the suicide may be triggered by an anniversary occurrence. In some of the cases cited above, it was the actual or feared attainment by the patient of the age the parent had reached at his or her death that set in motion suicidal activity. The anniversary brings back the trauma of the parent's death, and with this, the frustration, hostility, and guilt that served to feed the ambivalence that interfered with normal mourning. Instead an identification with the dead parent was fixated. In the instances in which mourning in childhood parent-loss situations can be worked out during psychoanalysis, the potential suicidal process may be converted into the more usual mourning reaction in the context of the analysis [4].

Not every childhood object loss results in an anniversary reaction, and not every anniversary reaction ends in suicide. Probably many individuals "live through" such anniversary crises without ever being conscious of them. Some may have spontaneous resolutions of these crises without treatment, while some are helped with treatment. Others who consider treatment may not link their need with mourning. Some individuals destroy themselves as part of the melancholic or symbiotic process, and some remain chronically depressive throughout their lives.

Before closing this discussion, it may be useful to call attention to the problem of when mourning is possible for the child. Dr. Morris Peltz has called to my attention the controversy among child analysts about the child's capacity to mourn. Some observers consider the reactions of infants to separation from significant objects as being very similar to the adult mourning process; others have raised questions as to when a child can comprehend the concept of death, including the idea of finality. Various ages have been suggested when such a comprehension can occur, varying from the 2- to 3-year-old to the early adolescent. Peltz believes that most children are incapable of an adult type mourning process but instead react with a variety of affective and cognitive responses, including anxiety, helplessness, rage, somatizations, magical thinking, denial, projection, splitting of the ego, displacements, regression, and repression. I would suggest we need further study of the evolution of the mourning process, not only in the Darwinian sense but as a developmental continuum in which various ego capacities appearing at particular times eventually become integrated into what we call the adult mourning process. Fixations, arrests of development of specific ego functions, or pathogenic traumas may then predispose the vulnerable adult to later consequences of interrupted or deviated mourning processes and can eventuate in anniversary suicides.

CONCLUSIONS

Correlation does not necessarily imply teleological, causal, or direct relationship. However, it can focus our attention on two coincidental events that may have significance and thus may lead to further investigations of this linkage. Among the cases I have described in this report, there were two actual suicides and an attempted self-destruction in a third patient that corresponded in time to the death ages of the lost parents. These parents died while the patients were children. It is suggested that the suicidal actions of these patients were anniversary reactions and that they represent manifestations of abnormal or incompleted mourning processes with pathological identifications. What time-age-event relationships are selected for the anniversary suicide is significant in terms of what has been the central conflict; in the cases in this chapter, the death of the parent was the nuclear event emphasized. When one elicits anamnestically the facts of parental death or suicide during the childhood of the patient, considerations of self-destruction by the patient when he reaches the "critical age" must be considered and dealt with analytically. Many of these potentially suicidal patients are long-standing partially compensated melancholics in whom past traumas are reawakened when the temporal-age identification with the deceased parent becomes coincidental. In an attempt to avoid this coincidence of fate, there frequently may be a distortion of time or age and a wish to keep time or age from moving the victim to his presumed lethal end. The actual mode of suicide may also be related to the type of personality organization of the victim, the amount of sadism inherent in the conflict that has been remobilized, the hostile identification with the deceased object, the method of death of the childhood figure, or the addictive-symbiotic wish of the victim to reunite with his fantasied object.

Suicide can and does occur in any diagnostic category and does not depend upon any single clinical constellation—in fact, it can occur in many who would be adjudged to be "normal." However, the "anniversary suicide" patients have certain unique descriptive features, which have been the focus of this report.

Frequently an external event may occur that serves as the releaser of more primitive ambivalent feelings in these patients. It is postulated that an internal trigger of this mechanism may be set off by the coincident-external temporal correspondence that symbolizes the past conflict relationship between the patient and the previously lost object. This concomitance in time serves to reawaken in the previously compensated individual a more overt and manifest pathological state in which suicide may occur. However, these symptoms may be limited to suicidal fantasies that are either overtly self-destructive or relate to fantasies of physical death (e.g., malignancy, heart attack) and need not be acted out in deed.

It may be that many supposedly endogenous depressive episodes, though unrelated to present and identifiable precipitants, are current reflections of anniversary-like responses to previous situations in which mourning did not occur, was abnormal, or was arrested. Careful clinical investigation is needed to understand these varied outcomes and their determinants.

REFERENCES

1. Abraham, K.   Notes on the Psycho-Analytical Investigation and Treatment of Manic-Depressive Insanity and Allied Conditions (1911). In *Selected Papers of Karl Abraham, M.D.*, transl. by D. Bryan and A. Strachey. New York: Basic Books, 1960. P. 137.
2. Abraham, K.   The First Pregenital Stage of the Libido (1916). In *Selected Papers of Karl Abraham, M.D.*, transl. by D. Bryan and A. Strachey. New York: Basic Books, 1960. P. 248.
3. Bibring, E.   The Mechanism of Depression. In P. Greenacre (Ed.), *Affective Disorders*. New York: International Universities Press, 1953. P. 13.
4. Fleming, J., and Altschul, S.   Activation of mourning and growth by psychoanalysis. *Int. J. Psychoanal.* 44:419, 1963.
5. Freud, S.   Instincts and Their Vicissitudes (1915). In *The Standard Edition of the Complete Psychological Works of Sigmund Freud*, transl. and ed. by J. Strachey with others. London: Hogarth and Institute of Psycho-Analysis, 1957. Vol. 14, p. 109.
6. Freud, S.   Thoughts on War and Death (1915). *Standard Edition*, 1957. Vol. 14, p. 273.
7. Freud, S.   Mourning and Melancholia (1917). *Standard Edition*. 1957. Vol. 14, p. 243.
8. Friedlander, K.   On the longing to die. *Int. J. Psychoanal.* 21:416, 1940.
9. Friedman, P. (Ed.)   *On Suicide: Discussions of the Vienna Psychoanalytic Society*, 1910. New York: International Universities Press, 1967.

10. Hilgard, J. R.   Anniversary reactions in parents precipitated by children. *Psychiatry* 16:73, 1953.
11. Hilgard, J. R.   Depressive and Psychotic States as Anniversaries to Sibling Death in Childhood. In E. Shneidman and M. Ortega (Eds.), *Aspects of Depression*. Boston: Little, Brown, 1969.
12. Hilgard, J. R., and Newman, M. F.   Anniversaries in mental illness. *Psychiatry* 22:113, 1959.
13. Menninger, K. A.   Psychoanalytic aspects of suicide. *Int. J. Psychoanal.* 14:376, 1933.
14. Moss, L. M., and Hamilton, D.M.   The psychotherapy of the suicidal patient. *Am. J. Psychiatry* 112:814, 1956.
15. Palmer, D. M.   Factors in suicidal attempts: Review of 25 consecutive cases. *J. Nerv. Ment. Dis.* 93:421, 1941.
16. Pollock, G. H.   Mourning and adaptation. *Int. J. Psychoanal.* 42: 341, 1961.
17. Pollock, G. H.   Childhood parent and sibling loss in adult patients: A comparative study. *Arch. Gen. Psychiatry* 7:295, 1962.
18. Pollock, G. H.   On symbiosis and symbiotic neurosis. *Int. J. Psychoanal.* 45:1, 1964.
19. Pollock, G. H.   Anniversary reactions, trauma and mourning. *Psychoanal. Q.* 24:347, 1970.
20. Pollock, G. H.   On Time and Anniversaries. In M. Kanzer (Ed.), *The Unconscious Today*. New York: International Universities Press, 1971.
21. Pollock, G. H.   Temporal anniversary manifestations: Hour, day, holiday. *Psychoanal. Q.* 40:123, 1971.
22. Pollock, G. H.   On time, death and immortality. *Psychoanal. Q.* 40: 435, 1971.
23. Pollock, C. II.   On mourning and anniversaries: The relationship of culturally constituted defensive systems to intra-psychic adaptive processes. *Is. Ann. Psychiatry* 10:9, 1972.
24. Pollock, G. H.   Psychoanalytic considerations of fertility and sexuality in contraception. *Is. Ann. Psychiatry* 10:203, 1972.
25. Pollock, G. H.   Bertha Pappenheim's pathological mourning: Possible effects of childhood sibling loss. *J. Am. Psychoanal. Assoc.* 20: 476, 1972. [See also, Bertha Pappenheim: Addenda to her case history. *J. Am. Psychoanal. Assoc.* 21:328, 1973.]
26. Pollock, G. H.   Mourning, immortality and utopia. *J. Am. Psychoanal. Assoc.*, in press.
27. Pollock, G. H.   Manifestations of Abnormal Mourning: Homicide and Suicide Following the Death of Another (1973). *The Annual of Psychoanalysis*, vol. 4, The Institute for Psychoanalysis, Chicago, in press.
28. Sandler, J., and Joffe, W. G.   Notes on childhood depression. *Int. J. Psychoanal.* 46:88, 1965.
29. Wall, J. H.   The psychiatric problem of suicide. *Am. J. Psychiatry* 101:404, 1944.
30. Zilboorg, G.   Differential diagnostic types of suicide. *Arch. Neurol. Psychiatry* 35:270, 1936.
31. Zilboorg, G.   Suicide among civilized and primitive races. *Am. J. Psychiatry* 92:1345, 1936.

16

Psychological Defense against Depression

MORTIMER OSTOW

That depressive illness is likely to occur in the case of individuals with a certain predisposing type of personality was suggested by Freud in *Mourning and Melancholia:* "the disposition to fall ill of melancholia (or some part of this disposition) lies in the predominance of the narcissistic type of object choice" [4]. Again, "This conflict due to ambivalence, which sometimes arises more from real experiences, sometimes more from constitutional factors, must not be overlooked among the preconditions of melancholia." Looked at another way, one may say that a certain type of pathological personality structure, which includes among its manifestations a tendency to ambivalence and an ability to establish object relations only on a narcissistic basis, is likely to invite recurrent attacks of depression. Later analysts have elaborated the description of the personality that is vulnerable to depressive illness.

This statement suggests a formulation of a natural history of depressive illness. A full description of that natural history would include much information that is not yet available. For example: What personality characteristics and pathological findings are we likely to encounter in the childhood of these future depressive individuals? Is the presumed primal depression always found? Is there a characteristic adolescent course? How do these potential depressives function as marriage partners and as parents?

It is the purpose of this chapter to describe a feature of the natural history of depressive illness, namely, the regular, sequential recurrence of certain clinical states preceding the actual decline into depression. Because the sequence is fairly constant, at least for a given patient, and because these clinical states regularly precede the relapse, and because they can be interpreted as tending to prevent the ultimate depressive outcome, I consider them defenses against depression.

The term *defense* is used in a specific, technical way in psychoanalysis. It designates a simple, primary process maneuver by means of which the ego protects itself against danger, whether the danger arises from importunate impulse, unwelcome percept, or intolerable affect. The type of maneuver I shall describe tends to protect the ego against lapse into illness in order to spare it the pain associated with that lapse. It may deter, defer, or prevent depression. In each case the maneuver yields a specific form of behavior or attitude.

In many instances the new behavior or attitude serves the defensive function assigned to it without appearing abnormal. In other instances the behavior or attitude assumes the form of a classic neurotic or psychotic syndrome or character disorder. Presumably an existing weakness in its own structure is exploited by the ego in its need to defend against the lapse into depression. For example, an individual struggling to protect himself against depression may experience anxiety if he leaves his home without a companion. Phenomenologically the condition must be labeled agoraphobia. Yet the dynamics differ from those that prevail in cases of true neurotic agoraphobia. The two conditions may be distinguished first by the fact that the dynamics do differ, and second by the fact that the antidepression agoraphobia will be effectively dissipated by the administration of antidepressant medication. Third, under careful psychoanalytic scrutiny one can detect behind the antidepression agoraphobia faint intimations of the threatening depression.

The idea that the depressive collapse is preceded by other maneuvers that seem to have a defensive function has been offered by Rado [9], who spoke of the rebellion that precedes depression, and by Fenichel [3], who described the acting out of neurotic impulses as an effort to forestall a threatening depression.

I shall describe here several defensive states and present them in the order in which they tend to occur spontaneously. In many patients, only one of these states is prominently visible and others are rudimentary or invisible. In a few patients two or more states are seen in clear succession. From patient to patient, the sequence is almost always the same. For a given patient, his individual pattern is repeated consistently from one episode to the next.

While the descriptions are meant to stand on their own merit as clinical observations, it is interesting to try to imagine the mechanisms that shape these phenomena. The precipitating factor for each episode of depression, while frequently invisible to the clinical psychiatrist, is usually discernible to the psychoanalyst. Such factors include loss of love, loss of the anaclitic love object, instinctual frustration, defeat, and narcissistic injury. The trigger does not seem to be specific for depression. In other patients, similar triggers precipitate other forms of illness. The distinction lies in the nature of the individual response, which is determined by preexisting personality structure.

Once the precipitating event has occurred, it triggers a disturbance of the inner psychic equilibrium. This disturbance sets in motion a sequence of events of which many are known, though their role and causal relation to each other is not well established. These events include an increase of ambivalence and a decrease of self-esteem. As a result of these changes the ego begins to lose its supply of libidinal energy. In the ultimate depressive state the manifestations of this energy deficiency are prominent, and they led Freud to the formulation (in *Mourning and Melancholia*) that the energy is absorbed into a psychic wound. It is this energy loss that is reversed by the psychic energizers (a term first used by myself and Kline [8]). We considered that term appropriate for two reasons. In the first place the administration of ample amounts of these substances does make large amounts of psychic energy available to the patient, and second, Freud's suggestion that in melancholia the ego's libido supply is not available would justify calling the chemical agent that undoes this condition an energizer. Since these defensive states that I describe are also eliminated by the psychic energizers, I infer that these too are elicited, if not by a deficiency of libidinal energy, then at least by the preconscious perception of a threatened depletion.

PARADOXICAL HYPERMOTIVATION

The first efforts to combat incipient depression frequently take the form of an increase in activity. This increase may be diffuse, or it may be confined to one or a small number of tendencies. In the latter case the specific activity selected is one that usually provides powerful sensual stimulation or gratification. For example, many of today's troubled young people become involved in sexual overindulgence, including promiscuity, homosexuality, and other forms of sexual deviation, and orgies. Incurring danger creates the stimulation of having to rise to an emergency. The wish to obtain such stimulation motivates some young people to provoke and encourage confrontations with authority. The fact that such confrontations serve a defensive psychic function is frequently obscured by their association with authentic social

protest movements that in many cases are popularly supported. However, those for whom this is an antidepression maneuver are found
more often in the front lines of danger than in the constructive coun-
cils. As the pathological need subsides, they usually lose interest in
the political activity. For example, one young man, active in the campus disturbances of 1968, ran from one confrontation with the police
to another, from campus to campus, to participate in the struggle. He
paid little attention to the political issues, some of which were at variance with each other, and explained all of his activity by employing
the currently popular slogans. In the midst of these struggles, he
would usually manage to find a young woman and indulge in an act
of intercourse. The excitement of the confrontations was able to revive libidinal desires that a strong underlying depressive tendency had
suppressed.

Drug abuse must be considered a form of sensual indulgence. In-
toxicating oneself with the substances commonly used obscures reality
with its frustrations and demands, attenuates the pain of defeat, and
replaces the perception of reality and its associated feelings of distress
with pleasant sensations or stimulation.

Under this same heading of paradoxical hypermotivation I would
include excessive work. The businessman who occupies himself constantly with business activities is clearly avoiding exchange of affection with family and friends. However, the need to work constantly,
to achieve and to be celebrated, admired, and envied, may also be
used as a device to defend against an underlying depression. When
such an individual does fall ill, it is said that he becomes ill as a result
of overwork, whereas in fact the overwork merely failed to protect
against the depression, which finally overtook him.

The evidence that these stimulating and sensual maneuvers do represent attempts to ward off depression is twofold. First, they are frequently discovered in the histories of individuals who present themselves for treatment of frank depression. Second, in the case of a few
patients who are observed in analysis for relatively long periods of
time, they can be seen to occur regularly when the patient starts his
descent toward depression. For example, a young man would dress in
his wife's underwear and imagine that women were masturbating him
against his will as he actually masturbated himself. He felt ashamed
of indulging in this perversion but was compelled to do so whenever
his wife turned away from him in anger. After a period in which he
sought solace in these activities, if there was no change in his wife's
behavior, he would generally slip into depression. It is clear that the
perversion made it possible for him to retain and identify with the
maternal object whom he is losing, but I wish to draw attention here

to the antidepression effect of the stimulation that the maneuver achieved.

It seems paradoxical that a threat of losing libidinal energy is met by activities that consume large amounts of energy. One must infer that the visible energies elicited for defense represent an emergency supply, made available to meet the emergency and to overcome the threat posed by the current pathogenic stress. Because excessive activity is elicited to combat a threatened loss of energy, I have called this state *paradoxical hypermotivation*. It is this reactive proliferation of emergency energies that creates the intense and irresistible drive that motivates the activities I include under that rubric. If this supposition is true, then the administration of psychic energizers should reduce the need for these extravagant activities and provide some tranquillity. I have not had the opportunity to test this hypothesis, because most individuals in this state of mind have an interest in seeing themselves as mentally normal and neither ask for nor accept treatment.

I believe it makes sense to include also hypomania and mania in the category of defense against depression by paradoxical hypermotivation. Freud [4] and his immediate followers tried to understand mania as the reaction that occurs when depression is lifted. However, Helene Deutsch [2], and Abraham [1] before her, detected that mania too seems to have to contend with a threat, and Deutsch specified that the defenses employed in mania are denial, projection, and identification. Lewin [5] subsequently elaborated the defensive function of elation. Whereas the depressed patient is persecuted by the lost love objects, whose images have been incorporated into the superego, the manic identifies with these objects in the ego.

It has been my impression, from clinical observation, that mania precedes depression rather than vice versa. That is, among those individuals with the manic diathesis, mania represents an attempt to deal with a pathogenic stress, and when the mania fails, depression ensues. This sequence is readily seen when the patient becomes ill only under the pressure of *recurrent* external stress. When the stress is applied, the person first becomes manic, and then, when the mania is defeated, he becomes depressed. On the other hand, when the stress is *constant* —for example when it is due to an inner inhibition that prevents him from meeting normal external demands—the patient may oscillate from mania to depression and back. Mania is the prime example of paradoxical hypermotivation, and as such it can be seen as the first phase in the process that ultimately ends in defensive depression.

If this argument is correct, then psychic energizers that combat depression should also combat mania. Such treatment has never been recommended. One disadvantage is that psychic energizers require a latent period of three to four weeks before they become effective; but in principle, I believe that they can overcome and prevent attacks of mania.

Case 1. A 57-year-old man who had experienced a number of episodes of depression previously was treated for the presenting episode with nialamide (Niamid, 250 mg per day) and was maintained on that dose for four months. At that point his wife, upon whom he was strongly dependent, became abusive and went off on a brief vacation without him. He became manic almost immediately; he felt excited, worked fast, drank a good deal of alcohol, and ate continually. He was unable to sleep. He denied that he missed his wife: "I'm so glad to have her gone." He indulged in petty thievery. His voice became hoarse from constant talking and shouting. He told me that he developed "telephonitis," making 30 or 40 calls a day. "I'm having the best time I've had in years." He gave away money and spent large sums in extravagant purchases. "I'm putting all of my dreams into action."

His mania continued for six weeks. At that point I increased the dose of nialamide to 300 mg per day. On the following day there was an abrupt change. He said, "All of us have thoughts of suicide, all our lives. My grandfather did it, my father did it, and I guess I'll do it . . . I don't like funerals." He brought in letters from his mother and some photographs of himself as a baby. "I'm not depressed, but I feel down a little. I feel very calm." When he left the office, he was weeping. He continued on the same dose thereafter and was neither manic nor depressed.

This case vignette demonstrates that treatment that is effective against depression is also effective against mania. I consider this observation a confirmation of my opinion that an episode of mania must be considered a form of defense against depression.

CLINGING

The next phase in the defense against depression is an attempt to reinforce the anaclitic relation with the primary love object or her representative. This attempt frequently takes the form of a clinging attachment. I referred above to a young man who indulged in transvestism when he felt threatened by his wife's withdrawal. He felt so ashamed of this behavior that it offered him little comfort. He then became obsequious and self-effacing, sometimes even weeping before his wife in an attempt to win her favor. The patient, whom I described moving from mania to depression, as he came down from his high, reread his mother's letters and wept. In this way he attempted to retrieve his mother's affection.

Clinging may become manifest in insatiable demands for physical proximity, for displays of affection, for frequent sexual gratification, in demand for gifts, money, and admiration, and in an increase in appetite. In general there is a craving for oral gratification. An aggressive component becomes visible in the extravagance and intensity of the demands upon the object, who soon becomes angry and sometimes finds himself, out of exasperation, forced to abandon the subject.

Clinging may take the form of turning to religion. The individual looks to God for protection and to the other members of the religious congregation and the clergyman for their personal interest in him.

Sentimentality often betrays the clinging defense against depression.

Case 2.   A man in his fifties who was struggling against depression, and who had previously disdained religion, sought comfort in the home of casual friends and accompanied them to religious services. There he found himself weeping in response to the congregational fellowship and family warmth he observed.

Weeping itself signals a wish for reconciliation with someone from whom one has been alienated. Therefore it is not infrequently seen during the clinging defense against depression.

Anticipatory guilt functions to discourage violation of superego standards. Actual guilt punishes and elicits a desire for atonement, that is, reconciliation with one's parents or their substitutes. The feeling of guilt is frequently elicited not by actual or even intended misbehavior but by misfortune. The ancients, and also many moderns, believe—as Job's friends did—that the occurrence of misfortune is a proof of misbehavior. This conviction is reinforced by the fact that the victim usually experiences a feeling of guilt and interprets the guilt as proof that he had misbehaved. The frankly depressed patient, for example, usually expresses feelings of guilt, and the enormity of the misbehavior to which he confesses matches the degree of his suffering. But in the process of descent into depression, the unconscious perception of the decrease in psychic energy elicits "signal guilt," which warns the prospective patient to conciliate his superego and current parental objects. There follows a series of activities designed to accomplish this goal, including renewed interest in religion, confessions of guilt, and efforts at atonement, including generosity, sacrifice, and consciously correct behavior. For example, the young man with the transvestite perversion, as he slipped further toward depression, prayed to God for salvation, accused himself of being too hostile toward his wife, and even blamed the analyst for encouraging him in that direction.

Because clinging betrays one's dependence, some individuals struggling with depression will behave in the opposite way: they assume a parental, caretaking role that denies their dependence and at the same time ingratiates them to others. For example, a man in his fifties who had suffered a personal tragedy suddenly left home, family, and occupation to devote himself full-time during World War II to rescuing fellow Jews from Europe. He had never previously felt or expressed any particular concern for the Jewish community. After a few months of work well done, he returned to his previous home and occupation. Another example of "negative clinging" is the immature, unmarried, often hysterical young woman who becomes pregnant and insists upon bearing her baby to prove that she is adult rather than the child she feels herself to be.

When the need to cling is intense and constant, it may take the form of a phobia, usually agoraphobia, sometimes acrophobia. Here it is not the fear of sexual temptation that elicits the phobia, as it is in the case of phobic neurosis, but the fear of losing contact with the parental love object in the first instance, or fear of falling, in the second. Among patients struggling against depression, the actual depressive collapse is often represented in dreams as falling or sliding uncontrollably down.

At times one finds in late adolescent or early adult life a normal or even pronounced adventurousness sometimes retrospectively recognized as counterphobic. Within a few years, however, the latter may be replaced by a phobia that severely restricts the life of the patient and of those around him. A few years later still, partly as a result of the phobic paralysis, depression may begin to develop, and when the patient is depressed, he becomes completely immobile. Chemotherapy with a psychic energizer, which dissipates the depression, will also dissolve that component of the phobia that represents clinging support against depression rather than anxiety hysteria [6].

Case 3. In her late teens and early twenties, a young woman went to an out-of-town college, was socially active and popular, and dated a good deal, though she avoided intercourse. She rejected a number of appropriate suitors, but in her middle twenties married a fine man who was successful in business. However, he was seriously impotent. In marriage she found intercourse a frightening experience and often developed vaginismus, which reinforced her husband's impotence; consequently their sex life during most of the marriage consisted only of mutual masturbation. For a number of years after marriage she was so phobic that she would leave the house only in a car driven by another person. She would not walk on the street for fear of dogs, and would not fly for fear of plane crashes. She would not drive for fear of having an accident. There was a brief postpartum depression following the birth of her second child and several years later a severe depression. She responded well to psychic energizer medication, which had to be continued over a number of years. Her agoraphobia and acrophobia remitted promptly, but fear of dogs and fear of driving have remitted only partially and slowly. I infer that the former two arose from defense against depression, while the latter two were symptoms of anxiety hysteria.

Among today's troubled youth we are encountering the phenomenon of religious conversion. The same individual, in many cases, who had hitherto lived a promiscuous sexual life, indulged in euphoretic drugs, rejected social and organizational responsibility, and cynically disavowed allegiance to traditional authority and standards of behavior, suddenly assumes a religious way of life that includes abstemiousness, rejection of drug abuse, and taking a responsible role in religious organizations. This abrupt reversal seems puzzling but it can easily be understood as an instance of sequential antidepression defenses.

Here the first attempt to deal with the frustrations and challenges of late adolescence and early adult life is the technique of paradoxical hypermotivation with sensual indulgence. Sensual pleasures are sought to dispel the pain of defeat and to provide stimulation that will override a depressive tendency. Simultaneously the culture, which usually interdicts such behavior and demands assumption of responsibility, is repudiated. Sooner or later this device fails because the activities that were once thrilling now pall and because, despite the fact that the young person consciously repudiates organized society, indulging in behavior that society condemns inevitably challenges his self-esteem. At this point he might feel himself sinking toward depression were he not able to seize upon another defensive device, in this case the clinging defense. Actually, by organizing themselves into communes and loose societies of antinomian individuals, these young people had invoked a clinging defense previously—that is, they had clung to each other. Now they join a very tightly organized group and thus draw comfort from the support of the organization. They assume a devotional attitude toward some god and to their leader, and they earn the approval and protection of the superego by their self-discipline and self-denial. The change in attitude is dramatic and utilizes the formal device of religious conversion. It is accompanied by fantasies of rebirth. It represents a shift from gratification of id impulses to gratification of superego demands.

The aggressive aspect of the ambivalence toward parents and society that was evident during the phase of sensual indulgence in the flaunting of standards and rejection of responsibility, becomes evident in the religious phase in the same way. It is true that they now cannot be accused of immoral or irreligious behavior, but their defiance persists in that the religion they join is usually one that is different from the one in which they were raised and to which their parents feel they owe allegiance. In fact it is common for the parents to become even more outraged than they had previously been. Hitherto the young people had rejected all the moral values of civilization and culture; now they reject only those of their parents and family of origin, provoking and teasing them by flaunting their preference for the god and family of strangers. To some extent, the ability of the religious position to protect them derives also from the fact that it permits them to continue to externalize the aggressive component of their ambivalence, whereas a clinging reconciliation with their parents requires internalizing the aggression, which in turn would facilitate the descent into depression.

ANGRY WITHDRAWAL

The clinging maneuver may fail to contain the depression. For example, the pathogenic stress may be too great, or the anaclitic object may become intolerant or lose interest. As the depressive threat intensifies, the patient then abruptly disengages from the anaclitic relation and retreats into solitude. He exhibits a generalized irritability. Dramatically and angrily he repudiates the object upon whom he has depended. The disengagement is frequently accompanied by fantasies of rebirth, which are patently meant to deny the inner awareness of being drawn further down to depression. If the patient is in psychoanalysis or psychotherapy, at this point he is likely to repudiate the therapist and withdraw from treatment. The angry withdrawal helps to defend against depression because it encourages the patient to externalize his aggression. Yet the fact that not all of the aggression has been externalized is indicated by the occasional resort to suicide. My favorite example of angry withdrawal is one that I have published elsewhere. It is the case cited earlier of the sentimental man in his fifties who was taken with his friends' religious observance. He kept a pet monkey. As he was becoming more depressed, he dreamed that his monkey had retreated to the corner of his cage and was bleeding from a bite on its wrist. When the patient attempted to reach into the cage to assist the monkey, the monkey bit out at him and prevented the rescue. At this point the patient himself was very angry, biting, and nasty, and kept everyone at a distance. On the day following the dream he left treatment in fury.

In some instances the withdrawal takes the form of a hysterical retreat, as in the following example.

Case 4.   A woman in her late forties who attempted suicide in the course of one of several depressions was later treated with a monoamine oxidase inhibitor, nialamide (Niamid). On each of several occasions it proved possible to alleviate the depression with a given dose of the medication. However, within weeks or even days there would be another quarrel with her husband, following which her depression would recur and could not be dissipated without raising the dose of medication significantly. Yet she could not bring herself to leave him. On one occasion in the course of such a quarrel, she threw a cupful of coffee at him and told him to leave the house. He went to live in a hotel. For a few days they communicated by telephone and visited back and forth. Her angry withdrawal alternated with the clinging attachment to him. After one unsatisfactory visit with her husband, she skipped her morning session and remained at home the rest of the day, having collapsed on the floor, weak and unable to move. The family physician found no organic basis for her disability. Late that evening she insisted that she had to come for her daily session. Although this hysterical paralysis had the effect of mobilizing family and friends around her, its major purpose was to distance herself from the real world in which she lived, reinforcing her separation from her husband and avoiding her therapist. It was similar in dynamics to the suicide attempt that had brought her into treatment in the first place.

Each time a given patient begins a descent into depression, he is likely to exhibit this sequence of defensive positions. The specific form that each defensive position takes, how long it lasts with respect to the duration of the others, and the relative prominence of each, varies from patient to patient but is fairly constant for any given individual. Frequently one of the phases is prominent and the others are traversed rapidly and silently; if the patient is not under close scrutiny, they might be missed. While each phase, when it prevails, is sufficiently distinctive that it can easily be recognized, nevertheless one often encounters overlap, especially at times when the situation is changing.

Case 3 Revisited. The phobic and depressed woman described in Case 3 at one point required a D and C (dilatation and curettage) for diagnostic purposes. It became necessary therefore to discontinue the monoamine oxidase inhibitor she was taking at the time, namely tranylcypromine (Parnate). The dose was decreased from its initial level of 40 mg per day by 10 mg each day starting Nov. 28. Dec. 1 was the first day she had no Parnate at all; on that day she reported a dream of sexual desire. On Dec. 2 she said, "I get so stimulated with people—I become cute and darling. I seem to get higher and higher instead of slumping." Here we see two days of paradoxical hypermotivation. On Dec. 3 she reported a "terrible, terrible loneliness." She was very angry with an associate with whom she had dealt on the previous day and said that she intended to be "brutal" to her. Then she admitted "I want to cry." On this day we see her weepy wish for a reconciliation and at the same time her inappropriate fury. On Dec. 4 she said she was no longer speaking to her husband. "I haven't felt so angry since I first married him." On Dec. 5 she said her husband was a mean man. "Why don't I forget him? I'd

be glad for a divorce if he gave me enough money. I feel very unloved."
On Dec. 6 the operation was performed; nialamide was begun on Dec. 7.
On Dec. 10 she reported, "It upset me to realize that when the medication was dropped, I became uncontrollably angry. Then after the operation I began to move toward melancholia. I was sad, inert, and pessimistic, but not angry." For three weeks most of her sessions dealt with
desires for reconciliation with her family and religious themes appropriate
to that time of the year. However, her concern with religion was considerably stronger than it ordinarily was even during December.

Note that the phases of paradoxical hypermotivation, clinging, and
angry withdrawal overlap to a certain extent. In this situation the
overlap is partially due to the great rapidity of the decline, and partially due to the fact that the transitions are often not very clear-cut.
However, the case vignette illustrates the sequence, the fact that it
was set in motion by discontinuing the administration of a psychic
energizer, and that the clinical picture was altered when medication
was resumed.

DEFINITIVE DEPRESSION AND ANGRY WITHDRAWAL

In the phase of definitive depression, elements of previous phases
can frequently be recognized. Components of the phase of paradoxical
hypermotivation or sensual indulgence, since it includes activities
that are utterly inconsistent with depression, are not likely to be
found. However, one may consider whether it would be proper to
include under that rubric the repudiation of all responsibilities, the
indulgence in idleness, the utter self-absorption, and what seems to be
an orgy of masochistic gratification.

On the other hand in definitive depression, components of the
clinging phase are easily seen. The feeling of guilt that occurs during
depression may be attributed to the need to account for one's misery.
However its loud assertion may be interpreted as an attempt at expia-
tion by confession, that is, an attempt to become reconciled to parents
and to God. Actual weeping seldom occurs in frank, well-developed
depression. It occurs more frequently in the clinging phase, on the
way down to depression, or on the way up. When it does occur during
depression, it represents a residue of the clinging phase. The inability
to venture out of the house represents a paralyzing agoraphobia in
which the individual clings to the home, if not to the love object.
Components of angry withdrawal are more visible than components
of the other phases. In definitive depression, however, the patient has
withdrawn and acknowledged defeat, whereas in angry withdrawal he
pretends to be withdrawing by choice. In fact in many instances the

diagnosis of depression is made by psychiatrists when the patient presents himself in the phase of angry withdrawal [7].

THE RECOVERY PROCESS

During recovery from depression, the sequence of changes is not regular. In Chapter 20 I give the sequence of changes encountered in a patient treated with a psychic energizer. There I saw on two occasions first the gradual appearance in consciousness of hostility to the love object, and second the resumption of libidinal motivation. In other cases the hostility has appeared only after the libidinal renewal.

The issue is further complicated by the fact that the process of recovery is usually interrupted by a number of brief relapses that can be considered a part of the recovery process. Each relapse activates one or more of the defensive positions considered earlier. Therefore the recovery process is likely to be marked by shifts in psychic state and fluctuations in intensity. These shifts and fluctuations are especially likely as the drug latency comes to an end and psychic energy supplies begin to build up.

I have described these defensive maneuvers as episodic events that are elicited successively when a patient is defeated by a pathogenic stress and starts to decline into depression. But there are some individuals who, because of constitutional vulnerability and continuing stress, must struggle against depression for years or perhaps the major portion of their adult life. These people may find one of these defensive positions especially congenial for them; then it becomes less a syndrome of illness and more a character trait. Even among these people, the intensity of the trait reflects the current intensity of the pathogenic stress. This relation becomes visible especially during the course of psychoanalysis.

There are individuals who periodically or continuously are driven to pursue sensual gratification, whether in the form of sexual indulgence, drug abuse, alcoholism, or tempting fate by dangerous activities. There are individuals who constantly display an active, cheery, energetic, hypomanic personality, who are constantly under the influence of visible drive. They sleep little, eat much, work hard, and do everything vigorously. Corresponding to the clinging phase, there are individuals who lead circumscribed lives, determined by the need to be close at all times to supporting love objects. Their clinging may be overt and declared, or concealed. Many marriages become essentially holding operations to sustain a dependent partner against depression. Some clingers conceal their dependence behind a facade of generosity, altruism, and caretaking. This facade disguises the clinging and thereby tends to spare the individual the humiliation and loss of self-esteem that clinging involves. At the same time it obligates others to supply friendship, appreciation, and gifts. The need to cling, as a character trait, may contribute to the motivation to live a religious life.

The phase of angry withdrawal is exemplified by individuals who display irritability, irascibility, and nastiness as enduring character traits. This attitude represents an attempt to strengthen self-esteem, which is threatened both by the depressive tendency and by the primary defensive attempt to cling. It is important for these individuals to demonstrate their independence at the cost of alienating family, friends, and fellow workers. Yet there remains a denied dependence on one or two love objects who continue to support them despite the abuse inflicted upon them. When these loyal individuals finally turn away, the prospective patient becomes definitively depressed.

None of the syndromes described is specific to the defense against depression. Impulse disorders, phobic inhibitions, and hysterical withdrawal all occur in other conditions too. What is emphasized in this chapter is that these maneuvers are regularly elicited in the sequence cited, by the inception of a process leading to depressive illness, and that the defensive maneuver can be resolved by the administration of an antidepression energizer. Psychic energizers will not remove these syndromes when they occur in other contexts.

Case 5. A young woman in her early twenties was first seen in a state of mild to moderate depression. She was unable to do her schoolwork. She clung tightly and desperately to her mother all day long; the poor woman scarcely had a moment of freedom or privacy. In addition, from time to time the patient would cut her legs with a razor blade to make them bleed. She had earlier been given thioridazine (Mellaril; 300 mg per day). To test whether that was causing the depression, I gradually reduced the dose of the drug and finally eliminated it. The depression lifted promptly, but the three major symptoms did not change. I then administered a monoamine oxidase inhibitor (Nardil) long enough to achieve clear evidence of energizing and euphoria. None of these three principal symptoms changed. Evidently, despite the fact that the patient had been rendered depressed by the thioridazine, that depression was not the essence of her problem.

From a diagnostic and therapeutic point of view, it becomes possible and helpful with respect to the syndromes I have described, to distinguish between those occurring in a neurotic or psychotic context and those occurring in a depressive context.

NARCISSISTIC TRANQUILLITY

There is a syndrome that occurs in patients subject to depression, at times when they are not depressed. It is a kind of metastable equilibrium that appears when the patient is subject to pathogenic stress but is able to resist it. For example, when a patient has been brought out of depression and maintained free of depression by psychic energizers but is still subject to the same stress that made him ill, the syndrome of narcissistic tranquillity is likely to appear. The patient finds himself eating constantly. He gains weight rapidly; however, the weight gain is greater even than that which would be appropriate to the increased intake. In other words, even when the patient diets stringently, he tends to gain weight with unusual ease. There is torpor that occurs sometime during the afternoon or early evening. There is an increase in sex drive, and in the absence of an appropriate object it leads to compulsive masturbation. There is a tendency to accumulate possessions.

It is interesting that this syndrome is the converse of the components of Selye's General Adaptation Syndrome [10], which includes sharp diminution of sexual desire, anorexia, weight loss, and general arousal. I believe that the syndrome of narcissistic tranquillity represents a state not of equilibrium but of response to a minor as distinguished from a major stress. If there were no stress, there would be no syndrome of either kind.

Narcissistic tranquillity occurs when a patient who was formerly depressed is supported by psychic energizers, or when a schizophrenic patient is held in remission by antipsychotic drugs, and he must face the precipitating stress once again. Because the patient is chemically protected, the external stress, from his point of view, becomes minor rather than major.

Narcissistic tranquillity also resembles the vacation syndrome that occurs fairly universally. People on vacation eat, gain weight, indulge more frequently than usual in sexual intercourse, nap during the day, and are inclined to purchase possessions. Here too, we may say that the vacationing individual has escaped the stress of daily life and replaced it with the minor stress of separation from home, family, and associates.

The interrelation between schizophrenia and depression is complex and depends upon the independent but sometimes concurrent constitutional vulnerability to each. I should like to note here only that depression and schizophrenia, for people who are predisposed to retreat to them, are alternative ways of escaping a pathogenic stress. Also, they are mutually exclusive for most, but not all such patients. The administration of an antipsychotic agent to a schizophrenic patient will undo the schizophrenia, but, pressed further, will force the patient, if he is at all vulnerable to it, into depression. Similarly, the administration of an antidepressant psychic energizer to a depressed patient will undo the depression, but, pressed further, will force the patient, if he is at all vulnerable, into a schizophrenic episode. In a certain sense, then, for many patients schizophrenia and depression act as defenses against each other. Within the range of normality, when the community offers it as an option, the individual who is challenged by pathogenic stress may select mystical withdrawal or a transcendental way of life as an alternative to depression. I shall not discuss the situation in which depression and schizophrenia coexist except to mention that they occasionally do, and the patient then requires a combination of antidepressant and antischizophrenic medication.

SUMMARY

Among patients susceptible to depression, exposure to a pathogenic stress initiates a process which may end in definitive depression, days, weeks, months, or years later. A sequence of separate stages can usually be recognized in this process, namely, paradoxical hypermotivation, clinging, and angry withdrawal. These positions may present as psychic states or as clinical syndromes; for example, impulsive, perverse or manic behavior, agoraphobia, or hysterical detachment. These positions may also present as character traits. The relative duration and prominence of each phase varies from individual to individual.

These syndromes resemble similar syndromes occurring in purely neurotic or psychotic contexts. However, they can be distinguished from the latter in that they occur in a sequence that, if the process is not arrested, terminates in clinical depression; and they are resolved by the administration of a psychic energizer.

Narcissistic tranquillity is a state that prevails when the formerly depressed or schizophrenic patient is protected by medication from these pathological states but still must confront an unresolved pathogenic stress.

Among predisposed patients, schizophrenia and depression function as alternative responses to pathogenic stress; removal of one by medication leaves the patient vulnerable to the other.

REFERENCES

1. Abraham, K. Notes on the Psycho-Analytical Investigation and Treatment of Manic-Depressive Insanity and Allied Conditions. In *Selected Papers of Karl Abraham, M.D.*, transl. by D. Bryan and A. Strachey. London: Hogarth Press, 1948.
2. Deutsch, H. Zur Psychologie der manisch-depressiven Zustande insbesondere der chronischen Hypomanie, *Int. Psychoanal. Z.* 19: 358, 1933.
3. Fenichel, O. *The Psychoanalytic Theory of Neurosis.* New York: Norton, 1945.
4. Freud, S. Mourning and Melancholia (1917). In *The Standard Edition of the Complete Psychological Works of Sigmund Freud,* transl. and ed. by J. Strachey with others. London: Hogarth and Institute of Psycho-Analysis, 1957. Vol. 14, p. 243.
5. Lewin, B. D. *The Psychoanalysis of Elation.* New York: Norton, 1945.
6. Ostow, M. *Drugs in Psychoanalysis and Psychotherapy.* New York: Basic Books, 1962.
7. Ostow, M. *The Psychology of Melancholy.* New York: Harper & Row, 1970.
8. Ostow, M., and Kline, N. S. The Psychic Action of Reserpine and Chlorpromazine. In N. S. Kline (Ed.), *Psychopharmacology Frontiers.* Boston: Little, Brown, 1959.
9. Rado, S. The problem of melancholia, *Int. J. Psychoanal.* 9:420, 1928.
10. Selye, H. Stress and psychiatry, *Am. J. Psychiatry,* 113:423, 1956.

17

Anhedonia and Depression in Schizophrenia*

ROY R. GRINKER, SR.

DEFINITIONS

A chapter devoted to discussing the relationship among three states would ordinarily begin with reasonably exact definitions of each. Unfortunately the terms in this case are global and vague and have fuzzy boundaries. For example, *depression* may refer to a symptom, a syndrome, or a nosological entity [11]. *Anhedonia* implies the absence of pleasure, a universal condition of all human lives at various times and under specific conditions.

From early infancy most humans smile, gurgle, and blabber with pleasure in response to satisfying stimuli. Later they develop a sense of pleasure expressed in laughter and appropriate bodily and facial movements. Some unfortunates are unable to experience pleasure, a condition termed anhedonia. They find little within themselves or in relation to others that excites them to a feeling of enjoyment; their facial expressions exhibit pleasureless boredom. They withdraw from contact with others and endure a painful sense of loneliness.

Anhedonia may be considered the zenith of depression because it is almost constant and is not related to internal or external dynamic or experiential conditions. In its depth depression may be associated with black despair at the worth of living, and the sufferer searches for a solution in suicide. The anhedonic knows only a joyless existence and rarely makes plans for a better life except through dependency on others.

* This work is supported in part by U.S. Public Health Service Grants MH-05519, MH-18991, and MH-19477 and State of Illinois Grants 131-13-RD and 218-12-RD.

This research is part of a program investigating schizophrenia that is being conducted jointly by the Psychosomatic and Psychiatric Institute of Michael Reese Hospital, the Department of Psychiatry, Pritzker School of Medicine, University of Chicago, and the Illinois State Psychiatric Institute.

Schizophrenia, wrote McFie Campbell, is "a Greek letter society, the conditions for admission to which are obscure; inclusion in and exclusion from the fraternity are determined by considerations which may vary from year to year and from place to place, and the directing board is not known" [2].

Meehl [13] has outlined a schizophrenic spectrum consisting of schizotaxic, schizotypic, and schizophrenic subtypes, the definition and boundaries of which are not clear. Some authors still write about borderline schizophrenics, despite the fact that the borderline syndrome [7] is not a phase of schizophrenia and persons either are schizophrenics or are not.

Clinical psychiatrists have observed unmistakable changes in the form and content of neuroses and psychoses during the last 20 years. The psychoses are shorter lasting, less detached from reality, and less dramatic. It has been suggested that the antischizophrenic and antidepressant drugs have affected the form and course of psychiatric entities. However, even the psychoses developing before the legitimate use of drugs were less dramatic than in earlier eras. In investigations of young first-break schizophrenics we have observed that the acute psychotic break is short-lived and that the subjects remember and honestly recount the details of their delusions or hallucinations. These patients reveal more affect than is usually described. They are depressed, lonely, and devoid of feelings of pleasure, with relatively little cognitive disturbance or associative slippage. They seem, in general, to recognize their social limitations and seriously attempt to adapt to their schizophrenic process.

The timing of the appearance of each state helps slightly in differentiating them. Only anhedonia seems to appear early in life and continue through acute psychotic disorganization and after, although in varying degrees. The absence of notable degrees of pleasure begins early in life, even before the competitive school years. Patients complain that they never really had fun and have difficulty remembering pleasurable incidents. The first sentences during an interview with young first-break schizophrenics reveal the plaintive, sad, soft, somewhat whiny voice that invites an almost irresistible desire on the part of the interviewer to touch, hold, and comfort his patient. Experienced psychotherapists recognize that such an instant positive countertransference is an obstacle rather than an asset in the treatment of a patient who needs help overcoming his intense dependency.

Depression appears somewhat later, in early adolescence and young adulthood, and seems to become manifest when life experiences have already been met with failure or incompetence. The depressed feeling may also occur during a breakdown or on reorganization from psychotic episodes, when the patient is faced with returning to the world of external reality (which is never easy to rejoin) and is aware of the developmental obstructions in his pathway.

Kayton [9] has described four phases in the clinical course during treatment of psychotic schizophrenics. Phase II, after the psychotic period of internal disorganization, he calls postpsychotic regression. There are feelings of loneliness, weakness, badness, emptiness, and many hypochondriacal concerns. Also there is impaired concentration, attention, and reasoning, with many long silences in therapeutic interviews. It is this phase of recovery that simulates and might be misinterpreted as depression. Yet most of these symptoms disappear during phase III, spontaneously or as a result of firmness and structure setting, although occasional periods of depression do occur:

With the beginning emotional investment in a more real, external good object there was an increasing vulnerability to disappointment and rejection. With a perceived rejection, or anger at the therapist or staff member, there was a fairly predictable sequence of events that could be discerned. First, there was a feeling of being totally deserted and alone. This was followed by intense self-abomination with feelings of worthlessness and being completely unlovable. In many instances, this was, in turn, followed by a temporary return of the bad objects. With the re-establishment of contact there would again be a disappearance of the bad object [9].

This postpsychotic depression is given various names, such as depressed-neurasthenia phase, and is said to last for a variable period of time but not to occur in all patients. There are conflicting views as to whether the postpsychotic regression, characterized by depression, presages a good outcome in the schizophrenic or is a necessary condition for recovery. An explanatory hypothesis is that the regression releases early infantile behaviors that have been inhibited and that going through this period again is a "corrective emotional experience." If so, it should be permitted for a time and not subjected to interpretations. How long a time to permit it is disputed currently and at present can be determined only by the judgment of the therapist or by a spontaneous shift in the patient's state toward improved socialization, sleeping, eating, and grooming.

The term schizophrenia covers a plurality of conditions still categorized to great extent according to the original Kraepelinian classification with modifications. There is, however, a spectrum of schizophrenias and schizotypic conditions, based on a variety of factors from biogenetic to sociogenic, including the neurotic overlay induced by special life experiences. As a result there is a bewildering array of symptom pictures, including those heavily loaded with biological defects (erroneously called process schizophrenia) and those with lesser loading who break down after severe challenge to self-esteem, loss of dependable objects, or competition above thresholds of competence (erroneously called reactive schizophrenia). In other words, the schizophrenias may be precipitated or become apparent or enter a psychotic phase at any age from childhood to middle life.

The characteristics of the so-called process and reactive schizophrenias are well summarized by Garmezy [3]. Sometimes the contrasting terms good- and poor-prognosis schizophrenia are used instead, relying on outcome as a deciding factor. However, Strauss and Carpenter [15] have shown recently that outcome studies using factors of rehospitalization, social contacts, employment, and symptoms cannot be correlated with diagnosis and prediction. The fact that process schizophrenia reveals many prepsychotic indicators and reveals no acute precipitation and that reactive schizophrenia shows a good developmental history and a sudden precipitation suggests a continuum of strong and weak biogenic predisposition. In summary, anhedonia, although appearing early, and depression, occurring at any time in the course of schizophrenia, are not discriminating factors as far as we now know.

RELATIONSHIPS AMONG ANHEDONIA, DEPRESSION, AND SCHIZOPHRENIA

Since timing of onset is of limited value in defining anhedonia, depression, and schizophrenia, I must utilize another method for putting them on a comparable basis without impugning causative significance—a systems theory [1]. To do this, an organizational, structural, or functional whole and its relation to its parts and its environment needs to be defined.

In this sense schizophrenia is a system or a polyvalent outcome of several variables held together in an organization that constitutes a form of attempted functional adaptation. The form should be considered as an end product that has a high degree of variability both within and between individuals. Causation cannot be attributed to either the parts or the organizing processes. Life challenges are necessary to move a predisposed individual into an overt schizophrenia or eventually into a psychosis. Thus, schizophrenia may be defined as a system or organization that develops and changes. Anhedonia and depression then become essential to the system as significant part-causes or as results of the schizophrenic organization as it develops over time.

Anhedonia and depression appear in dissimilar degrees in the five diagnostic subcategories of schizophrenia *tentatively* utilized in schizophrenic research [5]. Anhedonia appears, in order from least to most, in acute schizophrenia, schizophrenia with convulsions, schizo-affective states, paranoid schizophrenia, and chronic schizophrenia. The order for depression from least to most is convulsive, chronic, acute, schizo-affective, and paranoid schizophrenia.

The following factors indicate the characteristics of schizophrenic thinking, feeling, and behavior: strong dependency on others, confusion, delusions, hallucinations, social incompetence, loss of impulse control, and weak sense of identity and self-regard [5]. Anxiety is not focal and does not discriminate the types of schizophrenia. It may appear as a pervasive feeling of going insane or "going to pieces." Depression and thoughts of suicide may be manifested when psychotic thinking ameliorates, or depression may be associated with repeated experiences of incompetence and may appear later in the course of the patient's difficulties.

On the other hand, the pervasive sadness or boredom begins very early in life. This anhedonia is directly related to a feeling of emptiness, loneliness, and lack of capacity to love anyone. Attempts to relate to other persons are constantly met with failure, so depression and suicidal thoughts are secondary consequences. Recognizing that anhedonia is an early manifestation of the schizophrenic system and determines the fate of other parts of the system, we could speculate that it represents a psychological manifestation of a more basic biological factor. On the other hand, even more speculatively, anhedonia may constitute the feeling state accompanying the early introject of a bad object with no good offset.

No achievement seems to neutralize the feeling of sadness. Rado [14] stated that anhedonia is found not only in overt schizophrenias but also in schizoid personalities. Associated with inherited predisposition for anxiety, or acquired anxiety, the power of pleasure as an organizing principle for personality structure is deficient. Even hospitalized nonschizophrenics report periods of enjoyment in the past and also in their current hospitalization. Furthermore, the improved schizophrenics view their future with pessimism and hold little prospect for pleasure. In Rado's sense, anhedonia is constitutionally derived, that is, a genetic deficit prevents subjective positive reinforcement of socially accepted behaviors and speech, and according to Watson [17], deters learning.

Using psychophysical methods, Kayton and Koh [10] showed experimentally that schizophrenics' free recall of *pleasant* words was decidedly poorer than that of nonschizophrenics and healthy controls.

On the other hand, their recall of *unpleasant* words was no different from that of other subjects. Also, the schizophrenic showed a lesser tendency to utilize features of pleasantness in their mnemonic organization. These experiments supported the hypothesis that many schizophrenics are incapable of experiencing and utilizing pleasurable emotions.

Many definitions and descriptions of schizophrenia use the term "flat affect." This is a serious error because anhedonia and its associated loneliness are terrible affective states. As Rado states, anhedonia weakens motivation to love, joy, pride, desire, affection, and zest, leading to withdrawal and loneliness, with which there is intense suffering. In no way can this be considered a flat affect.

CASE VIGNETTES

Of the rating scales in the Schizophrenic State Inventory (S.S.I.), used in interviews of young schizophrenics, only the following two are significant for the thesis of this chapter (see [5] for the complete scale).

III. Pleasure
    0. Pleasure in accordance with external events.
    1. Occasional but rare pleasure in accordance with external events.
    2. Occasional pleasure but discordant with external events.
    3. Lack of humor.
    4. No convincing report of ever having fun.
    5. No joy, exuberance, or knowledge of shared happiness.
    6. Constant sadness or boredom.

(V.) B. Affect
    0. Affect consistent with reality.
    1. Affect changeable during the same thoughts.
    2. Affect shifting rapidly in intensity.
    3. Ambivalence of affect toward the same object existing simultaneously without a feeling of paradox.
    4. Affect not congruent with the situation.
    5. Flatness or maintenance of a singular affect, as in the angry paranoid.
    6. Uncontrolled affects such as violent rages; affects observed not consistent with affects reported.

The diagnostic data are collected by a semistructured clinical interview and tape-recorded. The topics discussed cover megalomania, use of drugs, suicidal depression, anhedonia, anxiety, anger, dependency, humor, defenses, sexual behavior and preference, future planning, and others. The tapes are played back to a research team of two psychiatrists, one psychologist, and one social worker, and the ratings are recorded on the S.S.I. A graphic profile for each patient's ratings is obtained for rapid reference.

Case 1. The patient, a 22-year-old male, was interviewed during his second admission to the hospital with the complaint: "I feel empty and hopeless." His pleasure rating was 6, indicating constant sadness and boredom (see also Figure 1). He "broke down" for the first time while

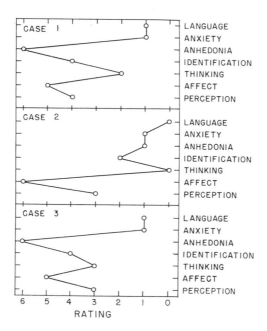

Figure 1. The three patients described in Cases 1, 2, and 3 when rated revealed the profiles shown. Cases 1 and 3 are high in anhedonia, with affect a little less high. Case 2 was high in affect and low in anhedonia. The relationship between these two items, however, is not reciprocal. In schizophrenics the affect may be, and usually is, depression only. Rarely is hypomania seen alone; it more often occurs along with depression, as in the manic-depressive syndrome. Data from Grinker [4].

in his second year of college. He became confused and lost control of himself. Sometimes in the middle of the night he would run around the block, screaming. He was a good student in high school, wanted to be top in his class and pressured himself to succeed. He uses no drugs. His family of 11 siblings contains no other disturbed person. All had high hopes for him, which he completely lacked. He is confused, often does not know who he is, and feels no love for anyone; he has never had sexual intercourse. He controls his confusion by returning to bed and then becomes extremely lonely. Again and again he attempts to be with people but gets confused. Fundamentally he is extremely dependent, looking at the interviewer with a beseeching expression, but he also fights to be independent. Television programs and movies seem to be real and related to him, and he has a number of hallucinations and delusions. At one time when these disappeared, he became depressed, with despair and hopelessness and thoughts of suicide, because his anxiety centers on "going insane" or inevitable lonely isolation.

Case 2. A 24-year-old single female patient has a high affect rating (affective inconsistency) precipitated by a deteriorating relationship with a man. She suddenly found herself in the hospital, out of touch with reality, but states that she is being tested biochemically for a regimen of lithium carbonate. Her first breakdown occurred at the age of 15 years; since then she had been in psychiatric treatment "on and off." Previous breakdowns occurred in adolescence, when her menstrual cycle was irregular and she feared that she could never be a woman. Another attack appeared without known cause, and another when she (erroneously) thought she was pregnant. She has had a number of depressions, with self-destructive behavior of banging her head against the wall and "purposely" failing in her activities. At other times she has "high" periods, for which lithium has been suggested, during which she frantically engages in continuous activity and talks incessantly. However, she has delusions that the Nazis and the Manson gang are after her, and she becomes frightened. Often she loses contact with reality—"flipping out," she calls it, with delusions and hallucinations and anxieties relating to impending death. She interposes the most serious statements with a peculiar laugh, even when relating how sad and isolated she has been. Although she has experienced well-documented hypomanic episodes and depressions, at the time of this report she is anxious, hallucinates, and has delusional thoughts.

Case 3. The patient, a 20-year-old female, was interviewed during her third week of hospitalization; before that she had been depressed for two weeks after a disappointment when her brother was divorced. Her troubles began at age 6 with a suicide attempt after being punished. Since then she has had a feeling of worthlessness and the expectation of a short and meaningless life. For the past 14 years of her life she has either been "high"—running about, excited, elated, and talking fast for periods of a few days to several months—or she has been depressed, with suicidal thoughts. Never has she felt in the "middle," between high and low. During depressions she paints with unhappy colors, mostly blue. In a self-portrait she painted her face blue. She feels that she has many friends and has enjoyed life but uses humor as a "cop-out," often overdoing it.

The patient cannot accept change easily (neophobia). There have been grave suspicions of others' motives. Periodically she hallucinates color flashes and figures, especially spiders, which she knows are not there. In general she has a continuous high level of anxiety and thoughts buzz rapidly through her head. When she hallucinates, she surrounds the figures of people with an imaginary picture frame from which she can turn away. There have been episodes of peculiar behavior termed "crazy" by her friends, but these she does not recall. No drugs are used. She feels that she never mourned for her deceased father and is constantly fighting a dependency on mother.

This patient reveals the thought disorder characterizing schizophrenia. She has rarely been on an even keel but rather is in either a manic or a depressive mood. The first paragraph suggests a diagnosis of manic-depressive psychosis, the second, schizophrenia. This young woman has clear evidences of schizophrenic thought disorders: the type of anxiety, delusions, hallucinations, and loss of sense of reality. But in addition she suffered from periods of hypomania and depressions associated with self-destructive behavior. The combination of such affective and cognitive disturbances has resulted in divergent diagnoses. American psychiatrists would more frequently call her schizophrenic, and the British, manic-depressive, 10 to 1 in either case. Most would hedge, diagnosing the condition as *schizo-affective*. This would be my tentative label, pending a long-term followup.

DISCUSSION

In my experience the schizophrenic thought disorder is not similar to that found in depressions, even in the so-called psychotic depressives, who are withdrawn and mute or who rock back and forth as they repetitively make the same complaints and ask the same questions, ignoring any answers. The differentiation between the cognitive dysfunction in depression and schizophrenia is not difficult.

The question arises whether the diagnosis of depressive or manic components in the schizophrenic syndrome might represent catatonic stupors or excitements in a mild form. I can only answer subjectively from clinical experience. Both depressive and manic attacks in schizophrenia apparently are truly affective disturbances in no way different from those seen in simple or bipolar depressive syndromes except of course for the schizophrenic thought disorders. The most commonly used diagnosis for patients who reveal combinations of depression and/or elation with schizophrenic thought disorder is schizo-affective schizophrenia, but the term good prognosis schizophrenia is also used.

McCabe et al. [12] conducted family studies of a group of schizo-affective schizophrenics. Criteria used in diagnosis were "illness of less than six months' duration, absence of a pre-existing diagnosis of psychiatric illness, a good premorbid personality," and "the presence of one of the following: catatonic traits, delusional depersonalization, passivity, symbolic disturbance, haptic hallucinations, special types of auditory hallucinations, other clear delusions which may not have shown clear symbolic disturbance, marked confusion with hallucinations, marked thought disorder." Their conclusions indicate an interesting genetic relationship between schizo-affective disorders and pure affective disorder:

> The schizo-affective families were found to have significantly less schizophrenia, neurosis, and overall psychiatric illness and significantly more affective disorder than schizophrenic families. Findings were consistent with previous studies comparing prognostically distinct groups which did not rely on blind interview and diagnosis of family members. The two groups were distinguishable both on the basis of prognosis and on the basis of family history. Schizo-affectives, although somewhat heterogeneous genetically, showed a strong familial relationship to the affective disorders.

Although their findings require confirmation, McCabe et al. state that the diagnosis of depression was found in 68 percent of good prognosis and 12 percent of poor prognosis schizophrenia. Mania was diagnosed in 46 percent of good prognosis and none in poor prognosis schizophrenia. Seventy-nine percent of all good prognosis schizophrenia had affective disorders. It would seem that a logical interpretation would consider that the affective component in good prognosis schizophrenics represents a capacity to react against rather than to accept the internal disorganization or the impact of the external stress, whatever it may be.

It seems clear that anhedonia and depression are separate parts of the schizophrenic system. Anhedonia appears early, usually long before the disease becomes apparent; hence it is dated by retrospective recall. It is associated in adolescence with feelings of emptiness and a feeling of loneliness and uncertain identity. Many patients cut themselves to feel pain or see blood in order to make sure that they are alive. These do not constitute suicide attempts. We can only speculate that anhedonia, if biogenetic, represents some disturbance in the pleasure centers of the brain or in the adrenergic conduction system.

Depression appears later and seems to represent a variety of reactions, such as feeling of impending disorganization, hopelessness and regression at the time of the breakdown, and the pessimism afterward of returning to the world of reality. Whereas anhedonia seems to represent a deficiency [8], depression is more likely a result of conflict or a defense. Manic and hypomanic attacks seem to constitute a last-ditch stand against an impending depression (as Ostow also suggests in Chapter 16). Yet depressions in schizophrenics may appear before any evidence of thought disorder, and I believe that youthful depressions should make one suspect the possibility of a schizophrenia in the process of becoming overtly recognizable.

Vaillant [16] considers that depression as an affect may indicate a good outcome, since it expresses an insight into the present and future. It presupposes the recognition that something is wrong. As one of my patients, who felt empty and devoid of feeling, stated, as she became depressed, "I have feelings now and therefore know that I am better." Patients who have a hereditary background of manic-depressive psychosis and whose symptoms suggest a psychotic depression seem to have a better outcome. Anhedonia represents no feelings —nothing is good; it does not progress, and if anything, has a poor prognosis.

The schizo-affective mixture and the frequent family history of affective disorders leads to the old question of a single disease entity, to which my experience does not lend credence. Still, schizophrenic probands often have a family history of multiple types of psychopathology. The only firm conclusion possible, until such time as faulty genes may be discovered, is that there are a variety of psychiatric conditions that sometimes occur in isolation and sometimes in combination. But the most common affective disorders in schizophrenia are anhedonia and depression, and sometimes hypomania. Thought disorders in schizophrenia are unique and unlike simple or bipolar depressions. Sometimes delinquent behavior in the young seems to be an attempt to cover up the loneliness and depression of the schizophrenic. Further knowledge of the role of anhedonia and depression in schizophrenia must await the results of long-term follow-up studies.

REFERENCES

1. von Bertalanffy, L. General systems theory: A critical review. *Yearbook of the Society for General Systems Theory*, 7:1, 1962.
2. Campbell, C. M. *Destiny and Disease in Mental Disorders with Special Reference to the Schizophrenic Psychosis.* New York: Norton, 1935.
3. Garmezy, N. Process and Reactive Schizophrenia: Some Conceptions and Issues. In M. M. Katz, J. O. Cole, and W. E. Barton (Eds.), *The Role and Methodology of Classification in Psychiatry and Psychopathology.* Washington, D.C.: U.S. Government Printing Office, 1968.
4. Grinker, R. R., Sr. The Relevance of General Systems Theory to Psychiatry. In D. Hamburg and Brodie (Eds.), *American Handbook of Psychiatry*, vol. 6. New York: Basic Books, in press.
5. Grinker, R. R., Sr., and Holzman, P. S. Schizophrenic pathology in young adults—A clinical study. *Arch. Gen. Psychiatry* 28:168, 1973.
6. Grinker, R. R., Sr. et al. *The Phenomena of Depressions.* New York: Hoeber, 1961.

7. Grinker, R. R., Sr., Werble, B., and Drye, R. C.   *The Borderline Syndrome*. New York: Basic Books, 1968.
8. Holzman, P.   *The Influence of Theoretical Models on the Treatment of the Schizophrenics*, in press.
9. Kayton, L.   Good outcome in young improved adult schizophrenics, *Arch. Gen. Psychiatry* 29:103, 1973.
10. Kayton, L., and Koh, S. D.   Pleasure-deficit in non-psychotic schizophrenics: Roche report. *Frontiers of Psychiatry* 3:17, 1973.
11. Lehmann, H. E.   Psychiatric concepts of depression: Nomenclature and classification. *Can. Psychiatr. Assoc. J., Special Supplement,* 4:1, 1959.
12. McCabe, M. S., et al.   Family studies in schizophrenia: A comparison of schizophrenic and schizo-affective families. *Am. J. Psychiatry* 128:1239, 1972.
13. Meehl, P.   Schizotaxis, schizotypy and schizophrenia. *Am. Psychol.* 17:827, 1962.
14. Rado, S.   *Psychoanalysis of Behavior: Collected Papers,* vol. 1. New York: Grune & Stratton, 1956.
15. Strauss, J. S., and Carpenter, W. T.   Prediction of outcome in schizophrenia. *Arch. Gen. Psychiatry* 27:739, 1972.
16. Vaillant, G. E.   The prediction of recovery in schizophrenia. *J. Nerv. Ment. Dis.* 135:534, 1962.
17. Watson, C. G.   Relationships of anhedonia to learning under various contingencies. *J. Abnorm. Psychol.* 80:43, 1972.

Treatment

IV

The three papers included in Part IV of the book have not only prac-
tical significance but also theoretical implications. Other chapters
dealing with clinical problems have made reference to therapeutic
approaches and difficulties, and in some instances the choice of ther-
apy has helped to clarify the psychopathology and thus has thrown
further light on theory. In this section, however, the focus is primarily
on treatment and the lessons to be learned from it. The first two
contributions concern themselves with the psychoanalysis of depres-
sive patients, calling attention to the often neglected fact that besides
being a method of investigation and self-development psychoanalysis
is, and always has been, a method of therapy.

A prerequisite for successful treatment is precise diagnostic and
prognostic evaluations of the patient within the framework of the
therapeutic method employed. With respect to psychoanalysis, for
instance, it is important for the therapist to construct what Greenson
[3] has called a working model of the particular patient's psyche in
terms of what is known of his development, his diagnosis, the etiologi-
cal factors involved in his illness, the characteristics of his mental ap-
paratus, his defense system, and his methods of mastering internal
and external anxieties and depressions. This particular working model
is then compared to other working models derived from the therapist's
experience and reading, making prognosis possible. The analyst must
remember, however, that his working model is highly flexible and
that during the course of psychoanalysis the factors responsible for
the depressive illness undergo changes that in turn affect the dynamic
constellation. The external result of such shifts is reflected in mood
and behavior changes in the patient. In a well-conducted analysis, the

426

evaluative process runs parallel with the analytic process in the mind of the analyst.

Psychoanalysts who analyze patients suffering from depressive disorders, as in all psychoanalytic treatment, focus on the developmental conflicts. Nor does the technique vary whether the depression stems from a symbiotic fixation of the mother or from a narcissistic conflict with marked fluctuations in self-esteem. Furthermore, because depression is a recurrent illness, its recurrence in the course of treatment could be brought about by factors that had not occurred before; accordingly, the depressive symptoms, whether psychic or somatic, may vary in severity and give varying prognostic indications. Indeed, "parameters" or variations in technique are introduced frequently and mostly intuitively in the analysis of every depressed patient.

The change in focus in the psychoanalytic treatment of depression, as represented in the next three chapters, can be best measured by comparing the authors' views with the views of Abraham fifty years ago when the main emphasis was on the libidinal aspects [1]. Abraham was characteristically cautious about making exaggerated claims for psychoanalysis but there were certain betterments it brought about, he thought, over and above the symptomatic relief furnished by other therapies. He had noticed significant reductions in the amount of narcissism and "negative attitude" and improvements in self-esteem and heterosexual genital interest. There were two therapeutic developments that were peculiar to the analytic situation: the patient's capacity for transference was enhanced by the analytic work, and the symptoms of the free interval, previously parathymic, became neurotic. The mental relief brought about by these improvements was often "quite astonishing." A good deal depended on when the analysis was undertaken, and in this he followed Freud's advice by instituting treatment when the patients were just coming out of the depressive state.

Because of her broad range of experience in treating depressive disorders, Jacobson in Chapter 20, is able to isolate specific problems that influence the general course of therapy. For example, she discusses the significance of the analyst's emotional attitude toward his patient in forecasting the development of transference and, consequently, the analyzability of the patient. In her view, countertransference is unavoidable and represents a dynamic factor in the treatment process. The inevitable idealization of the analyst by the depressive patient and the subsequent disappointment that goes along with this may create difficult, if not unsolvable, problems for the inexperienced therapist; but in competent and experienced hands, the appropriate management of these tendencies can help to further the progress of

treatment. Most analysts would probably agree that depressive pa-
tients are exquisitively sensitive to initial contacts and probably are
best treated by those with whom they empathically click and who, in
turn, respond warmly to them. In such cases the analyst walks a nar-
row line between accusations of seductiveness and rejection. Jacobson
reminds us that the analysis of depression is not without its anxieties
for the analyst, since suicide and psychotic breakdown are always
"just around the corner," but she is most reassuring in her final com-
ment that none of her patients have ever decompensated psychoti-
cally during analysis.

Anthony, in his analysis of two depressed adolescent girls of about
the same age, contrasts their personalities, their psychodynamics, and
the differing psychoanalytic processes involved in their treatment.
Like Jacobson, he views the countertransference, which also differs
with respect to the two patients, as the ongoing reaction of the analyst
to the patient—the natural outcome of his participation in the two-
body system—and not as a fault of the analyst. He also discusses the
activation or reactivation of depressive affects in the therapist as he is
gradually absorbed into the depressive constellation of the patient.

It is now generally accepted that the clinical use of drugs in de-
pression has brought about some very gratifying results. It seemed
important, therefore, to have a psychoanalyst experienced in both
forms of treatment describe the adjunctive use of chemotherapy in
psychoanalysis. Ostow groups the various chemical agents according
to their effectiveness as psychic energizers when there is a depletion
of energy and as tranquilizers when there is a "plethora of energy."
The links between psychoanalysis and pharmacology are evident. The
psychopharmacology appears to follow and to some extent substan-
tiate the theories emerging from neurochemical investigations de-
scribed in the early chapters. The energy depletion concept would
give support to the hypothesis of conservation-withdrawal. Within
the framework of this energy theory, Ostow explains the manic epi-
sode as a countervailing emergency supply for "defense" in the face of
a threatened depletion of energy. This "energy" theory differs in some
important respects from that of Wolpert, but the two hypotheses do
not exclude each other.

Ostow stresses the fact that the affective disorders originate in the
primary object relationship and that the depressive core is composed
of guilt, self-criticism, and loss of self-esteem. The meaning of chemo-
therapy to the patient's psychodynamics must then be understood
within this framework. What comes through in this chapter is the
way in which the experienced analyst makes full use of everything
that occurs in the analytic situation to further the analytic process.

The analyst who uses chemotherapy must be well acquainted with the indications for chemotherapy and well aware of the influence it might have on the analytic process. He must use this "chemical support" with sensitivity and sophistication. Like Jacobson, Ostow has reassuring comments for the inexperienced. In no case of his has antidepressant medication led to addiction and in no case has its discontinuance been resisted.

This is no place for the pharmacologically inept, since thorough knowledge and experience are necessary in deploying the drugs successfully; one should be fully acquainted with their effectiveness and their levels of reliability. Even in the most skilled hands, there are many unknowables in the way biochemical and physiological factors will behave in relation to the drug, and the result may be quite unexpected. The prescriber always has an obligation to observe very carefully the response to the drug and the presence of any unusual reactions. The prescribing psychoanalyst must know these basic pharmacological facts but must also be able to follow, analyze, and differentiate those elements of the patient's reaction that may be interpersonal or transference and to determine what to attribute to psychological factors and what to physical ones.

Chemotherapy cannot heal the aching mind of the depressive patient, but it may be potent in relieving him of the weight of his affective burden. As psychoanalysts, we have to realize that chemotherapy is not merely an adjunct to therapy but opens up new avenues for the observation of intrapsychic processes. The ideas contained in Ostow's chapter are so near to what Freud had in mind in the last decade of his life and so near to what we have had in mind as the purpose of this book that we quote directly from one of his letters: "The hope of the future here lies in organic chemistry or the access to it through endocrinology. This future is still far distant, but one should study analytically every case of psychosis because this knowledge will one day guide the chemical therapy" [emphasis added; 2, p. 480]. We, too, feel that the hope of the future lies in such a collaboration.

REFERENCES

1. Abraham, K. A Short Study of the Development of the Libido, Viewed in the Light of Mental Disorders. In *Selected Papers of Karl Abraham, M.D.* London: Hogarth Press, 1949.
2. Freud, S. Letters to M. B., January 15, 1930. Quoted in E. Jones, *The Life and Work of Sigmund Freud*, vol. 3. New York: Basic Books, 1957. P. 480.
3. Greenson, R. R. *The Technique and Practice of Psychoanalysis*, vol. 1. New York: International Universities Press, 1967.

18

The Psychoanalytic Treatment of Depressive Patients

EDITH JACOBSON

DIFFERENTIAL DIAGNOSIS IN RELATION TO TREATMENT

Not only all emotionally disturbed persons but also normal persons may occasionally suffer from depressive states; in patients undergoing psychoanalytic treatment these may even temporarily become worse in response to certain transference experiences, memory material, and interpretations. The analysis of such depressive reactions does not offer any particular treatment problems except in patients whose outstanding complaints revolve about their tendency to develop severe recurring, brief or long-lasting, depressive conditions. The analysis of such patients presents special technical problems, with which this chapter will deal.

Such severely depressed patients may be neurotic, borderline psychotic, or psychotic, but what they have in common is their narcissistic vulnerability, their tendency to react to disappointments and narcissistic injuries with intense feelings of hurt and hostility, resulting in more or less enduring states of depression, with loss of self-esteem and self-derogatory attitudes and behavior.

I tend to regard differential diagnostic considerations in general as very significant, but in severely depressive patients they are of special importance. When we are sure that the patient suffers from severe neurotic states of depression and we expect him to be accessible to analysis, we shall certainly suggest analytic treatment, if he can afford it. If in doubt we may accept him for a trial period. However, there are more cases than we like to admit in which we cannot be sure that our diagnostic judgment is valid.

Many years ago an eminent psychiatrist referred a female consultant to me for analytic treatment because after the death of her beloved aunt she had developed what he believed to be a severe neurotic

431

depression. During the treatment I discovered, to my surprise, that the patient suffered from a reactive depression but also that in spite of the clearly psychotic nature of her illness she was accessible to analytic treatment.

I followed up this case, which had turned my attention to the problem of depression, for over 30 years. Although this patient continued to have mild periods of depression, the therapeutic results were so good that they encouraged me to take a few other, carefully selected patients who suffered from periods of psychotic depression into analytic treatment and also some severely depressive neurotic, borderline psychotic, and even some schizophrenic patients.

My clinical observations led me to the conclusion that the differential diagnosis in some severely depressive patients is much more difficult than we usually believe. Of course, it is easy enough to diagnose a typical case of "endogenous depression" that presents all the familiar characteristic symptoms. But there are quite a number of cases of psychotic depression in which we are not sure whether they belong to the manic-depressive or the schizophrenic group. In other cases we need time to find out whether the patient is neurotic, borderline psychotic, or psychotic. But in severely depressive patients the diagnosis is significant because our choice of treatment depends on it. We have to decide whether this is a patient who should be hospitalized because of suicidal danger and get not only antidepressant drugs but even electric shock treatment, or whether the patient should get either supportive or psychoanalytically oriented psychotherapy or full analytic treatment.

There are no rules that can be applied with regard to these decisions. They depend on the individual case and one's own clinical judgment and experience. Moreover, there are definite differences of opinion regarding this matter among analysts. Some analysts are opposed to the analytic treatment not only of psychotics but even of borderline psychotics [4, 5]. Evidently, Kohut refers to schizophrenic patients or those verging on schizophrenia. He does not mention cases of simple or bipolar psychotic depression. At any rate, he is afraid of the danger of a regression during analysis that might provoke acute psychotic episodes. I personally believe that this depends on the technique applied in such cases, the analytic work on their special defenses, the timing and wording of the interpretations, the handling of transference, and the like.

I want to emphasize that none of the few psychotics or borderline psychotic patients I have analyzed ever developed psychotic episodes during treatment and that they showed good therapeutic results. However, this is not the place for a discussion of treatment problems in psychotics. We are concerned only with the therapeutic problems arising in the analysis of depressive conditions.

Depressive conditions originate in the special narcissistic disturbances that in many severely depressive patients relate to a borderline personality organization manifesting primitive defense mechanisms, primitive oral aggressive conflicts and extreme self-centeredness (so aptly described by Kernberg [4] and Kohut[5]). But neither of these authors refers specifically to the difficulties arising in the treatment of severely depressive patients.

What is so decisive from the standpoint of the analysis of depressive patients, and in particular of their transference problems, is their tendency to idealize or overrate the people to whom they are attached and, hence, to expect them to be, to do, and to give more than they realistically can. Their overexpectations are rooted in their special narcissistic type of relation to the persons to whom they are attached. It is significant that depressives who belong to the manic-depressive group do not want or tend to have symbiotic relations to their love objects. In contrast to schizophrenic or borderline psychotic patients, they do not suffer from fears or feelings of loss of identity. But in general depressive patients are inclined to turn the people they are close to into both their critical superego, on whose approval or disapproval they depend, and their ego-ideal, which represents what they themselves would like to be. Naturally, there are differences between the various types of depressive patients regarding their dependency on the love object and on the outside world in general [3]. Obsessive-compulsives, for example, who suffer from recurring depressions, may ward off their passive-dependent trends by an aggressive, rebellious independence, particularly with regard to their opinions or moral standards and their behavior. In contrast to psychotic depressives, they even rebel against their own superegos and their guilt feelings, as noted by Freud [1].

IDEALIZATION OF THE ANALYST
BY THE DEPRESSED PATIENT

In most severely depressive cases the patient begins the treatment with a visible idealization of the analyst.

Case 1. One such patient, a young analyst, told me that he had not wanted to go to his training analyst because this man had never written an important paper, which was, indeed, his own ambition. He admitted that this analyst had helped him in his love life, but not regarding his writing inhibitions. Hence the treatment ended with a postanalytic depression. In this case it turned out that the patient in seven years of analysis had never emotionally accepted certain interpretations. It is true that his analyst probably did not interpret defenses well enough and gave him too early interpretations referring to his infantile instinctual conflicts. But the essential point was the patient's complete derogation of his analyst, which he had never dared to express because, being a student, he was scared that he would be thrown out of the Institute. Hence, he seemingly submitted but complained about his analyst to others, including his supervising analyst. In spite of this he did not change analysts.

Only after his graduation did he come to me, and he faithfully repeated the pattern, though in a somewhat different way. He started off with an overidealization that was very unrealistic. He was one of those cases with whom one could not let the "idealizing" transference grow without touching it [5]. I pointed out to him very soon the extent to which he aggrandized and idealized me. He immediately brought up material that clearly showed that his transference revived his early relationship to his father. I did not analyze this memory material referring to his father except to show him soon how he had later felt severely disappointed in his father, who had once been a very successful man but went into a severe depression, became unable to work, and died of a coronary attack. His depressive conditions started after the loss of his father.

I showed the patient how he usually first idealized any colleagues who, unlike himself, had discussed or written a paper but then always found a good reason to be disappointed and finally derogated them to an extent they did not deserve. I emphasized that the time would come when he would feel disappointed in me and try to derogate me in the same way as he had with others.

What we can learn from this case is, first, that depressive patients should not be treated by an analyst whom they immediately reject or dislike or cannot relate to. Most often we can find this out during the first interview or interviews, i.e., before we start the analysis. In such a case we do better not to accept the patient for analysis because his initial rejection or hostility interferes with the treatment. I may add that in my experience depressives do better with analysts who have some natural warmth than with those who are emotionally detached or even have a negative countertransference.

Naturally, this does not mean that the analyst should be in any way seductive in his attitudes. Depressives frequently have the tendency to accuse the analyst alternatively of being too seductive and overly gratifying and of being too frustrating and rejecting. This cannot be avoided but must be carefully analyzed.

The analysand's initial feelings and the analyst's counterattitudes must be such that they allow the depressive patient to develop an idealizing transference. The early interpretation of such a patient's tendency first to aggrandize and idealize the analyst and then to feel disappointed in him is of great value for their further analysis because it prepares them for the negative transference that will make its appearance in the future.

These ambivalence conflicts are bound to develop in all depressives, but in many cases they may and must remain unconscious for a long time. This was not true in the case of the very narcissistic-ambivalent young analyst to whom I referred above. In the transference and otherwise he would quickly and suddenly swing from admiration with feelings of elation to derogation leading to depression, and in either state he would tend to deny the opposite feelings he had had in the past. Anyhow, with him, as with other severely depressive patients, the analysis of the negative transference is a very difficult problem, one to which I shall return.

Let me first underscore how careful we must be to understand certain differences between severely neurotic patients and psychotic depressives. No doubt in melancholic patients, their ideas of worthlessness or delusions of sinfulness reflect directly their complaints about their love object, whose faults are introjected into the self-image. This narcissistic identification is a primitive defense mechanism caused by their regression to early developmental stages. For this reason we do not find it in neurotic depressive patients, even though they also attempt to ward off their hostility by turning it to the self. The content of their self reproaches is not the same as that of their accusations. To be sure, the turning of aggression against the self is always a defensive device that intends to protect the love object and prevent the ego from any hostile impulses and actions toward the external world. The handling of this defense represents a difficult therapeutic problem in all severely depressive patients, especially when they have paranoid trends. This leads back to the difficult question how we should approach the negative transference in depressive patients.

MANAGEMENT OF THE NEGATIVE TRANSFERENCE
IN THE DEPRESSED PATIENT

I asked a young, gifted, very intelligent female supervisee, who wanted to discuss a compulsive depressive patient with me, about her ideas regarding the interpretation of the underlying hostility and sadism in such patients. She said: "You have to approach it as rapidly as you can." The opposite is true, but many inexperienced analysts do precisely what this beginner said, with very unfortunate results. As long as such patients are in a depressive mood and suffer from guilt feelings, they are unable to accept the fact that they have severe ambivalence conflicts. The interpretation of their underlying hostility can only raise their guilt feelings. In patients who suffer from periods of psychotic depression, reference to their ambivalence may sometimes not have such bad results, if you happen to see them first during the time preceding the depression. As Rado [6] pointed out, the patients are at that time very irritable or even frankly aggressive and complain about their partners and friends.

Case 2.   One patient, who suffered from attacks of involutional depression, would at this stage make bitter complaints to me about her husband's shortcomings, which were exaggerated but not entirely unreasonable. As she became depressed she began to express the same complaints about herself and suddenly stopped, saying: "I feel so confused, I no longer know whether I am talking about my husband or myself." This patient was not in analytic treatment but in a supportive psychotherapy with me. She could easily observe on her own that her depressive state was caused by her bitter complaints about her husband. At that point she told me that years ago, she had tried to run away from her husband. But after a disappointing love affair she had promptly returned to him.

This is characteristic of depressives. Unlike schizophrenics, who frequently do change therapists, true depressives are commonly unable to leave their love object and hence do not leave their therapists. The young analyst who complained about his training analyst to others stayed with him nevertheless for many years, though with good rationalizations. Only after he had been discharged by the analyst did he come to me for further treatment.

To return to the interpretation of the hostility conflicts in depressives, I would repeat that we must be very cautious and slow in our interpretations of the underlying hostility and death wishes, since they may intensify the depression and the feelings of guilt and even lead to suicidal impulses. Otherwise, as in so many masochistic patients, we may get "negative therapeutic results."

THE SPECIAL PROBLEM
OF THE PARANOID-DEPRESSIVE PATIENT

This problem of interpretation is even worse in paranoid-depressive patients, whose initial admiration may change rather suddenly into paranoid-hostile attitudes. If one points out the change and the provocativeness of the remarks, the patient may become both more provocatively aggressive and more depressed. One such patient, whose analyst had neglected to interpret her extremely masochistic behavior and constantly stressed her hostility, ended her treatment by making such hostile remarks that he threw her out, whereupon she went into a suicidal depression.

Of course, the analysis of paranoid patients is always a difficult task, one that I cannot discuss in this chapter. But I want to emphasize that analysts who tend to develop a negative countertransference to paranoid patients should not accept them for treatment. I have seen several cases in which the treatment went wrong because the analyst could not tolerate and handle the paranoid hostile transference. Unfortunately, paranoid patients have an uncanny talent for finding out their therapists' most vulnerable spots and, despite the "distance" required by the therapeutic procedure, get to know some of their weaknesses.

Case 3. One compulsive-depressive patient managed to discover that her very experienced analyst had an only child whom he loved very dearly. She also managed to notice that he himself was for some time in a depressed state. During a stage of very negative transference, which revived her bad relationship to her unpleasant father, she told him not only about his own depression that prevented him from helping her but also some very bad stories she had heard about his child. The analyst was so upset that instead of giving her the transference interpretation she needed, he talked about the wonderful qualities of his beloved child. Even later, he completely neglected interpretations of her transference reactions and soon stopped her treatment, telling her that the traumatic events of her first years of life made further analysis and improvement impossible. She went into treatment with another analyst, understood what she had done, and this time was able to undergo a proper analysis, which has not yet been completed but looks rather promising.

I may add that this case is also of interest because this patient's anxious-depressive states revolved exclusively around her professional efforts. At home, with her husband and children, when she was doing only housework, she felt no depression, and during her vacations she was very happy and quite free of anxiety. In fact, she loves her family and is fairly unambivalent toward them. As soon as she works in the field for which she was professionally trained, she becomes severely anxious and depressed, expecting failure. Her conflicts do not revolve about her love objects, that is, her husband and children, but about her "authorities." They represent the parents who had objected to her ambitious wishes to get professional training.

This example shows that the ambivalence conflicts of depressive patients need not necessarily be aroused by their partners or current love objects or, as with the young depressed psychiatrist, heterosexual love objects. In his case, like the woman just described, the depressive conflicts were aroused by his professional work and not by his wife, to whom he was happily married. Although his mother played a great role in his preoedipal conflicts, his depressive conflict was essentially a homosexual conflict.

Such differential reactions are of paramount importance for the analytic handling of depressive cases. The analyst may easily shift the focus from the specific objects on which the depressive conflicts are centered to objects that are not essential in the patient's ambivalence or inferiority and guilt feelings.

SIGNIFICANCE OF CURRENT LOVE OBJECT

Of course, in many or most depressive cases, the ambivalence toward the partner or the current love object plays the most significant part in the patient's depression. The complaints are often quite justified.

Case 4. A professional woman whom I treated many years ago suffered from a psychotic depression. Unfortunately I had to refer her to another psychiatrist for reasons of a severe physical illness. She reacted to this abandonment with such a severe depression that she had to get shock treatment. Although she was discharged as "cured," this patient committed suicide on the day on which she was supposed to return to me for further treatment. After her successful suicide her husband came to see me in a mildly hypomanic mood and admitted what she had told me and what he had always denied: that he had never been able to love her and had been glad to get rid of her. He could not tolerate her intellectual superiority. Only a brief time after her death he remarried, this time a simple, domestic girl with whom he happily lived ever after.

This unfortunate case contains an important warning. When we treat a patient with a psychotic depressive condition, we must be prepared to hospitalize him when he shows signs of suicidal impulses and not allow him to be discharged too early. Furthermore, we must pay attention to the patient's reports of the partner's feelings and attitudes toward him.

In other cases in which the patient's severe depression was caused by the partner's unloving behavior or cheating, I was able to get the latter into treatment.

Case 5. In the case of a female patient who suffered from a severe depressive condition, the husband's treatment ended in a divorce, with the surprising result that the former wife never had depressive conditions again.

Case 6. In another case the husband stopped cheating his wife and became so nice and attentive that the patient recovered from her very long-lasting depression and never relapsed again. In fact, she became so active that she went through a prolonged professional training related to the husband's activity, and then accepted and worked successfully in a professional job. She has never had another depression, except for one brief mild episode after the loss of her father and older sister. At that time, she did not even need any psychotherapy but took an antidepressant that was very helpful.

These cases are of a different category than those in which the patients, frequently females, make such masochistic choices of sexual partners that they are soon abandoned and react with a depression until another person turns up with whom the same story repeats itself. These are patients with a fate neurosis that leads to recurring states of depression.

Case 7.   One female patient, whose ambivalence to men prevented her from getting married, managed to get seduced by her married therapist, who started a brief affair with her and then abandoned her in a very unpleasant manner. This repeated her oedipal relationship with her father, who had been very seductive but rejected her abruptly when a boy was born. Only after her first treatment did she develop severe depressive states. Her major current conflicts and fantasies revolved about the former therapist. She actually refused to give him up as a love object, even though she constantly needed "a man," who represented a substitute penis. To her the loss of the therapist meant above all a castration, which revived intense infantile castration wishes toward men and made her unable to get orgastic gratification.

THE CASTRATION CONFLICT IN DEPRESSED WOMEN

Gero [2] correctly pointed out the significance of the castration conflict in depressive women. He regards this conflict as the reason for the greater frequency of depression in women than in men. This indicates why the thorough analysis of the female penis envy and castration conflict is of such special importance in the treatment of neurotic depressives. In my experience there are also male depressive patients in whose analysis the unconscious idea of being castrated plays an extraordinary part. This was the case, for example, in the young psychiatrist to whom I have repeatedly referred. In fact I found it very frequently in orphans and semiorphans who had lost their father at an early age, when they needed him most. They reacted to the object loss as to a castration because of the narcissistic nature of their relationship to the father. At the time of the loss such patients may react with a state of depression, and, remaining arrested at this stage, they may later on develop a great narcissistic vulnerability and predisposition for states of depression. These problems have to be understood, interpreted, and thoroughly worked through in the analysis of such patients.

INFANTILE CONFLICTS IN
SEVERELY DEPRESSED PATIENTS

Let me now turn to a more general analysis of infantile conflicts in severely depressive patients. I have spoken above about the necessity to approach their hostility conflicts very gradually, even though the analyst might call the patient's attention early to his idealizing transference and the likelihood of a disappointment in the future. This does not imply that we should go into the hostility, its infantile origins, and infantile conflict situations in general at an early stage of the analysis. However, even in the analysis of severely depressive or even borderline psychotic and psychotic patients, we should not hesitate to allow early infantile material finally to come to the surface. Not only does the analysis of early infantile material and preoedipal oral and anal conflicts not lead to a dangerous regression, but the opposite is true—it may lead to a remarkably good therapeutic result.

OBJECT RELATIONS AND IDENTIFICATIONS
IN DEPRESSED PATIENTS

Let me turn here to the analysis of the object relations and identifications, and of the guilt and inferiority conflicts of depressive patients. Of course these conflicts as such are commonly on the surface, except in hysterical patients, whose guilt feelings may be denied and may need time to come to awareness.

The infantile roots of the guilt, shame, and inferiority conflicts are hidden and must be only gradually uncovered and analyzed in connection with the patient's underlying or even manifestly ambivalent attitudes toward the parents and siblings, and their origins. This includes the analysis of the patient's identifications. The analysis of the latter is of particular significance in the case of patients with parents whose bad qualities had not lent themselves to idealization and hence to the building up of a stable superego and an ego-ideal modeled after them. Such patients tend to develop a reactive counterideal, i.e., an ego-ideal that is the opposite of what the parents had been like. Most such efforts, which are often quite conscious, are not fully successful because their ego-ideal, as it were, "dangles in the air." If such patients have at least grandparents or other relatives who can serve as models, they are better off. Usually they show a split in their ego identifications that is responsible for their depressive conditions. Their ego-ideal becomes too perfectionistic, and their superego is too strict and blames them profoundly for any attitudes that reveal their identification with the despised parents.

Case 8. A good example is the female patient to whom I briefly referred above. She was a young woman who had allowed herself to be seduced by her first analyst, whom she had initially greatly admired. She came from an unfortunate background. Her father was a professional man who had evidently married his wife mainly for financial reasons. Since he had been in the war, the patient had lived only with her mother until she was 3. The father had been very seductive with her, but when another child was born he turned away from her and gave all his attention to the second child because it was a boy. At the same time the girl began to notice that her parents frequently quarreled with each other, that her father became more and more withdrawn and involved in his work, and that her very domineering and possessive mother hated and constantly derogated her husband, men in general, her neighbors, and her own children. The child tried to get love from her mother by becoming very submissive and overly dependent on her. Unconsciously she became very critical and hostile to both parents, but particularly toward men. She built up a reactive ego-ideal and wanted to be a loving and understanding wife and mother but also to be a professional like her father. While her mother was very ambitious about her children and angry because the patient did not work hard enough, her father regarded her as unable to go into a profession. She passed her exams easily and made a professional career that aroused her father's envy. However, she was unable to get married because, like her mother, she could not love a man. She would like to "get a man's semen and have children," and since her first treatment has become rather promiscuous; she starts several relationships with men and then drops them. She has become fully aware of her rage and her castration wishes toward men, which are in such contrast to her wishes to become a loving wife and mother. Her inability to live up to her ideal standards and her identification with the mother, from whom she has detached herself, are in the center of her depressive conflicts. She feels she is "no better than her bad parents," who continue constantly to criticize both their children—their looks, their habits, their work—and talk even to others about their faults. The only person she loves is her younger brother, whom she tries to mother. In her work she also finds herself sometimes resembling her mother, which makes her depressed.

FREQUENCY OF SESSIONS WITH DEPRESSIVE PATIENTS

I should like to make some comments regarding the frequency of sessions with depressive patients. Some severely depressive patients tend to develop weekend and vacation depressions because they cannot tolerate the separation from the analyst and—being very demanding—expect more sessions per week than they can get. However, even in the case of psychotic depression one should not yield to their demands because this only increases their demandingness. In fact, we must never give either too much or too little. For example, to some depressives, who have difficulties speaking, one should not respond with complete, lasting silence; they cannot tolerate it. In such cases we must help them to speak. As for the amount of sessions, my observations have shown me that it is not the frequency of sessions that is so important but the analyst's responsive, warm, understanding attitudes. Moreover, in the case of psychotic depressives or manic-depressives we have to adapt to their psychomotor retardation or accelerated pace. I have usually given psychotic depressive patients sessions of 60 instead of 50 minutes. We have to consider the slowing of their thought processes, their speech, and their actions. At the end of their sessions they may, for instance, have difficulties in getting up and leaving.

SUMMARY

Let me briefly summarize my ideas on the psychoanalytic therapy of depressive patients. I pointed out that the major problem in their treatment is the handling of the transference, which in such cases is narcissistic in nature. These patients usually immediately develop a transference in which the analyst at first becomes the admired ideal parent or ego-ideal but later turns into the disappointing, rejecting parent or disapproving, overcritical superego figure. For that reason I commonly show the patient his idealization during the first phase of his positive transference and warn him regarding the disappointment he may experience in the future. This will be helpful for the analysis of his negative transference later on. I pointed out that in severe depressives we must approach the interpretation of their underlying hostility very slowly and carefully in order to avoid negative therapeutic reactions. I also indicated that we have to be very selective with regard to accepting psychotic depressive patients into analytic treatment, and that we have to consider and adapt to their psychomotor retardation.

I also gave special consideration to the fact that not in all depressives do the depressive conditions revolve around their love objects, but they may be caused by their work and their authorities. In the case of depressive conflicts centered on their partners, the analysis of these partners may be very helpful and may even prevent relapses in the future.

I emphasized that even in psychotic depressive cases we need not be afraid to let their preoedipal fantasy material come to the surface and that none of the psychotic or borderline psychotic patients I have had in analysis ever experienced a psychotic breakdown during the treatment (except, of course, patients with circular psychotic depressions who may reexperience depressive periods during their treatment). Finally, I stress that suicidal patients should be hospitalized and should get drug therapy or may even need shock treatment, but they can then return to their original psychiatrist for further therapy.

REFERENCES

1. Freud, S.   The Ego and the Id (1923). In *The Standard Edition of the Complete Psychological Works of Sigmund Freud*, transl. and ed. by J. Strachey with others. London: Hogarth and Institute of Psycho-Analysis, 1961. Vol. 19, p. 12.
2. Gero, G.   The construction of depression. *Int. J. Psychoanal.* 17:423, 1936.
3. Grinker, R. R., Sr.   On identification. *Int. J. Psychoanal.* 38:379, 1957.
4. Kernberg, O.   Factors in the psychoanalytic treatment of narcissistic personalities. *J. Am. Psychoanal. Assoc.*, 18:51, 1970.
5. Kohut, H.   *The Analysis of the Self.* New York: International Universities Press, 1971.
6. Rado, S.   The problem of melancholia. *Int. J. Psychoanal.* 9:420, 1928.

19

Two Contrasting Types of Adolescent Depression and Their Treatment *

E. JAMES ANTHONY

*I loved not, yet I longed to love; I searched for
something to love, in love with loving, and yet I
wanted not and abhorred myself for not wanting; in
me, I had a dearth of inward food, and the more
empty I was the more I loathed it. . . . And yet,
wretched me, I seemed to love to grieve.*

—*St. Augustine* [1]

ADOLESCENCE AND THE HUMAN EXISTENCE

The adolescent boy, who was later to become a bishop and then a
saint, put the problem of ambivalence at the very heart of his adolescent depression. He wanted very much to love, and he looked about
for something to love, but he could not find what he wanted, and he
could not want what he found. He was deprived of past supplies, "the
inward food," and remained empty and full of self-hate. Yet, he was
conscious that in the midst of his misery he was deriving some
peculiar enjoyment from being depressed. Augustine was describing
something of the predicament of the adolescent; caught between two
worlds, he feels imprisoned, as it were, within a developmental phase.

There are no better accounts of adolescent depression than those
given by gifted and introspective young people themselves. In their
diaries and autobiographies, they have spoken (to quote only a few)
of "the dumb and brutish trouble of adolescence," "the deadly despair and total emptiness," "the unspeakable melancholy," and "the
crushing, humiliating, bleak, and desolate joylessness." One of them
spoke of "the stifling sense of oppression and confinement, as if I
were in a prison house from which I could not burst . . . I thought
sometimes if only I could burst through the nameless constriction
that agonized me . . . ." These were, for many of these sensitive adolescents, the "oppressive" and "persecuting years." So commonly are
these moods described and so frequently do we meet with them in
accounts given by those undergoing apparently normal development,
that it would not be unduly extravagant to speak of the normal depression of adolescence, reflecting the difficulties and problems of

* Reprinted from *Journal of the American Psychoanalytic Association*, Vol. 18,
pp. 841–859, 1970, by permission of International Universities Press, Inc.

transition. In contrast, the clinical depressions of adolescence would tend to evolve out of developmental phases of childhood rather than those of adolescence itself, although, of course, the latter would add its own peculiar quota to the disturbance.

The differentiation of these two affective states—the normative and the clinical—is not always easy in practice because of overlapping where the one is superimposed on the other. However, the presence or absence of significant mood disturbances during previous childhood is of both diagnostic and prognostic importance. The normative variety is recognizable as an unstable interlude in an otherwise emotionally stable individual, whose future, like his past, is ordained to take a normative course. Moreover, it has a "reactive" quality to it, whereas the clinical depression, in addition to the "stage" upheavals during childhood development, has, on the whole, less meaningful connection to current experience except as a resonant or sensitized response to minimal provocation. More often it is a sadness "emanating from nowhere."

It is also of much interest to the therapist that many apparently acute depressions arising during this time are self-curative, stemming from some decisive act in the middle of much unhappy dithering, such as breaking away from parents, discovering a vocational interest, or doing something independently creative.

THE CLASSIC CASE

The clinical depression of adolescence, as described by an adolescent, had its clearest description by John Stuart Mill, who is of special importance to psychoanalysis, not only because Freud translated him when he was a medical student, but also because Freud was thought to have been influenced by Mill in his political attitudes. Ernest Jones [10] conceded that there was "much in common in the outlook of the two men," and I would suggest here that the common factor was the analytic tendency.

Mill was brought up with fanatic zeal by his father, who treated him from infancy as if he were nothing but pure, autonomous ego. His mother had no place in his life, and there is no mention of her in all the volumes of his writing. Although Freud admired him as "the man of the century who best managed to free himself from the domination of customary prejudices," he saw him as somewhat inhuman, as lacking a sense of the absurd, and of being "so prudish or so ethereal that one could never gather [from his autobiography] that human beings consist of men and women and that this distinction is the most significant one that exists." Freud pointed out that his own feelings about women, as exemplified in those directed toward his wife, were quite different—adored darlings in youth and loved wives in maturity.

Perhaps not surprisingly, in late adolescence Mill had a depressive breakdown and was overridden with guilt because of what it might mean to his father. "My education, which was wholly his work, had been conducted without any regard to the possibility of it ending in this result, and I saw no use in giving him the pain of thinking that all his plans had failed" [14]. Everything seemed utterly hopeless and dead within him until one day, by chance, he was reading a passage in a book in which the author told of his own father's death and of how he, then a mere boy, had made the sudden decision to take his father's place in the family. Mill found himself weeping, but from that moment his depression was relieved, and he was now able for the first time to be critical of his father's method.

He felt that his depression and breakdown had been due to his analytic tendency derived from his father. The compulsive dissection of all mental content could lead in time, he believed, to self-destruction:

I now saw that the habit of analysis has a tendency to wear away the feelings when no other mental habit is cultivated and the analysing spirit remains without its natural correctives. The very excellence of analysis is that it tends to weaken and undermine whatever is the result of emotion. We owe to analysis our clear knowledge of the permanent sequence in nature, the real connections between things. It is, therefore, favorable to clearsightedness but a perpetual worm at the root of the feelings and, above all, fearfully undermines all desires and pleasures. My father's education had failed to create these feelings in sufficient strength to resist the dissolving influence of analysis, while the whole course of my intellectual cultivation had made me precocious and premature analysis the inveterate habit of my mind [pp. 88-89].

Thus Mill realized that his mind was now "irretrievably analytic," but he did not want to be completely rid of the "power and practice of analysis" simply to have it corrected by joining it, with due balance, to "the cultivation of feelings." What he was pleading for here was the equal recognition of the emotional and cognitive, the abreactive and the analytic. The "self-cure" became possible when he could conceive of his father's death and the sudden cessation of his overriding influence.

Mill came to realize that he had lived life as half a person and that missing out on half of life's experiences and achievements was the traumatic event that had precipitated his breakdown. In his very cognitive fashion, he one day asked himself the crucial question as to whether he would be happy if all his present objectives in life were realized, and he was forced to answer "no." "At this, my heart sank in me; the whole foundation on which my life was constructed fell down . . . I seemed to have nothing left to live for." It is not unusual for the precipitating event, as for the curative event, to be clear-cut and dramatic in the case of an adolescent depression. With Mill, both events related manifestly to his father (his mother is conspicuous by her total emotional absence); he fell ill when he became aware that the realization of his father's aims in life would not satisfy him, and he regained his mental health (to the degree that this was possible) when he understood that the death of the father brought with it the growth of identity, autonomy, and responsibility for the son. In contrast, Freud's own self-analysis of his father's influence on his life led to the formulation of the oedipus complex but brought no depressive breakdown in its tracks.

Mill's case history is additionally fascinating because he would seem to be describing a special depressive syndrome of adolescence that one might call, for lack of a better term, an "analytic depression." Reduced to its common denominator, inherent in this syndrome is the concept that you cannot afford to take things to pieces until you have first learned to put the bits together as a whole and to "invest" this with feeling. There is also another aspect to this dynamic that has not yet received recognition in psychoanalysis. It is being increasingly noted that the pattern of affective disturbance may be related to the "cognitive style" of the individual, so that an analytic type of depression may be shaped by an analytic type of intelligence, and an amorphous depression by a more syncretic or global cognitive approach. (In this context, it is interesting to note that Wynne et al. [17] have found that an analytic intelligence predisposes to a paranoid type of schizophrenia, whereas the diffuse intelligence is conducive to hebephrenia. It is possible that cognitive style may also play a role in the differential development of obsessional versus the hysterical neuroses.)

THE GENESIS OF ADOLESCENT DEPRESSION

If depression were an easily recognizable phenomenon, it would not be too difficult to follow its vicissitudes during the course of development. Unfortunately, there has been some confusion in its usage. For some, depression is a simple, primary affect, like anxiety, called into being with every incidence of loss, either real or fantasied. For others, the primary affect is sadness, while depression is a compound affect which always originates in conflict. Those who deny that depression can be primary insist that it requires psychic structure and the process of internalization, which is not available to the infant. On the other hand, those who hold the first view think of it as an ego reaction which, with time and experience, becomes more accentuated and elaborate, in the same way as anxiety, which appears earlier on in life in a simple, undifferentiated form, and later, in the neuroses, is part of an internalized and structured organization.

A further confusion is added to the situation by those who wish to differentiate between depressive feeling, which everyone can have, and clinical depression, which only emerges at adolescence. In lieu of clinical depression, the child manifests what has come to be known as "depressive equivalents."

In a general review of adolescent depression, one is confronted, as in adult cases, with certain repetitive findings: narcissistic types of object relations, conflicts of ambivalence, lowering of self-esteem, regression to oral and anal fixation points, ego helplessness, aggression turned against the self-masochistic character structure, precipitation by object loss or narcissistic injury, and conflicts over shame and guilt. On more detailed inquiry, it becomes apparent that these characteristics are not always found in any individual case or in the same amount, and, therefore, the question arises as to whether there are different types of depression in adolescence, and, if so, whether they differ in kind or degree.

A number of other important questions arise at this point. First, is there a clinical depression in adolescence without developmental antecedents earlier in life? Second, if adolescent depression, in its clinical form, has precursors in childhood, can these be related to preoedipal or postoedipal depressive reactions or to preoedipal depressive or postoedipal depressive tendencies? It would be generally agreed today that variations in drive endowment may create marked differences in infants from the very beginning of life and that some of these may be conducive to a depressive proclivity. Several writers have emphasized the importance of the infantile experience for the development of later depression: the failure to master the depressive position [12]; the emergence of a depressive constellation [2]; the possible prodromal significance of "eight-month anxiety"; the actual loss of the parent as a statistically significant finding in later clinical depressions; and a basic depressive mood developing in some toddlers arising from experiences associated with toilet training, sibling birth, or the discovery of sex differences [13], and intensifying to a degree in which there is a depletion of basic trust [4], of confident expectation [2], of neutralized aggression [7], and of self-esteem [3] resulting in a sudden sense of helplessness and the laying down of a disposition to later depression or depressive-masochistic character formation.

Clinically, according to Mahler, this negative mood in the toddler (which may begin to swing in regular cycles) manifests itself in a hostile dependency on the mother, with increased "shadowing," constant protesting and demanding, provocative running away, refusal to accept any temporary maternal substitution, increasing angriness, and frequent severe temper tantrums.

There is increasing evidence that in some adolescent depressions (and the same is true of adult depression) the preoedipal history is fraught with clinical disturbances as described above. In addition, there may be other manifestations, already referred to as "depressive equivalents" [15, 16], for example, eating and sleeping disturbances, colic, crying, and head banging in the infant; temper tantrums and negativism and disobedience in the toddler; truancy, running away from home, accident proneness, and masochistic and antisocial behavior in the older child.

The depressive equivalents in adolescence, as manifested in boredom, restlessness, manic behavior, stimulation seeking, may oscillate with actual depression.

There is, however, a type of adolescent depression in which these preoedipal manifestations and equivalents are conspicuously absent; nor is there any history of a depressed mother complementing the child in the depressive position, the depressive constellation, the primal depression, or in the state of the basic depressive mood.

In the cases of latency depression described by Harrington and Hassan [6], none of the mothers were or had been depressed, and no emotional disturbances were ever reported in any of the siblings. The children up to the time of onset of their illness, between 8 and 11 years, were considered "good" children about whom there were never any complaints. They were described as helpful, kind, and sympathetic. The mother-child relationship was ostensibly satisfactory until the breakdown occurred, and the relationship with the father was extremely positive. Certain traumatic events changed the course of development, such as illness, accidents, or some disturbing experience at school. The changes of personality that resulted included an ambivalent dependence on the mother, open sibling jealousy, deterioration in school performance, and refusal to conform. Ego weakness and self-depreciation were present in all cases and were felt to be related to false and early identifications. A splitting of the function of mothering in the first two years of life had hindered the formation of strong feminine identifications.

A study of certain types of adolescent depression by Hunter [8] described a syndrome not unlike the one delineated by Harrington and Hassan. These cases were characterized by the fact that they all had had good experiences in the earliest years and had developed positive relationships with both their parents, thereby setting down what the author referred to as an intrapsychic root system conducive to future growth and stable emotional development. However, as in the latency cases, some specific trauma intervened to damage the root development, as a result of which a severe, intermittent, clinical depression emerged in adolescence associated with learning inhibitions, anxieties around intake, such as anorexia, bulimia, and addiction, and insecure sexual identity. Again, as in the cases described by Harrington and Hassan, these patients can and do make adequate relationships, although often tempestuous; in addition, they stay in treatment and have a good prognosis. If intelligent, they tend to use their intelligence to make their own way into a premature independence. However, they are basically insecure and profoundly dependent, and they cover this up with a display of rebellion and bravado which is really a protest. Their acting out and premature sexual activity is partly a cry for help, a defense against depression, and a search for a lost object. They tend to evoke counterdepressions in adults about them and also a great deal of rage, to which the adolescents respond with elation.

TWO CONTRASTING TYPES OF ADOLESCENT DEPRESSION

The central psychological problem in depression, according to Jacobson [9], is the narcissistic breakdown of the depressed person, resulting either in loss of self-esteem and feelings of helplessness, weakness, and inferiority, or in the development of a sense of moral worthlessness and sinfulness. She goes on to say that "it is important to decide which is the leading affect conflict, particularly in the treatment of adolescent depression."

A similar differentiation may be made of masochism, which is manifested clinically by dependency, guilt, the need for punishment, and the inhibition of aggression. There would appear to be two kinds of masochism, the one beginning in the preoedipal phase in which a sadistic mother produces a masochistic child, and the other, termed moral masochism, which has its origin in the oedipal conflict with regression to an earlier, passive, phallic phase. At some time in the course of development, the masochistic character is transformed into a depressive one because of the lowering of self-esteem or through object loss.

This would, therefore, lead to the possible delineation of two types of adolescent depression. In type one, the psychopathology would be mainly preoedipal and based on a marked symbiotic tie with the omnipotent, need-satisfying mother. The crucial problem has to do with discrepancies between the ego and ego ideal, with resulting changes in self-esteem. Shame, humiliation, inferiority, inadequacy, and weakness represent the major affects, and ego helplessness is the eventual outcome. The object relationships are narcissistic in type, and there is no clear separation between self and object. Orality is marked and dependency extreme. Identifications are primitive. The mother, in turn, tends to be sadistic, disparaging, reproachful, and deflating.

The type two depression is more oedipal in nature, with a great deal of guilt and moral masochism associated with a punitive superego. Whereas the ego ideal in type one links the condition to the mothering relationship (there is some indication that the ego ideal develops before the superego), the superego develops mainly out of the oedipal conflict. The hostility, intended for the parents, is deflected back on the self, and the self-depreciating trends are ultimately related to the wish to destroy the idealized image of the parents by whom the child feels betrayed. The feelings of self-disgust, brought about by disappointments at the breakdown of parental idealization, lead eventually to the aggression against the self in which both self and hated incorporated objects are annihilated, and death is the punishment for the wish to kill.

The type one depression tends to show a cyclical development which is usually absent in the type two depression. In addition, the type one depression can also be cut short in its less intense forms by the restoration of a lost object or approval by an idealized parent figure. The cycles relate to increases and reductions in the feelings of self-esteem. In one part of the cycle, self-esteem is high, verging on the grandiose, the mood is elated, and the patient feels himself above criticism. He eats well, gains weight, and preoccupies himself with his physical appearance. Following a narcissistic injury, he swings into a negative phase, characterized by low esteem, self-hate, and feelings of extreme helplessness. He regards himself as unloved and unlovable and may try to relieve his poor self-concept by searching for an object to love in his environment or resorting to some masochistic act.

THE TREATMENT COURSE OF
A TYPE ONE DEPRESSION

Case 1. Jane was a 16-year-old girl when she entered analysis. Her mother was a selfish, egoistic woman preoccupied with her own concerns and seemingly incapable of altruistic feelings. I would describe her as an "as if" character disorder. She divorced Jane's father when the girl was 7 years old because he had demanded more from her than she was prepared to give. She was exasperated throughout her daughter's infancy for the same reason and took every opportunity to escape from her mothering responsibilities. When the baby was 6 weeks old, she and her husband left for a long tour of Europe so that she could convalesce from childbirth. Consequently, Jane refused food and lost weight rapidly. Thereafter, she had constant problems with eating and sleeping, cried almost continually and resisted all methods of pacification.

As a toddler, her behavior was described by the mother as "intolerable." She could not leave her mother alone, and in spite of almost sadistic treatment attempted to cling to her. The mother described her as "shameless in her intrusiveness."

I first saw Jane at the age of 7, when she was already a sad looking child. Her parents had recently divorced, and her behavior had begun to change. From being clinging and demanding, she was now quiet, conforming, and compulsive. She practiced a number of rituals prior to bedtime which apparently mitigated a fearfulness that had been present since early life. She was a pretty girl, but so suspicious, stiff, and aloof that the image she projected was basically unattractive. She complained that she was always bored unless she was doing something, and in play therapy she came out with a princess fantasy that revealed how deeply self-absorbed she was. The theme of the story was restricted to her looking beautiful and wearing beautiful clothes and being constantly praised by everybody.

In the latter part of latency she began to put on weight, although when referred again in adolescence she had lost 65 pounds of the total gained and was obsessed with calories. Her depressions were now occurring at regular intervals and were quite severe. They often coincided with weekends, which she associated to the times her parents had left her when she was small. She was hypersensitive to rejection, separation, and loss, even in minimal amounts, and would be thrown into a state of utter helplessness.

At the beginning of treatment, Jane warned me that she occasionally got very depressed, and that she genuinely needed help. If I were not around then, she would find another doctor. We were soon caught up in a cycle of self-esteem. During certain days, she would come in elated and "bubbling," pouring out dreams and fantasies and amusing anecdotes, feeling pleased with herself and especially pleased with the way she looked. She was very interested in food and would even request candy during her sessions. Sooner or later, some girl would snub her or her mother would go out with a new boyfriend, and she would rapidly become depressed, tearful, slowed down in her reactions, and unable to speak except in an inaudible monotone. At such times, she spoke of hating herself because she was so inferior to others. She disliked going to school since her inadequacies would be known to everyone, and she would be overcome with shame. She talked of doing away with herself, because she was no good for anything.

There were several crises of self-esteem, since every interpretation, however tactfully and gently given, was understood as depreciating. During the negative phase of the cycle, she would attack me ferociously for my "uselessness," and would throw past interpretations in my face to demonstrate how bankrupt I was in understanding. And yet, she could not leave me alone. Following the session, she would go home and try to continue the session on the telephone. She would "shadow" me from my home to my office, and even followed me round a supermarket on one occasion to see, as she put it, what I bought in the way of food. Her attempts to control me at times amounted to tyranny, and I experienced it as oppressive. She tried hard to censor my communications, for, to use her expression, they got out of hand. "You can say whatever comes into your mind when you're with me, but you must never criticize me, because you know how sensitive I am and how people have criticized me in the past." At times, I found her behavior "intolerable."

A typical sequence in the therapeutic situation would take the following course. She would make some comment on the waste in time and money involved in seeing me every day, especially since I made her feel worse rather than better, and would then negotiate for coming in on Sunday since that was when her depression was greatest. I would interpret the nature of the ambivalent tie and her reaction to weekend separation. She would perceive this as a reproach and a criticism of her inadequacy and would bow her head in shame, reiterating endlessly in her saddest voice that she was no good and that she hated herself for being no good and that her mother despised her and now she could feel my contempt. I would point out that she was using me to humiliate and hurt herself and that in so doing she was treating me in much the same way that she had done her mother. Her response to this would be: "Then you don't really despise me and dislike me and I am really imagining it." This would make her feel better toward herself and toward me until the next cycle was set off.

For the early part of her treatment, guilt feelings appeared to play only a minor role, the major elements being fears of exposure, of being made to look silly in public, and of not having as good a face or figure as another girl. All of these intense affects were basically connected with shame and the failure to live up to some ideal that she had currently set herself. After reading a book by A. S. Neil, she constantly compared herself with the Summerhill child who was so self-assured, self-sufficient, and free from anxiety and depression. The Summerhill child experienced no pressures to live up to high standards. She wondered whether she should not apply for admission.

At the end of the first year, feelings of guilt began to invade the cycle. Interpretive "criticism" from me would generate enormous rage, and she would abuse me in anal terms. All of a sudden, she would stop, feeling that she had "hurt" me and that I would send her away, never to put up with her again. She would begin to look guilty, rather than ashamed, and confess to fantasies in which I would be killed in some way. She would

make strong efforts at reconciliation and restitution and would begin
mentioning some of the good things that I had done for her in the past.
It was quite an effort for her to overcompensate for her hostility, and it
would leave her weak and tired. Then she would plead with me to do
things for her, to help her with her homework because she was feeling so
poorly, and the push to greater dependence would continue until shame
reentered the cycle.

Psychodiagnostically, most of the evidence pointed to a personality
arrest at an early preoedipal-narcissistic level, showing characteristics of
shallowness, immaturity, and lack of consistency in her ego goals. Her
unrealistic ideals made her especially vulnerable to failure and loss of self-
esteem. During the stage of adolescence, all her early dependency conflicts, her lonesomeness, isolation, and confusion of purpose were remobilized and greatly intensified. In between her depressive bouts, she was a
typically masochistic character, courting suffering as if it were love.

Her earliest therapeutic aim was to become someone whom the analyst
might admire, and she would attempt to extract information on my
ideals. "I bet you adore those bubbling kids; they would be so much
nicer to talk to than me."

In the middle of the second year, her wish was openly to become like
my fantasied wife, who was beautiful, slim, self-assured, and never depressed. Her behavior would often become grossly artificial as she imitated
this imaginary character, but it helped to usher in rudimentary oedipal
concerns in which she would link me to her early memories of her father.
The symbiotic transference began to give place very gradually to a transference neurosis.

The countertransference evoked in the analyst by this type of patient takes many different forms. During her very helpless, hopeless,
and hapless periods, I would feel myself invaded by the gloom she
emitted, and the symbiotic nature of the relationship enhanced the
contagion. Sometimes the counterdepression would provoke an exaggerated display of professional good humor. The extreme sensitivity
of her self-esteem regulation made me think twice before I interpreted
anything that might imply an ego deficit of any sort. She accumulated
memories of such "criticism" and paraded them all in times of attack
to make me fully conscious of how often, according to her, I put my
foot in it. Her predominantly narcissistic mood of relating made me
feel like the proverbial cupboard, and occasionally I hungered for
some evidence of a more reciprocal relationship. She had little recourse to the gentle assimilation of identification and appeared to eat
me up and vomit me out with little consideration. I could feel within
myself some resistance to such cannibalism.

Working with Jane necessitated the constant use of what Glover
once referred to as the "analytic toilet," and in carrying this out, I
would sometimes be aware that her strongly masochistic attitudes and
behavior sometimes elicited an interpretation that, removed from its

context, sounded a little sadistic. I am reminded of her mother's telling me that she was the sort of child who made you hit her even when you did not want to do so at all. Nor was I reassured when my patient remarked one day that I was the only man in the world she could tolerate because I was not basically cruel.

The most subtle countertransference feelings were often aroused at the termination of a session. She approached every ending with anxiety, depression, anger, demandingness, and a refusal to leave. I found myself in some difficulties at times with announcing the end of the session (apologetically): "I'm afraid we have to stop now," or "I'm sorry but that's all for today," or, as on one occasion when I found her most oppressive and tyrannical, "You have to go now." It was, however, very difficult to terminate any session without generating a miniature depression.

While treating Jane, I was also analyzing a classically phobic child who was warm, cheerful, noncomplaining, and nondemanding, and my relief in going from Jane to him was such that I realized to what an extent I had developed some counteridentification with my depressed and depressing patient and had really become for a while a rather dismal therapist. It reminded me of Freud's amusing countertransference joke of a session between a priest and a dying insurance agent at the end of which the patient had not been converted but the priest was insured!

COURSE AND TREATMENT OF
TYPE TWO DEPRESSION

Case 2. The history, obtained with as much detail as possible from the parents, revealed nothing in the form of a preoedipal disturbance. The mother seemed to be a reasonably good mother with clearly differentiated images of her children. Mary was a likable girl with a wry sense of humor. During her happy periods, she was amiable and had a wide range of friends. She herself was aware that she latched onto them in an essentially unhealthy way insofar as she treated the loss of a single friend as the end of all possible existence and behaved very histrionically when this occurred. She became equally addicted to treatment so that termination was planned carefully almost a year ahead to offset any chance of suicidal behavior. There had been two suicide attempts prior to beginning treatment.

Her depressions began when she entered puberty, although there was some evidence of masochistic trends prior to this. For example, she seemed to have more accidents than she was statistically entitled to. Her depressions, which were not cyclical, were so intense as to raise the question of psychosis since her reality testing seemed impaired at the time. Guilt was a marked feature, and her sense of sinfulness very great. She herself spoke of her "guilt complex." There were no noticeable problems surrounding self-esteem nor in the area of identity. She was not in any sense an "outer-directed" person, and shame appeared to play no significant part in her neurosis.

Even between depressive episodes, there was a sad air about her, tinged with a note of pessimism. She managed to keep herself busy during the day, but at night loneliness and sadness would overcome her, and although she admitted that she sometimes enjoyed wallowing in these affects, she was occasionally alarmed by the wishes for death that accompanied them.

She dated her disorder from an attack of hepatitis which she had when she was 12 years of age. Things had never gone well since, and she had found her mother increasingly irritating and unsympathetic. She continued to retain a good relationship with her father and would still wrestle with him from time to time although she found kissing him "too stimulating."

She took to analysis as a duck takes to water and developed an instant transference in which the predominant fantasy was to be rescued by the analyst from some desert island where she was completely isolated and alone. The reunion would take various forms but in all of them we would end up having dinner together in a very elegant restaurant.

The transference fantasy was later elaborated in a number of "depressive games" that she played mostly by herself in my presence. One of them was like the peek-a-boo game of early childhood. She would remove her shoes, ask me to close my eyes, and then hide somewhere in the room. With the help of various nonverbal clues, hearing her breathe, hearing her move, etc., I was to guess where she was. Being found provided her with intense pleasure, and she obtained no satisfaction whatsoever if I failed. She was never ashamed of the immaturity involved in this behavior but would wonder constructively why she needed to play these games with me.

Whereas with Jane the transference was predominantly a two-body relationship, in the case of Mary it oscillated between a maternal and paternal transference so that at one time she would be overwhelmingly dependent on me and at another, giggly and seductive. She often wondered at my not getting angry with her when she teased me, and she recalled a time when she was younger when her father still spanked her and how mixed-up this made her feel.

During a period of transference love, she was very threatened by the intensity of her wish to be with the analyst. It distressed her to feel so possessive because she knew I had other patients. She mentioned that she did not need to be here all the time since she carried a picture of me in her mind and was able to discuss her problems equally with the picture. "It's even better because when you're inside me like that you don't interrupt." Her depression, stemming from oedipal disappointment, was much analyzed as she experienced it either as a deficiency (penis envy) or as deprivation (an empty inner space).

When we began to discuss termination, her depressive symptoms flared up, and she began to talk again of suicide. She mentioned that all her relationships in life had ended in disappointing ways. A typical pattern involved her becoming fond of someone who would tire of her and want to be rid of her. It had happened so often, and yet she could never quite get used to it. At other times she would get extremely angry that I was accepting termination so calmly and that I took her anger as a fact of life, while for her it caused the universe to explode. She wondered at my equanimity. I pointed out that she was denying me my feelings over termination because she was afraid to consider that I might have feelings about her. She was startled at the thought that I, too, might feel sad about losing her and seemed relieved.

Depression seemed to swamp all her feelings, and whereas during the nondepressed periods she had a considerable repertoire of affects, during a depressive episode she reacted as if there were nothing inside her at all. It was at these times of almost total emptiness that I would talk of the many things inside her that had accumulated during the period of treatment, which she would take away with her and which nobody could rob from her. She began to count the hours toward termination and said that she felt rather hopeless. A little later, she claimed that she had never been contented or happy since she was five years old. "It's almost as if my parents didn't give me something I terribly wanted, but I have no memory of what it is." In the same context, she added, "I just know in my bones that you're going to disappoint me." In the last session, she recalled her first visit. She said she was glad to have discovered such a "safe place," and perhaps it had made her strong enough to be alone by herself again. Although she might still get a little depressed from time to time, hopefully these depressions would be less severe. I said that it was natural to feel sad when parting from someone with whom you had been through so much. "But will you feel sad?" I said that I had two feelings, one of happiness that she was feeling better, that I had been able to help her in some way, and also some sadness because we would be separating. She said: "Your feeling even a little sad makes me able to go off without crying."

The countertransference in response to this type of depression is more libidinal in type. I would see two sides to her according to her mood. In her good, cheerful phase, I would envisage her as full of good things, her rich inner space flooded with positive objects of all kinds. She would seem to be the source of things which I could envy and yet admire. When, however, she became depressed, it almost seemed as if the good things drained from her. I would be more conscious then of her deficiencies, her castrated state and her ungivingness. The inner space, as Erikson [5] put it, is the center of despair in the woman, and its emptiness affects the man who is treating her. It is this kind of countertransference that conduces to the depressive contagion of the therapist. I also found myself at times reacting to her disappointment by disappointment at myself or in myself, and this would leave me despondent.

This second type of depression often has a precursory clinical depression during late latency, and occasionally the two are coterminous.

CONCLUSION

At the beginning of this paper, I described a general Weltschmertz, "a vast sorrow for the unrealizable and the indefinable" [11] that over-hang adolescence and to which the adolescent may respond to greater or lesser degree. I then went on to deal with those who entered the adolescent stage already highly sensitized to depressive reactions be-cause of preoedipal or oedipal experiences, and it is these adolescents who develop a well defined clinical depression. The more borderline and psychotic depressions stem from the preoedipal anlage possibly reinforced by strong constitutional elements. We have always to re-member, however, in any consideration of depression that it is in-evitable, ubiquitous, and expectable even in the most average environ-ment, and that a healthy person, according to Heinz Hartmann, must develop a capacity to suffer and to be depressed.

REFERENCES

1. Augustine, St.   Confessions of St. Augustine. Scranton, Pa.: Haddon Craftsmen, 1943.
2. Benedek, T. F.   Toward the biology of the depressive constellation. *J. Am. Psychoanal. Assoc.* 4:389, 1956.
3. Bibring, E.   The Mechanism of Depression. In P. Greenacre (Ed.), *Affective Disorders—Psychoanalytic Contributions to Their Study.* New York: International Universities Press, 1953. P. 13.
4. Erikson, E. H.   *Childhood and Society.* New York: Norton, 1950.
5. Erikson, E. H.   *Identity, Youth and Crisis.* New York: Norton, 1968.
6. Harrington, M., and Hassan, J.   Depression in girls during latency. *Br. J. Med. Psychol.* 31:43, 1958.
7. Hartmann, H.   Problems of Infantile Neurosis (1954). In *Essays on Ego Psychology.* New York: International Universities Press, 1964. P. 207.
8. Hunter, D.   Root Damaged Children. Paper presented at the meet-ing of the Medical Section of the British Psychological Society, Lon-don, 1970.
9. Jacobson, E.   Depression: The oedipus complex in the development of depressive mechanisms. *Psychoanal. Q.* 12:541, 1943.
10. Jones, E.   *The Life and Work of Sigmund Freud,* vol. 1. New York: Basic Books, 1953.
11. Kiell, N.   *The Adolescent Through Fiction.* New York: Interna-tional Universities Press, 1959.
12. Klein, M.   A Contribution to the Psychogenesis of Manic-Depressive States. In *Contributions to Psychoanalysis, 1921-1945.* New York: International Universities Press, 1948.

13. Mahler, M.   Notes on the Development of Basic Moods: The Depressive Affect. In R. M. Loewenstein et al. (Eds.), *Psychoanalysis— A General Psychology*. New York: International Universities Press, 1966. P. 152.
14. Mill, J. S.   *Autobiography of John Stuart Mill*. New York: Columbia University Press, 1948.
15. Sperling, M.   Equivalents of depression in children. *J. Hillside Hosp.*, 8:138, 1959.
16. Toolan, J.   Depression in children and adolescents. *Am. J. Orthopsychiatry* 32:404, 1962.
17. Wynne, L. C., et al.   Thought disorder and family relations of schizophrenics. *AMA Arch. Neurol. Psychiatry* 12:187, 1965.

20

Psychological Considerations in the Chemotherapy of Depression

MORTIMER OSTOW

The simple administration of antidepressant chemical agents, following the recommendations contained in package inserts, to depressed patients will yield gratifying relief in a significant number of cases. However, the psychiatrist who would like to offer more than symptomatic relief, and who realizes that the patient subject to depressive illness suffers from problems in object relations during the intervals between depressive episodes, would prefer to pursue a reasoned program of therapy that will not merely terminate the presenting episode of illness but will also tend to rectify the functioning of the interval personality and therefore also tend to discourage relapse. With that orientation, chemotherapy must be viewed as one therapeutic tool available for use in an overall therapeutic program that may also include psychotherapy, superficial or intensive, electric shock therapy, and recommendations for alterations of the patient's circumstances and *modus vivendi*.

To assess properly the potential role of chemotherapy in the management of the depressed patient, one must consider the natural history of the illness in general and in the presenting patient in particular. What kind of depressive episodes has he had in the past? How severe do they become and how long do they last? Does he neglect his work or contrive to get himself discharged from his position? How badly does he neglect or abuse his family? Does he become suicidal? Are his depressions seasonal? How resilient is he?

How severe was the stress that precipitated this episode? Is it continuing or has it subsided? How much of a role has stress played in previous incidents of depression? Is the stress something that was externally imposed? If so, was it an infrequent occurrence, such as the

461

death of someone loved or some special demand or frustration at work? Or is the stress a constant circumstance, for example, an insatiable spouse or a disappointing child? Is the stress, on the other hand, implicit in the patient's psychic disposition, for example, an inability to cope with the demands and expectations appropriate to adult life?

How old is the patient? Is the stress a function of his age? Is it aging itself that is creating the vulnerability to depression?

Is there a family history of depressive illness, or other mental illness? How did it respond to treatment? Is there a family history of suicide?

How has the patient responded to treatment in previous episodes, treatment by psychotherapy, or by drug therapy? Has he been willing to continue under therapeutic supervision after the individual episode remitted?

What is his attitude toward treatment? Does he desire and can he tolerate confrontation with reality, internal reality as well as external? Does he follow instructions reliably? Does he report changes in his mental state reliably?

What can be expected of the patient's family, his employers, his associates, and his friends? Will they cooperate with treatment or contribute to resistance? Will they encourage the patient to cooperate? Will they help to alleviate external stress?

What are the characteristics of the current episode? How depressed is the patient? How suicidal is he? Can he be treated at home or does he require hospitalization? How responsive is he likely to be to the psychotherapist's interest and to psychotherapy itself?

In formulating a treatment program, one must distinguish among various depressive states. There is, first, the true melancholic depression characterized by paralysis or inhibition due to inertia or agitation; a lack of resilience as indicated by failure to respond when the external stress lifts; a family history of depressive illness; and primary self-observation.

(One can distinguish three different varieties of self-observation. There is the self-observation that consists of viewing oneself in terms of his externally visible characteristics of behavior—for example, how he looks, how well he does his job, what his status is in the community. Such self-observation I call secondary self-observation. On the other hand, one may be concerned with how he feels, how worthy he is, whether he is optimistic or pessimistic, whether he feels energetic or inert, whether he feels wicked or virtuous. This concern with one's feeling tone I call primary self-observation. [The term tertiary self-observation may be used to refer to observations unconsciously made of oneself and then projected onto others.] In melancholic depression there is a good deal of primary self-observation associated with guilt, self-criticism, and self-deprecation.)

Second, there are nonmelancholic depressive states characterized by great anguish with suicidal rumination, but without inertia. There is often self-criticism but relatively little primary self-observation. When external stress is removed, the patient improves promptly.

Finally, there are clinical states that serve dynamically to defend against depression and that present as other illnesses, such as phobia, obsessive-compulsive states, hysteria, and varieties of schizophrenic illness.

In deciding whether the patient should have drug therapy, the psychiatrist is guided by the patient's current clinical state and by the treatment goals that the psychiatrist sets, taking into consideration such things as the patient's age, physical health, living and working conditions, and financial circumstances.

Of course there are certain overriding indications. For example, one will prefer the relatively rapid effect of drug therapy to the delayed and slow effect of psychotherapy when the patient is seriously suicidal. (If he is so suicidal that it is hazardous to wait until medication becomes effective, the patient may have to be hospitalized, given electric shock treatment, or both. In that case it might be well to start on medication at the same time in order to protect him from relapse after the daze of electric shock treatment has worn off.) Similarly, one will not wish to withhold drug therapy if the patient is suffering seriously, if he is seriously disabled, or if he is so disorganized that he cannot participate even in a psychotherapeutic procedure.

One may also decide that drug therapy is indicated if, for example, the patient is too old and external circumstances too fixed to permit influence by psychotherapy; if psychotherapeutic services are not available; or if the patient rejects psychotherapy, often because he cannot tolerate the idea that his illness betrays a defect in his interval personality function.

Drug therapy may be offered as an adjunct to psychotherapy. Frequently the depressed state produces a kind of psychic inertia that deprives the psychotherapy of the impetus it requires. Drug therapy may then be initiated to elicit the motivation to become engaged in object relations and in work, and therefore also in psychotherapy.

Preparation for the initiation of drug treatment depends on the circumstances. If the patient comes for help expecting to be given medication, then once the psychiatrist decides that it should indeed be administered as the only or the primary therapeutic modality, there is little problem with initiating the program. What is required is merely explaining to the patient the name of the therapeutic agent chosen, the nature of the improvement to look for, the time characteristics of the onset of improvement, side and toxic effects that might occur with instructions to report unusual symptoms at once, the probability of obtaining relief, and the program that will be followed while waiting for the treatment effect to appear, when the recovery begins, and what will be done if the drug selected should fail to produce the desired results. I usually explain that while success with chemotherapy is likely, it is impossible to know before trial which drug and what dose will be effective. I give the patient some idea of my plan of treatment and some general idea of the time period that will be required to achieve results.

On the other hand, the initiation of drug therapy becomes more problematic when it is introduced into an ongoing psychotherapy or psychoanalysis out of concern for the patient, the treatment, or both. It has been argued by some psychoanalysts that drug therapy is to be avoided because it contaminates the psychoanalytic process. If the patient's life is in danger, then the question of contaminating the psychoanalytic process becomes irrelevant. If depressive illness or schizophrenia has brought the psychoanalytic process to a halt, drug treatment in many instances can save it. It may also prevent the patient from leaving treatment in the case of either of these conditions.

Some psychoanalysts concede that these conditions are indeed proper clinical indications for administering medication but that medication nevertheless makes subsequent true analysis impossible. When he administers and monitors medication, the psychoanalyst does depart from the role of uninvolved interpreter, and he does become more personally involved in the patient's fate. By so doing he complies with the patient's wish that he be personally and genuinely concerned with his recovery. On the other hand, among patients I have seen who had previously been held in analysis without drug therapy during extended periods of depression, I have encountered bitterness against the analyst for withholding the relief that was so easily available. Therefore one could argue that to withhold medication when it would afford relief can be even more disruptive to the analysis. I believe that if the entire process of administering, regulating, and withdrawing medication is evaluated, the analytic process itself does not suffer.

One must consider what the true roles of analysis can be in the case of patients with depressive or schizophrenic diathesis. What is the prospect that by pure, uncontaminated analysis the patient will be enabled to advance to the point of reasonably and consistently appropriate behavior? On the other hand, what is the probability that the analyst can be even more helpful if he employs an analytic technique modified by drug therapy, guidance, advice, and education? Classic analysis was recommended by Freud as a treatment only for neurosis, not for depression or schizophrenia, and in the treatment of neurosis, drug therapy as we know it today can play only a small role. I infer that for treatment of depressive illness or schizophrenia, the classic purity of the analytic procedure is an irrelevant consideration.

When a patient has undertaken psychotherapy or analysis because of his conviction that his distress can be reversed by such a procedure, a recommendation made during the course of treatment to accept chemotherapy may be interpreted as an indication that the patient's illness is organic since he cannot be helped by purely psychological measures. In other words, the recommendation of drug therapy reinforces the usual hypochondria of depression. Under such circumstances, reassurance, explanation, and interpretation are required before treatment is actually begun.

In any case, introducing drug therapy may well be regarded by the patient as an intrusion into his analysis or psychotherapy. Therefore I usually raise the question, let the patient think about it for a few days, investigate and discuss the unconscious meaning of this intervention before actually prescribing medication.

Proper selection of the medication to be used, or of the sequence in which medications are to be introduced, may be vital for the success of the treatment. We could make the best selection if we knew how each of these chemical substances exerts its antidepressant effect. However, the ultimate chemical and physiological changes by which they combat depression are not definitively established. There are a number of hints of which biochemical systems may be involved, but the mechanisms have not been sufficiently elucidated to permit their use for predictive or prescribing purposes. One would think that the psychological processes that ensue when these drugs are introduced would by now be familiar to the clinician. But here too, no generally acceptable formulations have been devised.

When chlorpromazine and reserpine were introduced for the treatment of schizophrenia in the early 1950s, I suggested that these substances act by reducing the potential of dammed up psychic energy that presumably had brought about the psychotic state. I drew this inference from a number of observations. These substances, when given to normal individuals, or in excess dose to psychotics, tend to produce inertia. When given to susceptible individuals, they induce melancholic depression, characterized by a deficiency of available ego energy. A common side effect of each of these two chemical agents is a parkinsonian-like syndrome. Inertia is one of the most prominent and universal symptoms of parkinsonism. Nathan Kline and I presented this hypothesis in a paper read before the American Psychoanalytic Association in 1956 [2].

In the same paper, written before the discovery of the antidepressant potential of monoamine oxidase inhibitors and before the availability of tricyclic antidepressant agents, we considered the possibility that a "psychic energizer" substance might become available, and we tried to anticipate its properties. Our list included alleviation of melancholic depression, a reduction in the need for sleep, increase in appetite and sexual desire, intensification of behavior drives in general, speeding up of motor and intellectual activity, euphoria and optimism, and in large doses, psychosis. When the monoamine oxidase inhibitors and tricyclics became available, they exhibited just these properties. While some clinical phenomena require elaboration of this theory to a more complex structure, no facts that I have encountered make any other hypothesis more attractive, and I continue to bet on it. Nevertheless I must record that although the term psychic energizer has come into common use in psychiatry, relatively few of my colleagues are ready to assume that the psychic changes induced by these antidepressant and antipsychotic drugs pertain to the hypothetical energy constructs that Freud introduced.

States of relative deficiency of psychic energy, specifically libido, of which melancholic depression is the purest example, are characterized by preoccupation with death, pessimism, low self-esteem, self-criticism, and a lack of motivation that results in partial or complete inability to work or to pursue ordinary instinctual goals. These states are also characterized by the phenomenon I have called primary self-observation. I dwell on this function because it and lack of motivation and lack of resilience differentiate the state of energy depletion characteristic of melancholic depression from similar depressed states that are triggered by defeats and frustrations but that reverse readily when external stress is alleviated.

The monoamine oxidase inhibitors and the tricyclics seem to reverse states of energy depletion and therefore act as effective therapeutic agents in cases of melancholic depression and allied conditions. Under their influence the patient reverts to the state of mind that existed before the onset of the current episode of depression. But how do these agents affect the nonmelancholic depressed states, states that are created by frustration and produce personal anguish, weeping, suicidal tendencies, and occasionally even guilt and self-criticism but do not otherwise comply with the usual criteria of melancholia? In these states the dose frequently has to be advanced to the upper range of safety to be effective, because the medication must overcome the active resistance of a current stress. When the medication is offered in sufficient strength, the relative plethora of energy that it produces usually serves to overcome the misery and replace it with euphoria. However, by reinforcing motivation, it also produces a need to act, which, in the presence of stubborn external obstacles, becomes a need to "act out," often destructively.

In Chapter 16 I described certain clinical states that are brought about by the need to defend against impending depletion of libidinal energy. The observations on which these inferences are based are derived from patients who became depressed and recovered from depression under close clinical observation. That is, for each patient certain predepressive states and a fixed sequence in which they occur could be identified. The clinical proof of my inference that an identifiable clinical state represents a defense against depression is that this state can be reversed by the administration of energizing drugs.

Let us consider mania as a defense against depression. If it really serves that function, then it should be possible to treat and prevent the manic attack by using psychic energizers. I have seen no reports of the attempt to treat mania with psychic energizers. In the case of one manic-depressive patient whom I have treated, I found that I could abort incipient manic attacks by increasing the dose of psychic energizer medication on which he was being maintained to prevent depression. It is as if the threat of losing energy elicits a countervailing emergency supply. Replenishing the primary reservoir cancels the demand for this emergency supply.

The spontaneous manic attack is usually treated with a phenothiazine or other antipsychotic tranquilizer. Relatively large doses are usually required. To the psychiatrist it often seems that each increment in dose is met by a corresponding increase in excitement, until the dose becomes so large that the psychic apparatus is completely paralyzed. The manic's visible resistance to the tranquilizing medication can be explained as the reinforcement of his defense against depression. That defense is elicited when the threat of energy depletion is created by the administration of a tranquilizing chemical. The artificial mania that may be induced in the same subject by an overdose of psychic energizer is usually easily subdued by decreasing the dose of energizer, adding a small dose of tranquilizer, or both. These maneuvers merely alleviate the plethora of psychic energy caused by the overdose of energizer; they do not threaten to drive the energy level down below normal maintenance level.

One of the most frequent of the seemingly neurotic, antidepression, defensive states is agoraphobia. Even when it functions as an antide-pression defense, the clinical state superficially resembles classical anxiety hysteria. It differs only in that close questioning may disclose the self-criticism, guilt, and fear of death that betray the underlying depressive nucleus. There may also be a history of a previous depressive state. This syndrome can be greatly alleviated or overcome by the administration of a psychic energizer.

When an individual who has been attempting to sustain himself against a depressive pull feels that he is losing ground and is slipping further into depression, he becomes angrier and angrier at the individual or group upon whom he had depended, and ultimately, in fury, he turns away and retreats into solitude. The clinical manifestations include anger, withdrawal, and solitude, frequently associated with suicidal tendencies. This is not clinical depression. It lacks pessimism, guilt, self-criticism, and inertia. The clinical syndrome may take the form of hysteria or hysterical personality. Yet if the patient can be induced to accept treatment with the psychic energizers, the syndrome can usually be eliminated.

Even before the psychic energizers came into use, it was observed that some depressed patients were considerably helped by small doses of chlorpromazine (Thorazine). These are mostly agitated depressives; the inert depressives usually do not do well with this type of medication. Thioridazine (Mellaril) is a less powerful tranquilizer than chlorpromazine, and chlorprothixene (Taractan), while probably as effective an antipsychotic drug as either of the first two, in my opinion exerts a less powerful depressing effect. Thioridazine and chlorprothixene are both more useful for the treatment of agitated depression then chlorpromazine.

Despite the fact that the patient may obtain considerable relief from the use of these medications in some instances, the psychiatrist will hear indications of persisting guilt, self-criticism, low self-esteem, pessimism, and hypochondria that betray the persistent dynamic nucleus of depressive illness, even though the symptoms and overt manifestations of depression have been dissipated. It seems as though in these cases the patient complains of the agitation, and when that is remedied, he is considerably relieved. However, in many instances, not only does he feel better but he seems able, at least to some degree, to reconstitute.

The only explanatory formulation I can offer at this time, is that the agitation represents the reaction to self-directed hostility. These medications, in small doses, seem to be able to suppress the pathologically intense aggressive energies without exerting too much pressure against the libidinal energies. When the aggression is controlled, the dynamic structure of the depression is undermined, and, at least to some extent, libidinal energies are freed.

The concept of the dose-response curve has received little attention in the psychopharmacological literature, despite the fact that the antipsychotic drugs seem to be therapeutically effective over a much larger range of dosage than are drugs used in internal medicine or even the psychic energizers. What is even more interesting is that the nature of the drug action changes with its dosage. Above the low dose at which chlorpromazine, thioridazine, or chlorprothixene alleviates depressive illness, it no longer alleviates it and in many instances aggravates it. At a considerably higher dose, it may alleviate it once more. In other words, the dose-response curve with respect to the alleviation of agitated depression seems to be undulating. The dose-response curve with respect to the suppression of psychosis is quite different. I believe it rises rapidly and then, beyond a few hundred milligrams a day, probably flattens out. These phenomena have not been well established clinically, and no theory, either biochemical or psychological, has been established to explain them. It is my impression that these curves represent the resultant of the combined action of at least two different influences. I believe that these substances suppress both libidinal energies and aggressive energies independently and that the dose-response curves for these two actions differ one from the other. The inert depressive displays a deficit of both libidinal and aggressive energies. These three chemical agents that we have been discussing, which at every dose suppress both sets of energies, are ordinarily of little assistance to the inert depressive. The agitated depressive, on the other hand, seems to be troubled more by the plethora of aggressive energies that he cannot control, so a substance that attenuates these strongly and libidinal energies only mildly will be helpful. These three substances, in low dose, do just that. However, if they are given in higher dose, they attenuate both aggressive and libidinal energies and will make the patient worse rather than better. Unfortunately, we do not have good data on these dose-response curves. It is my impression that at very high doses—over 1000 mg a day—some depressed patients may be helped because there is another shift in the qualitative action of the drug. (For additional information, see Ostow [1].)

Thiothixene (Navane) in very small doses—1 or 2 mg a day—offers prompt and effective therapy for depression in a number of cases. The patients who respond to this therapy are depressed individuals who are active, and who offer classic complaints of depression, but who are not so seriously disabled that they cannot work. Often they complain of a sense of inner distress or agitation, though outwardly they do not seem agitated. They seem to be afraid that they may have to abandon their work but struggle to overcome the temptation to do so. This is not a well-known treatment. The drug is not recommended for this use by the manufacturer, but the results are striking.

The mechanism of action is obscure. This drug too exhibits an undulating dose-response curve: 1 or 2 mg of thiothixene per day may relieve depression; in the same individual 3 to 30 mg may intensify it, 30 to 70 mg may alleviate depression, and 70 to 100 mg may intensify it again; at very large doses it is likely that depression will be relieved once more. Again, not merely the intensity of the action but its quality depends upon the dose. The component that intensifies depression is doubtless the same one that produces the antipsychotic effect of all the thioxanthines and antipsychotic phenothiazines. However, the nature of the component that antagonizes depression is somewhat more puzzling. It may share some of the action I attributed above to chlorprothixene, namely reducing the intensity of aggresive impulses. If that were so, it should be as effective as chlorprothixene in alleviating agitated depression, and in my experience it is not. I suspect that the relevant action is the creation of some degree of detachment from reality and perhaps from the superego itself. This is obviously not sufficient to reverse depression in individuals who have already lost their resilience. It does provide relief for those who are still struggling against the stress of frustration or disappointment caused by external pressures or internal inhibitions.

If these two effects coexist, it means that one action of thiothixene, its depressive action, alleviates schizophrenic psychosis, while another action, which alleviates depression, might intensify schizophrenic detachment. A paranoid patient improved steadily as the dose of thiothixene was raised to 30 mg a day; When the dose exceeded that, his paranoia became worse and continued to intensify as the dose was raised progressively to 50 mg. I did not pursue it above that dose but suspect that I could have found a level at perhaps 100 mg at which the psychotic state would be suppressed once more.

Lithium is currently recommended as a treatment for mania and as a prophylactic to prevent the recurrence of manic attacks. Some investigators claim that it may be effective in preventing recurrent attacks of depressive illness. I have found that with doses less than those recommended for these prophylactic actions, some cases of true melancholic depression can be quickly resolved. In doses above that required for the treatment of depression, the lithium itself may become depressing. (A dose of 900 to 1200 mg a day is recommended for the prophylaxis of manic and depressive attacks. I find that in many cases 300 or 600 mg a day is sufficient to alleviate an attack of depression. Sometimes one must go higher, but the amount must be titrated because when the therapeutic amount is exceeded, a depressive influence ensues.) Here too, the psychological mechanism is not clear. I have the impression that in these small doses lithium acts to undo deviations of the ego's libido supply from normal, and in higher doses it drives the ego's libido supply down to levels associated with depression.

In selecting medication, one is guided by the characteristics of the illness, of the patient, and of the drug. Actually one does not select a drug so much as one constructs a program. The program includes what one does now in terms of drug therapy, psychotherapy, and environmental influence; and what one projects if things go well or if they go badly. This program may change from time to time, but the psychiatrist should at every point be prepared to change the therapeutic regimen in response to changes in the patient's clinical state. He should try to anticipate these changes and be prepared with plans for appropriate alterations in therapeutic regimen.

I distinguished above between true melancholic depression and nonmelancholic depressive states. This distinction may be important in selecting medication. The psychic energizers, because they produce euphoria, will combat all types of depression. However, if they are given to schizophrenic depressed patients, they have to be covered by an adequate amount of antipsychotic medication lest they trigger a psychotic episode. Lithium, on the other hand, will alleviate only melancholic depressions.

I know of no way to assess in advance how individual patients will respond to any of the psychic energizers, in terms of sensitivity to therapeutic effects or to noxious effects. Neither physical nor psychological characteristics seem correlated with these sensitivities. Often one finds that when another depressed member of the same family was treated with a psychic energizer, his response is duplicated by the patient. However, if the depressed patient has before him the example of one or more family members who are or have been ill, especially if they have done poorly, he will tend to identify with them and anticipate that he will do as badly or worse. The psychiatrist may wish to discourage such identification by using medications other than those used by the "bad example." While this consideration should not be overriding, when other options are available, it might be wise to honor it.

While the dose-response curve from individual to individual varies in a manner that up to now is unpredictable, once such a curve for a given patient has been established, it will be altered by the degree of stress affecting the patient. If the patient responds well to a given dose and is then subjected to an increase in stress—for example, by pressure from a difficult spouse or by a career disappointment—he may relapse while still on the same dose of medication. An increase in dose may then restore equilibrium. A further increase in stress may again require further increase in dose. Some patients ultimately become unresponsive to any dose. I have called this phenomenon "escape from antidepression control." When that happens, a course of electric shock therapy may restore the patient's sensitivity to antidepressant medication. There are no reliable data, but I suspect that some patients who are unresponsive to any other chemical approach may be helped by relatively large doses of thiothixene or any of the piperazine phenothiazines.

Noxious effects of medication must be considered in selecting therapeutic drugs. Many of the tricyclic compounds cannot be used by patients who have cardiac disease, and none can be used by patients with glaucoma (except with the consent of the treating opthalmologist) or partial urinary obstruction. Lithium cannot be used by patients who have renal disease.

From the psychological point of view, one should be prepared to find that side effects, even when there is no real threat to physical health, may lend verisimilitude to hypochondriacal delusions or fantasies. For example, a woman with a hypochondriacal obsession about her rectum and anus, clearly based on fantasies of anal masturbation, was unable to tolerate tricyclic energizers because the moderate constipation that they induced intensified her worry and agitation.

Having worked out with the patient his feelings about being given medication, the psychiatrist then devises the program of therapy. He cannot assume that the first drug selected will be successful, though it may be. If the drug is not successful, or if it must be discontinued because of side effects or toxicity, then the psychiatrist should be ready to replace it with another medication or procedure. One need not, at the outset, announce any anticipation of failure to the patient, but when the question of failure comes up, the psychiatrist should be able to assure the patient that reserve modalities are available and that the psychiatrist does indeed have an organized sequential program in mind.

When the transference is tinged with magic, then the medication becomes a magical potion. There are occasions when the psychiatrist may wish to encourage this illusion. For example, when the patient is desperately ill and requires maximum encouragement, the psychiatrist will demonstrate his professional concern and lend his magic to the medication if he personally gives the patient the pill rather than the prescription. When the patient is not desperately ill, one will probably wish to discourage the illusion of magic, if for no other reason than because it is unrealistic and conceals the negative component of the transference.

The patient must be informed about the medication. However, how much or how little information, or what specific information he should be given, depends upon his state of mind. He should always be told the name of the specific substance, and the pharmacist should be instructed to label the container with the name of the drug and the strength of the pill or the capsule.

It has not been sufficiently emphasized in promotional literature, at least until recently, that little if any therapeutic effect will be achieved by the administration of psychic energizers before three to four weeks in the case of the tricyclic substances, and before four to four and one-half weeks in the case of monoamine oxidase inhibitors. The patient must be cautioned about this latency lest he become discouraged at the delay in his improvement or unrealistically encouraged by an early placebo effect.

The patient should be informed that there may be some side effects, so that when they do occur they do not disturb him unduly, and so that he will report them promptly. I find it best not to tell the patient specifically what to look for lest he be too eager to find it. However, one can permit this only when the patient is seen so frequently that it is unlikely that side effects or the symptoms of toxic effects will escape the psychiatrist's attention. The less frequently the patient is seen, the more information he must be given about side effects.

To a large extent, the patient's response to drug therapy is a function of the transference currently prevailing. If the transference is positive, the patient is eager to respond well to medication, and this desire will reinforce the therapeutic effects of the drug and minimize its side effects. If the transference is negative, the patient will be eager to demonstrate that he is being poisoned rather than being helped. He will resist therapeutic effects and exaggerate side effects.

Transference, in turn, is influenced by response to the drug. If things go well, that is, if drug therapy succeeds with few or no side effects, transference is intensified and its magical quality is reinforced. If things go badly, the psychiatrist's actual failure will confirm the depressed patient's feeling that the parental figure upon whom he has been depending has let him down. In fact, failure may be used to confirm the patient's hypochondriacal belief that he cannot recover under any circumstances.

Being given a material substance to be swallowed is bound to stimulate oral fantasies within the transference. If a clinging tendency prevails in the transference, medication will be seen as gratification of the need to be fed by a good mother, and the drug will be endowed with magical therapeutic properties. Such a fantasy will reinforce the drug's pharmacological effect. One patient who recovered rapidly on a regimen including several varieties of medication dreamed that he was at a party in which there was a buffet table set with different varieties of cakes and cookies. A young woman dreamed of her pills as Life Savers. Obviously the oral fantasies sometimes take the form of fellatio. In this last example, the Life Savers were mingled with a whitish fluid that reminded the patient of semen.

Conversely, if the transference is negative, or if things go badly, the patient may come to feel that he is being poisoned. If the need to be fed and loved is so strong that it produces anxiety, the patient may resist medication, fearing that it might produce addiction. For example, a young woman with a tendency toward addiction developed visual hallucinations as a result of the anticholinergic effect of a tricyclic compound. A dream the following night revealed that she associated this experience with the hallucinations induced by LSD, which she had used in the past. She concluded that I was converting her into a "junkie," and this idea contributed to her resistance to treatment. If the depression is so severe that the patient has withdrawn from object relations, he may see medication as poison and resist it.

More generally, to the patient, accepting a drug to be swallowed implies an object relation. The patient's attitude toward the object relation determines his attitude toward the drug. Those eager to strengthen object relations in the transference will welcome the drug; those suspicious of object relations in the transference will suspect the drug; those incapable of object relations will reject the drug.

One encounters other variants of oral fantasies. Some individuals experience the administration of medication by the psychiatrist as impregnation. The feeling of rebirth and the sense of creativity that accompany recovery are then seen as the direct consequences of this impregnation. Other patients, under the influence of aggressive strivings, interpret the swallowing of medication as the fulfillment of incorporation fantasies. One woman who was both schizophrenic and depressed associated to her pills, which appeared manifestly in her dreams, both almonds, which her mother had fed her as a child, and "babies' penises," similar to that of her infant son.

During the initial waiting period (before the psychic energizer takes effect), one encourages the patient and offers whatever psychotherapeutic relief one can. I always give the patient a fixed date, approximately four weeks hence, before which he should not expect relief. During this latent period, one may also use any of the other medications I have mentioned. They act within a matter of a few days, and if they do not resolve the depression, they may at least ameliorate it. By the time one has finished trying these substances, one at a time, the latent period will have passed. Since side effects are likely to occur during this latency, the psychiatrist must be prepared to deal with them, that is, to encourage the patient to ignore them and to reassure him against possible hypochondriacal elaboration. If the situation is too urgent to permit this delay, one has a choice between intramuscular injection of imipramine (Tofranil) or amitriptyline (Elavil), or electric shock therapy.

Record keeping is a topic seldom spoken of among psychoanalysts. Some psychoanalysts keep no records; others keep meticulous records; most keep minimal records. There is seldom occasion in ordinary psychoanalytic procedures to refer to records, and most analysts who do keep records do so for research purposes. However, when drugs are administered, it is necessary to keep good records of what medication and what dose is taken each day; what changes are reported by the patient and observed by the psychiatrist; what changes may be inferred by psychoanalytic methods such as free association and dreams; what physical side effects are reported or observed. Without such records it is impossible to judge what the medication is doing, to regulate its dose, or to combine it with other medications. I have found it helpful, in addition to keeping brief written notations of the content of sessions, to record on graph paper a set of parameters of psychic function, alongside drug dosage. With such a record I can trace at a glance the fluctuations of a given symptom or parameter of psychic function and relate it to medication as well as to external events.

The analytic psychiatrist has a great advantage over his nonanalytic colleague in administering therapeutic drugs. He can detect preconscious changes before they become conscious and thereby avoid being deceived by the patient's denials. It not infrequently happens, for example, that a patient will declare that he is feeling quite well but in the same session will report a dream that clearly betrays to the analyst a depressive process. Usually in such instances, overt clinical relapse follows within hours or days. One patient told me that he was doing well and was pleased with himself but reported a dream in which he was attending a funeral. Another, who also reported freedom from symptoms, dreamed of a sick animal. Both patients relapsed within hours. Similarly, the analyst can detect resurgent hostility or fantasies of rebirth in dreams or associations before clinical improvement from depression becomes obvious to the patient.

The course of recovery induced by psychic energizers, whether tricyclic compounds or monoamine oxidase inhibitors, is slow enough to permit the psychotherapist to observe the schedule of recovery. This schedule remains remarkably constant from one episode of depression and recovery to another. In the case of one patient whom I observed in two such recovery sequences, the schedule was the following: after two and one-half to three weeks he first acknowledged the hostile components of his ambivalence to his wife, hitherto repressed. After three weeks he reported a resurgence of sexual desire and an interest in resuming object relations. Sadistic fantasies became conscious. After four weeks there was a resumption of sexual activity; there was a feeling of rebirth; and he displaced his sexual drive from his wife to extramarital partners. Generally as the patient recovers, hostility toward principal love objects becomes overt. Affectionate feelings reappear but are directed toward substitute objects or sometimes narcissistically toward oneself. Meanwhile the classic indicators of depression, guilt, self-criticism, pessimism, insomnia, and anorexia all disappear silently.

The sequence of changes gives us little information about the chain of causation, but it does confirm Freud's inference that in melancholia, hostility meant for the love object is redirected against the self. That is, the confirmation is demonstrated by the redirection of the hostility from the self toward the love object as the patient emerges from the melancholia. At the moment, I favor the idea that disappointment or frustration or stress produces a diminution in self-esteem. The latter increases dependent need and this in turn requires repression of overt hostility toward the anaclitic love object. When a psychic energizer restores libido to the ego, the dependency requirement is eliminated; rebirth fantasies ensue; and the patient feels free to display his anger against the love object, either because that object is responsible for the current frustration, or because the object, representing the omnipotent parent, has failed to protect the patient against the current stress.

When improvement is brought about by more rapidly acting chemicals, the disappearance of the feelings of distress becomes more prominent, while the externalization of the hostility and revival of libido occur more slowly and less dramatically.

When psychic energizer therapy is pushed too hard, one encounters a syndrome resembling mania, which I have called the libido plethora syndrome. The patient is overactive and overcommunicative, talking and writing incessantly. He considers himself omnipotent and omniscient. He is wildly and unrealistically optimistic. He exhibits overt hostility toward his proper love objects and readily accepts substitutes. Some patients even become frightened of the strength of their own instinctual drives. One woman in such a state, for example, experienced repeated and enjoyable orgasms during intercourse but nevertheless became so frightened by her insatiable need that she fled from her partner.

This state differs from true mania in that it quickly subsides in response to a reduction in the dose of psychic energizer, especially if a small amount of tranquilizing medication is added. In true mania, tranquilizing medication elicits at first a reactive tendency to become even higher and more agitated, since the mania serves to defend against depression and a drug that tends to increase the depressive tendency at first elicits an intensification of the defense against it. Enough tranquilizing medication must be given to overwhelm this defensive system before the mania is overcome.

It is interesting that in true, natural mania, with initial doses of tranquilizing medication, one can see depletion of the ego reservoir as manifested by inertia and sleepiness, while mental content remains manic. Several days are required on continuing medication before the poverty of the conscious ego penetrates to the drive representatives in the ego.

The consequence of failure of drug therapy depends upon the patient's state of mind. To the extent that the patient has seen the drug treatment as magical, its failure will leave the image of the analyst degraded. In other words, if the prospect of success was unrealistically based, then the fact of failure will be seen as unrealistically damaging. To forestall this possibility, the illusion of magic should be dealt with in the psychotherapeutic work at the outset. Obviously some degree of magic may be helpful in sustaining a despairing patient, but one must take into account also the fact that the magical quality is projected onto the analyst partly to cover a degraded image. Therefore in the event of a failure, when the magic disappears, nothing will be left to sustain either the treatment or the patient. The impact of failure of any given medication will be diminished if the patient has been assured beforehand that a program of therapy has been begun, no one element of which can be reliably promised to work. The patient can be assured that with the number and variety of drugs available, a large majority of patients can be helped. If none does help, the psychiatrist determines in advance whether he considers the situation sufficiently serious to warrant electric shock treatment.

The news that pharmacotherapy has failed does not, in my experience, intensify the depression, though it does seem to the patient to justify his pessimism. I have never seen a patient worse for the trial than he was previously.

Failure to recover *spontaneously* from depression is attributable to either the persistence of the pathogenic stress or a lack of resilience characteristic of melancholic depression. Thiothixene and the phenothiazines seem able to help the patient handle current stress so his response is less extreme and more appropriate. However, they may not help the patient who has slipped into inertia. The psychic energizers and lithium can restore resilience so a patient free of stress will recover. Even when the stress continues, a psychic energizer in sufficient dose might help the patient to overcome it.

Theoretically, if the pathogenic stress has disappeared and the depressive state has been resolved, the patient should be free to continue normally. For example, if a businessman becomes depressed as a result of a strike, after the strike is over and business has resumed, when he is brought out of depression, we should find no pathological behavior. Actually we seldom see such an outcome if we observe the patient carefully. We usually find that an individual who responds with depression to stress of a kind and degree that most individuals endure with pain but without becoming ill is likely to exhibit some impairment in his capacity for object relations even when he is at his best. The reason may be that the individual with depressive vulnerability— that is, with a volatile psychic energy supply—whether or not he actually becomes depressed, is likely to retain anaclitic dependency into adult life. This anaclitic attitude, though it can be camouflaged, seriously distorts object relations. (An exception to this generalization would be the adult who becomes depressed for the first time in the seventh decade of life or later as a result of the changes of aging; his depression does not reflect a lifelong vulnerability.) Accordingly, after the depression has been lifted, the patient will resume his usual abnormal pattern of object relations. He is also likely to wish to continue to deny the abnormality of this pattern and therefore to reject psychotherapy.

When the pathogenic stress continues, the depression may be resolved to some extent by thiothixene, or more powerfully by a psychic energizer. The dose required will usually be relatively high. In some instances the patient under stress may actually "escape the control of antidepression therapy," as I noted earlier. However, when the depression can be successfully overcome, the patient is forced once more to confront the stress under which he collapsed in the first place, without the refuge afforded by his illness. Therefore he will have to take other measures to contend with it. We have seen that in the course of recovery, aggression is redirected outward. This aggression will now be brought to bear to contend with the stressful situation. The patient may resist the stress more vigorously. For example, a businessman who became depressed repeatedly in the course of a running conflict with his associates, each time he recovered from depression, launched a new campaign to override and defeat his partner. The patient may turn away from the disappointing object. For example, when the depression occurs in the context of a bad marital relation, recovery from depression may encourage more vigorous opposition to the spouse and ultimate turning away by engaging in sexual affairs with others, by separation without divorce, or by divorce when a replacement has been found.

Depression often occurs in a young person who finds that he cannot meet social expectations for vocational and sexual responsibility. When he recovers from a depressive episode, the young person may withdraw even more vigorously than previously because the reinforced libidinal energies threaten to push him into situations that elicit anxiety. The withdrawal may take the form of literal seclusiveness, overinvolvement in nonserious activities, such as sports, or in an interminable program of academic studies leading to no appropriate advancement in status, or if there is a schizophrenic diathesis, an actual psychotic episode may ensue.

In cases in which chemical treatment of depression leaves the patient once more confronting an irresistible stress, it becomes important to limit the dose of psychic energizer medication so that the patient is not driven more vigorously than he can tolerate. It is helpful also to engage him in a psychotherapeutic procedure that will guide him, discourage acting out, and help him to overcome his inner inhibitions or to come to terms realistically with them and with external obstacles. If a schizophrenic retreat does ensue, it becomes necessary to complement the psychic energizer with an antipsychotic tranquilizer.

The recovered depressive who finds himself struggling to contend with a continuing pathogenic stress may exhibit the syndrome I have called narcissistic tranquility, characterized by bulimia, weight gain, hypersomnolence, increased sexual desire, and a tendency to accumulate possessions. This is a minor stress reaction as distinguished from psychosis or even acting out, which may be considered major reactions. Note that it is not the drug that produces the syndrome but the state of mind in which the patient finds himself.

I have never encountered a patient who resisted discontinuing antidepressant medication, and I have heard of only one patient who became addicted. The reason may be that the interval between the time the drug is taken and the time its antidepression effect is felt is so long that the immediate feeling of gratification, which promotes addiction, does not occur. On the contrary, most patients are eager to give up antidepressant medication, and some discontinue it before being instructed to do so. It is disturbing to their self-esteem to feel that their well-being depends upon chemical support.

When the antidepressant chemical support can safely be withdrawn is a function of the patient's vulnerability to depressive illness and the degree of stress currently prevailing. If the patient has become depressed as a result of a severe blow that no longer exists but has shown no previous propensity to depression, one may discontinue medication shortly after recovery occurs. It is usually wise to cut down the dose gradually. If the patient shows signs of relapse, medication can be resumed promptly and one will then not have to wait the usual three to four weeks' latency before its effect is felt. When the patient has exhibited a depressive diathesis in the past, and the pathogenic stress continues, whether the stress is internal or external, it may become necessary to continue medication indefinitely. Between these two extremes are the patients who become depressed recurrently when their defenses fail or when they are subject to recurrent stress. Shortly after a drug therapy program has relieved them of depression, medication may be stopped and they may be able to do without medication for months or years before breaking down again. Obviously when the patient is in psychoanalytic therapy, it becomes necessary to try to understand the meaning of continuing the medication or of removing it.

As mentioned earlier, certain syndromes that may present as neurosis, psychosis, or acting out behavior are really defenses against depression. These include some cases of agoraphobia, some cases of hysteria, some cases of schizophrenia, and some cases of angry withdrawal. These can be relieved by drugs that combat depression. The principles that govern the administration of drugs for depression, apply in these instances as well.

SUMMARY

Drug therapy can be used for treatment of depression with or without psychotherapy, but optimally with a maximum of psychotherapeutic assistance. Selection among the medications available can be guided by the presenting symptoms, but reliable prediction of effectiveness is not possible.

The fact of taking a chemical agent for treatment of a psychic disturbance influences the patient's image of himself and, if he is in psychotherapy or analysis, the transference as well. The side effects of these agents will also affect the self-image and the transference.

When the patient recovers from his depression, he may still have to contend with the pathogenic stress. His efforts may be self-defeating, and he will therefore profit if psychotherapeutic guidance is available.

REFERENCES

1. Ostow, M.   On the treatment of depression with tranquilizers, with a dissenting view of lithium therapy. *N.Y. State J. Med.*, in press.
2. Ostow, M., and Kline, N. S.   The Psychic Action of Reserpine and Chlorpromazine. In N. S. Kline, *Psychopharmacology Frontiers*. Boston: Little, Brown, 1959.

Toward a Theory
of Depression

Toward a Theory
That Encompasses Depression:
A Revision of Existing Causal Hypotheses
in Pychoanalysis

MICHAEL FRANZ BASCH

Depression as a clinical entity seems to have been familiar in all periods of recorded history. Seemingly, it may occur at any time during the human life span, and it has been attributed to other primates as well [26]. Depression has been termed an affect, an illness, a mood, a character style, a symptom, and a syndrome [6, 52]. In spite of its ubiquity and universality it remains undefined, and there exists no agreed upon theory that satisfactorily explains its manifestations.

Today, many theories of depression are based on the medical model for the infectious diseases. Hypotheses of this sort are designed to find or isolate the causal factor without which there would be no depression. This is an analogy to diseases such as tuberculosis, which, whatever other factors known and unknown may be involved in its occurrence, cannot exist in the absence of the tubercle bacillus. On this basis the evidence that depressive symptoms are alleviated variously by chemical, physical, psychological, and social means leads to the confusion of treatment and improvement with cause and effect and then to argument as to whether depression is a chemical, neurophysiological, or psychological illness. I believe that such debates miss the point. To me depression suggests a general system dysfunction rather than a unitary disease entity. For example, we do not speak of muscle weakness as an illness and look for its cause, nor do we try to understand the phenomenon on the basis of its clinical appearance. Rather, paresis and paralysis indicate dysfunctions of the skeletal muscle system that can be caused by neurological, traumatic, chemical, psychological, or genetic disease, and the presenting picture will vary depending on the nature and severity of the precipitating and associated factors. Similarly, depressed behavior and mood may appear alone or in combination with other signs and symptoms, has a wide range of intensity with effects ranging from total incapacity to almost unnoticed discomfort, and is precipitated by a variety of factors presumed to be causal. To confuse an end result called depression with an underlying specific disease and search for its cause hinders both understanding and treatment. Instead, it seems to me more promising to seek out the systemic pathology that represents the underlying common denominator of all depressions regardless of their precipitating cause. Of course this is not a new idea; Freud and others sought such general explanations on both the clinical and the more abstract hypothetical level. However, not till recently did psychology, philosophy, and neurophysiology reach a level of development that would permit such a formulation.

In this chapter I shall review some pertinent aspects of the problems related to establishing a general explanation for depression and the significance of current developments in science and scientific philosophy that have a bearing on this quest.

Current theories of psychological functioning based on studies of the development and processes of cognition, affect, and perception contradict those hypotheses used as the foundation for psychoanalytic metapsychology. As long as the causal explanation of depression in psychoanalysis depends on a fundamentally faulty model of mentation, it will remain unsatisfactory. It is therefore necessary to examine and correct many of the underlying explanatory principles adduced by psychoanalysis to explain its clinical findings in order to pave the way for the more specific task of suggesting an explanation for depression as a system dysfunction.

HISTORICAL PERSPECTIVE

Freud hypothesized in *Mourning and Melancholia* [24] that a real or symbolic loss of an ambivalently regarded object precipitated the lowered self-esteem and self-hatred observed in melancholic patients. In these cases the unconscious anger felt toward the lost object was turned on the self through regressive identification. Freud accepted Abraham's suggestion that such an outcome hinges on predisposing pathology at the oral stage of psychosexual development. Freud himself warned that his explanation was probably not satisfactory for all cases because he had studied only a small sample and his was a psychogenic explanation that did not take the probable somatic factors into account. Many psychoanalysts have taken Freud's lead and made significant contributions by exploring in great detail the nature and vicissitudes of the early trauma that predisposes to depressive pathology (see Chapter 6). It was also noted, however, that not all cases of psychogenic depression fit the prototype of *Mourning and Melancholia*. Accordingly, Bibring [10] advanced a more encompassing hypothesis. He suggests that depression is an indicator of intrasystemic ego pathology representing the ego's reaction of hopelessness when confronted by its inability to achieve significant, immutable, unconscious narcissistic goals. However, these need not be oral narcissistic goals exclusively. Bibring claims that in predisposed persons it is the loss of power by the ego at any stage of psychosexual development that renders life meaningless and lowers self-esteem. He does not contradict the earlier findings of Freud and others but includes them in a larger framework. This hypothesis also encompasses those depressions seemingly precipitated by organic disturbances [1]. By exhausting the ego, leaving it relatively incapacitated and therefore unable to strive for the fulfillment of its narcissistic goals, somatic factors can bring about the same intrasystemic ego situation, and potentially the same outcome, as is brought about by psychological conflict.

Using Bibring's criteria, not all depressed affect states would necessarily qualify as depressions in the dynamic sense. Freud himself had already suggested that the picture of melancholia could be produced simply by a narcissistic blow or by toxic factors [24]. Only if the dejected mood represents a conflict between firmly held goals and a hopelessness about achieving these would it be indicative of a depression. Normal mourning for example should not be called "simple depression," as it is so often labeled, for there is no dynamic conflict involved. Rather, there is a frustration due to missing an object through which and with which to reach one's goals, and when a new object has been found mourning terminates. What is mourned in normal grief is not inability but lack of opportunity to achieve one's goals when deprived of a suitable object. Only if a state of hopelessness about this situation supervenes does depression replace mourning. There are many psychological constellations that can promote moods of sadness, dejection, etc. Bibring's thesis implies that only if these are outcomes of loss of hope regarding unconscious narcissistic wishes may one attribute these moods to an underlying depression. Indeed, even the conscious feeling of loss of hope is not necessarily evidence of depression, since on the unconscious level it is quite possible that the complaint of hopelessness paradoxically expresses hope, with "hopelessness" seen as a means of enlisting help in achieving one's narcissistic needs.

Bibring's approach is very much in keeping with that of psychoanalysis generally, since his diagnosis of depression is based on an examination of unconscious factors rather than on the manifest content of the patient's association or other aspects of overt behavior or appearance. However, it is a clinical descriptive explanatory theory and not a causal explanatory theory [5]. His inferences and generalizations are made from, and their accuracy can in turn be tested through, the analytic observations of unconscious wishes, conflicts, and defenses. Such observations should not then have been used to serve, phoenix-like, as the explanation for their own existence, but that is what happened. Bibring, like Freud, uses causal language in speaking of the ego, treating it, as did Freud, as if it were an entity or an active principle underlying behavior. However, in practice, the word "ego" is used in psychoanalysis as a collective noun subsuming what Freud termed secondary process, i.e., adaptation to reality, behavior governed by delay, nonimpulsive functioning, age-appropriate maturity, etc. It is circular reasoning simply to reify such a collective noun and promote it to an explanatory principle that provides the substratum for the very findings it expresses collectively. Similarly, to say that the ego fails to meet its goals is to ask implicitly what this ego might be or what power it represents. Psychoanalysis, of course, attempts to solve this problem by using "ego" as a bridging term that also refers to a part of the nonanatomical mental apparatus postulated by Freud. But this is not an explanation; instead it creates a new problem: what might be the nature of this mental apparatus? In the case of depression, for example, organic factors such as toxins, anoxia, and cancer seem able to bring about depression, a psychological effect. If the mental apparatus is not the brain, what is the nature of the "leap" between the organic and the psychological? In other words, a search for causal explanations in psychology inevitably and immediately forces one to deal with the mind-brain problem.

The mind-body dichotomy has plagued science and philosophy since Descartes equated mind with consciousness and excluded thought and reason from the laws that governed the body. Freud was quite aware of the difficulty this posed for psychology and dealt with it repeatedly, but he was only partially successful in resolving it. On the clinical and methodological levels he did resolve it through his discovery of the psychoanalytic method, whose application demonstrated (1) that reason and thought, like all other natural events, can be examined scientifically and, at least post-dictively, can be seen to be determined by antecedent experience, and (2) that mental life was not equivalent or necessarily linked to consciousness. However, his so-called metapsychology, the hypotheses regarding the nature and operation of the system whose activity made mental life possible, was not equally successful in transcending the Cartesian separation between mind and brain.

Freud's theories regarding the manner in which thoughts originated and were processed were described in his *Project for a Scientific Psychology* [20]. As first formulated they were an attempt at a unitary theory for psychology in which mind and brain were treated as identical. Thought was equated with cortical activity, and meaning with the association of perceptual images at the neuronal synapse. Fear and moral conflict led to the formation of defensively distorted associations or to perceptual disavowal of painful or reprehensible experiences. Neuroses were the outward manifestations of such associations, and the task of the physician was to trace these and clarify them for the patient. The patient's understanding of the true meaning of defensive memory robbed the pathological associations of their power to control behavior and led to cure. Freud apparently found this theory unsatisfactory in many respects and did not publish it in his lifetime. Though he never abandoned his conviction that mind originated in brain, in 1900 [21] and thereafter his metapsychological efforts sought to deal with mind as a mental apparatus functionally independent of neuroanatomy and neurophysiology. In doing so Freud inadvertently reinstated the conceptual split between mind and body. Furthermore, he had not removed himself as far from neurology as he thought. Even though he declared it to be a nonmaterial construct, the mental apparatus betrays its true nature by functioning according to the nineteenth-century concept of brain physiology. Although now supposedly a psychic structure rather than a physical one, and powered by a psychic energy rather than a material one, the mental apparatus as portrayed in *The Interpretation of Dreams* [21], *The Unconscious* [23], and *The Ego and the Id* [25] remains in its structural essentials identical with the brain model of the *Project* [20]. Contrary to the generally accepted opinion in psychoanalysis, Freud's shift from the neurological model to the mental apparatus did not make much difference in resolving the difficulties of his causal explanatory theory. I believe that the basic problem with both forms of Freud's metapsychological models remains the same—they are inadequate to the function they are used to depict and therefore cannot support an acceptable theory of thinking.

MIND AND BRAIN

Even today many psychoanalysts, and other psychologists too, feel that a scientific explanation of behavior requires postulation of some generative apparatus whose operation accounts for the permanence of character, psychic determinism, and the laws of unconscious and conscious behavior. The alternative to a mental apparatus seems to be the unsatisfying "black box" approach of naive behaviorism, which equates behavior with what is public and overt, and eliminates private experience from consideration. A resolution of this issue is possible today through structuralism and the method of general systems theory. These disciplines have demonstrated that the ability to describe the world in a law-like manner depends on the relationship between events and not on their material embodiment. As long as a materialistic physics provided the paradigm for what was to be called scientific, reality was always represented by some thing. If the mind was not a material thing, then it had to be a nonmaterial "thing," a "mental apparatus" instead of a physical apparatus. Such a materialistic view has been shown to be inadequate; indeed, since Einstein, physics itself is structuralistic rather than materialistic in its philosophical outlook.

By examining the theories that Freud advanced to explain his findings, we may see how his constructs were limited by the scientific atmosphere in which he worked and by the absence of those concepts and that vocabulary needed to express his fundamental propositions in a valid manner. It is now possible to restate Freud's explanatory concepts so that they are in keeping with today's more encompassing scientific views, thereby making his clinical findings more meaningful for all fields investigating the human condition.

The Mental Apparatus

The separation of mind from body took place in psychoanalysis with Freud's postulation of a "mental apparatus." Through this device Freud hoped to free himself of the need to explain mental life neurologically while still creating a theoretical substructure that would enable him to categorize and explain his clinical findings systematically. Insofar as the postulation of a mental apparatus gave Freud personally the compromise he needed to pursue his work, while still believing that he was not straying from the norms of scientific rectitude, it may have been not only a necessary but a fortuitous step. As an acceptable explanation for mental life, however, the concept of a mental apparatus fails to accomplish its aim. It is now possible to demonstrate that Freud's original approach to the origin of mental life in the *Project* was correct and that mentation represents a function of the brain. On the level of clinical theory psychoanalysis has always stressed that structure is determined dynamically, i.e., through extant relationships. But now it is possible also to explain the mechanisms underlying this dynamic structure without having to resort to either physicalistic reductionism or fictitious psychic energic forces. However, the elimination of the topographic or topological distinction between mind and brain raises the specter of reductionism for those who have come to associate the distinction between psychology and other disciplines with the separation of mind from body. It is feared that in recognizing "mind" as a function of the brain, psychological activity becomes equated with neurophysiology, for example, with nerve impulses and brain waves per se. However, this is not the case.

It has become possible to formulate an organically based theory for the genesis of mental life that is not reductionistic and does not require the postulation of scientifically untenable entities or constructs, which Ryle [49] aptly calls "ghosts in the machine." "Brain" and "mind" are words that do not belong in the same universe of discourse. Operationally, "brain" indicates the *substrate* to which a number of biological functions are referred while "mind" designates *functions* which happen to (but need not necessarily) originate in the bodily substrate called the brain. To quote Ryle, " 'my mind' does not stand for another organ. It signifies my ability and proneness to do certain sorts of things" [p. 168], and, "to talk of a person's mind is not to talk of a repository which is permitted to house objects that something called 'the physical world' is forbidden to house; it is to talk of the person's abilities, liabilities and inclinations to do and undergo certain sorts of things, and of the doing and undergoing of these things in the ordinary world" [p. 199].

The brain supplies the fuel—the calories that make signal processing possible—and the molecular substrate in which message processing takes place. "Mind" is a word encompassing the vicissitudes of encoded patterns whose relationship form a nonmaterial structure based on, but not equated with, brain. Both mind and brain are real, i.e., are composed of stable relationships that allow predictions to be made and tested experimentally, but they belong to different orders of existence. Together mind and brain form a hierarchy in the general systems sense, not a unity.

It seems that perceptual stimulation in all other forms of life results in action of a muscular or glandular sort; in man alone may the ordering-abstracting activity of the brain be an end in itself. Message processing may itself be a signal leading to more message processing and not necessarily or primarily to muscular or glandular reactions. This is mentation (thinking), and it must be added to the reactions of contraction and secretion with which animals respond to messages.*

Psychology does not now study brain signals, i.e., the electromag-

---

* That thought is a function of the brain, organic and biological, rather than a "spiritual" entity, was postulated by the physician-philosopher Claude Bernard in the nineteenth century [32].

netic interactions of neurons as such, anymore than it did before. Psychology still focuses on "meaning," the dispositional effect that message processing has on the activity of the organism, and leaves to other sciences the investigation of how the physical signals and patterns involved are actually encoded and transmitted within the neural substrate. The error of a so-called behaviorist psychology limited to consensually validatable sensory observations is avoided if it is understood that the term behavior includes the potential for and tendencies toward reactions that do not necessarily terminate in observable autonomic and skeletal muscle phenomena. Psychoanalysis and its empathic use of the transference is the ideal method for investigating what MacKay [38] calls the brain's "matrix of conditional probabilities," the encoded potential for what might happen behaviorally in a given situation if certain messages were received. On a conscious level, wishes, hopes, ideas, and fantasies form the mental goal-directed activity from which a partial picture of the matrix of conditional probabilities may be obtained through introspection. The more accurate and broader grasp of mental behavior is obtained through the method of psychoanalysis, which reveals the matrix of conditional probabilities in all its ramifications in the transference neurosis.

Psychic Economics

In addition to understanding that the brain is the organ underlying psychological activity and that one need not postulate imaginary intermediaries like "mind" or "mental apparatus," it is also necessary to correct some still very common misconceptions about the nature of the brain's operations.

During Freud's time, even more so than today, mathematical quantification of sensory observation as practiced in the physics laboratory was the hallmark of scientific respectability, and Freud felt compelled to show that his researches could be expressed in that language [20]. This led to an unwarranted extrapolation of the entropic tendency of closed, inert systems to the living organism [29, 55] and the misapprehension (still current in psychoanalysis) that the brain seeks an equilibrium as close as possible to a stimulus-free "nirvana." Conceived in this fashion, the brain, left to its own devices, would follow the laws of thermodynamics and move from a state of high organization and unstable differentiation to an amorphous, stable steady state [62].

Freud's reliance on this axiom, his comparison of the brain and later the mental apparatus with systems seeking a stimulus-free or almost stimulus-free condition at all costs, had significant consequences. The fruitless task of trying to explain psychoanalytic clinical findings with explanations based on this notion already found Freud involved in page after page of complex, frustrating speculation, changing the format of his theories periodically but always openly dissatisfied with the results. We now know that the closed system concept of thermodynamics cannot adequately describe systems that show dynamic development proceeding from a less differentiated to a more complex state. Living systems are open systems, systems that temporarily defy the laws of thermodynamics, move toward greater complexity, and resist disintegration. Open systems do not just respond passively to intersystemic and intrasystemic changes but utilize these as signals that determine the nature of their response [9]. Open systems influence their environment by selective interaction and actively participate in shaping their own future. Behavior is another word for this activity of open systems. Small wonder then that psychoanalysis, which studies certain structures arising from the functioning of that most complex of open systems, the human brain, cannot depend for its causal theory on the thermodynamic model that was the paradigm for scientific explanation in Freud's day. Far from seeking a low-level equilibrium, it has been shown that the brain is continuously active in its totality and has a need for optimal stimulation. As the sensory deprivation experiments have shown, instead of welcoming a peaceful state, the brain engages in a veritable frenzy of activity in its search for stimuli and ends up by artificially providing them through fantasies, hallucinations, etc.

Another stumbling block in theory formation is the energic concept in thought processing. As Freud recognized, one of the characteristic features of neurotic thought is its overriding influence on behavior. In spite of all the common sense that can be brought to bear, the neurotic need demands fulfillment and will brook no interference. The economic point of view was developed to express the varying degrees of power that particular thoughts have on behavior. In Freud's day power was expressed in terms of energy. He first postulated in the *Project* that a certain amount of environmental energy entered the brain with each sensory stimulus and was converted to brain energy and attached to the thoughts corresponding to the particular perception. The idea that the strength of a thought depended on its energy charge was not discarded when Freud substituted the mental apparatus for the brain; brain energy became the "psychic energy" that powered the mental apparatus.

Psychic energy was considered a form of drive energy that represented the demands of the body's instinctual forces on the mind. Quantities of drive energy impinged on the mental apparatus, which, seeking the quiescent state, had to discharge this energy by finding opportunities to fulfill the drive's aim. In spite of its popularity as an explanation in psychoanalysis, the notion of a psychic energy has been shown to be scientifically untenable [34, 43, 48].

It is also not possible, as has sometimes been suggested [15], to reverse Freud's path and convert psychic energy back into brain energy to restore a unitary theory of mind and brain. Enough is known about the brain [17] to establish that it does not function as an energy transmitting or processing organ. The passage of nerve impulses is a propagation, not an energy transmission. That mentation proceeds by means of energy transformation is an untenable concept in the light of present day neurophysiological knowledge [29]; as Lashley has pointed out, there is no energy available for the transformation postulated by psychoanalytic metapsychology [15]. Like the computing automata that simulate some of its effects, the brain has signaling functions that *control* the systems that build up and expend energy, so called [12, 47].

The necessity for postulating an energy that represents the instincts and drives the mind is vitiated once the concept that the brain seeks nirvana is falsified; only a brain that seeks inactivity needs to be "driven" into action. Since the function of the brain, and its very structure, depend on the reception and ordering of stimuli, there is no more need to postulate driving forces for the brain than for any other organ of the body. Only the error of regarding the brain as an equivalent of the closed systems studied by nineteenth-century physics necessitated attributing "drive" potential to instincts. The name "drive" is a misnomer based on the misconception that the instincts, inherited patterns for ordering behavior and attaining those ends necessary for the survival of the species, must exert a force as well as a direction [4]. The work of Stechler and Carpenter [58], among others, shows that already at birth the infant tends to regulate his interaction with the environment and that such adaptation is not secondary to drive reduction. A viable alternative to a drive-energy theory of mentation is provided by communication theory and the quantification of the concept of information. This theory was only beginning to be developed at the end of the nineteenth century and was not available at the time Freud formulated his hypotheses on the origin and processing of thought.

The Genesis of Mind from Brain—the Ordering Function

It is now understood that what we call matter may be seen as an orderly state of molecular relationships that can be measured in terms of energy (energy being a quantitative measure of negentropy in the material world, i.e., the capacity for resisting randomness or entropy among molecules). "Matter" in this sense becomes an adjective that describes a negentropic, orderly, or structural relationship in the atomic world. Structure is not limited to order established by energy relationships; indeed, only inanimate, closed systems can be completely described in such terms. Open systems are structures based on relationships describing the vicissitudes of messages, not molecules, and mathematically expressed in units of information, not energy.

The brain is a specialized organ for receiving a limited range of signals from the environment, from the rest of the body, and from itself. By transmuting and ordering signals it transforms them into coded patterns that, when appropriately transmitted, serve as messages guiding the activity of the organism as a whole. Therefore, behavior is not determined by energy transformations within the brain but by the selective effect that signals have in activating and forming neural connections. This function is studied by communication theory, which quantifies in terms of information, not energy.

"Information," as used by communication theorists, is a statistical concept used to express the effect a coded signal has in reducing uncertainty in a receiver confronted by alternatives. The unit of measurement is called a bit and is defined operationally as that which reduces the number of alternatives by half [41]. Information is used as an empirical, quantitative measure of order in the sphere of communication, just as energy expresses a measure of order in the molecular world. The resolution of uncertainty by a message implies a disposition to action; a message, in controlling the utilization of the power of muscle contraction or glandular secretion, becomes itself a force [55]. For example, a red traffic signal resolves uncertainty in the driver and, by reducing the alternatives open to him in this situation, acts as an imperative to action, that is, it commands the expenditure of the muscle power needed to brake the car. A message exercises power since it not only resolves indecision but forces the implementation of one as opposed to another alternative. The message exercises this power because it acts either as a releaser mechanism, on the physiological level, or, on the psychological level, represents the reward or punishment that a suprasystem can transmit to the message receiving system [42].

Every living cell processes signals and creates order, i.e., extracts significance from the sequence of received signals and turns them into meaningful messages that determine activity. The brain carries this function to specialized heights. It does not just respond to signals in a phobic or tropic manner but seems to have the obligatory function of continuously abstracting, i.e., of registering and connecting sensory signals into figure-ground patterns. Reality consists of patterns of neural activity that reflect what signals have been received, the manner in which they have been connected with other signals past and present, and the reactions and interactions that have taken place as a result of the ordering activity.

It deserves to be emphasized that the sense receptors and the brain are presented with a myriad of *disconnected* impulses. It is the central nervous system that selects, collects, and connects these impulses into message patterns. In this sense, reality is the product of the brain's creative activity reflecting external conditions in such a manner as to, implicitly, make it possible to formulate predictions on which to base effective action. Insofar as structure, accident, or lack of training limits the central nervous system, reality too is limited for the individual or species concerned.

So-called sense data are the information that the brain derives from appropriate stimuli. Once direct stimulation is replaced by the inner stimulation of percept formation, it is brain activity itself that stimulates the effector portion of the brain. Percept formation shifts the emphasis for information transmission onto the "inner stimulation" of brain activity itself, the externally originating stimuli serving as building blocks for percept formation. The term "reality" is a verbal noun; like so many other terms, it refers to a function that has mistakenly been reified and externalized.

The process of perception refers to the ordering of signals into neural connections that form a permanent record of experience, making recognition and adaptation possible. As Arnheim [3] has clarified, perception is another name for the brain's abstracting and generalizing activity. Contrary to Freud's formulation that perception equals consciousness, we now know that perception is an unconscious, or better, not-conscious process [11]. The sensory experiences that we are aware of and mistakenly call "seeing," "hearing," etc., come after the fact of perception. Awareness of sensation arises only if what has been perceived by the brain is in some way ambiguous or requires confirmation. Consciousness seems to be a part of the perceptual feedback cycle by which those signals that do not fit or cannot be made to fit established patterns are recycled by the brain until they are either incorporated into the established order or form the basis for new patterns of abstraction. In other words, consciousness is not the equivalent of thought, a fact established by Freud clinically and now corroborated neurophysiologically. Consciousness is one aspect of problem-solving thought, i.e., that aspect of brain functioning that insures that signals that arouse attention but do not match existing patterns will not be disregarded until their significance, if any, for the organism becomes comprehensible.*

---

* There is no independent event called consciousness; consciousness is not a form of thought process, i.e., a separate electrochemical event. Brain consciousness is

HISTORY OF DEVELOPMENT OF
THINKING BEHAVIOR

Thought Formation in Freud's Writings

David Rapaport [45] points out that the basis of Freud's theory of thought development is embodied in the postulate of a wish-fulfilling hallucination of infancy. This hypothesis was already advanced in the *Project* [20] and remained unchanged in later works. Using the hunger drive as an example, it stated that the newborn infant lays down sensory images as he is exposed to need satisfaction. The visual image of some aspect of the breast becomes associated with the feeding experience, so when the baby becomes hungry again he initially conjures up that picture of the breast and begins to make sucking movements. This leads only to increasing frustration; he cries, and the mother then comes and feeds the child. Through such repeated experiences of trial and error, the baby eventually comes to differentiate between the hallucinated image and external reality, and learns to delay till the sensory quality of the latter is present. Eventually, under instinctual pressure, he associates sensory images of past experiences in order to bring about those conditions that were associated with satisfaction and to repeat the correct course of action that brought gratification. To describe the further development of thought, in the *Project* Freud utilized the hypothesis, already brought forward in *On Aphasia* [19], that images received and registered by the sensory-perceptual system of the brain were subjected to a process of association with other images, including images of words, and in this way an increasingly complex and sophisticated representation of reality was built up within the brain. Need and interest promoted the associational process, while fear, pain, and displeasure tended to block synaptic transmission or led to the making of false associative connections. Optimally, an adaptation to reality was possible that allowed for healthy gratification of inner tensions, especially sexual tensions; more often, however, emotional trauma during the immature, highly impressionistic years led to a nonadaptative picture of reality that made successful tension relief impossible. The concept of thought as a complex association of sensory images, especially those of words, remains fundamental to all subsequent theories of mentation suggested by Freud.

---

analogous to muscle contraction. Contraction is a phase of muscle action and there is no independent event called contraction, only muscle in a state of contraction. Contraction is the observable aspect of muscle action; similarly, consciousness is the potentially observable phase of brain functioning. Consciousness describes a brain state, just as contraction describes a muscle state.

Though he never referred to the *Project* in his published works, Freud's later speculations regarding the mechanisms of thought processing can only be understood in the light of their much more detailed exposition in the earlier work.

This series of hypotheses is often called the psychoanalytic theory of thought formation, implying thereby that it is in some way related to, and perhaps based on, the psychoanalytic method and its empirical findings. However, these hypotheses antedate Freud's discovery of the psychoanalytic method, and since the evidence of psychoanalysis is gathered from verbal persons, the concept of an infantile hallucination could not have been derived or inferred directly from psychoanalytic investigations. Furthermore, the psychoanalytic method reveals the *meaning* (the dispositional effect on behavior) of the activity of muscle, gland, and brain; it has no means of examining these activities as such. Freud's theories of the origin of thought and its later development, whether attributed to the brain or to the mental apparatus, are attempts to explain the substrate from which psychoanalytic findings stem; they are not psychoanalytic discoveries but speculations based on what Freud knew of nineteenth-century perceptual psychology and epistemology. It is necessary to stress this perhaps obvious point in order to make it clear that the corrections to Freud's explanation of the mental processes do not question a single *psychoanalytic* hypothesis; on the contrary, the necessary reformulation and revision of Freud's concept of mentation provides a more satisfactory setting for his clinical discoveries and the laws derived therefrom.

Imageless Thought

We know from the experimental evidence presented by Piaget and Inhelder [44], Vygotsky [60], Church [14], and others that the development of thought is not a simple progression from lesser to greater sophistication. The evidence is all against the idea that infantile thought before 16 to 18 months involves evocative recall of past experience. That representational activity in the form of sensory imaging is basic for thought formation, as Freud assumed, is not an acceptable postulate. Furthermore, the type of reasoning attributed to the infant by psychoanalysis is of the sort Piaget calls "propositional," which is not present until adolescence.

Church [14] reports that perception in infants and young children is not in terms of so-called sensory qualities, i.e., sound, color, taste, etc. Nor is their figure-ground differentiation atomistic, i.e., based on splitting reality into parts and wholes, inside and outside, self and others. Such constructs first appear around the age of 2 years and begin to be successfully manipulated by about 5 or 6 years of age.

Psychoanalysis, which places such emphasis on the early experiences of life, must take into account the stages in the development of thought. Here the psychoanalytic method is not applicable, and we must depend on the experiments of cognitive psychologists. The thrust of Piaget's findings is that nonreflective action, not recall through symbolic representation, is fundamental to learning. The first phase of development, from birth to about 16 months, is imageless and is termed the sensorimotor phase. Beginning with relatively simple inherited motor responses to sensory input, sensorimotor schema are developed and perfected through repetition. Although Piaget does not say so, these schema must be neural patterns of signal transmission. Such patterns are fundamental to all mentation. Church [14] calls them "frames of reference," "cognitive maps," or "schema of mobilization."

That particular sensory stimuli should set off specific reactions, such as sucking, presents no problem to neurophysiology. Neither does the fact that need-tension represented through chemically or electromagnetically encoded stimuli can set off the motor component of a sensorimotor schema without the stimulus from the gratifying object being present. The need for a "test of reality" that would promote delay between need and motor response until the environment is propitious for gratification does not require evocative recall of past experience through hallucination or imagination. Roughly speaking, all that needs to be assumed is that the experience of frustration when sucking is initiated in the absence of the breast leads to inhibitory facilitation between sensorimotor schema, so need can trigger sucking only when accompanied by the signals created by contact with the breast.* Coordination of eye-hand movements, imitations of observed activity, searching behavior, and integration of behavior as means to an end require only the increasing complexity of sensorimotor interaction and can develop without so-called image formation.

Neurologically encoded sensorimotor schema provide the familiar patterns with which new input to the brain is compared. They provide the perceptual set, as it is called, that permits action to be taken when a statistically sufficient likeness of pattern is present and heralds the expected total event. (It is the perceptual schema that supplies the nonvisualized aspect of objects seen head-on so that we need not check the totality once experience has taught us what to "expect"

---

* Precisely because the infant is *incapable* of representation of past experience, and therefore cannot hallucinate, his early attempts at pattern closure, when stimulated by need alone, become frustrating and lead to adaptive action. Were he able to hallucinate, he would die, since hallucinations put an end to need and are totally gratifying. Travelers who were about to die of thirst in the desert have testified to this phenomenon upon being rescued.

perceptually.) Lack of sufficient correspondence between the pattern aroused by need and the pattern derived from the surround initiates searching behavior until such correspondence is established. This is goal-seeking behavior. Even in later life we only believe we compare images to establish similarities; what is compared is the neurological activity set up by a new stimulus with that of past patterns established in the brain.* Further refinements of learning are all geared to making sensorimotor schema more effective for adaptation. All learning, however, is ultimately rooted in neurological sensorimotor patterns and is effected through them. The sensorimotor schema is the final common pathway for physiology, communications theory, and psychology. As a neural function a sensorimotor schema is a physiological event; as a signal pattern it belongs to communication theory; and insofar as it disposes to behavior it is of psychological concern. Far from being mutually contradictory, these fields of inquiry are intertwined and should never be thought of as being in opposition to one another. Discrepancies in their findings point to areas for further investigation and for interdisciplinary communication.

Sign-Directed Thinking

When stimulation of a particular sensorimotor pattern is able to set off or inhibit a complex reaction, semanticists call this "sign" behavior [35]. For example, Pavlov's famous experiments demonstrated the development of sign behavior in dogs. His animals learned to accept the part for the whole, that is, the sound of the bell as equivalent to the initial total experience of hearing the bell while seeing and smelling food. The bell served to set off the complex gastrointestinal preparations for digestion because the ringing sound had become a sign for food; it had become "reflex" behavior.

Unfortunately the term "reflex" connotes primitive, subcortical behavior; this is an error. It has recently been established that even the seemingly simple reflexes present at birth involve much more than the simple subcortical feedback loops postulated for them. Reflex behavior is not voluntary, but this does not mean it is carried out without the benefit of perceptual input and its evaluation. At first sign-directed behavior is established in the human infant through

---

* Pattern comparison, the basic activity of the brain, is a chemical-electromagnetic activity and has nothing to do with the subjective experience of imaging. Under special conditions the end results of the brain's activity may become conscious and assume image form; this is mistakenly called thinking. Sensory imaging is to thinking what the printout is to the computer; though the printout is in the form of numbers on a tape, this does not mean that the calculating activity itself was carried out with numbers; no more does the thinking process take place in sensory images.

activation of inherited behavior patterns, through chance experiences, or through conditioning by the mother. Later the infant himself develops adaptive sign-directed associations through trial and error experiments. Once a pattern of sign behavior has been thoroughly mastered, i.e., learned, it proceeds automatically when stimulated—it has become reflex behavior. The simplification made possible by reflex action is essential to survival; it is the manner in which highly complex activities can be carried out most effectively. The experienced pianist or automobile driver, having mastered his particular activity, is able to process and respond to many more signals quickly and efficiently than is the novice for whom the activity has not yet become "reflex." As will be mentioned again, the absence of conscious reflection is not an indicator of lack of complexity or of inferior thinking. Quite the contrary, consciousness of action indicates a lack of mastery that only further learning can raise to the level of reflex, that is, not-conscious activity. The reflex arc is a feedback mechanism, representing phylogenetic or ontogenetic integration of originally far more complex processes [36].

Motivation

A. T. W. Simeons [54] has pointed out that it is the old brain, not the neocortex, that initiates and coordinates the actual activity that supports attraction or avoidance behavior. The diencephalon, cerebellum, and brainstem precipitate and mesh the activities of the glands and muscles, and, as experiments with animals and experience with humans who have survived massive strokes show, the vital activities of the body can go on without the participation of the cortex, though the reverse is not true. According to Simeons the associational cortex is a complex of feedback loops whose activity prevents the older brain from overreacting to stimuli. The more primitive animals must respond directly to stimuli from the outside. In one way or another everything they perceive is significant for self-preservation or for the preservation of the species. The lower the animal is on the evolutionary scale, the more likely it is that every signal it receives is a sign initiating behavior of some sort. As animals become more independent of their environment, not all stimuli require a response. Not every potential danger is a real danger, nor does every inviting stimulus necessarily represent an achievable goal. The associational cortex developed as an organ that delayed response, i.e., delayed stimulation of the old brain, until signals could be further evaluated as to their significance. The primitive brain is the final common pathway for motivation of behavior, and once it is triggered, the reaction precipitated runs its course and will resist interference.

Instinctual behavior is the inherited self-preservative or reproductive behavior triggered by the diencephalon. Instincts do not behave as if they were substances like hormones, which initiate action; rather they act as dispositional patterns encoded in the old brain's "blueprint" for behavior geared to the preservation of the self and the species. Vis-à-vis the old brain, the cerebral cortex is a protective mechanism; it performs the function of the *Reizschutz* or stimulus barrier of which Freud spoke but which he assigned to the peripheral sense organs. However, it is not the cortex that needs to be sheltered from over-stimulation; rather, it is the total mobilization triggered by instinctual patterns that must not be unnecessarily activated, hence it is the old brain that requires shielding. Freud always emphasized how relatively minimal the strength of consciousness was compared to the driving might of the instincts, and how only linkage with instincts could produce the drivenness experienced in dreams, sexual behavior, and neurotic symptoms. What holds true for man holds true for other animals too in this case; only stimuli that address the instinctual behavior patterns insuring personal survival and reproduction can move the organism to activity,* or as Freud put it, only a wish, i.e., that which represents or is derived from the instincts, can move the mental apparatus. It should also be added that it is neither the cortex nor the conscious state that directly controls and opens the gateway to action; it is the diencephalon that provides the key to activity. Unless a percept can trigger the old brain, that percept is ineffectual, and only those percepts that seem to address themselves in some way to instinctual needs can precipitate a response from the organism via the old brain. However, to repeat, the hypothesis that learning and maturation is a matter of drive reduction, and secondary reinforcement, i.e., that man is born with a cauldron of primitive instinctual impulses that must be tamed and diverted to social ends has been proven false [58]. Similarly, the dual drive theory, the idea that all of behavior stems from either sexual or aggressive needs, has been disproven. Aggression is a form of behavior and not an instinct [18, 53], while the instinct for self-preservation and preservation of the species is not a unitary structure but is composed of numerous inborn goal-oriented behavior patterns including socially oriented ones that promote particular kinds of intraspecies contact and interaction [28, 57].

In the more primitive phyla, during various phases of the instinctual cycle, particular environmental stimuli evoke specific behavior. Mammals are both too complex and too mobile to be programmed quite so rigidly. Biologists speak of drive-governed behavior in mammals, by

---

* It should be noted that Freud's earlier division of instincts into sexual and self-preservative ones [22] corresponds exactly to the view put forward by Simeons.

which they mean that the inherited instinctual "blueprint" is more flexible and allows considerable latitude in the manner in which instinctual goals are attained. For example, mammals have a wide choice of foodstuffs and are not nearly as limited in what they may and must eat as are amphibians, reptiles, and insects. Should a dietary deficiency arise, they will become more alert to any and all nutriments containing the needed ingredient and are free to search for it far and wide. Similarly, during the period of sexual heat, if an appropriate and receptive partner is not available, homosexuality, masturbation, or miscegenation are alternative relief-seeking patterns for many mammals.

The fallacy of regarding "drives" as forces pushing or pulling an animal toward activity has been discussed previously. In mammals, even more than in other animals, drive patterns are guides that leave much room for developing optimal responses through learning from and by experience. Though mammals are born with some specifically programmed "reflex" behavior, a good portion of their adaptation depends on learning.

There are implications in the work of Simeons [54], Arnold [4], and Tomkins [59] that when correlated suggest that the foundation for one kind of learning lies in inherited reactions that are responsive to the intensity and duration of stimuli instead of to the qualitative (sensory) content of perception. For example, regardless of its origin, a sudden stimulus leads to an attitude of alertness and readiness to evaluate the situation; a more gradual rise in stimulation promotes interest in its source as evidenced by exploratory behavior; a massive rise in stimulus intensity, regardless of cause, promotes a pain reaction, and prolonged stimulation at such a high level creates active attempts to eliminate the stimulus through fight or flight behavior; on the contrary, a sudden decrease from high stimulus intensity brings relief and behavior appropriate to a state of contentment. These basic adaptive patterns become associated with the sensorimotor record of the organism's perception and of its reaction to experience. When such a sensorimotor pattern is recognized at a later time, the particular associated adaptive behavior, be it fight, flight, attraction, etc., is activated. This sequence of events exemplifies a learning in mammals that is based not on reflection but on activities under the control of the old brain and the autonomic nervous system.

It seems that the nonspecific autonomic adaptive mechanisms described above are an evolutionary advance that liberates mammals from too-rigid domination by instinctually programmed behavior. The instincts, or drives, still are the overall, cyclic behavior patterns serving self-preservation and reproduction, but they act not through inherited stimulus-response programs but through increasing or decreasing the sensitivity to various types of stimuli. This more flexible and sophisticated mechanism for drive gratification is an advantage in meeting the variety of relatively unpredictable circumstances, both internal and external, in which more advanced animals continuously find themselves.

Most mammals are born neurologically mature and with sufficiently developed muscle coordination to be able to engage in the various locomoting, seeking, finding, and feeding activities directed by the brain code. The combination of inborn behavioral programs responsive to being triggered by various sensations and the adaptive potential of the involuntary nervous system to stimulus intensity permits these creatures to adjust fairly quickly and successfully to life outside the womb. At first it seems as if human infants are in a very different situation from that of other newborn mammals. Man is born prematurely, so to speak, equipped neither with innate skeletal muscle avoidance mechanisms that would enable him to respond to and escape from danger nor with the muscle strength or coordination necessary to follow his mother, find her breast, and attach himself for feeding.

The tendency has been to look at the human infantile state as a relatively helpless one to which the mother responds instinctually with appropriate nurturing and protective behavior. The work of Silvan Tomkins seems to show that this view is only partially correct.* Tomkins alerts us to the fact that despite the general immaturity of the human infant, the mimetic musculature of the face is highly developed. These facial muscles are under the control of the involuntary nervous system and respond in a highly specific manner, Tomkins believes, to quantitative variations in stimulus gradients. He has described a series of eight behavioral continua identified by the particular muscles each brings into play: surprise-startle, interest-excitement, enjoyment-joy, distress-anguish, anger-rage, fear-terror, contempt-disgust, and shame-humiliation [59, vol. 1]. As environmental experiences become associatively linked to these fundamental reactions, their reoccurrence triggers the nervous system to react as it did originally by one or another attraction or avoidance behavior. New perceptions have their effect through being related to former experiences and their associated reactions. With development of the associative cortical functioning, the interaction between perception and the in-

---

* My colleague, E. V. Demos, in the course of her detailed and valuable criticism of this chapter, called my attention to a body of literature, including the work of Tomkins, with which I was unfamiliar and which, when I did acquaint myself with it, led me to a fundamental revision of my theoretical conceptualization of instincts and of affective behavior.

voluntary nervous system becomes increasingly complex, refined, and potentially modulated, so that in the older individual the basic interactions may no longer be so apparent. However, what holds true throughout is that perceptions do not stimulate drive-organized behavior patterns directly; drive needs and sensory stimuli act on the regulatory mechanism of the old brain, which responds to the patterns created by that interaction.

As his classifying labels suggest, Tomkins regards the basic subcortical reactions as emotional expressions. I think that in doing so he inadvertently detracts from the significance of his theory. As I have already implied, I believe that Tomkins' work explains the manner in which instinctual control of behavior is modified and transformed in the course of evolution to a mechanism more responsive to the needs of a complex and mobile organism. All mammals have taken this evolutionary step, but whereas other animals, born at a relatively mature stage of development, have executive capacity from the start, man, whose eventual brain size necessitates premature birth, can use his autonomic adaptive patterns at first only for communicative purposes. However, this handicap has been turned to an advantage. Through his mimetic responses to stimulus gradients, he has gained a significant degree of control over the "primary unit" as Benedek has termed the mother-child symbiosis [8]. Far from being a passive creature to be shaped by his mother, the infant forms a system with her, using her capabilities in the interest of his needs. Through his mimetic musculature he indicates whether he is optimally stimulated; if not, he sends signals that encourage the mother to search for and correct whatever is wrong. The mistake is, in my opinion, to consider joy, anger, interest, distress, or any other emotion, rather than the physiological condition, responsible for the infant's behavior. So-called affective behavior describes the basic quantitative aspect of drive-organized behavior, which becomes "affective" only when it is conceptualized symbolically much later in life and is experienced as an emotion or a feeling. (An analogy that might help to clarify the distinction I am making is the following: Children react to color long before the concept of color exists for them. To say that a little child "sees red" is an error. He is responding to the particular stimulus of a specific wavelength, an experience that some day he may learn to identify as "red." But even then his perception and reaction to that particular wavelength will remain independent of his conceptualization of that experience as one of color per se.)

Animals and human infants do not have emotions in the self-conscious sense, and, by the same token, adults may not respond emotionally to affective states. Though a particular situation may lead to what observers have no difficulty identifying as aggressive behavior, the individual manifesting that behavior may not be aware of any emotion or feeling of anger. Similarly, every psychoanalyst has had the experience of helping patients to "recognize" their emotions, that is, helping them to experience their attitudes toward the therapist in emotional form. The reason this is a confusing issue that seems to defy description and clarification is that the behavior usually called "emotional" subsumes all the responses of the subcortical nervous system to stimuli only one of which should properly be termed "emotional," i.e., becoming conscious of emotion, feeling, or mood. This confusion posed a problem for Freud, as it does for many others. He tried to clarify how it was that strictly speaking there could be no "unconscious feeling" [25], when the evidence was irrefutable that there was much behavior in analysis that seemed to be "emotional" yet was not conscious. The confusion can be eliminated once it is recognized that the term affective behavior (as commonly used in its wide sense) is synonymous not with emotion, feeling, or mood but with the nervous system's nonreflective, involuntary responses to stimulation.

A clinical example can be used to illustrate this point: A patient who had lost a parent during his infancy found himself after many years of analysis crying uncontrollably during a session in which the analyst had announced an impending vacation. It was quite likely that the man was reexperiencing some aspect of the reaction he had had to the loss of his father. A transference interpretation to that effect led to consciousness of emotions of sadness regarding the analyst's vacation and to experiencing sadness for the first time in relation to various seemingly trivial losses in late childhood and adolescence. In such a patient an episode of this sort is usually understood as representing the lifting of an emotional block formed at the time of the loss of the father. However, if infants do not have emotions, how do permanent scars of the sort just described form in the psychological structure to be manifested years later in the analytic transference? The infant had not responded to the symbolic significance of the death of his father but had suffered a narcissistic trauma through his mother's reaction to the death of her husband. It was her depression and inability to invest herself in her child for a time that created a situation in which the infant experienced repeated frustration and mounting tension that was not relieved. Neither as a child nor as an adult was this patient saddened or distressed when faced with loss or the threat of abandonment. His reaction to the analyst's vacation was not the result of "hidden" grief but was due to his inability to grieve. This patient had no capacity to deal with stress by experiencing emotional states and working them through. He either remained in full control of himself and the situation or he experienced an immobilizing and disorganizing total reaction of helplessness. His sobbing was not an object- or situation-directed message with symbolic significance ("I'll miss you," "Don't go," etc.) but the infant's automatic reaction to prolonged helplessness, a "to whom it may concern" type of distress signal. His anguished crying in the analysis was a reliving of his early autonomic reaction to the indescribable experience of being left helpless in the face of unrelieved tension; the more he cried the more hyperstimulated he became and there was no one who sought to soothe him. Only in the psychoanalysis did this "economic" symptom become transformed into an emotional one that he could then learn to describe and eventually work through. To reiterate, the initial behavior of such a patient has in the past been described as evidence of "blocked emotion." I believe this is not only incorrect but also obscures the practical issue, i.e., that the analysis of such a symptom requires that it first become transformed into its emotional equivalents. (The work of Kohut [31] describes the appropriate analytic stance to be taken in cases in which the degree of tension, rather than the content per se, is of primary importance.)

Symbol-Directed Thinking

Piaget's observations of sensorimotor development showed the increasingly complex, goal-directed activities made possible as the infant builds up a hierarchy of sensorimotor patterns encoding his encounters with and responses to the environment. These advances are based on the maturation of the nervous system and on increased motor coordination. They remain at the level of sign-ordered behavior, which, as mentioned, is carried out by matching encoded patterns with incoming percepts. Such an organization permits either the reoccurrence of some aspect of past experience to set off very complex behavior patterns or the recognition of some portion of a familiar routine to arouse sensory expectations that delay action or reaction until the next aspect of a familiar pattern registers. The increasingly adaptive capacity to respond to immediate experience, based on trial and error learning and reinforced by reward and punishment (so-called reality testing), remains a significant aspect of the maturational process, but it is not the upper level of man's achievement.

Abstraction of perceptual essence or form is an ability that is already involved in complex sign behavior. Many experiments have been done to show that mammals as a group have this capacity. For example, rats trained to jump toward a small black triangle for food will also jump toward large white triangles expecting a reward but not to a small black circle or a large white square. This shows that they have abstracted triangularity as an indicator of significance for behavior. However, though these animals will react to triangularity as an indicator of food, i.e., as a part of the total food experience, this abstraction does not *stand for* (re-present) food. No rat so trained will spontaneously build a triangle in order to make food appear or bring a triangle to the experimenter to induce him to bring food, or accept a triangle in lieu of food. On the contrary, animals trained to construct a triangle to obtain a reward will not react with expectation when presented with a picture of a triangle. Though triangularity has been abstracted as a sign *associated* with gratification, it does not serve as a symbol, i.e., it does not stand for or re-present a situation in such a way that it, rather than the experience it represents, is manipulated intracerebrally or interpersonally. As Susan Langer [35] has said, a sign evokes the action appropriate to the object signified, but a symbol arouses the conception of the object symbolized.

Man is the only animal that becomes able to function symbolically in the course of normal development. At about 18 months the human infant develops the capacity to utilize the record of his behavior encoded in sensorimotor schema symbolically, i.e., to re-present what has been experienced previously. The reason for stating that age 1½ to 2 years marks the beginning of symbolic life is that prior to that time there is no evidence for spontaneous recall to be found in the infant's behavior. Age 2 marks the appearance of imaginative play, imitation in the absence of a model, daytime fantasy, and nighttime dreams [44], all of which are activities requiring symbolic activity.* This indicates an evolutionary advance in kind, not just in degree, and its consequences for behavior are momentous. Physiologically no basic

---

* Only at this point would a wish-fulfilling hallucination become a possibility. Sensory imaging, whether voluntary or involuntary, is an activity of the brain based on symbolic function and recall, not on sign behavior and recognition. Prior to symbolism, only skeletal muscle and glandular wish-fulfilling reactions could be triggered through instinctual need patterns. For example, hunger might set off sucking movements. It may be clear that Freud's postulation of the wish-fulfilling hallucination was probably based on the erroneous notion that imaging was fundamental to and preceded thought. We now believe that sensory imagery is not essential for thought and that when it does arise it represents a consequence of the thought process and not its antecedent [44]. It should also be noted that the appearance of a REM electroencephalogram pattern during the sleep of infants, or lower animals for that matter, is not evidence that they are dreaming in the sense of imaging. All one may say is that dream imagery, when it does occur, is often associated with *waking* from a REM phase of sleep. Freud anticipated this when he said that insofar as we are dreaming (imaging) we are not asleep. The connection between REM sleep and manifest dream imagery is one of correlation and not one of cause and effect.

changes need be postulated with the advent of symboling activity. The sensorimotor schema remains the fundamental unit of behavior. Operationally, however, the development of symbolic capacity introduces a new influence on behavior. When one sensorimotor pattern can symbolize (stand for) another sensorimotor pattern, knowledge of former experiences can be recalled by the brain's activity. With symbolization the child can do more than just re-cognize, i.e., match stimuli in the here and now with established neural patterns; he can re-call (evoke) them and experience a mental life independent of the immediate situation. Whereas before recognition had made adaptation through duplication or multiplication of behavior possible, now, in addition, the division of experiences takes place. The potential for representation of an experience permits conceptualization in terms of past, present, and future, and the division of experience into objects and subject.

To understand psychological development and formulate a scientific psychology, we must assert that our manner of objectifying reality is based on our abstractions from, symbolization of, and reflection about our sensory experiences. The world of so-called material objects is a part of the symbolic world; it belongs to the world of ideas as much as do our dreams. It is through this symbolic capacity that a world of animate and inanimate objects, as well as an observing subject, becomes possible through reflection. This is not to deny that there is a reality apart from our reflections to which we react through perceptions, but this reality is one we never know directly. Each one of us creates the world anew, guided by our sensory capacities, conceptual ability, and the culturally determined figure-background permutations we are conditioned to make by our parents, teachers, and others.

Initially objects are not identified individually or combined in order that a universal class may be abstracted. Conceptualization of experience as a generality precedes conceptualization of individual objects. Indeed, the eventual existence of particulars is made possible only by the conceptualization of universals [3]. This capacity for generalization of experience, which Church [14] calls physiognomic perception, is based on the ability to extract and symbolize the essential form from the totality rather than building up a hierarchical classification atomistically (bit by bit). The presymbolic infant does not yet conceptualize a world filled with either whole or part objects; he exists without awareness of his experiences as experiences, i.e., without subjective awareness of self and others. The initial, preverbal, physiognomic, symbolic experiences are the roots for all future concept formation.

Because they present or re-present an experience rather than describing it, Langer [35] calls them presentational symbolisms as opposed to "discursive symbolism," which is a later development. Discursive symbolism does not present but rather describes an experience atomistically and sequentially by symbolizing its various aspects.

The formation of universal symbolic concepts antedates the use of speech; indeed, the development of language is based on the presence of symbolic concepts. Speech is at first only an adjunct to grasping, used to help get something, and only as conceptualization progresses is there a need for symbolic language. Rational verbal speech is a prime example of discursive symbolization. Its advantage for communicating particulars is obvious, but its failure to convey the totality of an experience in its presentational aspects is also well known.

Freud's study of the primary process, which he believed represented energy transformations, actually is an avenue for observing symbolic transformation. Conceptualization through analogy, metaphor, and synecdoche, which Freud termed the mechanisms of condensation and displacement, seems to be fundamental for presentational symbolism. Dream symbolism is a re-presentational intermediate step between presentational symbolism and the discursive symbolism of words, which Freud called the secondary process, in which various aspects of experience symbolized presentationally are given verbal names.

Man, as Bertalanffy [9] has pointed out, does not just live in the physical reality around him. The formation of a symbolic world, a world of concepts, creates a new environment in which a different relationship exists between the old and the new brain. Human infants and other mammals are governed by their involuntary response to stimulus intensity and the perceptual experiences associated with the basic autonomic responses through conditioning. Their perceptual function is an extension of drive patterns, registering what befalls them environmentally so that instinctual needs may be served optimally by the autonomic behavior patterns. With the advent of symbolic capacity the associational cortex is no longer limited to triggering sign-induced behavior. Now, instead of serving the old brain and its instinctual patterns of self-preservation and reproduction, the associational cortex through the symbolic function to a great extent controls the dispositional power of subcortical patterns. Henceforth any and all past, present, or projected future experiences may be endowed with symbolic instinctual (goal-directed) significance, regardless of whether or not there is a counterpart to that significance in the material reality. The importance of this for human behavior generally and psychopathology specifically will be clarified in the following sections.

DEPRESSION AS A DISORDER OF THE
BEHAVIORAL SYSTEM

Based on the foregoing discussion, depression will be shown to be a systemic disorder, a vicissitude of the interacting complexes whose activity gives rise to the conglomerate of goal-directed activity that we call thinking. However, before the implications of this hypothesis can be examined, another aspect of the behavioral system must be considered and certain concepts regarding development current in psychoanalysis must be reexamined. As Goldberg states in his review (see Chapter 6), our psychoanalytic conceptualizations of depression are all implicitly or explicitly "adultomorphic." For example, when analysts speak of the trauma in the oral phase as basic to depression, the infant is described as if he saw the world in terms of parts and objects, or self and others; as if he experienced moods and feelings; as if he made judgments regarding his experiences; as if he were capable of imaging and recall. We know from cognitive psychology [44, 60] that these complexities of mentation are not present in early life and that the goal-seeking, adaptive behavior of infants and young children is based on mechanisms different from that of adults. A closer study of development is necessary in order to see what the dysfunction called depression might signify at various levels of maturity.

Operationally the term mental illness refers to disturbances in the ordering function of the cerebral cortex. Since the ordering function derives its structure from the activity of the brain's feedback loops, mental illness can be precipitated both intersystemically and intrasystemically. Intersystemic failure of the brain's signal-processing function or failure of somatic systems in the hierarchy that influence the brain can create disturbances in behavior, so-called organic brain disease, by affecting the associational network or its ability to transmit signals. The aspects of mental illness usually called psychological, functional, or nonorganic, are those behavioral disturbances precipitated intrasystemically, that is, by disturbances in the symbolic significance of cortical signaling. Since depression can be precipitated by either intersystemic or intrasystemic brain dysfunction, the depressive syndrome is a mental illness but not necessarily a psychological illness. If "depression" is now used to designate a particular sort of malfunction in the ordering process that can be precipitated by a variety of disturbances in communication on the symbolic, sign, or signal transmission level, then, I hope to show, depression at various stages of life can be understood without resorting to adultomorphization or animism.

Depression at the Level of Sign-Directed Behavior

As was mentioned, depressions in infants are usually explained psychologically by adultomorphization, attributing to them the creation of a symbolic world by methods of thought processing that are far beyond their cortical capacities at the time. This is not necessary; the disturbance of ordering that may give rise to the depressions of infancy can be explained on a different basis.

ORDER

There is reason to believe [50] that prenatally the rhythm of the uterine environment, which reverberates to the mother's heartbeat, becomes the paradigm for ordering. Expulsion from the uterus temporarily disorganizes the rhythm to which the organism has become adapted, and it is postulated that this experience leaves a permanent neurologically encoded trace that serves as a prototype for all later anxiety, i.e., the threat of imminent disorder. For this reason birth is indeed the primal trauma, as Freud and Rank suggested years ago.

The infant is not endowed at birth with inherited patterns that permit independent adaptation, and even if the brain were more mature, the rest of the body could not respond to complex coordinating messages. Salk [50] has shown that when the mother starts to care for her baby shortly after birth she spontaneously holds the infant on the left side, closest to her heartbeat. The experience of parturition apparently serves as a releaser mechanism for an instinctual (diencephalic) behavior pattern by which the mother restores to the infant the familiar prenatal order of her cardiac rhythm. Too great a delay in the onset of the mother's caretaking function seems to vitiate the releaser effect, and the inexperienced mother may then not hold her infant in this manner. Comparison studies show that infants deprived of this experience respond adversely with irritability and a developmental lag.

Ordering is another word for the perceptual activity of the brain by which patterns ultimately or directly conducive to the survival of the individual and the species are formed or activated. The caretaking functions of the mother are carried out against the background of her heartbeat, and it seems reasonable to suppose that the infant's experience of the mother's body and her activities with him become neurologically associated with the primal ordering experience of her heartbeat. In this way the mother's activities with the child become the equivalent of order; so long as these are steady, reliable, and appropriate to the infant's needs, the mother-child system functions well.* It is not necessary to postulate that the child reacts to the mother's love or hate as such, only that the mother's emotional stance has either a positive or negative effect on the rhythmicity, reliability, and appropriate intensity of her caretaking function in terms of the pattern of stimulus gradients to which the infant is exposed.

STIMULUS HUNGER

Dependable care of his needs contributes to the infant's security and comfort through continuing a predictable rhythmicity somewhat replicating the existence in the womb. But, as Spitz [57] has documented, caretaking alone, no matter how dependable and technically sound, is not sufficient. If the energy discharge–nirvana theory of mental operation were true, infants exposed to the mechanical but efficient tending in orphanages of the type studied by Spitz should be contented, since their needs are met in an atmosphere of minimal stimulation. But, to reiterate the point made previously, it is not nirvana that the brain seeks but optimal stimulation. These infants become progressively irritable, withdrawn, and apathetic, and eventually marasmic unless the stimulation of mothering is reintroduced in time to arrest their downhill course. Far from thriving, these understimulated infants exhibit motor retardation and facial expressions resembling those of melancholic adults. Spitz termed this infantile syndrome, which has also been observed in infants of other primates [39, 63], anaclitic depression.

The accepted psychiatric view of depression is that it is primarily an affective (emotional) disorder caused by a loss of self-esteem and marked by a dejected appearance and motor and mental retardation. Certainly the infants described by Spitz were developmentally and motorically retarded, as demonstrated by their lack of response or inappropriate response to stimulation. But this state cannot be attributed to dejection based on loss of self-esteem or, as the Kleinians suggest, to the infant's fear of his own destructive anger, since such

---

* To say the infant needs "mothering" in addition to physical care begs the question of what that might entail in early infancy when the mother does not yet exist as a symbolic object. The psychological component seems to be related to the adequacy of message transaction between mother and infant. Insofar as the mother or mother surrogate creates an atmosphere in which what happens to and with the baby is related to the signals the baby sends out, the "mothering" component is supplied. Proper care of physical needs is "loving" insofar as it addresses itself to the needs the infant is communicating, and it lays the groundwork for a future reasonable accommodation between mother and baby. Throughout life, the feeling of controlling one's destiny to some reasonable extent is the essential psychological component of all aspects of life. The capacity to trust without being gullible involves the ability to relinquish that need temporarily and appropriately and is built on the security that one's messages do count, so this does not have to be tested continuously.

attitudes require conceptualization, including a symbolic concept of self, which is operationally not possible at that early age. A feeling or an emotion is always a self-conscious experience, that is, a state attributed to oneself. Since the "depressed" appearance of the infants precedes by years their capacity for symbolic representation of moods, feelings, etc., we are left to account for their appearance and their motor and mental retardation on other grounds. The so-called anaclitically depressed infants are infants who have to a significant extent been left out of the meaningful ordering system of the caretakers. Though properly fed, housed, and cleansed, they do not receive the organizing feedback of contact with the mother or mother surrogate that would continue to give them exposure to both her heartbeat and the narcissistically invested rhythmic caretaking, with the cooing, singing, talking, and caressing that takes place under such circumstances. These infants do not respond to the mother's love per se, that is, love in the symbolic sense. It is the mother's capacity for investing the infant symbolically with her narcissistic needs [7] that leads her to behave in a manner that conveys ordering rhythmicity through many sensory modalities of the infant while also providing the stimulus input for which the infant brain hungers. It seems that the motor and mental retardation of "depressed" infants is neither the result of sadness nor due to awareness of loss but may be a consequence of understimulation.

GOALS

The infant's ordering system is composed of the functional symbiosis [8] of his and his mother's brains, and if the mother fails in fulfilling her part of the message processing, the infant's part of the behavioral system ceases to function properly and eventually ceases to function at all. The retardation observed in anaclitically depressed infants can be understood as the consequence of this breakdown.

What differentiates a living, open, system from an inanimate, closed one is its internal goal-setting activity. Every living cell has optimal states toward which it strives through communication with its environment. Each cell is receptive to those particular chemical or electromagnetic changes in the surround that are significant for its enzyme system. These signals are received and become messages with "news value." With the reception of the message the alternatives open to the cell before stimulation are resolved in favor of one course of action, which is then instituted. If the activity in question enables the cell to perform its genetically designated function, its goal has been reached for that moment. (The cell of course does not have a "goal" in the self-conscious sense; it is we, the observers, who assign an aim to the system and equate closure of its feedback cycle with its "goal.")

More complex assemblies of cells have by virtue of their interaction established collective goals in addition to individual cellular goals. It is the goal-directed activity, the search for closure by means of signal-processing feedback loops, that transforms a collection of individual cells into a system. In the overall picture, the associational cerebral cortex is a part of the perceptual system. Its function is primarily one of inhibiting diencephalic activity, that is, permitting a triggering of action only when the inherited self-preservative and reproductive patterns are truly served. This function is carried out through pattern matching in the cortex. Only when the input sufficiently approximates significant message patterns will the cortex trigger the autonomic patterns that activate the muscles and glands. The perceptual goal of the cortex is therefore the creation or recreation and matching of message patterns. For the cortex the optimal or orderly state is one of transforming signals into patterns to be evaluated.

The infant brain, as has been mentioned, is not self-sufficient. Its orderly state depends on the mother's assistance in stimulating and carrying out pattern matching. Without the mother's stimulating activity, the infant brain has been deprived of the possibility for carrying out its normal activity of pattern formation and pattern matching. This means that its genetically determined function cannot be fulfilled, and it ceases to operate as a system, that is, as a "cell assembly" that extracts order from the environment. Since, as Dorpat [16] has shown, without the stimulation of sensory activity physiolocigal activity (which is dependent on messages from the diencephalon, brainstem, etc.) is impaired, the understimulated infant's appearance and retardation are consequences of the loss of messages from the cerebrum to the diencephalon and not to loss of either symbolic objects or self-esteem. In effect the infant who is unstimulated has been converted into a closed system, one that no longer maintains its individuality of function but inexorably approaches total disorganization and thermodynamic equilibrium with the environment, i.e., death. What we call depression, at least at the early infantile level, is a state in which signals no longer become informative messages, and that, by definition, marks the end of any open system.

Disorder as a Message

Anaclitic depression is the outcome of an extreme dysfunction in the mother-infant behavioral system that in milder form is necessarily part of all human development. So total is the dependence of the infant on the caretaking person that there inevitably come many times when the mother, no matter how empathic, fails to respond adequately in degree or kind to her baby's needs and precipitates a state of disorganization. The infant responds with anxiety, his crying and random kicking reflecting the disturbance of message processing and the inability to maintain order. His own cry raises the gradient of stimulus intensity to an uncomfortable level and leads him to cry even louder. Usually this cycle arouses the *mother's* symbolic identification with him, and she attributes to the child the unhappiness, sadness, or even depression that she would be feeling if she looked and behaved like that. Under reasonable circumstances she responds to "make him happy," which operationally means she does her level best to feed into the system and restore harmony. The infant's brain, busily engaged once again in perceptual figure-background ordering under optimal stimulus intensity, assumes the expressions that the mother adultomorphizes as representing "happiness." Not only are these temporary and reversible failures of empathy on the mother's part inevitable, they are the necessary stimulus to healthy psychological development. For, as Kohut [31] has described, it is in the failure of communication and the subsequent recovery between mother and child that new associations are formed and utilized fostering the child's maturation.

EXPECTATION

By stimulating the mother's narcissistic identification with his behavior, causing her to interpret it as his upset or sadness, the baby's response, to disorder is a signal, a negative feedback in the mother-child behavioral system that calls for corrective and restitutive response. Anaclitic depression eventuates only under those circumstances in which the mother-child system is or becomes nonfunctional. Ordinarily the behavior and appearance that accompany understimulation of the infant's brain have a dispositional effect on the mother's behavior. This not only restores organization but, as it is repeated over and over again, lays down a brain pattern of "expectation," i.e., the anticipation that restitution will follow disorganization. This is the beginning of what is later equated with "hope." By the same token, significant failure of this expectation, if it does not eventuate in anaclitic depression and death, could be presumed to lead to the encoded experience of mounting disorganization for which no help is forthcoming. This state makes an escape into isolation, regression, and apathy likely. The trauma at the oral stage unearthed in the analysis of depressed patients may very well lie in failure of the mother to respond effectively to the infant's need for a predictable, rhythmic environment that supports the brain's need for active creation and ordering of patterns. That this experience later becomes associated

with lowered self-esteem and ambivalence toward narcissistically significant objects is not in dispute, but one need not adultomorphize
the infant to explain the influence of the early experiences on an eventual psychological outcome.

PREDICTION

Looked at from the viewpoint of the encoding process, the function
of perception is the ordering of stimuli into re-cognizable figure-background configurations. Looked at from the viewpoint of the total
organism, the function of perception is adaptation through prediction.
In a sense every perception is an inference that a particular pattern
of stimulus intensity exists and this disposes to particular actions or
to inhibition of actions. The implied prediction is that if the percept
is accurate and the reaction efficient, certain consequences will follow.
(Again, the words perception, inference, prediction, consequence,
etc., refer to functions of the feedback loops of the neurological system and do not require postulation of self-conscious direction for the
system.)

In nonhuman animals born with instinctual patterns and adaptive
patterns already fairly well developed and correlated, the predictive
activity of perception is efficient but circumscribed and remains that
way for life. The animal's feedback system is not self-contained, it
depends on the environment for interaction and for closure. Therefore, implied in the brain's function is the "expectation" that the environment in which the animal functions holds the releaser stimuli
necessary to activate perception and reaction patterns. Too great a
deviation from the expected environment for which the animal's
brain is programmed makes feedback loop closure impossible, and
death supervenes. The situation for the human infant is radically
different. His incomplete development at birth and the paucity of
fixed, inherited response patterns leaves the human infant adaptively
dependent. In his relatively passive infantile state he is exposed to a
great number of stimuli which do not immediately release particular
behavior patterns, and he has the opportunity to exercise associative
cortical activity much more so than do the young of other species. As
has been outlined, at first the infant seems simply to respond to unmanageable failure in feedback loop function with evidence of disorganization that can be corrected by the intervention of mother's care
and interest. With maturation there is beginning independence from
the mother's behavioral system, and the infant is increasingly capable
of receiving stimuli and organizing and comparing sensorimotor patterns. The interaction of patterns becomes increasingly complex. The
activity patterns of the infant's own body, which involve a double

sensation, become contrasted to those patterns formed through stimulation which simply impinge on the body. The infant's developing
capacity for coordinating his whole body in goal-directed behavior at-
tests to the fact that patterns reflecting the body's boundaries (the
"body ego") are being established. Although he is increasingly capable
of organizing his activities and completing his feedback patterns, there
are many occasions when he is not successful, and the earlier established response to disorganization or threat of being unable to order
his self and his environment is triggered. Now it may be that the reaction of stress is once again a response to a disorganized state, or it may
express the frustration of being helpless to reach a closure that is adequately patterned. In any case, under reasonable circumstances the
mother continues to accept the child's reaction to disorder as a signal
for entering his feedback pattern and helping him to restore orderly
perception. Now the infant responds to the mother's ministrations by
forming sensorimotor patterns in which the sensory quality of mother's activity and her familiar appearance are linked with the comfort-
ing experience of reestablished order. He learns to identify the signals
she sends out as necessary for his ordering activities. Mother's absence
becomes linked with the encoded memory of the disorganized state
and produces anxiety. If restitution is not forthcoming, a "depressed
state" may eventuate.

The mother's presence, independent of the state of physical comfort, has become a sign for the orderly state and her absence a sign
for the panic of helplessness or goallessness or both. As is well known,
the greatest anxiety with strangers, i.e., not mother, occurs at about 8
months of age. The dysphoria experienced in the presence of strangers
results from the inability to complete sensorimotor schema and reestablish the orderly (pleasurable) state. Whereas at one time any adult
could serve to soothe, now the mother's presence is required because
the sensorimotor schemata are more complex and are attuned to the
specific pattern conveyed by the mother alone; this does not imply
that the concept of mother as object has been abstracted from the
infant's experience. As experiments have shown, it is the unfamiliarity of the experience, the physiognomic percept created by a strange
situation, that finds the infant's pattern matching inadequate and, in
effect, unable to predict with reasonable certainty what will happen
next [37, 56]. It is then that frustration, fear, and other signs of distress
serving as evidence of disorganization (anxiety) appear.*

* Psychoanalysts mistakenly speak of part object perception in infants, and of
object permanence, long before symbolic capacity is achieved, thereby confusing
progress in the complexity of transactional adaptation with the capacity for abstraction and symbol formation. Neither the dog who is distressed by his master's

If the interaction with mother is not restored within a reasonable time, the inability to predict what will happen paves the way for replacing irritability and anxiety with depression, i.e., with apathy, regression, and retarded behavior. There are experiments showing that even in lower mammals the inability to predict what will happen is a greater stress than painful stimulation; indeed, animals who can predict that they will be inevitably hurt by an electric shock fare better than those animals who can escape the painful stimulus but cannot predict its occurrence [30, 62]. At this stage of more advanced sensorimotor development the depressive syndrome is not due solely to understimulation, for the infant by now creates his own goals to a great extent. What is undermined by empathic failure at the advanced state of sensorimotor patterning development is perceptual expectations and, thereby, the ability to predict successfully what the next perception, i.e., the consequence of one's action, will be. Loss of the mother for the human infant, the loss of the perception of the nuances of mother's activity, is equivalent to the loss of the reasonable, expectable environment in which prediction is possible.

Whereas the so-called anaclitic depression may be attributed to understimulation of the brain, this form of depression is the result of failure to cope with the anxiety precipitated by overstimulation. Massive unfamiliarity and inconsistency in the perceptual input overwhelm the adaptive capacity of the pattern matching function. The depressive picture that may result can be explained as a consequence of the resulting failure of normal feedback to the rest of the body. Incidentally, this promotes a protective withdrawal from the unfamiliar input and an attempt at recovery.

Both types of depression in infancy are presymbolic and on an economic basis. It is the manner in which the pattern-matching function of the brain is affected that is important, not the nature of the percept per se.

It should again be emphasized that depression is a clinically significant syndrome representing the distortion of an otherwise average and expectable vicissitude of brain function. Whereas lower animals have from birth a sure but relatively inflexible encoded adaptational system, man is born in an almost totally uncertain but potentially flexible state. Devoid of adaptational action patterns, the human infant has great dependence on his autonomic ("affective") signaling patterns and their ability to engage his environment, i.e., his mother. What may terminate in depression, regression, and withdrawal is a failure of the behavioral system's establishment of effective goal-seek-

---

absence nor the 1-year-old child who cries when its mother is gone longs for an object per se.

ing patterns, which ordinarily stimulate the mother's identification with the infant and promote the feedback necessary to restore the ordering function of the infant's brain.

The Self-Concept and Symbol-Directed Behavior

It was mentioned earlier that the ability to reexperience and manipulate past events through activation of sensorimotor schema representing these occurrences permits man to isolate these symbolic representations and objectify them. That is, by isolating particular patterns of activity as figures against the ever-changing background of stimuli, holding them steady through recall, and giving them independent existence through projecting the symboling activity into the extracranial sphere man creates a world of objects.

Object formation is too often followed by inappropriate reification. It is important to reemphasize that "objects" are the result of symbolization. In a very limited number of cases a concept corresponds sufficiently with the invariances of energy relationships called "matter" to make reification of the object feasible. Thus our concepts of table, chair, and curtain lend themselves to material embodiment, "mother," "psychoanalyst," and "God" do not.* The latter represent functions, or structures composed of nonmolecular relationships.

Symbol formation and organization make reflection and fantasy possible; these activities can be used in the interest of protecting the lower brain and are a valuable evolutionary addition to the perceptual system, which is primarily a protective device, a system for delaying instinctually motivated action. Eventually, through a representation by means of symbols the whole gamut of perceptual activity, that is, expectations, registration and manipulation of sensations, and prediction, can be experienced both retrospectively and prospectively at small caloric cost to the total organism and without precipitating environmental reactions with which the organism would then have to deal. This action of reflection and fantasying, it should be emphasized, need not be self-conscious. Furthermore, the aspects that are made self-conscious as images, words, or sensory qualities should not be mistaken for the thinking process, as is so commonly done. Fan-

---

* The history of science that led to the misguided equation of reality with the material, and that made matter and its manipulation the paradigm of scientific endeavor, will not be discussed here. Suffice it to say that this misconception makes a scientific psychology a contradiction in terms. Since psychological activity is the only reality with which man is directly acquainted, a concept of science that excludes thought as behavior to be studied is rootless. The implications of this too-brief argument are clear: psychologists may not be hopeful that any continued effort to reduce psychology to the physics of sensory observation will succeed; rather, psychologists face the much greater challenge of participating in the elevation and revision of the concept of what shall be considered scientific.

tasy is an end result like running; fantasying is the outcome of thought processing, just as running is the outcome of coordinated muscle contraction.

Whereas on all other levels of life experience serves only to orient the organism's response in the here and now so that appropriate muscular or glandular activity can be instituted, in symboling animals the activity of the brain becomes an end in itself; reflection is added as a new form of behavior made possible by the re-presentational function. At the presymbolic level of the 8-month anxiety the mother does not exist for the infant as a concept but as a part of those sensorimotor recognition patterns associated with order. Her appearance and reappearance in his sensory environment activate those patterns originally created by the rhythmicity of her heartbeat prenatally and postnatally; and, similarly, her absence in the sensorium precipitates the irritability associated with failure of the ordering process. With presentational symbolism a concept equivalent to well-being, safety, and being cared for, is developed. Once this takes place, security need not be directly connected with mother's appearance or activities any more. Instead, as does indeed happen, the concept becomes attached to, i.e., objectified through, other experiences, which then stand for safety, order, etc. In this way toys, pets, familiar surroundings, other children and adults, acquire a meaning over and above their utilitarian function. Instead of merely signifying that particular conditions exist, they symbolize, i.e., stand for, those experiences with mother that originally signaled order. Once symboling capacity makes recall possible, the child lying in bed awake and afraid in the association-loosening darkness can recreate the sight of his mother's face, a memory which may soothe him not because it is linked to the perceptual experience of the person who is his mother but precisely because it is independent of that person. If the recall of his mother's face under the disorganizing strain of being in the dark served simply as a sign for mother, it would arouse his expectations of her imminent appearance and her absence would cause him to cry or go look for her. He would be comforted only when the sign function of his memory had been completed through reunion with mother. The symbolic representation of mother's face soothes because in recreating the experience of contact with mother it influences the diencephalic patterns directly by serving as a perception that stands for order, thereby eliminating anxiety and preventing activation of emergency responses.

The dispositional power of symboling activity and fantasy may also create difficulties, a vicissitude with which we psychoanalysts are only too familiar. The child in a dark room engaged, let us say, in some form of self-stimulating activity with which he has previously soothed himself successfully is now able to recall mother's or father's disapproving or tense face when he was observed by them in such a situation previously. The fact that neither parent can now observe him has significance on the sign level of behavior, but symbolically their disapproval and its representation directly activates the affective pattern associated with withdrawal of approval, by now the equivalent of abandonment and helplessness. This may again result in screaming, crying, or running to the parent, but now reunion with the parent does not immediately soothe the child. He continues to be terrified by the concept of being abandoned. It is the capacity for conceptualizing this horror that terrifies him and the reality of reunion itself does not immediately alter that realization. From then on the attraction and fear of conceptualization governs more and more of existence, giving rise to the aforementioned symbolic (conceptual) world [9].

THE INFANT AS A SYMBOLIC OBJECT

Considerable space has been given to emphasizing that the mother is not an object or part object for her infant during his sensorimotor phase of development. However, the infant's very existence depends on his being a symbolic object for his mother.

The infant as an object for his mother is the sum total of his mother's psychic involvement with him. For her the newborn infant is not the assemblage of cells that comprise his body, though that body is the target for much of the activity aroused by the meaning of her objectified concept "my baby." This is exemplified rather dramatically by the culturally sanctioned or tolerated infanticide in societies of the past where, for example, unwanted babies were abandoned to die. The sanctions of the culture were such that these infants were not permitted to become positive intrapsychic objects for their mothers and could therefore be left to perish. That is, in other times infants embodied different meaning and were therefore conceptualized differently by their mothers. Probably it is only in modern times when relative abundance and medical advances make a given infant's survival to adulthood a reasonable possibility that babies can be permitted to become so narcissistically meaningful [2].

THE SELF AS SYMBOLIC OBJECT

Perhaps the most important concept to be developed is the concept of self. The body ego, or the self on the sensorimotor level, is not exclusive to humans. All animals that have a central organ for correlating signal processing operate by ordering signals into figure-background patterns. Any animal that does not respond directly and simply to stimuli but engages in complex behavior must have a feedback mechanism that continuously compares the performance of the unit with the implicit task set by the original percept and controls the body in relation to the immediate past and to the goal to be achieved. For example, the lion hunting his prey requires a network of sensorimotor patterns that do not orient the body to the surround but evaluate the body's position in relation to its initial posture and to the end point or goal, i.e., the closure encoded in the behavioral plan. This figure-ground differentiation into self and not-self on the functional level does not imply that there is a concept of self. Only when human infants achieve symbolic capacity are the body boundary experiences objectified and raised to a conceptual, as opposed to a sensorimotor level of self. However, though based on the unique sensory combinations that accompany stimulation of the sensory nervous system by one's own actions and reactions, the conceptualized self is neither limited to nor identical with the body experience but transcends it and eventually encompasses it to a greater or lesser extent. Bronowski [13] has said correctly that what we in later life call our "self" is nothing less than the sum total of our experiences and the influence that these have on our behavior. The sense of uniqueness that each of us attaches to our consciousness of self is based on the fact that only we have experienced the world around us and our own brain activity in exactly the way we have experienced and coordinated it. If we accept the fact that this record of our behavior is in the first instance always a neurologically encoded record, then there is no problem in asserting, as psychoanalysis has always done, that our later behavior bears the imprint of former experiences and that, barring organic damage, nothing that a person has experienced is ever lost. This concept of self is of course not identical with self-awareness or self-consciousness. It is important to emphasize that the structure of symbolic self operates unconsciously, as does the earlier structure of self based on sign behavior and body boundaries. Consciousness of self or self-consciousness is not a structure but a symbolic activity useful in perceptual recycling and problem solving.

It is the imaging activity of reality testing that becomes symbolized as the verbal noun I. "I" never occurs alone. It is always "I am thinking (imaging)," "I am saying," "I am hearing," etc. During the act of perception one is not conscious of one's self; only if some failure to integrate stimuli smoothly occurs is the reality testing mechanism of sensory consciousness activated. It is the symbolization of the reflective activity, that is, the reflection on one's own reflections, that is objectified as "I," reified as "psyche," "spirit," or "soul," and projected inwardly as other reifications are projected toward the outside.

One's total self is much larger than "I" and in very important aspects is unknown, as psychoanalysis rightly maintains. One's "self" is not a static entity or structure any more than it is a thing. The concept of a permanent identity is based on the fact that the continuous pattern-matching activity of the brain calls attention to what has been experienced before and how it relates to what is being experienced at the moment.

SYMBOLIC ADAPTATION

The capacity for symbolic re-presentation introduces what Korzybski [33] calls time binding. It is this evolutionary step that has made man master of nature and has short-circuited the selective process of evolution itself. The communication of representations enables men to pass on to their fellows and to the next generation what they have learned without having to depend on the much slower process of genetic mutation to transmit those patterns that are superior in assuring survival. At the same time, however, the development of representation through symbols has altered the perceptual system's relationship to the lower brain and the drive patterns. Maruyama [40] describes two forms of feedback in causal systems: (1) those that oppose and correct deviations from a particular direction through negative feedback and (2) those that amplify deviations through positive feedback. In nonsymboling animals the cortex and lower brain act as a coordinated negative feedback system mutually adjusting any deviation from behavior in the direction of the ultimate goal of reproduction and survival of the species. In man the symboling subsystem of the cortical hierarchy functions as a positive feedback system that potentially enhances deviation from the standard interpretation of percepts. The manipulation of figure-ground configurations to yield new patterns is the source of man's creativity and inventiveness, but it also gives rise to perceptual inferences that do not reflect the danger-gratification situations of the immediate environment. The positive feedback mechanisms mentioned before serve to give the objects so created a life of their own; they do not simply re-present experience but generate experience.

Once the symboling subsystem has become operational, it serves, as do the muscular and glandular systems, as an outlet to be used for drive adaptation and affective gratification. Where before the threat of disorder activated anatomical systems in a search for restitution, now conceptualization, thinking in the narrow sense, is also used in the search for harmony. In this way conceptualization becomes a goal not for the perceptual system alone but for drive satisfaction as well. Indeed, it is in conceptualization that the child finds his first independence. The 2- or 3-year-old child has a comparatively sophisticated conceptual system while his skeletal muscle system is hardly effective yet for coping with danger or for obtaining the necessities of life. A child can combat the loss of hope that accompanies helplessness through organizing, usually idiosyncratically, what is happening to him. This gives him a feeling of power, since understanding equals control on the conceptual level. The fundamental classifications are based on presentational conceptualization and not on the later discursive symbolization of description. Presentational symbolism, precisely because it is not discursive, cannot be expressed directly in words. It follows the rules of topology, i.e., the mathematics of relationships, rather than the rules of grammar. Presentational symbolism continues throughout life to be the root of meaning, that is, dispositional power. Descriptive, discursive symbolism affects behavior only insofar as it represents and describes presentational symbolic constructs. Freud's great discovery was to penetrate the mystery of presentational symbolism, which he called primary process thinking, and to lay down rules for deciphering its manifestation in dreams, neuroses, and everyday waking life. By translating presentational symbolism into the everyday logic of discursive symbolism, called by Freud the secondary process, Freud taught us a new language, the language of meaning.

OBJECT RELATIONS

The power of concepts lies in their dispositional effects. Whereas a sign arouses perceptual expectation, a symbol awakens instinctual or affective tendencies. An "object relationship" describes a situation in which a particular symbolic construct can potentially evoke a response and dispose the organism toward some behavioral reaction. Two forms of relationship are possible depending on which drive patterns are triggered. These have been called object love and narcissism, two forms of object relations, and they undergo separate lines of development [31].

The difference between the two can be illustrated using the mother's relationship to her infant. Insofar as the psychic representation of her infant becomes an extension of the mother's fundamental need for care and affection, the infant becomes a significant narcissistic object for her, that is, the representation of her child mobilizes all her self-preservative instinctual patterns, which result in activities meant to preserve the child's physical well-being as well as the derivative emotional gratification that the mother herself experiences. Insofar as the concept of the child is one representing something separate, beyond and perhaps greater than the self-concept of the mother, it activates the reproductive, species-preserving, instinctual patterns, and makes the child the target of what psychoanalysts call object love.

Depression at the Symbolic Level of Development

Men living in organized communities in a machine age live primarily in the symbolic world. Most of the time their survival is not endangered by the forces of nature, nor are they hunted by other animals. Self-preservation for modern man means keeping the symbolic self intact. Fundamentally this involves his being able to receive and process messages accurately, and to understand and orient himself to their significance. Impairment of this operational ability creates narcissistic damage·because it affects the most important narcissistic object, i.e., the concept of self.

As was previously discussed, by learning to associate symbolic presentations with sexual and self-protective needs, the cortex can trigger the diencephalon and command a total organic response. As clinical examination shows, especially experiences related to infantile narcissistic frustration and gratification tend to become symbolic of sexual and self-preservative concerns. By symbolizing drive demands these experiences may come to dominate the behavior of the total organism. So, when we speak of man as living in a "symbolic world" we mean not just a world in which hypothetical entities are a possibility, but one in which life itself revolves around abstract concerns attached to mundane and in themselves insignificant events. For example, when a particular fantasy that has become central for the unconscious concept of self is shattered by some seemingly minor event, it may, like organic damage, impair message processing to the point where the self concept cannot be maintained. The resultant depression, due to symbolic loss, is evidence of the failure of the feedback process.

There is a significant difference between depression that occurs presymbolically and that which occurs later. Presymbolically the empathic response aroused in others by the signal aspect of the depressive syndrome results in the reestablishment of order and a reversal of pathology. Not so in depression at the symbolic level. Though the clinical picture is similar, support seems often to be of no avail in restoring the ordering process of a depression caused by symbolic loss. This is understandable once it is realized that it is the symbolic concept of self that has been impaired and that only when restitution or alterations have been made in the concept of self per se will the patient be able to respond to the efforts being made on his behalf by others.

The difference between mourning a loss and becoming depressed through it can now be explained. As Freud pointed out, the mourner grieves until he has found a new object. In structuralist terms, the mourner retains his goal on the symbolic level, but without an object he cannot attain it practically. The depressed person does not mourn an object, he bemoans a narcissistic loss, i.e., an injury to the self. On the symbolic level the dispositional effect of events, or their meaning, depends on the significance they have for the self-concept; once the self-concept is destroyed, life is meaningless because events can no longer arouse affective behavior. The depressed individual has lost the framework of the self-concept that served as the ordering principle for brain activity and, therefore, is not free to find new objects. As long as the symbolic system is functional, the capacity for resolution in fantasy and the flexibility of symbolism defend against the feeling of helplessness. Defeat, loss, and disappointment due to external circumstances do not bring about depression, though they may sadden their victim. It is only when a particular situation, person, or achievement is an essential part of the self-structure that a loss can precipitate depression by undoing the capacity for orderly processing of events. The feeling of helplessness vis-à-vis narcissistic goals that Bibring emphasizes as central to depression is due not to losing the possibility of fulfillment but to losing the capacity for organizing goal-directed behavior once the concept of self is no longer meaningful, that is, dispositionally effective.

PSYCHOSIS

Once the symbolic function is activated, the separation of the world into self and others becomes the focus for ordering experience. Failure to establish a stable concept of self interferes with the brain's message-processing activity and the maintenance of a viable organism.

The parents' emotional investment in the infant as a symbol of their narcissism lays the groundwork for the eventual development of the child's symbolic identity. Parental indifference or hatred creates an overload of negative affect in the early months of life. The self-concept that evolves under such circumstances is an unstable and defensively oriented one. The organism becomes geared more to minimizing stress than to enrichment through assimilating a multiplicity of experiences. Given such a fragile construct, the danger of fragmentation is great, and with stress a psychotic resolution may supervene in a final attempt to preserve the symbolic self and its ordering function on an idiosyncratic basis. The failure of such a psychotic solution reveals the depressive component seen behind all psychoses, that is, the inability to maintain the message-processing and pattern-matching activity necessary for the function of the open system. It is quite possible that there are genetic, organic predispositions that interfere with symbolic development and increase the probability that a psychotic state will eventuate regardless of the emotional climate of infancy.

The negative self-concept typically seen in psychotic patients is most clearly demonstrated in the so-called affective psychoses. The openly expressed sense of worthlessness and wish for death exemplifies the painful tension under which those patients labor whose self-concept does not enable them to draw narcissistic strength from others. It is quite likely that addictive personalities suffer a similar defect and depend on a chemical solution for an inner feeling of organization that human interaction cannot mediate.

The term "affective disorder" for depressive illness is, however, a misnomer insofar as it means these patients are overtly sad, distraught, weeping, etc. There are many individuals who are unable to engage in effective goal-directed behavior without being saddened; they do not cry or voice feelings of despair; they may even be manic; yet they are depressed in the systemic if not the phenomenological sense.

It is clinically confusing and theoretically incorrect to equate the emotions often associated with depression with the disorder itself. Indeed, insofar as a patient is aware of sadness, or is still crying and wailing, he is not totally depressed. Just as in infancy, these behaviors are reactions to the failure of the ordering process and are involuntary communications to members of the species to help correct a deficit. They are part of the anxiety created by the danger of disorganization and attempts to correct that condition. The presence of depression implies and is equivalent to the failure to get help with the ordering process and indicates a condition in which even the goal of calling for help is no longer possible. The inability to organize stimuli in keeping with the underlying drive patterns results in a situation in which the diencephalon and autonomic behavior patterns cannot be activated. Depression is the clinical evidence that the system is grinding to a halt, that messages are no longer being processed, that the input of stimuli is no longer informative, and that the negentropic balance of the organism cannot be maintained. Depression is therefore the syndrome in which the behavioral system is transformed from an open into a closed one; it indicates the death of the brain as a self-directing system and its reduction to a purely reactive organization subject to the laws of thermodynamics. The restoration of affective behaviors, i.e., despair, anguish, crying, and their symbolic concomitants, signals restitution and a resumption of the attempt at ordering activity. The psychotic attempts to restore the concept of self through delusions.

For example, the melancholic's feeling of worthlessness and the conviction that he deserves to die are his attempts to order the consequences of the dysfunction, not its cause. Through reasoning that his sins, real and imaginary, have brought down the punishment of depression upon him, the melancholic restores an ordering principle to his existence. These patients' notorious lack of response to psychological treatment can be understood as resistance to losing this new, albeit pathological, self-structure.

PSYCHONEUROSIS

Depression in the classic psychoneurotic case is a secondary occurrence only. These individuals are endowed with a strong and viable self-concept. Their symptoms are the result of a conflict between forbidden infantile wishes and the equally strong sanctions against acknowledging, much less fulfilling, such desires symbolically. Any depression that occurs in such patients is caused by their relative inability to continue their adaptation to the exigencies of present reality, preoccupied as they are with neurotic stress. A less stressful environment, a support of their defenses, or a resolution of the neurotic conflict through psychoanalysis all will restore the ordering capacity and ameliorate the depressive component in such patients.

CHARACTER DISORDER

Cases of so-called neurotic depression are more properly classified as depressions occurring in patients suffering from narcissistic character disorders. Although such patients have a stable self-concept, it remains on an immature level of narcissistic development [31] that is dominated by some form of an infantile sense of entitlement. Even average expectable disappointments and frustrations tend to undermine the unrealistic sense of grandiosity on which such patients' self-concept is based. No longer able to function unless their symbolic needs are met, these patients express a sense of futility and hopelessness about their existence that is often accompanied more by anger than by sadness. Nevertheless, they are depressed, as indicated by their inability to process messages in such a way that they elicit a positive affective response. Environmental gratification of needs or support of defenses in psychotherapy are restorative measures, but the final solution for such patients lies in the psychoanalytic examination and maturation of their infantile self-concept.

Signal Transmission and Depression

It is well known that various organic disturbances can generate depression. Any disturbance that interferes with the brain's reception, registration, and transmission of stimuli interferes with its ordering function and, *ipso facto*, with the concept of self. This explains how it is that a multitude of diseases in and out of the central nervous system may be accompanied by, or even have as their sole or initial symptom, a depressive reaction.

Similarly, disruption or drastic alteration of perceptual input may in predisposed individuals lead to depression. For example, a radical change in environment bombards the individual with signals that do not evoke past experiences in sufficient quantity to support the necessary continuous regeneration of the symbolic self. The traumatic situation may be a geographic dislocation, but more frequently it is a call for a symbolic shift, for instance: retirement at the end of the working life, or an incapacitating illness in a previously active individual. Such disorganizations precipitate anxiety, possibly marked by depersonalization and estrangement, which, if restitutive measures are not forthcoming, leads to a state in which goal setting is no longer effective and positive affect is not engaged, i.e., the patient has become depressed.

Allergic reactions to chemicals may also precipitate an interference with the perceptual function. The resulting estrangement, derealization, and depersonalization in some cases progresses to a depressive syndrome.

The phenomenology of depression, no matter what its cause may be, generally involves motor and mental retardation, irritability or apathy, and is often accompanied by an attitude of either hopelessness and helplessness or anger. It is important to be aware that the message-processing function whose failure is responsible for the disorder can be hampered at any level of the behavioral system. Only an examination in depth can establish whether dysfunction of signal, sign, or symbol processing has converted the brain from an open to a closed system.

CONCLUSION

A satisfactory causal explanatory theory of depression must consider the entire gamut of the depressive syndrome, must be independent of any given school of psychological thought or method of therapy, must go beyond clinical appearances, and should not contradict what has been properly established to be the case in other sciences. This necessitates construction of a theory of brain function that, while encompassing the clinical insights of psychoanalysis, significantly changes the nineteenth-century view of mental functioning heretofore accepted as the "metapsychology" of our field. This chapter is an attempt to formulate such a theory.

Utilizing the structuralist approach to the philosophy of science and the viewpoint of general systems theory, I have tried to demonstrate that depression refers to those consequences that follow from disturbances in the message-processing function of the brain and that depression should be considered a system dysfunction rather than a particular illness or clinical picture. The behavioral system generated by the brain's operation is an open one, which means that it sets its own goals on the basis of processing incoming stimuli and extracting their informational value. The systemic disturbance indicating that this process is no longer viable and that the system is converting from an open, transactional state into a closed, reactive position is properly called depression. This view makes it possible to understand how it is that multiple and diverse etiologies may precipitate depressive phenomenology and differentiates the nature of the disorganization giving rise to depression on the basis of the level at which the ordering function of the brain is disrupted.

There are of course many implications for the teaching and practice of clinical psychoanalysis in a systems approach to metapsychology that are not specifically related to the syndrome of depression, with which this chapter is primarily concerned. Though these implications are not taken up here, they have not been forgotten and will be the subject of future communications.

REFERENCES

1. Altschule, M. D. Nonpsychologic causes of depression. *Medical Science*, 16:36, 1965.
2. Aries, P. *Centuries of Childhood: A Social History of Family Life.* New York: Knopf, 1962.
3. Arnheim, R. *Visual Thinking.* London: Faber & Faber, 1969.
4. Arnold, M. B. *Emotion and Personality*, vol. 1. New York: Columbia University Press, 1960.
5. Basch, M. F. Psychoanalysis and theory formation. In *The Annual of Psychoanalysis*, vol. 1, ed. by The Institute for Psychoanalysis. New York: Quadrangle/New York Times Book Co., 1973.
6. Beck, A. T. *Depression: Causes and Treatment.* Philadelphia: University of Pennsylvania Press, 1967.
7. Benedek, T. Toward the biology of the depressive constellation. *J. Am. Psychoanal. Assoc.* 6:389, 1956.
8. Benedek, T. *Psychoanalytic Investigations: Selected Papers.* New York: Quadrangle/New York Times Book Co., 1973. P. 255.
9. Bertalanffy, L. v. *General System Theory: Foundations, Development, Applications.* New York: Braziller, 1968.

10. Bibring, E.   The Mechanism of Depression. In P. Greenacre (Ed.), *Affective Disorders*. New York: International Universities Press, 1953.
11. Brandt, H. F.   *The Psychology of Seeing*. New York: Philosophical Library, 1945.
12. Brazier, M. A. B.   How Can Models from Information Theory Be Used in Neurophysiology? In W. S. Fields and W. Abbott (Eds.), *Information Storage and Neural Control*. Springfield, Ill.: Thomas, 1963.
13. Bronowski, J.   *The Identity of Man*. Garden City, N.Y.: Doubleday, 1972.
14. Church, J.   *Language and the Discovery of Reality*. New York: Random House, 1961.
15. Colby, K. M., and Lashley, K. S.   An exchange of views on psychic energy and psychoanalysis. *Behav. Sci.* 2:231, 1957.
16. Dorpat, T. L.   Regulatory mechanisms of the perceptual apparatus on involuntary physiological actions. *J. Am. Psychoanal. Assoc.* 16: 319, 1968.
17. Eccles, J. D.   The physiology of imagination. *Sci. Am.* 199:135, 1958.
18. Eisenberg, L.   The human nature of human nature. *Science* 176: 123, 1972.
19. Freud, S.   *On Aphasia* (1891), transl. by E. Stengel. New York: International Universities Press, 1953.
20. Freud, S.   Project for a Scientific Psychology (1895). In *The Standard Edition of the Complete Psychological Works of Sigmund Freud*, transl. and ed. by J. Strachey with others. London: Hogarth and Institute of Psycho-Analysis, 1966. Vol. 1, p. 283.
21. Freud, S.   The Interpretation of Dreams (second part) (1900). *Standard Edition*. 1958. Vol. 5, p. 509.
22. Freud, S.   The Psycho-analytic View of Psychogenic Disturbances of Vision (1910). *Standard Edition*. 1957. Vol. 11, p. 209.
23. Freud, S.   The Unconscious (1915). *Standard Edition*. 1957. Vol. 14, p. 159.
24. Freud, S.   Mourning and Melancholia (1917 [1915]). *Standard Edition*. 1957. Vol. 14, p. 237.
25. Freud, S.   The Ego and the Id (1923). *Standard Edition*. 1961. Vol. 19, p. 3.
26. Goodall, J.   The behavior of chimpanzees in their natural habitat. *Am. J. Psychol.* 130:1, 1973.
27. Hall, E. T.   *The Silent Language*. New York: Doubleday, 1959.
28. Harlow, H. F., Harlow, M. K., and Suomi, S. J.   From thought to therapy: Lessons from a primate laboratory. *Am. Sc.* 59:538, 1971.
29. Holt, R. R.   A Review on Some of Freud's Biological Assumptions and Their Influence on His Theories. In N. S. Greenfield and W. C. Lewis (Eds.), *Psychoanalysis and Current Biological Thought*. Madison: University of Wisconsin Press, 1965.
30. Joffe, J. M., et al.   Control of their environment reduces emotionality in rats. *Science* 180:1383, 1973.
31. Kohut, H.   *The Analysis of the Self: A Systematic Approach to the Psychoanalytic Treatment of Narcissistic Personality Disorders*. New York: International Universities Press, 1971.

32. Kolakowski, L. *The Alienation of Reason.* New York: Doubleday, 1968.
33. Korzybski, A. *Science and Sanity* (3rd ed.). Lakeville, Conn.: International Non-Aristotelian Library Publishing, 1948.
34. Kubie, L. S. In panel on the concept of psychic energy, reported by A. H. Modell. *J. Am. Psychoanal. Assoc.* 11:605, 1963.
35. Langer, S. K. *Philosophy in a New Key* (2nd ed.). Cambridge, Mass.: Harvard University Press, 1951.
36. Langer, S. K. *Philosophical Sketches.* Baltimore, Md.: Johns Hopkins Press, 1962.
37. Littenberg, R., Tulkin, S. R., and Kagan, J. Cognitive components of separation anxiety. *Dev. Psychol.* 4:387, 1971.
38. MacKay, D. M. *Information, Mechanism and Meaning.* Cambridge, Mass.: M.I.T. Press, 1969.
39. McKinney, W. T., Jr., et al. Depression in primates. *Am. J. Psychol.* 127:1313, 1971.
40. Maruyama, M. The Second Cybernetics: Deviation-Amplifying Mutual Causal Processes. In W. Buckley (Ed.), *Modern Systems Research for the Behavioral Scientist.* Chicago: Aldine, 1968.
41. Miller, G. A. What Is Information Measurement? In W. Buckley (Ed.), *Modern Systems Research for the Behavioral Scientist.* Chicago: Aldine, 1968.
42. Miller, J. G. Living Systems: Basic Concepts. In W. Gray, et al. (Eds.), *General Systems Theory and Psychiatry.* Boston: Little, Brown, 1969.
43. Peterfreund, E. *Information, Systems and Psychoanalysis.* New York: International Universities Press, 1971.
44. Piaget, J., and Inhelder, B. *The Psychology of the Child.* New York: Basic Books, 1969.
45. Rapaport, D. *Organization and Pathology of Thought.* New York: Columbia University Press, 1951.
46. Rapoport, A. *Operational Philosophy.* New York: Harper & Row, 1953.
47. Rapoport, A. Technological Models of the Nervous System. In K. Sayre and F. J. Crosson (Eds.), *The Modeling of Mind: Computers and Intelligence.* Notre Dame, Ind.: University of Notre Dame Press, 1963.
48. Rosenblatt, A. D., and Thickstun, J. T. A study of the concept of psychic energy. *Int. J. Psychoanal.* 51:265, 1970.
49. Ryle, G. *The Concept of Mind.* New York: Barnes & Noble, 1949.
50. Salk, L. The role of the heartbeat in the relations between mother and infant. *Sci. Am.,* 228:24, 1973.
51. Schaffer, H. R., and Emerson, P. E. *The Development of Social Attachments in Infancy.* Monographs of the Society for Research in Child Development, Serial Number 94, Vol. 29, 1964.
52. Schmale, A. H. Depression as Affect, Character Style, and Symptom Formation. In R. R. Holt and E. Peterfreund (Eds.), *Psychoanalysis and Contemporary Science.* New York: Macmillan, 1972.
53. Scott, J. P. Biology and human aggression. *Am. J. Orthopsychiatry* 40:568, 1970.

54. Simeons, A. T. W. *Man's Presumptuous Brain*. New York: Dutton, 1962.
55. Singh, J. *Great Ideas in Information Theory, Language and Cybernetics*. New York: Dover, 1966.
56. Spelke, E., et al. Father interaction and separation protest. *Dev. Psychol.* 9:83, 1973.
57. Spitz, R. A. Hospitalism: A follow-up report on investigation described in Volume 1, 1945. *Psychoanal. Study Child* 2:113, 1946.
58. Stechler, G., and Carpenter, G. A Viewpoint on Early Affective Development, vol. 1. In J. Hellmuth (Ed.), *Exceptional Infant—The Normal Infant*. New York: Brunner/Mazel, 1967. P. 165.
59. Tomkins, S. S. *Affect, Imagery, Consciousness*. New York: Springer, 1962 (Vol. 1), 1963 (Vol. 2).
60. Vygotsky, L. S. *Thought and Language*. Cambridge, Mass.: M.I.T. Press, 1962.
61. Weiss, J. M. Psychological factors in stress and disease. *Sci. Am.* 226:104, 1972.
62. Wiener, N. *The Human Use of Human Beings*. Garden City, N.Y.: Doubleday, 1956.
63. Young, L. D., et al. Early stress and later response to separation in rhesus monkeys. *Am. J. Psychol.* 130:400, 1973.

Epilogue

As we look back over this book in its various parts, we cannot help but feel that the hypothesis stated in the Introduction has been confirmed in different ways by different contributors making use of different approaches. Depression does appear to be a universal experience, and the potential for developing depressive reactions does appear to be latent in everyone and manifest in some under certain conditions. By reason of this universality, depression has been compared with anxiety. Various authors in this symposium have examined the two systems and have found both likenesses and dissimilarities. Anxiety and depression have been described as basic affects, each with a normal range of expression that can become a clinical entity when predisposing factors or circumstances encourage it. The capacity to bear anxiety or depression and the tendency to become abnormally anxious or depressed may vary considerably from individual to individual depending on both intrinsic and extrinsic factors. A wide range of defenses is available within the individual to deal with excesses of either type of affect. The differences are equally striking: depression is not only a more negative type of experience than anxiety, it is more inward-turning. Zetzel [10] has suggested that depression is not built into the personality in the same way as anxiety and thus does not become a part of the organization of the self, but our own experience and understanding argues that it is as profoundly interwoven into the various levels of the mind. In characterological terms, the depressive person is not merely someone with a special proclivity toward depressive illness but more especially someone whose inveterate response to any and every problem of existence is "depressive." This is not to say that the two basic affects function in separate compart-

535

ments unrelated to each other. On the contrary, they are frequently seen in normal and clinical association and may replace each other in affective states from time to time. So-called anxiety-depression is perhaps the commonest of all clinical manifestations.

Depression has also been closely linked to the fluctuations in optimism and pessimism that occur throughout life. During childhood, as belief in the omnipotence of the self and of the parent decreases under the growing influence of the reality sense, optimism may give way to pessimism, especially if the child is disillusioned too rapidly or orally deprived inordinately. Depression has roots similar to those of pessimism, but unlike pessimism, it may collapse rapidly into helplessness and hopelessness. One can be pessimistic, rationally and reasonably, on the state of the world today without being depressed or giving up on it. Freud's attitude was often referred to as pessimistic,* especially in his later years, but he was not described as depressed or defeated.† To almost the end, his mind remained essentially open; the give and take between him and his intellectual and emotional environment never really stopped. The practice of looking on the dark side of things or expecting the worst outcome was closely attuned to reality in his case. The last 16 years of his life were passed in a day-to-day struggle with continual discomfort and pain.

This is not to say that pessimism is generally dissociated from depression. According to Beck [1], the reverse is true. He found that more than 78 percent of depressed patients give evidence of a "negative outlook" as compared with 22 percent of nondepressed patients and that this particular symptom has the highest correlation with the clinical rating of depression. A closer examination of Beck's study, however, suggests that a semantic problem may have been involved, since he appeared to use the terms pessimism, negative expectation,

---

* He also considered himself in this light. In a letter to Princess Maria Bonaparte two years before his death, he writes: "The moment one inquires about the sense or value of life one is sick, since objectively neither of them has any existence. In doing so one is only admitting a surplus of unsatisfied libido, *and then something else must happen, a sort of fermenting, for it to lead to grief and depression* [italics added]. These explanations of mine are certainly not on a grand scale, *perhaps because I am too pessimistic* [italics added]. There is going through my head an advertisement which I think is the boldest and most successful American one I know of. 'Why live when you can be buried for ten dollars?'" [6, p. 495]. It was this characteristic humor that seemed to preserve him from depression.

† This needs some qualification. When Freud was 38, he had some questionably anginal attacks, following which he became depressed. According to his physician, Max Schur, his "main reaction was a depressive mood entailing obsessive thoughts about how long he still had to live. . . . [It] interfered with the progress of his work. . . . It is inconceivable that when his mood was low, and progress in the treatment of his patients was slow, Freud was not beset by doubts about the validity of his findings" [8]. This was, however, the one and only reference made to depression during his long and often painful lifetime.

and hopelessness almost interchangeably, whereas they may refer to quite different states of mind. In fact, he may not have investigated the incidence of pessimism at all, and so a close relationship between depression and pessimism may not have been proven. He did discover, nevertheless, that what he labeled pessimism tends to cluster with a cognitive group of symptoms that includes a negative self-concept and a tendency to interpret experience negatively. In his view, pessimism was part of a predepressive constellation that renders the individual vulnerable to depressive illness. On the basis of these slender findings, supported by clinical impression, one could claim that pessimism can occur with or without depression and that there was some evidence that it, along with other factors, predisposed to depression.

It is a curious fact that one of the central experiences in life, namely sexuality, is rarely or only peripherally discussed in relationship to depression; it is true also of this particular book.* One can perhaps excuse this omission on the ground that it is far too complex an experience to be treated tangentially. In fact, it has so many motivations that its existential quality obtains for it no discussion, even by existentialist philosophers whose main preoccupation has been with anxiety, mental pain, deprivation, and misery. In contrast to the existential roots of depression, which are largely negative, Eros or libido is characterized by its positive motivational quality, whether in relation to psychological development or procreation. Disinterest in sex is reported in a majority of depressed patients, and Beck, in his investigations, found that the loss of libido correlated most highly with loss of appetite, loss of interest in other people, and a depressed mood. Occasionally, sexual desire appeared to be heightened when the patient was mildly depressed, but with moderate and severe depression not only was responsiveness nil but a pronounced aversion to any sexual activity developed. The motivations to love, to work, to play, and to think well of oneself are all frequent and heavy casualties in the depressive conflict.

On reviewing the contemporary world from a clinical point of view, one is impressed by the fact that the frequency of depressive disorders, both affective and psychosomatic, is on the increase and not only in countries in which technological civilization has reached destructive heights. To throw light on this development, we need to differentiate what represents human existence from what has become accepted as the "human condition." The first is ubiquitous and perpetual and

---

* However, in Chapter 14 the depressive condition is discussed in relation to the age-specific dominant conflict and to the way it manifests itself in the relationship between the sexes from adolescence through generative maturity to the final decline with aging.

governed by the laws of biology and psychobiology, whereas the second is merely the epiphenomenon of technology and is determined by the circumstance of time and place.

From the biology and psychobiology of human existence we can derive certain laws that are universally applicable. For example, the laws that regulate the cosmos are basically the same as those that regulate the physical, organismic, and even the interpersonal environment of the individual. Freud was led to postulate a universal law with regard to mental processes and termed it the principle of "repetition compulsion," the "compulsion" referring to the unavoidability of the repetition (and not any psychodynamic process) and the "repetition" relating to the final reduction of mental process, to which he gave the controversial name "death instinct." In the living, organic process, repetition constantly interacted with the positive, integrating, augmenting factor of life, Eros or libido. It is interesting to note that he deduced this repetition of instinctual process in mental life at a time when the laws of nature were not as widely known as they are today, and so for him the "repetition" was conceived within the closed system of the mind or "psychic apparatus," which he compared to a machine.

Prior to this momentous discovery (that had so much significance for the development of psychoanalysis), he had already opened up a new psychological world by differentiating the essence of what is experienced from what is not experienced or cannot be experienced in the domain of the unconscious, affording an endless clinical opportunity to collect, collate, and organize the systems that account for any experience.

A further seminal contribution was his postulation of a "stimulus barrier" that had developed imperceptibly over eons of time. The human cortex is normally protected against the onslaught of stimuli from the "booming, buzzing confusion" around it when this special screening device is functioning properly. Today, as never before, this functional barrier must perform efficiently if the mind is to be protected from continuous distraction. The amount of stimuli impinging on us, both physically and psychologically, has grown in pace with the uncontrolled proliferation of civilized living. There is an incessant barrage of information being disseminated through all the media and threatening the disintegration of even the most resistant minds.

The epiphenomenon of technology has so invaded every aspect of living that, like the sorcerer's apprentice, we are becoming inundated by it. Countermeasures so far have not succeeded in improving the material and psychological environment in which the next generation will grow up. The future outlook is not encouraging. It seems one can disturb the balance of nature with its built-in chain of relationships only at his own peril. In man's manipulation of his condition, a gain of advantage appears inexorably to be followed by a loss of advantage. Technology had promised a better world to live in, but now it is beginning to turn against its creators.

Psychiatrists, psychoanalysts, and other behavioral scientists have been investigating the deterioration in the life circumstances of individuals, families, and societies as a consequence of the Industrial Revolution. There can be no doubt that technological growth has made everyone increasingly aware of what they are doing to themselves and to their environment. It has brought about profound alterations in the "human condition," changing long established ways of life and the relationships between people (especially between the sexes). In the intrapsychic sphere, it has undermined the moral system of regulations and controls and the strength of the individual superego.

Attempts to mitigate or "cure" these developments have not been carried out systematically or collaboratively by the different approaches to depression. Neurophysiology has studied the roots of affective experience and expression, and neuropharmacology has tried to alleviate them. Psychiatrists have turned to different combinations of psychological, electroshock, and drug treatments, but they have found it difficult to increase the moral strength needed for lasting improvement.

Existentialists with a therapeutic bent, like Tillich [9], have long been aware of this same problem: what parts of human anguish are responsive to medically oriented treatment and what parts are not? In the Introduction a close look was taken at the way psychoanalysts saw themselves in relation to existentialism; now, as a contrast to this, the next step will be to examine how existentialists have seen themselves in relation to psychoanalysis.

Tillich has spoken of the gap that developed between existentialism and psychoanalysis after World War II as a result of Sartre's opposition to the concept of the unconscious and has suggested that existentialism, in its broader sense of creativity in all areas of life, did imply a very definite relationship. "Psychoanalysis," he insisted, "belongs fundamentally to the whole existentialist movement of the twentieth century." The two movements must be regarded as interdependent both in origin and in development.

It is a fact that psychoanalysis and existentialism have been connected with each other from the very beginning; they have mutually influenced each other in the most radical and profound ways. Everybody who has looked into the works of existentialist writers from Dostoyevsky on to the present will immediately agree that there is much deep psychological material in (them). . . . All this is understandable only if we see that there is a common root and intention in existentialism and psychoanalysis.

The common root that existentialism and psychoanalysis share is the protest against the increasing power of the philosophy of consciousness, which is itself a derivative of consciousness and technology. The history of industrial society could be understood as a "victory of the philosophy of consciousness over the philosophy of the unconscious." From the nineteenth to the twentieth century men were becoming increasingly lost in the mechanized universe and responding with anxiety, guilt, doubt, loneliness, emptiness, and meaninglessness. The existentialists, from Pascal onward, have protested vehemently against this estrangement from the natural world and the loss of subjectivity. These ontological intuitions were given substance by psychoanalysis: "Freud, in his discovery of the unconscious, rediscovered something that was known long before and had been used for many decades and even centuries to fight the victorious philosophy of consciousness. What Freud did was to give this protest a scientific, methodological foundation." Both existentialism and psychoanalysis chose to focus on man's alienation in the face of the new technology and on the symptoms of this estrangement. How could man continue to exist under such conditions, and what needed to be "healed"? The bringing together of existentialism and therapy in psychoanalysis not only introduced a new possibility of change but also indicated the relationship between disease—mental, physical, or psychosomatic—and man's existential predicament.

Tillich then raised the important question: "How is it possible that a being has a structure that produces psychosomatic diseases?" What aspects of the clinical picture relate to the universal predicament of existence and what aspects to the deterioration and distortion engendered by the "human condition"? Clearly the experience of loneliness, nothingness, and meaninglessness can be ascribed in large part to the brute fact of existence itself. The industrial society, on the other hand, has not only aggravated these existential feelings but has added loneliness, emptiness, and estrangement from oneself and his world. Existence predisposes to depression, the "human condition" to depressive illness and psychosomatic disorder.

According to Tillich, Freud was caught up in a paradox not of his own making. "His pessimism about the nature of man and his optimism about the possibilities of healing were never reconciled in him." Psychoanalysts after Freud may have missed or misunderstood the existentialist element in him and thereby lost an essential component of his thinking. "They have rejected the profound insight of Freud about existential libido and the death instinct and in so doing they have reduced and cut off from Freud what made him and still makes him the most profound of all the depth psychologists." There has been a loss of depth, a loss of the irrational, and a loss of contact with the unconscious. Cognitive knowledge interferes with the experience of depth, inhibiting intuition, and technique becomes a part of technology.

Tillich therefore divides the problem as is done here, into two parts: one dealing with human existence and the other with the "human condition." We can heal the illness, the psychosomatic irregularity, and the self-destructiveness, but it is extremely doubtful, he says, that psychoanalysis or existential therapy can heal the

fundamental existential presuppositions that lie behind the manifest disease. Many psychoanalysts try to do it. They try with their methods to overcome existential negativity, anxiety, estrangement, meaninglessness, or guilt. They deny that they are universal, that they are existential in this sense. They call all anxiety, all guilt, all emptiness, illnesses which can be overcome as any illness can be and they try to remove them. This is impossible.

At this point Tillich introduces theology as "an instrument of salvation" that lies over and beyond medical methods and involves the "healing of the center of the personality," but whether this *deus ex machina* can do the "impossible" is as much open to question as the efficacy of psychoanalysis. This is something that analysts have to consider as they examine their therapeutic instrument, ascertaining what it can do, what it cannot do, and what it is not meant to do. Although it has been repeatedly emphasized that psychoanalysis is a total experience and not simply a technique, it cannot be expected to match the collective efforts needed to change distorted modes of living within disorganized environments. What it can and often does do is to strengthen those aspects of interpersonal living that depend on intrapsychic functioning and thereby increase cohesiveness in the family and authenticity in the individual.

In the final chapter Basch attempts the difficult task of examining what is known and not known in this complex and confusing field and arriving at some synthesis. One is immediately struck by the scholarship, the order, the precision, and the logical clarity with which the general argument is constructed. The combination of a structuralist approach, a general systems framework, and insights derived from psychoanalysis provides not only an efficient, critical instrument of past and present concepts but opens up the exciting possibility of an overall theory.

Having defined the qualities that a causal explanation of depression must possess, he proceeds to demonstrate how his conception of a system disturbance in the goal-seeking aspect of brain function would help in understanding the pluralism presented by the disorder. He is concerned not only with creating an all-encompassing model but also with reviewing the deficiencies of past models. In the course of presenting this grammar of psychobiological science, he neatly demolishes some of the cherished Victorian models that are kept so nostalgically on our shelves and that we are all so reluctant to part with. The question whether "goallessness" provides the best of all possible models to date and reflects our present state of knowledge will be received with great interest by some and skepticism by others, but there is no doubt that the thesis represents a subtle creative effort at reaching beyond the current status. At the end of the reading, one is left with two significant impressions: (1) Basch's rejection of the adultomorphic interpretation of the infant's deprivational experiences and his attempt to correct this with the use of Piaget's developmental theory* and (2) his description of the way the depressive process transforms the mind from an open to a closed system. These seem to be valuable and lasting contributions.

In 1931, eight years before his death, Freud wrote a letter to Lou Andreas-Salomé admiring the psychoanalytical essay she had written, describing it as a "true synthesis . . . a true scientific one . . . where you transform back again into a living organism the collection of nerves, tendons and blood vessels into which the analytic knife has turned the body" [6, p. 483].

We have clearly not accomplished a "true synthesis" in this book because, in the present state of our knowledge, this could hardly be possible. But we share with Freud the need, after our analytic work, to "transform back again into a living organism" and to reconstruct the total person in terms of his total experience.

In these pages, we have viewed depression through the eyes of the geneticist, the endocrinologist, the neurochemist, the clinical anthropologist, the sociologist, and the psychoanalyst. We have constantly described it as an existential phenomenon, and we have done our best, along with our contributors, to describe and delineate the core attributes of the illness. It remains, nevertheless, a medical account as witnessed objectively from the outside. It might look as if we had failed to explore the essence of the experience itself by not inviting the depressed person himself to provide his own observations and introspections. In listening to him we might have been able to learn something of its existential nature at first hand. The reason for this

---

* See also Chapter 11, which embraces a similar point of view.

hiatus has less to do with us than with what is available; the literature is extremely sparse. Autobiography is not an easy task even for the healthy mind; self-revelation must be especially painful for a mind remitting from melancholia. Denial often plays a prominent role in the illness, and once it is over there is an understandable reluctance to revisit the suffering. Furthermore, the few who have attempted to document their experience on paper have met with limited success because so much of it appears to lie beyond verbal expression.

The following excerpts will demonstrate how difficult it is to communicate the feeling of mental pain in terms adequate to be understood. One can see how the effort to do so might drive the depressive further into self-isolation. Because of the universality of the affect, however, something does come through in sufficient amount to allow us to resonate sympathetically with some facet of the event.

The first account comes from William James [5]. It emphasizes the continuity between clinical and normal depression, the latter being known popularly as "an attack of conscience." "The normal process of life contains moments as bad as any of those which insane melancholy is filled with, moments in which radical evil gets its innings and takes its solid turn. The lunatic's visions of horror are all drawn from the material of daily fact."

Since depression, whether normal or pathological, exists as an everyday experience, James continued, it is important for every healthy-minded man to realize that it had a part to play in his systematic approach to life. This piece of insight did not come to him in his earlier depressions but emerged only after a great deal of pain and suffering. His description of a depressive attack can hardly be bettered:

While in this state of philosophic pessimism and general depression of spurts about my prospects, I went one evening into a dressing room in the twilight to procure some article that was there; when suddenly there fell upon me without any warning, just as if it came out of the darkness, a horrible fear of my own existence. . . . After this the universe was changed for me altogether. I awoke morning after morning with a horrible dread at the pit of my stomach, and with a sense of insecurity of life. . . . I remember wondering how other people could live, how I myself had ever lived, so unconscious of that pit of insecurity beneath the surface of life. . . .

The fact that James's father had suffered an almost identical attack at about the same age, raises the possibility of a dominant genetic factor in this case. James was able not only to bear his depressions without surrendering completely to them but even to put them to creative uses. To some extent these constituted attempts at self-therapy.

Custance [4] approached his experience with almost a clinical eye, as if he were at the same time observing himself undergoing the experience.

If I were asked to characterize in the briefest possible way the whole experience of the depressive phase, I would describe it as a total reaction of repulsion between those fundamental poles . . . , the "I" and the "not I." . . . Certainly it seems to me that my reactions in the depressive phase are crude . . . or "total." . . . There is little or no discrimination; everything is abhorrent to me, everything frightens me. My consciousness has, as it were, regressed to the earliest stage of the simple organism which, finding its environment unpleasant, wants to get away into the nothingness of annihilation, hence my suicidal tendencies. . . . Every unpleasant reaction or thought is magnified to the limit. . . . The sense of sin . . . is dominating and all-pervading.

Here the author documents his estrangement from an environment that takes on highly disagreeable qualities and his escape through withdrawal and regression from its demands. The need to get away is predominant and compelling.

Another striking symptom is the psychosomatic one of tiredness, fatigability, and loss of energy, which can be sudden and extreme.

I went to a grocery store to make some purchases. . . . Suddenly I realized that I did not have sufficient energy to go to the market, and that another depression was upon me. It was with the greatest difficulty that I ordered the goods, paid for them and came home. At these times my brain feels paralyzed. . . . I have the impulse to act, but it seems as if something shuts down and prohibits action [7].

In contrast to this inhibition, the older person goes to the other extreme and becomes grossly overactive. They may seem preoccupied and out of touch, but they are, in fact, very conscious of their surroundings. Feelings of rage are almost chronic. The agitation stems again from the need to escape disturbing thoughts that pursue the patient like the Furies.

In that state you seldom speak to anyone, and then only to snarl. A constant state of hostility would perhaps define the attitude. . . . I was perfectly aware at all times of everything that was going on around me and do not recall a single moment when I was confused or didn't know what I was doing. I do know that I was simply sick of living, that nothing interested me. . . . My frightful mental depression persisted. It was utterly impossible for me to dispel the gloom. . . . The power to work, the will to work was temporarily gone. . . . Life had lost its savor. . . . I just didn't want to get well. I would much rather be dead. . . . It was thoughts like these that produced agitation; that compelled me to walk unceasingly and breathlessly all my waking hours. . . . I went at breakneck speed; I would say five miles per hour would be a conservative estimate. For two years . . . not eight hours but twelve hours a day. If you are fond of figures you can multiply . . . and you get a very respectable total of 43,800 miles for my two years' performance [2].

These individuals do their best to express the almost inexpressible, and certainly some parts of the experience come through very clearly, especially the pain and suffering entailed. In his great study, *The Anatomy of Melancholy*, Burton [3] wrote that the suffering of the melancholic constituted

the cream of human adversity, the quintessence, the upshot; all other diseases are but flea-bitings. . . . They are in great pain and horror of mind, distraction of soul, restless, full of continual fears, cares, torments, anxieties, they can neither eat, drink, nor sleep for them, take no rest, neither at bed nor yet at board, will any rest despair afford.

This description can hardly be bettered even by the experienced clinician. It summarizes, for all time, the essential ingredients that make up the experience of depression in any epoch of human history: the loss of energy, the sense of worthlessness, the self-reproach, the feelings of helplessness, and the utter and hopeless despair. In spite of the vast changes that have occurred since the seventeenth century, melancholic man has remained constant to himself. This is why one can label it, so confidently, an existential experience.

In spite of all the vicissitudes of human existence and the "human condition," the human spirit, like Samson Agonistes, continues to struggle tenaciously, to battle against often overwhelming odds, and to find hope again "on the far side of despair."

We cannot bring this work to a close without recapturing an image of Freud's that reveals something of his quality and his continued "openness to life." This was perhaps the element that staved off depression. He had acquired a horrible disease in middle life that had to be treated and operated on over and over again; his whole existence was on sufferance. Yet, in the midst of this he was able to write this to a correspondent: "Life is not easy at my age, but spring is beautiful, and so is love" [6]. There can hardly be a better example of hopefulness in the face of almost impossible conditions. It gives all of us hope.

REFERENCES

1. Beck, A. T. *Depression.* New York: Harper & Row, 1967.
2. Brown, H. C. *A Mind Mislaid.* New York: E. P. Dutton, 1937.
3. Burton, R. *The Anatomy of Melancholy.* New York: Farras and Rinehart, 1927.

4. Custance, J. *Wisdom, Madness and Folly*. New York: Pellegrini and Cudahy, 1952.
5. James, W. *The Varieties of Religious Experience*. New York: Longmans, 1902.
6. Jones, E. *The Life and Work of Sigmund Freud*, vol. 3. New York: Basic Books, 1957.
7. Reid, E. C. Autopsychology of the manic-depressive. *J. Nerv. Ment. Dis.* 37:606, 1910.
8. Schur, M. *Freud: Living and Dying*. New York: International Universities Press, 1972.
9. Tillich, P. The Theological Significance of Existentialism and Psychoanalysis. In *Theology of Culture*. New York: Oxford University Press, 1959.
10. Zetzel, E. R. Depression and the Incapacity To Bear It. In M. Schur. (Ed.), *Drives, Affects, Behavior*, vol. 2. New York: International Universities Press, 1965.

Index

Index

Abraham, Karl, 120, 126, 150, 200, 202, 206, 229, 245, 250, 289, 342, 346, 350, 373, 427
  theories of
    on etiological factors in melancholia, 201
    on mourning, 371
    on orality in depression, 128–129
    on pure mania, 201–202
Active-engaging, 183
  function of, 184
Activity, increase in. See Paradoxical hypermotivation, in defense against depression
Actual neurosis
  examples of, 204
  physiological considerations in, 204–205
  symptoms of, 205
Acute depressive illness, symptoms of, 264
Adaptation, symbolic, 524–525
Adaptive regulation
  affective disorders and, biochemical theory on, 60–62
  catecholamine hypothesis and, 59–60
Addison's disease, 22
  depression and, 45–46

Adjustment, social, related to depression, 107
Adolescence
  confusion in, 345
  defined, 345
  developmental phase of
    identity confusion in, 347
    potential for depression in, 347–348
    psychodynamic motivation, 346
    psychosocial factors in, 347
  extension of, 349
Adolescent depression
  ambivalence and, 445
  clinical depression in, 459
  contrasting types of, 451–452
    type one, 452
      course and treatment of, 453–456
    type two, 452
      course and treatment of, 456–459
  description of, 446–448
  diagnosis of, 317
  genesis of, 448–451
  mood disturbances in, 445–446
  mourning process in, 320–322
  object loss and, 226
  recognition of loss in, 317–318
  self-curing of, 446
  sources of, 349

549